Educational Handicap, Public Policy, and Social History

Educational Handicap, Public Policy, and Social History

A Broadened Perspective
on Mental Retardation

SEYMOUR B. SARASON
AND
JOHN DORIS

THE FREE PRESS
A Division of Macmillan Publishing Co., Inc.
NEW YORK

Collier Macmillan Publishers
LONDON

Copyright © 1979 by The Free Press

A Division of Macmillan Publishing Co., Inc.

The Free Press
A Division of Macmillan Publishing Co., Inc.
866 Third Avenue, New York, N.Y. 10022

Collier Macmillan Canada, Ltd.

Library of Congress Catalog Card Number: 78-3203

Printed in the United States of America

printing number

1 2 3 4 5 6 7 8 9 10

Library of Congress Cataloging in Publication Data

Library of Congress Cataloging in Publication Data

Sarason, Seymour Bernard
  Educational handicap, public policy, and social
history.

  Includes index.
  1. Mentally handicapped--United States. 2. Mentally
handicapped--Education--United States. 3. United
States--Social policy. I. Doris, John
joint author. II. Title.
HV3006.A4S32   362.3'0973   78-3203
ISBN 0-02-927920-8

Passages from the following works have been quoted here by permission of the author(s) and/or publishers:

A. J. Sameroff, "Concepts of Humanity in Primary Prevention." Paper prepared for the Vermont Conference on the Primary Prevention of Psychopathology, Burlington, Vermont, June 1975.

F. K. Grossman, *Brothers and Sisters of Retarded Children: An Exploratory Study*. Syracuse, N. Y.: Syracuse University Press, 1972.

Harlan Lane, *The Wild Boy of Aveyron*. Cambridge, Mass.: Harvard University Press, 1976.

S. B. Sarason, *The Psychological Sense of Community*. San Francisco: Jossey-Bass, 1974.

E. Zigler and D. Balla, "Impact of Institutional Experience on the Behavior and Development of Retarded Persons." *American Journal of Mental Deficiency*, 1977, *82*, 1-11.

G. E. Blom, "Principles of Normalization: A Case Study." Unpublished paper available from author, Department of Child Psychiatry, Michigan State University, East Lansing, Michigan 48823.

W. Wolfensberger and R. A. Kurtz (eds.), *Management of the Family of the Mentally Retarded*. Follett Educational Corporation, 1969.

A. P. Matheny and J. Vernick, "Parents of the Mentally Retarded Child: Emotionally Overwhelmed or Informationally Deprived?." In J. J. Dempsey (ed.), *Community Services for Retarded Children*. Baltimore: University Park Press, 1975.

B. P. Berkowitz and A. M. Graziano, "Training Parents as Behavior Therapists: A Review." *Behavior Research and Therapy*, 1972, *10*, 297-317.

W. Wolfensberger, *The Principle of Normalization in Human Services*. Toronto: National Institute of Mental Retardation, 1972.

B. Blatt, *Exodus from Pandemonium*. Boston: Allyn & Bacon, 1970.

J. W. Sanders, *Education of an Urban Minority: Catholics in Chicago, 1833-1965*. Oxford University Press, 1977.

L. Covello, *The Heart Is the Teacher*. New York: McGraw-Hill Book Co., Inc., 1958.

L. D. Wald, "Education and the Arts." *International Council for Exceptional Children Review*, February 1935, 1 (3), 82-87.

J. R. Mercer, "Sociological Perspectives on Mental Retardation." In H. C. Haywood (ed.), *Social-Cultural Aspects of Mental Retardation*. New York: Appleton-Century-Crofts, 1970.

J. R. Mercer, "A Policy Statement on Assessment Procedures and the Rights of Children." *Harvard Educational Review*, 1974, *44* (1), 125-141.

J. C. Loehlin, G. Lindzey, and J. N. Spuhler, *Race Differences in Intelligence*. San Francisco: W. H. Freeman & Co., 1975.

L. Covello, *The Social Background of the Italo-American School Child*. Leiden: E. J. Brill, 1967 (copyright F. Cordasco, West New York, N.J.).

J. J. Gallagher, "Why the Government Breaks Its Promises." *New York University Education Quarterly*, 1975, 22-27.

J. J. Gallagher, "The Special Education Contract for Mildly Handicapped Children." *Exceptional Children*, March 1972, 527-535.

S. B. Sarason, M. Levine, I. Goldenberg, D. Cherlin, and E. Bennett, *Psychology in Community Settings*. New York: John Wiley, 1966.

S. B. Sarason, C. Carroll, K. Maton, S. Cohen, and E. Lorentz, *Human Services and Resources Networks*. San Francisco: Jossey-Bass, 1977.

To Marje and Esther

Contents

Preface

THE FIELD OF MENTAL RETARDATION (indeed, those of all handicapping conditions in general) has changed remarkably in the past two decades. The changes are of such variety and force, of such potential significance, and are taking place with such speed, that one is hard put to account for them, let alone to judge where they are taking us. In fact, one can no longer count on reading the professional journals to keep up with what is going on or is in the offing. Almost daily, the newspapers contain summaries of court decisions and proposed legislation that will affect existing practices, attitudes, and public policies. The one thing that can be said with certainty is that handicapped people have, so to speak, come out of the closet. More correctly, they have been propelled out of the closet, often by forces over which they have no control. These forces have gained speed and mass and can best be characterized as a "movement." Like most movements they are comprised of diverse and even conflicting and contradictory tendencies.

The day is past when one can write a conventional textbook on mental retardation replete with definitions, descriptions of clinical syndromes, tests and diagnostic criteria, and suggestions for educational and institutional placement and programming. This is not to say that these features are unimportant, but rather that recent changes in our society and public policy have exposed what has always been true but drastically underemphasized: the definition of, attitudes toward, and programs for mentally retarded people have always been a function of the nature of our society and its history. Mental retardation is not a "thing" but an invented concept suffused with social values, tradition, intended and unintended prejudice and derogation—all reflecting the dominant characteristics of our society and its history. And like most inventions there have been numerous efforts to "improve" them, the improvements again reflecting changes in the society. Most people like to believe that we know more about mental retardation, and can do more for those to whom that label is appended, because of more and better knowledge derived from research. That belief is not fully warranted. The fact is that the revolutionary changes the field has undergone in recent decades have to do more with court decisions, and legislation inspired or required by those decisions, than anything else. But that statement has to be understood in the context of larger and more potent social forces that characterized the turbulent sixties. Racial strife and discrimination, the twin cancer of poverty, heightened sensitivity to civil rights, the women's liberation movement, the rights of patients—these and other issues, surfacing in and out of our courts and legislatures, guaranteed that some of the so-called basic conceptions about mental retardation would be challenged. And they were with momentous consequences, the outlines of which—let alone their substances—are by no means clear.

Precisely because mental retardation is a socially invented concept, the people who have "it" have to be seen in relation to those who do not have "it." And to understand that relation demands that we come to terms with how we understand our society to be structured; the diverse values that power it; the ways those values are institutionalized; the cultural "shoulds and oughts" that seem so natural, right, and proper (but may not be); and the threads of continuity that tie the present to the past. Each generation or era tends to see itself as unique and is more aware of discontinuities than of continuities with its history. In large measure, this book is an effort to expose the dangers of the ahistorical stance. It is now a cliché to say that different societies define and manage behavioral deviance differently, but it is not yet a cliché to say that we rarely take it seriously to the point where we inquire about why we are different. What is there in our past that set the stage for the present? How different is that past from the present? And if that past turns out to have important similarities to the present, what have we learned about us and our society? Basic to this book is the belief that if we want to understand the concept of mental retardation and those who are called mentally retarded, we have to understand ourselves and our society in historical terms. History is not a discontinuous stream; man divides history by use of dates, events, and labels and in the process relegates to museum status much of what has shaped and continues to shape him. It is, we hope, not an indulgence of immodest presumption to say that the contents of this book are needed as much as the usual contents of introductory texts by those who are entering the field. And, of course, we hope that this book will be helpful to people who are so immersed on a daily basis with matters of policy, programs, management, and education that they have difficulty taking distance from what they are doing and how they are thinking. If it is hard for anyone to keep track of all that is happening in the field of mental retardation, it is all too easy to overlook, if not to downgrade, the challenges that social history contains. And, finally, this book is intended for those people, professional or lay, who continue to see mental retardation as a "strange" field that cannot possibly illuminate the nature of our society. However much the field of mental retardation has changed, it is still true that the bulk of people in fields directly or indirectly relevant to mental retardation (e.g., psychology, medicine, sociology, political science, history) see it as too "special" to have general significance. Parochialism and the ahistorical stance are, unfortunately, highly correlated.

We are grateful to Carolyn Perry for bearing with us with such grace as she typed this manuscript and the numerous changes it went through. We also appreciate the time and facilities made available to us by our respective universities, especially Yale's Institution for Social and Policy Studies, that not only encourages collaborative efforts but also provides the material support for them.

Educational Handicap,
Public Policy, and
Social History

1

Plan of the Book

WE HEAR THAT WE LIVE in a fast-changing world and the basis of this assertion seems compellingly true. It is not our intention to deny validity to the assertion when we suggest that many changes have not taken place as quickly as believed. For example, before World War II, it was said that when one got married, it was forever. Religion and civil law supported such a view. But at the same time, divorces, extramarital affairs, and desertions indicated a discrepancy between what people said and what they did. If one went by marriage and divorce statistics, let alone the pronouncements of civic and religious leaders, one might have concluded that the traditional institution of marriage had a solid foundation capable of resisting change. However, if one went beyond the conventional statistics to examine how people experienced marriage, how they sought to maintain and circumvent its spirit and form, one might have been less secure about marriage in the future as a carbon copy of the present.

We become aware of change after its dynamics have already had an affect. Awareness further accelerates the pace and shape of the change, and when that change becomes "obvious" there is the tendency to proclaim that the world was, so to speak, born yesterday. We become ahistorical or, worse yet, antihistorical. The danger in all of this is not in ignoring history but in our lack of respect for it; we devalue one of the most obvious "lessons" of historical writing: Beware of those who in proclaiming the birth of a new world blithely assume that the old world will lie down and die; tradition, custom, and practice are not easily unlearned. Those who proclaim a new world cannot confront the fact that parts of the old world have been silently absorbed by them.

In planning this book we anticipated several problems, although we predicted their interrelatedness far better than their level of difficulty. The first problem had to do with recent versus long-term history. How can we discuss the recent history of mental retardation without relating it to what may seem to be ancient history? If we began with long-term history, without the reader knowing the recent history, would not our account cause the

1

reader to ask why he or she is being asked to wade through material that seems tangential or irrelevant?

These questions get more complicated as a consequence of another problem: Do we start by emphasizing recent changes or, in the effort to help the reader distinguish types, degrees, and quality change, do we concentrate on what *needs* to change if the optimistic spirit of the new era is not to be replaced by pessimism and disillusionment? There have been in recent decades changes of sea-swell proportions in the field of mental retardation but that should not blind us to the ways our thinking and practices continue to bear the imprint of the "old days."

We have no desire to be seen as cynics or temperamental wet blankets but neither do we want to contribute to unwarranted optimism and a confusion between change and progress. If this were not complicated enough, we still have to deal with the fact that what has happened in the field of mental retardation cannot be understood without looking at the changes that have taken place among racial and ethnic minorities, handicapped people and others who have felt disadvantaged.

Although the 1954 desegregation decision did not deal directly with mental retardation, the striking down of the "separate but equal" clause by the Supreme Court came to have enormous consequences for mentally retarded people. The argument that separate but equal facilities insidiously affected both black and white children was not lost on some people who had similarly viewed the consequences of special classes. Mental retardation, like so much else in our society, became food for legal and judicial thought. When the National Association for Retarded *Children* changed its name to the National Association for Retarded *Citizens*, it signified a social change that had already begun to take place: a heightened sensitivity to individual rights and constitutional guarantees, and a willingness to go into the courts to clarify and protect these rights. One could argue (Sarason and Doris 1969) that it has been the case that the definition, perception, and reaction to mentally retarded people have always reflected society at a particular time but never has that been as explicit as in recent decades.

The final problem we anticipated was a consequence of the decision that this book make no attempt to be encyclopedic but rather concentrate on several topics and issues we regard as crucial in two ways. First, there are issues one takes a stand on even without realizing what assumptions are implicit in that stand. Second, there are issues that our culture, social history, and professionalism make extraordinarily difficult for us to articulate, let alone recognize. When we begin to do so we see that culture and tradition insure continuity but also that they put blinders on our perception of alternatives. Culture is a double-edged sword: it is at the same time our ally and our adversary. This is not a book to indoctrinate the student into the field but rather to sensitize the student to the dangers of indoctrination, to recognize that mental retardation is not only about "them" but about "us" as well, and to challenge the student to come to grips with the fact that we are historical beings shaped by a past and drawn to a future in a present we can only comprehend when it has become the past.

If we were writing for ourselves, the organizational problems this book seemed to present would not be thorny. We would take a historical approach in which we would emphasize what we regarded as crucial issues. But such linearity made sense only because in starting in the past we already knew the end of the story. There are many people, however, who not only do not know that past but a good deal of the present scene as well. For them, what would make sense to us would be a bore.

What was decisive in our decision about how to organize this book was the realization that one of the issues we were interested in would not be illuminated by a historical approach, if only because even today it has not received the attention it deserves. We refer to the fact that the diagnostic process is always initiated because a social context has in some way been disrupted. The nature and consequences of this obvious fact are taken up in Chapter 2. This chapter attempts to show how the failure to see the concept of mental retardation as a social invention, plus the discrepancy in emphasis on the *individual* in contrast to the social context, have had enormously mischievous consequences for diagnosis, research, and practice. Toward the end of that chapter we draw heavily on the writings and research of Sameroff, especially in regard to how his transactional model clarifies some long-standing puzzles in atypical development. As important as what he clarifies in the research literature is his claim that prevailing concepts of developmental anomalies unwittingly lead to regarding persons as things: Something is wrong with the child and what is wrong will remain wrong.

In Chapter 3 we pursue the transactional approach not only because it is antithetical to conceptions and practices that continue to dominate the field of mental retardation but because it opens up new vistas and possibilities. For example, we point out that definitions of intelligence and therefore mental retardation have hardly reflected a transactional way of thinking. That inadequacy is not easy to remedy because it requires us to change our ways of thinking. We have to give up thinking of intelligence as a characteristic of individuals and, instead, learn how to pose questions in a transactional context; in other words, to observe a transaction and not an *individual*.

In the last two decades there has been a veritable revolution in our understanding of the newborn's cognitive capacities. That would never have been possible if the transactional nature of the newborn's existence had not been taken seriously. In the field of mental retardation we still look at the individual in the same way we used to look at the newborn, and nowhere is this more clear than in diagnosis. It may come as a surprise to some to learn that this was an issue Alfred Binet understood quite well, although the Termans and the Goddards who followed him used his methods without his assumptions. In the realm of human behavior, the need to define and measure always reflects dominant social needs as the society at the time perceives them; and these perceptions are inevitably colored by moral or value judgments. Those who regard the diagnostic process as objective, value free, and independent of society simplify their lives at the expense of understanding the fact that diagnosis is sanctioned by society. They also fail to see the possibilities of the transactional model.

In Chapter 4 we take up more directly the social context of diagnosis, the implications of which are rarely drawn and acted upon. The diagnostic process tends to be carried out as if only *one* individual required assessment and help, as if the locus of the problem inhered in the person and the consequences of the problem are of secondary significance, however upsetting or disruptive to others. There is always more than one character in the diagnostic drama and it is the diagnostician's task to make sense of how the web of their relationships has altered as a result of events. We discuss this with two cases that illustrate the significance of several questions. How will each of the parents react to and interpret the implications of the child's condition? How will each perceive the other's reaction? What are the immediate consequences that they see themselves facing as a couple? How should they react to the "retarded" infant? What special problems may arise? *From a transactional approach the diagnosis has developmental consequences but the quantity and quality of these consequences will always be a function of the total social-interpersonal context of which the child is a part.* If in practice the concept of diagnosis is seen as taking place in regard only to the child, even though the developmental implications of the diagnosis will inevitably be shaped by a larger context, it says more about the weight of tradition than about requirements for helpful action. The transactional approach requires unlearning habits of perceiving that rivet attention on the child with the social-interpersonal context relegated to the background.

In Chapter 5 we look at what happens when the diagnostic process is not carried out from a transactional perspective, and to illustrate the consequences we use Heller's novel, *Something Happened*, in which a profoundly retarded child has equally profound effects on all members of a family who, in turn, create a social-interpersonal context that rules out any positive developmental advance by the child. *Something Happened* is fiction but it is faithful to what frequently occurs in reality. In contrast, we examine Itard's classic description of how he set up and nurtured an environment in which *The Wild Boy of Aveyron* could develop. Itard's sensitivity to the social context reflects a transactional approach and is in marked contrast to much of today's separatism between diagnosis and program planning. Heller's artistry brings to the fore the fact that the sense of aging is *not* a function of chronology but of events and experiences that make one feel that the best of life has passed and the future is a downhill slide. This concern with the passage of time and a foreboding future—those obsessive thoughts about one's death and its consequences for one's kin—are almost never absent in parents of retarded children. Indeed, historically speaking, these parents as a group knew about the poignancy of the aging process long before it became a topic of public concern.

The belief that mentally retarded individuals should live in the community rather than be segregated in large residential institutions has gained currency only in recent decades. In Chapter 6 we look into this change in public policy and attitude from two standpoints. We first examine certain aspects of medicare and how federal legislation spawned a nursing home industry that was to take care of many older people who were burdens to their families. Then came the nursing home scandals and the beginning of a reversal in public policy in order to keep senior citizens in the community. The nursing home scandals were in all respects similar to Blatt's (1966, 1970, 1975, 1977) exposés of institutions for the mentally retarded.

We then view the issues of institutionalization and community living by examining recent federal legislation regarding "intermediate care facilities" for the mentally retarded, legislation intended to maximize their return to community living. However well intended, we find this legislation wanting in a number of respects, and we are driven to the conclusion that the forces working against community acceptance and placement of retarded individuals are subtle and pervasive. This, we point out, cannot be understood in terms of evil intentions or organized conspiracy but by the degree to which segregation of "deviant people" is prepotent in our society. Custom and prejudice in our thinking and behavior do not change quickly.

What should be the ingredients of a community program? This is a question we take up in Chapter 7, limiting ourselves to three ingredients that deserve more attention than they have received. The first has to do with the inadequacies of medical training and how these inadequacies manufacture problems. This is not because physicians are less motivated or more callous than other people but rather because their training poorly sensitizes them to the social-interpersonal context of diagnosis and program planning. It equally ill prepares them in regard to community facilities and placements. Physicians are important "gatekeepers" in our society, especially in regard to the mentally retarded, and it is our contention that in the development of a valid and comprehensive community orientation we cannot afford to continue to overlook the inadequacies of medical training.

The second ingredient we discuss has to do with home-community relationships. Although the concept of community programs for mentally retarded people does not preclude a focus on services within home and neighborhood, most of these programs require the child and family to travel to the site. The risks in such a requirement are several and we point out that recent research indicates rather clearly the superiority in outcomes of home based, parent-implemented programs. The third ingredient is advocacy. At the same time that it has become fashionable, it has become a function delegated to those who were largely responsible for the need in the first place.

This is a point that Wolfensberger originally made in his pioneer writings on advocacy but it has been deftly sidestepped by the policymakers.

Up until Chapter 8 our discussion and case examples largely concern what used to be called the mentally defective child: the child who had neurological and motor deficits suggestive of a damaged central nervous system. But these children, who can be found at all socioeconomic levels, have always been a relatively small minority of those put into the category of the mentally retarded. Indeed, it used to be the practice (as it still is with the World Health Organization) to distinguish between mental deficiency and mental retardation, the latter being reserved for that very large group of individuals whose presenting "symptoms" were early school failure, a low intelligence test score, and a cultural milieu that today we would call disadvantaged and disorganized. The child's "condition" seemed to run in the family and it was the practice to use the label "familial," meaning an interaction between "poor stock" and "subcultural" level and style of life. And there was no doubt that subcultural did not only mean a different kind of cultural milieu but an inferior one socially unacceptable to the dominant culture. One could use the Kallikaks and Jukes as "classic," albeit extreme, examples.

From the time that special classes began, they were largely populated by "subcultural" children from minority groups. Not the blacks, Chicanos, or Hispanics of today but primarily the children of the "new immigration" from southern and eastern Europe. What went unnoticed was that the retardation was diagnosed in the school, and it was automatically assumed that the low quality and level of cognitive functioning had also characterized the child's preschool development. It was not until much later that this assumption was called into question and the alternative question posed as to what extent this condition was caused by the culture and structure of the school. Here the assumption is not that the problem lies in the inherent limitations of the child but that the culture and structure of the school makes it unresponsive to the ethnic, cultural, and socioeconomic differences among the pupils it purports to serve.

The more we got into the origins and composition of special classes, the more impressed we became with the consequences of the emergence of universal compulsory education, because wrapped up in the fierce controversies surrounding compulsory education as public policy were many of the same social issues we are still dealing with and which have a mighty impact on our schools. Today, when we think about the major issues in public education we would put high on the list the problems "caused by" cultural and racial minorities, but that has been the case from the early years of our republic. Today we think of blacks, Chicanos, and Hispanics. In the 19th century it was the Irish, Germans, and Italians who were the minorities society regarded as inferior, culturally strange, disruptive of the social calm, and potentially capable of ruining the country. And not far from the center of these concerns was religious conflict.

It became apparent to us that for a better understanding of universal compulsory education and its consequences, and of the context from which special classes emerged, we had to discuss the origins of the "common" school, and Chapters 8 through 12 attempt to deal with aspects of the relevant social history. Some readers may find themselves puzzled at the contents of these chapters, ranging as they do from education in the Colonial days, to the waves of immigration, to the religion-school wars, to anti-Catholicism, to the development of the Catholic parochial school system — and the way in which all of these had an impact on ever enlarging school systems seeking pedagogical-administrative solutions to their problems. But that history is absolutely essential to anyone who seeks to understand how the problems of today are related to the past. Far from being dead history, the contents of these chapters help explain why problems endure over the centuries, and how our habits of thinking play a part.

The common school as we shall endeavor to demonstrate in those chapters was to a large extent devised as a cure for the ills of society — poverty, crime, delinquency, and immorality. Curricula were chosen to develop the cognitive skills, and the moral and ethical character that would, according to the leading thought of the time, ensure citizens capable of participating in a complex, ever more industrialized society as productive, law-abiding, and socially responsible members. The methods of instruction were dictated not only by the prevalent theories of knowledge, philosophies of education, and psychologies of childhood but by the available science and technology of instruction, and by the availability of human and financial resources. Curricula and methods were implemented in organizational settings growing ever more complex as the nineteenth century advanced from the one-room school to the mammoth physical plant of the urban school with teachers numbered in the scores and pupils in the thousands, from the essentially local district school board administrative control to the administrative complexity of state-wide educational bureaucracies. In the end, the massive ills of society had dictated the massive therapeutic intervention known as the common school system.

But the therapeutic regimen of the schools had an unforeseen effect. It was based on the assumption that all children of a given age were essentially the same for purposes of instruction. It ignored the environmentally determined differences among children of different social classes, of different cultural and ethnic groups. It ignored the individual differences — both environmentally and genetically determined — in physical, cognitive, and temperamental traits that exist in any and all groups of children. The result of the obliviousness to the differences among children in the design of the lock-step, class-graded, common school system — once compulsory education forced all children into the school — was a threatened breakdown of the system.

This was especially so in the large city school system with overcrowded classes and the individual heterogeneity of the students exaggerated by the cultural differences of various ethnic groups. This threatened breakdown of the instructional system of the common school was avoided only by diagnosing all children who did not fit into the standard pupil pattern of the system as either intellectually, morally, or culturally defective. Once so diagnosed the child could be segregated into a special education class of one type or another and the system would remain intact to function as designed. It is to this development of a segregated educational system within the common school system that we concern ourselves in Chapters 13, 14 and 15.

In Chapter 13 we see how educators responded to the presence of these non-standard type students that were forced upon them by the compulsory education laws. They devised segregated classes and schools that were to be the respositories for all the varied kinds of children that could not fit into the regular class without creating *problems* for the system. Thus to a large extent the concern was primarily with the preservation of the system.

Nevertheless, there was often genuine concern for these nonstandard students themselves which was in part as we indicate in Chapter 14 a reflection of the expanding social-work role of the school as it struggled with the problems of urban life and mass immigration. This concern for the welfare of the student led to the diagnosis of the different kinds of *problems* presented by these children and the setting up of different kinds of special classes with the mentally subnormal constituting one of the largest of these special groupings and the one of particular interest to us. The growth of special education for the mentally subnormal and the problems of curriculum development and the training of teachers for this group prior to World War II is the concern of Chapter 15.

In Chapter 16 we take note of the growing concerns in regard to the efficacy of special education for the mentally subnormal child that began to develop following World War II. In particular we note the challenge raised by minority groups that found their children overrepresented in special education classes. The validity of the diagnostic procedures that assigned children to special education classes then leads us to a consideration of the overrepresentation of different minority groups in the special education classes in the first decades of this century—particularly that of the children of Italian immigrants. Along with this overrepresentation of Italian children in special education classes, we present evidence for their higher rates of school failure and dropout that persisted up until the Second World War.

In addition we note that the consensus findings of numerous IQ studies undertaken in the 1920s was that the Italian children obtained average IQ scores of 85, not very different from those obtained by black children in those investigations and generally noticeably below other ethnic groups. The picture is very much like that obtained for some of our racial and ethnic minorities in the present day. We are led to speculate on what this historical perspective implies for the nature-nurture controversy in relation to racial and ethnic factors and to question the extent to which the school itself is a factor in the development of that form of mental subnormality which we designate as familial retardation.

Chapter 17 discusses an apparently distinctive phase in the history of mental retardation and special education. The passage of Public Law 94–142, the mainstreaming legislation, like the Supreme Court 1954 desegregation decision which preceded it, gave concrete form not only to constitutional principles but to particular values. Mainstreaming reflects a policy that is opposed to removing children from the regular classroom and segregating them in special classes. Put positively, mainstreaming seeks heterogeneity in the classroom in order for children to perceive, understand, and tolerate diversity within their midst. Mainstreaming as a concept is rooted in law, social history, philosophy, and pedagogy. That legislation, concerning all handicapping conditions, was intended to radically alter the school's perception of its diverse student population as well as its administrative procedures and practices.

Consistent with the thrust of previous chapters, we see how conceptions about the nature of mental retardation reflect changes in the larger society in that this public law takes on its full meaning only when viewed in light of the current emphasis on the rights of the individual, due process, and the role of discrimination in our major social institutions. We stress the fact that it has been the courts through which these social changes have been brought about and not through a changed public consciousness. One must expect, therefore, that long-standing institutional practices and attitudes, as well as the attitudes of the general public, will not bend so easily to the requirements for true mainstreaming. What has been inculcated over the decades into the minds of people does not become transformed by legislative fiat, a point our historical review amply confirms.

In Chapter 17 we describe the kinds of resistances mainstreaming seems to be engendering and, although the legislation is too recent to warrant any firm judgment about its implementation, we attempt an assessment if only because so many people misjudge the gulf between theory and practice, between legislative intent and everyday practice. If our assessment is not a very happy one, it is due less to cynicism on our part and more to respect for the weight of tradition to subvert the forces for change.

The chapter on mainstreaming raises a question that occupied center stage in our account of the origins of the common school and special classes. It is *the* question, and rightly so: *What are schools for?* (Chapter 18). At different times in our history, that question has been answered in rhetoric that was usually discrepant with practice. Briefly, the answer has been that schools are places where children can acquire and develop cognitive knowledge and skills and, no less important, learn to act on the values and principles of democratic living. Unfortunately, in practice a major function of schools has been to determine the capabilities of students and to so organize the schools that children of different capabilities do not interfere with each other's educational growth: In other words, *the perceived limits of capabilities are the major criterion for determining with whom they live in schools. At its root, this rests on production-achievement as the major criterion for judging people.*

This criterion went virtually unchallenged until the 1954 desegregation decision and the passage of Public Law 94-142. Mainstreaming puts back on the discussion table the question of how we want to live together. What are schools for? How shall we judge them? If we want to change them, what are the major obstacles and what constitutes a realistic time perspective for overcoming them? The myth of homogeneity, as well as difficulty in confronting the axiom that resources are always limited, are among the major obstacles we examine. Only in recent years have we been forced to recognize that resources are always limited; this fact has to be directly confronted when we attempt to lessen the gulf between what we proclaim and what we do. In implementing the mainstreaming legislation—to the extent that we want to avoid confirmation of the maxim that the more things change the more they remain the same—we will have to better understand why we continue to avoid the fact that resources are limited. This is not peculiar to the field of mental retardation. It is general in our society, but that says that mental retardation—as we know it, define it, and deal with it—bears the imprint of the larger society.

From this brief overview of the contents of this book the reader will see that we do not regard the field of mental retardation as comprehensible apart from moral and ethical values as they have emerged in the course of social history. In fact, one way of reading that history suggests that to the extent that people saw mental retardation as a congeries of conditions whose manifestations were independent of time and place, as a set of philosophical questions and cultural considerations of dubious relevance, and as certain people who, even though they were unproductive, could and should be humanely housed in segregated settings—to the extent that these perceptions held sway they guaranteed that someone would come along to expose the tragedy of man's unwitting inhumanity to man. However the reader may regard this book, he or she is not likely to deny that the issues we have addressed have to be conceptually absorbed if one is not to be overwhelmed by an ocean of facts that can effectively drown the truth.

2

Mental Retardation: Social Invention and Transactional Phenomenon

MENTAL RETARDATION is not a thing you can see or touch or define in terms of shape and substance. It is a concept serving two major purposes: to separate a group of people; and to justify social action in regard to those who are set apart. The setting apart may not be a physical separation but may be conceptualized in ways justifying special attention and action.

When we label people as mentally retarded, it already reflects the fact that society has regarded them as "different" in ways that the society says requires special action. We are always labeling people. But not all labels are closely tied to action. For example, we can label people as thin, forgetting that thinness is an abstraction implying social judgments of good and bad, healthy and unhealthy. In thus labeling people as "thin" there may be no conscious implication that we should do anything for or about them. But if we are unaware of how labels reflect value judgments, indicating how our perceptions and conceptions are tied to what society says is good and bad, we have only to reflect on how society uses the label "fat" people. Thinness is "good," fatness is "bad." Fat people *should* try to reduce and we *ought* to help them. Although thin and fat can be defined by operations unconnected with value judgments, in our daily lives we use the terms with implied "shoulds" and "oughts" suggesting the need for action. There is nothing wrong in this as long as we recognize that our conceptions contain value judgments rooted in a society at a particular time.

As we shall see, the concept of mental retardation has been a troublesome one precisely because of the failure to recognize the degree to which it carries meanings far more revealing of "us" than of those whom we categorize as mentally retarded. This point has been made by numerous writers (Blatt, 1970; Braginsky and Braginsky, 1971; Dexter, 1964; Goffman, 1963; Hurley, 1969;). Bogdan's and Taylor's (1976) paper makes the same point, illustrating it with a poignant case presentation. Mercer's (1973) book deals at

11

length with the issues in labeling people as mentally retarded. Some writers (Gallagher, 1972; Kolstoe, 1972) have pointed out that labeling can have positive consequences, especially where it heightens social awareness of the scope of a problem and leads to new public policies to remedy neglect.

We would maintain that the issue is not "to label or not to label." Labeling is a human characteristic and to say "no labeling" is like commanding the sun not to rise. It is the failure to recognize the arbitrary features of labels and to assume uncritically that labels are more revealing of the labeled than of the labeler that leads to problems. As Bogdan and Taylor (1976) put it:

> If one wishes to understand the term *holy water,* one should not study the properties of the water, but rather the assumptions and beliefs of the people who use it. That is, holy water derives its meaning from those who attribute a special essence to it (Szasz, 1974).
>
> Similarly, the meaning of the term *mental retardation* depends on those who use it to describe the cognitive states of other people. As some have argued, mental retardation is a social construction or a concept which exists in the minds of the "judges" rather than in the minds of the "judged." A mentally retarded person is one who has been labeled as such according to rather arbitrarily created and applied criteria.
>
> *Retardate,* and other such clinical labels, suggests generalizations about the nature of men and women to whom the term has been applied. We assume that the mentally retarded possess common characteristics that allow them to be unambiguously distinguished from all others. We explain their behavior by special theories. It is as though humanity can be divided into two groups, the "normal" and the "retarded."

Take, for example, the statement "she is a woman." This is essentially a diagnostic statement on the basis of observable anatomical characteristics. Ordinarily, we do not take into account the fact that some men have bigger breasts than some women, or that some men have bodily contours we ordinarily associate with those of women. And if we go beyond the anatomical to physiological-endocrinological functioning, we find further overlap. Ordinarily, we have no trouble making the diagnosis and, indeed, we are not even aware we have made the diagnosis. But what do we learn about our diagnostic process when we are proved wrong? How many older people complain that they are having trouble distinguishing between young men and women because of the trend toward unisex clothing and hairstyling? What the complaints indicate is that the judgments we make about sexual category imply a good deal more than anatomical factors. It would not occur to anyone to blame a woman for having big breasts, or a man for not having big breasts, but it does occur to many people to blame them for dress they consider strange and unseemly.

When we use the term mental retardation, we tend to be unaware of the perceptions and attitudes toward the people we have put in this category as reflections of our culture rather than inherent or objective characteristics of these people. This is an obvious point but it is surprising and disturbing how the label mental retardation is pinned on people as if the process has been solely concerned with data free from the effects of culture, tradition, habit, and morality.

There has also been the tendency to describe mentally retarded people as "children." This designation was rooted not only in society's conceptions of social and intellectual behavior but also meant to justify society's actions in protecting and segregating these people. When the extent to which the concept of mental retardation was tied to uncritically accepted value judgments began to be sensed, the fiction that mental retardation was a purely scientific concept was exposed. When the National Association for Retarded *Children* changed its name to the National Association for Retarded *Citizens*, it signaled the societal change that was taking place.

We like to believe that when we apply the concept of mental retardation, we are uninfluenced by time, place, and society. The fact that this is an untenable belief is suggested by several considerations. First, over the centuries, description and explanation of people who were called mentally retarded have varied as a function of time, place, and society. This, of course, does not mean that the past must dictate the future. But, at the very least, knowledge of the past should give pause to those eager to believe that the concept of mental retardation they are using is coldly impersonal and scientific. Second, as a concept, mental retardation implies a decision about action, and this always reflects the society's view at a particular time about what is right or wrong, appropriate or inappropriate. Over time, a society does change its views toward those it regards as special or different: e.g., homosexuals, the elderly, children, women, alcoholics, or any individuals representing minority groups within that society. Third, within scientific and scholarly traditions, the one belief that seems not to change is that the more you know the more you need to know. This belief should make one suspicious of a stance that says that our present concepts and actions will require no revision. As a social or scientific concept, mental retardation has undergone dramatic change and there is every reason to believe that this process will continue.

Strangeness, Differences, and Action

We may identify a person as strange without feeling we must do something; we may consider the matter as nobody's business. This view already reflects a judgment, a social value governing action. What is the more frequent situation is that we think that somebody else should do something about the strange person, someone with special knowledge who would know what to do. Strangeness does more than pique our curiosity; it bothers us. We want to understand the strangeness either because it interferes in some way with our activities or we want to be helpful to the strange person.

When we perceive someone as being different we do not necessarily think of the person as strange. For example, if you are a third grade teacher who, shortly after the beginning of the school year, finds that one of the pupils is reading Shakespeare and likes to solve problems in advanced geometry, you are likely to see that child as different rather than strange. You are also likely to be intrigued and positively attracted to the child, perhaps even delighted that you have a little genius to brighten your working hours. And you are not likely to feel the need to understand the child. You accept the child. But how are you likely to feel if the pupil tells you, directly or indirectly, that your interest is not appreciated and that the pupil would prefer to be left alone. Calling this behavior "different" is appropriate but obviously incomplete as a summary of your reaction. The child's behavior would strike you as strange not because it is different but because it presents you with the problem of how to think. Whereas you initially regarded the child positively, you now see the child in negative terms. In both instances our perceptions and actions are influenced by societal norms and our sense of understanding and competency. The characteristic of strangeness is not inherent in the child but derives from the interaction of the child, the place, the teacher, and features of the larger society. When we say the child is strange, we mean that we regard something about the child as "foreign" in some way. And to the extent that we are in a role requiring us to act in regard to others, as the teacher with the child, strange and puzzling behavior will engender negative feelings in us. We do not take kindly to those who complicate our lives. We tolerate both different and strange people as long as they do not interfere with our activities.

What we are suggesting is that our characterizations of other people and how we act in regard to them always reflect time, place, and societal values. There are, however, two unfortunate consequences. First, we tend to see our thoughts and actions as "caused" by the individual "out there" as if we were responding only to objective characteristics of the person. Second, we are unprepared for, indeed resist, new ways of thinking and acting that suggest that our view of reality might be faulty.

To illustrate these points, let us imagine that we are attending a meeting in 1950 to discuss how to render better services to mentally retarded individuals. There is general agreement that among the major ways of improving conditions would be more and better special classes and residential institutions. It would not be quite correct to say there was general agreement because the condition we call mental retardation requires us to set up segregated, protected places in which the adverse consequences of limitations of the condition are kept to a minimum. In other words, we do not create these places because we are punitive or because it makes life easier for us, but rather because individuals and the condition *require* such places. The nature of external reality *dictates* what we *must* do.

Now let us imagine that someone gets up at the meeting and says, "I disagree. I think we are being inhumane and unjust. We would like to believe that we are doing the only thing we can do, as if we had no alternatives, as if mental retardation were a characteristic uninfluenced by the values and organization of society. When we say that mentally retarded individuals *need* these places, we are blind to the fact that that is the way we have set things up. Why can't mentally retarded individuals be in regular classrooms? Why can't they be integrated into our communities instead of being sent to residential institutions? Why are these institutions usually in the middle of nowhere? I submit that mental retardation says as much about us as about them. We created the concept as much to preserve our *status quo*, to keep them as far away as possible, as to help them. We say that mentally retarded individuals have characteristics A, B, and C, and then we proceed to fulfill our self-serving prophecies. Can it be that we don't want to realize this? Can it be that when we say that they would be happier with 'their own kind,' we are saying they are foreign to us as human beings?"

The person who would have said this in 1950 would have been viewed as strange, and most of those listening to this person's "rantings" would have hooted the speaker into silence or left the meeting. Twenty-five years later these rantings became public policy. Yes, we now say, every effort should be made to integrate mentally retarded individuals into the regular classroom, and to keep them in the natural social community rather than institutions in which what they learn and experience almost guarantees that they will be unable to live in their homes and communities.

What happened to mental retardation? Did the nature of the condition change? Or did *we* and our *society* change in how we view mentally retarded individuals? The answer is that our society has changed. We have given up an old concept and created a new one, and this would not have been possible unless we recognized that mental retardation is a concept reflecting time, place, and society.

Action → Diagnosis → Action

Another way of clarifying how our conception of mental retardation reflects the nature of our society is by asking a deceptively simple question: Under what conditions does diagnosis take place? We have all had the experience of not feeling well; we have had a severe headache, a burning sensation in our stomach, or we could not sleep. There was a time in our society when people had remedies they had learned about from others, "home" remedies from people's social experience. So, even though people tended to be their own healers, their definition of illness and cure reflected a social component.

The diagnostic process is always a consequence of somebody saying that someone has something wrong with him. We put it in this way because frequently it is not the individual who decides to initiate the process. This is the case with children, but there are also times when adults are forced by pressure from others or by legal action to participate in the process. In all of these instances people individually or society in general communicate four ideas: something may be wrong with someone; our lives are being affected; we should find out the source of the trouble; and we should come up with solutions to alter the individual's status and allow us to experience our lives in the way we wish.

Although the diagnostic process is initiated for the welfare of an individual, we should not overlook that the lives of others have been adversely affected and they wish to change the course of events. They are, so to speak, hurting. The diagnostic process is not a response to the fact that an individual has symptoms A, B, or C, but to the reactions of those around him to those symptoms. These reactions always reflect socially influenced judgments which are time-bound.

Take, for example, a third grade teacher who discovers that one of the pupils can hardly recognize the letters of the alphabet. The teacher's initial reaction is likely to be a mixture of anger and puzzlement. Why have they given me a pupil who is so far behind in reading? What will I be able to do to help this child? The teacher decides to make a special effort to help the child but in the process begins to feel guilty about how much time this child requires. There are other children in the class with other types of problems who could benefit from special help. Furthermore, the teacher is becoming discouraged by the child's rate of learning. To cap it all, the child seems unable to form relationships with other children. Needless to say, the teacher begins to think there is something seriously wrong with the child and somebody had better find out what the trouble is. The child is strange and the total situation is upsetting. So the teacher refers the child for diagnostic study. This is a very shortened version of a complicated but familiar story but the point is that characteristics of the child did not lead directly to referral for diagnostic study but the interaction between those characteristics and the teacher. It is when the teacher's feelings of frustration mount, that the referral begins to be considered. So when we say that something is wrong with the child, we are incorrect if we intend to convey by such a statement that the problem inheres *in* the child. To say that is to say that the child would act and be reacted to in the same way in all situations. That is obvious nonsense. What would be more correct would be to say that what is perceived as the usual organization, activities, and goals of the classroom have been upset and someone in that situation has identified the source. These characteristics of classroom organization, activities, and goals are expressions of social values, traditions, and expectations.

What if the diagnostic study is carried out and the child is considered mentally retarded? It used to be the case that this meant it was in the best interests of the child to be removed from the regular classroom and placed in a special class, or special school, or some other special setting. These recommendations were in the "best interest of the child," and the fact that it was also considered in the best interest of the others in that classroom was usually not mentioned.

Diagnosis is not an empty exercise or ritual; it is a process arising from troubled social interactions and it is the basis for further action to eliminate the trouble. We place much emphasis on the fact that the diagnostic process is never initiated because an *individual* is a "problem" but rather because a social context has in some way been disrupted. The thrust of our emphasis can be illustrated in the difference between two statements: That person is a woman. That person has social characteristic X *because* she is a woman. The second statement "explains" the characteristic by reference to another characteristic of the person that is indisputable, thereby completely obscuring how the social characteristic is ultimately determined. So, it is only when women begin to act in ways opposite to that social characteristic that we realize how much of our conception of "women" was a cultural invention justifying, so to speak, the *status quo*. We also begin to realize that these kinds of cultural inventions have been a source of injustice.

Today there are many people who would object strenuously to removal of the child from the regular classroom and would buttress their argument in terms of the moral and educational development of the so-called normal children in that classroom. Today there are many schools "mainstreaming" mentally retarded children in opposition to the practice of placing them in small tributaries leading to isolation. What has changed? The nature of mental retardation or our ways of acting toward children who are so labeled? It should be obvious that mental retardation is not a "thing," not a set of characteristics inherent *in* an individual, but a concept that both describes and judges interactions of an individual, a social context, and the culturally determined values, traditions, and expectations that give shape and substance to that context at a particular time.

The Social Significance of Mental Retardation

The field of mental retardation is a good window through which to look at our society. No one would deny that our understanding of our society has changed by virtue of having been forced to look at it from various perspectives, such as through the eyes of various minority groups. We do not have to agree with any of these perspectives to recognize that their very existence says something significant about our society. This is no less true in the field of mental retardation. We have already indicated that changes in conceptions of and reactions to mentally retarded individuals are indicative of major societal changes. When we study mental retardation we are studying our own society and how and why it changes. When we ask why conceptions of mental retardation have changed, why public schools have been forced to develop programs for mentally retarded individuals who heretofore were not "eligible," why living in the community is now preferred to institutional placement, why law and the courts have come to play a crucial role in regard to mentally retarded individuals, why families with mentally retarded individuals differ markedly in coping with their problems—when we ask these questions, we are not only talking about mental retardation but about the nature, structure, and traditions of our society. We shall be discussing these issues throughout this book, but it may be helpful here to provide a particularly illuminating example.

In 1843, Dorothea Dix gave her famous speech on the inhumane conditions in the "humane" institutions of Massachusetts to the assembled state legislature. In 1967, Dr. Burton Blatt gave essentially the same speech to the same legislature! At the least, the two occasions should sensitize us to the difference between change and progress. The fact is that a lot of things have changed in a century, and a lot of well-meaning people have devoted themselves to improving the residential care of the mentally retarded as well as other dependent or handicapped groups, but the end result was another instance of the more things change the more they remain the same. To understand why this was so we cannot restrict our focus to mentally retarded people, the residential institution, and those who administered it. The very existence of these institutions (creations of government) bespoke widely held attitudes and values about what was "right and proper", i.e., what a just and humane society should do for handicapped people. No one has consciously sought to create conditions that were sadistic and evil, and yet time and again the end results were inhumane. Is part of the answer in the attitude that mentally retarded people were hopeless, helpless, and needed to be in protected settings, preferably as far as possible from "normal" society? Was this geographical separation society's way of not having to see "strange" people, some of whom literally looked strange? Is part of the answer in the implications of the view that these people were a burden, perhaps divinely ordained, on a sinful society? Is it in the view that the problem was custodial-medical and therefore not capable of being evaluated by the general public? The questions are many and the answers complex. So, when we discuss mental retardation we are talking about a concept that not only is a creation of that society but also illuminates that society as much as it does the objects of its concerns.

This is not peculiar to mental retardation. Take, for example, the change in society's view of alcoholism. The accepted view had always been that alcoholism was the moral weakness of individuals for whom sympathy was the last reaction a moral and religious society could justify. Alcoholism was a personal, family tragedy that had to be kept a secret if one wanted to avoid the scorn of a righteous society. In short, society not only defined alcoholism but took actions consistent with that definition. Today, our views are different and we look back at earlier times with an attitude of superiority because we say we now know that alcoholism is both a social and individual problem. Far from regarding it as a moral problem we are now told that it is a *disease,* one to which some people have a predisposition which may or may not be expressed, depending on social factors. The attitude of superiority is justified only to the extent that we have come to recognize the role of societal factors. But is it possible that defining alcoholism as a disease is society's way of adapting to the fact that millions of people have a drinking problem? In other words, by defining alcoholism as a disease, the role of our society in contributing to the ever increasing frequency of alcoholism is downplayed by defining the problem and its solution so that the spotlight is put on the relationship between alcoholics and professionals. As a consequence, the question of how our society should change is hardly confronted. It is safe to predict that several decades from now society will regard our present conceptions as no less naïve than we now regard those of several decades ago.

If the field of mental retardation is a window through which to study our society, not many people have taken advantage of it. It is certainly true that there are far more people interested in mental retardation than ever before. Educational programs of diverse kinds have escalated in number, as has research. Yet it is surprising how few people have concentrated on what mental retardation tells us about our society. There are at least two reasons for this. The first is that most people concentrate on how to help the mentally retarded individual. Such efforts can only be applauded, but we must recognize that such a concentration tends to divert attention away from the larger social context. The second reason is that those disciplines (e.g., sociology, anthropology) whose central concern is the nature of society have hardly had contact with the field of mental retardation. These disciplines have developed an enormous interest in psychologically troubled people, namely, so-called normal people whose lives have become disrupted and disrupting. But this interest in personal disorder has hardly been extended to the mentally retarded. This is not an oversight but reflects the history and traditions of these fields. This is but another way of saying that the values and priorities which characterize these fields reflect in their own ways values and priorities of our society, and mental retardation is far down on the priority lists. And yet, from any theoretical standpoint, there are no grounds for asserting that the field of mental retardation is less good a window through which to look on society than those provided by problems higher on the priority list. Indeed, one could argue that precisely because mental retardation has historically been low on the priority lists—a reject in the social science academic community—that it may lead us to some of the more illuminating insights into the nature of our society. What a society does not pay attention to can be no less revealing of that society than what it does pay attention to, as blacks and women can attest.

The Transactional Approach

If mental retardation as a concept inevitably reflects society at a particular time, how do we conceptualize its social nature so that we avoid the harm of an approach that sees mental retardation as characteristics of individuals? How do we approach the problem so that we can direct our efforts at remediation more broadly and successfully? Let us start with a paper by A. J. Sameroff in which he incisively illuminates the issues.

It has been estimated (Babson and Benson, 1971) that each year 300,000 children are born in the United States who will have varying degrees of mental retardation. In most cases, as Sameroff notes, the retardation cannot be ascribed to clearly genetic factors or signs of clear anatomical damage. This has long puzzled investigators who believe in the traditional "medical model."

> From this point of view, if a disorder exists, there should be some clear factor in the patient's history, preferably biological, which led to this disorder. If this factor could not be found, it was presumed that the diagnostic techniques were not yet sufficiently sophisticated to detect it. Such reasoning led Gesell and Amatruda (1941) to propose the concept of minimal cerebral injury as the perinatal cause of the learning disorder effect. The reason for not being able to show the existence of such injury is because it is, by definition, minimal, that is, undetectable. Pasamanick and Knobloch (1961) expanded the range of deviant developmental outcomes thought to result from minor central nervous system dysfunctions caused by damage to the fetus or newborn child. Their results led these authors to propose a "continuum of reproductive casualty." The term casualty referred to a range of minor motor, perceptual, intellectual, learning and behavioral disabilities found in children. In a review of their studies, Pasamanick and Knobloch (1966) reported that five later disorders were significantly associated with greater numbers of complications of pregnancy and prematurity. These included cerebral palsy, epilepsy, mental deficiency, behavioral disorders, and reading disabilities. In the comparisons, between groups of children with these disorders and controls, those having the most serious condition, e.g., cerebral palsy, were more sharply differentiated from control groups in the number of obstetrical complications than were those children who had the milder disorders, for example, reading disabilities.
>
> Retrospective studies such as those of Pasamanick and Knobloch have im-

plicated at least three factors in early development as related to later disorder: (1) anoxia, (2) prematurity, and (3) delivery complications [Sameroff 1975, pp. 4-5].

Sameroff points out that most of the studies implicating some form of brain damage as an etiological factor were retrospective in nature in that the investigator had already identified the people with the condition and then looked back into their early history to find "the cause." There are very serious methodological problems in retrospective studies, among the most important of which is that only those who have the later disorder are ever studied. Sameroff, therefore, pays special attention to recent prospective studies in which relatively large numbers of infants who had asphyxia at birth were followed up. The results are surprising to those who hold to the view that biological factors must be *the* most important, because these studies demonstrate that perinatal complications only influence later development on children raised in poor environmental conditions.

> How are we to understand a situation where perinatal complications only influence later development in children raised in poor environmental conditions? Even the retrospective data of Pasamanick, Knobloch, and Lilienfeld found that the proportion of infants having some complication increased from 5% in the white upper social stratum, to 15% in the lowest white socioeconomic group, to 51% among all non-whites. These data imply that the biological outcomes of pregnancy are worse for those in poorer environments. These outcomes are clearly not the result of the delivery complications themselves, since children with identical complications, raised in good environmental situations, show no consequences of these problems. It is also clearly not the result of the environmental situation, since children in these studies without complications raised in the poor environments did not show the same deviant outcomes evidenced by their affected neighbors [Sameroff 1975, p. 11].

Sameroff then proposes a transactional model in which a key feature is not only the effects of caretakers on a child but the effects of the child on the caretakers. We have long been aware that characteristics of parents impinge upon children, but it is only in recent decades that research (Thomas, Chess, and Birch, 1968) has demonstrated that characteristics of children affect parents. This is a two-way street called transaction.

Using the transactional model, Sameroff and Chandler (1975) were able to clarify some of the mechanisms behind child abuse: Not all abusive parents abuse *all* of their children, and not all parents with characteristics of abusive parents have abused their children. "It appears that certain children are selected for battering, or rather that certain children tend to elicit abusive behavior from their parents."* Klein and Stern (1971) found that many abused children had been born prematurely or had significant medical

*On July 10, 1977, on the CBS-TV program *Sixty Minutes,* parents who had abused their children were interviewed. Although no special note was made of it, it was clear that several of the parents abused one and not all of their children and that the parents were aware of this and could give reasons for their selectivity.

illnesses during infancy which may have served to deplete their parents' positive emotional resources. The fact that abusive parents have been found to be less intelligent, more aggressive, impulsive, immature, self-centered, tense and more self-critical than non-abusive parents does not ensure that they will abuse children. Sameroff concludes: "It appears that only when this kind of parent *transacts* with a child who is seen as making greater than ordinary caretaking demands that the parent becomes abusive. The child with the appropriate characteristics is necessary to complete the system."

Sameroff then goes on to describe the Rochester longitudinal study he is conducting with Melvin Zax (Sameroff & Zax, 1973). The reader is urged to consult this work because it reveals how many different factors have to be comprehended when one takes the transactional model seriously. More crucial than the number of factors is how from the perspective of the transactional approach one can see how such concepts as educational and economic status lose their abstract quality and take on a living reality. Instead of seeing only a *child,* one is always dealing with a social and interpersonal drama that unfolds over many acts having no intermissions.

> The continuum of reproductive casualty which was earlier thought to explain significant aspects of later developmental deviancy has been shown above to be an empty concept unless related to the subsequent caretaking environment in which the child is raised. Sameroff and Chandler (1975) have proposed that a new concept which they labeled the "continuum of caretaking casualty" is necessary to fully appreciate the developmental implications of perinatal complications. The continuum of caretaking casualty refers to a range of environments into which infants are introduced. At one end of the continuum the environment is so adaptive to the needs of the child that even the most distressed infant can achieve an adequate developmental outcome, while at the other extreme the environment is so disordered through emotional, financial, and social distress that even the best of infants can come to a bad end. The mother who can appreciate her child's development at a high level of sophistication is better equipped to make qualitative changes in her treatment of the child as the child's activities and requirements change with age. The mother who is restricted to more primitive levels of viewing her offspring enmeshes the child at later stages in obsolete social and affective relationships formed during infancy. [Sameroff 1975, pp. 25-26].

In presenting Sameroff's discussion we omitted saying why he wrote the paper, and that omission needs to be rectified now because it speaks to a truly basic issue.

He asks: "What does it mean to be a person?", and he notes that two answers are that a person is a "thing" and a person is a "human being." Obviously, he says, the answer is self-evident, "since none would admit or support the idea that people are things." And why not? Because, he says, there are two concepts of thingness that are objectionable: (a) "that if a thing doesn't work right it is because it is made wrong, and (b) that things don't change." *The thrust of his entire paper is to show that in fact our prevailing concepts of developmental anomalies unwittingly lead to regarding persons as things: something is wrong with the child and what is wrong will stay wrong.*

> When people are treated as if a constitutional or genetic deficit remains as an unchanging characteristic they are being treated as a thing. When any abnormality in functioning is treated as intrinsic to that person and taken out of the social and cultural context in which that person is living, that person is being treated as a thing. The ethical considerations of such depersonalization can be left to the humanists. Of concern here is the hard data of medical and psychological research. There has yet to be demonstrated a causal connection between a constitutional variable and any personality or intellectual developmental outcome. This may sound like a strong statement, but it characterizes the developmental data from myriads of longitudinal studies. Whenever retrospective research has pointed to a variable which was thought to be causal to some adverse behavioral outcome, prospective research has shown that individuals with exactly the same characteristics or experience have not had the adverse outcome. Whether the variable be poor genes, birth complications, or even psychosexual trauma, individuals with these same characteristics have shown not only a lack of later deviancy but often an increased competence (Garmezy, 1974). Why is it then that in the face of this negative data we continue to believe that premature children, difficult children, or handicapped children will all have poor developmental outcomes? I would suggest it is because we here do not have the necessary developmental perspective. As long as we believe that labels are received rather than given we will be confronted with this problem. When we come to see that not only is the label something we have attributed to the child but also the initial ingredient in a self-fulfilling prophecy, will we really come to the heart of primary prevention [Sameroff 1975, pp. 28-29].

Sameroff's conclusions are based on his quest to understand some longstanding clinical and research puzzles. His classifications have enormous significance for the field of mental retardation, especially in regard to actions we take toward those we label as mentally retarded. He is a researcher and theoretician but to those in roles requiring action there is the task of pursuing the implications of what he has said so well. Two questions immediately confront us. What are the implications of his position for defining mental retardation? What should be the relationship of the definition to the diagnostic process and remedial action? These questions we take up in the next chapter.

3

Definition, Diagnosis, and Action in Light of a Transactional Approach

A MODEST-SIZED BOOK would be required to describe the change in the definition of mental retardation in this century. On the surface, at least, controversy about definition centered on two issues. One of these has been the relative contributions of heredity and environment. Intelligence is almost always defined without formal reference to the relative contributions of heredity and environment. But what is striking from a historical perspective is that the appropriateness of these definitions becomes the center of attention whenever a heredity-environment controversy occurs. This was true at the turn of the century when the eugenics movement became fashionable; when somewhat later there was concern about the intelligence of immigrant groups; when intelligence test scores of soldiers in World War I were analyzed and publicized; when in the thirties research on the intelligence of identical and fraternal twins became the subject of academic and public debate; and when in the later thirties the effects of preschool programs on intelligence produced another debate. Definitions of intelligence were not hard to come by and they seemed to have both clarity and cogency, until their implications for social action became apparent.*

The most recent chapter on this aspect of the controversy erupted following Jensen's (1969) monograph in which he concluded that blacks did more poorly than whites on intelligence tests and in school achievement because of genetic differences. Criticisms of Jensen were of two sorts: his methodology, data, and statistical assumptions were faulty; and he grossly underestimated the effects of unfavorable past and present social conditions. With one exception, these criticisms were strikingly similar to those made in regard to Goddard's (1912) study of the Kallikak family. The exception was that more of

---

*For an extended historical discussion of this point, the reader should consult Chase's (1977) *The Legacy of Malthus: The Social Costs of the New Scientific Racism.*

Jensen's critics agreed with him that the heredity-environment dichotomy was a meaningful one, in that there was no basis for denying that whatever intelligence was, it was not exempt from genetic influences. Jensen's mistake, his critics said, was in misevaluating the relative contributions of genetic and environmental factors.

Sameroff's formulation of the transactional approach suggests that Jensen and many of his critics were conceptually misguided in exactly the same way that researchers and clinicians were, in regard to children with delivery and perinatal complications. The concept of a "continuum of reproductive casualty" assumed that children born with biological vulnerabilities later had intellectual difficulties; thus the central importance of the early vulnerabilities was underlined (Sameroff 1975). Sameroff not only emphasized what had long been known—that such a concept left many cases unexplained—but on the basis of studies by himself and others, he was able to show that the transactional formulation was both necessary and productive. It was necessary because it parsimoniously explained the heretofore puzzling exceptions to traditional formulations, and, productive, because it radically opened new paths to the study of people. From the transactional perspective, heredity and environment are never dichotomous. It can even be misleading to say they "interact" because that is more often than not interpreted in terms of effects of heredity *on* environment just as for so long we have paid attention to the effects of parents *on* children and virtually ignored the influence of children on parents. The transactional approach is always a two-way street. There is nothing in the transactional formulation that denies the existence and influence of genetic processes or the existence of a socially structured context populated by diverse people.

What it does deny is the logic of focusing on one or the other. They are different sides of the same coin. What follows from the transactional approach in regard to the Jensen controversy is the conclusion that the studies relevant to explaining black-white intellectual differences have not been done. That is to say, a definition of "intelligence" or intellectual retardation in terms of its nature and origins is at this point a dubious achievement at the least, and at worst another conceptual disaster. The immediate task is not one of definition but of studying the complexities of transactions over time with people, not a child or "things," in center stage, and from which we get a clearer delineation of the plot. Plots are always transactional.

Is it not both noteworthy and strange that to our knowledge there is not a single longitudinal study of a mentally retarded child that even begins to reflect a transactional approach? There are scores of studies in which mentally retarded infants and young children have been tested over a period of years, as Sameroff and others have pointed out. But collecting and analyzing test scores are a far cry from the transactional approach. We would contend that the absence of relevant studies is a reflection of definitions based on a concept of defect that attributes the characteristic to an *individual*, i.e., "something" in or about him. That is as justified as saying that stubbornness is a characteristic of an individual, something he carries around with him and emits to everyone in any and all situations as if he had been born that way. So, if an infant or young child is labeled as mentally retarded, he has "it." The "it" becomes the focus of interest and all else fades into the background. Mental retardation is not an "it." The Braginskys (1971) have put it well:

> what happens over and over is that the social factors seemed so vital are viewed solely in terms of their relationship to putative defects inside the retardate's head; not only intellectual defects, but emotional, interpersonal, motivational ones as well. The social variables, once assimilated into a defect model, are interpreted as etiological factors or "causes" of the deficiency, rather than being analyzed and understood in their own right [p. 28].

The Braginskys, like Sameroff, vehemently criticize traditional concepts and definitions, and present a number of ingenious and intriguing studies leading them to conclude that:

> the concept of mental retardation must be discarded entirely. It has no scientific value whatever, merely serving to obfuscate and distort the meaning of the behavior of the rejected child. It has no humanitarian value, but instead stigmatizes and victimizes youngsters for social events over which they have little or no control. Moreover, this concept has led to enormous expenditures of time, effort, and money in a useless search for psychic factors when the real problems exist in society [p. 176].

Let us now turn to another aspect of the Jensen controversy that illustrates the intimate relationship of definition, the search for causes, and societal actions and reactions. It would perhaps be more correct to say that controversy about definition and causes always peaks after the society reacts adversely to some of its policies. It is not fortuitous, for example, that the Jensen monograph was stimulated by widespread disappointment about the failure of compensatory education programs to produce higher IQs, higher educational achievement, and a lower incidence of mental retardation among blacks.

Having reviewed scores of studies, Jensen concluded that blacks were genetically different from whites in those cognitive processes required for traversing our educational system successfully. And if blacks did not do as well as whites on intelligence tests, it was because these tests were such good predictors of school achievement. Jensen's critics did not dispute either that blacks generally did more poorly on intelligence tests, or that the incidence of mental retardation among blacks was higher. What many critics objected to was Jensen's way of defining intelligence by test scores and, significantly, the implications of his conclusions for social policy. Obviously, if one agreed with Jensen one could not recommend continuation of compensatory programs in their customary form. The controversy was heated and multifaceted.

Two aspects of Jensen's monograph were given less attention than they deserved. The first was that the scores of studies Jensen reviewed were based on widespread acceptance of certain conceptions and definitions of intelligence and subnormal functioning. Jensen did not invent these conceptions; he was merely reflecting a widespread acceptance of certain theories and practices. So why the furor? What Jensen did was confront his critics with a choice: accept my conclusions or come up with a theory that explains the facts better. For the most part the critics were mired in the same conceptual morass as Jensen. They too defined intelligence as an "it" and if someone did not have "it" or very much of "it," that was, so to speak, *his* problem. The fact is that no critic could or did present a sophisticated transactional alternative, as Sameroff later did.

The other aspect of the controversy that was ignored was the ahistorical flavor of the criticisms. It could have been pointed out, as Sarason and Doris (1969) did at some length, that the same controversy with much the same arguments and polarizations took place in regard to different immigrant groups: Jews, Hungarians, Italians, and Russians. In 1913 and 1917, Goddard conducted studies of these immigrants and concluded that 80 percent were feebleminded! Later he reduced the estimate to 50 percent. Listen to Goddard address himself to the skeptical reader:

> Doubtless the thought in every reader's mind is the same as in ours, that it is impossible that half of such a group of immigrants could be feeble-minded, but we know that it is never wise to discard a scientific result because of apparent absurdity. Many a scientific discovery has seemed at first glance absurd. We can only arrive at the truth by fairly and conscientiously analyzing the data [Goddard 1917, p. 266].

After welcoming these immigrants to our shores, our society began to have doubts about the wisdom of its actions, and the movement to change the laws in order to restrict the quotas for Mediterranean people and increase quotas for Nordic people gained steam. It took more than four decades and a world war against an enemy committed to Nordic supremacy before the immigration laws were relaxed. But it was not only foreigners who were considered a threat to the quality of the natural intelligence; the poor, black and white, were always on trial for not having enough of "it."

When the compensatory programs begun in the sixties did not have the desired consequences, one could have predicted that there would be a backlash in the form of "blaming the victim" (Ryan, 1971). And one could also have predicted that another controversy would center on the definition of intelligence, the meaning of mental subnormality, and the relative importance of nature and nurture. If only we had a better definition of "it," if only we had better measures for "it," if only we better understood how genes determine the nature and limits of cognitive processes. If only our sampling procedures for population studies were less biased and more rigorous. If only our statistical theories and procedures were less controversial and better developed. If only we had better methods for isolating and measuring the impact of environmental variables. If only the controversy could be kept out of the crossfire of social and political warfare and cooly studied by dispassionate scientists committed to the truth. If only we could look at the facts uncontaminated by personal commitments or prejudices—the number of ifs were many.

Those who were pro-Jensen maintained that they were looking reality in the face, and disliking what they saw was irrelevant to acceptance of the truth. Those who were contra-Jensen maintained that he was looking at one aspect of reality to the neglect of others, and that what he considered reality had some of the characteristics of an inkblot. Surprisingly, no one seriously pursued Sameroff's question: Regardless of which side you are on, how do you explain the exceptions? Jensen could say that exceptions are plausible on the basis of what we know from genetic theory and studies in that they were exceptions because of something inside *them.* His critics could be gratified at the exceptions but they had no way of pursuing their potential significance.

Let us examine these issues from another vantage point. William James once said that to the newborn the world is a big, buzzing, blooming confusion. That made sense, especially if one had spent time observing infants in the first week of life. Their visual-perceptual apparatus was too underdeveloped to permit discrimination of form. Whatever characteristics this apparatus required to perceive form were absent; the organism lacked "what it takes." It took quite a while for investigators to ask if this conclusion was due to our lack of understanding and our failure to observe the transactions between the infant and its stimulus fields. Put in another way, the question to be asked was: if we do not understand the transactions between the infant and its perceptual world, if we have not learned to structure and manipulate those transactions, were we then justified in "blaming the infant" for not being able to discriminate form? When researchers began to examine in ingenious detail infant response to different shapes and forms—when it became possible to observe and manipulate this kind of transaction—it was established that in their earliest days infants were capable of making perceptual discriminations. What had previously been considered a characteristic of the infant turned out to be the result of our failure to take transactional approach seriously.

Transactional concepts are certainly not new and we emphasize Sameroff's work not only because it bears so directly on the purposes of this book but also because he has taken such an approach with such illuminating consequences. One could argue that one of Freud's major contributions was his transactional conception of the relationship between analyst and analysand. His concepts of transference and countertransference could only derive from a transactional view of relationships. The transactional approach, though not new, is antithetical to conceptions and practices that continue to dominate the field of mental retardation. Definitions of intelligence and, therefore, mental retardation have hardly reflected a transactional way of thinking. That inadequacy is not easy to remedy because it literally requires us to change our ways of perceiving. We must give up thinking of intelligence as a characteristic of individuals and, instead, learn how to pose questions in a transactional context.

We must observe a transaction and not an individual. For example, Sameroff (1975) reviewed studies on how the behavior of infants and very young children changed when a parent entered the room. In all of these studies one gets all kinds of descriptions about the child's behavior but nothing is ever said about the behavior of the parents. It is as if nothing in the behavior of the parent constitutes part of the transactional context for the child except mere presence.

We are not opposed to definitions in principle, but we are opposed to the lack of recognition that definitions tell us what to exclude as well as what to include. The thrust of this discussion is that by virtue of what definitions of intelligence and mental retardation have excluded, they have contributed to confusion and fruitless controversy. One can live with confusion and fruitless controversy were it not for the fact that these definitions give rise to techniques for measurement which in turn are used to determine policies that will affect the lives of people. In the areas with which we are concerned definitions have not been empty exercises. The quest for clear and rigorous definition was a consequence of society's need to act and to deal with what it had come to see as a problem. And if the definitions changed over time, it was less because of new knowledge and more because societal attitudes toward the problem had changed.

As we pointed out before with the changing definition of alcoholism, the change is far less because of new knowledge that has been gained and far more because of society's altered perception about the extent of the problem and the inadequacies of its past ways of reacting to it. And if that altered perception in turn reflects how health professionals have told the society how to define the problem, we should not blithely assume that their advice was based on compelling data or prejudice-free conceptions.*

Thus far, we have discussed how definitions about intelligence have been related to periodic debates on the relative contributions of heredity and environment to intelligence and mental retardation. Let us now turn to a second and related issue about definitions of intelligence: How do you measure it?

---

*The reader who is interested in pursuing these issues in another field should become acquainted with the writings of Szasz (1970, 1974, 1977), a psychiatrist and psychoanalyst. His argument is that the concept of mental illness is a social invention that serves to justify and perpetuate unwarranted diagnostic and custodial practices. There is a good deal of conceptual and moral overlap between what Szasz has written and the major themes of the present book.

The Pressures for Measurement

Controversy about the nature of intelligence has usually led to the development of new ways of measuring it. When critics pointed out that procedures requiring individuals to comprehend and reply in a certain language gave a distorted and narrow picture of intelligence, nonverbal tests were developed. When critics noted that there were aspects of intelligence that could be better assessed by observing individuals in normal social-developmental tasks or situations rather than relying exclusively on problem-solving in the usual test situation, we got Doll's (1935) Vineland Social Maturity scale. This scale was not meant to supplant intelligence tests such as the Binet or its descendants, but to reflect better the scope and manifestations of intelligence. When other critics pointed out that intelligence did not stop developing in adolescence as the early intelligence tests seemed to suggest, new tests such as the Wechsler Adult Intelligence Scale (1958) appeared and tried to reflect the cogency of this criticism. A plethora of new tests emerged when applications from the burgeoning field of statistical theory and analysis demonstrated that the most frequently used tests were inadequately sampling what they said they were sampling; and that they were also sampling intellectual "factors" of which the test developers were not aware.

Guilford (1956) was a leader in this attack on conventional definitions and measurement of intelligence. In part because of Guilford's massive criticisms of existing conceptions and tests, tests of creativity were developed to remedy the almost complete neglect of this factor in the most widely used intelligence tests. And in response to the criticism that existing tests of intelligence were permeated by cultural material and values, "culture fair" or "culture free" tests appeared.

Anyone who sets for himself the task of collecting, describing, and critiquing intelligence tests either currently in use or advertised for use has staked out at least half of a career. In the face of such a bewildering array of tests, conceptions, and criticisms, it is understandable if one concludes that far from being naked the emperor not only has a surfeit of clothes but he is wearing them all at the same time. This is said to suggest that as one gets overwhelmed perusing test after test and tries to organize the various underlying conceptions into some coherent framework, one may well conclude that the concept of intelligence has all the characteristics of an inkblot onto which people have projected meanings on the basis of which they wish to urge other people to see what they see, to "measure" it in the same way they do. In fact, the situation is so analogous to a Tower of Babel that one is justified in thinking that Jensen's monograph and the ensuing controversy have been either monumental obfuscation of issues or equally monumental presumption. As a colleague once put it:

You would think that when people talk about the relative contributions of heredity and environment to intelligence, there was a fair agreement about what intelligence is and how you measure it. We should be thankful to Jensen that he managed, unwittingly, to teach us otherwise. Whatever criticisms have been directed at Jensen in regard to definition and measurement of intelligence can also be directed at most of his critics.

Let us try to take a small step out of this confusion by asking: Why would anyone want to define and measure intelligence? This may seem to be a question to which there should be a relatively simple answer, until one asks a second question: Why is it that attempts to formally define and measure intelligence are very recent in human history? How did we get along without such attempts? What gave sanction to such attempts? To most readers the name Alfred Binet is a familiar one. They may know that his was the first standardized intelligence test to receive international recognition and acceptance. In the United States, in particular, his tests had quite an impact and he was paid the compliment, if not of slavish imitation, of acknowledgement that what he did provided the basis for later versions of the "Binet." Goddard, Kuhlmann, Terman—these figures who played such a crucial role in transforming and developing Binet's tests, and in seeking public acceptance of them—never denied their debt to Binet. Unfortunately, by acknowledging Binet's accomplishments they were right for the wrong reasons.

Binet had many intellectual interests which ran counter to the prevailing academic orientations of his time. It was not so much that the procedures or substance of his research were atypical but rather his fascination with the question of individual differences. For example, in 1903, he did long and painstaking experiments on tactile thresholds, which was then a fashionable and conventional research area. But, unlike others, Binet was fascinated by the variety of individual differences he observed, even in such a simple process as determining tactile thresholds. Binet understood that to the activity of an individual's taking in sensations there must be added the inseparable process that is:

> properly called judgment . . . with its operations of *inventiveness, adjustment,* and *realization* that cut into the sensation and modify it profoundly. . . . The stimulus receives the imprint of each personality. . . . External perception does not dominate us; it is rather *we, intelligence,* that dominate it [Binet quoted by Wolf, 1973, p. 160].

Contained in that statement is the spirit of the transactional approach: the individual is not only affected by external stimuli but affects those stimuli. In 1903 Binet saw intelligence not as a thing, or an amount, or something "inside" a person, but an active transaction between individual and external stimuli. It is reading too much into Binet to say that he understood the implications of a transactional approach. He saw the issues far more clearly in relation to things than to human transactions, but he grasped the principle that each of us seeks to change our world at the same time we are changed by it.

> We are a bundle of tendencies; and it is the resultant of all of them that is expressed in our acts. . . . It is, then, this totality that must be evaluated. . . . The mind is one, despite the multiplicity of its faculties; it possesses one essential function to which all the others are subordinated. . . . Considered independently from phenomena of sensitivity, emotion, and will, *the intelligence is before all a process of knowing that is directed toward the external world, that works to reconstruct it in its entirety, by means of the little fragments that are given to us.* . . . Since all this ends up in inventing, we call the whole work an *invention,* which is made after a *comprehension* . . . that necessitates a *direction.* . . . It must be judged in relation to the end pursued; therefore, we must add *criticism.* Comprehension, inventiveness, direction, and criticism: intelligence is contained in these four words [Binet quoted by Wolf, pp. 204–205; emphasis in original].

When Binet says "this totality must be evaluated," he was reflecting that although we may have words like intelligence and personality, they do not refer to separable processes. Binet fought the "faculty psychology" of his time on two bases: it separated processes that in reality were inseparable, and it rendered hopeless explanations for individual differences. In the quest to divine the different faculties of the mind, the psychology of Binet's time managed the difficult feat of not studying people.

For Binet intelligence was not a fixed amount, a constant, or some Platonic bounded essence. Intelligence was "educable." He advocated a "mental orthopedics" that:

> teaches children to observe better, to listen better, to retain and to judge better; they gain self-confidence, emulation, perseverance, the desire to succeed and all the excellent feelings that accompany action; they should especially be taught to will with more intensity; to will, this is indeed the key to all education [Binet quoted by Wolf, p. 207].

As Wolf rightly notes:

> Even as early as 1896 he [Binet] was seeking ways to determine "the organization of intellectual functions in different cultural milieus, including national cultures, [and] socioeconomic levels." He also sought to know what might be the effects of "typical problem-solving styles . . . or response styles" on mental organization when in 1903 he made the masterful study of his daughters' habitual orientations of thought. Furthermore, his certainties about the pervasive nature of the emotions on intellectual acts can be translated into the current belief that "the separation between abilities and personality traits is artificial and the two domains need to be rejoined in interpreting an individual's test scores." His penchant for improvement strongly suggests that he would have deplored "the built-in inertia of tests," perhaps especially of his own. Indeed, the fact that so many of his ideas emerge as important problems a half-century after his death underlines the unhappy conclusion that his disciples often failed to appreciate, perhaps even to

understand, the real bases for Binet's psychological methods and thought. [Wolf, pp. 217-218].

Wolf is quite correct in saying that Binet's disciples often failed to appreciate the real bases for his methods and thought. The fact is that Binet's "followers," particularly in the United States, were caught up in a confusion between technology and science, between measurement and meaningful rigor, between method and substance. The particular means whereby one studied a problem became so absorbing and complex that it was not long before the original problem was drowned in a sea of measurements. Seizing upon the need for measurement, they were blind to the complex issues which alone could give significance to their efforts. Binet had all kinds of qualms about a possible pseudo-precision in his scale, but never could Binet be accused of denigrating precise measurement. His qualms stemmed from the strong belief that his scale lacked the substance and scope required by his conception of intelligence in action.

How could such a belief withstand the Goddards and the Termans whose concerns for rigor and precision in measurement were uncluttered by the thoughtfulness of a Binet? If American psychology celebrated Terman and his achievements, it was because his work had all the apparent trappings of the scientific mind: standardization of procedures, precision in measurement, quantification, replicability, and validity. Binet may have originated the scale but it was an American scientist who *really* developed its potential. Was not what Terman did scientific progress?

Among those who participated in the development of intelligence tests, it is unlikely that anyone rivals Binet for his firsthand, investigative experiences with diverse populations. One may wonder how many and what types of people Terman himself studied. This is not intended as an *argumentum ad hominem* but rather to suggest that the overevaluation of technique and measurement is a dangerous business, usually with two victims: the investigated and the investigator. That has not been an infrequent occurrence in American psychology.

These critical comments require that we emphasize two other characteristics of Binet. The first is that he understood that neither the definition and measurement, nor judgments of intelligence were independent of society. Intelligence was action and transaction and it never developed in a social vacuum. And society acts on its judgments, usually unaware of how permeated with the culture these judgments are. The concept of intelligence is given a mythical objectivity as if it were independent of the culture.

The second of Binet's characteristics we emphasize is his sensitivity to injustice in the service of societal traditions and the status quo. We all know that Binet was asked by the French government to develop means for identifying mentally retarded children in the public schools and to recommend educational programs. One of the truly illuminating aspects of Wolf's book is the description of Binet's role in forcing the authorities to act. Long before he was commissioned by the authorities, he had been publicly expressing his moral indignation concerning the educational neglect and maltreatment of mentally retarded children. Far from denigrating the mentally retarded, or viewing them as a source of pollution in the educational milieu, Binet fought for the retarded child to be treated no less humanely than other children. Binet was quite an organizer of effective pressure groups. In seeking to bring about change, Binet was forcing society to recognize that morality, as well as intelligence, as the society defined them, were interrelated in ways that society preferred not to confront. Lest this sound too general or fuzzy, let us listen to the following from Wolf (1973):

> Along with the warnings about pitfalls in selecting special class pupils, Binet added others of a completely different nature: there were teachers, he said, who would try to get rid of annoying pupils by recommending them for these classes; others who were unconvinced that the backward students were anything other than lazy; teachers of special classes who would retain pupils now ready to return to regular classes, in order to maintain their enrollment levels; parents who wished to "protect" their children, or, on the other hand, who wanted to take advantage of getting rid of them in special residential schools, and so on. In other words, he had found mixed motivations for the "identification" of children for special education [p. 306].

These words describe a man who knew that far from being an "it" inside a person, intelligence was action, comprised of people, a social structure, traditions, and values. Binet not only understood the culture of the school but also how that culture shaped the actions and status of those who were in it, for good or for bad. If Binet considered intelligence as "educable" — rather than a fixed amount of a "thing" — it was not because he thought there were no limits or individual variations in potential; rather his conception of intelligence was one in which there was constant interplay between "inside" and "outside." And in the case of the school that interplay could have adverse affects. For Binet, special classes were not an end in themselves because he knew how their existence could be used, wittingly or unwittingly, to produce interplays of an adverse sort for individuals. Like the traditional conceptions of intelligence, special classes existed in and were shaped by their surroundings; they did not have an independent existence.

In addition to being a superb observer, Binet was also a splendid clinician for whom the diagnostic process centered on the individual and his surroundings. Diagnosis was not for administrative purposes but for the beginning of a remedial process that never lost sight of the fact that it was a process in which one sought to understand and change the nature of interplays between the individual and his surroundings. To change the *site* of the interplays was easy. To change their *nature* was another matter because that involved taking "mental orthopedics" seriously. This is another way of saying that we take individual differences seriously.

For Alfred Binet the major function of testing was its basis for educational planning and practice. Binet was not a tester; he was a developmental psychologist whose work had to have practical consequences for the education of children. He worked in schools, he worked with teachers, he worked with parents, and he organized what today we would call community organizations. He was a scientist, but he was also an activist. He was a researcher, but he was also a clinician. The center around which all of these roles were organized was the individual and the most important question was how to educate. Binet took individual differences seriously, and that is the reason he took a dim view of premature quantification—he knew very well that a score on his scale obscured the fact that the scale was far from comprehensive, and that what it left out was of practical significance for what one planned for children.

Binet in *his* role as a psychologist did not restrict himself to testing and report writing. Testing was not an end itself but rather a beginning which would end in the classroom. How would Binet have reacted to a situation where the school psychologist rarely went into a classroom either before or after testing a child? Could he have conceived of the not-infrequent situation where the school psychologist is unwelcome in the classroom? Would he have understood how it can happen that the school psychologist might not even know the consequences of testing, or that teachers might never see the report? Would he have understood why the school psychologist exists primarily to perform some administrative-legal functions—a dispatcher into this or that special class or program, or into this or that school—rather than as someone vitally concerned with what happens to *individuals?* Would Binet, who was such an acute observer and interpreter of individual differences, have supported a role primarily concerned with norms, groupings, and scores? Would Binet, who seemed to have an understanding of the tensions and special interests that characterize the school and adversely affect the fate of a child, have looked kindly on a school psychology which was narrow in function and power?

We have not dwelt at some length on Binet to correct the record. Theta Wolf's book has done that. Our aim has been to underline that the movement to define and measure intelligence reflected societal needs. It did not just happen. It was an effort to react to a newly perceived social issue. Society determined that intelligence should be formally defined and measured. Binet in this respect reflected his times, but it is ironic that those same times distorted his conceptions, accepting his methods and ignoring his thoughts and values, all in the service of what appeared to be objective, value-free scientific method and progress.

The difference between what Binet stood for and how he was interpreted can be illustrated by analogy. Several decades ago the world's record for running the mile was several seconds above four minutes. Each time the record was lowered by a fraction of a second one could always count on some people saying that the ultimate had been achieved. If those people had been told that in the not too distant future the sub-four minute mile would be a frequent occurrence, they would have reacted with disbelief. How do we explain what happened in the intervening decades? For one thing, there had to be people who believed that the record could be lowered and that more penetrating experimentation with the task, leading to new conceptions of training, would provide the key. Obviously, they believed there were limits but, equally, they did not believe that existing knowledge justified the conclusion that those limits had been reached. They developed, so to speak, a "sporting orthopedics."

Binet viewed intelligence in action in much the same way. The task was not to determine what an individual could or could not do but rather to understand the individual so that one had a basis for changing conditions in order to favorably alter his performance. Binet was not a rampant optimist or an indiscriminate environmentalist. Intelligence was forged and manifested by action, by commerce with an environment never the same for two people or even for one person over time. If we understood the dynamics of that commerce we would be on the road to altering that commerce in ways more favorable to the individual.

At the end of the previous chapter, we raised two questions: why define intelligence and mental retardation? Why measure them? We can now formulate an answer: in the realm of human behavior and actions, the need to define and measure always reflects dominant social needs as the society at the time perceives them, and these perceptions are inevitably colored by moral or value judgments. Neither the substance of definitions nor the types of measuring devices to which they give rise are neutral, dispassionate affairs, although the effectiveness with which the culture transmits these dominant perceptions to us ordinarily obscures how rooted in the culture we and the definitions are. What we take to be "natural" and objective is not free from the influences of social time and place. What we are taught to consider as enduringly objective and realistic about people in general and certain groups in particular turns out to have "subjective" features against the recognition of which we as individuals and society as a collectivity ordinarily erect strong barriers.

The definition and measurement of intelligence and mental retardation are clear examples of what we just said, but they are by no means the only ones. For example, in the last ten years there has been a veritable explosion of publications describing, criticizing, and reformulating the nature of sex differences (Maccoby and Jacklin, 1974). What is the "essential" nature of women? What is the "essential" nature of men? What is the relation of time, place, and era to perceived differences between them? For centuries those questions received seemingly clear answers, ordained not by society but by the dynamics and vagaries of human evolution. There were always some people, however, for whom these answers, far from being clear or valid, were blatantly prejudicial and reflected social rather than biological evolution.

Today, of course, these answers are under assault precisely because our definitions and methods of assessing maleness and femaleness were far more valid reflections of our culture and society than of the "essences" of the two sexes. And the more investigations of sex differences have been done, the less our certainty about how we should think. So, in her review of the Maccoby and Jacklin book, Block (1976) states:

> Early assessments of sex differences by Maccoby and others also evaluated the empirical literature and reached conclusions quite different from those embodied in the current Maccoby and Jacklin appraisal. The erosion in the evidence for sex differences over the past decade raises questions both puzzling and profound.

The same situation characterizes our definition and assessment of "normal" and "abnormal" sexuality. Money (1976) has put it well:

> Periodic changes in scientific theory are irregular and follow unascertained laws of the sociology of knowledge. Sexual theory in psychology and psychiatry is at present in the throes of an intellectual earthquake. The shifting tectonic plates that generated this social earthquake have been the black liberation movement in the United States, the women's liberation movement in western culture, the gay liberation movement in Europe and the United States, and the Cultural Revolution of Red Guard youth in China. The fixed tectonic plate against which the shifting ones collided is the movement, mostly within communism, whereby political dissidence may be equated with psychopathology, and dissidents are given a psychiatric nosological label and locked away as though in prison.

> In the United States, the psychiatric revolt against nosological labeling in its extreme form declares that there are no psychiatric disorders, but only stigmatizing and pejorative labels whereby society imposes its intolerance of idiosyncracy, eccentricity, and nonconformity.

As another example, take the radical transformations that have occurred among religious people as to the nature of God and man. By their very nature religions stand for immutable truths providing man-made explanations for why things are and have become what they are, and yet if anything is obvious it is how mutable religion has been in the cauldron of society.

As a final example, there is the fascination that people have had with Itard's *The Wild Boy of Aveyron* (1932), first published in 1801. The subject of his study was a boy, eleven or twelve years of age, who for a period of years presumably had been living in the woods having no contact with other people. On one occasion he had been seen completely naked seeking acorns and roots to eat. In 1799, he was seized by three sportsmen. He was brought to Paris and seen by the famous authorities of the day. Some pronounced him an incurable idiot, others thought him a fake, while others saw him as an example of what man would be like if deprived of language. The boy, Victor, was the center of controversy on two grounds. In those days of the Enlightenment when the forces of research were waging war against religion and superstition, and the perfectibility of man was thought to be both possible and in sight,

Victor represented a challenge to competing conceptions of the nature of man. Also, if Victor could be trained and educated, the results would throw light on these competing conceptions. Itard believed that Victor's condition was due to lack of intercourse with people. His book is an enthralling account of his work with Victor. Why in the intervening scores of decades have so many people analyzed and reanalyzed Itard's account? (The most recent and most comprehensive analysis was in 1976 by Lane.)

The reasons are many but certainly among the most influential is that each era develops its conception of the nature of man and his abilities and feels called upon to reinterpret Itard's educational-therapeutic efforts and demonstrate how Itard was a prisoner of *his* times. The account of Victor has some of the characteristics of an inkblot in that each era seems to project onto the account its distinctive conceptions. What was true for Itard and his times is no less true for us and our times. This should be neither disheartening nor surprising when it is the nature of man and his abilities that is in the spotlight.

Mental retardation is a concept indicating that by the performance standards of his or her social context an individual is judged inadequate; this inadequacy is sufficiently troublesome to those in that context to warrant actions to achieve three purposes: to keep performance standards intact, to reduce or eliminate the discomfort of those who are troubled by the individual's inadequacy, and to be helpful to the individual as help is defined by the moral-ethical values of that social context. In practice, the source of the individual's inadequacy is seen as within him, some kind of mental inadequacy preventing him or her from meeting performance standards deemed necessary, fair, and normal by that social context. At different times in the life of that social context the concept of mental retardation may change, and radically, as performance standards are perceived differently, as any or all of the purposes of action are reformulated, and as the relationship between the source of inadequacy in the individual and the social context undergoes change. It is ironic and instructive how quickly the societal picture changes during wartime. For example, during World War II, women, old people, physically handicapped individuals; and many so-called mentally retarded people (including some in institutions) found employment opportunities that were closed to them during peacetime. When the needs of society change, especially as they do with the onset of a war, society's accustomed way of defining and responding to certain groups can change dramatically. When the war situation is over, there is usually a partial reversion to the old ways.

Mental retardation is quintessentially a social rather than an individual concept implicating the individual and his social context. It is not an etiological concept illuminating the transactions specifically accounting either for the individual's perceived inadequacy or for the characteristics of the social context. It is a concept developed in response to perceived social problems and used to justify action. Perhaps the most frequent action taken in the social context is the process we call diagnosis, the attempt to describe, understand, and assess as a basis for action.

Diagnosis is a pathology-oriented process activated by someone who thinks something is wrong with somebody else. As we shall see in the next chapter, the perspective we have adopted casts the diagnostic process in a more problematic light than we ordinarily see it. Precisely because it is action, the diagnostic process allows us to intuit the springs of action which, not surprisingly, reveal the role of tradition and value judgments. It is a process in which objectivity and precision are sought, but it is a process permeated with personal values and judgments.

4

The Social Context
of Diagnosis

ORDINARILY WE THINK of clinical diagnosis as a process geared to making an assessment of an individual who has come for help. It has often been said that the *sine qua non* of the clinician is that he does his best on the basis of his knowledge and experience to help another person with his or her problems, and the nature of the help derives from a searching attempt to organize data and observation about the nature, significance, and probable course of the individual's symptoms. Diagnosis is a serious affair precisely because it is the basis for recommended action that will influence the life of a human being. This characterization of diagnosis holds regardless of whether the person comes on his own to the clinician or is brought by others.

However, when a child is brought by others to the clinician the diagnostic process perforce has two parts: a first one during which the clinician focuses directly on "the patient," and a second part in which the clinician seeks information from those who brought the individual. Because the information these people provide reflect far more than "facts" about the child—inevitably reflecting the personal-familial impact of the child—the diagnostic process is a social one in that it involves more than an *individual*. This is obvious enough but as we shall soon see the implications of the social context of diagnosis are rarely drawn and acted upon. The entire diagnostic process tends to be carried out as if only *one* individual required assessment and help, as if the locus of the problem inhered "in" him or her; whatever the consequences of "his" problem, they are of secondary significance, however upsetting or disruptive to others.

Diagnosis is seen as a drama having a beginning and an end, with several acts in between. Like all drama, however, it soon becomes obvious that we are witnessing events, thoughts, and interactions related to the past, present, and future. As a production a drama does have a beginning and an end, but by the end the audience knows that there is no end just as it learned that there really was no one beginning point. Similarly, by the end of the diagnostic drama, the cast of characters is pointed to a future shaped by

40

knowledge about the near and distant past. The analogy between the diagnostic process and a theatrical drama is that there is a cast of characters whose lives are interrelated. There is more than one character in the cast and it is the diagnostician's task to make sense of how the web of relationships has altered as a result of events. The question, of course, is what makes "sense," — what convinces us that we understand why things happened as they did to produce the dilemmas of choice in action.

Let us discuss the social context of diagnosis, of its "dramatic" qualities, with an example using a small cast of characters.

A Retarded Newborn

Alice and Harold have been married for five years. Alice has been a schoolteacher and her husband a graduate student in anthropology. When they married they knew they could not have a child for several years and that Alice would have to work until Harold finished his doctorate and had a job. Alice never saw herself as a full-time mother and housewife but she was prepared, depending on circumstances and economics, to be at home until their child was of nursery school age. Both of them came from modest-sized families with modest financial resources. Their families lived in very different parts of the country quite far from the couple. Two years before their child was born Harold was nearing the end of his graduate work and had good reason to believe that he would receive a university position. The question in their minds was whether to have their first child before they moved or after they were settled in the city where Harold's position would be. Alice was then thirty-one years of age, and Harold, twenty-nine. Both, particularly Alice, were anxious about the effects of her age on childbearing and wished to try to have a child as soon as possible. Harold felt that the turmoil that was to be expected in moving with a very young child argued against Alice's understandable anxiety and desire. Besides, he argued, if the child were born during the crucial phases of dissertation writing, he could be helpful to Alice but perhaps at the expense of not finishing his dissertation on time. As it turned out, their decision to try to have the child early foundered on the fact that Alice did not conceive until five months before they were to move. Four months after they had settled into their new quarters they became the parents of a girl. The delivery was uneventful.

There was, however, a "problem" of which neither Harold nor Alice were aware. That is to say, this was not a problem the parents were bringing to the pediatrician but rather one that the latter discerned very soon after the child's birth. The infant's cries were weak, some expected reflexes were absent, and she had trouble sucking and taking nourishment. No one "symptom" was flagrant but in combination they made the pediatrician quite uneasy. He was convinced that something was radically wrong although the symptoms fell into no recognizable or established syndrome.

The pediatrician was quite upset. Why? That may seem like a silly question, but how one answers it has enormous consequences, not the least of which involves what we traditionally mean by diagnosis. Many things were bothering him about the infant: What caused the child's condition? Why did her listlessness and unresponsiveness persist? For how long should he keep the infant for observation in the hospital nursery? In his discussions with the parents he had no basis for assuming that something untoward had happened to the mother or that their genetic history should be suspect. If, as the pediatrician feared, this was a retarded infant, how serious would the retardation be? His guess was that the retardation was and would be of a serious degree.

In truth, the pediatrician was less bothered by these questions than by others: What should I tell the parents? When? How much? With what degree of certainty? How would the parents react? How do I handle the inevitable tears and despair? And all those questions about how to react to the child? What a shame and mess! Two nice people like that to have a retarded child! These questions and reactions are no less diagnostic in nature than those asked only about the infant. But they are not about neurological, developmental data. They are about a social-interpersonal situation that will obviously be changed drastically when knowledge about one of the cast is communicated to the others. What is bothering the pediatrician is that he feels far less secure and competent to handle *that* kind of diagnosis than when he focuses only on the infant. He can look at the infant, test her reflexes, get laboratory data on biological-chemical functioning, alert nurses to a special kind of record-keeping, try different types of stimulation, and bring in consultants to check his diagnostic formulation.

But how does one diagnose what kind of parents one is dealing with as a basis for action? Now, if we were to ask the pediatrician what he meant by diagnosis, he would describe for us what he did that led to his diagnosis of the infant. He would not label the questions he had about the parents as similarly reflecting a diagnostic process, one no less thorny and complex than "physical" diagnosis. He would see his task, albeit an unpleasant one, as communicating a diagnosis about the infant. The consequences of that communication, the basis on which it is justified, as well as its implicit connection with a picture of the future, are not conceptualized as a diagnostic process. We shall have more to say about this in later chapters. Suffice it to say here that physicians proudly proclaim that their expertise is in relation to a patient, or a part of the patient, not to the social-familial context in which patients play out their lives. We prize specialization highly, but it takes an instance such as we have described to realize that in restricting the conception of diagnosis to a process between a professional and a patient we pay a high price. Such a conception does not mirror the realities of social living, even though conventional practice does violence and injustice to those realities.

Let us now turn to some of the ways pediatricians, or any other type of professional, communicate the diagnosis of mental retardation to the infant's parents. Our interest here is to elucidate some of the characteristics and effects of their social diagnosis, such as their assessment of the past, present, and future of a social context, and how that assessment justifies their definition of help.

1. The "whole" truth. The physician feels obligated to tell the parents precisely what his diagnostic conclusions are and that in his judgment the child will always be retarded. Parents, he feels, should know the truth and begin the difficult process of coming to grips with it and choosing among alternatives for action. It is the physician's job to answer all questions about what to do and how to do it, but it is the parents who must make final decisions. The physician is never neutral; he knows what he would do if he were in the parent's place but he must refrain from influencing decisions. There are no data about how well these physicians maintain neutrality. There are physicians who deliberately eschew neutrality for two reasons: They assume they know what is best and they believe that in these crisis situations parents are unable to make decisions rationally. So, if the physician believes the child should go home with the parents, he will say so, even though the parents feel otherwise. Similarly, if he believes that for the good of the parents and future children, the child should be institutionalized, he will say so, usually cataloguing the obstacles to normal living in rearing such a child. And, let us not forget, there are physicians who, in very severe cases of retardation, will suggest that no special efforts be made to keep the infant alive.

2. The "partial" truth. Here the physician tells the parents that the child does not seem to be normal but it is far too early to tell to what degree, if any, the infant's development will continue to be problematic. "Let's play it by ear and see what happens." The most frequent basis for this stance is that parents have to learn by direct experience the degree and consequences of the child's impairments. By learning the truth in this way they will make their own decisions, and in the long run that is far more healthy than following other people's recommendations or having to be persuaded to consider a particular course of action.

3. Conceal the truth. If by the time the mother and infant are ready to leave the hospital the family has not raised questions about the infant's developmental status, some physicians will say little or nothing and wait to see what is brought up at the first office or hospital check-up. Here too, the belief is that it is best to deal with issues arising from parents' experience.

If the appropriate studies were available, we could undoubtedly come up with finer descriptions and categories, but our experience indicates that for our purposes in this chapter, little is lost. *Behind all the ways physicians view the retarded infant is the assumption that it creates a social-interpersonal disaster. This "diagnosis" says far more about the value systems of our society than it does about the retarded infant.* There are cultures that would not view this infant in such catastrophic terms, and even within our own culture families differ in how much of a catastrophe they would perceive. The fact that the physicians' view does reflect a widely accepted set of values must not obscure its consequences: the turmoil it engenders in the physician, and the effects of this on his actions and definition of help. It is fair to say that the view of the modal physician stems far more directly from *his* value system than it does from anything we would dignify as social-interpersonal diagnosis.

On their own, Alice and Harold surmised by the fifth day that something was wrong but, nevertheless, when the pediatrician told them of the diagnosis of severe retardation it had predictably catastrophic effects. After all, here were two highly educated, professional people who had the usual plans and fantasies about what their child would be. Like so many of us in our society they set great store on educational achievement, professional status, and independent living. To be told that their child would be unable to go the "onward and upward" route was bitter news. They (Harold particularly) quickly came to see the possible implications for their daily lives and professional careers. Understandably, they were beginning to mourn the death of *their* plans and fantasies, and only secondarily were they concerned with their infant's fate.

This in no way should be construed as criticism of Alice and Harold but rather as a demonstration of how the diagnosis of individual retardation takes place and alters an ongoing set of relationships. From the very beginning, the diagnostic process is social and cultural in nature and consequence. If it is traditionally presented as an objective process uncontaminated by judgment and values, not suffused with feeling and cultural givens, it is not the first time that we have been led to confuse description with reality. As long as we restrict our conception of diagnosis to that which one individual "does" in regard to another, we cannot appreciate how from beginning to end everyone in the drama, especially the diagnostician, is sensitive to its social context. His sensitivity, however, rarely extends to the recognition that the criteria with which he is familiar for individual diagnosis should also hold for his inevitable but rarely formulated social-interpersonal diagnosis.

Conventional individual diagnosis involves more than observing, collecting facts, and making judgments according to standardized scales. In instances where serious pathology is suspected the diagnostician will seek ways to deliberately intervene (e.g., biologically, chemically, surgically) in order to better ascertain the stability and validity of the individual's symptoms. He will perform experiments, so to speak, to find out the conditions under which the individual's status can be desirably altered. His diagnosis does not rest on conditions as they are but also on what they might be through strategic efforts at manipulation. In the case of Alice and Harold's infant, the pediatrician tried numerous strategies aimed at altering the infant's sluggish behavior and he was able to bring about and sustain some improvement, albeit slight. One might characterize this diagnostic process as one which assesses the extent of the discrepancy between what is and should be and seeks to determine how influenceable that discrepancy is. The aim of diagnosis is not to append a label on someone but to formulate the nature of symptom relationships that can serve as a basis for helpful action. The boundaries between diagnosis and treatment are far more in our language than they are in the realities of practice and action.

The Diagnosis of a Social-Interpersonal Catastrophe

The pediatrician predicted rightly that Alice and Harold would react as though faced with a catastrophe. This prediction rested less on any knowledge about their personalities or their interpersonal relationships than it did on society's reaction to mentally retarded individuals, of which his own reaction was typical. Let us now try to address some of the questions which this type of diagnosis raises, bearing in mind that the aim is to obtain information that can serve as a basis for help—not stemming only from kindness or sympathy but from as intimate knowledge as can be gained about the parents and their social context. How will each of the parents react to and interpret the significance of the child's condition? How will each perceive the other's reaction, and what are the immediate consequences that they see themselves facing as a couple? Put another way, how will their perceptions of themselves as individuals and as a couple change? A second set of issues concerns their sense of competence as parents: How should they react to the infant? What special precautions should they take? What special problems may arise and who may be available to help if something goes wrong? A third set of questions concerns the future: Will the child be able to walk and talk, go to school? Will special help be needed and be available? Will all our children be this way? Should we have other children? When? What will be the effect of this child on the others?

Parents who take their first child home from the hospital are apprehensive, but relieved and happy. When that child is retarded, however, anxiety and depression suffuse everything. The thrust of the diagnostic questions stated above (and there are many more) is how to understand *and* interrelate the answers so that helpful actions can be taken. *Just as the pediatrician and his hospital colleagues searchingly sought over a period of days to get answers to questions about the infant's status and behavior in order to alter her condition or to prevent it from deteriorating, precisely the same task and process is required to deal with the social-interpersonal context. Indeed, whatever im-*

plications the diagnosis of the infant has for her development will depend on how the diagnosis of the social-interpersonal context is conceived and handled. This last point deserves emphasis: the diagnosis of the infant's condition has developmental consequences but the quality and quantity of those consequences will always be a function of the total social-interpersonal context of which the infant is a part.

If in practice the concept of diagnosis is seen as taking place only in regard to the infant, even though the developmental implications of the diagnosis will inevitably be shaped by a larger context, it says more about the weight of tradition than about requirements for helpful action. Unfortunately, this constricting view of diagnosis has profound and upsetting consequences. For example, consider the fact that the diagnosis of the infant did not take place at one point in time but rather evolved over a period of days in which data was collected and careful observations made.

When we say that diagnosis is a process, we mean that it is a series of actions and checks taking place over time and, not infrequently, involving interventions and treatments that give a more secure base to diagnosis. Similarly, diagnosis and treatment of the social-interpersonal context is an ongoing process that should not terminate when the mother and infant leave the hospital, to be resumed at the first office or hospital visit, or to be changed as a function of telephone calls from parent to physician. After all, from the moment the family leaves the hospital the quality and quantity of interactions within that social unit take on a fateful and changing character that is far from predictable. And what is at stake is no less than the direction of change in the lives of three interrelated human beings. The sad fact is that the diagnosis of the social-interpersonal context almost never is carried out in the sustained, painstaking, probing manner that characterized the diagnosis of the infant's condition. In point of fact we know amazingly little in these instances about what goes on, less because so much is going on and more because our conceptions and practices are inappropriately neglectful of the issues.

In the case of Alice and Harold the first few weeks were a nightmare. But as the father said: "You wake up from nightmares." A pediatrician once said with humor that the hardest job with parents of their first newborn was to convince them that their child would live. One function of humor is to allay anxiety, and pediatricians are not without anxiety but the strength of it is as nothing compared to that in parents. When that newborn is clearly retarded, the anxiety is usually exponentially more persistent and disabling. Harold came to one of the authors one week after the infant had been brought home, plying him with all sorts of questions which neither he nor his wife could ask the pediatrician because they were "personal" and not "medical" questions. One did not have to be all that sophisticated to conclude that these personal questions not only illustrated how the parents were being affected by the infant but, no less important, how the infant was probably being affected by the parents.

There are three major points of similarity in principle between what we have said about the social context of diagnosis and Sameroff's elaboration of the interaction hypothesis in the previous chapters. The first is that the fates of the parents and infant emerge from a common web of interacting relationships. Even before its birth the infant is not only biologically but psychologically in that web as the fantasies of parents would attest. The second similarity is in the possibility that the "match" between the characteristics of any two actors in the cast of three can be mutually destructive. The third similarity is in the fact that any form of intervention and prediction about one actor, independent of the others, is incomplete, misleading, and possibly harmful.

The basic reason for diagnosis is to be helpful; it is not an empty exercise or ritual, but a process society sanctions for the welfare of people. Therefore, when the diagnostic process explicitly or implicitly focuses on one individual in the social drama—*that* individual becomes figure and the others become background—it unwittingly but inevitably restricts the degree of help the individual may require, at the same time that it restricts the help the others may need even more drastically.

Within three years after the birth of their child, Alice and Harold were in the process of arranging a divorce and placement of their daughter. One could say that this came about *because* the child was retarded but that of course does not explain why similar disruptions do not take place in other families. One could say that more important than retardation was the fact that the child was *seriously* retarded and probably presented overwhelming management problems. But here too one can point to comparable instances where family disruption was surprisingly minimal. These types of explanations reflect an oversimple and, indeed, incorrect conception of causation and diagnosis. To illustrate: If a child with an IQ of 180 takes a neighbor's cat and strangles it, we would not say it was *because* he had an IQ of 180. If, however, the child had an IQ of 60, many people would say he did it *because* of an IQ of 60. The fact is that there are many children with very high and very low IQs who have never performed such an act.

We cannot say that what happened to Alice, Harold, and their child could have been prevented. What we do say is that the degree and quality of destructiveness that characterized the social-interpersonal drama could have been lessened. But that possibility could only have been realized to any degree if the diagnostic process had taken the social context seriously instead of seeing it as background and the infant as foreground. And to take it seriously would have meant to be sensitive to the fact that from the moment the infant was taken home the lives of all were interlocked, in the present and future.

Let us turn to another case which, although strange and dramatic, has the virtue of illuminating the issues surrounding the nature and function of diagnosis. Cynthia was four-and-a-half years of age when she was first seen by a psychologist. A friend of the grandparent arranged for the psychological evaluation. Cynthia was a resident of a private "nursery" where she had been placed at the age of two. The parents had been divorced, neither the father nor grandparent had ever visited her. The mother, who lived in another part of the country, visited Cynthia once a year during a shopping expedition to the east coast. All that the psychologist knew prior to his visit was that the child had been diagnosed as retarded and that a question had been raised about the advisability of a different placement. Before seeing her, the psychologist arranged a meeting with the nursery's pediatrician who reported that Cynthia had clear signs of central nervous system dysfunction and was obviously retarded. But her level of functioning was well above that of other residents and that was why another institutional placement seemed advisable. It was only when he visited the nursery that the psychologist learned that Cynthia was the only ambulatory resident and that the recommendation for another placement had been made to the grandparent by the nurse.

Cynthia was a strange-looking child: her head seemed to come to a point; she was very awkward motorically; her speech was not easy to comprehend; and she had a very animated facial expression. The nurse reported that Cynthia had been outside the nursery a handful of times. She enjoyed going to the nurse's home but on the couple of occasions when she had accompanied the nurse to a local store Cynthia panicked and the shopping had to be terminated.

One did not have to be a psychologist to determine that Cynthia was not a "normal" four-and-a-half year year old child. Although it was understandable why the nurse and pediatrician were recommending another institutional placement, it was equally clear that neither of them comprehended the significance of Cynthia's social-interpersonal context. The fact was that the nurse, psychologically speaking, was Cynthia's mother, the only adult with whom she had a sustained, loving, reciprocating relationship. There literally was no other adult on this earth with whom Cynthia had what could be dignified as a relationship. And the nurse acted and felt as a mother to the child.

The question was not why and to what extent Cynthia was retarded, but why in these surroundings did she function as well as she did? How did one justify separating this child from her "mother" and what might be the consequences? How could one separate the intellectual stimulation Cynthia needed from her needs as a child to be loved, dependent, and secure in a feeling of interpersonal continuity? In short, for the psychologist there were two diagnostic questions: What had been and what would be in the best interests of the child?

It has to be emphasized that any question about the child's intellectual-developmental history and status could not be answered independent of the social-interpersonal context. In the very nature of the case such questions could not be answered in any definitive way. One could only speculate about what the child experienced in the two years before she was placed in the nursery; the parents and grandparent were unavailable to provide information. Why the maternal grandparent, who was paying all of the financial costs and received periodic reports, never visited Cynthia could not be determined! There was no basis for a secure judgment about the rate of the child's development since she had entered the nursery. The only really secure judgment one could make was that Cynthia had a surrogate mother and to separate the two could be catastrophic for a child who was psychologically fragile.

So what to do? What would be helpful? In his report the psychologist described two residential settings that would be appropriate for the child, but he asserted that *under no condition should a placement be made unless Cynthia was accompanied by the nurse who would have to be prepared to stay with her until she adapted to the new setting.* If this could not be arranged, the price Cynthia would pay could be unconscionably great. In submitting his report to the grandparent, the psychologist had little hope that his recommendations would be followed.

But Cynthia did not go into another institution. Somewhat more than a year after I first saw Cynthia I received a letter from the grandmother informing me that for the past year Cynthia had gone to live with the nurse who had been prevailed upon to resign her job and devote all her time to Cynthia. The nurse had placed Cynthia in a nursery school where she had done very well. In fact, the nursery school felt that Cynthia was ready for first grade but there was a question whether this was a desirable promotion from the standpoint of personality maturity. I was asked if I would make another visit and evaluation.

I read the letter with dismay because I assumed that someone was selling the grandmother a bill of goods. I could not believe that the Cynthia I had seen somewhat more than a year ago—the child who had such a history of atypical development—was the girl being described in the letter.

When I arrived at the garden apartment to which the nurse had moved with Cynthia, I was greeted by the child who spoke as clearly as one could wish, comprehended all that I said and carried on a clear conversation with me. I took a walk with her through the development during which she greeted and was greeted by what seemed to be hundreds of children. When we returned to the apartment we talked about school. I determined that she knew all the letters of the alphabet by sight regardless of the order in which they were presented. She also had a grasp of simple number concepts. When I began some formal testing she, as on my previous visit, became visibly uncomfortable and indicated that she would prefer doing something else. I persisted with enough Wechsler performance tasks to determine that she could function within normal limits.

I do not want to give the impression that Cynthia had changed markedly in all respects. She certainly was not a graceful child, and one was still struck by her peculiarly shaped head. Although she spoke clearly and carried on meaningful conversations, affective expression seemed on the flat side. For the purposes of the present discussion the important thing is that a dramatic change in psychological behavior had occurred over a period somewhat longer than a year [Sarason, 1964, pp. 26-27].

We did not present Cynthia in order to contrast the outcome with that of Alice, Harold, and their infant daughter, but rather to illustrate a difference in conception of the focus of the diagnostic focus.

The Diagnostic Focus

The reader may have already discerned an association between our conception of the diagnostic focus and Sameroff's interpretation of research findings on the development of children with developmental disabilities (Chapters 2 and 3). It may also have occurred to the reader that what we and Sameroff have proposed is really quite obvious. After all, the idea that to assess and help any individual, to judge and predict possible courses of development, require the most careful study of his or her social-interpersonal context seems obvious enough. But, as Sameroff's writings and our own position reveal, the tendency to ignore the obvious is quite frequent and strong. It may be more correct to say that we are all prone to act in ways quite discrepant with our verbally stated conceptions. Nowhere is this more clear than in diagnostic practice with mentally retarded individuals. The idea that one diagnoses *individuals* and not *individuals in social-interpersonal contexts*—that one's obligation is primarily to help an *individual* and only secondarily those who are involved with and related to him—has unwittingly caused much grief. To unlearn this way of looking at diagnosis is not easy, witness, as Sameroff points out, how long it took researchers to start taking the concept of transaction seriously.

At its root diagnosis is a socially sanctioned process serving a helping function. And precisely because diagnosis is socially approved we have to expect that it will change in certain respects as the society changes. It will change as new knowledge is gained but it will also change as society's views of right and wrong, fair and unfair, helpful and unhelpful change. For example, it used to be that no one would think of questioning the right of the diagnostician to proceed as he or she saw fit in terms of procedures or even recommendations. But that is beginning to change as people insist on being informed not only about what will be done and why, but also about possible consequences. Increasingly, people are not presenting themselves as passive objects to be studied, examined, and manipulated, as if they had neither the right to question nor the intelligence to comprehend.

Within the past decade there has been an exponential increase in the number and variety of diagnostic-therapeutic issues that have come up for judicial review. Malpractice, the right of informed consent, and the rights of children are only some of the controversial issues reflecting a change in people's attitudes toward the diagnostic-therapeutic process. It is our experience that powering this change in public attitude is a poorly formulated but nevertheless deeply felt resentment toward the shortcomings of the diagnostic process: its narrow, impersonal, and too often demeaning character. And few groups have felt this narrowness more keenly than parents of retarded children.

The point we are stressing is of such importance that we shall illustrate it by a problem familiar to most readers. How is help defined in instances where an individual has been found to have cancer? How is help defined in terms of the individual? How is it defined in terms of the family? As in the case of mental retardation one does not need an active imagination to know that cancer is experienced as a social-interpersonal catastrophe. How, then, does the diagnosing physician conceptualize and react to such a catastrophe? Farber's (1977) study provides an answer. Farber was able, with the consent of patients and two physicians, to observe office visits of cancer patients at different stages of the disease. Three clear findings emerged:

1. The physicians were adept at avoiding dealing with the patients' psychological status and questions.
2. The physicians rarely dealt, and then only indirectly, with the familial consequences of the patients' condition.
3. Twice as much time (19 minutes) was spent with patients of the highest social class as compared with the time (9 minutes) spent with those from the lowest social class. Even when less extreme social class comparisons were done, the results were much the same.

In the case of these two physicians, it would be erroneous to conclude that they conceptualized the diagnostic-helping process in the most narrow, individualistic terms; such a conclusion is justified in terms of what they *do*. On the level of conceptualization, however, they were quite aware of and troubled by the obvious fact that they *should* be dealing with far more than narrow medical diagnosis and treatment, in that cancer in our society is inevitably a biological, psychological, familial complexity requiring its own diagnostic and therapeutic rationale. Indeed, these physicians agreed to the study because they knew there was a discrepancy between their practices and their understanding, and in this respect they were very unusual physicians. But like so many others, they were victims of a training and tradition that, whatever the virtues, reinforced tunnel vision.

In the paragraph above when we were describing how the two physicians felt, we said that they recognized that they "*should* be dealing with far more than narrow medical diagnosis and treatment." In italicizing the word "should," we were emphasizing the moral-ethical aspect of diagnosis. Wittingly or unwittingly, the public is led to believe that diagnosis is a wholly dispassionate, scientific, no-stone-left-unturned process based on perfected procedures that provide facts upon which a formulation can be made and a rational treatment undertaken. This is only partially true, as any diagnostician will attest. Pervading the process is not only awareness of the role of judgment but also the sense of obligation, the keenly felt imperative to do no harm and to be as helpful as possible. The moral dilemmas and conflicts arise when the diagnostician feels inadequate to understand and deal with the social-interpersonal consequences of a condition, and when he perceives a discrepancy between what he does and what he should do.

These are upsetting perceptions which too many diagnosticians defend against by rationalizing lack of time, the healing power of time, and the responsibility of families to learn by experience and to make their own decisions. But these rationalizations obscure a significant factor which cannot be overestimated because, at the same time that it helps explain the origins of the moral conflict, it also illuminates why the diagnostic focus tends to be so narrow. We refer here to the fact that diagnosticians are clinicians whose training ill prepares them to think in preventive terms. Faced, as in the case of Alice and Harold, with a social-interpersonal context containing all kinds of potential onslaughts on a satisfying future, the diagnostician not only is unable to conceptualize the substance of these onslaughts but also the necessity to prevent their full impact. Clinicians feel comfortable dealing with problems that are manifest, which is why they rivet on the afflicted individual. They are far from comfortable thinking about, let alone dealing with, the potential problems of those surrounding the afflicted individual.

This would not be so distressing were it not for the fact that the afflicted individual is inevitably affected by what happens to those around. It is literally an example of adding insult to injury. There is a world of difference between a diagnostic focus rooted in a preventative-public health model and one reflecting the clinical, problem-oriented tradition. It took a long time for the significance of this difference to be recognized in the field of mental health. Up until shortly after World War II, diagnosis and treatment of personal problems concerned an *individual*. But once the conceptual inadequacies as well as the fact of a relatively low level of treatment success were confronted, treatment of families became both frequent and fashionable. Family therapy rests on acceptance of the fact that the status of one member of the family cannot be diagnosed or treated apart from diagnosis and treatment of the family as a social unit (Ackerman 1959, Minuchin 1974). Unfortunately, this rationale, which has demonstrated its worth in the psychotherapeutic area, has had little influence in the field of mental retardation. That this rationale has indubitable practical worth and consequences can be seen by discussing Grossman's (1972) intriguing and careful study of the normal siblings of retarded children. It is not fortuitous that one of the factors propelling her to study normal siblings of retarded children was her experience with family therapy, especially with one family having an institutionalized retarded child and another atypical child who had been referred to Dr. Grossman (1972, p. 7).

Grossman's conceptual approach and clinical goals are contained in the following statement:

> enormous differences exist from family to family in how members react to, and cope with, the presence of a handicapped child. Many variations seem to involve social-class differences in values and perspectives (e.g., Felzen, 1970). However, dealing with children with similar handicaps within any given social class makes it obvious that families vary tremendously, both in the way they cope and in their effectiveness in dealing with issues raised by the handicap.
>
> In addition to supporting our own view that a family's response is not intrinsic to the handicap itself and therefore inevitable, this variation suggests the possibility of learning much more about how and why some families are able to cope in ways that provide valuable growth experience for all members of the family, while others are damaged or limited by the experience.
>
> In our search for knowledge about how families might cope successfully with retardation, our interest was drawn to a less studied component of the social system affected by and itself influencing the retardation of a child. We began to wonder about the effects on the normal brothers and sisters in these families. For example, we wondered if, for some normal children, the experience of growing up with a retarded sibling might be a positive experience, and felt that if we could find such children, we might be able to learn from them how to be more helpful to other children with a handicapped brother or sister. More generally, we were curious about some specific effects of growing up with a retarded sibling, such as how this influenced the normal boy's or girl's curiosity or self-concept or feelings toward his or her parents.
>
> We also felt that a family's response to the presence of a handicapped child must have similarities to the family's reactions to any other unexpected event, or to a serious disappointment. That is, the problems associated with mental retardation seemed to us to be related to a host of more general social and psychological problems. Consequently, study of the former issues promised to shed some light on these broader questions [pp. 4-6].*

Grossman studied two groups of college students with retarded siblings. One group was from an Ivy League school and the other from a community university. There was also a control group of matched students who had only normal siblings. Here are some of the highlights of Grossman's findings:

*Grossman makes the important point that "emphasis on the importance of social and psychological factors in determining the effect of a handicap on an individual and his social world is not unique to retardation" (p. 4). She relates her work to those of earlier investigations of handicapping conditions such as deafness, blindness, facial deformities, and motor impairments. (Ausubel, 1952; Hanks and Hanks, 1948; Macgregor, Abel, Bryt, Louer, and Weissman, 1953; Meyerson, 1948; Wright, 1960). Wright's book (1960) is still the best single source for understanding the social-ecological consequences of handicapping conditions. Together with Farber's (1960, 1963, 1964, 1968) and Grossman's studies in mental retardation, this literature provides a solid conceptual and empirical base for the position we have taken on what should constitute the diagnostic focus.

We found a surprising number of brothers and sisters of retarded children who appeared to us to have benefited in some way from the experiences of growing up with a handicapped sibling. These students seemed to us more tolerant, more compassionate, more aware of prejudice and its consequences; sometimes more focused, both occupationally and personally, than comparable young adults without such experiences. We also found many students who seemed damaged: students who were bitterly resentful of the family's situation, guilty about their rage at their parents and at the retarded sibling, fearful that they themselves might be defective or tainted; sometimes truly deprived of the time and resources they needed to develop because every support the family had to give was used in the care of the handicapped child.

Although, in our study, about as many students seemed to have benefited as were harmed, we suspect we would find many more in the latter category in any unselected group of college-age brothers and sisters of handicapped children; our sample was almost unavoidably heavily biased toward those who had coped to some extent with the retardation and its meaning and consequence for themselves and for their families [pp. 176-177].

For both men and women siblings in the private university "the extent to which their mothers and fathers were seen as accepting the retarded child and his or her handicap related most strongly to the young people's own ability to deal adaptively with the meaning of the handicap to themselves and their own lives. . . . in virtually all of the research findings, the more the retarded child was physically handicapped or had physical stigmata, the better adjusted the sib was to the handicap. This result seemed closely tied to the entire family's greater clarity about, and comfort with, a visible defect in the child, in contrast to their discomfort and uncertainty with retarded children who showed no visible evidence of defects" [pp. 177-178].

The families of students from the community university, unlike those from the Ivy League school,

lacked the financial resources to pay for assistance in dealing with H's retardation; they either received services through the local community program or they did without them. Further, the role-expectations they had for a son or daughter in a family were very different; the girls were expected to take a major share of the responsibility in caring for the other children, including a retarded one, while the boys were not expected to provide such help. When they were younger, these women spent far more time than the men with their retarded siblings, both as playmates and as babysitters.

The women consequently were greatly influenced by characteristics of H that directly affected their relationship with that child. Most strongly, the less the child was *physically* impaired, and presumably the less his or her physical dependence, the better the Community U women were able to cope adaptively with the child and the handicap. On the other hand, for these women, the more H's *retardation*, the better their coping. The pain of seeing a mildly retarded brother or sister struggling with an awareness of his or her handicap seemed to make this most difficult for these young women. [p. 179].

The clinical material strongly suggests that the normal brother or sister in a two-child family feels a great deal of pressure to achieve or more generally to make up to the parents for their disappointment over the retarded child. This effect seems strongest when the retarded child is a son [p. 182].

Reports in the literature on the effects of religion on a family's acceptance of a retarded child suggest that Catholic parents are, in comparison to Protestant and Jewish parents, more accepting of the retarded child (Adams, F. K., 1966; Kirk and Bateman, 1964; Stubblefield, 1965; Zuk, Miller, Bartrum, and Kling, 1961). Other investigators (Ehlers, 1966; Felzen, 1970; Stone, 1967) did not find such a relationship. In Grossman's study the anecdotal evidence suggested "that Catholic families at least make *more* use of religion in coming to terms with the retarded child's handicap than do Protestant and Jewish families." However, Grossman could discern no clear relationships between parentally inspired religious explanations and the siblings' ability to adapt to the retarded child's handicap.

Before presenting Grossman's study, we had largely limited our discussion of diagnosis to the parents and the retarded child. Her findings and discussion confirm, of course, the significance of parental reactions and attitudes and the diagnostic importance of understanding and dealing with them. Her decisive contribution, however, is how she illuminates the role of the normal siblings, especially as that role is affected not only by parental attitudes but by characteristics of the retardate. And the consequences are not always adverse, in contrast to the expectations of the professionals and the general public! And yet, we must pay heed to Grossman's caution that if she had chosen an unselected sample of normal sibs rather than a volunteer sample of college students, the frequency of adverse affects would probably have been larger. Nevertheless, the implications of her study on the context of diagnosis—its thrust, scope, and relation to help and remediation—require no further emphasis.

Two final notes on Grossman's study. She attempted to ferret out the effects of the retardate child on the normal sib. The assumption was that the development of the normal sib was not independent of the relationship to the retarded child. The same assumption is no less true for the development of the retarded child, and again we are back to Sameroff's interaction hypothesis! We also wish to emphasize the roles of social class and economic factors in the familial reaction to and management of the retarded child. Money, as Grossman suggests, cannot buy happiness but in many of her cases financial resources had the effect of diluting the strength of potentially adverse forces. We shall have more to say about this in later chapters.

Technical Considerations in Diagnosis

The techniques of diagnosis too often are confused with diagnosis itself and they become ends rather than means, partial descriptions isolated from the social context, and obstacles to productive thinking. The case of Keith and his family is illustrative of what we mean. Keith was the second of two children. His mother had a doctorate in history, and the father was a highly regarded physician. One month after Keith's birth it was obvious that something was wrong. He was hospitalized for extensive observation and testing and the diagnostic conclusion was that he had extensive brain damage. It says something about the parents, especially the father, that they questioned the validity of the diagnostic findings and the gloomy picture they implied. The father would not deny that the neurological, radiological, and developmental examinations showed abnormalities, but he would make two assertions: The bleak interpretations of the technical findings were not fully warranted, and one should try various medications to compensate for Keith's biological defects. Needless to say, these assertions were greeted either with respectful silence or mild disagreement.

The fact is that the father was a very strange man who before Keith's birth was regarded as brilliant but "a nut." It occasioned no surprise when the parents took Keith for examination to a medical center in another state. Their diagnostic report was essentially the same but far more explicit about the child's gloomy future course, and the parental reaction was in no way different than to the first diagnostic report.

When Keith was two years of age, the father asked a psychologist to evaluate the child. The psychologist, an acquaintance of the father, was reluctant because he knew of the earlier findings, and he also considered the father a queer person. But the father was insistent and the psychologist agreed to visit the home and observe the child. At age two, Keith could not walk but he could get around on all fours with amazing speed. He was constantly in motion, although his activity rarely seemed related to what was going on around him. He could not talk and seemed unresponsive to efforts to engage his attention. The psychologist told the parents that Keith was obviously seriously retarded and that in light of earlier diagnostic findings he could hold out no hope that at maturity Keith's degree of retardation would be other than it was now. Again the father insisted that nothing was being done, pharmacologically, to try to remedy the child's psychological status. He was not about "to give up."

Let us put into our own words what the father was saying: "I have been given a lot of facts. I know what x-rays of the brain showed. I know that the neurological examination shows indisputable signs of central nervous system dysfunction. And I know that behaviorally and psychologically Keith is far behind children his age. Each of you specialists has done your thing and you are telling me the way things *are* as you see them by virtue of your techniques. But is a diagnosis a collection of facts? Does your responsibility end when you have given me technical findings? It may be a fact that on the basis of your techniques Keith's developmental quotient is around 50. That is a technical fact, and you pin labels on him: brain-injured, seriously retarded, etc. But isn't the sole purpose in employing your techniques to determine the universe of possibilities that should be considered in an effort to improve his condition? I have gotten no concrete suggestions at all and nobody seems to want to experiment. Is it that hopeless? Or is it that you have neither the courage nor imagination to try new things? Do you know so much about cases like Keith that you can write him off as hopeless? There is a big difference between the facts and the truth, and you have only given me the facts. You seem unable to test the validity of the conclusions you have drawn from the facts. You have only done half of your job, the technical part, the easy part. You stop where I as a parent want you to proceed. Specifically, concretely, in detail, what should we do or try?"

This physician-parent had spotted the jugular in the diagnosis of mental retardation: the tendency to amass technical facts and append jawbreaking labels. Isn't it strange that we go to fantastic lengths in terms of time, energy, money, research, and technology to keep a dying person alive at the same time that the Keiths of this world are so frequently "written off"?

Some clinicians would reply to Keith's father by saying: "You are right. Diagnosis can only be justified as the basis for helpful action, and we are not being helpful, or minimally so, when we tell you what our technical procedures have uncovered. The fact is that we don't know how to help Keith, how to repair his brain, or to give him something which will make him more attentive. We simply don't know anything that can give you help and hope." Diagnosis is more than description, test scores, and labels, and in conceding the argument to Keith's father these clinicians are only reflecting what is obvious: Diagnosis is a socially sanctioned and valued process precisely because its goal is to be helpful. It is more than an exercise in technique and fact finding.

Let us return to Keith about whose later development we know, unfortunately, nothing except that he turned out to be an ostensibly normal young man who was graduated from college. and that several years after he was seen by the psychologist the father committed suicide under rather bizarre circumstances. We say "unfortunately" for obvious reasons: Was anything special done with and to this child by the father? How can we account for this amazingly favorable outcome? In what respect were faulty conclusions drawn from the large number of diagnostic facts that were amassed? We must caution the reader that we did not present Keith to derogate the diagnostic techniques used or even the validity of the facts to which they gave rise. Keith did have a damaged brain, the course of his development up until at least the age of two years was grossly atypical, and the conclusions that were drawn did reflect the status of knowledge at the time. The people who saw him were not incompetent. Even if Keith's later development had been in line with predictions, we still would be justified in emphasizing the difference between diagnosis as fact finding, on the one hand, and diagnosis as fact finding leading to intended helpful actions, on the other hand. Because we do not know how to be helpful says as much about us as it does about the retarded person.

There is a vast difference between hopelessness powered by certainty and hopelessness powered by humbleness. It was the former rather than the latter to which Keith's father seemed to be reacting. If we did not present Keith's case to disparage diagnostic techniques, neither did we present it, or Cynthia's, to justify optimism. The significance of these kinds of cases is the force they give to the obligation, societally determined and sanctioned, to use one's energies and ingenuity for remediation, however modest the expectations. If we then fail to be helpful, we at least cannot be accused of having indulged in the dynamics of the self-fulfilling prophecy. And, let us not forget, when we fail, it often says as much about our inadequacies and ignorance as it does about the unremediable nature of the afflicted individual's condition. Diagnosis is at its root a moral endeavor.

5

The Family's View
of the Future

WHEN PARENTS HAVE A CHILD their lives are forever changed and at the time of birth the changes they foresee are almost always positive. They may be aware of but do not dwell on the complications and obligations that can introduce stress in their lives. Economic, psychological, sexual, physical, and recreational areas of functioning may be adversely affected by having to care for the developing child. The point is that even when a child is developing according to norms, the balance between satisfactions and dissatisfactions, between personal freedom and frustration, changes for all members of the family.

Several decades ago, one would have said that the balance in the relationship between positive and negative factors was clearly in favor of the positive. Today, however, with the dramatic increase in the rate of divorce it is obvious that marriage and the family have become more fragile institutions. This, of course, in no way implies that this increase is due in large part to the stresses engendered by rearing children, but it does suggest that the attitudes and expectations people bring to marriage decrease their tolerance to frustration. And when we bear in mind that, increasingly, women as well as men are planning lifelong working careers, the problems surrounding child rearing can be expected to put added burdens on family stability. All of this is by way of saying that fantasy and reality, great expectations and the restrictions of marriage and family, are polarities that few families seem to balance satisfactorily.

If what we have said characterizes the family with "normal" children, we would expect that the vulnerability of a family would become greater when it confronts the task of rearing a retarded child. The fact is that this expectation cannot be demonstrated by data because the relevant studies have not been done. Grossman's study, which we discussed in the previous chapter, did indicate that many brothers and sisters seemed to have benefited by the fact that they had a retarded sib. But she cautioned that the number of these instances would probably be far less on a percentage basis if she had chosen her subjects in a way more representative of the population of families with retarded children. Also, Grossman studied only the normal sibs and it was from them that she obtained an indirect and admittedly incomplete picture of family dynamics. And, as she emphasizes, social-economic factors played an important role, a point we shall return to later. There is still another factor that should temper expectations, and that is the development in the past two decades of community programs that never existed before and have enabled families to cope better with their retarded children.

One would expect that the study done in the fifties by the Carvers (1972) of the dispiriting and disabling consequences for families with retarded children would be inapplicable to the current scene. Although this may be true, our experience suggests that it is less true than some people would like us to believe. There can be no doubt that the recent changes in society's verbal expressions about the needs and rights of retarded children and their families, accompanied as these have been by dramatic increases in public funds for a wide array of programs and services, have been helpful to families. But just as we should not uncritically accept the belief that the presence of a retarded child in a family has only catastrophic effects, we should not smugly assume that increased funding and programs have dramatically and positively altered the experience of families. The history of the field of mental retardation contains too many instances where progress was confused with increased expenditures or public resolves to give more than lip service to the idea of humane treatment. In 1843, Dorothea Dix gave her famous, searing address to the Massachusetts legislature, detailing the inhumane conditions of the state's "humane" institutions. We like to believe that in the century following that address the conditions she described were eliminated, and humaneness restored to its appropriate governing role in this sphere of human affairs. In 1967, Burton Blatt described similar conditions to the same legislature. There is a difference between change and progress!

"Something Happened"

Something Happened is a novel by Joseph Heller, published in 1974 to wide critical acclaim. The major themes of the book are by no means new: the driven, competitive, materialistic, married, Don Juanish American male whose personal and familial instability and disintegration increase as he climbs the ladder of "success." The book is an indictment of many aspects of our society and, although it describes a tragedy, it does contain, as one would expect from the author of *Catch-22*, zany and comical moments. By the end of the story the narrator and the central character, Slocum, is a prematurely aged, empty, lost soul bereft of any social intimacies or anchors. To those around him Slocum is still whole, but he is going to pieces. How this came about is beyond our purposes here. Suffice it to say that Heller, as a serious novelist, gives no simple cause and effect explanation. Indeed, novelists tend to take the transactional approach more seriously than other students of human behavior and, therefore, do not easily fall prey to simple cause and effect explanations. One way of describing a novel is that it is a diagnosis of social context based on the transactional principle.

What is relevant to our purpose is that Slocum is the father of three children one of whom is Derek, brain damaged and mentally retarded from birth. What picture is drawn about Derek's perceived effects on the family as .a unit and on each of its members as individuals? Not surprising, the clearest picture we get is Slocum. To say that he is ambivalent toward the child is misleading because that would obscure the fact that his negative feelings are stronger than his positive ones. He is, of course, guilt-ridden because of his feelings; he admits his dislike for the child, but only to himself. When he reviews the birth of the child; the dry, insensitive way in which Derek's diagnosis was communicated; the maddening unhelpfulness of the physicians; his early attempts to interact with the child and the lack of responsiveness Derek could give in return; the kind and quality of person the family hired to take care of Derek; Slocum's unwillingness to interact with families who also had a retarded child; his wife's complete unwillingness to consider institutionalizing the child; the worry about what would happen to Derek if something happened to Slocum and his wife—these ruminations exacerbate other keenly felt personal disappointments and inadequacies. Slocum would rather have Derek dead, not because Slocum is a hateful or sadistic person but because the child is such an obvious reminder of almost all of the father's vulnerabilities. Derek was not a "cause" but an addition to a social-familial context, to a web of interrelationships the strands of which varied considerably in strength, durability, and historical origins.

We are given less detail about the reactions of Slocum's wife to Derek. Her personal slide downhill, social withdrawal, and alcoholism are not attributed only to Derek, to whom she seems to have a religious, protective but aloof attitude. As for Derek's two siblings, the one thing we are told is that the sister worries that Derek's presence in the family may interfere with her social attractiveness to males. All in all, what comes through in the novel is a family where the members increasingly become strangers to each other. Derek is seen by them as an object who is "there": empty, unresponsive, unconnected.

What about Derek? What kind of *person* is he? We are told next to nothing. It is as if no one inside or outside the family ever focused on Derek as a human being deserving special thought and attention. From the moment Derek's condition was "diagnosed," the world seemed to give up on him. Since money was no problem, Derek received "care"; there was always hired help to be with him. He had custodians, but there is not the faintest suggestion that anyone was devoted to him as a human being with some capability, however modest, for development. And so the author leaves the reader with the impression that Derek was what he was because of his "condition," as if he did not inevitably reflect how he was perceived and treated. The self-fulfilling prophecy claimed another victim.

Something Happened is fiction but it is faithful to what frequently occurs in reality in several important respects. First, the impact of the retarded child on the family has to be seen in terms of the existing strengths and weaknesses of the marital relationship. Second, the developmental fate of the retarded child has to be understood in light of the marital relationship. Third, no member of the family escapes the impact of the retarded individual, be it positive, negative, or, more likely, both. Fourth, the family tends to view proffered help as inadequate, ineffective, and even inappropriate. Fifth, there are forces in our society that engender and reinforce personal isolation and feelings of loneliness so that when a personal or family tragedy occurs it tends to aggravate these feelings.

When we talk about the retarded child we must never forget that that child is in a particular family in a particular society at a particular time. There are societies quite different from ours and it is not surprising, therefore, that in some of them a Derek would be perceived by the family and the social surroundings in a fashion opposite to that described in Heller's novel. To understand the significance of this point, the reader is urged to read Eaton and Weil's (1955) study of Hutterite society.

Aging and the Passage of Time

Near the end of *Something Happened,* immediately after another unsatisfying attempt by Slocum to establish rapport with his favorite child, Derek's male sib, Slocum says to himself:

> My memory's failing, my bladder is weak, my arches are falling, my tonsils and adenoids are gone, and my jawbone is rotting, and now my little boy wants to cast me away and leave me behind for reasons he won't give me. What else will I have? My job? When I am fifty-five, I will have nothing more to look forward to than Arthur Baron's job and reaching sixty-five. When I am sixty-five, I will have nothing more to look forward to than reaching seventy-five, or dying before then. And when I am seventy-five, I will have nothing more to look forward to than dying before eighty-five, or geriatric care in a nursing home. I will have to take enemas. (Will I have to be dressed in double-layer waterproof undershorts designed especially for incontinent gentlemen?) I will be incontinent. I don't want to live longer than eighty-five, and I don't want to die sooner than a hundred and eighty-six.
>
> Oh, my father—why have you done this to me?
>
> I want him back [pp. 523-524].

For Slocum the future, like the present, is oppressive and prolonged. Throughout the novel Slocum fears that tomorrow will be like today, and next year like this one. He does not, understandably, reach for the future. Instead, he longs for a past where he did not have to protect others, but others protected him. It is as if he feels that his life is over and the future will be mere existence, a kind of penance for past misdeeds. Slocum feels old, very old, and psychologically he is like some aged people who wait, sometimes eagerly, to meet death. It would, as we have emphasized, be mindless to attribute Slocum's view of the future to the fact and consequences of Derek's retardation. Derek is but one strand, albeit an important one, in the fabric of Slocum's social living that suffuses the future with anxiety, loneliness, and pathetic dependence. The point is that Heller is describing well how a person's sense of the passage of time is one of the core ingredients of the sense of aging. The sense of aging is *not* a function of chronological age (Becker 1973; Sarason 1977) but can be experienced because of events and experiences that make one feel that the best of life has passed and the future is a downhill slide. *This concern with the passage of time and a foreboding future—those obsessive thoughts about one's death and its consequences for one's kin—are almost never absent in parents of retarded children. Indeed, historically speaking, these parents as a group knew about the poignancy of the aging process long before it became a topic of public concern.*

This is what Heller's artistry has shown. When Slocum was told about Derek's retardation, it was like throwing a bomb in a smoldering volcano. Suddenly, his accustomed view of the future changed. It no longer was an endless upward and onward course but more like a mine field in which he was trapped. He was hemmed in and that was the way it was always going to be. And what if he died? Where would Derek go? Who would take care of him? And when Slocum fantasied about how nice it would be if they put Derek into an institution where they could visit him a couple of times a year, and then they could forget him, it indicated how dearly Slocum wanted to reexperience the old sense of the future, a future toward which one willingly goes. But these fantasies only emphasized the bitter reality.

We are not suggesting that what happened to Slocum and his family is a representative story. What our experience clearly suggests, however, is that what they thought and felt would be found in the internal dialogues of members of families with retarded children. Our society approves of expressions of love toward our children, not hate or ambivalence. We are expected to give priority to our children's needs over our own, to deny ourselves self-expression and self-fulfillment in order to insure that our children's need for untrammeled growth will be met.

Some parents can follow society's dictates and contain the negative side of their ambivalence at no great cost. The negative side is there but it does not become unduly disruptive to self or others. Other parents follow society's dictates but at the high cost of their sense of well-being and family integration, and the Slocums are only one of many types who fall into this group. And then there are those parents (like Cynthia and Harold, and Keith's parents) who reject society's dictates, with massive disruptions to existing relationships. What is common to all of these parents, because of how mental retardation is perceived in our society, is that they are confronted with the task of accommodating an altered future, with its consequences and quality, preceded by upset, mourning, grief, and the extension of the sense of isolation.

We have been concentrating on parental reaction for two reasons. First, these parents are coping with one of the most difficult experiences people in our society can have. That may sound obvious enough but the obvious is not always taken seriously, as we have been at pains to stress in earlier chapters. Second, focusing on them illuminates the enormous difference between the experience of the normal and retarded infant and young child. The gleeful, doting parents approach, touch, manipulate, hug the normal infant, concerned, perhaps, that they are too intrusive and may "spoil" the child, "spoil" meaning that the child may come to think that the world exists only to fulfill his or her needs. The parents seize, rightly or wrongly, on any action that suggests that their child may be precocious. They know he is normal, they would like him to be supernormal. Rarely is one human being so aware of, responsive, indulgent, and selfless to another human being as in the parent-infant relationship.

But what about the parents of a retarded infant? Preoccupied with their own altered needs, plagued with anxiety, guilt, and anger, searching the past for reasons and the present for hope, they cannot evade the knowledge that planning and hoping are frail needs on which to restructure lives. Experiencing those too frequent, piercing reminders that by virtue of someone coming into their lives a good deal has gone out of it and they must bury treasured hopes and fantasies—caught up in this swirl of personal despair, it is the rare parent who can respond unanxiously, spontaneously, and competently to the infant. When you are absorbed with yourself and your future, a limit is set to what you can be aware of and respond to in others. To give of yourself to someone else when you feel you need so much of it for yourself is extraordinarily difficult, if not impossible.

Matters are usually made worse by the professionals who communicate the fateful diagnosis to the parents. For one thing, they confuse communicating the diagnosis with being helpful. It does not follow that if diagnosticians were more sensitive and competent with social-familial diagnosis and, therefore, understood better the difference between communicating a diagnosis and being helpful, they would *always* be able to be helpful. That is not the issue, but rather the failure of diagnosticians to recognize and feel a responsibility for those who comprise the social-familial context. For another thing, they usually discuss the infant as if it were a thing rather than a human being, a damaged or incomplete object toward whom the usual parental response will not have productive consequences.

The infant can become an object of fear, a strange puzzle the parents cannot figure out. The parents have been given a diagnosis but no guidelines or specific directions about how to think and act in the course of days and nights. We stressed earlier the significance of parental coping with an altered *personal* future. The difficulty of that deeply personal and private task is increased by parental inability to imagine what the child will be like in the future. Will the child walk, talk, laugh, respond, play, go to school? Will the child look different? The questions are endless; in reality the number of questions is finite but they are asked and unanswered endlessly. Behind these questions is an assumption that professionals too often have instilled in parents: *The answers to questions about the child's future will be determined exclusively or largely by the nature of the child's condition, and minimally or far less by the transactions between parents and child.* That is to say, the condition will unravel itself, and parents and others who participate in the child's rearing are more like bystanders watching a predetermined developmental unfolding. This, of course, is conceptual nonsense and in flat contradiction to experience and research, but, unfortunately, that has not prevented the acceptance of this unwarranted assumption in clinical diagnosis and action.

Optimism and the Future

How do we account for the recurring interest in a case study that was begun at the end of the eighteenth century and completed and written up at the beginning of the nineteenth century? Why has it been a source of fascination and controversy for almost two centuries by different people to illustrate different points? We are referring, of course, to Itard's *Wild Boy of Aveyron.* In 1976, a new book by Harlan Lane on Itard's work was published, bringing together for the first time new and old documents about the case. It is a book that deserves careful reading.

The story begins one day in 1797, in the fifth year of the new French Republic, when peasants in the region of Lacaune, in south central France, spied a naked boy fleeing through the woods called La Bassine. Curiosity aroused, they lay in wait on the following days and finally saw him again searching for acorns and roots. In 1798 he was sighted again by woodsmen and, despite violent resistance, taken to the village of Lacaune, where his arrival created a sensation. He was put on display several times in the public square, but the crowd's curiosity was quickly satisfied by the sight of the filthy mute urchin and, under relaxed surveillance, he was able to escape into the forest.

Over the next fifteen months, the wild boy was seen from time to time in the fields on the edge of the forest, digging up potatoes and turnips, which he ate on the spot or occasionally carried off. Several lairs were found and attributed to him, including one with a bed of leaves and moss. Then, on July 25, 1799, three hunters spotted him in the same woods, gave chase, and succeeded in dislodging him from a tree. Tied up tight, he was led back to Lacaune and entrusted to the care of an old widow. This devoted guardian, one of her contemporaries recounts, dressed him in a sort of gown to hide his nakedness and offered him various foods, including raw and cooked meat, which he always refused. He did accept acorns, chestnuts, walnuts, and potatoes, always sniffing them before putting them in his mouth. When not eating or sleeping, he prowled from door to door and window to window seeking to escape. After eight days, he succeeded.

This time the wild boy did not return to the forest. Climbing the nearby mountains he gained the broad plateau between Lacaune and Roquecézière, in the department of Aveyron. Through the autumn, and into a particularly cold winter, he wandered over this elevated and sparsely populated region, entering occasionally into farmhouses where he was fed. When given potatoes, he threw them into the coals of the hearth, retrieving and eating them only a few minutes later. During the day, he was seen swimming and drinking in streams, climbing trees, running at great speed on all fours, digging for roots and bulbs in the fields; and, when the wind blew from the Midi, turning toward the sky he rendered up deep cries and great bursts of laughter. Finally, working his way down the mountain along the course of the Lavergne and Vernoubre rivers, he arrived on the outskirts of the village of Saint-Sernin. Encouraged perhaps by the treatment he had received from the farmers on the plateau, urged on perhaps by hunger, he approached the workshop of the dyer Vidal. It was seven o'clock in the morning, January 8, 1800. The boy slipped across the threshold into a new life, and into a new era in the education of man [pp. 6-7].

For our purposes here we can do no better than to give Lane's succinct, moving, and personal beginning pages of his first chapter:

The Luxembourg Gardens are an island of calm, of lawns, gravel paths, fountains, and statues, in the heart of left-bank Paris. On a summer's day in 1800, two young Frenchmen from the provinces met there for the first time and joined together their lives and futures. Although neither could have said so, each was engaged in a search whose success required the other.

The first young man was well but not elegantly dressed in a long coat, drawn in at the waist, with full lapels. His curly hair fell in locks over a slanting forehead; his aquiline nose extended the plane almost as far as his jutting chin. Tightly drawn wide lips and large, dark brown eyes completed the Mediterranean features, set off by a broad white collar that rose funnel-like from his frilly white shirt. Jean-Marc-Gaspard Itard was twenty-six and had just become a doctor. He had left the barren village at the foot of the French Alps where he was raised and had come to Paris in search of a place for himself in the new social order that had emerged from the chaos of the Revolution. Paris at this time was vibrant: painting, theater, music, and literature were flourishing, abetted by the glittering salons of the very rich, the rendezvous of the intellectual and social elite. Medicine was surging ahead; it had become possible to protect people against disease by giving them some of the disease itself, although no one really knew why. One of Itard's teachers, Philippe Pinel, had just written the first book on psychiatric diagnosis, and had dramatically ordered inmates of the city's insane asylums to be unchained. The first anthropological society was formed, while expeditions returned with the flora, fauna, and inhabitants of Africa, Indonesia, and the New World, to the delight and fascination of naturalists, anatomists, and, above all, philosophers. Itard had left the relative isolation of the provinces in search of this excitement of senses and mind, to share in it, even to contribute to it if he could. His alliance with the strange boy rocking back and forth in front of him would surely bring him public attention; it might admit him to the ranks of the great doctors and philosophers of his time, or it might destroy his career right at its beginning.

The boy was twelve or thirteen years old, but only four-and-a-half feet tall. Light-complexioned, his face was spotted with traces of smallpox and marked with several small scars, on his eyebrow, on his chin, on both cheeks. Like Itard, he had dark deep-set eyes, long eyelashes, chestnut brown hair, and a long pointed nose; unlike Itard, the boy's hair was straight, his chin receding, his face round and childlike. His head jutted forward on a long graceful neck, which was disfigured by a thick scar slashed across his voice box. He was clothed only in a loose-fitting gray robe resembling a nightshirt, belted with a large leather strap. The boy said nothing; he appeared to be deaf. He gazed distantly across the open spaces of the gardens, without focusing on Itard or, for that matter, on anything else. That same day, he had ended a grueling week-long journey. By order of the Minister of the Interior, Napoleon Bonaparte's brother, Lucien, the boy had come to Paris from a forest region in the province of Aveyron in southern France. This journey was the latest development in his search, which began a year before when he clambered out of the forests, worked his way across an elevated plateau in the bitterest winter in recent memory, and entered a farmhouse on the edge of a hamlet. He exchanged the freedom and isolation of his life in the forests of Aveyron, where he had run wild, for captivity and the company of men in society. He came without a name, so he was called the Wild Boy of Aveyron.

Perhaps Itard knew better than the savants of his time, who expected to see in the boy the incarnation of Rousseau's "noble savage," man in the pure state of nature; perhaps he did not. What he saw, he wrote later, was "a disgustingly dirty child affected with spasmodic movements, and often convulsions, who swayed back and forth ceaselessly like certain animals in a zoo, who bit and scratched those who opposed him, who showed no affection for those who took care of him; and who was, in short, indifferent to everything and attentive to nothing." The society of the eighteenth century had held both young men at bay, depriving the first of the best it had to offer, depriving the second of everything. Itard sought to master the ultimate skills of his culture—trained observation, persuasive language, social grace—the boy, their rudiments. So be it: they would help each other. Educating the boy would be a test of the new science of mental medicine and a proof of philosophy's new empiricist theory of knowledge. It would give still more justification for social reform by showing how utterly man depends on society for all that he is and can be. If the effort succeeded, the nineteenth century would give them their proper place, where the eighteenth had not.

Much more than a century later, nearly two, I sat in the Luxembourg Gardens and wondered about the two young men who had met there. Off to my left, the National Institute for Deaf-Mutes, where Itard had taken the wild boy to live and to learn. There, in his efforts to train him, Itard created a whole new approach to education, centered on the pupil, closely adapted to his developing needs and abilities, seconded by instructional devices—an approach we have accepted so thoroughly as our ideal that we scarcely imagine any other or credit anyone with its discovery. Behind me, the Sorbonne, where Itard had defended the possibility of educating the boy against the judgment of the great philosophers and doctors of the time, who contended that the boy was left in the wild because he was an idiot, not an idiot because he was left in the wild. Behind me, and farther north, the Academy of Medicine, where Itard read his historic reports on methods for teaching the deaf and the retarded to speak—methods he had developed with the wild boy. In front of me and to the south, the Hospital for Incurables, where Itard's student, Edouard Séguin, set out to prove that idiots were educable, contrary to unanimous medical opinion where George Sumner came to see Itard's methods in action, bringing them back to America to start the education of the retarded there; where, finally, Maria Montessori came, to end by extending Itard's methods to the education of the normal preschool child as well as the handicapped.

Thinking of these places close at hand, where the drama of Dr. Itard and the wild boy took place, shaping the lives of countless children up through my own time, imagining the excitement of another time when men affirmed, "Yes, the deaf *can* speak, the retarded *can* learn," when they believed that the only sure limit to a child's knowledge is his society's ignorance, when they were convinced, as I am, of the perfectibility of man—thinking of these times and places one summer afternoon in the Luxembourg Gardens, I decided to begin my own search, to find Itard and the wild boy. I retraced their steps, gathering copies of letters and documents as I went. The town hall in Rodez and the regional archives for Aveyron, the boiler-room "archives" and library of the National Institute for the Deaf, the dusty attics of the Sorbonne and School of Medicine (with the priceless view of Paris rooftops accorded only to students and cleaning ladies), the opulent quarters of the National Archives and the Academy of Medicine, the corridors of the hospitals Bicêtre and Val-de-Grâce, a dozen other places but especially the cavernous hushed reading rooms of the National Library: these were my joyful haunts in every spare minute for two years.

Here is the outcome—a moving story about how a man and a boy helped each other in the search for knowledge, and how that search changed their lives and ours [pp. 3-6].

We shall not be concerned here with the more obvious points of interest in the Itard-Victor saga: how the whole affair was rooted in competing philosophies of the time; the enormous changes it represented in man's view of man; the fantastic degree of thought, planning, persistence, experimentation, and devotion that characterized the efforts of Itard and his helpers; the wide discrepancy between the goals sought and attained; and how that discrepancy was interpreted by competing theorists.

Victor never became "normal"—far from it. But the difference in Victor before and after his encounters with Itard was vast. Two points deserve emphasis. The first is the relationship between optimism and results. Itard did not see Victor as a victim of a "condition" that doomed him, but rather as a victim of a lack of normal social intercourse. If Victor could be enticed to participate in normal social relationships in an ambience of love, support, and stimulation, his dormant capabilities would become manifest. From Itard's standpoint there was a future for Victor, but that future depended on how Itard met the pedagogical problem: How to stimulate, motivate, sustain, and build upon Victor's existing behavioral repertoire? *The challenge was Itard's!* If he failed, it would say as much about his inadequacies as Victor's limitations. What a contrast to a view of the future we see so frequently today in regard to Victor-like infants!

The second point deserving emphasis is as subtle as it has been undiscussed. Itard was not only a diagnostician, but a participant and superviser in Victor's daily life. He did not give advice, he implemented it. He *knew* Victor as few, if any, clinicians today know their patients. Itard structured Victor's social context. And if an approach or technique did not work, *he* tried another. Itard's optimism was grounded in a point of view that made it seem natural to experiment, persist, be patient, and loving. If Itard failed, it was a magnificent failure. He demonstrated what willing and total involvement can achieve when the odds against you seem overwhelmingly high. That, in our opinion, is why his work will always be a chapter in the history of individual accomplishment.

When we look at how parents of retarded infants and young children are "helped" by the diagnosticians we can begin to understand why a parent (like Slocum) may have raging anger for those who help. How many of these diagnosticians have been in the home to observe, advise, and demonstrate? In our experience, the answer is zero.

But there are parents who are like Itard, except they do not write about it. For example, there is the story of David. He was carried into the institution in which he would spend the rest of his life in a man's arms. It appeared as if the man were carrying a young but somewhat large grown child. That young child was chronologically a young man with cerebral palsy involving all of his extremities; he never seemed at rest because of athetosis, and his speech for all practical purposes was unintelligible because when he tried to respond, the uncontrollable body movements would become exacerbated. He was as handicapped a case of cerebral palsy as we had ever seen. His mother had recently died and his father had died when he was a young child, so there was no one at home to take care of him. Understandably, but wrongly, he seemed on initial impression to be severely retarded.

There was, we thought, no reason to evaluate him quickly, and he was placed in a building for the severely retarded. Three weeks later the admitting psychologist met the staff aide in charge of that building and when he was asked how David was doing, the reply was: "He's a real smart fellow." The psychologist was skeptical and this must have shown in his facial expression because the aide said: "Come on over and I'll prove it to you." David was lying in the seat of the wheelchair, gnarled, in motion, saliva dripping from his mouth and becoming more of a stream when the psychologist approached with a routine greeting to which David seemed to want to make a reply. Quite a sight! The aide gave the psychologist a large checkerboard that had accompanied David to the institution, and in each of the squares was a large letter of the alphabet. "Ask him a question requiring a one-word answer, then run your finger slowly across the checkerboard. When David wants you to stop at the first letter of the answer he'll let you know, and then do that for the second letter of the answer, and so on." David, it turned out, was a very smart young man!

How had these parents reared David? How had his mother, confronted with such a severely handicapped infant, managed to reach the child? There are many more questions but there are no answers. His case record was unrevealing except that he had been diagnosed as mentally retarded and, therefore, eligible to be placed in an institution for retarded children. How smart David was is really not the issue, and it is indulging the nit-picking tendency to make an issue of what label one should pin on him. The important questions are: Why was this mother, Itard-like, optimistic? What permitted her to shape a future that few others would have allowed themselves to imagine? What kept *her* going?

Cautions and Significances

Up to this point we have been discussing infants and young children who had indisputable central nervous system defects. That is to say, something was seriously wrong, although it does not follow that these defects are invariably associated with what is called mental retardation. An individual can have indisputable brain dysfunction (e.g., epilepsy) and be perfectly "normal." Indeed, some of these individuals have been shapers of our civilization. Because of the case examples we have used thus far, the stance we have taken can be misunderstood. Several cautions are in order:

1. Brain dysfunction at birth can drastically limit both the pace and level of an individual's development.
2. The limits on development may be drastic regardless of how the social context is organized or the energies expended.
3. Our knowledge and experience in the relationships between brain dysfunction and the course of development are meagre, subject to various explanations, and puzzling.
4. What we think we know derives from cases that may be atypical in one or another unknown ways or from data that completely ignored the

transactional relationships between the individual and his social context.

With these cautions in mind, we would maintain that the significance of these cases is three-fold. First, from a narrow, scientific research point of view these cases should force us to recognize how little systematic effort has been used to experiment with new ideas and techniques; not with the often unrealistic goal of "curing" but simply and boldly to challenge existing theories and practices about brain behavior-social context relationships. Second, such effort could contribute to a better understanding of the nature of our society precisely because this effort would both reflect and challenge tradition. It would seek new knowledge in an approved no-holds-barred fashion, and it would explicitly challenge how our culture defines our reality and our conception of the nature of man. Third is the moral issue. As a society, what obligation should we assume to help afflicted individuals, even if the degree of accomplishment in no way erases the obvious gulf between them and us. Do we make such an effort for them, for us, or for them and us?

At its root, science is a moral endeavor, although it has taken a long time for this to receive general recognition. For example, it is only in recent decades that scientists have been forced to recognize that in pursuit of new knowledge of human behavior they could not "use" people as subjects in a *carte blanche* manner. Society rebelled against many scientists' implicit morality that permitted them to do things with people as if the justification for their procedures had a superior claim over the rights, welfare, and feelings of people. The reader should consult Katz (1972) and Shore and Golann (1973).

In our society we do not practice infanticide, although allowing "hopeless" infants to die is by no means unheard of, even though it is kept from public knowledge. This is another example of the intimate tie between morality and practice. But a society that makes infanticide both illegal and immoral cannot escape defining the nature and scope of its responsibility to these infants and their families. We shall have more to say about these issues in later chapters. We now turn to another aspect that throws further light on the determinants of the future perspectives of these families.

Community Services and the Psychological Sense of Community

Far more often than not, aloneness and isolation characterize the feelings of the family, especially the parents. The intervals between dispiriting thoughts about the retarded young child are not long. Sometimes, the scope of parental socialization is narrowed considerably but even when not, there is the piercing knowledge that they are alone with their problems. We are no longer a society in which one can count on extended families living near each other, or on having one's neighbors as friends, or on belonging to a church from which help is spontaneously forthcoming. Loneliness, anomie, alienation—these words have come to reflect what plagues people generally in our society (Nisbet, 1970; Sarason, 1974).

The family with a retarded young child knows these feelings only too well. But families begin to adapt to their problems, and the word adapt is used neutrally. They begin to cope in good or bad fashion depending on what criteria one employs. They continue to mourn the death of past hopes while at the same time trying to envision and shape a future. They want and need advice and help to prepare for that future. They ply themselves and their physicians with all sorts of questions about that future but the answers inevitably are vague because of reluctance to be too specific about what services the child may require or benefit from in the future. They may feel reassured when told that mental retardation has finally been accorded the attention it never had, and that diverse programs and services are now available.

They may even join the local chapter of the National Association of Retarded Citizens. Our experience suggests, however, that they are not likely to join until the child is well beyond infancy. If they do join, they may experience that sense of community with others that may otherwise be absent. However, very few physicians urge parents to join for what psychological and social benefits they, the parents, may derive. Whether parents even hear about the parents' group appears to be a matter of chance.

It is not many months after the child's birth that certain questions can begin to take on an obsessional quality. Broadly speaking, they may be termed social-educational questions. Will the child be able to walk, talk, go to school, learn to read? Will he or she have playmates or is the child doomed to a life of isolation? Will the child require a special school or program? What about a nursery school? Would the child be better off in a residential institution? Public or private? How does one determine quality? Where are these special schoolf and institutions? How do I determine what is best for the child, given the fact that I have conflicting feelings? Should we have another child? When, and what will that mean for us as a family? Will it be fair to this and the next child? Some of these questions seek clarification of alternatives involved in decision-making, and others are exquisitely and agonizingly personal-moral in nature, but they are all pointed to a cloudy, anxious, puzzling future. And, for the most part, they are questions that rarely have a satisfactory forum for discussion. They tend to remain private and festering.

Bruner (1972) pointed out that "there is no known human culture that is not marked by reciprocal help in times of danger and trouble, by food sharing, by communal nurturance for the young or disabled and by the sharing of knowledge and implements for expressing skill." Human cultures, however, differ markedly in the quantity and quality of the reciprocity, and in the case of our own culture, unfortunately, the troubled family with a young retarded child experiences little of the reciprocity that comes from the sense that one is an integral part of a larger community. On the contrary, many of these parents conclude that they live in a cold, uncaring world indifferent to the dangers and troubles of its inhabitants.

What happens when the child becomes somewhat older and the questions above take on an unavoidable urgency? What community services and programs are available and how does a "match" between them and the needs of the family come about? It used to be that this question was not a difficult one to answer because the options a family had to consider were relatively few: institutionalization or a special class *if* one were available and the criteria for acceptance could be met. Today, as a result of organized parent pressures, increased public funding, and court decisions, there are more services and programs available. In our large urban centers there may be scores of services and programs, public or private, although even the private depend on grants from public agencies. In a moderate-sized community and its environs there can be as many as twenty to thirty discrete programs and agencies providing some kind of service to mentally retarded individuals and families.

For example, in an area containing about a quarter of a million people, London (1977) found twenty agencies and programs providing some sort of explicit service. In each of these agencies she interviewed an administrator in relation to four questions: What services were they rendering; How well informed were they about other services and programs; How much cooperation and sharing of information and staff existed among these agencies; What was the quality of agency interrelationships? The results were staggeringly discouraging. Here are some of the clearest findings:

1. Less than a handful of these agencies had any kind of meaningful relationship with the state department of mental retardation and its satellite offices, programs, and settings. They had surprisingly little knowledge of the nature and scope of the state's programs, resources, and responsibilities. One could look at that in another way: the state department did not seem to have taken the initiative to establish some kind of cooperative arrangement between it and the agencies.

2. Not one community agency had any real knowledge about more than three or four other community agencies, and some of that information was either obsolete or wrong. Some community agencies, amazingly, had no real knowledge of any other community agency or program.

3. Cooperation of any kind among agencies was, for all practical purposes, nonexistent. This was also true for the relationship between school system programs, and community agencies.

4. Agencies tended to be very critical of each other.

5. Every agency bemoaned the lack of cooperation.

6. Every agency uttered the universal complaint: They did not have the

resources either to meet the demands made of them or to give service according to the highest qualitative standards.

It would be illegitimate to come to any conclusions about the quality of services and the programs. That was not the point of London's study. The major significance of her findings is the picture we get of fragmentation, unrelatedness, and ignorance of existing community services. *If these are valid characterizations of community agencies under the leadership of highly trained, knowledgeable professionals, what can one predict about the experience of parents who are seeking community resources in order to make informed choices?*

Parental experiences are of two types. There are parents who never get a sense of the variety of programs and services that exist, and they seek out the one program that "somebody" told them about. There are parents who try to find out what exists, become frustrated at their inability to get the kind of information they want, and end up angry at themselves and the world. In short, many parents see themselves in relation to programs and services in much the same way as agencies do. In the case of parents, though, they feel far more alone as they try to manage the present in order to make a more desirable future likely. This does not distinguish parents of retarded individuals from those with normal young children.

Parents are future-oriented, but in the case of parents of retarded children they are always in the position of trying "to cut their losses," that is keeping a difficult situation in the present from becoming more so in the future. It is by no means rare to hear these parents labeled as "anxious, demanding, and controlling." The use of these labels is sometimes, of course, justified but many times their use reflects an insensitivity to the degree to which the parental view of the present and future is suffused, and realistically so, with anxiety and the sense of aloneness.

When someone is ill and a physician is called, we make two assumptions: He will do his best to be helpful, and in the event he concludes that the services of other professionals are needed he will tell us and help us make appropriate arrangements. For example, he may call the hospital to find out if a bed is available, alert the admitting service and the laboratories, and secure the services of other colleagues he deems necessary. Put in another way: We count on the physician not only to know what facilities exist, and to tell us what he thinks needs to be done but, crucially, that he will assume supervisory responsibility for the entire process.

In the case of the retarded infant or young child, no one assumes that kind of role in relation to community programs and agencies. Generally speaking, physicians know little about existing programs and agencies, although they are by no means alone in this respect. However, given the relationship of physicians to the family, they are potentially in the best position to render the most help. Their inability to exploit that potentiality may be understandable in terms of the limitations of their training and the pressures of a medical practice, but that should not prevent us from recognizing the significance of missed opportunities. We shall have more to say about this in later chapters.

Some Socioeconomic Differences

Grossman (1972) found that socioeconomic differences among families were related to how brothers and sisters seemed to have been affected by their retarded siblings. It obviously makes a difference if a family can afford to hire extra household help, possess ample living space, or as was true in a number of Grossman's cases, place the child in a private institution. Being relatively free from financial worry, however, does not guarantee family tranquillity depending as that does on parental attitudes. As Heller demonstrated so well in *Something Happened,* the Slocum family had financial security and yet they were tragic figures. It could also be argued that because of the correlation between income and education, the more affluent families are better able to obtain whatever information and services they feel they need. One of the most significant differences between rich and poor people is in their ability to exploit "the system." And yet, the more highly educated the parents the greater the expectations for their children and, therefore, they may experience their retarded child as a greater disappointment. It may be more correct to say that the fact that families differ widely in economic resources does not permit us blithely to assume that the depth and consequences of the psychological wound are radically different.

Rich or poor, parents with young retarded children are anxious about the future and that anxiety can be put in the form of plaguing questions. Are we doing the *right* thing? Is our child getting the best available help, and how will we feel in the future if we learn that we did not make the best choices? What will happen to our child when we are gone? People do not like to contemplate their own death, and if we are forced to do so as the years go on, it is not because we like to. Parents with young retarded children feel compelled to confront the possible consequences of their own death; this is another way of saying that they are forced to confront the long-term future long before other people their age.

It was not too many decades ago that parents with severely retarded children had very few options about how to care for the child. One of these options was institutional placement. Affluent parents tended to place the child in a private setting. The financial costs were considerable so that if a family had moderate means it could place the child there only at a great sacrifice. Private placement was out of the question for the family of low income and even for many with above average incomes. The only placement available to them was the state institution.

People have always been inclined to believe that the quality of care in a private institution is better than that in the state institution. Private institutions were smaller; by virtue of being profit-making, they were disposed to be more sensitive to the needs and attitudes of parents, in contrast to the large, bureaucratized state institution. In light of the class of parents to which they catered, the private institution was able to be more selective about the quality of its staff. And, almost always, the private institution appeared esthetically more pleasing than the usual, formidable and depressing buildings of the state institution. It was hard to tell some of these state institutions from one's mental picture of a prison.

Belief in the superiority of the private institution was probably justified, although in our experience the degree of superiority was always less than touted. This belief had upsetting consequences for those families who could not afford the private setting. After all, if one believes, rightly or wrongly, that one's child is getting second-rate care, it is not a thought that is easy to live with.

But for parents with a child in the state institution there was one considerable benefit: in the event of the parents' death the individual would continue to be taken care of. This was not necessarily the case for families with children in private settings, unless they happened to be that wealthy and willing to endow, so to speak, their child's care in perpetuity. Few were that wealthy or willing, especially if it meant drastically reducing what the other siblings would inherit. It could get very complicated, indeed, for parents and siblings each of whom in different ways was trying to secure a satisfactory future.

In the past two decades there have been two major changes in attitudes. One factor has been the rise and influence of parent groups seeking an increase in the variety of community programs and services enabling parents to keep their child at home. In earlier days institutionalization as often as not had been the reluctant choice of parents who saw no other option. A second, related factor has been the public recognition of the scandalous conditions in institutions. Inhumane conditions were more characteristic of the public than the private institution—and institutions for the mentally retarded were by no means unique in their conditions—but a generalized, deeply negative attitude toward all boarding institutions was aroused in people. These two factors converged to make it easier for parents of young retarded children to keep them in the community.

"Mentally retarded individuals can and should remain in their homes and community"—this new societal attitude became a matter of public policy. But this attitudinal change has added a new aspect to an old problem. If the child remains at home and is entered in one or more educational-community programs, the parents are again faced with an old question: Who *in the com-*

munity will care for our child when we are gone? And this question is given force as parents learn that satisfactory program options for the maturing retarded individuals hardly exist. In many communities they do not exist at all. Parents may be prepared to keep their child at home or in some community setting as long as they live but at the same time they know that living in the community is subject to risks and dangers. They also believe that these risks would be less than in a state institution.

The fact is that the risks and dangers are different; one set is not "better" than the other. The point, however, is that we rather grossly mislead ourselves, run the risk of being seen as dense, and dilute our effectiveness if we underestimate the centrality of concern for the future in the lives of parents of retarded individuals.

In this and the previous chapters, our focus has been primarily though not exclusively psychological in emphasizing what happens to parents and families—their feelings, expectations, frustrations—when confronted with the knowledge that their child has been called retarded. We saw, however, that there are several major limitations to psychological oversimplification. One of these limitations is the tendency to think in cause and effect terms. For example, far more has been written about how parents have been affected by the child than about how children have been affected by parents, whereas in reality we are not dealing with separable processes. This limitation is not merely psychological but is in itself a reflection of certain characteristics of a society that has always demeaned the worth of the retarded child.

Psychology, neither in theory nor practice, operates in a social vacuum, but directly or indirectly reflects the larger society. And in our society the retarded child has always been a second-class human being for whom one should have pity, and toward whom one should be humane, but for whom society has no use. As a concept mental retardation will always reflect characteristics of a society at a particular time, and this means that we need more than psychology to understand the concept of mental retardation. So, to talk about mental retardation without comprehending how much of its history is in the living present is like talking about racial issues as if they are products of today or the recent past. To talk about mental retardation without confronting the fact that we are not homogeneous in social class, and that we are a very heterogeneous society in a cultural sense, is like talking about people as if they did not vary in age, size, gender, race, and religion. And, finally, to talk about mental retardation without comprehending why and how it has become embroiled in legislation, public policy, and the courts, is like trying to understand a school system independent of these same instrumentalities and their history.

As we pointed out earlier, changes in recent public policy toward people labeled as mentally retarded have been one manifestation of changes taking place in our society. Indeed, one could argue that changes in the concept of mental retardation have been a consequence of these other changes. In the chapters that follow we therefore shift our focus from the individual and the family. We shall look at the relationship between changes in public policy and the structure and traditions of institutions serving mentally retarded people. Personality factors, interpersonal dynamics, and individual developmental considerations will be less in the foreground as we look at various types of institutions, the formation and implementation of public policies, group conflicts stemming from different traditions and vested interests, and the ubiquitous dynamics of economics.

6

Old People, Intermediate Care Facilities, and Mentally Retarded Residents

THE BELIEF THAT mentally retarded individuals can live in the community rather than being segregated in large residential institutions has gained currency only in recent decades. The concept of mainstreaming in schools is the most recent manifestation of the belief that mentally retarded individuals should experience mainstreaming in all areas of living. If mainstreaming in schools is being variously interpreted, it is in part because the more general concept of mainstreaming lacks general agreement. This could hardly be otherwise considering how new the concept of community living for mentally retarded people is in our society. In this chapter we shall scrutinize this concept from several vantage points: What it reflects and how it is related to current changes in our society; how it varies from the standpoint of individual development; the role of political-administrative-legal factors; and the influence of economic considerations.

Medicare, Senior Citizens, and Nursing Homes

Although we shall not be discussing mental retardation in this section we shall be describing events and social changes in an attempt to counter the tendency to see the field of mental retardation as unique in its substantive issues and place in society. It is our contention that one can never fully grasp the social and cultural significances of the field of mental retardation unless one sees it in relation to other dependent and handicapped groups in our society. Unfortunately, the tendency to specialization has been an obstacle to the recognition of communalities among different dependent groups in terms of society's reaction to them.

If today we are beginning to see these communalities (Bogdan and Biklen, 1977), it is due less to the contribution of the specialists and more to principles contained in court decisions. For example, the 1954 desegregation decisions did more to direct people's attention to the way society discriminated against a variety of minority groups than did the writings of researchers and theorists. The fact that Public Law 94-142 concerned *all* handicapped children, and that section 504 of the federal Rehabilitation Act of 1973 was to prevent discrimination to *any* handicapped person, reflects the relatively recent recognition that society had very similar ways of responding to differently labeled handicapped groups. A young colleague of ours who had worked for several years with mentally retarded individuals decided to gain experience in the geriatric field. When she told us about her decision, she said, "But I know nothing about aging and I don't know where to begin." It did not take us long to convince her that the problems she had encountered in trying to help mentally retarded individuals would be met again in the field of aging: "writing people off"; expecting little of people and responding to them in ways that would prove the point; the tendency to segregate; and looking at people through the distorting lens of labels rather than in terms of their individuality. We have paid quite a price for training narrow specialists.

When the history of this century is written, there is no doubt that the Great Depression of the thirties will be viewed as a turning point in the organization of our society. Those who did not experience the Great Depression will have difficulty comprehending how it affected the thinking and lives of citizens of subsequent generations. The most obvious consequence of this cataclysmic period was the degree to which the relation of the individual to the state changed. Before the Depression, the rhetoric was "rugged individualism" and "that government is best which rules the least." Just as in the twenties and most of the thirties the national sentiment had been isolationism toward the affairs of the world, it was also widely believed that the federal government had no business interfering in the affairs of individuals or assuming any responsibility for citizens who for one reason or another were unable either to care or provide for themselves. If you were sick, dependent, and old, it was too bad, but that was no business of the federal government. It was a local affair, but even there, citizens and local officialdom were reluctant to render assistance. It was not only that the locality viewed its public wards as failures; this was the view the public ward had of him or herself. It was literally inconceivable to most people that government should as a matter of policy be concerned with the personal welfare of its citizens unless, of course, they were a physical or health danger to the surrounding community. But even in these instances, local and state governments had laws seeking reimbursement from the individual or his family. It would be unfair to interpret such laws as symptomatic of a cruel, insensitive society, because we would then be judging it by our present-day outlook. In those days, the bulk of the citizenry regarded it as right and natural that those who "took" from public monies had an obligation to repay, and if they could not, it was only "proper" that the family should be obligated to do so. Ideologically speaking, the government owed its citizens nothing.

There were some exceptions such as the blind, but they were, to say the least, minimal in scope. Even as late as the sixth decade of this century, the state of Connecticut had legislation which sought reimbursement to the state from relatives of individuals who were receiving state aid. The interested reader should consult the recent book by Robert and Rosemary Stevens, *Welfare Medicine in America* (1974), which confirms our central point that entrusting the welfare of people to centralized government is an invitation to social disaster.

What happened to older people who for reasons of health or finances could not sustain an independent existence? On a percentage basis very few became residents of "poor houses." For one thing these facilities were small, but far more decisive was the view that dependent, aged people were responsibilities of their children. To place one's aged parents in a public institution was both embarrassing and shameful. This was even the case where money was no problem. To place one's parents was "to give them away." Somehow the bulk of families managed to maintain sick and aged parents in the community, which meant keeping them as part of a network of family, friends, and neighborhood. The truth is that we hardly know the variety of ways in which this was accomplished, or the consequences for all concerned. In that pre-Great Depression era old people were not a designated group from the standpoint of society or legislation.

The Great Depression set in motion the dynamics of social change. Of all the legislation dealing with the social and economic catastrophe, none was more important than the Social Security Act of 1935. A "retirement test" provision was designed to encourage older workers to retire and make jobs available for the many unemployed younger workers. One could say that for the first time society was singling out older people for special treatment. From one standpoint the provision could be viewed as humane in that a step was being taken to give older people some financial protection. Unfortunately, for most aged people the level of protection was pitifully inadequate. It is not hyperbole to say that to the extent the law was intended to encourage older workers to leave the work force, it was not only singling them out for special treatment, but it was also implying that their worth to society was less than that of other groups. They were, so to speak, disposable items: With one hand society gave, with the other it took away.

The law did no less than to create a separate class of citizens who by virtue of an age criterion could be restricted in the full use of their capabilities. Before the act, becoming old was for most people a difficult experience. After the act, the potential for making it more difficult was increased. During the Great Depression young workers were pitted against older ones. The need to hide one's age became a matter not only of personal vanity but of survival in the work world as well. Slowly but surely the older person's status and sense of worth were beginning to erode as a function of public policy.

The beginning of World War II in Europe, and somewhat later our entry in the war, terminated the Great Depression. Ironically, the needs of the armed services for young people meant that the obstacles to older people entering or remaining in the work force were removed. Older people gained renewed worth! They were needed. But only as long as the war lasted. This was also the case for women as well as physically and mentally handicapped people. During the war years, individuals in training schools for the retarded were placed in the armed forces or into the work arena, and many more who ordinarily would have been placed in these institutions also entered the armed services or easily found gainful employment. What the war years so clearly demonstrated was how the transient needs of a society can force it to give new roles and opportunities to groups that are denied them in peacetime, exposing in the process how the denials stem more from societal prejudices than from limitations possessed by the individuals. An excellent discussion of what happened during the war years in regard to uneducated, illiterate, or low test-scoring people, is contained in Ginzberg and Bray's *The Uneducated* (1953).

Soon after the end of World War II, pressure began to mount for some form of national health insurance. In President Truman's second term he proposed a form of health insurance; the pressures stemmed from several sources. First, it was obvious that many citizens could not afford good medical care, and in some regions they were, for all practical purposes, receiving no medical care. Second, many families saw their financial resources depleted and were forced to go into debt because of sustained illness to one of its members. Third, the number of older people in the population was increasing and that meant that there would be more need for medical service because older people have more illnesses and infirmities. It was also the case that many of these aging people were financially unable to purchase services. This put increased financial pressure on the families of these aging citizens as well as on the welfare budgets of local communities. Fourth, medical care costs were beginning to skyrocket. Fifth, unless the initiative came from the federal government, efforts to protect people against medical catastrophes were not likely to be equitable in their consequences.

There was more recognition than heretofore that although serious illness happened to *individuals,* it always had pervasive consequences for the *family.* The number of older people was growing and their life expectancy was increasing, as well as chances of experiencing chronic, debilitating diseases. In combination, these factors increased the pressure on children, kin, and others who bore responsibility for older, sick, dependent people. The pressure was further exacerbated in that after World War II, sub-units of families, tended not to live near each other. The relatives of older people tended no longer to live in the same neighborhood or even the same city or state. We had become a truly mobile society, and few people predicted what this could mean for older people in need of support and care.

What this feature of our society exposed was the absence of community services that to some extent, at least, could substitute for what used to be family functions and responsibilities. The community, as a political-geographical entity, was slowly recognizing that within its midst were people who were coming to be seen as a "class" — and labeled "older," "aged," "senior citizens" — with special problems for which something had to be done. This meant financial help and a "place" where they could be cared for when they could no longer care for themselves in daily living. What went unnoticed in this development of community consciousness was that emphasis was unreflectively being given to the need for special "places," segregated places, rather than services that might prevent or delay placement in a special place.

What range of services could be made available to older people in their own residences that would either allow them to remain in the community or even strengthen their community ties? That question received hardly any attention. It was not the first time that society, having identified and labeled a group of its citizens who presented problems, gave priority to the role of residential segregation.

The passage of the Medicare, and later the Medicaid, legislation spawned the nursing home industry. Put in another way, the legislation contained financial incentives to families and communities to place many older people in nursing homes. More correctly, the legislation contained very little to enable or encourage old, dependent people to remain in the community. Nursing homes became big business and the major problem seemed to be that they could not be built in numbers sufficient to meet the immediate and projected demand.

We said earlier that as our society became aware of the plight of old people the problem was seen largely as that of individuals and not of a family or neighborhood or community network of social relationships. Medicare legislation reinforced this view by its medical focus. The word *Medi*care, the term "*nursing* home," the growth of the medical specialty of geriatrics — these were more than reflections of illness or patient-doctor, patient-hospital conceptions. They were the basis for public policies that however well meaning placed the problem in the field of medicine, and diverted attention away from the social-familial-community context. These were policies that in a very deliberate way were concerned with the diagnosis and treatment of illness and infirmity, rather than their social origins and concomitants, that is, the social psychological fabric of which each of us is a part. As someone once said: "We treated old people less in terms of what *they* needed or wanted, and more in terms of what *we* knew *we* could do for them." It's like the joke of the ill person who goes to a physician in the dead of winter for an examination after which he is told to go home, take off all of his clothes, stand in front of an open window, and breathe deeply for a half hour. "But," says the patient, "if I do that, I'll get pneumonia." To which the physician replies: "*That* I know how to treat."

It took only a few years after the Medicare and Medicaid legislation for the adverse consequences of public policy to become glaringly obvious. Not surprisingly, the disenchantment started with the fact that implementation of these policies was economically staggering. With the effort to cut back on expenditures came the era of nursing home scandals. The reader who wishes to become familiar with the details of the nursing home scandals should consult published reports of the subcommittee on long-term care of the special committee on aging of the U.S. Senate. The details are only somewhat different from what Blatt (1966, 1970, 1975, 1976, 1977) has described about institutions for the mentally retarded. And, as we shall see later in this chapter when we discuss Zigler's two decades of research on institutions and their retarded residents, the problem has not been money or size of staff but the failure to make the boundaries between institution and community permeable.

In wake of the nursing home scandals the mass media bombarded us with instances of how tarnished the "golden years" could be. It also became evident that not every person put into a nursing home needed to be there if a range of supportive community services had been available. In short, the problem began to be redefined less in terms of an illness or hospital-nursing home model and more in terms of community responsibility, diversity of services, and maintenance in the context of a person's family and friendship networks.

The Self-Defeating Consequences of the Residential Institution

It is ironic that at the same time that residential segregation became a major thrust in programs for older people, its self-defeating consequences began to be exposed in regard to mentally retarded people. The latter development had several sources. The first was that the costs for building and maintaining new institutions had escalated considerably; the second source was the slowly dawning realization that the traditional institution, whatever its rationale, becomes custodial in nature and therefore generates the need for more institutions. A third source was the conception that attempts had to be made to prevent the need for families to institutionalize a retarded member. There were many families who reluctantly resorted to institutionalization because their communities lacked educational or day care programs that would help them keep the retarded person in the home.

Somehow, the new thinking went, we must move in new directions by putting services and programs in the communities, not by building new institutions that in essence said to these communities: "*We* will take care of *your* problems. Send them to us, we will do our magic, and some day we will send them back to you." A new message was being formulated: Mentally retarded people can be maintained in the community if we develop appropriate services and programs, and if the community begins to accept more active responsibility. Neither from the standpoint of economics or humanity can we continue to isolate these people psychologically and geographically from the natural community. As a case in point, a number of years ago the state of Connecticut adopted the policy that it would never again build a large residential institution for mentally retarded individuals. This policy was adopted fifteen years after building its second such institution in 1941. That institution, the Southbury Training School, was for some time an international showcase because of its striking architectural features, country setting, commitment to being an educational rather than a custodial setting, and its objective of returning its residents as quickly as possible to the community (Sarason, Grossman, and Zitnay, 1972). The educational emphasis was a response to the fact that Southbury had been built to take care of the waiting list of the other and much older training school. Needless to say, things did not work out as they were supposed to, and it was not long before Southbury had its own waiting list and had settled into familiar institutional traditions.

However, some far-seeing individuals at Southbury realized the self-defeating nature of the large institution placed in the middle of nowhere. It was obvious to them that as pressure would grow to build a third institution there would also develop a strong resistance based on purely economic consideration; it had cost nine million dollars to build Southbury, and a comparable facility built within the past decade would cost fifty or more millions. Instead, it was proposed and accepted that the state be divided into small regions, each having a regional center strategically located near population centers. Each would have very few beds; its major thrust would be to avoid institutionalization by developing day programs for non-resident children, supporting and strengthening existing community programs, and providing various home services. A major selling point was that by building a community orientation into the regional center concept, vast economies could be effected. And what skeptic could be unmoved by the threat of having to spend millions upon millions to build another Southbury?

Four assumptions were crucial to the hoped-for success of the regional center concept:

1. An institution was necessary because there were individuals requiring full-time care but it would be a very small institution in terms of beds.
2. The need to plan programs for its full-time residents would not interfere with the development of programs and services for scores of nonresidents. Indeed, one of the consequences of the community thrust would be to reduce the pressure for beds.

3. It would be possible for the regional center to educate and stimulate community forces to see that responsibility had to be shared for their retarded citizens—that it was not only the state's responsibility.
4. All of the above would demonstrate that the regional center concept was economically superior to past practices.

The regional center concept pioneered in Connecticut had a major national impact. It is important, therefore, to report two of the findings from a study by McClellan (1973) who did a painstaking economic analysis of one of these regional centers. First, the actual costs of a regional center are at least 39 percent more than its yearly budget from the state would suggest. The second finding was that on a per capita basis the amount of money spent to maintain the residential program was almost four times the amount devoted to day-care and community services for nonresidents.

In other words, there was precious little going for the "community thrust." This means that the number of nonresidents that can be accepted into programs at the center is limited, and that the kinds of programs in the community, *not* at the regional center, which could maximize the chances that the nonresident could live productively in the community are very limited, indeed virtually nonexistent. Furthermore, the inability to develop work and social living programs in the natural community for the nonresidents has adverse affects on the fate of the more than half of the residents who are capable of living and working in the community. The bulk of these residents are at the regional center not because they require an institution but because appropriate working and living programs in the community have not yet been developed for them, and their stay in residence will be prolonged as long as these community programs are not available.

It is more likely that when residents are returned to the community it will not necessarily be in a setting appropriate to their needs such as a group home, but in one that happens to be available, such as a foster home, however questionable in the individual case. The consequences for residents and nonresidents are predictable on the basis of the discrepancy between levels of financial support for residential and community programs. One does not have to know the particular institution to make these predictions; one only has to know the size of the discrepancy in support, and the larger the discrepancy the sadder the situation.

Let us now turn to aspects of the "prehistory" of the regional center that McClellan studied, in regard to which one of the writers, Seymour B. Sarason, had been intimately involved.

While the regional center was being built there was no staff to speak of—only the newly appointed superintendent and his secretary. However, the superintendent had informally picked some of his key staff members, and for the year before the regional center opened they met fairly regularly for planning purposes. These meetings were held at the Yale Psycho-Educational Clinic, with which the regional center was to have a close working tie. I was director of the clinic and had long been working in the field of mental retardation. The conceptual basis for the tie between the clinic and the regional center was that both were committed to the idea that mental retardation was a community responsibility. To the extent that the regional center was seen as the major source of programs, services, and funding, and to the extent that community talent and resources (latent and actual) were not developed and organized to man and maintain a wide variety of programs and services, the regional center would be regarded as a failure. The population to be served was a very heterogeneous one in terms of level and needs, and this required a greater variety of services and settings than one agency could possibly provide.

The suggestion was made that we approach the problem by dealing first with the emergency waiting list: those individuals for whom institutionalization was considered essential, not tomorrow or today but yesterday. There was no institution yet and there would not be one for at least a year. What help could we be to the individuals (and their families) on this emergency waiting list? What resources in the community could we bring to bear to be helpful? From the time we began to work with the individuals on the waiting list only the superintendent was paid by the state; everyone else volunteered time. We secured the help of the clergymen, students, community agency personnel, the visiting nurse association, school personnel, and an assortment of interested citizens, physicians, and so forth. The persons we sought out for help depended on the nature of the problem, where the individual lived, and the agencies that had had contact with the case. We viewed ourselves as "talent scouts" and as prodders of social agencies to assume meaningful responsibility for individuals who because of the label "mentally retarded" were not considered appropriate for these agencies, even though their services were very much needed by the retarded individual and his family. It was no secret that many social agencies had little or nothing to do with mental retardation either because they felt they had no expertise in this field or because they did not regard it as interesting or fruitful—this latter opinion being the cause for their lack of knowledge. This was as true for public agencies (local and state) as for private agencies.

We quickly found that individuals on the emergency waiting list were there not because they required institutional care but because a variety of community services and programs (such as group homes, homemaker services, parent education and counseling, baby-sitting help, marital counseling) were not available or, if available, were unknown to the family. Some of these families were requesting institutionalization because they had been told that it was the best course of action, and not because they personally desired it. There was not a single case, regardless of severity, for which an alternative to institutionalization was not possible, if community resources, actual and potential, could be utilized. *This does not mean that these alternatives would or could solve all problems in the individual case.* But neither could institutionalization, as we so well know. What struck us forcefully was that these alternatives would *create* fewer major social problems than institutionalization would (or has). Indeed, in the process of developing some of these alternatives we found many people in the community grateful for the opportunity to be helpful, to be part of something that brought new knowledge and challenge into their lives. Whatever we were able to do in conjunction with these people was in large measure due to a feeling of community we communicated to and instilled in them. We needed them, even though they had no special knowledge or skills. We were prepared to help them help us. In some quarters this was not viewed with approbation because we were using "untrained" people, which could be harmful—a suffocating professional view that justifies nothing.

It needs to be emphasized that in approaching the families on the emergency waiting list we did not have beds to offer, and since it would have been ridiculous to predict when the new regional center building would be ready for occupancy, we could not say when their retarded child could be admitted. What we could offer them was our willingness to be helpful now. In short, whatever we could do was not presented as a substitute for what they had been told was the best course of action—institutionalization. As a consequence, the families cooperated with us.

These were exciting months for everyone. *They were also disturbing because we began to see that we did not need the regional center.* If the millions that were going into buildings were made available to us we could develop scores of programs and settings in *and* by the community, and in ways that would bring new meaning into the lives of many people. Our disturbance deepened the closer we came to the opening date because we found ourselves forced to think about institutional programs, modes of staffing, recruitment, and the host of other issues and problems that are consequences of opening a new and complicated institution. At the last meeting held at Yale Psycho-Educational Clinic, someone said: "The regional center has seen its best days." It was a comment that mirrored accurately the vague dysphoric feeling of everyone at the meeting.

No one doubted that from that point on the community thrust would take second place to what went on within the walls of the regional center. We were going to struggle against this, but as time went on it was apparent that we would not be successful. The enabling legislation, the nature of budget allocations, the preoccupation with filling beds and determining their per capita costs, state-dictated staffing patterns, job descriptions—an examination of these and other factors made it all too clear that the major justification for the regional center was to provide beds. Put in another way, the regional center was embedded in a state legislative-judicial-administrative apparatus and tradition that was geared to build and maintain institutions. (The same, of course, is true for the mental hospitals and youth correctional settings.) If through some miracle the state was prevented from building more institutions, and was required to phase out existing ones, only then could one grasp how much of state government existed because of institutions. Is it any wonder that the suggestion that institutions are not necessary, that they defeat the purposes for which they were built, that they dilute the sense of community responsibility, and that they produce all the evil consequences of segregation are not looked upon kindly by the state apparatus? [Sarason 1974, p. 233]

A note of caution. Although we must be critical of the regional center concept, there can be no doubt that from a moral and social-historical perspective the concept represents a step forward in its goal to keep individuals within the fabric of community living and prevent the insidious consequences of physical and social segregation. That is no small advance.

The fact remains, however, that precisely because the concept required an institution for its base, albeit a small institution, meant that in practice priority would be given to those who lived within its walls. Thus, the institution becomes inward-looking and walled-off from the surrounding community. One must grant that this happens somewhat less than in the case of older and larger institutions built away from the centers of population, but that is the point: we are dealing with a difference of degree and not with a departure from traditional ways of thinking. The history of human services institutions—be they for the aged, or mentally retarded, or mentally disordered—supports the conclusion that they slowly but surely become places where insensitivity, stifling custodialism, low morale, and even brutality come to be dominant characteristics. For the history of these institutions the reader should consult Wolfensberger (1972) and Rothman (1971). To get the flavor of a particular period that illustrates the problems of all periods one should read Jarvis's 1855 report *Insanity and Idiocy in Massachusetts. Report of the Commission on Lunacy* and Grob's excellent introduction to it (1971).

Intermediate Care Facilities

In this section we shall further pursue the ways in which an institution obscures the problem of clarifying what should be meant by a "community program." Further discussion is necessary because, as a result of a 1971 amendment to Title XIX of the Social Security Act, federal support for "intermediate care facilities" for mentally retarded individuals and certain other needy segments of the population was authorized. This support for a new class of residential institutions lightens the financial outlays of states because it permits parts of existing institutions housing eligible individuals to be categorized as intermediate care facilities (ICF). In order to comprehend this new development, we shall briefly summarize a document prepared for the federal government at Tulane University. The *Surveyor Course Manual* is meant for state officials who would have responsibility for meeting regulations for ICFs. The manual, 304 pages, and the accompanying course of one week are unusually comprehensive and intensive. The purposes of the 1971 amendment may be seen in the following:

Discussion of the Title XIX amendment relating to ICFs-MR in the Senate Committee on Finance prior to its passage underscored the Committee's interest in institutions whose primary objective is the active provision of rehabilitative, education and training services to enhance the capacity of mentally retarded individuals to care for themselves or to engage in employment. Public institutions whose primary objective is the provision of health services or rehabilitative services to the mentally retarded should be subject to Federal (financial) participation under adequate safeguards. The amendment, therefore,

> defined such facilities as intermediate care facilities if . . . the institution meets standards of either health services, rehabilitation services or a combination of the two that are set forth by the Secretary of Health, Education, and Welfare . . . (and if) these standards are sufficient to achieve the purposes and to distinguish such facilities from those which are primarily residential.

A second condition underlying the amendment is that the individual in such an institution, who is mentally retarded, has been determined to need and is actually receiving the health or rehabilitation services which the institutions set forth as being provided. Through this legislation both public and private facilities may participate as providers of services in an ICF-MR under the Title XIX [Tulane U., p. 10].

States that elect to provide ICF-MR services may reimburse as providers only those facilities that meet the requirements in regulations that were published in the Federal Register on January 17, 1974, and became effective on March 18, 1974. In developing these standards, HEW took a number of factors into consideration. Among these are the intent of Congress to assure the individuals are receiving more than custodial care or room and board, to improve institutional care and services to individuals with mental retardation, as well as persons with related conditions, and to provide adequate safeguard for Federal funds expended. In addition, the President has announced a goal of reducing by one-third the number of mentally retarded persons in institutions. The regulations were designed to foster this goal [Tulane U., p. 13].

As a result, it was the goal of HEW to design a set of standards and requirements to ensure that the institution provides a range of services adequate to help its residents develop maximum independent living capabilities and to return to the community at the earliest possible time [Tulane U., p. 13].

The training manual is a remarkable document. Aside from the fact that it is clearly written, it does not oversimplify the complexity of issues surrounding history, diagnosis, institutionalization, the rise and misuse of drugs and treatments, etc. It leaves no doubt in the minds of those who will be creating or supervising the ICF what a major difference is between a custodial and habilitative attitude.

> A shift from the custodial to the habilitative philosophy implies the involvement of the family as an important, and in some instances the primary force in the treatment process. Residential living should not mean that the family is shut out of the process. Sometimes it occurs that the mentally retarded person who is "put away" in an institution comes to be thought of as dead by the family who put him there. They mourn him and then they disengage themselves emotionally and psychologically from him, unless there is a viable and consistent means available to keep the relationship between the individual and his family intact and constructive. Perhaps this single aspect of the whole philosophical shift is the most important. The family is becoming a much more integral part of the active treatment

process and the family is included as a living and vital force in the resident's life. If indeed the goal of upgrading services to the developmentally disabled is to be realized, then the family should always play a direct role in whatever services are provided [Tulane U., p. 44].

Permeating the entire manual is an exquisite sensitivity to what it means to interact with a person, not a label. In these days of cynicism it is inspiring to read a document that does not pander to ignorance or prejudice, and does not avoid seamy history. Unfortunately, despite its many virtues the manual is deficient in one important respect and self-contradictory in another; in tandem they force one to an unpleasant conclusion. Although the major justification for the ICF is "to ensure that the institution provides a range of services adequate to help its residents develop maximum independent capabilities and to return to the community at the earliest possible time," the manual is about what should happen *within* the confines of the ICF. Nothing is said about how this should be related to the community. How should return to the community be brought about? What should be the role of the community *in* ICF, or the role of the parents in the process and the transition? Why will the ICF not have the same fate of the institutions it seeks to supplant?

Let us not blithely assume that those who created the older type institution had intentions less humane than ours and, limiting ourselves to the past forty years, that they did not accept the rhetoric of returning people to community living. No group of people could have been more accepting of the goal of returning people to the community than those who created the Southbury Training School in 1941 (Sarason, 1972), and that effort influenced all institutions built since. And, as we have seen, the regional centers devised as means to correct the inadequacies and failures of the Southbury Training School have little of the community thrust in them. Why should the ICF have a different fate?

The manual gives a partial and negative answer: There is so much absorption with what should happen within the institution, so much emphasis on meeting federal regulations for federal support, and keeping records, that the elaboration of a community orientation is absent. Furthermore, the failure to examine the details of funding and budgets and how they relate to a community orientation is an omission that forces one to be skeptical about how the ICF will meet its stated purposes. It is similar to what happens so frequently in Congress when it passes legislation authorizing a program, but then does not fund it.

In the 304-page manual approximately five pages are devoted to brief descriptions of desirable, community-based facilities such as temporary crisis or respite care, sheltered living, apartment training, and foster placement. The manual notes that very few of those who are presently institutionalized "are now benefiting from [these] new and innovative alternative residential settings" (p. 48). It is also true that very few noninstitutionalized people benefit from these alternative residential settings. There is a very definite social class factor, for example, in who can afford to take advantage of training programs for apartment living.

In creating ICFs, it is the expectation that these alternative settings will increasingly be places to which ICF residents will go. The adjective "intermediate" connotes the image of a way station on the road to community living. We are informed in the manual that most ICFs will be created in existing "public centralized institutions."

> These institutions may be as large as a small town with 2,000 to 3,000 or more residents, or may be as small as a facility housing 35-50 residents. The larger institutions will have as residents retarded individuals of every age and description. In such a setting, the implementation of even a seemingly minor regulation may require extensive administrative actions. Small institutions often have more specialized populations, and in some respects, change can be facilitated more rapidly in a small setting than it can in a large one.
>
> While there are more private facilities for mentally handicapped people than there are public facilities, there are relatively few mentally retarded persons in private facilities. The private facility may, however, apply for certification as an ICF-MR facility, and the same regulations must be met as with public facilities [Tulane U., p. 47].

What the manual is saying, and subsequent events have amply confirmed, is that existing institutions, or parts of them, will be *converted* to meet the stated purposes of the ICF. The immediate consequence of this, of course, is to reduce the state's costs for maintaining these institutions. The federal government will contribute to the maintenance of the ICF. But we are confronted with this question: By what kind of alchemy will these existing institutions, or parts of them, be transformed from noncommunity to community orientation? What have these institutions been doing up until now? What prevented them from having a community thrust? And why should they be any different in the future? Heal and Gollay (1977) reported that a major difference between those deinstitutionalized individuals who remained in the community and those who had to be returned to the institution was that the former had more community services available to them. But they also report that returnees had a higher proportion of their services provided by the institution for ten of a possible eleven services; nonreturnees had the greater proportion of their services provided by community agencies for ten of the possible eleven services. These are striking findings because they again imply the inadequacy of the institution's community orientation. In our experience, institutional personnel do not know how to effectively utilize existing community resources.

From the standpoint of the states, the legislation is an economic boon. But in our discussions with state officials they view the legislation as a laudable effort to "humanize" their institutions rather than as a mandate to move large segments of their population into community settings. This despite the fact that all past efforts to humanize these institutions have largely failed, and that in regard to a community orientation the discrepancy between rhetoric and practice remains. To the extent that the manual focuses on what should happen within the institution, it unwittingly postpones confronting the implications of that fact.

Far from being possible vehicles for solving problems, these institutions are the problem. They reflect and perpetuate the segregation mentality, the major consequence of which is the erection of barriers between the community and the institution. These institutions are like ghettos; over time those within and without feel comfortable staying apart, colluding, so to speak, in the fiction that this is the best and most "natural" state of affairs. Until, of course, the scandals and exposés destroy the fiction.

Let us not scapegoat institutions which, after all, exist as an expression of attitudes and policies of the larger society. This is a point about which the writers of the manual are well aware.

> A shift is beginning to take place away from the community rejection of retarded persons to a more active community involvement with them. Slowly but surely many communities are reassessing the responsibility they have to meet the special needs of retarded persons. Many of the obstacles are being eliminated through education, but others are being overcome by confrontation with the issues. As group homes are opened, for example, court suits are sometimes brought by citizens concerned about their welfare and property values. In most instances, group homes have been upheld in the courts, and their residents have proved themselves quite able to function as good and responsible neighbors. Before the new points of view and approaches can work, the society, from related professionals in the scientific community to the neighbor across the street, must be able to know, understand, and cooperate with the process of change. Other segments of the service-providing system cannot function well unless the community accepts the retarded person back into its midst.
>
> The residential care circumstances that many mentally retarded persons find themselves in today reflect a compromise, representing a deviation from the optimal plan of retaining the child with special needs within the family, with his parent and sibling growth and support experience backed up by dependable and intelligent community programs and opportunities. The services of the future will hopefully provide all relevant habilitative components, including educational, social, recreational, employment, and general counselling elements, which represent society's acknowledgment of the handicapped person's right to needed services [Tulane U., p. 45].

This clear statement of fact and morality has implications that need explanation. The statement is factual in pointing to community resistance to accommodating and maintaining mentally retarded people in community residences. And the statement is moral in that it criticizes these sources of resistance and justifies the actions of those who seek to confront these issues. What the writers of the manual could have said is that those who have been courageous enough to confront the issues (through courts and legislation), to deal with the community not as suppliants but as seekers of fair treatment, have *not* been our institutional leaders or the heads of our state agencies but rather private citizens. And, not infrequently, to the extent that these citizens have been successful, it has been despite rather than with the active help of those responsible for our institutions.

Precisely because our institutions are public, and, therefore, inevitably part of the political system, a massive constraint is put on the willingness and capability of institutional leaders and heads of state agencies to confront the community in an assertive fashion. The institution literally is intended to serve the community, not to upset it, and heads of public institutions and agencies know this well. This helps explain why over the course of the decades these institutions have never changed from within but rather from the courageous actions of "outsiders" beholden only to the truth as they saw it. Why the ICF should be expected to have a different fate is hard to understand, if only because the ICF, as the manual makes clear, will largely though not exclusively, be cosmetically changed parts of existing institutions.

The reader is urged to consult Scull's (1977) recent book on the origins and history of the "decarceration" movement. He argues that historically the anti-institutional movements only met with success when the economic burden of institutions was more than public officials and policy makers considered feasible. They were in favor of decarceration not on moral grounds, or because they knew how to develop and sustain more productive community programs, but rather because they thought decarceration would be cheaper. Scull's indictment of the decarceration movement does not rest on any belief in the superiority of institutions but on the gross oversimplification of the real problems that decarceration poses and to the solution of which the proponents of decarceration have had amazingly little to offer. In short, when decarceration is powered primarily by economic considerations, a new set of evils replaces the old one. Scull's indictment of decarceration programs is based on a reanalysis of studies purporting to show their superiority to institutional programs. Consistent with our own position, Scull emphasizes several major sources of obstacle to decarceration: the administrative-bureaucratic mentality embedded in the apparatus of the state, the self-seeking and self-protective traditions of professionalism, community resistance, and the structure and traditions of a highly complex and production-oriented industrial society.

In a recent paper, in part briefly summarizing twenty years of research by Zigler and his associates, Zigler and Balla (1977) make a number of incisive points about the impact of institutional experience on retarded people. The first of these points is that variations in the quantity and quality of social stimulation before institutionalization can affect behavior many years after institutionalization. The second point is that:

those individuals who had experienced greater preinstitutional social deprivation were more responsive to social reinforcement than less deprived children. Of special interest was our finding that the retarded individuals who maintained contact with their parents or parent-surrogates either by being visited at the institution or by going home on vacations were more likely to display the type of autonomous behavior characteristic of nonretarded children. Thus, we found clear empirical evidence that an institutional policy of encouraging many contacts with the community does promote psychological growth [Zigler and Balla, 1977, p. 4].

The significance of the second point is in its relationship to the findings of the King, Raynes, and Tizard (1971) study which demonstrated that far more important than size of institution was whether the institution was resident-oriented or institution-oriented.

The third point was based on a searching comprehensive study of resident care practices in 166 *living units* from 19 institutions in the United States and 11 institutions in a Scandanavian country. They found that living units in the Scandanavian country were more resident-oriented than were living units in the United States. They also found that "Large living-unit size and level of retardation were found to be predictive of institution-oriented care practices. Cost per resident per day, number of aides per resident, or number of professional staff *did not* predict care practices [pp. 6–7]."

> The lack of association of either financial or human factors — as measured by cost per resident per day and by number of aides and professional staff per resident, respectively — came as a considerable surprise to us. Apparently, simply increasing expenditures or personnel will not necessarily guarantee better care for retarded persons. Rather, it is how these personnel are utilized in the settings. The finding that living-unit size was predictive of care practices is of special practical interest. One way of creating more humane settings for institutionalized retarded persons may well be to design living units small enough so that each resident is, of necessity, seen as an individual. It is encouraging to note that it may be possible to pursue such a policy with existing resources. The reader will recall that the most resident-oriented care practices were found in group homes, which were operated at less cost than either the regional centers or the large central institutions. It may well be that part of the lower cost for group homes can be accounted for by the fact that these facilities, for the most part, serve mildly retarded residents who require less care and supervision. However, as mentioned above, number of aides or professional staff per resident were not found to be predictive of care practices.
>
> We did find one exception to the general lack of association of such "human variables" as number of aides per resident and employee-turnover rate and care practices. In group homes in the United States, low employee-turnover rate and a high ratio of professional staff per resident were found to be predictive of more resident-oriented care practices. It may well be that such human factors as continuity of staffing can only become operative in certain settings [Zigler and Balla 1977, p. 7].

The fourth point is based on a unique study in that it took into account both care practices and the actual behavior of the residents.

There were no differences between persons residing in central institutions and persons residing in regional centers on any of our behavioral measures. This lack of findings was of some surprise in view of the fact that the average size of the large central institutions was 1,633, while the average size of the regional centers was 111. The central institutions also housed more residents per living unit and had a higher employee-turnover rate. The cost per resident per day was twice as high in the regional centers as in the central institutions. The number of aides per resident was twice as high in the regional centers as in the central institutions. The proportion of professional staff per resident and the number of volunteer hours per resident per year was almost six times as great in the regional centers as in the central institutions. Such findings lend credence to the view that simply increasing cost and/or increasing staff will not, in and of itself, ensure greater behavioral competency on the part of residents in institutions. The findings also suggest that more intensive efforts need to be made to discover what particular kinds of programs enhance the behavioral competency of residents in institutions. The mere placement of a retarded person in a regional center did not seem to suffice as a means for increasing competency [Zigler and Balla 1977, p. 8].

Zigler and Balla go on to speculate how the characteristics of institutional living units can be inimical to the behavior of retarded people. And they conclude their important article with these words (italics ours):

In conclusion, if there is a consistent theme to this 20 years of work on the effects of institutionalization on retarded persons, it is a continuing and increasing emphasis on the social-policy implications of our research. We are convinced that any comprehensive program of research must take into account not only the behavioral functioning of residents but the quality of life they experience, *the extent to which they maintain contact with the community, and whether they are successfully discharged to community placement.* We believe that only by means of such a multifaceted research program will it be eventually possible to determine empirically the optimal residential setting at the optimal cost [Zigler and Balla 1977, p. 10].

So the degree to which institutions will change in hoped-for ways will be determined not only by how they shift from institution-oriented to resident-oriented attitudes and practices, but also how the boundaries between institution and community become more permeable. The fact has to be faced that one of the consequences of a community orientation is to question the need for institutions, or at the very least to drastically reduce their importance in public policy. That implied threat will not be viewed favorably by the people whose work and livelihood depend on the existence of these institutions. Nor will it be greeted enthusiastically by all segments in our communities. This point needs underlining and cannot, as Scull (1977) emphasizes, be avoided. "Normalization" in the lives of handicapped individuals will not be accomplished by reiterating the moral basis for normalization. Normalization poses real problems and obstacles rooted in the fabric of our society and to proceed as if that were not true is naive in the extreme. Ignorance is no less justified than immorality, especially when ignorance stands a good chance of creating a new immorality.

Community Attitudes

It is too easy to scapegoat the residential institution by leaving the impression that their inadequacies or evils only arise from their internal dynamics. As we said earlier, and the ICF manual illustrates, the segregating institution is a socially sanctioned and supported vehicle. In this section we shall begin our discussion of community attitudes by discussing a most unusual "case" that illuminates several things: negative community attitudes; changes in a positive direction; and the significance of these attitudes for our understanding of the developmental potentialities of those people society labels as mentally retarded. If the case is unusual, it is because the writer, Dr. Gaston Blom, is a very unusual person: a psychoanalyst, professor of child psychiatry, and professor of education at Michigan State University. What is more unusual than this combination is that Dr. Blom is a most unusual human being possessed of that degree of courage that leads society to confront its accustomed ways of thinking and acting.

Let us begin where Dr. Blom begins:

On April 25th of this year, just three weeks ago Heather, age 21, and Wayne, age 25, were married in a small church ceremony. In attendance were Heather's mother and father, a friend from the tea room of the Department store where Heather worked, Wayne's boss from the restaurant where he worked, and the family minister. Wayne's mother refused to attend since she was opposed to the marriage and his father is divorced and has no contact with his son.

You may immediately wonder why such an episode has any particular significance. Do not many young men and women get married at this age, sometimes against a parent's wishes? Is this then not a normal event? Of course the answer to these two questions are yes. However, when I add that Heather and Wayne are young people handicapped by fates over which they had no control nor did their parents, a story begins to evolve. It is a story which Heather and her family want me to share with others who can learn from their experiences. As her mother put it—"she has helped us and I hope will continue to help others." Heather advanced in a world that tended to oppose and question her rights to as normal a life as possible.

For two years I shared Heather's inner feelings about herself and her past and current experiences with the outside world as her therapist and friend and also tried to be helpful in dealing with many realistic issues. I had the support and confidence of her parents in these endeavors with a greater willingness on the part of Heather's mother to take risks. For me the story was a sensitive and moving venture in areas where I had little experience and limited help from theoretical conceptualization. I tried to facilitate what felt right and to oppose what seemed wrong and in that process received support, indifference, and opposition from various agencies and professionals. I also slowly became Wayne's friend of the present and I say slowly because initially his trust in me as a man and particularly as a psychiatrist was limited. The love relationship of these two young people was a convincing one and to support in realistic ways its fulfillment came naturally. So I want to share my part in this story with the hope that as professionals we can provide appropriate help and advocacy to handicapped people and their families individually and collectively—of making available patterns and conditions of everyday life which are as close as possible to the norms and patterns of the mainstream of society.

Heather, the child of professional parents, was born when her mother was thirty-nine years of age at which age the incidence of Down's syndrome (mongolism) is about 1 in 660 births. And Heather had the syndrome. In 1954, when Heather was born, the mother knew that institutionalization was the most frequent recommendation in these cases but she "couldn't go through with it." Fortunately, Heather's pediatrician favored home care, and Heather grew up as a regular member of the family.

The precipitating factor which brought Heather to Dr. Blom was a psychological evaluation when she was 18 years of age "to bring her records into conformity with state regulations and to determine eligibility for continuing participation in a work-study program."

A pediatric friend asked if I would do a psychiatric evaluation on Heather who was then almost 19 years old. Her mother had a number of concerns: (1) was she psychotic, (2) how disturbed was she, (3) what were her future adjustment possibilities, and (4) what recommendations could be given to facilitate her adaptation. The questions about psychosis and severity of emotional disturbance had arisen suddenly from a school conference a month previously where the parents were told about the results of "routine psychological testing" done twelve months previously in 1972. Twelve months is a long time to delay in sharing and communicating findings of such an ominous nature, regardless of their reliability. Again this was evidence that the normalization principle was not being practiced—i.e. the principle being that human management professions, as Wolfensberger calls us (Wolfensberger, 1972), did not use means as normative as possible to establish or maintain behaviors and characteristics that were culturally normative as possible. Understandably the parents were frightened and confused but had sufficient ego strength to question the psychological interpretations. Heather's mother knew she was sad and troubled but had every reason to doubt that Heather was psychotic. Previous experiences with professionals had given her good reasons to question them at times and rely on her own judgement, intuition, and values—beginning with the obstetrician. As mother wrote—"I remember seeing Heather in the bassinet in the delivery room and remarking that she looked a little mongoloid. Dr. U. thought I was a rejecting mother for this comment." In another part of a developmental questionnaire she wrote about the pregnancy—"I also worried about Down syndrome especially since I was over 35 years. We didn't know about its relation to chromosomes at that time in 1954." However, in a letter to me mother also said positively—"M. G. was Heather's pediatrician until she died. She was a great help to me when Heather was born since she favored home care rather than institutionalization (which was common then—and which I knew I couldn't go through with)."

As for Wayne, his family physician reported that he had a traumatic birth which resulted in stunted growth and slow development. He is an only child from an unhappy marriage which resulted in divorce. Although his father is living, on his mother's advice he has told people that is father is dead. Wayne's mother has fostered his dependency on her, opposed his relationship to Heather, and has actively resisted all attempts by various people to discuss the relationship and her feelings. Wayne is judged to be mildly retarded but he does have a driver's license, driving only with his mother present.

Several things are remarkable about Dr. Blom's account. Dominating the account is Heather herself: imaginative, sensitive, verbal, engaging, persistent, and troubled. Knowing that she has Down's syndrome we are simply not prepared for Dr. Blom's description of her and her interactions with him over sixty-six sessions. If we are not prepared, it says as much about us as it does about Heather. When someone looks "odd" and that oddness is supposed to be associated with intellectual and interpersonal inadequacies, we are surprised when that person does not fit our preconceptions. Indeed, Dr. Blom is quite sensitive to the possibility that his account may be seen by some people as a distortion of the true state of affairs.

> Perhaps, Dr. Blom, you are not objective enough and too emotionally involved—the implication being that you can't be both objective and emotional. But let me cite some statements from a revised 1976 edition of a well known textbook on mental retardation (Robinson and Robinson, 1976). In a discussion of Down's syndrome these authors indicate that retardation is usually moderate to severe; IQs range from 40-54 but can vary widely; "affected persons rarely marry and their libido is said to be diminished"; "emotional disturbance in retarded persons often is more a social phenomenon than an intrapsychic problem"; consultation with parents and teachers should be the emphasis in psychological efforts.

In this connection, let us listen to part of a report from a pediatric geneticist to whom Dr. Blom had sent Heather and Wayne for counseling about sterilization.

> My meeting with Heather and her fiancee was most informal and intimate. They were, as you know, a delightful couple. I had the impression that both were slow but probably borderline. One felt innocence but also character. On occasion there was the use of words and phrases that were not fully understood, the kind of thing a precocious child who has grown up in too adult an atmosphere might say. None of this is meant to detract. I have never seen anyone with Down syndrome as able to cope and relate as Heather.
>
> When I asked them why they came, Heather did most of the talking and said that they were in love and wanted to get married. She knew she had Down syndrome and understood that her children might have it. Since she did not want her

children to have the problems she had, she felt she should be sterilized. We discussed this and mentioned the roughly 50% risk that any child she bore would also have Down syndrome. Wayne was concerned lest the projected surgery would be painful and unpleasant and offered to be sterilized himself. We discussed that. He brought up the fact that his mother was not in favor of either the match or of vasectomy. We discussed the fact that the risk was Heather's and that we did not know his risk for retarded children. I supported them in their desires, agreeing that they might have a problem with the added burden of a child. I referred Heather to Dr. D. and offered to see them again if they wished. I only heard from them again by a Christmas card from Heather [several months later].

A second remarkable feature of Dr. Blom's account concerns Heather's parents who obviously had been crucial in her rearing. Clearly they regarded Heather as an independent human being who had to be given every opportunity to experience normal living, and if that meant taking risks, that was a problem inherent in rearing any child. This, of course, was in marked contrast to the attitude and practices of Wayne's mother as well as of school personnel and other professionals with whom Heather had contact. Whereas Heather's parents reacted to her as a unique individual, the community reacted to her in terms of labels.

The third remarkable feature is Dr. Blom himself. Like Heather's parents, he "saw" past her looks and labels, and in a manner quite atypical of professionals he actively helped her in regard to many endeavors.

Over the course of two years I saw Heather sixty-six times, eight of them being shared with Wayne as their relationship developed. I saw the parents about ten times. There were also meetings with school staff, association for retarded citizen staff, child advocates, and a number of occasions when I saw Heather in places other than my office—searching together for music companies who would transcribe her tapes at a reasonable price, having lunch with her at the tea room where she worked, and visiting her at the hospital when she had a sterilization procedure.

Let me first tell you about some of the expressive aspects of the therapy even though a great deal of work was also spent on planning and choices, information about plans, and feelings about plans. As you know the best made plans also with "normal" people do not always go smoothly!

Beginning with the second interview Heather would regularly write a list of problems in a book, which became her therapy book. These were the problems she wanted to discuss as well as take off points for associated concerns and problems. If I became too pressing or when Heather became too uncomfortable, she would say "OK, well" and go back to the list.

The list in the second interview consisted of:

1. Watergate is on my mind
2. How to hold a conversation without being interrupted
3. Work at Goodwill
4. Drug addicts and police
5. Make new friends

6. Two uncles died
7. Newer generation

This list of topics got us into her conservative fundamentalistic values—beliefs in the president who is head of our country and can't be wrong, police as friends and protectors, and the newer generation destroying the image of God. While I was not always in agreement with her belief system, it became clear that they served a security motive and that relativism made her uncomfortable and anxious. There was some indication over the two years that as her self esteem improved and the anxieties about death and anger diminished, Heather seemed more flexible in her values and more accepting of wrongdoing in thoughts and actions for herself and others. At her graduation ceremony from high school a young man streaked through the audience and as she told me about it she laughed saying—"he was as naked as a Jay Bird." Work at Goodwill Industries as one of her work study assignments (study was usually the weaker part) made her uncomfortable because of all the deformed and crippled people. She was anxious, cried, felt sorry for them, but didn't want to see them. As you might have expected she eventually talked with feeling about her handicaps—her sadness, anger, blame of parents, envy of others including her sisters, and the guilt such feelings engendered. Slowly she accepted my gentle encouragement that she did not have to use big words but use her own that were very acceptable. Later on with her parents she was willing to accept not understanding situations—"I'm not that smart, but—"

Heather used her problem lists for quite a while but as she felt better about herself, the problems were fewer or she would not bring her therapy book because "I didn't have many problems this week." She brought her poems and transcribed song readings with background music. She was an avid country music fan, listening to KLAK and expressing love for Johnny Cash and his family. She gave me three of his books to read and I became highly informed about his life, activities, and songs. On one occasion she actually shook his hand when he arrived at the airport for a concert he was to give. She also went to the concert with a friend of the family. On another occasion she decided to enter a country music contest and asked me to help her transcribe one of her tapes in the form prescribed by the contest. I was reluctant and tried to discourage her by indicating we both enjoyed her music but I did not think it was good enough. After my hemming and hawing, Heather finally admonished me by saying—"it doesn't do any harm to try—what if I do fail!" I agreed with her and then she said, "OK let's go right now." Whereupon I made some phone calls and we explored some music shops together and finally got the tapes transcribed using her employment money to pay for it.

Her relationship to Wayne developed only a few months after these steps were unsuccessful and quickly became one of love. Heather shared with me their love notes and their secret meetings after work every day. I never had the occasion to question its genuineness. It took several weeks before I met Wayne. One afternoon he came with Heather to a Friday afternoon session which was arranged by her. He understandably felt awkward and uneasy and asked me in an inquisitory tone why Heather was seeing a psychiatrist. I explained that Heather was not crazy but had problems that were helped by talking. He then wanted to know when treatment would end. It was not until some time later he could acknowledge jealousy about Heather's warm feelings for me and his wish to have her share with him exclusively. I recognized the legitimacy of his feelings and wishes. Wayne was at times puzzled by my acceptance. He gradually saw me as a substitute parent for both of them and could share his concerns about his mother. It was hard for him to believe that advocates and legal assistance were available to help realize his wish to consummate his relationship in marriage. Wayne was quite frightened by the power he attributed to his mother—her custody, her threats to legally classify him as incompetent. He had anxieties about separation and independence too. He used Heather's parents somewhat as his own parents and at times thought of moving in with them if he was thrown out or just had to leave. This concerned the parents who questioned this possibility. As father put it—more bluntly and realistically, "I was worried about having one dependent upon us but having two is too much and going too far." In retrospect his firmness and definiteness at many times, while not always appreciated, were helpful in establishing the reality of what Heather and Wayne wanted. Father was somewhat a skeptic towards many of the endeavors but his love for his daughter was very real and he could allow himself to be convinced where other fathers might continue to oppose.

Many attempts were made to contact Wayne's mother through phone and letter by Heather's parents without success. One letter from her seemed to shut the door on further communication. Wayne's family physician was reluctant to become involved in counseling her. It was at this point that child advocates were involved through the offices of the local association for retarded citizens. An experienced, likeable, and sensitive young couple met Heather and Wayne through my aegis with a view towards providing a relationship, support and advice in their efforts to live independently and be married.

What are the significances of Dr. Blom's account? From one standpoint it could be argued that the major significance is that he had to write it. This is testimony not only of how unaccustomed the community is to dealing with the issues that brought Heather to Dr. Blom but also as a contrast to more frequent community attitudes and practices that work so effectively against normalization. However, from another standpoint it could be argued that the account testifies to a change in community attitudes and practices in that Heather did have a school program; there was a Dr. Blom and a pediatric geneticist, advocates and other supportive services; and no legal or civil rights barriers to the marriage.

Twenty or more years ago it would have been highly unlikely that Heather's parents and Dr. Blom could have been able "to pull it off," and let us not forget that the marriage took place despite the objections of Wayne's mother and school personnel. Put in another way, the community today tolerates and, to a lesser extent, accepts mentally retarded people in its midst more than in the recent past. That is quite a contrast to the days when institutionalization or some other form of social isolation and segregation were the community's chief modes of response.

But how justified are we in stressing the change? An Associated Press report (*New Haven Register,* October 8, 1976) had the following large-lettered headline: "Retarded Couple Make Success of Marriage that 'Couldn't Work'." The article described the objections the young couple encountered. They met at a workshop (Fresno, California) for handicapped people, fell in love, and wished to marry. "Workshop officials there discouraged them from marrying, as did friends and relatives. But a friend took them to get blood tests and a marriage license, and a justice of the peace performed the ceremony. Seventeen states ban marriages among retarded people, but California is not among them." The couple does have the aid and advice of a social worker who said: "Their arrangement is not something I would recommend for all mentally disabled people, but they seemed to have handled it rather well." When an article like that is in the mass media, it suggests that there has been some change in regard to community attitudes to and understanding of mental retardation, but, similarly, it indicates how far we have to go before such marriage will not be considered newsworthy.

How many parents have the personal strengths and the financial resources to help their children in the way Heather's parents did? How many Dr. Bloms are there? How many parents could afford to pay a Dr. Blom for sixty-six sessions? In our experience, the answer to all these questions is: very, very few. So, although one cannot doubt that there has been a positive change in the community's attitude toward mentally retarded people, the fact remains that the change has been in greater toleration than in acceptance. And by acceptance we mean an effort to incorporate them as individuals and not as members of a labeled group, to introduce no barrier to whatever degree of social normalization of which they are capable, to refrain from reacting to them stereotypically.

On April 30, 1976, Stanley Meyers, former Commissioner for Mental Retardation in Pennsylvania, gave a talk to a convention of the Ohio Association for Retarded Citizens. What his talk meant to the parents is indicated by the fact that they decided to publish the talk and give it wide circulation. His talk was entitled "Have you killed a retarded child recently?" Here is an excerpt:

> In order to define the environment we will be discussing during this presentation, I would like to return with you to elementary school. There, your teacher or parents (if you were fortunate enough) had you look up words to discover their meanings.
>
> When arrangements were being made for this presentation, your staff asked me what the title of this talk would be. I responded, "Do you want controversy, or do you want pap?" "What would the pap be"? *What's the good of Islands of Excellence if you don't have the bridge to get there?* "Let's be controversial," they answered.
>
> Therefore, the first definition from the *Random House Dictionary* is "P-A-P Pap: (1) soft food for infants or invalids (2) an idea, talk, book or like, lacking substance or real value." I am not here to give you pap. Let's add one "p" to pap and we get P-A-P-P which is an acronym for Parents, Administrators, Professionals and Politicians.
>
> The title of this talk is: "Have You Killed A Retarded Child Recently?"

Attitude Is A Weapon

From the *Harrisburg Patriot,* on Monday, April 5, 1976, the following quote is taken from an editorial: "The commonwealth must soon adopt some form of legislation for power plant site selection and to be fair about it, some incentives must be built in for communities burdened by the power stations. Like prisons, homes for the retarded, and waste disposal facilities, power plants have become unwelcome, however necessary in many communities. The reasons are obvious."

Most people visualize killing as an act which generally includes a knife, a gun, a rope, a car, hands, etc. This type of killing—which actually tends to be overkill—is done by attitude. Murder of the mind; the pen is mightier than the sword. This is the environment of killing and the environment of society's attitudes about which I am talking.

Attitude is an insidious, murderous weapon. The attitude of the Harrisburg editorial writer, a professional, has killed a retarded child.

On December 24, 1975, Michael was born, a Down's Syndrome child—uncomplicated. On January 5, 1976, twelve days later, a request for institutionalization into a state facility of 1,500 residents was received in the Office of Mental Retardation. On follow up with the family, it became apparent it was not the immediate desire of the family, but the advice of the father's parents and a professional clinician, two parts of the PAPP acronym, which resulted in the request. Have you killed a retarded child recently?

Cases like Michael are by no means rare today, and, unfortunately, the community attitudes reflected in the editorial are the rule rather than the exception. Heather needed to be written up precisely because she is an exception. Prevailing community attitudes made residential institutions into dumping grounds and also make it so difficult today for families to strive for normalization for their mentally retarded members. The significance of Heather's case is not *in* Heather but in the attitudes that, so to speak, surrounded her in her family and in her interactions with Dr. Blom. From birth, Heather's family believed in Heather's capacity to "grow"; they were supported in this belief by an unusual pediatrician and at a crucial time in Heather's life they found a most unusual psychcatrist.

The combination of people and attitudes is very rare, but what is not rare is the underlying principle of the self-fulfilling prophecy. We are used to examples where the self-fulfilling prophecy operates to produce predicted inadequate behavior. We think individuals are incapable, react to them as if they are incapable, and when in fact they turn out to be incapable, we glory in our ability to prognosticate. But Heather's case demonstrates the positive way the self-fulfilling prophecy can work: Heather's family believed she could be a "person"; they acted accordingly, and Dr. Blom's account gives us the results.

And the same could be said for Dr. Blom: he treated her with the respect and seriousness he would have for any of his therapeutic patients. He did not predetermine what he would take up with her and he was prepared to side with her against the prejudices of others. As a result, he learned much and Heather gained a great deal. One would not have to use all the fingers of one hand to count the therapists who would have established a similar relationship with a Heather.

At the end of his account Blom raises a question of momentous significance, a question that involves the nature and vicissitudes of the relationship between the individual and society. He notes that in the two published diaries (Seagoe, 1964; Hunt, 1967) of people with Down's syndrome there was an unusual development of reading and writing abilities. In both cases this was a function of extraordinary efforts on the part of the parents. Blom then rightly comments that in both cases the parents seemed to have tunnel vision in regard to their child's feelings and potentialities, shaping them, so to speak, according to their own needs and feelings. The parents accomplished a great deal; they were in their own way unusually devoted, loving, and protective, but the end result was socially isolated, unhappy, extremely constricted sons incapable of anything like an independent psychological and social existence. Heather presents a very different picture.

> Heather communicated her conflicts, anxieties, and concerns directly as well as through her diary, poetry, and songs. Her parents, particularly mother, were able to take risks towards realistic independence. From social isolation, loneliness, and imaginary friends Heather advanced to a real love relationship with a handicapped young man. Depression, anger, dependence, sexuality, and conflicts with school, work, and other aspects of the outside world were dealt with in therapy through discussion, planning, and advice. Decisions were worked through about work, marriage, having children, sterilization, and appropriate independence. Schooling, work, agency assistance and advice, professional consultation, and child advocates assisted in a psychoeducational program.
>
> Heather experienced rigidities, inflexibilities, and stereotypes about her handicap. She advanced in a world that tended to oppose and question her rights to as normal a life as possible. Although married, her rights have as yet not been fully realized. Some generalizations can be made from Heather and her family about reactions to handicapping conditions and what handicapped people experience, positively and negatively, from social institutions and their professional representatives. In retrospect I may have been too critical of school professionals since one could be equally critical of other human service professionals, their professional disciplines, and the social institutions in which they work. It should be recognized that we professionals function in social sanctioned roles in spite of individual and collective efforts to the contrary. Most fundamentally this means that criticism should also be leveled towards a society which still views handicaps as a form of deviance. Deviance is socially defined as being significantly different from others in an important aspect that is negatively valued. As a consequence labels, attitudes, beliefs, expectancies, and social treatments develop which should be challenged and questioned.
>
> Heather, her family, and the author present this story to make the issues in

normalization more vivid to those who experience handicap and to those who are their helpers. In Heather's most recent letter she wrote—"i and Wayne will be thinking about you when you Give my story and i personally thank-you for lisening to me and knowing my ups and downs. and helping us Both with our Problems and how to face the world. of Love—Heather and Wayne."

The questions Blom is raising may be put the following way: the development of any human being is always a function of the interrelationships of the person, the family, and the characteristics of the society in which they live. And the characteristics of that society are always time-bound so that when the society changes the individuals in it think and act differently than before. Heather is not understandable only in terms of Heather and her family. Heather and her family live at a certain time in our society, when perceptions about people labeled as mentally retarded are slowly changing, "permitting" these people to enter the normal social world at the same time that it continues to erect obstacles to entering that world.

We are still largely a society that segregates those who seem deviant. This effectively prevents us from recognizing that the attitudes justifying segregation, be it in residential institutions or in community programs, have played a role in exacerbating the conditions surrounding the segregated person. Why is Heather's case unusual? Because Heather's parents were unusual? Because her case is a positive indication of a social change? Or is it because in addition to all of these factors Heather's case reminds us how far we have yet to go, how she is the exception and not the rule. Despite all that we think we have learned about human development our ignorance gives us no comfort and we find that our conceptions of an individual's potentials are always outcroppings of time-bound societal structures and attitudes.

7

Some Underemphasized Ingredients of a Community Program

IN 1969, WOLFENSBERGER AND KURTZ edited a book of readings entitled *Management of the Family of the Mentally Retarded.* It is well worth the reader's attention not only because of its comprehensiveness and portrayal of rapid changes in attitudes, practices, and services, but also for the healthy skepticism the editors express about foundations for the new developments. Indeed, from the vantage point of a decade later one must admire the editors' courage and foresight in expressing some doubts, as in the following quotation:

> It has taken many years to move toward compassionate and scientifically-based understanding of parents and their retarded children. Because long neglect has been followed by sudden and extensive interest, mental retardation has been called the Cinderella of the handicapping conditions. Some say that we would still be in a mental retardation dark age if not for President Kennedy's stimulating interest in the problem. Although this spark was late in coming, it may have come at an optimal time, since premature ideas usually do not result in meaningful social action programs. On the other hand, a more evolutionary, rather than the current revolutionary, development would have been desirable, as we must now establish patterns of action and services without having the necessary empirical underpinnings [p. 1].

Let us focus discussion at the point at which the family is told that their infant or very young child is mentally retarded. Recent research, our own clinical experience, and the Wolfensberger and Kurtz book justify starting with this event because it is the litmus test of the degree to which changing community attitudes and professional practices appropriately influence how this difficult task is carried out. This is not to say that how this task is met is fateful for all else that follows, but simply that it is a window from which one can glimpse how the nature of our contemporary communities influence the actors in this unfolding drama.

Communicating the Diagnosis

Consider the following two instances: minutes after a mother has delivered her child, and still groggy and dazed from the experience, she is told that her child has mongolism. The second instance is that of a mother who has come for the first time to a pediatric clinic a few weeks after delivery; in the hall she meets her doctor who in the process of saying hello and continuing down the hall tells her that her child is mentally retarded. Both instances took place in 1976 in a prestigious medical center.

We cannot say with what frequency such instances occur but let us hopefully assume they are not frequent. But that assumption has to be reviewed in light of the caution by Wolfensberger and Kurtz that we have an insecure empirical basis for developing programs. Contained in their book are several articles by physicians about communicating diagnoses to parents, and in general they reflect a sensitivity quite in contrast to the instances above. These physicians, however, like Dr. Blom in the previous chapter, are not average physicians, a conclusion substantiated by numerous parental accounts of their experience with physicians.

In the entire literature on this difficult task there is no attention to a factor that we know is very influential in the quality of the family-professional relationship, a factor illustrated in the two instances above. We refer to differences in social class and education between professional and patient. In the instances above, both mothers were of lower social class status and we can assume that that was not an irrelevant factor in how the diagnosis was communicated. We can also assume that such instances would be quite rare where the family and the physicians were of similar social class background.

The reader will recall Farber's (1977) study of the length and quality of the relationship between cancer patients and their physicians (see Chapter 4). In that study physicians spent significantly more time with patients of a social class background similar to their own, and they seemed far more at ease. Farber also found that patients of a social class similar to that of the physician sought and received more information than lower class patients who were more intimidated by their perception of the physician as someone who does the questioning.

The way in which the communication of the diagnosis is handled in part reflects the fact that ours is a society in which social class status varies considerably. As important, the awareness that this is the case not only structures relationships between classes but is colored by mutual perceptions that contain a large dose of error and prejudice. "Community attitudes" are at play in the communication of the diagnosis and if for no other reason it must be a starting point for discussion of a community program. The issues are made more complex by the fact that professionals, physicians particularly, are given and accept an elevated status that creates a gulf between them and those they serve.

We need not dwell on the many ways in which widely differing social classes differ in where they receive medical services, from whom, and with what degree of sensitivity and respect. Nor do we have to recite the litany of abuses that stems from the system of welfare medicine in this country. Stevens and Stevens (1974) have documented in great detail the relative failure of welfare medicine. The question that needs to be asked is not if the diagnosis of mental retardation is communicated differently to people of different social classes but the nature of the differences and their consequences. In Wolfensberger and Kurtz (1969) there are many articles by parents on their experience with physicians who communicated the diagnosis to them but these are obviously educated parents. Indeed, from 1950, when the National Association for Retarded Children (Citizens) was formed, the leadership, and most of the membership were middle to upper class people. Even so, the thrust of their accounts about how they were given the diagnosis of mental retardation is clearly in the direction of dissatisfaction and this has been no small factor behind their efforts to improve the education and training of medical students and physicians about the field of mental retardation.

It is only in the past two decades that a public policy in relation to health has emerged and this would not have happened were it not for the social turmoil surrounding civil rights, discrimination against ethnic and racial minorities, poverty, the maldistribution of health services, and the failure of the health professions to give serious attention to certain problems that were highly related to social class and race, such as lead poisoning, sickle cell anemia, malnutrition, and prematurity. In regard to mental health, for example, it could no longer be denied that the bulk of mental health professionals spent most of their time, and earned large sums of money, treating white, middle and upper class people.

But the indictment of the health professions went beyond matters of neglect and omission. From within and without the professions, serious questions were raised about the capacity of these professional personnel to learn to deal with populations and problems foreign to their background and experience. As never before, there was recognition that differences in social class, ethnicity, and race between professional and client were differences that made a difference. It was not simply a matter of mandating services; the heart of the issue was whether the quality of the services would change. It is our surmise that when Wolfensberger and Kurtz (1969) caution against unbridled enthusiasm about mental retardation emerging from its Cinderella-like status, they are raising the same question.

In the past, not only family management, but also management of the retarded generally has been based on the disease model. Surprisingly, this disease model was not only adopted by medical practitioners, but also by social, behavioral, and even educational personnel. Mental retardation was defined as a "disease"; retardates (and even their parents) were widely referred to as "patients"; management, even if purely social or educational in nature, was interpreted as "treatment" or "therapy"; residential facilities, even if lacking a single full-time physician, were called "hospitals"; and living units of such facilities were labeled "wards." The lower-class, mildly retarded were said to "suffer from" cultural deprivation, as if from a disease. Since mental retardation was conceptualized as a disease, its treatment was seen to be analogous to treatment in medicine, and the concept of "cure" was widely utilized. Many workers in the field even defined mental retardation as being "incurable." Those who believed that treatments for mental retardation might be discovered looked forward to treatments that would be analogous to medical treatments. Thus, many held the hope that an operation would be developed or a pill would be discovered that would "heal" the "patient." Revascularization operations and the glutamic acid studies are typical examples, and even the 1963 President's Panel Report spoke in terms of "intellectual vitamins" when referring to early environmental stimulation [p. 512].

Considering the low state of current knowledge and the prospects for the future, we would like to propose that the time has arrived for programmatic high-quality research on family management and related topics . . . [p. 515].

What is the relationship of such variables as parental agreement, age, and socioeconomic status to optimal case evaluation; to type of evaluation feedback, to amount, extent, duration, spacing and type of counseling; and to use of resources? When is individual and when is group management preferable? What type of group management (e.g. fact-oriented, or therapeutically oriented) is most effective with different types of parents? what are optimal management structures and techniques for various types of groups? Is diagnostic feedback most effective in a single concentrated session, or should it be spaced-out over time? If the latter, what is the optimal spacing for most or for certain types of parents? Such a listing of unanswered but significant questions could be continued at some length [p. 516].

In questioning the "disease" model and including cultural factors and socioeconomic status as important variables, Wolfensberger and Kurtz reflected the times. Mental retardation was in a new ballpark but these authors were essentially asking whether the rules of the game would be different. Unfortunately, the questions they deemed significant have with some exceptions we will note later largely gone unstudied. And among those that have been ignored are the ways in which the communication of the diagnosis varies with social class status. Our own experience and observations of this problem have led us to the following conclusions:

1. The lower the social class of the family the more likely the communication of the diagnosis takes place in a hospital outpatient clinic which is usually crowded and noisy, with privacy not always possible.

2. The physician communicating the diagnosis almost always feels under time pressure and sometimes will terminate the discussion by referring the family to another professional, usually a social worker, or a psychologist.

3. It is by no means infrequent that the diagnosis will be communicated only to the mother, the father usually being at work. The physician communicating the diagnosis may not be the one with whom the family had contact when the child was born or on the occasion of initial clinic contacts.

4. There is a strong tendency on the part of the physician to assume that families that appear to be of a lower social status, or with a language barrier, are incapable of comprehending the nature and implications of the diagnosis. This assumption is acted on in ways that produce the consequences of the negative self-fulfilling prophecy. And yet, some of these families are sensitive to the physician's obvious difficulty in communicating the diagnosis to them.

The fact that physicians and other professionals react differently to families of different social class backgrounds is not surprising. Nor should these differences obscure another fact. Generally speaking, families of similar status to the physician report dissatisfaction with the way the communication of the diagnosis was handled. It could be argued that the nature of the diagnosis is so difficult to accept, requiring accommodation to frustrated hopes and fantasies, that it is no wonder families are dissatisfied with their professional contacts and thus project onto the professionals inadequacies and inaccurate motivations. There is truth to this argument but it cuts two ways. On the one hand, it is an extremely difficult situation for families and one has to expect that their resistance to the nature and implications of the diagnosis can cause irrational and unrealistic behavior. On the other hand, it is such a difficult situation for the physician to handle well that one has to ask what training prepared him or her for these occasions. As we shall see in the next section, there is very little in the education and training of the physician to reassure us that the physician feels adequate to the task.

The Training of the Physician

By the time the student finishes medical school, he or she is painfully aware of three reactions. The first is the wide discrepancy between how competent the student expected to feel and does feel. (This is not unusual for students graduating from any professional school.) The second reaction exacerbates the first and it was well put by a medical student: "From the moment a medical student puts on the white coat he becomes aware that other people accord him a status and respect he has not earned. It is a feeling that doesn't go away. You are always acting a degree of competence you do not feel." The third reaction is that time is a very precious commodity the distribution of which must be carefully controlled, so that one cannot allow *a* patient or *an* activity unduly to upset one's manifold responsibilities. Of the three reactions, of course, it is the third that is especially communicated to patients.

As a consequence, the patient-physician relationship is structured primarily to allow the physician to obtain and communicate information. The underlying assumption is that in providing the information the physician is being helpful. This assumption is frequently valid, except in those instances in which the information has ramifying effects on the lives of the patients and those with whom he is intimately related. In these instances, providing information, or primarily limiting one's self to providing information, far from being helpful, sets off thoughts, feelings, and actions that expose the limitations of sheer information.

These are very difficult situations that require of the physician a sensitivity to the ramifications, a willingness to be helpful in regard to them, a sense of adequacy about being helpful, and the willingness to give the time to be helpful in ways that ramifications require. More often than not, the physician is sensitive to the ramifications and would like to be helpful in regard to them. Unfortunately, more often than not the combination of time pressures and the feeling of inadequacy about how to be helpful forces the physician to stay within the confines of information giving. We are all familiar with the argument that the physician must steel himself against overinvolvement with the miseries of his patients if he is to maintain his own stability.

What this argument obscures is its relationship to the pressures of time and the sense of inadequacy about how to deal with these miseries. It has been noted (Fuchs, 1975) that most of the problems with which the physician deals cannot be *cured* and that the major function and effect of his actions is in communicating a *caring* attitude. Part of the explanation for the rising resentment toward physicians is the feeling that they are not discharging their caring function. But here a distinction must be made between whether physicians care and how they reflect the caring attitude. In our experience most physicians do care but their training ill prepares them for acting appropriately on their feelings. And when the shortcomings of their training are combined with major alterations in the profession as a result of changes in the larger society, it is no wonder that there is growing resentment both on the part of the public and the physicians.

One of the shortcomings of medical training can be compared to the training of educational personnel. In the case of teachers there is one function they perform for which they receive no training and that is dealing with parents and other individuals and groups from the community (Sarason, Davidson, and Blatt, 1962). One can justify giving no preparation for this task if one assumes it requires an ability that is already possessed by all human beings, or that it is such an unimportant function that it does not deserve special training. Both assumptions are clearly untenable. Similarly, administrative personnel in our schools spend a large percentage of time arranging meetings. It is an open secret that most of these meetings are dull, unproductive or counterproductive, or all of these. And yet, in their education and training administrators had not been exposed to how one should conduct meetings.

The situation is no different with physicians in regard to how one relates to patients. The student is supervised in conducting physical examinations and obtaining a history relevant to the presenting symptoms, but gets next to nothing in regard to interpersonal sensitivity, to the truism of dealing with a person and not a complex of bodily symptoms, and to the difference between providing information and being helpful. No one is more keenly aware of this than the beginning medical student, and no one more quickly learns that his supervisors will not reward him for his efforts to understand the *person*. The physician learns that the caring function is very narrowly defined and that time pressures are an excellent excuse for justifying the narrowness. It is also true that in this age of specialization one cares more and more about less and less of a person. One way of characterizing the period since World War II is by calling it the Age of Psychology or the Age of Mental Health (Sarason, 1977). Within our universities the departments of psychology and psychiatry have enjoyed quick growth and power. And yet, in terms of training physicians their imprint has been minimally recognizable. Neither in terms of time nor intensity of supervision is the budding physician fine-tuned as a psychological observer and interactor. He is molded into a role that makes caring and follow through on such, a luxury. And to the extent that the physician does care and act appropriately it is not because of his training but despite it.

This may be seen to be a harsh assessment but the literature and our own experience suggest that it is a realistic description. At the very least, it gives added force to Wolfensberger and Kurtz's caution that in planning programs in mental retardation we are lacking an empirical foundation. This is particularly true when one seeks the rationale behind proposed community programs for mentally retarded people. One looks in vain for an explanation for the lack of focus on one of the more important "gatekeepers," the physician, who so frequently is the communicator of the diagnosis to parents. Whatever the reasons, the role cannot be ignored or glossed over, if for no other reason than experience indicates that the handling of this admittedly difficult task is no cause for reassurance. Let us pursue the matter further.

Medical school is not a place where one learns anything in depth. Depth of knowledge and the fine tuning of skills become possible during postgraduate training. It is in pediatric training that the physician is exposed to diagnostic, etiological, and treatment aspects of the many conditions associated with mental retardation. It is strange that although historically there has been a close tie between the fields of psychiatry and mental retardation through governmental administration as well as in institutions, the training of psychiatrists in mental retardation can be described as a form of tokenism. As a psychiatrist once said: "Mental retardation simply does not have the sex appeal of schizophrenia, depression, and the neuroses." Compared to the pediatrician the psychiatrist's exposure to mental retardation is narrow and slight. Even so, there are certain characteristics of the pediatrician's training although by no means peculiar to it that have to be recognized.

For all practical purposes, the pediatrician receives little or no formal training in the skills of observing or affecting human behavior, and this is as true for the individual as it is for the family. There can be no doubt that compared to two or more decades ago the pediatrician in training is more aware of psychological or personality factors, as well as of the organization intricacies and dynamics of family life. However, this awareness is less a function of training than it is a consequence of the Age of Psychology ushered in by World War II. That is to say, we became a society absorbed by "psychology," and this manifested itself in all segments of society.

Nowhere was this more clear than in matters concerned with parenting and child development. The phenomenal sales and impact of advice-giving books for parents is a post-World War II phenomenon. But there is a big difference between knowledge and interest, and action consistent with them. This is particularly true when one is dealing with serious developmental atypicalities inevitably having ramifying effects within and beyond the family.

These are very difficult affairs that literally put everyone, including the physician, under stress. And if we know anything about stress it is that it tends to constrict awareness, affect adversely the amount and quality of information one needs and obtains, and lead one to terminate one's presence in the situation. When the stress inherent in the situation is compounded by one's own feelings of inadequacy about dealing with it, the stage is set for misinterpretations. It is the initiation of a process that creates distance between the physician and the family. What we are describing here is identical to what happens between the physician and the terminally ill patient and his or her family (Kübler-Ross, 1970; Farber, 1977). We have had nurses describe to us how the dying patient becomes socially isolated in the hospital because the staff feels so uncomfortable, inadequate, and fearful in the patient's presence. It is a reaction to stress; while it serves to "protect" the staff, it exacerbates the loneliness of the patient.

The communication of the diagnosis is not a one-to-one situation but a family one, as we have stressed in earlier chapters, and that is precisely the orientation the pediatrician does not have. Furthermore, the word "communicate" here usually means a one-time, unilaterally directed message: the physician, so to speak, transmits information. If we have learned anything about communication of the diagnosis of mental retardation it is that *everyone* concerned is under stress and flooded with questions. We are not dealing with "information" but with interlocking lives undergoing great change. We are not dealing with a one-time communication but the beginning of a process during which people's perceptions of themselves in relationship to the others and to the child will be altered. The pediatrician's formal training simply does not prepare him or her for how to think and deal with this process; this fact has not been confronted directly in discussions of a community orientation and community services. In the past two decades schools, residential institutions, legislatures, and communities have been criticized for errors of omission and commission in responding to the needs of mentally retarded people and their families. Yet, despite the fact that there has long been recognition of the inadequacies of the physician's training to deal with families, those inadequacies have not been similarly addressed.

The second inadequacy of the physician's training involves the physician's woeful lack of information about community resources. To illustrate the nature and significance of this inadequacy we turn to a study by Hassler (1965) on the allocation of training time among psychiatric residents. It is important to note that the study was done in the mid-sixties when most major community agencies were being forced to be more responsive to community needs and change (Sarason 1974), and the field of psychiatry was under more pressure than most to adopt a community orientation. Table 1 presents a summary of Hassler's findings. It is obvious from the table that very little time was allocated to community experience and orientation. There is no reason to believe that the situation has changed. There is good reason to believe that the subsequent psychiatric debacle in the community is in part traceable to the inadequacies of training.

There is no comparable study for pediatricians or other physicians who play a role early in the development of the retarded person. Our own knowledge of medical training suggests, unfortunately, that the situation in psychiatry is typical. Indeed, it may even be somewhat better than it is in pediatrics. Generally speaking, pediatricians have little knowledge about services and programs in the community, and the situation is even worse if one restricts this statement to knowledge based on the pediatrician's firsthand experience with these programs. Yet, in any moderate-sized community there are usually infant stimulation programs, nursery schools for retarded children, various public school programs, and a variety of agencies and associations with programs specially designed for young retarded individuals. And the same is true for the older retardate. In metropolitan New Haven, for example, there are literally scores of agencies and programs for retarded individuals, and New Haven is a moderate-sized metropolitan area. This is not surprising when one considers the dramatic increase in funding for services and programs in the past two decades by federal, state, and local authorities.

**TABLE 1.   Current Training Time as Reported by
Psychiatric Residents (Percent Distribution)**

1 person = 0.8%

Training Areas	Much Time	Some Time	Little Time	No Time	No Response
1. Intensive depth psychotherapy	59.1	25.8	9.2	5.0	0.8
2. Consultation theory and techniques	13.3	39.2	32.5	15.0	—
3. Clinical diagnostic skills	34.2	52.5	11.7	0.8	0.8
4. Concepts of allied social science	1.7	19.2	55.8	22.5	0.8
5. Clinical research	6.7	16.7	29.2	45.8	1.7
6. Administration	22.5	16.7	32.5	28.3	—
7. Experience in training and teaching	5.0	31.7	35.8	25.8	1.7
8. Short-term or crisis therapy	12.5	31.7	35.0	20.8	—
9. Psychopharmacology or chemotherapy	10.0	24.2	43.3	20.8	1.7
10. Community organization or knowledge of community agencies	0.8	16.7	54.1	28.3	—
11. Clinical neurology	3.3	12.5	23.3	60.8	—
12. Epidemiology or ecology	—	—	25.0	74.1	0.8
13. Action research or program evaluation	1.7	5.8	12.5	79.1	0.8
14. Public-health principles or techniques	—	—	18.3	81.6	—
15. Neuroanatomy or neuro-physiology	—	10.0	11.7	78.3	—
16. Mental-health education	0.8	3.3	33.3	61.6	0.8
17. Knowledge of individual psychodynamics	75.8	17.5	6.7	—	—
18. Knowledge of family or group psychodynamics	24.2	49.1	22.5	4.2	—

Source: Hassler 1965.

The point of all this is that the process by which the diagnosis of mental retardation is communicated, digested, and absorbed is one distinguished by question-asking. Initially, the questions are of the why kind: Why is our child this way, is it hereditary, what did we do wrong during pregnancy? These questions are soon superseded by questions about what the family should do, what the child will be like, and what services and programs exist for the child now and over the long term? A great deal has been written about the emotional reaction of families to the diagnosis but what has been underemphasized is the relation between the family's need for support and reassurance and the flood of concrete questions about services and programs.

Parents of normal children would not think of asking: Will there be a nursery school for our child? Can we get babysitters? Will our child have anyone to play with? Are there summer programs and camps? What will happen in school? Will there be a place for our child to live in the community? Parents of a very young retarded child ask these and related questions because they have been rudely confronted with the fact that their knowledge of their community is very incomplete. As important, they find themselves thinking, often in an obsessive way, beyond today, tomorrow, next week, next year.

What parents need and want is information about community programs and services that addresses all of these questions. The problem is complicated by the fact that parents frequently feel that they should only raise the "here and now" kinds of questions as well as by the fact that the physician is content to stay with these kinds of questions. It has been argued by physicians that one should only deal with the questions actually raised by the family, and not to burden them with too much too fast. This is a tenable position only if communication of the diagnosis is viewed as a short-term process, and one assumes that the questions asked are all of the important ones in the minds of the parents.

What physicians generally are insensitive to is how their manner makes it difficult for parents to ask questions they fear will be seen as in some way irrelevant (Farber, 1977). If we have learned anything from Freud, it is that what goes on in any meaningful interaction is a function of the personal style and set of *all* the participants, not just the "patients."

A more legitimate argument has to do with the fact that the physician is frequently uncertain about the nature and extent of the young child's condition and about the future course of development. The physician is therefore reluctant to commit himself. But this argument misses the point that as soon as parents are alerted to their child's atypicalities they are drawn to questions that go beyond the present. If these questions do not surface in their discussions with the physician, and if the physician does not deal directly with them, the questions will be answered by the parents themselves or by other sources. And the answers, like the answers young children give to sexual questions parents will not deal with, can be problem-producing.

The physician's capacity to be helpful to families is limited to the extent of his knowledge of community programs and services. The consequences of this inadequacy are compounded by the fact that families want not only information but also judgments about the *quality* of the available services. Because programs and services exist in no way testifies to their quality, something that families of retarded children have long known. Although there has been an exponential increase in community programs and services in recent decades one should not be lulled into a confusion between quantity and quality. If the pediatrician's training and experience do not permit him to express judgments, if his knowledge is not firsthand but based on rumor, or agency labels, if he is simply unaware of what exists in the community, it is obvious that he not only limits his helpfulness but increases the chances that what he says will be wrong and harmful.

To the families of young retarded children the physician is the gatekeeper to community programs and services, and for that reason alone discussions of a comprehensive community program cannot gloss over his preparation for that role. It could be argued that there is a practical limit both to what can be incorporated into medical training and to the scope of the responsibilities of the practicing physicians. But that argument concedes the point that these limits may be having untoward effects. It could be pointed out that in hospitals and clinics the responsibilities are divided among physicians, psychologists, and social workers, with the explicit goal of one supplementing the skills of the others. Before commenting on this division of labor, we give below the rationale employed in one clinical setting. The mean age of the children being evaluated was four years, which is older than those around whom we have centered our discussion. Nevertheless, it makes an important point.

> The clinical setting in which this study was carried out is one in which military dependents below the age of seven years are evaluated for suspected mental retardation. Routine diagnostic practices include a home visit by a social worker and a nurse, and medical and behavioral procedures carried out at the clinic. After the evaluation, which requires about two days per family, the child's case is discussed by the staff. Both parents are then given the clinical information and recommendations by a pediatrician during a session lasting from one to two hours.
>
> For the purposes of this study, additional procedures were added; these will be described in some detail since the findings underscore the conclusions presented in this paper.
>
> Prior to the initial visit to the clinic, the social worker interviewed *both* parents in their home for one to two hours. During this period he first administered, independently to each parent, a questionnaire which could be completed in five minutes. On this pre-clinic questionnaire the parents were asked to subscribe to items in content areas about: (1) the expected grade level of the child's future educational achievement, (2) the expected degree of future independence as an adult. (3) the expected degree of success in maintaining a family, and (4) the expected level or type of occupation for which the child could be proficient as an adult.
>
> The social worker then obtained medical and social information pertinent to the clinical evaluation. Although the first impression of the stability of the family unit was gained during this session, little or no time was spent trying to discuss feelings and emotions centered about the child.
>
> Since it was the feeling of the authors that the "major item we had to sell to both parents was information," the social worker made it quite clear that we would discuss with the parents everything that we would find out about their child. Further, the parents were told that they would be present during all aspects of the evaluation and that they should feel free to ask questions of each staff member encountered. The social worker suggested that the parents should not hesitate to put pressure on the staff members to communicate with them about their child. In discussing the communication process with the parents, the social worker indicated that, as with any group of people, some staff members would be

better "communicators" than others and that some would be more willing to communicate than others. The parents were encouraged to let the social worker know about any communication problems and told that he would "manage" the communication process until the parents were satisfied. (The establishment of the social worker as an "Evaluation Manager" *for this study* was an attempt to assure ourselves and the parents that a frequent experience with physicians at clinics — the parents being given unclear, little or no information — would not occur.) Finally, the social worker made it clear that, despite any difficulties of communication encountered by the parents during the evaluation, they would be given a final integration of the information during the counseling session [Mathany and Vernick, 1975, p. 516].

The initial home visit of one to two hours, the inclusion of both parents at all aspects of the evaluation, the recognition that staff members differ as "communicators," the urging of parents to question and pressure — in combination, these features come close to being unique for clinic and hospital practice. Efficiency and helpfulness may be the major justifications for the division of labor in clinics and hospitals but the inability to face up to the inadequacies of professional training subverts the intentions of the division of labor. Matheny and Vernick (1975) put it well:

> More often than we would want to believe, counseling also fails because of the counselor. The counselor's difficulties — inexperience in communication techniques, hesitancy to give "bad news," protection or "sheltering" of the family, pursuit of the parents' having a positive image of him, and lack of expertise with or confidence in diagnostic information — interfere with his role as an effective communicator (or teacher). Moreover, the consequences of the counselor's difficulties are likely to be attributed to difficulties in the parents when they return to the clinic or go elsewhere. By this process, the parents' continued ignorance can easily be described as psychopathology, and indeed it may become so.
>
> Having a retarded child is a unique learning experience for almost all parents. The guidelines for parental behaviors and expectations are altered; the knowledge gained from having other children in the home or acquired from neighbors is of limited usefulness. Consequently, parents become confused. In the face of this confusion the parents, whether overwrought or calm, will be seeking information for new guidelines and expectations. We are convinced, on the basis of this preliminary study, that many parents can be helped to learn appropriate guidelines for action and expectations when we place the primary emphasis on effective communication rather than on effective short-term psychotherapy [p. 84].

How one approaches the family in regard to the diagnosis of mental retardation is one of the litmus tests of a community orientation: perceiving and treating the family as a unit; being sensitive to the many questions they will be asking for which "ordinary" living has not prepared them; assuming the responsibility to learn about resources in the larger community; and discharging this responsibility in a way so as to enable one to spot and remedy deficiencies in community resources. A community orientation is an active process in which one's horizons go far beyond a family or the existing order of services. It is not an orientation that is learned in clinical training. A community orientation is not defined by how one "looks at" the community but rather how one is "in" that community; how one seeks to experience those aspects of the community that will, positively or negatively, impinge upon families with retarded children. One cannot experience these aspects by remaining in one's office, clinic, or hospital. Unfortunately, professional training tends to inculcate a parochial rather than a community orientation.

In a paper given at a working conference on the needs of people disabled early in life, Cohen (1977), a pediatrician, stated:

> The implications of these studies of maternal-infant interaction for the development of services are significant and rank next to prenatal and neonatal services in the hierarchy of preventive measures. Programs to deal with these issues must stress the training of clinicians to recognize pertinent psycho-social factors and provide anticipatory guidance. Brazelton (1975), Senn (1947) and Wessell (1963) have pointed out the value of prenatal visits to prospective parents. These visits enable the clinician to deal not only with medical questions but also with parental expectations, anxieties, and pertinent child-rearing techniques. Next, at the time of birth, nursing procedures must be structured to nurture effective bonding by fostering close parental contact with infants. In the case of the high risk or sick infant requiring special nursing care, providing staff time to counsel and support parents could mitigate the adverse effects of separation and normalize the long-term, intra-familial relationship. Such early in-hospital support, coupled with a home support program through trained visiting nurses or home aides, will have a long-range benefit of deterring subsequent adverse effects. These could range from the extremes of potential child abuse (Kempe 1971; Kempe and Helfer 1972) to indifference, rejection and development of significant emotional problems, or to the eventual attitudes on the part of families with a handicapped child, as described by Bronfenbrenner (1974), that determine whether the child will be encouraged, trained and supported at home, or relegated to alternative residential care settings. With these long-range implications in mind, there is obvious benefit in programs that enable behavioral scientists to study and clinicians to apply methods of supporting families and dealing with parents. The interpretation of infant's behavior to parents, along with insight into their reactions, can help to avoid the inevitable strain that results in chronic disruption of intra-familial interactions.

Putting these recommendations into the realm of training and practice should be a very high priority, as Cohen indicates, but this will not take place until the training of personnel is seen in the context of a community and preventive orientation. It is not fortuitous that the subtitle of Cohen's paper is "Implications for Public Policy."

The Relationship between Home and Community

It used to be that most people died at home and the funeral was also conducted there. Today, most people die in a hospital and the funeral is held in a funeral "parlor." We are not judging this change but using it to illustrate a more general phenomenon of social change: Geographically speaking, most of the experiences that can mightily influence the life of a family take place outside of the home. Babies are born in hospitals; they are brought to clinics and doctors' offices; they may be brought to special settings for training and rehabilitative services; and the parents may go to a variety of other places for information and guidance. Today, this seems both "natural" and efficient.

We are beginning to learn that, as in the case of all major social changes, we are paying a price. Today, policymakers are painfully aware that past programs for aged people vastly underestimated the significance of home and family-centered services. That is to say, they failed to understand the daily needs and problems of older people from the time they arose in the morning to when they went to sleep at night. Therefore, the policymakers and the professionals from whom they sought advice could not ask: What services could be provided in the home that would make life more tolerable, capitalize on the desire for independence, and maintain family ties? As long as older people were seen in doctors' offices, clinics, and hospitals—on other people's turf—there was the tendency to see deficiencies and not potentialities, to be overprotective rather than to accord others the right to take risks, to overvalue the advantages of segregation, and to undervalue the advantages of sustaining family and neighborhood living.

What happens when one starts with the assumption that services have to be based on a knowledge of the home setting in order to bring to it appropriate community services? We urge the reader to study the monograph-sized testimony of Daphne Krause, Director of the Minneapolis Age and Opportunity Center before a congressional committee (Krause, 1975). It is one of the best descriptions of a community orientation and what it can accomplish when attention is focused on the individual or family in the home.

Although the concept of community programs for mentally retarded people obviously does not preclude a focus on services within the home and neighborhood, most of these programs require the child and family to travel to the program site. This emphasis runs several risks:

1. The failure to know the home setting firsthand in its social and physical aspects can limit the relevance of recommendations to the family. Since these recommendations are based in part on parental reports of the home setting, they will always reflect an unknown degree of distortion.
2. The picture of the dynamics of family living gained from interviews cannot be assumed to be free from interviewee *and* interviewer bias, and these biases can either underestimate or overestimate the presence and strength of problems. It is interesting to note that Erik Erikson (1950) always tried to visit and eat with the family of a child he was considering taking on in psychotherapy. We are not suggesting that retarded individuals be viewed routinely as "patients," but rather that

one can learn a great deal from spending time in the home setting (Sarason, et al., 1966, ch. 23).

3. In our experience, the failure to gain familiarity with the home setting can obscure sources of strength and positive motivations.

To illustrate the above we turn to studies by Yepsen and Cianci (1946, 1947) that are noteworthy for three reasons. They were pioneer studies not given the attention they deserved; they were done at a time when institutionalization was the prepotent recommendation; and the results were startling. In 1943, the state of New Jersey developed a Home Training Program for retarded people. More specifically, it was developed to aid parents of profoundly retarded individuals who could not be admitted to custodial institutions because of the lack of facilities. As Yepsen and Cianci (1946) pointed out:

> Vacancies in institutions providing custodial care because of the very limited mental development of the patients admitted usually occur only in case of death. The turnover is, therefore, slight and the waiting lists increase from year to year instead of decreasing. This means that there are many children in every state of limited ability who never receive any training and whose chance of ever being admitted into an institution is very slight [p. 22].

The following statement by Yepsen and Cianci bears repetition because it was made long before its substance became fashionable:

> The problem is fundamentally one of education and training of children and parents. It was the belief of this Department that the work should be carried out by a person trained as a teacher who will consider the problem from the teacher's point of view and uses teaching methods. The philosophy which governs this work is simple. The teacher in order to be successful in his work must have the firm conviction that every child regardless of his mental level is entitled to as much training and education as will aid him in developing to his maximum capacity. He must also believe that the parents of these children are entitled to every consideration and aid which will help them lead a normal life, and most important of all, he must truly believe in home training as a means of making the child adjustable in the family. He must discard the idea that every feeble-minded child must be taken out of the community and put into an institution. This last statement cannot be emphasized enough for there are still many well-meaning people who influence and misguide parents into believing that the institution is the ultimate and only solution to the problem presented by the mentally deficient child [pp. 22-23].

The function of the teacher in the home was twofold: (1) to work with the child in order to effect elementary habit-training, speech, self-help, emotional control, and play activities aimed at developing muscular coordination; and (2) to guide the parent in the handling of the child.

> Such parents need to be guided in the right attitude and they must be made to realize that the time spent in training the child is time well spent. Parents are given simple directions on how to proceed in establishing these correct habit pat-

terns and advantages which will result in this training are pointed out to them. The mother must be advised that teaching these children will be a long time process and can be accomplished only by a systematic established routine [Yepsen and Cianci].

As a result of this home-based program the following was found:

	BEFORE HOME TRAINING	AFTER HOME TRAINING
No. of parents who wanted child in institution	17	6
No. of parents who did not want child in an institution	5	18
Undecided	2	0
	24	24

[Yepsen and Cianci 1946, p. 26]

The reader will recall from the previous chapter that twenty-five years later, Sarason, Grossman, and Zitnay (1972) reported similar findings with families with retarded individuals on an emergency waiting list for institutionalization. We cannot resist the temptation to suggest that the major significance of these studies is in illustrating what can happen when professionals are *forced* to change their accustomed ways of thinking and practicing. In both studies, institutionalization could only be in the distant future and so the question became one of how to marshall resources into the home. What the professionals learned was that many families had strengths and motivations which, interacting with the new aid and encouragement heretofore unrecognized, could be productively developed.

In recent years there has been increasing recognition of the significance of home based services in the form of research studies focused on the effects of early intervention. With no exception they have confirmed the practical importance of a home based service. For example, Garber (1975) summarizes findings from the Wisconsin longitudinal study:

Evidence for changes having occurred in the mother's behavior because of her involvement in the maternal rehabilitation program appears in our measure of "locus of control." Locus of control gives an indication of how the mother views her ability to control her life. We found the Experimental mothers showed a greater tendency to an internal locus of control, indicating she felt more in control of environmental consequences. Such feelings of control are transmitted to the child, whose self-confidence is thereby enhanced.

Such changes in the mother's attitudes are significant because they signal not only an increased sensitivity both to their needs and the needs of their families, but indicate an increased receptivity to the suggestions of respected and responsible outsiders. There can now be, therefore, more hope for these parents to make use of community resources.

Thus, it seems that as a result of the long term family rehabilitation effort of families with a retarded mother, there has been a change in the motivation of these families to seek out, participate in, and profit from the rehabilitation program, together with continued guidance by the parent coordinator, has effected the changes observed in the mothers, including job and homemaking skills. The mothers have shown significant changes in self-concept; they are more positive and more self-confident, and they have shown an increased sensitivity to the needs of their children in terms of nutritional and health care [p. 289].

There will continue to be controversy surrounding the nature and the degree of impact of home-based services on the development of the child. It should occasion no surprise if there are differing opinions about effects, when these studies differ in intensiveness, comprehensiveness, when the intervention began, populations studied, and choice of variables and initial condition of the child. And, we must point out, in the case of very young children having indisputable central nervous system malfunctioning, we are far from understanding the universe of alternatives for home-based interventions. Yet, no one has ever argued against such interventions as a necessary and significant means of supporting and helping families qua families. One could argue that even if all the studies ever done had not demonstrated any meaningful impact on the child, it did not speak against helping families as families, in much the same way that no one would argue against a family with a terminally ill member receiving help and support.

Programs for providing help in the home to families with terminally ill members have sprung up by the scores in the past decade, and more are on the way. Obviously, their justification is not in the hope of reversing the course of a terminal illness but in diluting the destructive impact of the situation on family health and relationships. One of the first of these programs was started in New Haven by a nurse, a minister, a pediatrician, and a surgeon. From our knowledge of this home based program, it has literally been a boon to many families. This is one of those instances where the saying "the operation was a success but the patient died" is high praise indeed.

There is another body of research, stimulated by behavior modification approaches, that has illuminated the usefulness of home-based services as well as the role of the parent as "educator or therapist." When one recognizes that behavior modification rests on the "here and now" situational context with a particular kind of behavior, it was almost inevitable that in using these approaches the parents, family, and home would become a site for intervention. Berkowitz and Graziano (1972) put it well:

This approach attempts to overcome some major limitations of traditional child psychotherapy, at least as seen by behavior therapists, i.e. traditional therapy is seen as an essentially "artificial" situation, occupying only a small portion of the child's life and possibly only having incidental relation to it. The therapist operating in an isolated office might never directly observe parent-child interaction in its natural environment (Hawkins, Peterson, Schweid, and Bijou, 1966) or the behavior which brings the child to the clinician (e.g. anorexia, stealing, school phobia, which are periodic and rarely occur during therapy contact; Russo, 1964). The therapist's data, then, are usually limited to his one-hour, weekly cross sectional slice of the total reality of his young client's life, and to the retrospective and often unreliable reports of parents not trained in behavioral observation. Further, as pointed out by Russo (1964) and Hawkins *et al.* (1966), the therapist rarely makes useful, "practical" suggestions. He believes this to be of less importance than psychodynamic material and, not knowing relevant environmental details, his suggestions may be so technical or general that parents, teachers, and even other therapists are unable to translate them into specific behavior. Some parents, overwhelmed and unable to cope with the demands of a disturbing child receive little practical guidance from the therapist, and find no ebbing of their feelings of helplessness, rage, and literal hate (Holland, 1969; Patterson, McNeal, Hawkins and Phelps, 1967). A large area of research is suggested here concerning the functioning of such powerfully negative feelings and attitudes in complex behavior chains leading to and/or from the disturbing behavior of both children and adults. Such intense parental feelings may occasion significant further disorganization in the family's life. Thus, the direct and practical coping with the everyday realities of the disorganized family situation may be an important therapeutic need currently unmet by psychodynamic therapists who deal with inferences and not behavior . . . .

Despite such developments, the main direction of therapy has traditionally deemphasized the child's natural environment (Hawkins *et al.*, 1966) which is composed primarily of his family (Watson, 1928; Guthrie, 1938; Ackerman, 1959; and Straughan, 1964). Peine (1969) notes that most of a child's behavior is maintained by its effects upon the natural environment and can be most effectively modified by changing the reinforcing contingencies supplied by the social agents who live with the child. Thus, this approach assumes that: (1) a child's maladaptive behavior has been acquired in his natural environment and can best be changed by modifying that environment: and (2) the maintenance of newly-developed adaptive behavior also depends upon successful modification in the natural environment. If the natural environment is not modified, new, adaptive behavior developed in a clinic may be extinguished at home and maladaptive behavior which has been extinguished or in some way decreased in a clinic may be reinstated at home [pp. 297-298].

Although Berkowitz and Graziano's review of the literature is not restricted to studies of mentally retarded individuals and their parents, the thrust of their summary statement gives added force to what we have been saying:

The focus on parents-as-therapists opens a large area of research and development in clinical treatment methodology, ranging from basic and theoretical questions to highly practical, applied problems. The professional must provide more in the way of well validated methods of behavior change, as well as develop more successful and efficient approaches to training parents. Areas in need of investigation include: (1) the development of possible predictive measures of the extent of parental success; (2) further development and validation of a "family systems" framework of therapeutic intervention; (3) the development of more precise and meaningful measures of parental and child behavior change in the broader sense of at-titudinal and interactional variables; and (4) investigation of its preventive value, i.e. do disturbed children whose parents were trained in behavior modification have significantly fewer problems in the future than children whose parents were not so trained? Throughout the present paper, an attempt was made to illustrate appropriate research areas.

In light of the available evidence, there is little doubt that behavioral tech-niques can be effectively applied to children's problem behaviors through the training of their parents. The direct and practical coping with the everyday realities of the disorganized family's situation may be an important therapeutic need currently not met by most child therapists. This entire development provides a new framework for clinical intervention, which, in addition to therapeutic value, has important implications for future use in a systematic and prevention-oriented model of mental health intervention [p. 315].

In the light of the *research* studies that have been done one might assume that they would have had a significant impact on *clinical* and community *agency* practice. This is far from what has actually happened. It is still largely the case that the professionals and agencies do not provide a home based service. It could be argued that a major obstacle is the increased time such an orientation would require, but this is not very convincing. For one thing, aside from the behaviorally oriented psychologists, the theoretical and practical foundations of the training of most professionals ill prepares them for providing home based services. Second, if the significances of the existing research were truly appreciated, one would have expected that clinicians and community agencies would have sought means to deal with issues of time and limited resources, especially as funding for community programs has in-creased so dramatically over the past two decades.

Professions and community agencies never change quickly. They are rooted in history and tradition. And the form that professional training takes is always highly related to the economic expectations of those who seek to be practitioners. In short, professional training does not change quickly in response to new theories and research findings. This is by no means "all bad" when one considers that most theories deserve extinction and most research findings do not stand up under replication.

But, as Berkowitz and Graziano pointed out so well, this is not the case with the use of parents and home based services. Since the Berkowitz and Graziano review paper, the work of Baker and his colleagues (1972, 1973a, 1973b, 1976a, 1976b, 1976c, 1977) and Heifetz (1975, 1976, 1977) require special note not only because of the seriousness with which they view the role and potentialities of parents and the home setting but also because of the practical import of their findings. What is especially intriguing is the development and evaluation by Baker and his colleagues of skill teaching manuals to be used by parents in the areas of self-help, speech and language, play skills, and behavior problem management. In fact, skill gains were found to be as great when parents had only manuals as teaching guides as when they had more extensive professional supervision. (Baker, Heifetz, and Brightman, 1973; Baker and Heifetz, 1976). Heifetz (1975) has stated the thrust of this parent-oriented approach well:

> the prospect of involving the parents directly in providing educational services adds a novel and hopeful dimension. Instead of being exclusively at the receiving end of a hopelessly undermanned service system, parents now have the potential of becoming service deliverers themselves. *As para-professionals they can function within the system as "middlemen" between the professionals and their children.* And the professionals need not be restricted to the small area of influence which they could cover as providers of direct services to the children; by becoming trainers of parents as service agents, the professionals can serve a much wider clientele.
>
> The key to this more powerful and efficient service delivery system is the availability of *effective educational techniques which are readily learned by parents and other para-professionals* [pp. 4175-4176].

For all practical purposes, community programming in mental retardation hardly orients itself to practical, home based services. This is not to say that what has been developed is not needed but rather that it has glaringly failed to deal with families *qua* families in their natural environment. A family is a mini-community the parts of which cannot be seen in isolation from each other without drastically limiting one's capacity to be helpful. A community program that focuses on individuals not only limits the help it can provide to those individuals but is prevented from seeing sources of strength in that natural environment that can positively alter the quality of family functioning.

Murray Levine (1969) has succinctly stated five postulates of community psychology practice:

> 1. A problem arises in a setting or in a situation; some factor in the situation in which the problem manifests itself either causes, triggers, exacerbates, or maintains the problem.
> 2. A problem arises in a situation because there is some element in the social setting that blocks effective problem-solving behavior on the part of those charged with carrying out the functions and achieving the goals of the setting.
> 3. Effective help has to be located strategically preferably in the very situation involved and at the time at which the problem manifests itself.
> 4. The goals or values of the helping agent or the helping service must be consistent with the goals and values of the setting in which the problem is manifested.
> 5. The form of help should have the potential for being established on a systematic basis, using the natural resources of the setting, or through introducing resources which can become institutionalized as part of the setting [pp. 209-220].

These are simple but powerful statements. If taken seriously, they would transform many of the services for mentally retarded individuals and their families. Once stated they seem obvious, but it is surprising how frequently the obvious is ignored.

Citizen Advocacy

One could characterize the last decade or so as the Age of Advocacy. Or, as one student put it: "Wouldn't it be more correct to call it the Age of Indecent Exposure because it seems that we have done far more exposing how different groups are not getting a fair shake than in getting them a fair shake." This may be unduly cynical because it underestimates the significance of the spreading recognition that the rights and needs of many groups may be unsatisfied or abused. If one is a pessimist, it is easy to look at the need for advocacy and conclude that callousness and wickedness rule the world. If one is an optimist, one looks at the plethora of advocacy proposals and movements and takes satisfaction from their existence. In June of 1977, we received at least two dozen pieces of promotional literature in the mail dealing with books, organizations, and legislation concerned with advocacy. And if one took into account newspaper and other mass media vehicles, the score would be a good deal higher. It is beyond the scope of this section to survey the literature or to describe the myriad forms that advocacy has taken. Our goal is a far more narrow one but, we believe, concerns an issue that is fateful for the future of this well-intentioned movement.

Wolfensberger (1972) is one of the pioneers in the theory and practice of advocacy. His description of advocacy is refreshingly unambiguous:

> First of all, in citizen advocacy, competent citizen volunteers represent—as if they were their own—the interests of other individuals who are in some way impaired, handicapped, or disadvantaged. Secondly, this relationship is structured on an individualized one-to-one, or at least one-to-a-few, basis. Thirdly, many of these relationships will be established on a sustained and often life-long basis. Fourthly, the functions of the advocate will be highly differentiated in order to meet a wide range of "protégé" needs, while only providing the minimal amount of protection that is needed. Fifthly, the efforts of the volunteer advocates will be coordinated and supported by a citizen advocacy office.
>
> Advocacy roles can range from minor to major, from formal to informal, and from short-term to long-term or even life-long. Formal advocacy roles might include adoptive parenthood, guardianship, and trusteeship for property. Informal roles include friend, guide, and what we have called "guide-advocacy." Some advocacy roles emphasize close relationships, and exchange of affection and concern. Others are more involved with practical problem-solving. Many roles fulfill both types of need.
>
> Perhaps the most "perfect" type of advocacy occurs when a citizen chooses to adopt and perhaps even rear a handicapped and/or neglected child. A less demanding role would be to provide transportation, clothes, counsel, or other practical assistance to the handicapped child of a family who loves and accepts the child, but lacks the means to solve the child's problems. An advocate could make certain that a person gets the education, training, and other services which the

community has a responsibility to provide. Advocates could sponsor children without (adequate) family ties by visiting them, giving them gifts, or taking them on trips or to entertainments. Handicapped adults can be assisted in such practical matters as managing money, finding and maintaining living quarters, securing jobs, and learning how to use transportation services. Citizen advocates can give friendship and emotional support to the lonely and neglected by offering companionship, and by sharing worship or the observance of holidays and special occasions.

There is a vast number of persons who are in particular need of individualized citizen advocacy: hundreds of thousands of residents of our mental, penal, and corrective institutions, and of homes for the aged. Many of these persons will also need individualized citizen assistance upon their return to open communities, as will almost all of those who reside in sheltered settings within the community, where even highly dedicated agency personnel must relate to so many persons. For example, an advocate for a young retarded adult or emotionally disturbed person can contribute much to the successful adjustment of his protégé, keeping him out of trouble, teaching him how to use his free time well, and offering advice and support in time of stress and crisis. In some cases, advocates and young persons of the same age who are being rehabilitated could live together in apartments, sharing skills and fellowship, and making more normal, adjusted living possible. (A small program similar to this is currently being operated in Omaha.) Persons once rejected by society for inappropriate action can be assisted to make acceptable social and job contacts in the community by their individual citizen advocates.

Many parents of retarded or physically disabled children look after the interests of their own child as long as they are able, but have great fears and misgivings about their child's future when they are no longer healthy or living. Citizen advocacy could be the means of providing attention to such a retarded or physically handicapped person, and of preserving the overall type and quality of life that he enjoyed with his real parents [p. 218].

Wolfensberger cautions that volunteer efforts of the citizen advocacy type require a stable coordinating mechanism that serves the function of attracting, selecting, orienting, guiding, and reinforcing citizen advocates. When Wolfensberger articulated his ideas in 1966, he met all kinds of resistance. It was rejected as too "idealistic and unworkable." Wolfensberger proceeded to set up two very successful programs. Those efforts played an important role in crystallizing what was then an emerging but inchoate sentiment about the need of different groups for advocates. His ideas and programs had significance far beyond the field of mental retardation and, as he says, it was an accident of history that these initial programs were tested in that field.

Although Wolfensberger has been duly recognized for his contributions, it is obvious that most advocacy programs have been developed by people who read Wolfensberger in a very selective way, if at all. The fact is that Wolfensberger did not casually choose the word *citizen* in the phrase citizen advocacy. He is quite clear that citizen advocacy is a role, program, or vehicle *independent* of government, institutions, and human services agencies.

The rationale for such independence is no mystery: *The moral morass which spawned the need for advocacy reflected the inter-connections of government, institutions, and a wide variety of human services agencies both public and private; the failure to deal with abuse and the denial of rights; the many conflicts of interest that caused injustice to be overlooked; and the long history of failure to lengthen the intervals between well-documented scandals—these are precisely the factors that explain Wolfensberger's plea for independent citizen advocacy as a crucial ingredient in community planning.*

The concept of separation of powers goes back a long way in our national history, and the constitution that was forged in 1787 reflected, among other things, an exquisite sensitivity to the dangers of government powers, the need for balancing such powers, and the importance of an independent judiciary (Rossiter, 1966). It is fair to say that among the factors that made the 1787 convention such a protracted and difficult affair was the question: How do you keep public officialdom honest and responsible? The founding fathers were not cynics but they had had bitter experience in their own lifetimes with the insensitivities and excesses of government. They knew history too well to expect that government could be given the sole responsibility to protect the freedom of its citizens. Citizens had the responsibility to protect themselves against their own government; they could not assume there was an identity of interests between citizen and government. Indeed, they had to assume that there were many sources of conflict between interests. So, when Wolfensberger argues for citizen advocacy and cautions against the dangers of entrusting the advocacy role to government, he not only has political history on his side but also the history of our "humane" institutions.

In the past decade the concept of advocacy has become fashionable and embedded in many pieces of legislation, federal and state. In fact, one of the features of federal legislation requires states to have an advocacy plan and office as a condition for receiving money. There are two distressing aspects to these developments. The first is that many agencies have arrogated to themselves the title of advocate. Second, there seems little or no recognition of the predictable dilemmas consequent to allowing established agencies or their representatives to be "advocates." When requirements of advocacy jeopardize agency relationships, when one has to turn the spotlight of justice on one's own agency, on what outcome will the reader give odds? Yet, with very few exceptions, "official" advocacy programs are the responsibility of those agencies that were caught in the moral morass that gave such force to the concept of advocacy.

One exception we know of is the Massachusetts advocacy program against child abuse. It gives functions and power to citizen groups who are chosen by public elections in the different regions. Massachusetts has numerous advocacy programs (e.g. for the mentally ill, the mentally retarded) but the one above is the only one which places the advocacy role "outside" of government. Biklen's (1974) *Let Our Children Go; An Organizing Manual for Ad-*

vocates and Parents is consistent with Wolfensberger's emphasis and contains many practical suggestions to help individuals and groups who are advocates avoid the traps that beset "official" advocates.

As a result of federal developmental disabilities legislation, each state has had to come up with a plan for advocacy. In one state, a planning group was convened by the chief officer of the state department of mental retardation. It was a mixture of state employees, some representatives of the more traditional social service agencies, representatives of parent groups, and a few "unaffiliated" individuals. Suffice it to say, in this example it was egregiously clear from the outset that the commissioner would have the final say on the advocacy program. The commissioner was not being arbitrary because according to the federal legislation he could come up with any advocacy program he deemed appropriate. The commissioner could have made the advocacy program relatively independent of the state apparatus, but he did not. How many people in that position want an independent watchdog? After many meetings the planning group came up with the following recommendations:

1. There should be a fifteen-member board consisting of five people representing the interests of the physically handicapped, five for the developmentally disabled, and five members at large.
2. The board will have policymaking responsibility and power.
3. The director of the program will be chosen by the board and his or her chief function would be to implement board policy.

It was no secret that some of the planning group wanted the board to be as independent of the political process as possible and to place responsibility with citizens rather than state or community agencies interconnected with governmental functions. This is not to say that the planning group went as far as it could toward such a goal but rather went as far as thought "practical." And that is the point. Created as this board was by public officials who were part of the problem with which the board was trying to deal, some of the members quickly saw that there would be resistance to a truly independent advocacy function. The worst fears of the planning group were realized. By the time their recommendations were digested by the governor's office and then locked in legislative and administrative concrete, it was the governor who would choose the director and the advocacy board. Therefore, the director would have the most important policy role, not only because he or she would be responsible to the governor but also because the board would be likewise appointed. It is axiomatic in political life that what you cannot control can control you, and is to be avoided. This in no way should be interpreted as a derogation of people in public life but simply as an acceptance of what it means to enter political life. Let us bear in mind that this is no less true for the world of private business and industry. When it is said that we should put our trust in laws and not men, it is because so much of human history has taught us that over time principles are more trustworthy than motivations.

In concluding this section we give part of the preface written by one of us (Sarason) to Blatt's *Exodus from Pandemonium* (1970). It was a book written after Blatt and Kaplan's (1966) *Christmas in Purgatory,* a photographic essay exposing conditions in residential institutions for mentally retarded individuals in several states. Among its numerous virtues, *Exodus from Pandemonium,* which is a series of reflections by Blatt on his experiences as Deputy Commissioner for Mental Retardation in Massachusetts, describes the obstacles to advocacy by people within the state apparatus seeking reform and justice. The preface was written in 1969, well before the nursing home scandals became standard fare in the media. At that time Sarason was not acquainted with Wolfensberger's work on advocacy, and it is therefore interesting that he also emphasizes the independence of the advocate.

> A couple of years ago it became necessary for me to become acquainted with nursing homes for the aged. As the reader probably knows, there has been a fantastic number of these facilities built in recent years primarily because of the medicare program. They are very modern, well-equipped settings and many more of them are being and will be erected. Psychologically speaking, however, they are hell-holes in which patients languish until death. From the standpoint of the patient, life is silent and usually in bed. The patient is completely and cringingly dependent on others for all or most of his needs, and any display of anger or complaint is viewed either as a personality defect or the consequence of senility. The actual amount of patient-staff contact, visual or physical, during a day is amazingly slight. These conditions are not due to deliberate human abuse. When one talks to the staff one gets two responses which are identical to what Dr. Blatt describes in the case of those who care for the mentally retarded in our institutions. First, the shortage of personnel is acknowledged (since these facilities are *businesses,* there is no likelihood that more personnel will be hired because that would obviously cut profits). Second, and somewhat in contradiction to the first, it is stated that there is not much one can do for these old people. The self-fulfilling prophecy is always at work!
>
> I was describing these conditions to an undergraduate class, which is not a group one should expect to get personally upset by what happens to old people. They had some kind of intellectual appreciation but it was and could be no more than that. As I said to them: "You get all upset about what you think is wrong with your education—and you should. You have a burning sense of injustice about racial discrimination—and you should. You and others spend a lot of your time tutoring ghetto children—and you should. You demonstrate about the senseless loss of life in wars—and you should. But the aged in our euphemistically labeled nursing homes or convalescent hospitals is not a group you know about or can feel for or have an interest in or towards whom you have the kind of obligation you feel with other groups." This was not said critically but as a statement of fact relevant to something of deep concern to them: man's inhumanity to man. Following this particular class, one of the students asked if he could do his research paper on convalescent hospitals. As luck would have it, he had complete access to a new con-

valescent hospital and he proposed to spend three weeks there, dividing his time among the three shifts. He was also a photography bug. He did a study which, unfortunately, cannot be published. He presented his data and pictures to the class. What is noteworthy is that although the students were shook up, the student who did the study was far more upset than anyone else. Like Dr. Blatt he experienced the hell-hole and was aware that his words (and even his pictures) could not communicate the depth of his feelings.

There is a saying that war is too important to be left to the generals. In a similar vein I would maintain that the care of dependent children and adults is too important to be left to the professionals, and Dr. Blatt's account amply confirms this. It is not that professionals are evil people or that they do not want to do what is right. It is just that they are people. Their knowledge and expertise notwithstanding, they can be blind to injustice and their unwitting role in it. They can make virtue out of necessity and thereby accept evil. They are torn between personal comfort and security, on the one hand, and the consequences of not conforming on the other hand. They can pledge allegiance to the symbols of objectivity at the same time that they can discredit an opinion not because of its content but because of the status of the utterer. They may know how power corrupts but not see the process in themselves. Like the rest of humanity the professional person, especially if he is in an important administrative position, needs to be controlled against himself, for his sake as well as for those in his overall care. This control function is not now being carried out in the central administration in our state capitols, or by boards of trustees of our institutions. Although "public control" is supposed to be exercised via boards of trustees or visitors, the fact is they (unwittingly) serve the purpose of window dressing. If my own experience is any guide, and Dr. Blatt's account certainly does not contradict it, boards of trustees are the least knowledgeable about what goes on in the institutions for which they have responsibility.

We have to think of new ways whereby representatives of communities take more direct responsibility for the life of our institutions. There are different ways and bases by which these representatives can be chosen. However, in my opinion, they should have one major function: several times each year, and each time at a different time of the day, they should appear unannounced at the institution, have immediate access to anyone and to any part of the institution, make whatever observations they deem necessary, ask whatever questions they think relevant, and following the visit write a report, copies of which should be submitted to those in charge of the institution, central office, and parent organizations, and elected officials. This report should be considered a public document. My suggestion is not meant to supplant any existing mechanism or procedure; rather it is an attempt to develop a mechanism completely independent of the existing structure.

There are problems, known and unknown, with this suggestion. I have offered it here as a basis for discussion. There will be numerous objections to it and they will be of three kinds. The first of these objections will concern the effects of these visits and reports on institutional morale; the second will revolve around issues of knowledgeability and professional expertise; the third objection will involve maintaining that there is nothing basically wrong with present arrangements except for insufficient funds to do what is needed. The first two objections are given no support whatever by Dr. Blatt's account, i.e., morale cannot be much lower than it is, and the performance of our professionals (both as leaders and treaters) is not something to cause us to do gyrations of enthusiasm. As for the third reaction, it is unlikely that one can point to an instance of institutional human abuse for which the expenditure of public monies had other than the most transient beneficial effects, if it had any such effects at all. In all of these instances there have been two major consequences: the system which produced or maintained the human abuse was not tampered with, and many people felt virtuous because it was so easy to confuse spending money with righting wrongs.

But why pick on the professionals? Is it not true, as Dr. Blatt makes quite clear, that professional groups are by no means the cause of the conditions and that in a sense all of us play a role? I agree completely with Dr. Blatt and that was implied in my statement that there is no one problem and no one solution. But I start with the professionals for the reason that by law or administrative regulation our institutions are in the care of various professional groups. They are in the driver's seat but drivers, be they of the real or symbolic variety, must never be allowed to determine the rules of the road [pp. xi-xiv].

On May 31, 1977, Blatt gave his presidential address to the American Association on Mental Deficiency in New Orleans. It was, in part, a follow-up photographic essay on the institutions he had visited a decade earlier. There was less filth, there were better-clothed people and more games and equipment. But in terms of stimulation and educational programming, the use of equipment, and staff–patient interaction, little or nothing had changed. The more things changed the more they remained the same!

The motivation for advocacy, however clear and unexceptionable, is compromised as soon as it encounters the crossfires of the political system. This is what Wolfensberger cautioned against and it powered the citizen-community programs he so successfully mounted. Unless the advocacy function is assumed by the community it would be unrealistic to expect that those who need advocacy will be protected to the degree that they deserve. Advocacy frequently requires forthrightness, militancy, and selflessness. An advocate is not only *for* someone but in the world of realities he or she will be *against* practices and some people. The advocate function is not an easy one to discharge under any plan. It is not a panacea for the prevention of inequities and outright immorality. At its worst it is empty ritual, a victim of rhetoric and self-interest, a mockery. At its best it puts responsibility where it belongs: on independent citizens, willing to put meaning in their lives by helping others obtain what is coming to them, and sensitive to the fact that they or others dear to them may some day need an advocate.

8

The Interaction of
Our Schools and Mental
Subnormality in the Light
of Social History.
An Introduction

IN THE PREVIOUS CHAPTERS we considered the entire class of the mentally sub-normal who, keeping in mind our previous cautions about diagnostic criteria, show significant impairment in adaptive behavior, and have subaverage intellectual functioning measuring one or more standard deviations below the mean I.Q. score on a standard intelligence test (Grossman 1973).

Diagnosis, intervention, and public policy have been considered broadly and often with special reference to subclasses of the mentally subnormal who are moderately, severely, or profoundly retarded, i.e., those for whom the traditional prescription was so often the residential institution, those with I.Q.s ranging from the low fifties downward, and those who were more likely to show neurological or physiological lesions. We felt that the diagnostic process, family impact, therapeutic intervention, professional training, and the development of community programs could often be made more dramatically clear utilizing these more severely handicapped cases.

But the fact is that by far the preponderant number of the mentally retarded do not fall into the more severely retarded categories and are not diagnosed at birth or in early infancy. They are rather the children who are diagnosed as mentally retarded after starting school. After leaving school they melt back into the general population in not inconsiderable numbers, undistinguished by the label of mental retardation.

The issues of diagnosis, intervention, professional training, and public policy are no less relevant to this larger subclass of mild retardation. But since these children are less likely to have obvious physical handicap, and since they are less likely to be identified before they enter school, they need some special and extensive consideration on their own.

It is important to bear in mind that the diagnostic process and identification of these children is peculiarly related to the functioning of the school. Secondly, intervention programs on their behalf are part and parcel of public education. Finally, public policies related to them are often specifically in the form of educational policies. Therefore, they cannot be considered independently of our public school system.

In the diagnostic and remedial work of the schools these children are generally classified as *educably retarded*. Their IQs are roughly in the range of 50 to 75, and they stand in contrast to that other school classification of the *trainable retarded* who are moderately or severely retarded children such as we discussed in earlier chapters. These *educably retarded* children constitute some 2 percent of the school age population, and they may be further subdivided into two groups on the basis of etiology. The smaller group of educable retardates, comprising about 10 percent of the total, are those where the mild degree of retardation is accompanied by neurological, physical, or emotional handicap, factors which presumably contribute to, if they do not determine, the retardation in its entirety. Those in the larger group, comprising 90 percent of the total, are known as *familial retardates*. The criteria for the diagnosis of *familial retardation* include, in addition to a mild degree of retardation, the existence in the family line of at least one other individual similarly retarded and an absence of specific causal factors such as a genetic error or an environmentally determined insult to the central nervous system. In addition, familial retardation is so invariably accompanied by environmental conditions existing in the lowest socioeconomic classes that this too has been suggested as a criterion for diagnosis (Dunn 1973).

Since these familial retarded children constitute the bulk of the educably retarded children, it is a group whose specific characteristics must be kept in mind when we consider the role of the school in relation to the mentally subnormal child. Insofar as the processes of identification, classification, and intervention take place in the school it is necessary to ask: Are these processes equally valid for the familial retarded, for the educably retarded with known neurological, physical or emotional handicap, as well as for the more severe forms of retardation represented by the trainable child? This is a question to which we shall briefly address ourselves at this point but which should remain in the reader's consciousness throughout the remainder of this book.

The Schools and the Educably Retarded Child

Our recognition of the intimate relationship between the functioning of the school system and the identification of the educably retarded child made us aware of the need for some historical perspective on the development of special education programs in our public schools. As we began our literature search of those origins we quickly realized that our developing perception of the educably retarded child and the public school needed to broaden into a wider perspective that encompassed not only the retarded and the schools but the schools and the larger society. We noted that in the latter half of the 19th century, the schools, endeavoring to provide for the efficient and economically feasible instruction of ever growing numbers of pupils, were forced to adopt class-graded instruction in which schooling was provided in sequential yearly units for children grouped approximately by age and degree of academic achievement. In that same era, for a number of reasons involving child welfare, the politics of labor and industrial relations, and the presumed curative effects of education for social problems, the various states also adopted and enforced ever more stringent compulsory education laws. Such laws kept within the educational system those children who for one or another reason were apparently unable to pass through the newly developed class-graded schools with normal rates of progress.

These two educational developments that called for a lock-step progression of pupils through class-graded schools, and forced attendance of all children within a given age range, immediately confronted the educator with the problem that not all children were capable of maintaining the necessary rate of progress required by the lockstep instructional system. And yet all children had to attend school. Various adjustments in the class-graded system were called for. Obvious remedies for the less severe problems were retention in grade or demotion for children not keeping up with their class, and the development of various tracking systems. For those children unable to keep pace even with such adjustments on the part of the system it was necessary to set up special ungraded classes where the requirement of lock-step progression could be completely suspended. At first, all children who fell too far behind their age mates were placed into such classes regardless of the cause, be it behavioral adjustment or scholastic ability. Eventually different kinds of special classes evolved. Truants and behavior problems were sorted into correctional classes and the ungraded classes were reserved for what we would now classify as the educably retarded child.

A third factor of note for which we felt there was evidence in the literature of the time was that a disproportionate number of children failing to move through the grades in normal progression were members of minority groups. Thus, in Leonard Ayres's (1909) study of retardation and elimination of pupils in our city school systems there is the report of a 1908 investigation of the comparative success of children of different nationalities in a number of New York City schools. Twenty thousand pupil records were classified according to whether the children were of normal age for their grade or whether they were markedly retarded. The study has a number of methodological flaws, such as a lack of control for the age of starting school. Nevertheless what is readily apparent is that different national groups showed differential rates of retardation. Although German children showed slightly less retardation than American children, Irish and Italian children showed almost twice the retardation rate of the former two (Ayres 1909, p. 107).

Similarly, in 1921, Elizabeth Farrell surveyed the nationality of children in the ungraded or special education classes of New York City and determined that 75 percent of the 4,771 children on whom data were obtained were of foreign-born parentage. Unfortunately, she did not present data on the proportion of children with foreign-born parents in the regular classes and since this was a time in the history of the New York City school system in which the children of immigrants constituted the majority of the pupil population one cannot assume that immigrant children as a whole were over represented in the ungraded classes. However, she does present data from the Census of 1920 suggesting that certain ethnic groups, notably the Italian, were markedly overrepresented in these special classes.

Looking at the interaction of the immigrant child, the schools, and the larger culture as they existed in the early decades of this century, we are also mindful of the recent challenges to special class placement made by minority groups in the 1970s. These groups, particularly Spanish-speaking Americans and blacks, noting the disproportionate representation of their children in the special education classes, questioned not the abilities of their children but the system that could end up with a sorting of the children that apparently reflected the racial and ethnic biases obviously present in the larger society. There followed a number of successful court challenges (Goldstein, *et al.*, 1975; Ross, *et al.* 1971; Kirp, 1974) which are still effecting our educational system in ways which we will discuss later in this book.

With such a parallel between the immigrant children at the turn of the century and the black and Spanish-speaking children in the latter half of the century, we began to wonder what there might be about the educational system in its aims, methods, and organization to account for the difficulty of minority groups in our public schools.

A Possible Hereditarian Explanation

Of course, in narrowing our concern to the public school system we were focusing on only one part of a global environmental explanation and we were not readily enough impressed with the possibility that the placement of these minority group children was determined by their "natural" abilities. Such an explanation was as available at the turn of the century as it is now. Then and now the assumption was not unfashionable that the differences in natural ability that determined the school success of some children and the failure of others were hereditarily determined.

In an earlier volume (Sarason and Doris 1969) we dealt at length with the historical origins of theories of the hereditary transmission of this natural ability. We noted the 19th century popularity of Morel's theory of degeneration as an explanation for both mental illness and mental retardation. This theory assumed that such "degenerations" or deviations from the normal were transmissible by heredity. In their various forms of epilepsy, psychosis, mental subnormality, moral degeneracy and alcoholism, they adhered to a family line becoming more severe in succeeding generations and eventually leading to the extinction of that family.

A more sophisticated theory developed with the work of Francis Galton. In his influential study on *Hereditary Genius* in 1869, Galton had systematically, and with the apparent corroboration of much pedigree data, advanced the thesis that natural ability (by which he meant the combination of "intellect, zeal and power of work" necessary for achievement) is inherited. Galton's interest in traits of intellect, character, and physical skill led him to propose a theory of hereditary transmission that postulated a blending of parental traits. He further proposed that such continuously variable traits were distributed in the population in the form of an approximately normal curve. Individuals possessing an average amount of the trait occurred most frequently, and individuals with greater or lesser amounts occurred less and less frequently insofar as they deviated from the average. This is a model of the inheritance and distribution of intellectual ability that with the modifications of Mendelism is still current today.

We noted in that earlier volume how such theories of heredity joined with the developing sciences of psychometrics and the societal theories of Social Darwinism to foster the development of the eugenics movement, racism, restrictions on immigration, and agitation for the institutionalization and sterilization of the retarded. Our examination of these interactions of science, values, and social action programs led us to express our concern about the uncritical application of science to social problems, a concern which was later elaborated in direct connection with the concept of familial retardation (Doris 1970). That occasion presented itself in the form of George Albee's (1970) proposal to change national priorities for research in mental retardation. Albee objected to governmental emphasis on bio-medical research in the area of mental retardation and advocated a shift in emphasis to educational, social, and habilitative approaches in research centers located outside the bio-medical orbit.

The rationale for Albee's proposal lay in his assumption that the largest component in the spectrum of mental subnormality consisted of those cases of mild retardation in which no medical disorder was implicated. This is the group of cases that we have been discussing within the category of familial retardation. The stance that such cases are not, properly speaking, a medical problem is readily defensible and we have no quarrel with Albee on that score or on his equally valid inference that there should be a more realistic balance in the apportionment of research funds between bio-medical research, on the one hand, and educational, behavioral, and social science research on the other.

Where we found ourselves in sharp disagreement with Albee was in his etiological explanation of this large group of mildly retarded individuals we are calling the familial retarded. For Albee has adopted the kind of explanation proffered by Galton, adopted in modified Mendelian form by American eugenicists such as Davenport, East, and Goddard, and revised and updated by Cyril Burt, Sheldon Reed, Arthur Jensen, and others. This explanation in its modern form assumes that intelligence is determined by a polygenic inheritance in which a number of genes determine the quantitative expression of the trait in additive and interacting fashion. It is believed that the relatively larpe number of genes whose allelic forms contribute to the sum total of intelligence account for the fact that this trait appears to be continuously variable in its expression. The differences between successive individuals in a large population ranked from greatest to least are for practical purposes negligibly small and the frequency distribution of the whole approximates the normal Gaussian curve. For Albee and others who hold such a model of the inheritance of intelligence and who choose to assume that this genetic determination is relatively little influenced by environment, the etiological explanation of the familial retardate poses no problem:

> basic intelligence is inherited in a normal polygenic way, like many other measurable human characteristics dependent on structural factors, and . . . today, tomorrow, next year, and for the next century, some 2-½ percent of all children born will be mentally deficient because of the normal interaction of these polygenic factors [Albee 1970, p. 141].

Albee cites Zigler in a more explicit etiological statement on familial retardation:

> From the polygenic model advanced by the geneticists, we deduce that the distribution of intelligence is characterized by a bisymmetrical bell-shaped curve. . . . Once one adopts the position that the familial retardate is not defective or pathological but is essentially a normal individual of low intelligence, then the familial retardate no longer represents a mystery but, rather, is viewed as a particular manifestation of the general developmental process [Zigler cited in Albee 1970, p. 141].

We have great difficulty in assuming that the familial retardate represents the taii end of a distribution determined by "the normal interaction of polygenic factors," and we would again argue our understanding of the matter as we already have.

In the study of any trait that has an hereditable component, be it the color of seed coats in peas or intelligence in man, a distinction must be made between the genotype and the phenotype. The *phenotype* is determined by observation and measurement of the trait in question. The *genotype* is inferred partly from observation and measurement of the trait and also from an examination of the trait as it appears in the ancestral and filial generations. In the case of a major gene, the phenomena of dominance may prevent one from directly inferring a genotype from an observed phenotype. In addition, different genes or combinations of genes can result in the same phenotype. Thus, albinism in man is usually transmitted via a recessive gene, but exceptional pedigrees have suggested that some forms of albinism are transmitted via dominant genes and still others by different kinds of recessive genes. Again, the expressivity and penetrance characteristics of a gene may result in the same genotype being associated with different phenotypes. For example, in a pedigree of genetically determined polydactyly (the presence of supernumerary digits) carriers of the dominant gene determining the defect may show the defect on different hands, to a different degree, or not at all. More importantly for the present discussion, environmental factors can make similar genotypes into different phenotypes and dissimilar genotypes into similar phenotypes. Thus, cretinism may be the result or a genetic defect or a lack of iodine in the diet (Stern 1960).

In the case of a polygenetic trait such as height, a tall strain is smaller under deleterious environmental conditions than under average conditions. Conversely, a genetically determined dwarf strain raised under optimal conditions might be taller than it would be under average environmental conditions. It is therefore possible to create a situation in which a genetically taller strain raised under deleterious conditions produces a phenotypical group of individuals that is considerably smaller on the average than a genetically smaller strain raised under optimal conditions.

Bearing in mind these complex relationships between phenotype and genotype, we can now consider the case of intelligence in man. The phenotypical distribution of intelligence in man is easy enough to obtain, provided we can agree on a suitable measure of that trait we call intelligence. Such a metric might be IQ scores, teachers' ratings, judgments of social effectiveness, etc. If we use any one of the standard intelligence tests and measure a population similar to that on which the test was standardized, we are likely to obtain a distribution that very closely approximates the normal curve.

Thus, if we selected the Stanford-Binet or the Wechsler Intelligence Scale for Children as our measure and tested a large random sample of American school age children, there is little doubt that the phenotypical trait of intelligence for that population — as defined by the IQ scores — would be distributed in the form of the normal curve. However, it is worth noting that the trait of intelligence might not distribute itself normally if we chose another metric. In fact, the distribution of scores obtained with other instruments might give us curves departing radically from the normal curve. For some theoretical or practical applications, these different curves could conceivably provide us with even more useful discriminations of intellectual ability.

The genotypical (hereditarily determined) distribution of intelligence is not observable in the same sense that a set of IQ scores is observable. Rather, it is a theoretical distribution derived from our knowledge of genetics and our attempts to use that knowledge to explain the distribution of the hereditable variance of that trait which we call intelligence.

Although the earliest attempts to apply Mendelian genetics to the inheritance of intelligence considered only a single gene factor (East 1927), greater sophistication led to the abandonment of this model. In recent years, different genetic models have been formulated, but they all assume the model must be polygenic. They may differ as to whether or not major genes and modifiers are involved, the number of genetic loci, or whether the gene pairs need to be equal and additive, but the assumption of the interaction of multiple genes would appear to be a sine qua non (Burt and Howard 1956; Fuller and Thompson 1960).

Let us assume, as Albee, Reed, and some others do, that a polygenetic model is adequate to explain that part of the variance in intelligence that is hereditable. Let us further assume, as some do, that the polygenetic model consists of a rather large number of different genotypes, whose frequency is distributed in the form of the normal curve.*

Now we are dealing with two different distributions—one of phenotypes and one of genotypes—and if we are willing to grant all of the assumptions made above, they are both normal distributions, and we may make the final assumption that each adequately describes the distribution for which it was designed. The *phenotypical distribution* describes the observed distribution of a trait which we measure by means of IQ scores and which we assume has both an hereditable and an environmental component. The *genotypical distribution* describes the distribution of that part of the variance of the trait of intelligence which is hereditable.

In considering any argument that stresses the hereditary component in familial retardation, it is important to bear in mind the distinction between these two distributions and the possible relationships that may exist between them. We have no difficulty in accepting the fact that when one measures intelligence by IQ scores, the lower end of that phenotypical distribution is composed to a considerable extent of the scores obtained by "familial retardates." We are also willing to entertain the hypothesis that there may be an hereditable component of IQ scores which is adequately described by a

*Burt (1956, 1958) maintains that his data on the distribution of intelligence scores depart significantly from the perfect normal curve with an excess of cases at both extremes. This influenced the design of his genotypical model, leading him to assume a number of major genes causing large deviations in intelligence, as well as multiple genes having small, similar and cumulative effects on intelligence. This work nicely illustrates how a genetic model is designed to provide a theoretical genotypical distribution that will match the characteristics of the obtained phenotypical distribution which, as far as it goes, is perfectly sound scientific procedure. The next step, not yet performed as far as we know, is to demonstrate that the genotypical model has predictive or explanatory power that goes beyond the distribution of phenotypical scores for which it was designed.

polygenic model whose genotypes distribute themselves in a rough approximation of a normal distribution.

Where we would differ from such as Reed and Reed (1965), Zigler (1967), and Albee (1970) is in the assumption that if one knows the individuals who compose the lower end of the phenotypical distribution, then one could place them on the theorical distribution of genotypes, and that placement would be at the lower end of the genotypical distribution. If, as we believe, you cannot make that assumption for a human population — where environments are neither uniform nor randomly assigned — then you cannot assume that the familial retardates placed in the tail end of the phenotypical distribution of IQ tests or any other behavioral measure would similarly be located in the tail end of the theoretical genotypical distribution.

Everything that is known about plant and animal genetics indicates that such an assumption would be gratuitous. The tail end of the genotypical distribution is solely determined by hereditary factors. The tail end of the phenotypical distribution is determined by the interaction of heredity and environment. *In human populations, environments are not uniform and there is no guarantee that the poor environments have been assigned to the poor genotypes and good environments to good genotypes; for all we know, the reverse may be the case.*

We have no doubt that the Reeds, Zigler, and Albee would readily agree that there cannot be an identity of individual assignment upon the two distributions and that the effects of environment on a given theoretical genotype might move it closer or further away from the phenotypical mean. But what we think they must accept is that the variance attributable to the environment in the determination of the phenotypical curve is relatively small, and that for all practical purposes the total variance in the phenotypical curve is pretty much accounted for by variance in the genotypical curve. While they might be able to conceive of a hereditary-environmental model in which this did not hold for the upper ranges of the two curves, they must certainly maintain this, at least, for the lower end of the two curves. Otherwise, how could they maintain that the familial retardates found in the lower end of the IQ distribution are accounted for by the lower end of the assumed genotypical distribution?

But what are the environmental factors which the Reeds and Albee must assume to be so ineffective, especially at the lower end of the distributions? Would socioeconomic class be one? In the United States, there is considerable evidence for a positive correlation between socioeconomic level and IQ score (Sarason and Gladwin 1958). There are many ways in which this environmental factor could exert its influence. At one extreme might be the higher quality of the formal educational system in which the upper-class child develops; at the other extreme, as argued by Knobloch and Pasamanick (1960), there might be the greater risk of trauma or malnutrition for the developing central nervous system of the infant in the lower socioeconomic class. But if one denies that environmental factors are powerful enough to account for the obtained correlation between IQ and socioeconomic class, one is left with the alternative hypothesis that it is genetic differences that determine the correlation.

Since the lower socioeconomic classes are disproportionately representative of certain racial and ethnic groups, a corollary of the genetic causation hypothesis would seem to be that these groups are also hereditarily endowed with lower IQs. We know those who would argue that such groups are at a lower socioeconomic level because as groups they are not equipped with the intellectual capacity to improve their lot. On the other hand, there are those who would reject the genetic causation hypothesis and argue that certain racial and ethnic groups are at lower socioeconomic levels because environments of human groups are neither uniform nor randomly assigned. Rather, certain historical and cultural factors have placed certain groups and individuals at economic and social disadvantages.

We are obviously dealing with the unresolved aspects of the nature-nurture controversy, a controversy which has been going on in this country for over sixty years with varying degrees of intensity. The pertinent literature is voluminous and there is no need to present even a brief synopsis of it here. In such a mass of conflicting data and theories, with an extraordinary range in the quality of the research, any expert has an exceptional opportunity to influence the selection of data that he will put together to argue for or against the effectiveness of environmental factors in modifying the underlying genotypes. For further consideration of this point we refer the reader to the Sarason and Doris (1969) discussion of sociopolitical factors in science in which they take particular note of Pastore's (1949) study of the relationship of the political liberalism or conservatism of scientists and their position in regard to the nature-nurture controversy. Similarly informative is the Sherwood and Nataupsky (1968) study on predicting the conclusions of negro-white intelligence research from the biographical characteristics of the investigator.

As far as we are concerned, the evidence is of such ambiguity that one is perfectly free to assume that in the correlation of social class and IQ the causation is from IQ to social class, or social class to IQ, or that both IQ and social class membership reflect the effect of some third variable. Perhaps, in any individual case or group of cases, any one of the three alternatives could be applicable, while it may be completely inapplicable in other cases.

It should now be evident why we object to Dr. Albee's argument that the familial retardate represents the lower end of the distribution of a polygenetically determined distribution of intelligence. Insofar as we can evaluate the scientific evidence, we must conclude that it is a debatable hypothesis needing further investigation. The available evidence certainly does not warrant the implementation of social action programs, whether they be concerned with where we spend our limited resources, as Albee would argue, or whether we should implement eugenic programs for the elimination of retardation, as the Reeds would argue, or whether we should change the aims and methods of our educational program as Jensen (1969) has argued.

Environmental Factors

If one assumes, as we do, that there is neither sufficient evidence nor compelling argument to ascribe the familial retardation identified in the schools to a polygenetic factor, then one must look for an explanation in the prenatal or postnatal environment or in an interaction of genetic and environmental factors. If we were to draw up a list of possible environmental or interacting nature-nurture factors that could determine familial retardation, we would need to stipulate that these factors, either by their quality or by the degree to which they were effective, should produce a mild form of mental retardation without evidence of neurological lesion; they should also occur more frequently in lower class family lineages. *If these conditions obtained, then such environmentally-determined retardation would be indistinguishable from the hypothesized polygenetically-determined familial retardation.*

Is it likely that such environmental factors acting either independently or interacting with susceptible genomes could cause mild retardation to accumulate in certain family lines within the lower socioeconomic classes? We believe there is evidence to suggest that there are in fact a considerable number of such factors embedded in chronic, cross-generational poverty. First of all, there are factors that are known to result in varying degrees of insult to the central nervous system ranging from death through gross neurological impairment with profound retardation to the mildest degree of cognitive or emotional impairment in which latter case were it not for the fact that the condition followed upon known neurological stress it would not be attributed to impaired neurological functioning. (The discussion of minimal brain damage in Sarason and Doris (1969) gives evidence for this point.)

These varying degrees of insult, as determined by the same factor, may be due to the intensity, the duration, or the developmental period in which the factor was at work. What is relevant in the causation of familial retardation is that in some families these factors are differentially present and of such intensity and duration that they have occasion to affect more than one member in a family line with similar degrees of mild retardation without demonstrable neurological lesions. Let us look at one such factor solely for illustrative purposes rather than conclusive argument, in order to demonstrate how an accumulation of such lines of familial retardation might occur.

Lead is a toxic agent which if ingested, absorbed through the skin, or inhaled in sufficient quantity can result in death or in varying degrees of neurological impairment, chronic or transient, depending upon the amount of toxin acting upon the central nervous system. According to Chisolm (1970) the clinical manifestations in children vary with the age of the child and the amount of lead ingested. Acute encephalopathy is most common at 15 to 30 months of age while intoxication without encephalopathy in this age group is usually in the form of hyperirritability or aggressive behavior disturbance. In the two- to five-year-old, unrecognized lead poisoning "may present with a convulsive disorder indistinguishable from the pattern of idiopathic epilepsy, chronic hyperkinetic behavior disorder, or mental retardation, or the picture may be suggestive of degenerative cerebral disease" (Chisolm 1970, pp. 600-601). Chisolm's assertion of a relationship between unrecognized lead poisoning and mental retardation is reiterated in Needleman's (1975) review of the neurological implications of subclinical lead intoxication in which he particularly calls attention to the following studies.

Perlstein and Attala (1966) reported on 59 children whose lead poisoning had gone unrecognized prior to an inadvertent discovery or who were identified only subsequent to the diagnosis of a clinically active case of lead poisoning in a sibling. These 59 children had no symptoms at the time of their pickup, yet five of them (9 percent) were mentally retarded. The suspicion of a causal relationship between their previously undetected lead poisoning and this high incidence of mental retardation would appear not unwarranted.

Less strongly suggestive but provocative is the finding of Moncrief et al. (1964) that of 210 institutionalized children with mental retardation 45 percent had elevated lead blood levels as compared with 2.5 percent for normal controls. But here one has to consider the possibility that the eating of lead paint chips follows rather than precedes mental retardation. Nevertheless, let us grant that cases of mental retardation due to unrecognized lead poisoning are rare, even though some physicians assume that tens of thousands or even hundreds of thousands of children in susceptible age ranges are yearly subject to lead exposure resulting in toxic blood levels and that the bulk of these cases go unidentified (Goyer 1971; Roffman and Finberg 1969).

We are not interested in how many cases of mental retardation due to lead poisoning may go unidentified as instances of environmentally determined retardation, but whether when such cases exist there is the possibility that they might be misidentified as familial retardation. Now, if such unrecognized poisoning does occur and if it results in a mild form of retardation, there is no question that it is very likely to have another characteristic of familial retardation—occurence in the lower socioeconomic class—since the exposure of children to lead paint is most likely to occur in run-down ghetto housing. In fact, surveys have shown that 10 to 25 percent or more of children in the age range of 12 to 36 months, residing in old deteriorated urban housing have evidence of increased lead absorption and that 2 to 5 percent have manifestations compatible with intoxication (Chisolm 1970).

Next we need to ask if it is a mild form of retardation with its etiology unrecognized, is it likely to have the clinching characteristic of familial retardation? Will it occur in more than one child in a family? The possibility would seem not unlikely. All the children would be exposed to the same rundown, lead-contaminated family housing. Of course, not all families in equally run-down housing have children with lead blood levels above the point of toxicity and that is because not all children ingest the flakes of peeling paint that contain the lead.

Physicians refer to the ingestion of inedible substances as pica and we may assume that children differ in the strength of their oral drives and hence their tendency to develop pica. Nevertheless, pica is undoubtedly affected by the social context. Lourie (1963) and his associates have emphasized the role of pica as a substitute gratification in cases of inadequate mothering, and it is known that older children tend to indoctrinate their younger siblings in the habit. Hence, the total family social dynamics may help explain the common finding of multiple cases of lead poisoning in the same household. But what if in such a lower socioeconomic family the lead poisoning goes undetected, as is often the case, and yet two or more children have mild forms of retardation as a sequela to toxicity? Would they not be considered cases of familial retardation and would not the proponent of hereditary factors feel comfortable in adducing such children as fitting a polygenetic etiology?

We readily grant that lead poisoning operating in an occult fashion such as we have just described could not account for anything but a minute fraction of the large mass of familial retardates. *We wished, however, to show how a known toxic agent in the environment could in fact have a hidden effect upon the incidence of familial retardation. What is especially important from our point of view was to indicate how such an environmental agent lies embedded in and is potentiated by chronic, cross-generational poverty.* For the children of the poor are so differentially housed and so poorly provided with medical care as compared to those children above the poverty line that they are differentially prone to lead poisoning. The middle-class child with pica, whether as the result of high oral drives, inadequate mothering, or sibling example, is just unlikely to ingest the pre-1940 paints with their high lead content; and should he ingest lead he is much more likely to receive appropriate diagnostic and therapeutic attention.

If one grants the possibility of some small increase in the incidence of familial retardation due to the interaction of two environmental variables. one specific, lead, and the other global, poverty, then the question can be raised as to how often that global variable of poverty—which is a defining characteristic of familial retardation—either contains within itself or potentiates specific variables that cause mild degrees of mental retardation unaccompanied by demonstrable neurological lesion? For a suggestive answer we might refer to Birch and Gussow's *Disadvantaged Children* (1970), in which their review of various health and nutritional factors embedded in poverty leads them to conclude that from conception until death the poor are "at differential risk with respect to a whole spectrum of physical hazards any one of which may be productive of intellectual deficit and intellectual failure" (p. 10).

In their extensive review of various prenatal, perinatal, and postnatal factors that effect the physical and intellectual growth and development of children, they make use of a model first suggested by Lilienfeld and Parkhurst (1951).

> There appears to exist a relationship between stillbirths, neonatal deaths and cerebral palsy. The pattern of factors, such as complications of pregnancy, prematurity, etc., which influence infant loss seems to behave in a similar manner with regard to cerebral palsy. On the basis of these related patterns, it is possible to broaden the concept of 'reproductive wastage' to include cerebral palsy and possibly other related disorders. One might postulate the existence of a 'continuum of reproductive wastage' which can be subdivided into lethal and sublethal manifestations. The lethal component includes abortions, stillbirths and neonatal deaths. The sublethal component includes cerebral palsy and, possibly, other disabilities. Although this concept has never been stated as such, insofar as the present authors are aware, it has been implied previously by those investigators who have emphasized the role of cerebral hemorrhage in the etiology of cerebral palsy. These workers felt that the cerebral palsy group represents those infants who have survived the lethal effect of the hemorrhage. It has also been implied by Ingalls and Gordon in their epidemiological investigations of such conditions as mongolism and is probably equivalent to their concept of disease described as the "biological gradient of disease." It would appear that other congenital stigmata, such as malformations, mental deficiency, etc., should be similarly investigated in an attempt to delineate possible antecedent factors [p. 278].

For our present argument it is of interest that Lilienfeld and Parkhurst recognized that the biological factors with which they were concerned did not operate in a vacuum and that they were specifically aware of the interaction of these biological factors with poverty.

> At this point it would be well to emphasize that the various factors that are apparently involved in producing this "continuum of reproductive wastage" are, in turn, probably the result of a complex of biosocial factors. There is, no doubt, an interplay of both genetic and environmental (both socio-economic and intrauterine) factors. The various factors of pregnancy and parturition probably represent specific manifestations of this biosocial complex [Lilienfeld and Parkhurst 1951, p. 278].

This model of reproductive wastage was subsequently elaborated by the work of Lilienfeld and Pasamanick and their various colleagues and in a more fully elaborated form was presented by Knoblock and Pasamanick (1959).

Some time ago we constructed the hypothesis of a "continuum of reproductive casualty" which has been investigated in a series of retrospective and anterospective epidemiologic studies. According to this hypothesis, there is a lethal component of cerebral damage which results in fetal and neonatal deaths and a sublethal component which gives rise to a series of clinical neuropsychiatric syndromes depending on the degree and location of the damage. We have found that these abnormalities range from the more obvious disabilities, such as cerebral palsy, epilepsy, and mental deficiency, through the learning and behavioral difficulties, such as reading disabilities, tics, and the behavior disorders of childhood, probably as a result of cerebral disorganization after minimal cerebral damage. The retrospective investigations have indicated that three prenatal and perinatal factors appear to be most highly associated with the components of this continuum; namely, prematurity, toxemia, and bleeding during pregnancy. In the retrospective study of children with behavior disorders, this association was found to be particularly high in the hyperactive, confused and disorganized group [p. 1384].

Starting with a discussion of the support for a hypothesis of a continuum of reproductive casualty resulting from nutritional, health, and medical care factors operative during pregnancy and delivery, Birch and Gussow (1970) adduce evidence from numerous studies for an extended hypothesis of *a continuum of neurological and/or cognitive deficit* in the children of poverty. This continuum of deficit results from nutritional and health factors operative not only during pregnancy and delivery but operative prior to conception in the growth and development of the mother that prepares her more or less adequately for parturition, and operative in the postnatal life of the infant in ways that more or less adequately support normal neurological and cognitive growth and development. In the various studies reviewed by Birch and Gussow it is apparent that the specific nutritional and health factors that correlate with neurological and cognitive deficit in the child are embedded within the more global factor of poverty. In addition, it is important to recognize that not only does poverty predispose the infant to the action of specific adverse developmental factors such as prematurity or illness but that the continued presence of the infant in an environment of poverty reduces its ability to recover from the original hazardous exposure.

Birch and Gussow (1970) and Ricciuti (1977) cite a number of studies indicating a "dual risk" when factors of prematurity, low birth weight, or perinatal complications occur in an adverse socioeconomic environment. In summarizing such studies on low birth weight, Ricciuti (1977) notes:

Some of the best illustrations of important interactions between biological and social influences on psychological development are provided by studies of the effects of low birth weight on subsequent intellectual functioning (Francis-Williams and Davies 1974; Braine, *et al.,* 1966). Drillien's well known work for example (1964), showed very clearly that at every age from 12 months to 5 years the likelihood of sub-normal intellectual development occurring in infants of very low birth weight (under 1500 grams) was substantially greater for children in the lower socio-economic groups than for those in the upper-middle groups. In the latter case, at 4 years of age the IQ's of very low birth weight babies were essentially normal (97 compared with 110 for normal controls), whereas in the lower social groups these low birth weight children had a mean IQ of 63, compared with 95 for the controls. The recently reported National Child Development Study (Davie, *et al.*, 1972) also provides clear evidence of the "dual risk" implied by low birth weight combined with an unfavorable socio-economic environment. When "full term" infants with gestation ages 37 weeks or later were classified according to birth weight percentiles for gestation age, there was a substantial increase in the likelihood of "educational backwardness" in school at age seven for infants in the lowest percentile groups (below the 10th percentile). It is particularly interesting to note that this effect was much more marked in working class than in middle class groups, with by far the highest incidence of educational backwardness (nearly 17%) occurring in 5th or later born children in the working class, with birth weights in the lowest 5 percent for gestation age. If these "small for date" babies were first born in middle class families, the prevalence rate dropped to 1.5 percent [165-166].

In summarizing studies on prematurity, Birch and Gussow (1970) similarly note:

> It would appear, then, that there is a differential risk associated with prematurity in terms of the social class in which it occurs, and that the interactions between prematurity and environment are complexly mediated and affect the prospects of the premature child both before and after birth. When added to the stresses of being poor and lower-class, premature birth is a cumulative condition of risk — so far as measurable IQ is concerned — not merely uncompensated for by events succeeding natality, but exacerbated by the adverse circumstances in which the lower-class child lived [pp. 64-65].

This "dual risk" factor, which Birch and Ricciuti note, should remind the reader of our earlier discussion of Sameroff's interaction model which holds that any prediction of long range developmental outcomes must include information on the child's caretaking environment as well as his constitutional make-up. In fact, Sameroff and Chandler (1975) proposed the concept of a *continuum of caretaking casualty* to incorporate the environmental risk factors leading toward poor developmental outcomes. This concept is the interactive counterpart of Pasamanick's *continuum of reproductive casualty*. This consideration of health and nutritional factors in poverty indicates how as in our case of lead poisoning specific environmental variables can cause a differential incidence of not only extreme neurological deficit but mild forms of intellectual impairment in the lower socioeconomic classes. When such cases of mild intellectual impairment occur in lower class children without a recognition of their environmental cause — and on the basis of our own years of working with school systems we can attest to the generally limited investigation of causal factors when a child is presented for possible placement in an educable class — it requires only the additional characteristic of being present in more than one member of the family in order to be designated familial retardation.

It is not hard to imagine how this additional clinching characteristic of familial retardation could come about. A woman of the lower socioeconomic class with a chronic state of ill health that endangers the fetal development of a given pregnancy is not likely to pose less danger during succeeding pregnancies. In fact, we may expect that in conditions of poverty, the mother's health is likely to deteriorate with succeeding pregnancies. Similarly, a family whose economic status is so precarious as to deprive a given infant of adequate nutrition and health care is apt to be even less capable of caring for the nutritional and health care needs of succeeding children. Thus an accumulation of familial cases could occur by the operation of various specific factors operating within the global factor of poverty.

We do not maintain that this argument attributing familial retardation to environmental factors operating within an adverse socioeconomic environment is any more compelling than the arguments advanced for a polygenetic etiology of familial retardation. But we do think it is cogent enough to give one pause before accepting a polygenetic theory of inherited mental ability as a general explanation for familial retardation. We would go at least one step further and hazard the guess that environmental and genetic variables contribute to the incidence of familial retardation both independently and in interaction, as when a somewhat lower inherited potential for cognitive functioning is further affected by an adverse socioeconomic setting. Furthermore, we are impelled to go one step still further and recognize that environmental variables such as we have been considering, added to genetic variables, do not exhaust the universe of possible factors determining the incidence of familial retardation.

The Cultural Factors

Another group of factors that could be hypothesized as contributing to familial retardation we might term cultural differences. In contrast to the environmental factors just discussed — where physical and biological agents are in the foreground as the immediate cause of cognitive and learning deficiencies and where psychological and social factors serve only to enhance or potentiate those physical and biological agents — we would now consider psychological and social factors that have either a direct effect upon cognitive functioning or an effect upon personality factors that interact with that cognitive functioning.

In making this distinction we are aware that other authors using terms such as cultural or social deprivation intend to designate that conglomorate of biological, physical, psychological, and social factors that exists within the environment of poverty. We choose to make some rough demarcation between the biological and physical factors discussed in the previous section and the psychological and social variables which we wish to discuss in this section. In part, we make this distinction because the effects of the physical and biological factors on the efficiency of cognitive function is more direct and ascertainable even if we must make allowances for their interaction with Sameroff's continuum of caretaking casualty. In addition, we feel that the presumed deleterious effect of psychological and social factors on cognitive efficiency depends on whether we measure the efficiency as it functions in a culture of poverty or whether we measure it in a middle-class setting of school or work.

The hypothesization of such psychological and social factors became increasingly current in the 1950s and 1960s, and was an attempt to explain the observed negative correlation between socioeconomic class and cognitive functioning as measured by such indices as standardized tests and educational progress. The argument here proceeds along the lines that normal cognitive functioning in the later stages of development requires an appropriately stimulating social and psychological environment during the earlier stages of development. Studies on dogs, rats, and monkeys demonstrate that in lower animals if the young are deprived of maternal care or social and psychological stimulation, they grow up with various kinds of disturbances in their cognitive, emotional, and social functioning. Studies on human infants raised in institutional settings bereft of social and psychological stimulation can also be adduced to indicate that such deprivation results in impaired cognitive and social functioning. Conversely, studies such as those of Skeels (1966), or Clarke and Clarke (1953), suggest that increased levels of stimulation and care can enhance the cognitive development of children in at least some circumstances. An introduction to the extensive literature in this field is provided by Newton and Levine (1968), particularly, in the chapters by O'Connor, Casler, and Bronfenbrenner.

From this empirical base the argument can then be advanced that since children in the lower socioeconomic classes show scholastic retardation and learning difficulties, with accompanying low scores on standardized tests, the inference is reasonable that they too must have suffered a deprivation of psychological and social stimulation in early childhood. The factors in lower socioeconomic class life that might cause such deprivation have been postulated as including family disorganization, absent fathers, working mothers, a lack of parenting skills, an excess number of children resulting in less individualized care, an impoverished language environment, a deficiency of sensorimotor stimulation in infancy, etc.

In recent years this purported relationship between psychological and social deprivation within the poverty subcultures and cognitive and learning deficits as reflected in school performance has undergone challenge (Leacock 1971; Horowitz and Paden 1973; Ginsburg 1972). Tulkin's (1972) analysis of the concept of cultural deprivation criticizes it on three accounts. First, the concept of cultural deprivation makes it easy for social scientists to overlook the importance of the processes by which environmental experiences influence development. To use a status variable such as class or race membership as a correlate of performance on a specific developmental or intellectual task does not further an understanding of the actual processes by which environmental factors influence behavior. What we need to understand is what specific factors in the status variable may effect development for good or for ill. Second, in discussing the deprivation in a subcultural population, many authors appear to discount the importance of cultural relativism. Here Tulkin utilizes material from Gans's (1962) study of Italian-American culture in Boston's West-End, and the controversy over the adequacy of black English as a vehicle for cognitive development, to indicate the importance of placing observations on specific cultural factors within their whole integrated cultural context. Failure to do so leads to a misunderstanding and devaluation of the subculture and well-intentioned, but perhaps destructive, efforts on the part of the majority culture to transform the minority subculture into a replica of itself. Tulkin (1972) challenges this approach noting that:

> Cultural relativism and success in "schools and industry," however, are not mutually exclusive. It is possible to teach children the skills needed for articulation with the majority culture, while encouraging them to develop a pride in their own family or cultural heritage, and to utilize the particular skills which their own socialization has strengthened. A majority culture can, however, promote a narrow definition of success in order to ensure that the power of the society remain in the hands of a relatively select group within the society. Thus, by maintaining that any deviation from the white middle-class norm represents cultural deprivation, the white middle class is guarding its position as *the* source of culture—and power—in this nation. Cultural deprivation, then, is not just a psychological or educational issue; it is also very much a political issue [p. 331].

Finally, Tulkin argues that the majority culture, "by its tolerance for social, political, and economic inequality, actually contributes to the development, in some subgroups, of the very characteristics which it considers 'depriving'." Here he considers such obvious faults in the system as inadequate medical care for the poor and the realities of life in a poverty subculture that engender chronic hopelessness and despair.

The School Itself as a Factor in Determining Familial Retardation

In all the alternative explanations of familial retardation that we have considered to this point, there is one common feature. In every case, the assumption exists that the familial retardate exists prior to entry into school. Yet, since the familial retardate is generally not identified prior to school entrance and often disappears from view upon leaving school, it would seem logical that one should be forced to examine the possibility that the school itself is a factor in the development of familial retardation. This would not suggest that the school is the only factor in the causation of familial retardation. As we have tried to indicate in our examination of other alternative explanations, each has a certain plausibility and it seems reasonable that such factors as polygenetic inheritance, or the physical, biological, psychological, and social hazards in poverty should each contribute a share to the total incidence of familial retardation. But the hypothesis that we should like the reader to entertain is that a major factor in the determination of familial retardation is the educational system itself.

Suggestions of such a hypothesis have been advanced by various authors in connection with the problem of educational failure in poverty populations (Fantini 1969; Horowitz and Paden 1973; Clark 1968). But we would like to consider it at length. Such a consideration will often seem indirect, focusing as it must not specifically on familial retardation and the school but upon the much broader context of the interaction of the larger society, its subcultures, and its schools.

There is a certain irony in accusing schools of having a major role in creating the problem of familial retardation within our society. For the common school, as we shall endeavor to demonstrate in subsequent chapters, was to a large extent devised in the course of the nineteenth century as a cure for the ills of society: poverty, crime, delinquency, and immorality. The content of the curriculum was chosen to develop the cognitive skills and the moral and ethical character that would, according to the leading thought of the time, ensure citizens capable of participating in a complex, industrialized society as productive, law-abiding, and socially responsible members. The methods of instruction were dictated not only by the prevailing theories of knowledge, philosophies of education, and psychologies of childhood, but by the available science and technology of instruction, and by the availability of human and financial resources. Curricula and methods were implemented in organizational settings growing ever more complex as the nineteenth century advanced from the one-room rural school to the mammoth physical plant of the urban school, with teachers numbered in the scores and pupils in the thousands, from the essentially local district school board administrative control to the administrative complexity of state-wide educational bureaucracies. In the end, the massive ills of society had dictated the massive therapeutic intervention known as the common school system.

To the extent that it is appropriate to view the common school as a prescribed cure for the ills of society, we maintain that a considerable proportion of mental retardation encompassed by the term "educably retarded" can be viewed as an iatrogenic disease. By that we mean, just as the administration of certain medications in the treatment of physical disease can cause the appearance of new disease related to the nature of the medication and to the patient's idiopathic response to it, irrespective of its effect upon the original disorder for which it was prescribed, so, in like manner, a considerable part of the problem of educably retarded children derives from the way in which we have devised our educational system. To the extent that we have ignored cultural differences, differences in patterns and tempos of learning, social and affective differences in the temperaments of children, to the extent that we have set goals of achievement for individual children that are either unrealistically high or low, we have ensured the development of that educationally disordered child, with cognitive and social handicaps, that we relegate to the special classroom.

This is not to deny a continuum of competence that may be based on genetic and environmental factors acting together and independent of the educational environment in which society attempts to develop and measure competence. It is to state that the continuum of competence, cognitive and social, existing prior to entry into school becomes distorted by the very system that society has devised for the development and measurement of competence. And that the distortion is of such a nature that individual social and ethnic class differences interact with the categorical rigidities of curriculum, methods of instruction, and administrative organization to sort out the children not solely in terms of the constitutional and environmentally determined differences existing prior to school entry, but to a large extent independently of such preschool individual differences.

If this were not so, then we would not understand the difficulty that investigators have in attempting to identify familial retardation prior to school-entry age. Nor would we understand why the special education classes from their very beginning have been disproportionately composed of subcultural minorities and why over time these minorities, in proportion as they have made it in the larger society, have reduced their numbers in the special education classes where they have in turn been replaced by the more recently arrived minorities in our urban ghettos.

If our contention that familial retardation is in large part an iatrogenic disorder is correct, then we have no problem in supplying explanations for the above conundrums. We are not surprised that the teachers of the first special education classes at the turn of the century noted a disproportionate representation of Italian, and other ethnic groups among their pupils. We feel that it was inevitable that blacks, Puerto Ricans, and Mexican-Americans would predominate in the special education classes of our urban schools of today. Nor are we surprised that Pintner (1932) could summarize the results of some seventeen studies of intelligence differences between "Italian" and "American" school children in this country by indicating a range of group means from 76 to a 100 with a mid-point of 87 for the "Italian" children and a range of 85 to a 109 with a mid-point of 102 for the "American" children—figures that are prescient of those reported by Shuey in her 1966 summary of the hundreds of studies on black and white differences in intelligence.

Rather than express surprise at these gleanings we would rather formulate the questions they so obviously pose. What has happened to those Italian children with a mean IQ of approximately 85? Did they grow up to pass on their genes and their cultural disadvantages to their children? If so, where are the studies in *today's* psychological and sociological literature pondering the educational and social problems posed by the Italian children and their mean 85 IQ? If such Italian children no longer exist, is it meaningful to wonder in learned journals heavy with statistics about the problem of the black child and his 85 IQ or the Chicano child and his special class placement? Or should we for the moment put aside the subtle arguments on the various heritability coefficients, and the political rhetoric on the existence of racial and class differences in cognitive functioning, and simply try to understand our educational system and its relation to mental retardation and the larger society? It is with the conviction that the answer to the latter question should be in the affirmative that we will undertake a brief history of the development of the common school. We will attempt to understand the problems to which such development addressed itself, the adequacy of its answers, the inevitableness with which the logic of its development led to the identification of the educably retarded child and the appropriateness of its special education programs. In such a review we hope that the reader will not be unmindful of our previous discussion of the problems of definition, diagnosis, intervention, and training of professionals in the area of mental retardation. We have focused on the child and the existing social context that defines the problem. The issues we addressed are persistent and, to a considerable extent, transcend our educational system. But now we wish to understand the specific interaction of our educational system and the educationally retarded child in ways which both broaden and narrow the issues of definition, diagnosis, intervention, and training. To achieve this we will first require an understanding of the history of our educational system and how its development inevitably affected the definition and the diagnosis of mental retardation as well as the strategies of intervention and the training of professionals.

We must prepare the reader for the fact that in the next several chapters it will appear as if we are saying little or nothing about mental retardation and special education. The reader may ask these questions: Why is it important to understand the development of the public schools beginning in the colonial period? Why should one know the developing rationale for age-graded classrooms or the factors leading to universal compulsory education? Why go into detail about the role of religion, ethnicity, and immigration in shaping the public schools?

It is necessary because we tend to be ahistorical in our thinking. When we endeavor to make a change in our schools, we fail to recognize that the *structure* of our schools was developed in relation to earlier societal problems, and that these structural characteristics will be effective obstacles to our efforts at change. Indeed, as we have suggested, the structure may not be part of the solution but the problem itself. Second, most people would assert that among the major problems in our society the education of blacks, Chicanos, Hispanics, and handicapped people is pressing and perplexing, and that the "track record" of the schools in meeting the needs of these groups gives no great cause for optimism.

From a historical point of view we are dealing with the latest version of an old story: the conflictful interaction between the culturally-religiously-ethnically dominant groups and those who are different and newly arrived. The substance of the problem has changed as have the actors in the social drama but that is no warrant for an ahistorical stance. This is not to say that if one knows history, one can easily distill lessons for the present. But it is to say that if one adopts a historical perspective, one is less likely to come up with oversimple proposals, and more likely to adopt a more realistic perspective about institutional and societal change (Sarason 1973).

More importantly, one is less likely to see the problems in narrow educational terms but rather in the continuous stream of the history of our society. For too long the field of mental retardation has been special, in that it has been concerned with people who are "different," with the difference residing *in them*. Only in recent years has there been general acceptance of the idea that our concept of mental retardation bears the imprint of our society and its distinguishing features, e.g., ethnicity, religion, social class, and economic status. It is this recognition that requires us to look back at social history in an attempt to see two things more clearly: the ways these distinguishing societal features shaped our schools, and how this shaping set the stage for the emergence of special education. Why did special education emerge when it did and not fifty years earlier or fifty years later? The answer does not lie in an examination of schools but in the ways the structure of the schools was forged in response to a fast-growing population, floods of immigrants, ethnocentrism, resistance to assimilation, urban poverty, and social disorganization, and, finally, the victory of the forces for compulsory education.

So, in the next several chapters the reader will not find very much on mental retardation and special education, but a good deal on how our public schools took shape. From time to time we shall point out parallels with today's scene, and we have no doubt that the reader will see other parallels. For example, when we talk about immigrant groups like the Germans, Irish, and Italians in the context of *their* experience of the nineteenth century, the reader will see communalities between these immigrants and the blacks, Chicanos, and Hispanics of today. Our society today is obviously different from what it was in the nineteenth century, but the differences must not obscure continuities that appear in different guises at different times. The reader who regards history as a collection of dead people and forgotten issues (a kind of museum of dead conceptual relics) may wish to skip the next few chapters. To such a reader we can quote George Santayana: "Those who do not remember the past are condemned to repeat it."

9

Emergence of the Common School: Aims, Quick Growth, and Organizational Changes

SPECIAL EDUCATION OF the mentally subnormal in public schools in the United States began in the late nineteenth century, largely as an outgrowth of the attempt to institute free, universal, compulsory education. To understand, then, the origins of our special education programs and the specific effects which those origins were to have upon subsequent developments requires some consideration of the general development of public school education in the nineteenth century.

The ideal of free, universal, compulsory education developed more or less simultaneously in various countries of western civilization. It derived in large part from the social problems arising from industrialization, urbanization, poverty, class, and cultural differences. These social problems were shared throughout western civilization and accounted for the similar and simultaneous development of educational programs in autocratic Prussia, monarchial England and republican United States. This similarity of problems and response is attested to by the ease with which these countries borrowed educational innovations from one another. However, there were some national differences not only in the educational systems developed but in the problems faced and the assumptions underlying the professed ideal.

It is reasonable to suppose that the assumption prevailed that free, universal education offered a remedy for the major social ills accompanying the development of the modern industrial state. But the American educational ideal was further buttressed by assumptions about democracy's need for a literate, educated citizenry in which each member was of equal worth and possessed of equal potential for contribution to society. These particular assumptions were of course not universally held, as our revisionist historians are likely to remind us. Nevertheless, they served as a rationale for free public education, and were not without impact on the way our American educational institutions developed and are still developing.

There were also significant differences in the nature of the socioeconomic problems facing Europe and America. Like Europe, America was changing from a predominantly agrarian economy to one more and more dominated by industry. But in the accompanying urbanization and population growth, America outstripped Europe to the point that quantitative differences had qualitative effects. Thus in the nineteenth century America's population growth rate exceeded that of Europe by a factor of six or seven. Europe had a long history of urban development with its accompanying problems. In 1800, the United States had no city population in excess of 61,000; by the end of the century, 38 cities had populations in excess of 100,000, and three had grown beyond the million mark. Add to this the fact that this population growth was due in large part to the immigration of culturally diverse peoples often arriving in the new country without more than the clothes on their backs and bundles of hand-carried personal effects, and the size of the socioeconomic problems are compounded several times over.

The differences in socioeconomic problems, coupled with cultural conditions, made for differences in the way various countries organized their systems of free public education. In fact, even within the borders of the United States varied socioeconomic factors, historical origins in diverse colonial traditions, and distinct cultural heritages made for notable differences in the development of educational institutions.

Full consideration of these national and international differences in economic and social conditions, in ideologies, and in the educational systems they influenced would be essential for any thorough history of nineteenth century education. But for our limited purpose, we shall selectively choose the educational developments of the nineteenth century, focusing principally on the United States with even more narrow vision on the northeast and with partiality to developments within New York City. And we shall do this as if we were dealing with a uniform and simple evolutionary development — which simply did not exist. Our aim in selective simplification has its rationale in an attempt to understand the development of special education programs in the twentieth century. A selective and simplified history of general public school education in the nineteenth century will add a necessary complexity to our perception of the development of special education; it is for the sake of that increased complexity of perception, which we hope will further more adequate problem solving, that we present a brief view of nineteenth-century developments of elementary education in its ideals, its theory, and its practice. This will provide the background for understanding the ideals, the theory, and the practice of special education as it began in the public schools toward the close of the nineteenth century. Then we will be able to pursue in some detail the development of special education in the twentieth century and to assess the problems that confront it today.

Early National Education and Its Colonial Origins

The development of education in the early years of the republic was in itself no product of spontaneous generation. Its origins were in colonial education and it was influenced not only by the general socioeconomic development of America but by the ideas, philosophies, and practices of European educators.

It has been customary to cite the Massachusetts Law of 1647 to emphasize the religious motivation in the establishment of those schools that were to be the forerunners of our present public school systems. In the preamble to that law it is recognized as "one cheife proiect of ye ould deluder, Satan, to keepe men from the knowledge of ye Scriptures," and in remedy the law provided that every township of fifty householders or more shall, "appoint one wthin their towne to teach all such children as shall resort to him to write & reade, whose wages shall be paid eithr by ye parents or mastrs of such children, or by ye inhabitants in genrall. . . ." An additonal provision of the law called for larger towns to maintain grammar schools to prepare youths for the university — the primary source for the educated clergy (Cubberly 1934b, pp. 18-19).

If we think of this concern with universal elementary education as designed simply to provide the means of a personal salvation by access to the scriptures we are probably defining religious means and ends much too narrowly. For in the Puritan theocracy religion infused the government of the state, and the relationship between education and governance was obvious to the Puritan mind.

Following Wertenbaker (1947), we note in William Hubbard's sermon of 1676: "It was well replied by an officer of the state to a nobleman that made small account of learning in the education of his son, aiming at no higher learning than to be able to ride a horse or fly a hawk, that if it were so, then noblemen's sons must be content that mean men's children should govern the kingdom." In Hubbard's view, New England was in need of experienced, broadly educated men "acquainted with the affairs of the world abroad, as well as with the laws and customs of their own people" (p. 140).

Urian Oakes, renowned preacher and one time president of Colonial Harvard, put the matter even more forcefully, "The fall of schools and contempt of learning will make way for rudeness, ignorance, want of able instruments to manage church and state affairs, irreligion and ruin to this poor country. . . . Think not that the commonwealth of learning may languish, and yet our civil and ecclesiastical state be maintained in good plight and condition" (p. 140).

Although Calvinistic Massachusetts was most consistent in applying the principle that elementary education should serve religious needs, the essentially religious basis for the establishment of elementary schools prevailed in all the colonies. The instructional materials of the schools were themselves basically religious texts. The hornbook used to teach the alphabet to children consisted in one of its popular forms of a wooden paddle to which a sheet of paper was affixed bearing the alphabet, syllables, and the Lord's Prayer. For protection from childish fingers the paper itself was covered with a sheet of transparent horn (Tuer 1897, Littlefield 1965).

Catechisms presenting religious dogma in question and answer form, Psalters containing favorite Psalms, and the Bible itself were the earliest textbooks. Later, English primers and, beginning about 1690, the famous New England Primer were introduced. The New England Primer, the most common textbook in the colonies of the eighteenth century, opened with a listing of the alphabet, syllables, and spelling words followed by a picture alphabet with accompanying rhymes. Thus, next to the letter A would be a small engraving of Adam and Eve standing before the Tree of Knowledge accompanied by the rhyme:

> In Adam's fall
> We sinned all.

The rest of the Primer in its various editions would consist of sundry moral and religious exhortations, the Lord's Prayer, the Creed, the ten commandments and, perhaps, a catechism.

In the transition from the colonial to the postrevolutionary era this religious motivation for universal elementary education was gradually replaced by the expressed need for providing educated citizenry as the foundation of republican government. This was reflected in the increasingly secular nature of the books utilized for instruction in the schools. But this change in rationale for the establishment of schools was not as radical as it first appeared. In both cases the welfare of the individual whether it was called "salvation," or the "pursuit of happiness," and the welfare of the state, theocratic oligarchy or republican, were assumed to be inextricably bound up with education. The perennial problem for education, then and now, was how to balance its assigned commitment to the welfare of the individual and the welfare of the state.

In the establishment of the colonial schools there were, as Cremin (1951) points out, two principal traditions of support. The first of these, deriving from our English heritage and individualistic in its nature, he calls the tradition of philanthropy. It held that the provision for the child's education was the right and duty of the individual family; such a tradition fostered the development of private schools. The community was to be held responsible only for the children of those families too poor to provide from their own resources. For such children, charity schools might be established by church, community, or private philanthropy.

The other tradition of support represented in the educational legislation of the Massachusetts Bay Colony was that of *collectivism*. In this tradition, although the parent was free to provide private education if he so wished, the town government was assigned the responsibility for providing at least elementary public education, available to all that might seek it; an education that was basically supported by public funds even though families that could afford it might be required to pay special assessments. Generally speaking, the collective tradition of Massachusetts prevailed in the New England colonies and philanthropic tradition in the middle and southern colonies.

With different patterns of support and varying socioeconomic and cultural conditions both within and among the colonies, the structure and organization of elementary education of colonial times does not permit brief description without distortion. Couple with this the fact that provisions for elementary education were evolving over time, and the task multiplies in difficulty. But for our purposes it may only be necessary to touch upon some general characteristics of colonial schooling as they existed just prior to the revolution and as they survived into the beginnings of the nationalist period.

These general characteristics should be sufficient to enable us to appreciate the immensity of the problem that faced the school men of the nineteenth century as they sought to develop the common school system in face of an ever increasing population that was constantly shifting geographically — centrifugally moving ever westward while it centripetally condensed from farm through village to city. We note that a population of five and a third million in 1800 had grown to nearly 76 million in 1900. This represents a growth factor in excess of 14 during a period in which the population of Europe no more than doubled.

The centripetal shift during this century is indicated by a growth in the urban population from approximately 6 percent to 40 percent of the total population. Add to this the multicultural, multiracial makeup of the people, and the shifting patterns due to changes in immigrant flow. At the same time the economic base of the society was moving from primarily agriculture to a mixture of agriculture and industry with the latter growing ever more important in terms of the working force involved and the wealth produced. With this in mind, we are better prepared to appreciate the successes and the failures of the educational system that evolved.

In general, elementary education in those times that preceded the rapid socioeconomic changes of the nineteenth century was characterized by untrained teachers, poor equipment, and grossly inefficient methods of instruction. The curriculum was extremely narrow with reading, writing, and some exposure to arithmetic computation the primary fare. Books were scarce, typically each child bringing as a text whatever might be available in his home. Paper was in short supply. Teaching might be done by any literate adult desirous of adding to income by part-time operation of a school — by a farmer with time to spare in the long winter months, a clergyman in one of his multifaceted functions, or a college student during vacation periods. Recitations were modeled after home instruction, with one or two children at a time while the remainder without books or supplies would fidget waiting their turn. Schoolmasters spent inordinate time making and repairing quill pens, preparing specimens of writing for the children to copy, and setting sums for arithmetic. It has been estimated that as much as two-thirds of the school time was wasted by this combination of poor equipment and methods. Letter perfect memorization, from the alphabet through the catechism to the computational rule of three, was both the aim and the test of learning. Discipline was harsh. The physical setting was Spartan and stark; typical were backless benches without desks, and writing surfaces made of slanted boards pegged to the sides of the room (Parker 1970, Johnson 1925, Littlefield 1965).

Schools during this period and well into the nineteenth century were often in two sessions: a summer session usually taught by women and attended by girls and younger children of both sexes; and the winter session more often taught by men and attended more often by older boys.

Thanks particularly to the work of Barnard and his mid-century *American Journal of Education* a considerable amount of biographical reminiscence of these early schools exist. Noah Webster who contributed so much to the changing of the schools in that period recalls his own educational experience in a letter to Barnard dated in March of 1840:

> You desire me to give you some information as to the mode of instruction in common schools when I was young, or before the Revolution. . . . When I was young, the books used were chiefly or wholly Dilworth's Spelling Books, the Psalter, Testament and Bible. No geography was studied before the publication of Dr. Morse's small books on that subject, about the year 1786 or 1787. No history was read, as far as my knowledge extends, for there was no abridged history of the United States. Except the books above mentioned, no book for reading was used before the publication of the Third Part of my Institute, in 1785. In some of the early editions of that book, I introduced short notices of the geography and history of the United States, and these led to more enlarged descriptions of the country. . . .
>
> Before the Revolution, and for some years after, no slates were used in common schools: all writing and the operations in arithmetic were on paper. The teacher wrote the copies and gave the sums in arithmetic; few or none of the pupils having any books as a guide. Such was the condition of the schools in which I received my early education [Webster 1840].

The spellers that Webster refers to began to replace the primers as elementary reading books in the latter half of the eighteenth century.

Webster's own speller, first published in 1783, was to become the most famous of all American schoolbooks, and dominated the field through much of the nineteenth century. Johnson (1925) estimated that at the time of Webster's death in 1842 over a million copies were being sold annually with a total of 24 million in print. During the earlier decades of the Republic, it was the chief text for the first two or three years of schooling.

A glance at the 1831 edition tells much about the education of the time. It opens with a didactic essay on the analysis of sounds in the English language, alerting the student and teacher to both regularities and ir-regularities between spelling and sound, and providing a pronunciation guide. Then follows the alphabet with a listing of the letters and their names, a list of syllables, numerous tables of spelling words beginning with words of one syllable and with tables of longer words helpfully syllabified and accompanied by guides to accentuation. Most importantly, different vowel sounds represented by the same letter were so grouped and keyed in the lists that the student would not go astray, and several typographic devices such as italiciz-ing mute vowels were introduced as further aids to the student. (Such typographic devices have had recent revival in a number of our modern introductory reading systems of which the Distar may be taken as an example.) After some twenty-five pages of spelling lists, the lists become interspersed with reading lessons consisting of disconnected sentences or paragraphs or moral exhortation, a few illustrated fables, and uplifting anecdotes. The final section of the book consists not in the religious catechism of the New England Primer but in a "moral catechism" dealing with various virtues and vices (Webster 1962).

The delay in the introduction of connected reading material into the speller reminds us that reading during this period was taught by the synthetic method, proceeding from alphabet to syllable to word. The method is as old as Greek civilization and may be assumed particularly adapted to the phonetic accuracy of the Greek alphabet for rendering the ancient Grecian tongue (Matthews 1966). The English alphabet bears no such fortunate rela-tionship to the spoken word and hence the need for Webster's elaborate and complicated guide for pronunciation of the written word, with its heavy burden on the memory function.

It was not until the middle of the nineteenth century that the analytic or word-to-meaning methods became widely known with the resultant tugs of war between the proponents of the various one-best-ways to teach reading. But returning to Webster's approach, it is of interest that the combination of ethical and moral precepts with reading instruction, which is apt to strike us as quaint, also had precedent among the Greeks, who set before the boy learning to write copies approving virtue and respect for the gods (Matthews 1966).

Society would seem to always assume that in the education of the young the mastery of skills should be blended with the development of character. In fact, we shall see that in the view of those advocating the development of the common schools in the early and middle nineteenth century, and of those who proposed the development of special education at the end of the century, the formation of character was often a more compelling argument than the development of skills.

The synthetic method of learning to read features prominently in the reminiscences of many who attended these early schools; one is struck with the degree to which education involved the memorization of words and texts. Direct contact with, observation of, and reflection upon concrete objects were not to become a feature of American education until the Pestalozzian movement reached us in the middle and latter half of the century.

Henry Clarke Wright, abolitionist and reformer, grew up in frontier country just south of the Mohawk Valley in upstate New York. His autobiography gives a vivid account of schooling in the early years of the Republic.

> My first recollection of a school house are of an old log building, rudely put together; a huge fireplace, with a mighty chimney of stones, loosely piled together; a floor of boards, rough, and not nailed down; and standing on the bank of a rapid brook, not a stone's throw from a grove of huge hemlock trees . . .
>
> I remember, too, the stupid process of learning the alphabet, and to put letters into syllables, and syllables into words, and words into sentences. I could not then understand the difficulty, but I know it was a practice calculated to disgust children with all books and book learning. The children that were learning the alphabet were called up, two or three at a time; the teacher held the book before them, and pointed with a knife to the first letter and said A. Then the children repeated A after her. Then she pointed to B, and told the children to say B, and they said B, with their eyes, perhaps, fixed on the floor, or turned askance at some other scholar, or half asleep. So the process went on to the last letter. Then the children sat down, and there we had to sit, with nothing to do; no pictures to look at, no slates and pencils to draw the figures of the letters, nothing in the world to rouse stupidity or instruct ignorance; and not a single familiar object or thing associated with the letters, syllables and words that we had to say over. In this way, I was thoroughly drilled into the art of saying over letters, syllables and words, and spelling them, without exciting one emotion, or one thought of persons and things as they existed around me. No wonder we all broke forth from such a place at recess, and when school was dismissed, with an irrepressible shout of joy at our momentary deliverance. It has often been a doubt in my mind, if my school and book learning during my childhood did me more good than harm. I know it did me a great harm. I do not know that it did me much good.
>
> During the period of my childhood, from about five to twelve years of age, I was kept at school, on the average about eight months per year; about five months in summer, under female teachers, and the other months in winter, always under male teachers. In spite of the disgusting and untoward circumstances attending the schools and manner of teaching, I became fond of going to school and of study; though the study did little else for me but to exercise and strengthen my memory. It did nothing to teach me how to think, to reflect on what I felt within

me, or saw or heard about me; nothing to rouse, invigorate, and discipline my affections or my intellect. . . [Wright 1849, pp. 46-48].

The contrast between this frontier school and the village school of more settled regions was not marked. Samuel G. Goodrich who under his own name and under the pseudonym of Peter Parley wrote numerous popular textbooks in the middle of the 19th century recalled in his *Recollections of a Life Time* (1859) his own childhood education in Ridgefield, Connecticut, at the very beginning of the century.

The school-house itself consisted of rough, unpainted clapboards, upon a wooden frame. It was plastered within, and contained two apartments—a little entry, taken out of the corner for a wardrobe, and the school-room proper. The chimney was of stone and pointed with mortar . . . . In winter, the battle for life with green fizzling fuel, which was brought in sled lengths and cut up by the scholars was a stern one. Not unfrequently, the wood, gushing with sap as it was, chanced to be out, and as there was no living without fire, the thermometer being ten or twenty degrees below zero, the school was dismissed. . . .

It was the custom at this place, to have a woman's school in the summer months, and this was attended only by young children. It was, in fact, what we now call a primary or infant school. In winter, a man was employed as teacher, and then the girls and boys of the neighborhood, up to the age of eighteen, or even twenty, were among the pupils. It was not uncommon, at this season, to have forty scholars crowded into this little building.

I was about six years old when I first went to school . . . . I think we had seventeen scholars—boys and girls—mostly of my own age. . . . The school being organized we were all seated upon benches made of what were called *slabs*—that is, boards having the exterior or rounded part of the log on one side: as they were useless for other purposes, these were converted into school-benches, the rounded part down. . . .

The children were called up, one by one, to Aunt Delight, who set on a low chair, and required each, as a preliminary, to make his manners, consisting of a small sudden nod or jerk of the head. She then placed the spelling-book—which was Dilworth's—before the pupil, and with a buck-handled penknife pointed, one by one, to the letters of the alphabet, saying, "What's that?". . . .

I believe I achieved the alphabet that summer, but my after progress, for a long time, I do not remember. Two years later I went to the winter-school at the same place, kept my Lewis Olmstead—a man who had a call for plowing, mowing, carting manure, &c., in summer, and for teaching school in the winter. . . .

The next step of my progress which is marked in my memory, is the spelling of words of two syllables. I did not go very regularly to school but by the time I was ten years old I had learned to write, and had made a little progress in arithmetic. There was not a grammar, a geography, or a history or any kind in the school. Reading, writing, and arithmetic were the only things taught, and these very indifferently—not wholly from the stupidity of the teacher but because he had forty scholars, and the standards of the age required no more than he performed [Goodrich 1859, pp. 33-38].

During this period some of the cities did offer more highly differentiated and organized educational programs. Boston, for example, had Dame schools, operated privately by women who took children into their homes to teach them the elements of reading before they entered the English grammar or reading schools as they were alternatively called. In the grammar school children were instructed in reading and spelling, English grammar, and composition. In writing schools—operated independently from the reading schools even if housed in the same building—the children were taught writing and arithmetic. The Latin schools, entered at a later age, prepared the boys for college.

Despite the complexity in the Boston School System, methods and contents of instruction in the lower levels did not differ much from the district schools of the village and countryside. This is attested to by the reminiscences of Henry K. Oliver (1876):

> In the year 1805, or thereabouts, being then something under five years of age, I was first placed under educational influence, consigned to the care of one Mr. Hayslop, who, with his wife and widowed daughter, one Mrs. Hurley, kept school in an old building, long since demolished, standing on the northerly corner of Franklin and Washington streets. . . . By him was I taught A, B, C, D, E, F, G, my a, b, abs, and my e, b, ebs, after the old, old way,—praised because ancestral,—the old gentleman holding an old book in his old hand, and pointing, with an old pin, to the old letters, on the old page, and making each of us chicks repeat their several names, till we could tell them at sight, though we did not know what it was all for. We must have been a bright set, excellent of memory, for by this excellent old method . . . we were not more than four or five weeks in acquiring complete knowledge of the twenty-six arbitrary marks constituting the English Alphabet. . . .
>
> From this school I was removed to another, Madam Tileston's in Hanover below Salem Street, of the same general character, where I was taught elementary reading and spelling, after the same ancestral fashion;—that is, I received about twenty minutes of instruction each half day, and as school was kept three hundred and sixty minutes daily, I had the privilege of forty minutes' worth of teaching, and three hundred and twenty minutes' worth of sitting still, (if I could), which I could not,—playing, whispering, and general waste of time, though occasionally a picture book relieved the dreary monotony. . . .
>
> There were no schools systematically graded; there were no blackboards; there were no globes, nor other ordinary school apparatus in schools I attended. I never saw a full-sized map, nor illustrative picture of any sort suspended aginst the school walls. . . .
>
> Though vividly recollecting very many school incidents, there are some matters of which I have no remembrance whatever. I do not remember that my powers of perception or observation were ever awakened, or drawn out, or cultivated. I do not remember that my attention was ever called to the consideration of any object, great or small, in the great world into which I had been born, or in the little world by which I was surrounded. I saw the great Solar Eclipse in the forenoon of June 16th, 1806,—when my father's hens went to roost in the barn, and the cows on Boston Common gathered at the gate to start for home, . . . but nobody ever

told me by what means that great and unwonted obscurity came to pass, — ere the sun had reached high noon, — or how it was that the sun of that day twice left the earth in darkness. . . .

You will, therefore, see the object-teaching, now most wisely considered to be of the very highest importance, was then not only ignored, but was not even thought of . . . [pp. 209–213].

Oliver's reference to object-teaching concerns the Pestallozian method of oral teaching and observation of events and objects in the child's world. This method was to cause a major revolutionary change in nineteenth century education, and we shall need to discuss it later not only for its importance in the development of general education but because of its close relationship to the kinds of developments that were taking place in the education of retarded children during the same period by such pioneers as Itard (1962) and Seguin (1866).

The above description of the late colonial and early national schools illustrates several major problems that nineteenth century school men had to struggle with: inefficient use of instructional time; limited and inadequate instructional methods; scarce and inferior instructional materials; and poorly trained teachers. Major characteristics of the schools were individual recitations, a paucity of books and writing materials, an excessive reliance on learning through the printed word, a single schoolroom with children ranging from 4 through 20 years of age working in a variety of subject matters at different skill levels, and teachers whose sole preparation may have been the completion of a similar course of study in the common school.

Obviously, such a school system was working under handicaps in endeavoring to produce the educated citizenry deemed necessary for the development of a free republic. While the worst of these conditions did not prevail in all schools and at all times, it is nonetheless true that as late as the 1840s Henry Barnard, in his official reports on education in Connecticut and Rhode Island, depicted the continuing prevalence of such conditions (Brubacher 1965). These problems had also been encountered in the development of education in Europe, and solutions proposed and tried from this body of theory and practice were borrowed freely by American schoolmen of the nineteenth century.

The Substitution of Simultaneous for Individual Instruction

Comenius, the seventeenth-century Moravian bishop, proponent of a blending of religious and secular education taught in the vernacular, had advocated in his *Great Didactic* (1896) the substitution of class or simultaneous instruction for individual instruction, the grading of schools, the use of oral teaching, the study of objects and things, and the primacy of understanding over memorization. Although these instructional principles had no direct influence on the elementary education of his time, they did accurately forecast future developments.

Jean-Baptiste De La Salle (1651–1719), founder of the teaching order of the Brethern of Christian Schools, was one of the major figures in the actual production of change in educational practices. Two of the important features of the schools De La Salle founded for the instruction of the children of the poor were grading and simultaneous instruction, the former necessitated by the latter. There were nine grades of instruction. The first grade learned the alphabet, the second proceeded to syllables, the third worked from a primer of syllables and words, the next used a book of connected discourse, and the highest grades were devoted to arithmetic, Latin, and the mastery of writing. Within higher grades, sections of beginning and advanced students further homogenized the instructional groups.

Simultaneous teaching was facilitated by the use of wall charts of the alphabet, syllables, and numerals with a blackboard of special service for the teaching of arithmetic. In learning the alphabet and syllables, the children were seated before the wall charts, and the teacher indicated with a pointer the letters and syllables he wished pronounced. One child read aloud while the others were required to repeat in a low voice what they had heard. Similarly in the reading lessons, one pupil read aloud while the others followed silently in their own books. The teacher was admonished by De La Salle to check that the others were indeed following. The next child called upon to read was expected to take up precisely where his schoolmate had left off. In other lessons, the attentiveness to the recitation of one pupil was ensured by the teacher questioning his schoolmates on their understanding of the recitation. Again, while one pupil worked on an arithmetic problem on the blackboard, the others followed knowing they might be called upon for their understanding of the operation involved or to correct a mistake (De La Salle 1935).

These methods of De La Salle have a simplicity about them that belies the revolutionary change they made in the instructional methods of the time. In *The History of Modern Elementary Education,* Parker (1970) was to maintain that, "The schools of the Christian Brethren were without doubt the most effective elementary schools in existence before the French Revolution" (p. 100).

This simultaneous method of teaching with further elaboration in the schools of Europe was to be gradually taken over into the American education system during the nineteenth century. But progress was slow and as late as 1835, Theodore Dwight Jr., in a lecture before the American Institute of Instruction, was to lament that in the district schools it was still general practice to teach by the *individual system.* In at least some instances the introduction of the simultaneous method was to be facilitated by its amalgam with another revolutionary European method of instruction, namely, the monitorial system. Such was certainly the case with the introduction of the Lancastrian monitorial system in New York City in 1806 (Bourne 1870, p. 9). The monitorial system of instruction, developed independently by Andrew Bell and Joseph Lancaster about 1800, achieved a remarkable success in a short time, spreading from England to the continent and to North and South America (Kaestle 1973b).

The monitorial method of instruction actually had more ancient roots than Bell and Lancaster. In his chapter on the "Principles of Conciseness and Rapidity in Teaching," Comenius (1896) had outlined many of the essential features of a monitorial system. In Comenius's view, the teaching of several hundred scholars at once was not only possible but essential. To achieve this he recommended that the whole class be divided into groups of about ten, under a scholar of higher rank who in turn would be under a still higher scholar. These leaders would hear the lessons and inspect the work of their respective divisions (Comenius 1896). Experiments with such systems were made in Europe from the sixteenth century on and in at least one instance in seventeenth-century America (Barnard 1855-56, p.307).

What is of interest is the explosive development of monitorial systems of instruction in the early part of the nineteenth century. It might be surmised that their spread in America was due at least in part to the rapid growth of cities with large numbers of children whose parents could not afford private schooling. The Lancastrian monitorial system provided for the simultaneous instruction of anywhere from 200 to 1,000 students within the confines of a single large schoolroom with one schoolmaster. The obvious economy of such a system made it ideally suited to the provision of education in charity schools for the indigent children of the cities. In fact, it was in part Joseph Lancaster's endeavor to open wide his school to children who could not afford to pay his usual small fees that caused him to devise a monitorial system. Within a few short years of its founding in London in 1798, Lancaster's school with himself as the only schoolmaster had 700 boys in attendance.

This extraordinary economy of instruction was achieved by ability grouping, simultaneous instruction of groups, and the use of more advanced students as group instructors. Coupled with this was the ingenious employment of instructional materials that facilitated simultaneous teaching. In Lancaster's own words:

> To promote emulation, and facilitate learning, the whole school is arranged into classes, and a monitor appointed to each class. A class consists of any number of boys whose proficiency is on a par: these may all be classed and taught together. If the class is small, one monitor may teach it; if large, it may still continue the same class, but with more or less assistant monitors, who, under the direction of the principle monitor, are to teach the subdivisions of the class. If only four or six boys should be found in a school, who are learning the same thing, as A, B, C, ab. &c. Addition, Subtraction, &c. I think it would be advantageous for them to pursue their studies after the manner of a class. If the number of boys studying the same lesson, in any school, should amount to six, their proficiency will be nearly doubled by being classed, and studying in conjunction [1806, p. 40].

In the first class the pupils were seated on a bench placed before a table on which sand was smoothly spread within an enclosed area. Boys who knew the alphabet were seated next to those who did not and as the first boy traced letters in the sand with his finger, the others copied. This method, borrowed from Bell's system, is of interest not only in demonstrating the monitorial principle with even the youngest children but also for the ingenuity involved in providing cheap instructional materials and for the combination of learning to write with learning to read, a practice recommended by Comenius but not at all typical of those times when it was assumed a child should not be introduced to writing until he had mastered reading. As with De La Salle, wall charts of letters and numerals were placed around the room and utilized by monitors working simultaneously with ten or twelve children.

In the second class, children learned to print words and syllables on the sand tables to the dictation of monitors. In this class they were also introduced to writing on slates. Lancaster documented the great saving that could be made by substituting slates for paper in writing exercises. At higher levels, to save the costs of books and to facilitate simultaneous instruction, Lancaster provided for the printing of a book upon cards with type three times normal size. Before such cards, mounted on the wall, monitored groups would assemble and the children would take turns reading successive lines, sentences, or paragraphs. In recognition of uneven skill patterns, monitored groups were reshuffled as they went from their reading to their arithmetic exercises and again each group was relatively homogeneous in its skill level in the particular subject being studied. The promotion of children from one class to another was also a function of the monitors. A given monitor was selected to be inspector general of reading and his function would be to examine the children in each group to determine when their accomplishment was sufficient for them to pass on to the next higher class.

In addition to emulation which Lancaster felt was induced by simultaneous teaching, he provided motivation for his students by awarding small prizes and honors. As Lancaster conducted his school, the student monitors received no pay but were rewarded by the honor attached to their select roles. In addition, Lancaster justified the employment of monitors in that the monitorial function facilitated the child's own development of skills—an argument that Comenius had also made for the value of a monitorial system. In fact, Lancaster proposed that the monitorial system be utilized as a means of teacher training and undertook raising funds to further than end.

The Free School Society: The Emergence of the "Urban Crisis"

The Lancastrian system of education was introduced in New York City by the Free School Society about the very time that Oliver (1876) began his schooling in Boston in the "old, old way," receiving "the privilege of forty minutes' worth of teaching, and three hundred and twenty minutes' worth of sitting still." The Free School Society had been founded in 1805 by a group of civic leaders for the purpose of providing a school for the education of such poor children as were not attending sectarian charity schools. As may be remembered, the Colony and State of New York, unlike Massachusetts, followed the philanthropic tradition of support and in 1805 all but a few of the 141 teachers employed in New York City were in private schools. The handful of exceptions were in the parochial charity schools, the African Free Schools founded by the Manumission Society, and in a school founded by the Female Association for poor white girls (Boese 1869).

In a public appeal for funds and support, the Free School Society delineated the problem and the remedy:

> While the various religious and benevolent societies in this city, with a spirit of charity and zeal which the precepts and example of the Divine Author or our religion could alone aspire, amply provide for the education of such poor children as belong to their respective associations, there still remains a large number living in total neglect of religious and moral instruction, and unacquainted with the common rudiments of learning, essentially requisite for the due management of the ordinary business of life. This neglect may be imputed either to the extreme indigence of the parents of such children, their intemperance and vice; or to a blind indifference to the best interest of their offspring. The consequences must be obvious to the most careless observer. Children thus brought up in ignorance, and amidst the contagion of bad example, are in imminent danger of ruin; and too many of them, it is to be feared, instead of being useful members of the community, will become the burden and pests of society. Early instruction and fixed habits of industry, decency and order, are the surest safeguards of virtuous conduct; and when parents are either unable or unwilling to bestow the necessary attention on the education of their children, it becomes the duty of the public, and of individuals, who have the power, to assist them in the discharge of this important obligation. It is in vain that laws are made for the punishment of crimes, or that good men attempt to stem the torrent of irreligion and vice, if the evil is not checked at its source; and the means of prevention, by the salutary discipline of early education seasonably applied. It is certainly in the power of the opulent and the charitable, by a timely and judicious interposition of their influence and aid, if not wholly to prevent, at least to diminish, the pernicious effects resulting from the neglected education of the children of the poor [Bourne 1870, pp. 6–7].

In this portrayal of the problem and its solution are assumptions about the relationship of poverty, vice, and crime, on the one hand, and religion and education, on the other hand, that are worth clarifying for the light they throw upon the motivation of the founders of the Free School Society. Indeed that motivation was similar to what fostered much of the educational developments here and abroad throughout the nineteenth century, including the special education programs that developed toward the end of the century.

To understand the motivation we must look at the socioeconomic conditions and social problems that confronted the city of New York in the period following the revolution and preceding the Civil War. Within this period, from 1805 to 1853, the active work of the Free School, or Public School Society, took place. The problems New York City faced in this period were similar to those of the other developing American cities, particularly Boston, Philadelphia, and Baltimore. They were problems associated with urbanization and industrialization. In that sense they were the same problems confronted in Europe but they were compounded in the New World by the constant immigration of culturally dissimilar peoples.

Therefore, though we will be using New York as our illustration of the relationship between socioeconomic conditions and the development of educational programs, much of our picture is relevant to the rest of the United States, particularly the Northeast; it is also related to developments in Europe. This latter relationship is emphasized because later when we study specific developments in special education we will note how European developments in special education preceded those in the United States and indeed were models for developments in the United States.

Some of the socioeconomic conditions and their interrelationships with the development of education in New York City have been detailed by Mohl (1971), Schneider (1938), and Kaestle (1973b). Relying principally on their descriptions, particularly that of Mohl, the following sketch may be drawn.

Shortly after the evacuation of the British occupation forces in 1783, the population was estimated at about 12,000; by 1800, it was over 60,000; in 1825, it was in excess of 160,000; and by 1850, it had passed the half-million mark. Within this growing population there were increasing numbers of poor, as well as unacculturated immigrants. Residential segregation along economic lines had begun by the turn of the century, and by the second decade major slums existed within the confines of the city. The expanding economy of trade and manufacture on which the city survived was subject to recurrent depressions set off or aggravated by the embargo acts of Jefferson's Administration, the War of 1812, financial panics associated with the speculation in western lands, and later in this period by overexpansion in cotton production in the South. In the early 1800s, widespread epidemics of yellow fever periodically caused the economy of the city to grind to a halt as those who could afford it — as much as one-third of the population in the epidemic of 1805 — fled the city; shops and businesses closed as the poor and the working classes were left behind to shift for themselves.

The degree of poverty and distress is succinctly recorded by statistics on private and public charitable and relief efforts. Public charity in this period took the form either of complete support in the form of residence in the almshouse for the aged, the infirm, and orphaned and those so destitute as to be without even the minimum of shelter, or outdoor relief in the form of donations of firewood in the bitter winters, and food, clothing, credit, and cash to those deemed in sufficient need by the city inspectors. This public relief was supported by the efforts of churches and private organizations functioning along similar lines. A miscellaneous selection of the available statistics indicates that in a single year following the War of 1812, over 19,000 needy persons, or one-fifth the city's population, received public assistance. In February of 1817, investigators estimated that 15,000 persons depended on public or private charity.

From the years 1798 to 1816, the number of almshouse paupers were by conservative estimate 1.5 percent of the total population. In January of 1838, in the midst of the country's severest and most sustained depression prior to 1929, Horace Greeley in his weekly newspaper estimated that one-third of the 200,000 wage earners in the city were wholly or in large part unemployed. Not without reason did he repeatedly urge the immigrant and the unemployed to "Go West!" to the land of opportunity! In 1847, it was estimated that one-fourth of the population received some form of charity, and in the severe winter of 1854-55, 31 percent of the city's population was considered destitute. The cost of the public relief efforts are indicated by the fact that from the close of the revolution until after 1825, the social welfare costs constituted one-fourth to one-fifth of the city's total budget.

Enough has been cited to indicate that in the first half of the nineteenth century, the problems of New York City were the problems of the American city as they existed throughout the latter half of the nineteenth century and down into our own times. Indeed the magnitude of the statistics of relief efforts are jarringly similar to those appearing in the metropolitan news of today.

It is within the foregoing socioeconomic context with its chronic poverty and recurrent waves of unemployment that the Free School Society began and developed its educational program. In the public appeal for support that we quoted previously, the Society gave its perception of poverty and allied social conditions. Noteworthy in this perception is the conjuction of poverty with intemperence, vice, and crime, constituting an "increasing and alarming evil." The remedy to this growing evil was seen as religion and education. These perceptions of the founders of the Society were, as Raymond Mohl has documented in his study of *Poverty, in New York 1783–1825* (1971), common to the times. Though there were undoubtedly "the deserving poor," worthy of charity, poverty, in large part was seen as a moral evil fostered by irreligion, ignorance, and the vices of alcoholism, improvidence, and sloth. Parents given to such ways could only raise children by means of their own bad example. The school—imbued with broad, generally agreed upon, nonsectarian principles of Christianity—could interpose itself between the parent and the child and by means of character training and the abolition of ignorance break the transmission of poverty and vice across the generations.

This perception of poverty and vice and the preventive roles of religion and education was not limited to the supporters of free schools in New York

City. Evidence of it can be adduced for other parts of the country. But the relatively advanced state of the city's urbanization may have made such motivation more prominent than in other sections of the country. At any rate, Thaddeus Stevens, an effective political leader of the abolitionists and one of the congressional sponsors of the 14th amendment, in 1835 argued for the support of common schools before the Pennsylvania legislature.

> Many complain of this tax [for the support of free schools], not so much on account of its amount, as because it is for the benefit of others and not themselves. This is a mistake; it is for their own benefit, inasmuch as it perpetuates the Government and insures the due administration of the laws under which they live, and by which their lives and property are protected. Why do they not urge the same objection against all other taxes? The industrious, thrifty, rich farmer pays a heavy county tax to support criminal courts, build jails, and pay sheriffs and jail keepers, and yet probably he never has, and never will have, any personal use of either. He never gets the worth of his money by being tried for a crime before the court, by being allowed the privilege of the jail on conviction, or receiving an equivalent from the sheriff or his hangman officers! He cheerfully pays the tax which is necessary to support and punish convicts, but loudly complains of that which goes to prevent his fellow-being from becoming a criminal, and to obviate the necessity of those humiliating institutions [Finegan 1921, p. 61].

In the irony of Steven's argument there is a specific and a general premise: education prevents crime, and education perpetuates government and ensures the due administration of laws. It is not unusual these days for historians of education to point out the class interests motivating the supporters of free education in the nineteenth century. Those of property and power in the socioeconomic system have reason to preserve the status quo, to offer palliatives for social ills rather than basic remedies. If poverty is seen as a moral evil resulting from the inadequacies of the poor themselves rather than as a deficiency of the socioeconomic system, one may undertake measures of relief that will in no way threaten the system. We shall return to this aspect of the motivation for the founding of free schools — partly because it is a dominant theme in the development of special education programs at the end of the century — but for the moment let us simply assume that it was one component in the overall complex of motives, idealistic and self-serving, that motivated the members of the Free School Society.

The Free School Society assumed its burden of fighting poverty and vice in 1806 with the opening of its first school. To assure the maximum effect of its charitable dollar it instituted a Lancastrian system of education. The members of the society, including its first president, De Witt Clinton, were most optimistic about the ability of the Lancastrian system to solve the problem of cheap, effective, mass education. Throughout its history, albeit with some modifications, it maintained a monitorial system in its schools.

The first school of the Society was an instant success and within the year attendance was over 150, necessitating a move to larger quarters. Soon, still larger quarters were necessary and it was obvious that the resources of philanthropy were inadequate to the task that the Society had assumed. Petition to the city resulted in the gift of a building known as the "Old Arsenal" and a contribution toward the renovations necessary to provide a school room for five hundred pupils (Boese 1869).

Legislation providing funds for the partial support of common schools was passed by the New York State Legislature in 1795, and again in 1805, but not until 1812 did state legislation reflect deep involvement in the provision of common school education. Legislation of that year provided for the establishment of school districts throughout the state with a system of school inspection and control at local and state levels. At the apex of the organization was the office of state superintendent of common schools, the first office of its kind in any state. State funds, local taxes, and assessments upon parents with ability to pay, were the sources of support. This pattern of organization and support for the common schools was similar to that being developed in other states during the first half of the nineteenth century. It is this pattern of public support and control of elementary education in schools open to all that constitutes the essential features of the common school system as the term is most often used.

The Free School Society was a striking anomaly in the development of this pattern. By its successful solicitation of increasingly available school funds from the state and city, the Society ensured that its schools would in effect become the common school system of New York City despite the fact that control of the schools was vested in a self-selected corporate body not directly responsible to the public. For several decades the Society was successful in obtaining from the state and the city the lion's share of these funds for public elementary education. It succeeded in doing this in part because it maintained that it offered a nonsectarian education open to all. In fact, to emphasize its expanding mission of education for all the city's children, the name of the society was changed in 1826 to the Public School Society and for a brief period tuition charges were made for those families that could afford them. Among other benefits it was hoped that tuition charges would reduce the opprobrium attached to sending one's children to a charity school. The society had felt that many poor children were kept from attending the schools by the parents' refusal to accept charity in any guise. In addition, it was hoped by some members of the society that the intermingling of the children of the different classes would reduce the class antagonisms which had become an increasing problem of urban life. In the Annual Report of the Free School Society of 1825, this latter issue was addressed as follows:

> Our free schools have conferred the blessings of education upon a large number of the children of the poor, but still it is to be lamented that a description of public school is wanting amongst us, where the rich and the poor may meet together; where the wall of partition, which now seems to be raised between them, may be removed; where kindlier feelings between the children of these respective classes

may be begotten; where the indigent may be excited to emulate the cleanliness, decorum and mental improvement of those in better circumstances; and where the children of our wealthiest citizens will have an opportunity of witnessing and sympathizing, more than they do, with the wants and privations of their fellows of the same age [Kaestle 1973a, p. 85].

There is no direct evidence whether or not the intermingling of the classes reduced social antagonisms. Although the schools of the Public School Society remained open to all regardless of family income, the tuition scheme was dropped as being unworkable; in the opinion of some, it fostered class differences with the children able to pay looking down upon those who could not, and the latter chagrined and mortified (Boese 1869).

Kaestle (1973b) has argued that the egalitarian stance of the Society may have been influenced by the example of the New England Common schools whose collective tradition of support was conducive to the view of education as a right for all children, not as a gift of charity to the poor. However, he sees as a more important motivation the rivalry of the Society with the Bethel Baptist Church whose expanding school system, admitting children of all persuasions, was challenging the Society's special position in relation to public funds for erecting schools within the city.

In the previously described legislation of 1812, which organized the statewide system of common schools, the provision of state funds had been limited to the support of teachers' salaries, with the construction and maintainance of school buildings being assigned to local resources. In 1817, special legislation was passed with the provision that if the Free School Society had surplus monies after the payment of ample compensation to the teachers—a surplus easily provided, thanks to the economics of the Lancastrian monitorial system—such funds could be used for "the instruction of schoolmasters on the Lancastrian plan, to the erection of buildings for schools, and to all the needful purposes of a common school education, and to no other purposes whatever" (Palmer 1905, p. 38). This preferential treatment of the Society in the utilization of school funds, plus several direct grants from the state for building costs, permitted accelerated expansion of the Free Schools.

In 1822, the Bethel Baptist Church sought and received similar preferential treatment for its own charity schools which were ostensibly open to children of all denominations and hence eligible for sharing the common school funds. Among other issues that arose was concern that school buildings erected by such means would be used by the churches for purposes other than the education of the poor. The Free School Society therefore petitioned the legislature for the repeal of the special act in favor of the Bethel Baptist Church. While some church schools supported the petition of the Society, other churches sought to have the preferential considerations extended to their own schools. In 1824, the State Legislature responded with legislation providing that the entire matter of distribution of the school fund for New York City should be in the hands of its Common Council.

In 1825, the Council passed an ordinance providing that religious societies should not share in the Common School Fund but that the distribution of funds should be restricted to the Free School Society, the Mechanics' Society, the Orphan Asylum Society, and the African Free Schools. Except for the competition of the pay schools, the Society was now effectively in control of elementary education in New York City. A number of innovations in the Society's programs during these expansionist years are of note in that they highlight problems of education that persist to our day, with solutions that we are likely to consider modern.

One of the most notable of these was the establishment of infant schools for children ranging in age from 18 months to six years. In 1827, at the suggestion of De Witt Clinton, a number of women founded the Infant School Society for the purpose of establishing an infant school patterned after those recently introduced in England; the aim was avowedly for moral and character training. In addition, Bourne, the historian of the Public School Society, points out there was concern "growing out of the fact that children of laborers were often left at home, locked up in the absence of parents, and in danger of fire or other accidents, or left to roam in the streets, exposed to casualties and corrupting influences" (1870, p. 658).

Shortly after the establishment of the first infant school in the basement of the Canal Street Presbyterian Church, the Public School Society was petitioned for the use of their school basements for the establishment of additional infant schools. The Society appointed a committee to investigate and this committee responded with a very favorable report.

> The infant school in Canal Street has on register one hundred and seventy children of both sexes, and from about two to six years of age, the latter being the limit at which any was received. The number in attendance varies from fifty to one hundred. There are two female teachers, a principal, and one assistant, employed at salaries of $200 each. The children are allowed to come early in the morning, and to remain till near dark, bringing their dinner with them, or to attend during the usual school hours only. The essence of the system pursued in the school appears to be a judicious combination of instruction and amusement, and that both shall be calculated to form and elicit *ideas*, rather than mere literal knowledge, though this is by no means neglected. The children are evidently happy and interested in their employments, and the scene is altogether deeply engaging to the best feelings of humanity. The opinion of the first directress and teachers is, that the same plan may be advantageously adopted in a school of two or three hundred children; and the English Reports inform us of schools of the latter number now in successful operation [Bourne 1870, pp. 660-661].

The report goes on to compare this infant school with the junior department in one of its own Lancastrian schools in which the children were only slightly older, ranging in age from three to eight years of age.

> On comparison of the mode of instruction adopted in the two schools, your committee are of opinion that the infant school system, as applied to children of such

tender years, is decidedly preferable; the one being the mere course of common instruction in the knowledge of letters and words, the other including the first, and
extending its views to what is of much greater importance—the knowledge of
things and ideas, with moral maxims and scriptural instruction; the whole illustrated by visible objects and verbal explanations calculated to excite the attention and interest the feelings of the infant mind. From this view of the subject,
your committee are led to the conclusion that it is expedient that infant schools be
gradually established throughout the city; and the question only remains, whether
this shall be done by the already organized Infant School Society of ladies, and to
whom the credit and honor are due for having first, and by persevering exertions,
introduced this system into this city, or by the Public School Society [Bourne 1870,
p. 661].

As a result of this report, the infant school program was introduced into
the Junior or Primary departments of the public schools; female teachers
were employed for the instruction of these younger children and female as
well as male students admitted. The school committees of the various schools
operated by the Society were supplemented by subcommittees of ladies who
were entitled to nominate the teachers and the monitors. By 1844, the Society was operating fifty-six primary schools for white children and five for
black children, with a total enrollment of 8,970 pupils.

These primary schools are of interest in that they arose in response to a
perceived need for the training, care, and protection of the children of the
poor working classes. In some respects they reflect the same problem definition and solution as our own modern day-care and preschool programs.
Other important aspects of these schools are the acceptance of the assumption that women are more suitable teachers for the youngest children, and
that the Lancastrian educational system was not ideally suited to the
youngest pupils. The teaching methods utilized in the Infant School were, in
fact, with their emphasis on knowledge of things and ideas, a variety of the
Pestalozzian methods.

Immigration and the Public School Society

Another innovation of the Society during these years—although an abortive one—is of special interest because it focused on the social problem of the
immigrant family.

In 1837, the Board of the Public School System became concerned with
the increasing numbers of German immigrant children for whom there was
no provision for education in their own language and who were barred from
participation in the public school program by their ignorance of English.
The Board therefore established a primary school program for the instruction of German children in the English language. The object of the program

was to prepare the children for participation in the regular public school program, and attendance at the special German school was to be limited to twelve months. As it turned out, the German children were reluctant to transfer from their special school to the regular schools and the teacher sought to extend their instruction beyond the basic mastery of English. In 1843, when it was proposed that similar Italian schools be established, the Primary School Committee of the Society reported negatively on the proposal in terms that throw light upon the way in which the immigrant populations were viewed by the Society and the Society's perception of its educational mission toward the immigrants. In summary, the report argued as follows:

> 1. The desired object can be better attained by the attendance of the Italian children at our primary schools; for experience proves that a foreign language can be more readily acquired by a person in attending a school where his own language is unknown, "necessity" being the most speedy and thorough teacher.
> 2. In educating children in our schools, it is intended to give them habits and feelings adapted to our institutions and Government; and when a foreigner adopts our country as his home, it is expected that he should subscribe to our forms, and particularly to our system of education, which is intimately and inseparably connected with our forms of government.
> 3. When foreigners are in the habit of congregating together, they retain their peculiar national customs, prejudices, and feelings; they therefore remain much longer unsettled, and are not as good members of society as they would otherwise be. This is apparent to all who are acquainted with our German school. Children attending that school, as is well known, retain their national costume, manners, and feelings; while those German children who mingle promiscuously in other schools, lose all trace of nationality.
> 4. Children, like adults, are clannish. It is difficult to conduct a school composed of foreigners, with a foreign teacher, without exciting continual prejudices between it and our other schools.
>
> Finally, information has been obtained which induces the committee to believe that the more intelligent class of Italians do not desire such a school, and that, like most of the better class of Germans, they would prefer that those of their countrymen who come here with good intentions should be Americanized as speedily as possible. This result, in the opinion of this committee, will be most easily and promptly attained by the attendance of their children at our primary schools [Bourne 1870, p. 529].

The committee report was adopted and Italian schools were not established. Depending upon one's assumptions and value systems, this committee report could be read either as a reasonable evaluation of two alternative approaches to the education of the immigrant child with the cognitive weight of the argument against special immigrant schools, or as the subtle but reprehensible expression of calloused nativist attitudes toward the problems of the immigrant. Was it unreasonable for the Public School Society to assume that "in educating children in our schools, it is intended to give them habits and feelings adapted to our own institutions and government?" As we have previously indicated, from the ancient Greeks through the Puritan founding fathers to the schoolmen of the 19th century, this was a prevalent assumption. If we reject that assumption, do we limit education to the inculcation of skills devoid of a context of beliefs, feelings, and attitudes that constitute a value system?

All societies—especially to the degree that they are complex societies—will have some diversity of value systems. Insofar as different functions exist in a society and as various groups and individuals become specialized for the more effective fulfillment of those functions, there will be a diversity of special value systems. The farmer, the laborer, the manufacturer, the lawyer, the physician, the teacher cannot have a complete overlap in shared feelings, attitudes, and beliefs; even more strikingly will this be true for the poor versus the privileged classes, and the various religious, ethnic, and racial groups.

One might even argue that diversity in value systems is a necessary precondition for society's survival. The specialized functions cannot be realized without individuals who possess divergent value systems necessary for the performance of those functions and whose value systems in turn are reinforced by the very exercise of those functions. The value system of the teacher that would prize the sharing of knowledge would be a handicap in the competitive marketplace. A reverence for life which might be an asset to a physician might be a handicap to a soldier's function. And insofar as a society is called upon to change in order to survive, a multiplicity of value systems will be an asset rather than a handicap. Like the geneticist's concept of hybrid vigor, a multiple value system gives reserves to draw upon as conditions change and call for new responses upon the part of the culture.

Yet, in a pluralistic society surely the point can be reached where multiplicity of value systems fractionates, disperses, and vitiates the cohesiveness required for the communal actions necessary for survival. There must be some irreducible commonality of shared values if the society as a whole is to survive.

The problem for the society at large is to determine the balance of plurality and commonality. How do we ensure that the range of acceptable balances will exist? What will be the role of the schools in this? Such a problem obviously permits no definitive solution. It is a dynamic, persistent concatenation of goals more or less irreconcilable, of means more or less inadequate, and by the very limits of our nature each of us approaches such a problem-solving task with defective vision and fallible judgment. Pooling our perceptions and judgments does no more to improve our problem-solving attempts than it does to limit the excesses of our errors—a poor comfort but the best that may be available.

At any rate, the Public School Society in its narrow class-limited perceptions and judgments did not see the complexity of the problem and the inadequacy of its solutions. This led to the demise of what with all its shortcomings was not an ignoble attempt to meet the educational needs of New York City in the first half of the nineteenth century. That the Public School Society and the privileged classes from which its membership was drawn did not accurately perceive the issues posed by immigration can be easily documented by the more extreme nativist statements appearing in the documentary records of this period. But such documentation should be accompanied by some reference to the magnitude and the complexity of the social and economic impact of the mass immigration prior to the Civil War. An awareness of the social and economic impact permits us to better understand the misperceptions and faulty judgments of the Public School Society and the class interests represented on its Board. Condemnation may gratify the heart but understanding may permit us to face analogous problems of our own day with greater sophistication.

10

Immigration and Educational Problems in the Nineteenth Century

IN THE OFTEN myopic view we have of our cultural history, we have a tendency to see contemporary social problems as unique and of larger magnitude than those past generations faced. The children of immigrants thrown upon our shore immediately prior to World War I are still among us. An old Jewish grandmother tells us of her joy at the stricter enforcement of child labor and compulsory education laws prior to World War I. "Now, they had to let me go to school!" "They" included the amorphous society which gave and took away opportunities as well as the family which adjusted economic needs and traditional values within the new land.

"When I was a boy we spoke only Italian at home and in the neighborhood. In the school we couldn't understand," and so an Italian grandfather recreates his childhood for us and to a degree we understand. To a greater extent, we can grasp the educational problems posed by the even more recent migrations of black and Spanish-speaking minorities into our cities following the World Wars; these problems are still chafing and unsolved.

But the problems are not new; they were there prior to the Civil War. Differences exist in terms of the uniqueness of the various ethnic and racial groups and the changing society in which migrations occurred. But the differences do not make the comparisons less relevant; rather they make them more relevant in that they highlight important variables that might otherwise be overlooked. In this framework, then, we think it worthwhile to give a brief synopsis of immigration and its interaction with social and educational problems prior to the Civil War and in the period in which the Common School system was developed.

The Old Immigration

Around World War I the nativists urging immigration exclusion, made much of the difference between the old immigration from northern and western Europe and the then current immigration from southern and eastern Europe. The industry and natural virtues of the former were contrasted with the indolence, ignorance, vice, and criminality of the latter. If one consults the historical record, however, it appears that before 1882—the date at which the federal government assumed control of immigration and which Abbott (1926) views as a convenient cut-off date between the old and new immigration—the nativist saw no such industry and virtue in the "old" immigrant. In fact, perception of the immigrant, old and new, and responses to him are strikingly similar in the two periods and not at all unlike those elicited by the black and Spanish-speaking migrants to our cities following World War II.

Reviewing the constancy of the pejorative view of the newcomer, we note that ethnic diversity was built into the very foundations of the American Colonies. The English in Massachusetts and Virginia, the Swedes in Delaware, and the Dutch in New York—separate political entities at first—were forcibly amalgamated in the course of the seventeenth century.

But the unity of British rule did little to restrict further colonization to the English. In fact, the mercantile theories of the time, emphasizing the relationship between the population and wealth of a nation, caused the English to discourage emigration from the mother country to the colonies. On the other hand, proprietors, anxious to exploit the wealth of the new lands imported black slaves into the southern colonies and brought over French Huguenots in an attempt to establish silk and wine industries in the Carolinas. The British Government itself settled Palatine Germans in the Hudson Valley in hopes of establishing an industry for the production of naval stores; and Penn's "holy experiment" attracted German pietists into his utopian wilderness (Jones 1960). In such fashion the population in 1790 came to stand at approximately 3.2 million white and 800,000 nonwhite, with only 61 percent of the white population being of English origin (U.S. Bureau of Census 1965; Cole 1968).

But these foundations of ethnic diversity did little to ensure ethnic harmony. The foreigner was generally welcomed only when his labor or his numbers contributed to the economic well-being or safety of those who were already here. Otherwise he was frequently seen as a threat to the established society. Thus the Scotch-Irish with their Presbyterianism, poverty, and rough ways were not welcomed by the Congregationalists of Massachusetts, but were invited to the frontiers of Pennsylvania and Carolina where they might serve as buffers against French and Indian attack (Jones 1960).

This general colonial ambivalence is nicely displayed in the correspondence of Benjamin Franklin to Peter Collinson in 1753.

I am perfectly of your mind, that measures of great temper are necessary with the Germans; and am not without apprehensions that, through their indiscretion, or ours, or both, great disorders may one day arise among us. Those who come hither are generally the most stupid of their own nation, and . . . it is almost impossible to remove any prejudices they may entertain . . . . Not being used to liberty, they know not how to make modest use of it. And as Kolben says of the young Hottentots, that they are not esteemed men until they have shown their manhood by *beating their mothers*, so these seem not to think themselves free, till they can feel their liberty in abusing and insulting their teachers . . . unless the stream of their importation could be turned aside from this to other colonies, as you very judiciously propose, they will soon so outnumber us that all the advantages we have will, in my opinion, be not able to preserve our language, and even our government will become precarious. . . . Yet I am not for refusing to admit them entirely into our colonies. All that seems to me necessary is, to distribute them more equally, mix them with the English, establish English schools where they are now too thick settled, and take some care to prevent the practice, lately fallen into by some of the shipowners, of sweeping the German gaols to make up the number of their passengers. I say I am not against the admission of Germans in general, for they have their virtues. Their industry and frugality are exemplary. They are excellent husbandmen, and contribute greatly to the improvement of a country [Abbott 1926, pp. 415–416].

In the selection of documents that Edith Abbott has brought together in her *Historical Aspects of the Immigration Problem* (1926), there is ample evidence that Franklin's ambivalence toward the immigrant was not unique for either Colonial or subsequent times throughout the period of the old immigration. As in the case of Franklin, the ambivalent attitudes often coexisted in the same individual or group. At other times the individual or group spoke with relatively unalloyed rejection or acceptance. In either case, the sum total of social attitudes toward the newcomer was highly ambivalent.

Samuel B. Morse, developer of the telegraph, spoke of immigration as "the *momentous* evil that threatens us from *Foreign Conspiracy*" (1835; italics in original). In his perception, the despotic governments of Europe sought to destroy American liberty and democracy by unloading upon our shores their paupers, criminals, and social outcasts. In the forefront of the conspiracy were the ignorant Catholic immigrants led by their scheming Jesuit priests.

In contrast, the Reverend Edward Everett Hale, author of that paean of patriotism *The Man without a Country*, spoke feelingly of the Irish emigration which was "the dispersion, after its last defeat, of a great race of men, which, in one way or another, has been undergoing defeat for centuries. In the order of history it is our duty to receive the scattered fugitives, give them welcome, absorb them into our own society, and make of them what we can" (Abbott 1926, p. 462).

In its Convention of 1845, the Native American Party made in interesting distinction between the immigration of former years "recruited chiefly from the victims of political oppression, or the active and intelligent mercantile adventurers of other lands" and the more recent immigration of "the feeble, the imbecile, the idle, and intractable" sent from Europe at the public and private expense of numerous societies and corporate bodies, "thus relieving themselves of the burdens resulting from the vices of the European social systems by availing themselves of the generous errors of our own." The nativist of 1845 apparently had the same abhorrence of current immigration, and the same nostalgic view of the immigrant of former years that the nativist of the decades surrounding World War I was to have of "new" versus the "old" (Abbott 1926, pp. 746-747).

On the other hand, from the Emigration Society of Philadelphia founded in 1794 to the Immigrants' Protective League at Hull House in the Chicago of the 1890s, other Americans organized for the support and defense of the immigrant.

The nativist's rejection of the immigrant throughout our history always had a ready rationale in correlating immigration with poverty, crime, and immorality. And if the nativist was often naive in attributing social problems to the nature and character of the immigrant himself, and in heaping upon him the obloquy of indolence, stupidity, and moral degeneracy, it is equally naive to ignore or deny the correlations and to assume that the abolition of bigotry and the diffusion of goodwill among the nativists would have solved the problem. In either case, the judgment upon the immigrant or upon the nativist is one of moral indignation that contributes little to solution of the underlying social problems.

But it may not be without some value to look at these correlations of immigration poverty and crime as they appeared in the first half of the nineteenth century, to note how they were perceived by the public, and to look at the responses they evoked from those involved in public education.

From 1783 to 1819, the total immigration to the United States has been estimated at 250,000. In subsequent years, due to the economic conditions in Europe and to the cheapening of passenger rates, there was a marked acceleration of immigration, with a total of approximately five million immigrants entering the United States from 1820 to 1860. In that latter year, of a total white population of approximately 27 million approximately four million were foreign-born.

Although precise data are not available, the predominant immigrant groups in the early years of the Republic were apparently Scotch-Irish, German, and English. By 1820, when more precise statistics became available, Ireland, Great Britain, and Germany sustained the immigrant flow in that order. Ireland maintained its lead—with the Southern Irish dominating over Ulster—well into the 1850s. Then the German contribution, which had outstripped Great Britain in the 1830s, took the lead from Ireland and maintained it until close to the turn of the century when the "new" immigration took over.

From 1851 to 1854, the two peak immigration years prior to the Civil War, the annual Irish immigration fell from approximately 221,000 to 101,000, while the German immigration rose from 72,000 to 215,000. Together, they accounted for approximately 75 percent of the total immigration in those years (U.S. Bureau of Census 1965).

As early as 1795, when immigration was only a trickle, the immigrant was seen in association with poverty. The report of the Commissioners of the almshouse in New York City noted in that year that 44 percent of the 622 paupers housed in that institution were of immigrant stock, and foreigners approximated a third of the almshouse paupers throughout the period of 1798 to 1816 (Mohl 1971). Nor was New York unique. A Boston Common Council Document of 1835 gives data for the almshouse residents in the preceding year for New York, Philadelphia, Baltimore, and Boston, from which it may be seen that the percentage of foreign paupers ranged from 42 to 61 percent (Abbott 1926, p. 572). A congressional report of 1855 cites census data of 1850 to indicate that of 134,972 paupers supported in all the states in the prior year, 68,538 were foreigners (Abbott 1926, p. 607).

Schneider's (1938) account of public welfare in New York State from 1609 to 1866 gives ample explanation for the poverty of the immigrant during this period. The majority left Europe under economic duress, barely able to pay passage on ships where disease was often rampant and rations short. They arrived jobless and homeless, not infrequently in periods of economic recession, with considerable numbers ill and malnourished from the journey. The scant resources that they might possess made them fair game for swindlers, extortioners, boardinghouse racketeers, and common thieves who lay in wait for them at the port of entry. Before 1847, no effective state legislation was designed to protect the immigrant. Not until 1854 did federal legislation require minimum rations per passenger on the immigrant ships, and not till the 1880s did the federal government seriously involve itself in helping the immigrant in his efforts to adjust to his new environment. Such corrective and supportive legislation came about only gradually against the protest of powerful interests such as the steamship companies, transportation brokers, real estate interests, and employers of labor. Small wonder that of the millions that arrived thousands found their way to to almshouses (Schneider 1938, pp. 296–97).

Factors such as those cited by Schneider might offer sufficient explanation for the disproportionate representation of foreign-born in the occupancy of almshouses but what confused the issue and supported the nativist alarms was the undeniable practice of many European municipalities and private corporations assisting the emigration of the poor to relieve their own tax burden (Schneider 1938, Abbott 1926, Jones 1960). In one of the more flagrant instances a group of immigrants arrived at New York in 1839, still wearing the uniform of the Edinburgh almshouse (Schneider 1938, p. 298). Jones's (1960) review of immigration confirms the fact that the English ratepayers, Irish landlords, German municipalities, British trade unions, and

American employers for various reasons did assist the emigration of the impoverished, the jobless, and the pauper. However, his overall assessment maintains:

> the number and variety of such agencies should not be allowed to obscure the fact that, even in aggregate, they dispatched only a small fraction of the immigrants who arrived in the United States during this period. The mass immigration of the nineteenth century originated as a self-directed, unassisted movement, and this character it retained throughout [p. 116].

Schneider is undoubtedly right that the preponderance of foreign inmates in the almshouse was more the result of the interaction of American socioeconomic conditions with the unplanned arrival of the immigrant rather than the result of factors inherent in the immigrant himself. But the social fact was that the atypical flagrant case presented in the journals such as *Niles Weekly Register,* or the books and tracts of a Samuel B. Morse (1835) or a Samuel Busey (1856, 1969) became the stereotype that inflamed public opinion.

As with pauperism so with crime — with an even older history of abuse on the part of European governments. It is estimated that in the course of the eighteenth century, when the English Parliament created the new legal punishment of transportation to overseas colonies, Britain shipped a minimum of 30,000 felons to the New World, the majority to Virginia and Maryland (Jones 1960). In addition, European states and municipalities were not adverse to offering pardons to those criminals that would emigrate to America — a practice that continued well past the middle of the nineteenth century. The Congressional Globe of that later period includes several lengthy congressional debates on the problem. James Cooper, addressing the Senate in 1855, noted the arrival of a vessel in New York with 150 paupers and some 15 convicts still in chains (Abbott 1926, p. 601). In 1866, Sumner presented to the Senate evidence that a chief justice of Hanover, Germany had pardoned a thief, a robber, and an arsonist on condition of their migration to America; even more outrageously, a highway robber and murderer condemned to death had his punishment commuted to migration to America (Abbott 1926, pp. 642–43).

Jones properly points out that this exportation of criminals contributed only a trickle to the flow of immigrants and in fact most of the convicts had been convicted of minor offenses. But this patent abuse of the hospitality of the New World was fuel to the indignation of the nativists who had no scarcity of data demonstrating the proneness of criminality in the immigrant once he arrived in America. In 1848, a Special Committe report to the Legislature of Massachusetts revealed that in the period 1841–45, two-thirds of the inmates in the state prisons were foreigners (Abbott 1926, p. 585).

James Cooper's previously noted speech to the U.S. Senate reviewed the census of 1850 to indicate that in the penitentiaries and prisons of the various states the ratio of foreign to native inmates was on the order of six to one (Abbott 1926, p. 605). In 1856, Samuel Busey's *Immigration: Its Evils and Consequences* (1969) used the same census data to indicate that of the number of persons convicted of crimes in the year ending June 30, 1850, there was one conviction for every 154 foreigners but only one for every 1,619 natives (p. 117).

Although the nativist was greatly alarmed at the burden of crime and pauperism that immigration placed upon the Republic, the still greater danger was, as Samuel Busey pointed out, the political danger. The quickly naturalized foreigners — and in this there were scandalous if rare instances of immigrants led from the wharf to the polling places — voted the will of corrupt politicians, or even banded together to vote in bloc their antidemocratic or radical prejudices. Again Busey used the census to portray the danger. In 1850, foreigners constituted 11.46 percent of the whole free population — and immigration was rapidly accelerating; but what made the foreign vote formidable was its unequal distribution. Examining the data from the previous presidential election, Busey concluded that in fifteen of the thirty states the foreign-born voters constituted from one-half to one-seventh of the voters. In Busey's view, it would be not long before the immigrant vote would have the strength to amend the constitution itself and then what "odious and oppressive feature may be engrafted upon the Constitution bequeathed to us by our forefathers?" (p. 141). He adduced further figures to show that in fourteen states the foreign vote exceeded the majority by which Pierce exceeded Scott in the presidential election of 1852 and argued that "if even *one-half* of the foreign vote had been given to General Scott, he rather than General Pierce would have been elected!" (Busey 1969, p. 146; italics in original).

What were the characteristics of this immigrant population that wielded such formidable and growing political power? In addition to the pauperism and criminality, Busey again with the help of the census data showed the relative lack of "intelligence" of the foreign-born. Whereas the proportion of illiterate or uneducated in the native population was 1 in 22, among the foreign-born it was 1 in 12.

> So far as a knowledge of our institutions is concerned, the entire foreign population may be, and should be classed as ignorant, illiterate, and uneducated; for the experience of the past, has most clearly proved their ignorance of Republican institutions constitutes the most grievous and dangerous evil of foreign immigration. But notwithstanding the ratio of foreign illiterate is nearly double that of the native, yet the ratio of children between five and fifteen years of age, being taught in our schools bears the same relative proportion among the native and foreign. The percent, of native white children in the schools is 82.25, of the foreign 47.00. This is a most important fact. Our schools are open to all, free to all, and in most of the States free of expense to the parent or child, yet the foreign population refuse to avail themselves of these advantages, refuse the offer of a free government, to educate their offspring. It is not only important but alarming; it envinces

the tenacity with which this class of our population adheres to the habits, customs, and superstitions which characterize foreign countries, and unfits them for the exercise of political franchises in this [Busey 1856, p. 129].

As the roots of antiforeignism can be traced back to Colonial times so with anti-Catholicsim. Although the founding of many of the colonies and plantations in the New World had been undertaken by groups seeking freedom of worship, it would be incorrect to assume that these founding fathers — with the lone exception of Roger Williams — advocated religious toleration. The Puritans of the Massachusetts Bay Colony rejected and persecuted the Anabaptists and the Quakers. Almost everywhere, the Catholic, the Jew, and the Freethinker were proscribed. Maryland, founded by Lord Baltimore as a refuge for persecuted English Catholics, was by the standards of time most tolerant and mingled therein were Catholics, Presbyterians, Anabaptists, and Quakers with the laws of the Colony protecting these sects from calumniating one another. Nevertheless, Unitarians and Jews were banned; and in the latter part of the seventeenth century, as Protestants achieved ascendency, Catholics themselves were prevented from holding civil office and there began a campaign of calumny and slander against the Catholic priesthood (Stokes, 1950).

Established religions were prevalent in the New England and the Southern colonies and everywhere, with the lone exception of Rhode Island, minority sects were subject to legal restrictions on their civil rights.

This state of affairs continued into National times and William Marnell (1964) has argued that the adoption of the first amendment — with its clause that "Congress shall make no law respecting an establishment of religion, or prohibiting the free exercise thereof" — was in no way the product of a secular philosophy. Rather it was a compromise among the states that were concerned about maintaining their own religious establishments without federal interference. That such was the case is attested to by the various state constitutions that came into being shortly after the revolution.

Several of the states used either test oaths or specified religious qualifications to exclude Catholics or Jews from holding public office. Only gradually during the first half of the nineteenth century were these constitutional provisions modified or removed. After a long, bitter political fight the requirement of belief in the Christian religion for holding office was removed from the Maryland constitution in 1826; and not until 1844 did revision of the state constitution permit Catholics and other non-Protestants to hold elective office in New Jersey. In New York the right to citizenship itself was limited until 1806 by requiring that all persons naturalized by the state take an oath abjuring foreign allegiance, and subjection in all matters "ecclesiastical as well as civil" — a device aimed particularly at the Catholic immigrant with his spiritual allegiance to Rome (Stokes 1950, Marnell 1964).

While legal restrictions of Catholics and other minority religious groups were being removed during the first half of the nineteenth century, at the same time there was a growth of overt religious intolerance in the social and political sphere. This anomaly might be explained by the fact that when civil restrictions on Catholics and other groups were written into state constitutions the Catholics were essentially a small minority without political power or voice. In 1790, they had numbered less than 1 percent of the population. By 1820, just as the immigration was beginning to soar, they amounted to 2 percent of the population and in 1870, had increased more than fivefold to approximately 11 percent of the total population. As with immigrants in general, this population was distributed unevenly, with major concentrations in the large urban centers, particularly in the northeast. It might be surmised that as Catholics increased in numbers the injustice of depriving them of citizenship rights and political office became more apparent, especially when state constitutions with such restrictions were compared with those that did not. On the other hand, as their numbers increased the social and economic problems associated with the Catholic immigrant become more apparent and caused prejudicial social reactions.

The attack on the Catholic immigrant couched in political terms by such writers as Morse (1835) and Busey (1969) was joined by an attack couched in terms of moral obloquy. This took the form of the convent exposé literature which became so prevalent during this period. The most flamboyant of these publications was the notorious *Awful Disclosures of Maria Monk,* which appeared in 1835. Posing as a nun who had escaped from the Hotel Dieu convent in Montreal, Maria Monk claimed that a priest had fathered her illegitimate child. Her tale told of licentious practices between priests and nuns and of the murder and burial in the convent basement of the infant progeny of these illicit relationships. Her story was written with embellishments and prepared for publication by a group of unscrupulous clergymen. It was an immediate sensation and the controversy that swirled about it provided long-lasting publicity. The anti-Catholic press proclaimed its truth and even the more responsible elements in the Protestant community were inclined to give it credence.

A number of skeptical Protestant leaders, however, took an active role in discrediting the book. Among these was William L. Stone, a New York newspaper editor who made a detailed examination of the Hotel Dieu nunnery and found not only a lack of evidence in support of Maria Monk's contentions but also physical evidence that the description of the convent in her book was an obvious fabrication. The very gates through which she purported to make her escape proved nonexistent. Maria Monk's Protestant mother testified that her child had never been in the convent and this statement agreed with the one that Stone obtained from the convent.

A subsequent fabrication by Maria Monk of her abduction by priests in New York and her conveyence to a Catholic Asylum in Philadelphia was again unmasked by a group of lay Protestants and ministers. However, in spite of this discredit, such was the tenor of the times that Maria Monk's book continued in popularity, and its fabrications were used in the political campaigns of the 1850s by the Know-Nothing party, in a virulent attack upon Catholic immigrants. By the Civil War, it had sold over 300,000 copies (Billington 1936, 1938; Myers 1943).

It is possible that these gratuitous attacks reinforced in the Irish Catholic immigrant the very traits of isolation and clannishness which the nativist purported to deplore and may have added to the immigrant's difficulty in assimilation. Certainly they were not calculated to modify Protestant attitudes that would in any way aid the immigrant.

At any rate, this period was characterized by a self-conscious growth of political power and deployment of that power on the part of the Catholic immigrants. This in turn caused equal reaction from the other side and the period from 1830 to the Civil War was characterized by friction and even outright violence between groups.

Among the most serious incidents of violence were the riots of 1844 in the Philadelphia area and those occuring in St. Louis, Missouri, and Louisville, Kentucky, in the mid-1850s. In the Philadelphia riots of May and July 1844, several Catholic churches and schools were burned plus scores of Irish homes. The known dead on both sides exceeded 40 with many more seriously wounded. Significantly, the St. Louis and Louisville riots occurred at election times when Know-Nothing propaganda aimed at foreigners was particularly in evidence. In St. Louis, in August of 1854, ten were killed, dozens seriously wounded and scores of Irish homes looted and destroyed in four days of rioting. Louisville's "Bloody Monday" in August of 1855 resulted in the death of more than a score with several hundred wounded (Billington 1938, Myers 1943, McAvoy 1969).

In these civil disorders the anti-Catholic theme in the nativist movement was stridently in the fore but other issues — such as economic conflict between indigenous artisans and cheap immigrant labor, a general concern with the assimilability of large masses of foreigners with different life styles and value systems, and growing political conflict as the newcomers became politically organized — were prominent, and in themselves would probably have been sufficient to foster the development of a nativist movement. It should also be noted in balance that Scisco (1901) and Handlin (1941) have pointed out liberal and reform components that existed within the nativist movements in New York and Massachusetts.

Religion, Ethnicity, and the Great School Controversies

For our purposes the emphasis on the anti-Catholic component in nativism has particular relevance because it influenced the clash between the nativists and the Catholics in the great school controversies of the period.

This in turn led to further polarization of Catholic and Protestant views on the role of the common school in the education of the young and the development of the citizen—a polarization not yet completely resolved.

In New York City this clash took place between the Public School Society, protective of its near exclusive right to common school funds, and the Catholic schools desirous of obtaining a share of the funds. As may be remembered, in 1825 a request from the Bethel Grove Baptist Church for the right to use such funds for the erection of school buildings had been rejected by the City Council at the instigation of the Public School Society; it, with all other churches, lost the previously enjoyed right to receive support for the operating expenses of their charity schools. There the matter might have rested, with the Public School Society, for all practical purposes, the provider of common school education in New York City, but for the tremendous influx of Irish Catholic immigrants in the 1820s and 1830s.

The poor, ignorant children of these immigrants should have been the target group for the idealistic, uplifting aims of the Public School Society. However, the Public School Society sought to uplift by ways and means that were at best irritatingly insensitive and at worst callously indifferent to the needs, perceptions, and sensibilities of the immigrants. If religion was uplifting then religion would be in the school albeit in a nonsectarian form that all reasonable Protestants could find acceptable. If Catholics viewed the enforced reading of the Protestant version of the Bible as reason enough to keep their children from attending the schools then it was their narrow prejudice and intransigence. Parents who neglected the education of their children should be coerced by civil penalities and privations into sending their children to school.

From the point of view of the Irish-Catholic immigrant prostrate on the bottom of the socioeconomic heap, the church was both comforter and champion, the source of identity and pride. He was not likely to be indifferent to nativist attacks upon his religion. He resented the defamations of the church and clergy that were present in the schoolbooks of the time.

Even if there were not Protestant teaching in the public schools the philosophy of the Catholic church would have had difficulty accepting a purely secular education. In that respect, it was no different than many of the conservative Protestants of the time, and even liberal Protestant leaders sought not a secular education in the schools but a nonsectarian education, i.e., one that was acceptable to the generality of Protestants. That Protestants were split over nonsectarian versus conformist religious education is attested to by the bitter attacks that many churchmen made upon Horace Mann's efforts to reduce sectarian influence in the Massachusetts schools during this same period.

At any rate, the Catholic hierarchy had already decided to build its own parochial school system. But a church consisting largely of impoverished immigrants was in no position to support development of schools to meet its needs; and there was no question but that the Catholic schools of New York were overcrowded and poorly equipped. And so the church was unable to accept the generalized Protestant education of the public schools but financially could not provide for the educational needs of its children. A double bind from the point of view of the Catholic immigrant, a pseudo-problem from the point of view of the supporters of the Public School Society who in today's jargon could not see its own "institutional" prejudice.

The Catholics, desirous of obtaining some relief for their financial difficulties via access to the public school funds, therefore, saw in Governor Seward's 1840 message to the legislature encouragement for the pressing of such a claim. Seward had visited the public schools of New York City in 1838, and although favorably impressed by those institutions, he was deeply disturbed by the large numbers of Irish and German Catholic children not attending any school at all. He shared with many of his generation the conviction that political democracy and social equality necessitated an educated citizenry. In his 1840 message he expressed his concern:

> The children of foreigners, found in great numbers in our populous cities and towns, and in the vicinity of our public works, are too often deprived of the advantages of our system of public education, in consequence of prejudices arising from difference of language or religion. It ought never to be forgotten that the public welfare is as deeply concerned in their education as in that of our own children. I do not hesitate, therefore, to recommend the establishment of schools, in which they may be instructed by teachers speaking the same language with themselves, and professing the same faith. There would be no inequality in such a measure, since it happens from the force of circumstances, if not from choice, that the responsibilities of education are in most instances confided by us to native citizens; and occasions seldom offer for a trial of our magnanimity by committing that trust to persons differing from ourselves in language or religion.
>
> Since we have opened our country, and all its fulness, to the oppressed of every nation, we should evince wisdom equal to such generosity, by qualifying their children for the high responsibilities of citizenship [Bourne 1870, p. 179].

Seward's perception of a relationship between the failure of immigrant children to attend the public schools and the cultural differences that existed between the children and the school unfortunately was not shared by the majority of educators and legislators of the nineteenth century or indeed the twentieth century. Yet, we suspect that supporting evidence was often readily enough available.

Troen's account of the attendance of black children at the segregated schools of St. Louis indicates how quickly attendance increased once the school board decided to replace the white teachers with black. "From 1876 the year before black teachers were hired, through 1880, enrollment had more than doubled, from about 1,500 to more than 3,600 pupils, even though the city's black population had remained constant" (Troen 1975, p. 92). William Torrey Harris, then superintendent of the St. Louis system, directly attributed the increase to the changeover to black teachers and Troen indicates that what had taken place prior to the changeover was in effect a boycott of the public schools unaccompanied by the public demonstrations and legal protests that occurred in later decades in other cities.

At any rate, the trustees of the seven or eight Catholic churches that maintained free schools were quick to accept Governor Seward's apparent invitation and they petitioned the Common Council for a portion of the school funds. This precipitated what has been described as the first of "The Great School Wars" of New York City (Ravitch, 1974). In quick response, the Public School Society sent a remonstrance to the Common Council objecting to the Catholic petition as "unconstitutional and inexpedient." Another detailed remonstrance was prepared for general distribution in order to arouse public opposition to the Catholic petition. An argument was drawn to demonstrate that the 97 schools of the society with their 20,000 enrollment were the right and proper recipients of common school funds and any diversion to church schools would be a fatal check to the cause of general education (Bourne, 1870).

Amid rapidly growing public controversy the Catholic application was rejected. This action instead of quieting the issue only increased the debate. Catholic leaders raised objection to numerous defamatory passages appearing in the textbooks of the Public School Society. Recognizing their vulnerability on this score the Society made efforts at accommodation. The Catholics took the stance that they did not intend to cooperate in removing objectionable passages when they had no assurance that such passages might not reappear. The issues were broadened. The Catholics seized upon the antinomies posed by nonsectarian religious education in the public schools.

Nonsectarian religious education was the professed aim of the Public School Society. It was the aim of Horace Mann in his fight to reform the Massachusetts school system. It was in fact the general belief of the times as it had been the belief of the Puritan forefathers that education and religion were inseparable in the preparation for citizenship. The years had modified this belief as we noted in comparing schoolbooks such as the *New England Primer* and the later *Spelling Book* of Noah Webster. Religious catechisms had given way to moral and ethical catechisms and the early McGuffey Readers just coming into vogue were increasingly secular in content. However, the latter included versifications of the Ten Commandments and the Lord's Prayer and, in subtle but pervasive ways, fostered the general tenets of conservative Christianity (McGuffey 1879, Minnich 1936, Mosier 1947).

On the other hand, even as the secularization of textbooks proceeded, the American Bible Society pledged itself—with notable success—to work zealously for the reading of the scriptures in every classroom in the nation. Catholic objections to Bible reading in the schools was one of the major issues leading to the Philadelphia riots of 1844 and in subsequent years there were scattered instances of Catholic children subjected to physical punishment and expulsion for refusing to participate in the reading of the Protestant Bible within the public schools (Billington 1938).

In this climate of religious conflict the Catholics of New York challenged the state professing the freedom of religion while it fostered the daily reading of the Protestant Bible in its common schools. If the state were not to favor one set of religious beliefs over another, or to confuse the children by the simultaneous presentation of all religions with their irreconcilable differences, then the only logical position was to offer a completely secular education. That such a position was not reached until the Supreme Court decision of 1963 outlawing the reading of the Bible in public schools attests to the strength of the earlier American conviction that religion is inseparable from public school education.

In 1840, the Protestants were certainly not ready to accept the logical implications of the separation of state and church which they publicly professed. Nor could the Catholics themselves accept complete secularization of education as an appropriate solution to the dilemma; hence, the call for church schools supported at least in part by state funds. The Public School Society and its supporters saw this as a threat to the very existence of a common school system.

Throughout the summer and fall of 1840, the issue continued to agitate the Catholics and in October the matter was again before the Common Council. At the invitation of the Council the proponents of both sides debated the issues at great length. Representatives of the Public School Society were supported by a number of ministers of various concerned Protestant Churches. The Catholic side was championed by the outspoken and forceful Bishop Hughes. The application was again turned down and the Catholics, under Hughes's leadership, elected to fight the issue at state level where the sympathetic Seward might have influence. In his 1841 message to the legislature, Seward referred to the interrelated problems of immigration, poverty, and crime, singled out education as the ameliorative agent, complimented the excellent public schools of the city of New York but noted that there were still 30,000 children growing up in ignorance and vice.

> Others may be content with a system that erects free schools and offers gratuitous instruction; but I trust I shall be allowed to entertain the opinion, that no system is perfect which does not accomplish what it proposes; that our system, therefore, is deficient in comprehensiveness in the exact proportion of the children that it leaves uneducated; that knowledge, however acquired, is better than ignorance; and that neither error, accident, nor prejudice, ought to be permitted to deprive the State of the education of her citizens. Cherishing such opinions, I could not enjoy the consciousness of having discharged my duty, if any effort had been omitted which was calculated to bring within the schools all who are destined to exercise the rights of citizenship; nor shall I feel the system is perfect, or liberty safe, until that object be accomplished. . . . I solicit their education less from sympathy,

than because the welfare of the State demands it, and cannot dispense with it [Bourne 1870, p. 355].

The Catholic petitions to the legislature were balanced by petitions opposing any diversion of the school funds from their lawful objects. The matter was referred to John C. Spencer, Secretary of State and *ex officio* Superintendent of the Schools. He presented a report which helped shift the focus of the issue. Commending the efforts of the Public School Society, he nevertheless maintained that less than half of the school age children of the city were receiving the benefits of education despite the object of obtaining the education of the greatest possible number. Reviewing the petitions, he argued that it was in principle undesirable and in practice impossible to separate religion and education.

It is believed to be an error to suppose that the absence of all religious instruction, if it were practicable, is a mode of avoiding sectarianism. On the contrary, it would be in itself sectarian, because it would be consonant to the views of a particular class, and opposed to the views of other classes. Those who reject creeds, and resist all efforts to infuse them into the minds of the young before they have arrived at a maturity of judgment which may enable them to form their own opinions, would be gratified by a system which so fully accomplishes their purposes. But there are those who hold contrary opinions, and who insist on guarding the young against the influences of their own passions, and the contagion of vice, by implanting in their minds and hearts those elements of faith which are held by this class to be the indispensable foundations of moral principles. This description of persons regard neutrality and indifferences as the most insidious forms of hostility [Bourne 1870, pp. 365-366].

The solution of the dilemma for Spencer was the principle of nonintervention as embodied in the common school law which applied to all of the state with the exception of the city of New York.

No officer, among the thousands having charge of our common schools, thinks of interposing by any authoritative direction, respecting the nature or extent of moral or religious instruction to be given in the schools. Its whole control is left to the free and unrestricted action of the people themselves, in their several districts. The law provides for the organization of districts, the election of officers, and the literary and moral qualification of teachers, and leaves all else to the regulation of those for whose benefit the system is devised. The practical consequence is, that each district suits itself, by having such religious instruction in its schools as is congenial to the opinions of its inhabitants; and the records of this department have been searched in vain for an instance of complaint of any abuse of this authority, in any of the schools out of the city of New York [Bourne 1870, pp. 363-364].

The difficulties in New York City were the result of the violation of this principle of nonintervention. The Public School Society attempted to encompass the education of the entire city instead of operating within the small units of local school districts as did the rest of the state. Religious instruction in the schools or the complete abandonment of religious instruction could not be accomplished in a population in excess of 300,000 without offense to many. There was the further anomaly that a private corporation such as the Public School Society should be entrusted with the discharge of an important function of government without a direct and immediate responsibility to the people.

The solution Spencer saw would involve in part the extension of the general school laws of the state to the city, with a commissioner of common schools in each ward. The schools of the Public Schools Society, other schools receiving public money, and any district schools that would be established would be under the jurisdiction of elected commissioners.

Ravitch (1974) in discussing the implications of Spencer's report notes that: "The issue, then, was larger than whether or not there would be religious instruction in the public schools; it was, instead, a question of who would control the schools and whether there would be any constraints on their power" (p. 61).

Under Hughes's leadership, the Irish increased their political pressure and demonstrated the effectiveness of their endorsement of candidates for political office. The result was that in the spring of 1842 a state law was enacted that essentially provided for the extension of the general school law of the state to the city. Each ward of the city was to be considered as a town and elect its own school commissioners, inspectors, and trustees. In short, the principle of decentralization and "local" control was the key, a principle that only in recent decades has been resurrected as an antidote to centralized, bureaucratic control.

The commissioners of the various wards would collectively constitute the Board of Education of the City of New York. The schools of the Public School Society, as well as those other incorporated societies receiving public funds, were allowed to remain under the management of their own trustees but subject to the jurisdiction of the commissioners of the wards in which they were located. Provisions were also made for the establishment of district schools within the wards as need would arise. In addition, the law specifically prohibited the distribution of public school monies to schools "in which any religious sectarian doctrine or tenet shall be taught, inculcated, or practiced" (Bourne 1870, pp. 521–25).

With these changes, the growth of the Public School Society gradually came to a halt and the development of a system of district schools began within the city. For a while, the two systems of ward schools and public schools existed side by side. Difficulties and conflicts arose and in 1853 it was agreed by the trustees of the Society and the Board of Education that the two systems should be consolidated; by an act of the legislature the properties of the Society were turned over to the city and the Public School Society was dissolved (Bourne 1870).

Although the Public School Society had been defeated in the struggle of 1840–42 in that it lost its power to function independently of state and public control, the Catholics had not carried the field. The law's prohibition of the use of public school monies for sectarian schools foreclosed the possibility of financial relief that they had initially sought. Even on the issue of Bible reading in the public schools they had not won their point, in spite of the legal prohibition against sectarian teaching. Prior to the passage of the law, the state superintendent of common schools had recommended the daily reading of the Bible in the schools and the practice continued. A Catholic petition to the Board of Education in 1843 asking for prohibition of that practice was rejected. The Board argued that the Bible in itself, without note or comment, was not a sectarian book and that reading from it could not be prohibited under state law.

For the Catholics there was a defeat in one sense but a challenge in another. Certainly, it bolstered the argument of Bishop Hughes that the real solution for the Catholics could only be achieved by pushing ahead with their own school program. Throughout the protracted, acrimonious, and riotous struggle, Hughes had been a highly controversial figure. Ravitch (1974) noted that with Hughes's leadership, the Catholics had broadened their offensive beyond a contest for public funds.

> Under Hughes' direction, the Catholics fought for their self-respect and the respect of their fellow citizens. There was nothing Hughes could do about poverty and discrimination in the immediate present, but he wanted politicians and everyone else to know that Catholics intended to stand up for their rights. As militant blacks over a century later raised the banner of black power, so Hughes sought to unify and assert Catholic power [p. 46].

This analogy obviously has limitations but it is nonetheless capable of enhancing our understanding of the plight of the Irish immigrant and his children in the 1840s and the black ghetto migrant and his children in the 1960s. One needs to take care not to make a too facile equation between the social status of the two groups or the cultural resources available to them in their time of struggle; and certainly the social-cultural-economic milieu in which the stuggle took place radically altered from 1840 to 1960. But in both instances an urban minority group was statistically associated with poverty, crime, and social disorganization. And what was a larger struggle for political, social, and economic rights became focused on the schools. What is particularly interesting is that when the struggle focused on the school it led to accelerated polarization of the attitudes of the majority and minority social groups.

Hughes and his tactics were taken to task by the nativists of his time who deplored his contentiousness, his arrogance, his chauvinistic rhetoric, and his bullying use of political power. Even some Catholic historians and sociologists of our own time have, in the revisionist spirit of the age, questioned his contribution to the Catholic cause.

Andrew Greeley (1967) has stated that, "At precisely the time when the crises of the immigration period were most severe, Hughes' influence can only be considered a major disaster," and he refers to David O'Brien's indictment of Hughes.

> he is convicted of using the issue to unite the Catholic population under his leadership, to destroy the lay trustees within the Church and the Public School Society without. He helped force the non-sectarian education he decried onto his Protestant fellow citizens and then strove to remove even generalized religious instruction from the schools. The Catholic school system now seemed more necessary than ever to protect the immigrants against the hostility which Hughes and others helped to intensify. He added fuel to the fire of nativism by engaging in politics and denouncing both Protestant and public education. Remaining loyal to his primary responsibility, the spiritual welfare of his flock as he saw it, he did little to assist his immigrant followers to understand their surroundings and to live in peace with their neighbors. He taught them that a strong, militant and politically united Catholic bloc could defend its interests, but he neglected to instruct them in the requirements of the common good [O'Brien 1966, p. 314].

The Irish under Hughes probably did increase their insularity and evoke further rejection by the majority culture, a rejection reified in subsequent years by the activities of the Know-Nothing party in the 1850s, the American Protective Association in the 1890s, and the second Ku Klux Klan in the 1920s, the latter's campaign of hate being commodius enough to encompass Catholic, Jew, black and foreign-born alike.

But it is also likely that Hughes's leadership helped the Catholics recognize the effectiveness of organized political clout — a lesson which every minority needs to learn, at least once. One may also wonder if desirable social change does not require the occasional stimulus of the militant leader. His dramatic rhetoric may easily drown the voice of reason but he can agitate the passions which motivate the desire for change. If his extreme stance evokes counter positions of intransigence, it yet sometimes provides the room to maneuver a compromise when reason at last is heard.

The Disadvantaged Minority

Putting aside the issues of leadership and tactics in social conflict, it is the underlying problem of the disadvantaged minority in the schools that deserves our closer attention. Lodged between the individual and the modern state is the family and assorted social institutions and the subcultures, large and small. In a reciprocal and interdependent exchange of goods and services, rights and obligations, ideas and affects, the various units of social organization are bound together. It has been maintained that the simplest of these social units, the family, has the function of raising the next generation and ensuring that it in turn will be motivated to raise the succeeding generation. We note that this function is effected by the provision of care and protection which fosters physical growth and development and by the inculcation of skills and values that ensure that the next generation will in turn be successful in rearing the succeeding generation.

But long ago in the history of the human race the decision was made that the raising of children was, to paraphrase Clemenceau on war and generals, too important a matter to be left in the hands of parents. The family may well be the primary and most efficient socializer yet discovered, but the larger social units, particularly the state, cannot allow the family unlimited discretion in standards of protection and care or in the nature of the skills and values to be transmitted. They would do so only at the risk of their own demise. Therefore not only the family but the larger social units including the state have a stake in the rearing of the next generation and they participate in such rearing by supplementing or supplanting the family as the need arises.

In an ideal society, the social units at all levels from family to state would participate harmoniously in this function of rearing the next generation with mutual support and aid. Perhaps in a simple, static society the ideal is even approached. But in a complex society undergoing rapid historical change, such as America in the nineteenth and twentieth centuries, the values of families, subcultures, institutions, and state are likely to be in considerable discordance; and the function of rearing the next generation cannot be carried out by the cooperating social units without considerable conflict.

Since the larger society utilizes the school as its most direct and formal vehicle for inculcating skills and values, it follows that clashes of values among the various social units participating in the rearing of children are apt to become focused upon the school. The children, the objects of concern, are then unhappily caught in the middle. The family, the subculture, will not support the school in its functions. The larger society, certain in its values as to what should be taught and how it should be taught, assumes that the fault lies with the children, the families, the subculture, and not with the schools. The children stay away or are kept away, with family and community acquiescence, if not outright support; and if attending under pressure, they are not motivated to meaningful participation. The supporters of the schools are dismayed, if not virtuously indignant. That such is the case for our own times we leave for later argument. To a considerable extent, such was the case for the immigrant children of the nineteent century.

Faced with the children of poverty and prejudice, the Public School Society "intended to give them habits and feelings adapted to our institutions and Government," and like the generality of American schoolmen of this time, took little account of the feelings and habits which the children had

formed within their immigrant subculture. Subsequently, and perhaps consequently, a nativist like Busey could note that while nationwide 82 percent of
the native white children attended school, only 47 percent of the children of
immigrants attended. He could declaim that such data evinced "the tenacity
with which this class of our population adheres to the habits, customs, and
superstitions which characterize foreign countries, and unfits them for the
exercise of political franchise in this" (Busey 1969, p. 129).

It is possible, as Greeley (1967) has done, to challenge the rhetoric of
Hughes concerning the danger to his flock of sectarian Protestantism in the
public schools when only 300 Catholic children attended those schools
whereas 5,000 were in parochial schools. But that would miss the real point,
which was that 12,000 Catholic children were not attending any school.
Seward rightly addressed that issue when he said in his message of 1841:

> I trust that I shall be allowed to entertain the opinion, that no system is perfect
> which does not accomplish what it proposes; that our system, therefore, is defi-
> cient in comprehensiveness in the exact proportion of the children it leaves
> uneducated; that knowledge, however acquired, is better than ignorance; and
> that neither error, accident, nor prejudice, ought to be permitted to deprive the
> State of the education of her citizens [Bourne 1870, p. 355].

He was right again when he stated in his message of 1842:

> I cannot overcome my regret that every suggestion of amendment encounters so
> much opposition from those who defend the public school system of the
> metropolis, as to show that, in their judgment, it can admit of no modification,
> either from tenderness to the consciences or regard to the civil rights of those ag-
> grieved, or even for the reclamation of those for whose culture the state has so
> munificiently provided; as if society must conform itself to the public schools, in-
> stead of the public schools adapting themselves to the exigencies of society [Bourne
> 1870, p. 499].

Therefore, the attack on the Public School Society—though one might
grant its opportunistic and self-seeking components—was not without warrant. The Society had taken to itself the task of educating the poor and for
several decades had made meritorious progress. But as it became increasingly
obvious that its efforts were not likely to achieve an adequate degree of success, it proved itself unable to assess the difficulty, propose new solutions, or
allow others to share its mission. Instead it reacted defensively. For others to
become involved in the task would lead to an inefficient division of public
funds and "the important cause of general education would receive a fatal
check" (Bourne 1870, p. 184). If the children did not attend the schools, the
cause should be sought in the parents and the children themselves. In its 27th
annual report, the Society called attention to the problems of truancy and
nonattendance at its schools and noted that:

> In a Government like ours, "founded on the principle that the only true sover-

eignty is the will of the people," universal education is acknowledged by all to be not only of the first importance, but necessary to the permanency of our free institutions. If, then, persons are found so reckless of the best interests of their children, and so indifferent to the public good, as to withhold from them that instruction without which they cannot beneficially discharge those civil and political duties which devolve on them in after life, it becomes a serious and important question whether so much of the natural right of controlling their children may not be alienated as is necessary to qualify them for usefulness, and render them safe and consistent members of the political body. The expediency of such a measure would be confined pretty much—perhaps entirely—to large seaport towns, and, in its practical operation, would be found to affect but a few native citizens. The number of families arriving in this city almost daily from Europe is so great as to require some measure of the kind; for the means heretofore used to induce the attendance of their children at the public schools have proved insufficient [Bourne 1870, pp. 153-154].

Presumably, the use of coercion was less repugnant because "in its practical operation" its effect would fall only upon the immigrant classes. At any rate, at the instigation of the Society, the Common Council of the city passed a resolution to the effect that all persons—whether immigrants or otherwise—having children in charge capable of receiving instruction and between the ages of five and twelve years should send such children to schools designated by the Trustees of the Public School Society. Failing to comply with the resolution, "all such persons must consider themselves without the pale of public charities, and not entitled, in case of misfortune, to receive public favor" (Bourne 1870, p. 154). Thus the Society's response to nonattendance was not to assess and modify its own operation with an aim of improving its acceptability to the immigrant, but rather to coerce the immigrant.

The Public School Society, proudly conscious of its decades of accomplishment, had great difficulty in seeing where it had fallen short. Insofar as it would admit to some degree of failure in its self-appointed mission to educate the poor, it sought the cause of failure outside itself. Hughes and Seward on their side had a better perception of the size of the failure but with too narrow a vision they identified the source of the problem solely within the Society itself.

In part that was true but even if the Society had been more sympathetic to the immigrant culture it sought to edify, the problem would have still been only partially resolved. A greater willingness to undertake the initial education of the German or Italian child in his native tongue would have demonstrated a willingness to ease the transition of the immigrant child to his new culture. An understanding of the depth and sensitivity of religious differences could have forestalled the problem posed by biased textbooks or sectless Protestant religious exercises. Such accommodations might have headed off the attack. But can the leaders of the Society be blamed for refusing to see the desirability of such compromises when the state school systems themselves only gradually and reluctantly faced up to the problems of such cultural differences during the course of the next century? Even today such accommodations lag behind the need.

But such accommodations on the part of the school can only ameliorate the problem. The issue is broader. What Hughes and Seward did not focus upon was that aspect of the difficulty that lies outside the Public School Society and within the larger society itself. The intransigence of the Public School Society was in all likelihood but a contributing cause to the problem of nonattendance. The root of the difficulty more likely lay in those aspects of poverty and social disorganization that directly contribute to nonattendance or ineffectual performance even with school attendance.

A free school is not enough when the basics of physical care do not provide the children with the health and energy for adequate participation in the school programs, when the economic contribution which the children can provide to the home directly aids in the family's subsistence, or when the disorganization of home and community life do not support and facilitate the socialization of the school programs. It would seem apparent that if the state is, as it must be, committed to participation in the rearing of children, it must design its schools to attract and hold willing students and it must promote the socioeconomic conditions that permit families and communities to participate in the efforts of the school. The provision of a building and a teaching staff is only the first and easiest step.

Viewed in this light, the school war of the 1840s can be assessed not as a confrontation between the Catholics and the Public School Society but as a self-confrontation of conflicting ideals within the larger society. On the one hand was the ideal of universal education to provide the appropriate skills and values necessary for full social, political, and economic participation within the society; on the other hand was the ideal of social and economic freedoms which the Constitution and its evolving interpretations provided.

The society, if it is to continue to exist, must have a certain degree of political, social, and economic coherence. The school with its skill and value training for all children is an obvious vehicle for attaining that end. If at the same time the society advocates social and economic freedom for individuals, families, and subcultures, the stage is set for either destructive conflict or a Hegelian dialectic of values.

The destructive aspect of the Catholic challenge to the Public School Society is apparent enough in the way in which it undoubtedly fanned the fires of religious and ethnic conflict. The Hegelian dialectic of values may be less obvious but we believe that there were long-term consequences which can probably be adjudged instrumental in aiding the larger society to reconcile its ideals in a more harmonious synthesis.

As we have noted, the compromise arrived at by the legislature did not immediately result in removing Protestant teaching from the schools. But the law did legalize the ideal that public school monies were not to be distributed to schools "in which any religious sectarian doctrine or tenet shall be taught, inculcated, or practiced" (Bourne 1870, p. 529).

In discussing the secularization of the schools, Leo Pfeffer (1958) had noted that the struggle in New York City was part of a nationwide struggle of Catholics for their right of conscience.

> In community after community Catholic parents, on the urging of their priests, forbade their children to participate in Protestant religious instruction or exercise in public schools. This they did notwithstanding the harassment and even persecution often visited upon their children by Protestant public school authorities. They went further. At the urging of their priests, they frequently went to court to challenge the legality of Protestant Bible instruction in the public schools.
>
> Naturally, their goal was not the secularization of education; that concept was as unacceptable to Catholicism then as it is today. Their goal was to obtain for their parochial schools the same financial support out of tax-raised funds received by what they called the "Protestant public schools." The validity of their grievance could hardly be disputed by any but the most rabid anti-Catholic nativists and Know-Nothingers. The result was that American Protestantism was faced with the alternative of agreeing to state financing of Catholic teaching in Catholic schools or accepting the elimination of pan-Protestant teaching from state-financed schools. The choice was difficult but one which could not be evaded. . . . Faced with the unescapable dilemma, it chose what it considered the lesser evil; it accepted the elimination of pan-Protestantism from the schools. The secularization of American public education thus came about through a peculiar triple alliance of secular humanism, Roman Catholicsim, and dissent within Protestant dissent. It is not only politics that makes strange bedfellows [p. 66].

In viewing the secularization of American public education as a more harmonious synthesis of conflicting values, we are not maintaining that secularism in itself is a desideratum in the education of the young. We feel that Spencer had a point when he reported to the legislature in 1841 that:

> It is believed to be an error to suppose that the absence of all religious instruction, if it were practicable, is a mode of avoiding sectarianism. On the contrary, it would be in itself sectarian, because it would be consonant to the views of a particular class, and opposed to the views of other classes. Those who reject creeds . . . would be gratified by a system which so fully accomplishes their purposes [Bourne 1870, p. 365].

But the overriding issue is that when there is a multiplicity of religious values, religious training in the common school can only be a source of conflict and confusion. The barring of religious instruction from the common school then permits the state to focus on the training of values and skills that are generally acceptable to the society regardless of religious differences. Although this barring of religious instruction from the publicly supported common school appears to have the consensual support of the American people, we would feel remiss if we did not call the reader's attention to the fact that some authors (McCluskey 1962, Phenix 1955) have raised serious questions as to whether we have really removed religion from the school or simply substituted a different kind of religion, in the form of the democratic humanism of John Dewey.

For Phenix this new kind of religion would "include belief in the self-sufficiency and autonomy of man, in human society as the arbiter of morality and the master of its own destiny, and in the sole reliability of natural scientific inquiry to provide knowledge. [p. 30]" This scientific naturalism is in Phenix's view as dogmatic a faith as that which it replaced. One might not wish to grant all of Phenix's argument but he is right that there is an underlying set of assumptions and value judgments—whether or not one wishes to term it a religion—that both supports the public school system and is propagated by it. To the extent—and we personally hold that the extent is considerable—that these assumptions and value judgments are not recognized and made explicit, we would agree with Phenix that this "common faith of public education needs to be recognized for what it is, made explicit, criticized and reconstructed" (p. 30).

Perhaps some of the difficulty our minorities of today have in coping with the public school system is that they are forced to deal with a system in which the underlying assumptions and value judgments are not recognized and made explicit. In that respect the Catholics in their struggle with the overt pan-Protestantism of the nineteenth century common school may actually have had an advantage.

11

The Catholic Parochial School System and the Emergence of Compulsory Education

PRECISELY BECAUSE WE are so aware of how our urban school systems are trying to cope with poverty, ethnic and racial diversity, and language and reading problems, it is appropriate to discuss how these same problems surfaced in the schools of the nineteenth century. Although not in the forefront, there were two "secondary" issues: What was "normal" educational progress, and what factors contributed to or interfered with an individual's educational progress?

If what today we call special education did not, for all practical purposes, exist in the schools of the nineteenth century, that should not be taken to mean that the stage was not being set for the later problem of how to deal with educational "misfits," nonlearners, and others with labels associated with poverty, race, ethnicity, and language use and comprehension. Given the popular, nativist view that the immigrant poor were intellectually inferior, and that their behavior and achievements in and out of schools were proof positive for that stance, it is not surprising that when special education was born, its classrooms were populated by the same minority groups that had participated in the school-religion wars.

If only to remind ourselves that contemporary problems in our schools have a long history, we shall begin this chapter with a brief discussion of the factors that led to the development of the Catholic parochial school system. The reader must bear in mind that the development of this system was determined in large part as a reaction to the forces advocating universal compulsory education. And, as we pointed out in an earlier chapter, it was the ultimate success of these forces that brought in its wake the problem of what to do with children who could not adjust to the age-graded classroom. If special education was not in the forefront of the controversies surrounding universal compulsory education, it emerged from the background with the

207

advent of compulsory education. And when it did emerge, it largely concerned cultural, ethnic, religious, and racial minorities.

The Catholic Parochial School System

In our sketch of the Catholic parochial school system* we shall not have interest in it as a religious educational system in which "ultimate values" are contrasted to those prevailing in the public schools. Rather, we are interested in it as the educational system of a cultural minority. As such, we shall indulge in unavoidable distortions that will be as objectionable to a Catholic historian of his schools as our treatment of the development of the common schools is likely to be to the public school historian. But as our interest in the development of the common school derives from our concern for understanding the development of special education programs, so our interest in the education of cultural minorities derives from our concern about the interaction between the problems of minorities and special education programs as they developed around the turn of the century and continue today.

Therefore, we are not so much interested in why the Catholics built an independent school system as to why any cultural minority should choose to build a separate school system. In looking at the Catholic school system we will try to discern the kinds of needs that a separate, independent school system might satisfy for any cultural minority whether it be Catholic, Lutheran, Hassidic, Amish, or Black Muslim. What is gained and what is lost when a cultural minority chooses to go such a route? We would even like to raise the question as to whether a separate school system is the only alternative open to a minority desirous of maintaining its particular value system intact, or whether the state in its public schools must pay the price of homogenized values in order to minimize conflict in the schools?

From the historical point of view there may be a certain naiveté in putting the question in the form: Why did the Catholics build an independent school system? In modern European and American history the role of the church in education is rooted deeper than that of the state, and Bernard Bailyn (1960) has pointed out that the distinction between public and private education was quite meaningless throughout most of the Colonial period. Indeed, the support of the Church Charity schools of New York City by public funds indicates that this lack of distinction continued into the national period; nor was New York City unique. Richard Gabel's (1937) study of the use of public funds for church and private schools indicates not only that such schools were widely supported by the state in the colonial period but that support in-

---

*The Catholic school system at the elementary and secondary level includes the parish supported or parochial school, diocesan schools, and private schools operated by various religious orders. We shall, as is customary, refer to the conglomerate as parochial schools.

creased during the national period up until about 1820, despite the development of the state-sponsored common school during these latter years.

Since denominational schools did share in public school funds and since the tradition of the Christian churches was predominantly one of involvement in the schooling of the young, the question might be more aptly phrased: why did the majority of the Christian churches in America turn over the young to the state? According to Curran's (1954) account, the secularization of the elementary public schools was not assented to by the Protestant churches without some soul-searching and anguish of spirit. This was particularly true in the case of the older denominations such as the Episcopal, Lutheran, and Calvinist churches.

Not only did these older churches resist the loss of denominationalism and the secularization of the public schools, they at times flirted with the establishment of their own parochial school systems. This occured most notably in the decades immediately prior to the Civil War when the secular drift of the newly developing common schools had become increasingly obvious. Among the older churches, the Presbyterians made one of the more concerted efforts, founding several hundred parochial schools in 1845–1871. But these schools like most others set up by the major denominations—with the sole exception of the Lutheran schools—were destined to fade away in the years following the war. The survival of the Lutheran schools, particularly those of the Missouri Synod, is particularly interesting in that these schools served not only to transmit religious values but also a rather distinct minority culture encapsulated in its own Germanic language (Stokes 1950). This ethnic factor was also to play a role in the development and survival of the Catholic schools.

Curran's (1954) analysis of the American Protestant surrender of the church's historic role in popular education suggests the interaction of varied causes and a different pattern of causes for different denominations. There were the logistical problems of small congregations, geographically dispersed membership, lack of trained teachers, and money. Added to this was a lack of single-minded, dedicated leadership, and a membership already accustomed to the use of the rapidly multiplying public schools with their not unacceptable pan-Protestant ambience. But the factor influencing the Protestant rejection of the Christian church's traditional role in education that is of most interest to us because of its direct effect upon the development of the Catholic school system is the growth of anti-Catholicism in this pre-Civil War period.

Jorgensen (1963) elaborates on this latter thesis of Curran's, noting that a serious weakness in the histories of the common school movement is the neglect of its inextricable tie to contemporary anti-Catholicism. In this interaction between anti-Catholicism and the common school movement, Catholic objections to Protestant teaching in the public schools were seen as an attack not only on the schools but on Protestantism and even the Republic itself. Particularly outraged were the newer Evangelical sects of Methodists and Baptists who, lacking the long tradition of educational involvement of the older denominations, were quick to adopt the state common schools as their own. These sects were soon joined by Congregationalists who felt that the public schools were a legacy from their "Puritan ancestors."

> The defense of the public schools against alleged Catholic attacks thus became the *leitmotif* of educational discussions in these denominations, and they embraced the public school movement with militant enthusiasm. The historical claims of the church in the field of education seemed to be forgotten, as their spokesmen ardently championed the rights of the state. And it was not long before they reached the only logical conclusions which could ensue from this type of reasoning: that elementary education should be the monopoly of the state, that only public schools were truly "American," that all children should be compelled to attend the state schools, and that denominational schools should not be allowed to exist [Jorgensen 1963, p. 412].

In assessing this thesis of an "inextricable" bond between the development of the common school movement and anti-Catholicism we think it important to keep in mind Scisco's (1901) contention that during that period in our history when immigration was dominated by the Irish and Germans, the two aspects of nativism—antiforeignism and anti-Catholicism—were essentially one. Animus toward Catholics may have had deep roots extending back to the religious wars of Europe, it may have been fed by paranoid fears of Popish plots or the militant rhetoric of Catholic clerics such as Hughes, but we doubt that anti-Catholicism would have had such pervasiveness and intensity in the pre-Civil War period were it not for the identifiction of Catholicism with all the social turmoil associated with mass immigration. It was that identification which permitted the Protestant native to see in Catholicism not only a threat to his dearly held religious beliefs but to the very foundations of social order and civic life.

At the risk of deflecting the reader's attention from our line of argument we feel it important to warn against any single factor analysis of nativism. Higham (1958), in his attempt to correct the historians overemphasis on ideological issues, has formulated other sociological aspects of the nativist movement including the struggle for status among the various contending ethnic groups. Further complicating but illluminating our understanding of nativism, Davis (1960) extends the term from opposition to immigration to include the anti-Mason and anti-Mormon movements of the Jacksonian era. Indicating the similarity in the stereotypes held, the attitudes toward, and the attacks upon all three groups by the alarmed defenders of native traditions, he suggests that:

> When the images of different enemies conform to a similar pattern, it is highly probable that this pattern reflects important tensions within a given culture. The themes of nativist literature suggest that its authors simplified problems of per-

sonal insecurity and adjustment to bewildering social change by trying to unite Americans of diverse political, religious and economic interest against a common enemy [pp. 213-214].

This psychological approach is of course not incompatible with either Higham's sociological analysis or a historical account of Catholic and Protestant ideologically based antipathies. We also feel that Davis's analysis of the psychosocial components of nativism could profitably be used to analyze the Catholic minority's attitudes toward Protestant religion and culture of this period. In that, it would help explain the motivation of many Catholics to insulate themselves by building their own parochial school system.

As Catholics attacked the schools for their pan-Protestantism, the Protestant denominations for the large part rallied to the schools' support even if that meant ceding to the state the traditional right of the Christian church to educate its young. This was done willingly enough when the state retained a generalized Protestant teaching in the school, was questioned by some when the secular drift became more apparent, but was eventually accepted as inevitable and even desirable.

So in 1889, the National Council of the Congregationalist Churches could take the position that since the Catholics were establishing parochial schools which threatened to undermine the public school system:

> Resolved, That we will firmly and constantly resist every such effort on the part of the Roman Catholic hierarchy to overturn one of our fundamental institutions.
> Resolved, That regarding the common public schools as the agency best calculated to unify and make homogeneous the various nationalities that make up our diverse population, we look upon the establishment of parochial schools, where the children of foreigners are instructed by their teachers and priests, as just cause for apprehension and a menace to the best interests of our country.
> Resolved, That to the last we will withstand the effort to appropriate the public school funds to sectarian purposes, and will insist upon free common school education for the whole American people [Cited in Curran 1954, pp. 57-58].

Thus there was a complicated interaction in which a preexisting mixture of anti-Catholic and antiforeign attitudes galvanized Protestant support for the common school which the Catholics had attacked. At the same time, the attack evoked further anti-Catholicism and consolidated it with the preexisting attitudes. This anti-Catholic reaction on the part of considerable numbers in the Protestant community served to convince many Catholics that they were indeed in an alien and hostile culture. They would fight for their rights in the public schools where and when they could; they would build their own protected parochial school enclaves as their resources and ingenuity would permit. It was a strategy not at all unlike that appearing among the urban black minorities in the 1960s and 1970s: pressing for desegregation of the public schools and at the same time building as best they could their own school enclaves whether independent private schools such as those established by the Black Muslims or public schools under black neighborhood control.

The motivation pattern for the Catholics in the nineteenth century was, of course, complex. One must grant that purely religious motivation—the dedication to "ultimate values"—was the predominant motivation for considerable numbers of the clergy and laity alike. But there is reason to question whether that would have been sufficient in itself to cause an impoverished immigrant society to take on the heavy financial burden of building an independent school system. Certainly, among the older Protestant denominations there was also dedication to the "ultimate values" of Christianity, and this was coupled with possession of more economic resources than those available to the immigrant, and yet most of these churches made only desultory attempts at establishing parochial schools.

It is certainly true that the Catholics had some special assets in the form of a more organized and hierarchially structured clergy, and access to the European religious teaching orders for cadres of trained and dedicated classroom teachers who would undertake their assigned tasks for no more pay than their scant sustenance. Thus, in terms of personnel the Catholics did have some resources not readily available to most of the Protestant denominations. But it can be argued that the most important consideration must have been the ethnic factor. Indeed, the ethnic factor may be seen in the very development of the American immigrant churches themselves, let alone in the efforts of these immigrant churches to develop parochial schools.

Oscar Handlin's account of the experience of the immigrant, which he vividly portrays in *The Uprooted* (1951), lays much stress on the importance of religion and church membership in the adjustment of life in the New World. Among the stresses of this unfamiliar scene, the church offered the immigrant a sense of identity and worth, of psychological and sociological security. The church was not just the embodiment of his religious aspirations, it was the hub of his social and cultural world. The sense of identity, worth, and security it provided was likely to be in proportion to the stresses encountered in his new life. To the extent that the immigrant was poor, rejected, and despised by the native American, the church had more to offer him in the form of spiritual solace and social support. It can be imagined that for many of the immigrants the church was more dear to them than it had been in their homeland.

Small wonder, then, that when the Catholic church found itself in increasingly frequent confrontation with the larger Protestant culture, its poor immigrant adherents rallied to its support and gave their mite to advance the cause of a parochial school sytem. But it must not be thought that leadership of the parochial school movement came only from the clergy. In fact, despite the directives of the church councils, the Catholic clergy was not all of one mind on the desirability of a parochial school system, especially when resources spent there were not available for other pressing needs of a rapidly expanding church membership. Both Burns (1969) and Cross (1965) call attention to instances in which the laity's desire for parochial schools arose independently or even in spite of clerical leadership. Again we would suspect the presence of the ethnic factor supporting and reinforcing whatever there was in the way of religious motivation.

In assessing this ethnic factor it must be kept in mind that the Catholic church in America, almost from its inception, has been a church of diverse ethnic groups. The English may have dominated the church in the eighteenth century, but the French, German, and Irish were present. The Irish and Germans may have dominated the church in the nineteenth century but there were large influxes of Italian, Eastern European and French-Canadian Catholics, particularly in the latter half of the century. Of course, as the borders of the country expanded, there were the additions of French and particularly Spanish-speaking Catholics. The story of these diverse ethnic groups adjusting to one another within the framework of the Catholic church not only attests to the importance of ethnic factors in the development of parishes and parochial schools, but also provides support for the triple melting pot thesis that the major religious communities in the United States—Protestant, Catholic, and Jewish—served as three separate melting pots in the assimilation of the immigrant (Herberg 1955).

Weber's (1915-16) account of the development of these early national churches within the Catholic community indicates how strongly ethnic factors influenced the establishment of churches and schools. In 1787, the German Catholics of Philadelphia established a school and subsequently informed John Carroll, Prefect Apostolic and later America's first Catholic Bishop, that they, wishing "to keep up their respective nation and language . . . are fully determined to build and erect another new place of divine worship for the better convenience and accommodation of Catholics of all nations, particularly the Germans" (p. 426).

This first of the national churches, opening in 1789, was to break away in schism from the rest of the church in the United States in 1796. Joining itself with German Catholics from Baltimore who were seeking to build their own national church, petition was made to the Holy See for the creation of the new diocese with a German Bishop for Catholics of that nationality. Rome refused the request but the difficulties between the German Catholic churches and their American Bishop did not cease. Thwarted by the trustees in attempting to exercise his ecclesiastical right of appointment of pastors for the Baltimore Church, Carroll was finally forced to resort to civil suit. This schism resolved in the early 1800s, and the building of national German churches proceeded with greater harmony and cooperation between German communities and ecclesiastical authorities. However, the issue of greater freedom and independence for such churches was not dead and it continued in the nineteenth century reaching a climax in the Cahensly controversy of the 1890s (Barry 1953).

The conflict between Carroll and the German churches was part of the larger rash of trustee controversies of the early national period in which Bishops found themselves at odds with the trustees of the parishes under their jurisdiction, particularly in matters relating to the appointment of pastors. In accounts of these controversies, it is interesting to note that although important and complicated issues of ecclesiastical control and property rights were involved, ethnic rivalries often played a fundamental role in precipitating the disputes—German congregations versus American bishops, Irish Catholics against French bishops, and ultimately Irish bishops against other ethnic congregations (McAvoy 1969, Handlin 1951, Stokes 1950). These trustee problems were gradually resolved during the course of the nineteenth century but the ethnic factors that had interacted with the legal issues of canon and civil law remained.

The French Canadian migration into New England in the latter half of the nineteenth century is particularly instructive of the importance of the church and the parochial school to an immigrant people. These French Canadians, according to Mason Wade (1950), used the term "survivance" to designate the threefold concept of preservation of religion, language, and customs; and the means of "survivance," in their view, was the national church with its associated parochial school. The French Canadians struggled for "survivance" not only against native Protestants but against their Irish coreligionists as well. The Irish immigrant, scorned by the Yankee as a foreign papist, in turn looked down upon the still more foreign French Canadians who could not even speak English, and who shared with all late arriving immigrants the economically threatening trait of working harder and longer for less pay.

Despite the common faith, differences in religious customs, language, and temperament were of such degree that many of the Canadians ceased practicing their religion rather than attend the Irish-dominated Catholic churches. As soon as they were numerous in any community they opted for their own churches with French-speaking priests accompanied usually by an array of parochial schools, convents, religious and national societies, and a French press. In analyzing these Irish and French Canadian antipathies, Wade notes that the Irish Catholics having in the previous decades borne the brunt of the nativist attacks were loathe to promote the establishment of national parishes with foreign language schools. They opted for rapid Americanization of foreign-born Catholics in the expectation that this would ease anti-Catholic feeling. On the other hand, the French Canadians concerned with "survivance" were zealous in the founding of parochial schools and rejected the leadership of what they called the "Irish assimilators" (Wade 1950).

Like the French Canadians, the Germans throughout the nineteenth century also opted for national parishes in order to ensure the survival of their language and culture.* In his analysis of the origins of the Catholic parochial schools in America, Robert Cross (1965) notes the greater zeal of German Catholics in comparison to Irish Catholics in the founding of parochial schools and attributes it in part to the fact that for the Irish such schools were not needed to preserve the ethnic language. But ethnic motivations were not absent in the Irish. Peter Rossi and Alice Rossi in their study of parochial schools speculate as to why of all the denominations, the Roman Catholic and German Lutheran were alone successful in establishing school systems serving a mass clientele.

> To begin with, in both cases, more than denominational purity was at stake. In each case very self-conscious ethnic groups were identified with each denomination: the Irish and Germans in the case of the Roman Catholics, and the Germans alone in the case of the Lutheran Church. In each case the church was a major point of identification with the old country, and the strength of identification was augmented by experience in the new land. Both the Irish and the Lutherans had some experience in maintaining their church under unfavorable conditions, the Orthodox Lutherans against a reformed state church in Germany and the Irish against the established church of Ireland. The Irish particularly had developed the institutions for maintaining their church in a hostile environment and had also evolved customs favoring heavy financial support of church activities. In addition, each group brought with it an experienced religious cadre, and when established in this country quickly set up organizations for the recruitment and training of future cadres [Rossi and Rossi 1957, pp. 171–172].

Supplementing the ethnic identification factor indicated in the above, their argument also suggests an ethnic isolation factor.

> While the rural isolation of the German Lutherans helped them to maintain a viable denominational school system, the urban Irish Catholic schools derived a similar strength from their position on the bottom of the urban heap. The anti-Catholic movements of the nineteenth century helped to maintain the strong attachment of the Irish to the Roman Catholic Church. The German Catholics benefited from very much the same geographical isolation as the Lutherans [Rossi and Rossi 1957, p. 172].

---

*On the editorial page of the *New York Times* of December 12, 1977, were letters to the editor under the headline "On Bilingualism. The Importance of a Child's Roots." One letter was from a Catholic priest, a sociologist from Fordham University; the other from a member of the New York City Board of Education who is Puerto Rican. Both letters speak to the issues of language, culture and education in terms identical to those described above, with the big difference that these issues are now far less controversial than they were in the nineteenth century. The Catholic priest-sociologist states:

> Inculcating in the child a respect for his own cultural background must be an essential, not a marginal, component of the programs. It is the secure child with a sense of identity and self-confidence who learns well. If the learning of anything, including English, appears as a process to convert a child from his own way of life to another, it may result in a demeaning of the self and a resistance to the learning of English or anything else. The whole history of immigrant adjustment to American life makes this clear.

The isolation of the Irish at the bottom of the socioeconomic heap deserves some further elaboration. In a way their poverty became part of their ethnicity by ensuring their isolation from the larger society and by adding to purely ethnic traits the social behavioral traits that are likely to accompany poverty. In similar fashion, in the twentieth century, the poverty of the black, the Puerto Rican, and the Chicano becomes correlated with their racial and ethnic status.

There can be no question but that poverty can be a deterring factor in a group's attempt to build its own school system and thus Cross (1965) had attributed the greater zeal of the Germans in building schools not only to their desire to preserve their language but to the fact that they were by and large better off economically than the Irish. But the French Canadians pushed for schools in New England when their better-off Irish coreligionists did not. We would expect that the anomaly might be due to the fact that when poverty through its isolating effect reinforces the ethnicity of a group, instead of acting as a deterrent it may actually prove to be a factor in the motivation for a parochial school system.

From this perspective it is interesting to record some of Archbishop Ireland's observations on his difficulty in attempting to build a parochial school system in the Minnesota of the 1890s.

> In every parish there is a certain number of Catholics of better condition who desire higher associations for their children than they can make in the parochial school. Into the parochial school are gathered all the children of the masses of the poorest emigrants. They come in their simplicity and poverty with the rough manners of their parents from the lanes and tenements of the city. All their associations are with the children of the streets, and the destiny of most of them is to take their fathers' place in the factories and workshops. In private schools or in the schools of the State are gathered the children of the influential classes of the community, of those persons who control the social, financial, commercial and political interests of the town. It is with the children of such persons that Catholics of the better condition in the United States and of higher hopes for their family wish their children to associate, so that when they go out from school to begin their life their manners will be refined and their friends will be found in the banking and commercial houses of the city and not on the streets or in the workshops.
>
> I do not say that this disposition is right or that it would not be better for them to renounce it in view of the greater benefit of parochial training. I only wish to assert that such is the fact, and in an ambitious and wealthy community like America, a very obstinate and widespread one [Reilly 1943, p. 259].

Again, noting that there was very little sympathy for the parochial school among the upper classes of Catholics and that some pastors, in order to enforce attendance in their parochial schools, often resort to spiritual censures, Archbishop Ireland recalled:

> A Vicar General of a very flourishing diocese in the Eastern States informed me that when a pastor undertakes to erect a parochial school he meets with three

classes of persons in his parish: the upper class which he cannot force, the middle class which he is able to force, and the poor people who are in favor of it [Reilly 1944, p. 260].

It seems not unreasonable to suppose that these socioeconomic divisions of the Catholic classes were correlated with degrees of ethnic identification, with the recent immigrant element in the lower socioeconomic levels and the older assimilated groups represented more in the higher socioeconomic classes. If that be granted, the greater desire of the poorer Catholics for parochial schools would again attest to the importance of the ethnic factor.

However much might be the exact weight that one wishes to attach to this ethnic factor in the establishment of churches and parochial schools, it seems unquestionable that it must have been a considerable factor. If nothing else, the number of national parishes existing during the flood tide of immigration in the early 1900s would attest to that. According to data presented by James Burns (1969), it would appear that in the first decade of the twentieth century there were approximately five million Catholic parishoners over the age of nine years enrolled in national parishes in which a foreign language was used exclusively or jointly with English in the conduct of church services. This number constituted approximately one-third of the total Catholic Church membership at that time.

These parishes, which included German, French, Italian, Polish, Bohemian, Lithuanian, and Slovak, among others, often supported parochial schools in which the native tongue was used for part if not all of the instruction, particularly in the lower grades. Thus in 1906, of 188 French parishes, 161 supported parochial schools attended by some 63,000 children. Similarly, in the same year, 408 Polish parishes supported 293 schools enrolling 98,126 children.*

The German parishes, which were the most numerous of the national parishes during this period, had a total membership in excess of 1.5 million. Yet despite the fact that the German parishes excelled other national groups in the building of schools, Burns (1969) does not bother to list their enrollment. For by this time German language instruction had come to assume only a minor role in the German schools and with but some exceptions they could no longer be considered real "German" schools. Burns's explanation of this is of interest in that it advocates the melting pot function of the Church considerably before Herberg's (1955) more extensive discussion of that function for the major church groups in American society. Noting the similarity to policies advocated by Governor Seward, Burns (1969) maintained:

> The Church has seen to it that children of Catholic immigrants, speaking a foreign language, have been provided with teachers who were of the same faith and could

---

*Sanders's recent study of Catholic education in Chicago indicates that as late as 1930, 56 percent of Chicago's Catholics belonged to national churches and 53 percent of Catholic school pupils attended ethnic schools (Sanders 1977, p. 105).

speak the same tongue. And the result has been, unquestionably, such as the great statesman [Seward] anticipated. The process of assimilation has gone on quietly, smoothly, rapidly. There has been no friction no reaction. The movement has proceeded along the lines of natural growth. Schools which began with practically all the teaching in a foreign language have become, after one generation or two at the most, schools in which practically all the teaching is done in English . . . .there could be no clearer evidence of the thoroughness of the work of assimilation effected in the Catholic school than the fact that the German or Polish young man, removed by but two generations — and sometimes by only one — from his immigrant ancestry, has become the strongest advocate of the use of English in his children's school [p. 295].

Burns recognized that the chief factor making for this assimilation was of course the general American environment — with its language, customs, and institutions — in which the immigrant found himself. But among other important factors Burns lists, paradoxical as it might seem, the Catholic foreign language school itself, and he quotes Cardinal Gibbons to support his contention that the stress of assimilation was eased by the foreign language school:

Our Catholic schools afford a much easier pathway for the foreigner to enter the American life than is the case in the public school. There the child must enter at once upon the use of the English language — perhaps under the guidance of one who does not know the habits and customs of the immigrant child, and hence cannot enter into complete sympathy with his work . . . . In the Catholic school they come under the instruction of those who know the respective languages, and can understand their peculiar idioms of thought and speech. With the English language as a constantly enlarging part of their course, they are gradually, almost unconsciously, brought into complete sympathy with American ideals, and readily adapt themselves to American manners and customs. This assimilation is constantly going on in our Catholic schools, and is quite an important factor in our national development [Burns 1969, pp. 298-299].

But Burns and the Cardinal may give too rosy a view of the church's role in assimilation if one takes them to mean that policies for assimilating the immigrant were preplanned, harmoniously adopted, and smoothly put into effect. Reilly's (1943) monograph on the school controversy of 1891-1893, Barry's (1953) account of the role of German Catholics in the American church, and Sanders' (1977) account of ethnic issues in the archdiocese of Chicago indicate that the policies which in retrospect can be seen as having aided the assimilation of the immigrant were only arrived at with considerable politicking and infighting among the various ethnic groups and their champions and with much confused communication and working at cross purposes among the hierarchy.

Sanders's study (1977) is of further interest to us in that while he focuses on a single archdiocese his perception of the roles of ethnic factors, poverty, and social discrimination in motivating the building of Chicago's parochial school system is not very different from that which we have perceived on the national scene. In fact, in the epilogue to his study, Sanders summarizes his views in a way that reflects much of our own perception of the social dynamics behind the growth of our nation's dual system of coexisting public and parochial education.

Recent research on the nineteenth-century evolution of urban school systems in the United States has tended to stress a single theme — that the public school served to control assimilation of the immigrant into the American urban-industrial way of life. With the social power of family, church, and apprenticeship having been weakened in the process of urbanization and industrialization, the school seemed a potential resource of last resort in the face of urban crime, unrest, and general social change attributed to the immigrant influence. Contrary to the myth created by its protagonists' rhetoric, the common school functioned not merely to provide opportunity for the common man but also to teach him his place. Though the common or public school may not have aimed at oppression, as the radical revisionists contend, it did exercise social control. It served at least as the battleground between society's guardians and those against whose contamination they sought to guard themselves. . . .

This less flattering theme in the otherwise noble history of public education has no doubt suffered from exaggeration and excessive attention in the heady aftermath of recent discovery. Its recognition in recent educational historiography, nevertheless, admirably underlines the essential cultural difference between public and Catholic schooling in the nineteenth- and early twentieth-century city. As the public school moved toward centralization and bureaucratic control, the Catholic system, despite the Church's reputation for centralized authority and bureaucratic structure, remained singularly untouched. Aside from enforcing religious orthodoxy in its schools, the Catholic Church in Chicago exercised no central control at all. It allowed the maximum possible local diversity and, as it turns out, each ethnic, cultural, and educational group flourished. Thus, the Catholic Church, as expressed in its school system, emerges as a nineteenth century exemplar of internal social tolerance and permissiveness in a society than condemned it as intolerant and undemocratic. This seeming paradox resolves itself when the reasons that lay behind the public school's quest for centralized bureaucracy on the one hand and the Catholic school's intentional avoidance of it on the other are compared. The public school, as a symbol of established mores — not merely Protestant in original orientation, but Anglo-Saxon and middle class as well — stood to a degree as a truly organized effort by the established to impose their values on those they saw as deviant. To the established, creation of the "one best system" followed logically from a belief in the one best way of life. But Catholic schools, as expressions of the deviant, originated from and thrived on rejection of that belief, first in its religious dimension, and then in its broader cultural and socioeconomic ramifications. Thus, as public schools centralized to secure cultural homogeneity, Catholic schools, as an early expression of counter-culture rights and beliefs, deliberately reveled in hopeless — or glorious — diversity. Further, in catering to the culturally diverse, the parochial school appears to have functioned in sympathetic vibration with the Catholic, immigrant, alien poor, whereas the public school, as the increasingly bureaucratized agent of a dominant culture, could not. The intense hostility often expressed by public school advocates to parochial eduction most probably stemmed not merely from its divergent religious orientations but much more from the general threat it posed to their vision of a thoroughly homogenous society in America. Conversely, the intense devotion to parochial schooling on the part of many Catholics most probably stemmed not merely from religious belief but from the Catholic's recognition of his image as an alien in the city [Sanders 1977, pp. 225-27].

While we can accept much of this argument we would again have strong reservation if it means to imply—as did Burns and Cardinal Gibbons—a conscious adoption on the part of the Catholic hierarchy of a program of "internal social tolerance and permissiveness." There is too much evidence even in Sanders's own account of the archdiocese of Chicago as well as from numerous other dioceses throughout the nation of clashes of schismatic proportion between ethnic minorities and their diocesan leadership. We suspect that the tolerance and permissiveness were more the result of a pragmatic adjustment on the part of church leaders who recognized that if they were to preserve the "ultimate value" of unity on essential dogma it was necessary to permit wide latitude in the development and functioning of national churches and schools.

At any rate, what appears to us as really important about the rise of parochial school systems such as that developed by the Catholics—and their coexistence and rivalry with the common school system—is that they forced society to confront directly many vital questions about the conflicting rights of the family, cultural minorities, and the state, in relation to the education of children.

Education: To Whom Does It Belong?

In the early nineteenth century America, the right of the parent to determine the education of the child—formal as well as informal—went without serious challenge. It was a right assumed inherent in natural law. Similarly, the role of church in education was generally accepted whether defended as part of the divine mission of teaching and spreading the gospel, or as part of the church's general concern with the spiritual and moral well-being of the community. On the other hand, the role of the state—a complex one that was about to begin an extensive and prolific growth—was not so clearly defined.

In early colonial times, according to Bailyn (1960), the educational system and the role of the state in relationship to it had been based on the English model. In that model much of the education was primarily informal and conducted in the family and the community which together provided "instruction and discipline in work and in the conduct of life" (p. 18). Secondary, although indispensable, was the formal pedagogy of the schools where the church played a major role. The role of the state in this formal education was forceful but indirect:

> It was exhortatory, empowering, supervisory, regulatory; it was with rare exceptions, neither initiating nor sustaining. Support for schools and universities was almost universally from private benefaction, usually in the form of land endowments; public taxation was rare and where it existed, local and temporary [Bailyn 1960, p. 20].

But for various economic and cultural reasons indicated by Bailyn, the English educational system did not work in the New World and, by the end of the colonial period, the educational system and its economic basis had undergone revolutionary change. The change from the old European-style extended family, that was geographically contained and socioeconomically fixed toward the new, more nuclear, and mobile family, had been accompanied by a relative decrease in the importance of the informal education provided by family and community and an increase in the importance of formal schooling. Further, where land was plentiful and capital scarce, endowment funds were not a reliable economic basis on which to build educational institutions. Increasingly, in addition to tuition, support came from current and repeated donations in the form of taxes, individual, family or community gifts, all of which contributed to the growth of external control for the educational enterprise.

These changes in the colonial period inevitably set the stage for a reexamination of the rights, privileges, and obligations of family, community, church, and state in relationship to the education of the child. We indicated earlier how the rationale for schooling gradually shifted from the religious motivation of early colonial times to the argument of a need to prepare the future citizens of the new republic for their civic and social responsibilities. Accompanying that shift was a growing assertion of the necessity of the state to provide education and of the state's right to compel and to control the education of the young. We noted how the Protestant churches in the course of the nineteenth century acquiesced to the assertion of these expanding rights of the state in the development of the common school system. The Catholics, however, chose a more challenging attitude toward the rights of the state in matters of education. These challenges reached their peak shortly before the turn of the century and are of special interest because the issues they raised continued to live on in the twentieth century. In fact, in view of the increasing concern with the education of minorities in the sixties and seventies, one might argue that the issues of state versus family and cultural rights in education are of increasing importance.

To the Catholic church, the parents' right to educate the young is primary, as based upon natural law. The right of the church to educate in matters of religion is a divine commission. The right of the church to educate in the secular realm is derived from its right to educate in the spiritual realm insofar as the impartation of natural knowledge might facilitate and support the development of spiritual knowledge. This logic of the Catholic Church's position on family and church rights in the education of the young is not very different from that held by Protestants in the colonial and early national period. Where the two religious communities began to diverge was as the state began to move more actively onto the educational scene and the assertion of its rights began to conflict with those of church and family.

Where the Protestant churches moved more or less quickly to grant the right of the state to provide and then to control education during the period of the development of the common school system, the Catholics gave ground slowly. The Catholics would not grant the state's right to provide education if such provisions were exclusively pan-Protestant or secular. If it could not prevent the exercise of such asserted rights then it would provide its own Catholic education in its own schools. This burden was difficult but at least it safeguarded their most basic values, religious or cultural as the case might be. If the state was to move from exercising a right to provide education to a right to control education, the safety of the parochial school was threatened. With control, could not the state throttle the very attempt of the Catholics to transmit their cultural and spiritual values to their children? Had not the Penal Laws that the English imposed in Ireland forbidden Catholic schools and even denied the right of Catholics to function as schoolmasters? Had not Prussia under Bismarck restricted the educational right and freedom of Catholics and even enacted laws to place the training of priests under government supervision? And if there were not these cultural memories, did not the recent schemes of the nativists suggest that such was possible in America during the latter decades of the nineteenth century?

In 1874, California enacted a law making it an offense for a parent to send a child to a private school without first obtaining permission from the public board of education. In 1887, a bill was introduced in the Massachusetts legislature that sought control over private schools with provision for inspection and annual approval by the school committee. It was defeated only by determined resistance by Catholics and concerned non-Catholics such as President Eliot of Harvard. In 1889, a bill in the Massachusetts legislature again sought control over parochial schools and would place strictures on the use of foreign languages in such schools. In 1890, a less stringent bill was passed in Wisconsin which did not abolish foreign languages from parochial schools but did insist on the use of English for certain subjects (Reilly 1943, pp. 44, 45). Illinois, in 1889, passed the Edwards Law which stipulated that the compulsory school attendence requirement could be satisfied only in those schools that were approved by the local board of education. In addition it banned the use of foreign languages as a medium for instruction in the schools. German Lutherans were to join Catholics in opposition to this law (Sanders 1977, pp. 34, 235).

Reilly (1943) indicates that prior to the 1890s, no Catholic leader had publicly asserted the right of the state to educate. In fact, he maintained that prior to the common school revival of the 1840s, neither did the non-Catholics publically uphold the state's right to teach. At any rate, after the common school revival it was in the Catholic camp where one was likely to encounter public denial of the state's right to teach. This was not to deny the state the right to act in loco parentis when the parents neglected or were unable to provide for the education of the child. Nor did it deny the state a role in founding, endowing, and supporting schools so long as that did not entail a dictation or interference in the education or discipline of the school. But education as a specific, proper, and prior right was reserved to the family and to the church.

However, by 1890, the social and economic changes accompanying the development of a modern industrial, highly urbanized state necessitated some clarification of the Catholic stance toward the state's role in education. It was obvious that the state, through its support and control of the common school, dominated the educational scene. It was equally obvious that the state with compulsory education laws as an opening wedge was moving toward the regulation of all elementary education, public, private, and parochial as well. Coupled with this was the complex issue of state support for parochial schools. For despite the increasing number of state constitutions that prohibited such support, preceding and following the Civil War, many communities in such states as New York, Massachusetts, and Minnesota had succeeded in finding ways of offering support to parochial school systems (Gabel 1937, Burns 1969). This support was welcomed by some "Americanizing" bishops and resisted by conservative Irish and German church leaders who felt that acceptance of such support would eventually lead to complete control of parochial education by the state. With a changed cast of characters this division of opinion continues on today's parochial school scene.

In 1891, Thomas Bouquillon, a professor of moral theology at the newly founded Catholic University of America, attempted, at the request of his ecclesiastical superiors, to provide the necessary clarification of the Catholic position in a pamphlet entitled: *Education: To Whom Does It Belong?* The argument set forth was not accepted without challenge by the Catholics themselves but the issues it considers have interest that transcend that of Catholic theology and philosophy for they deal with the individual, the family, the subculture, and the state in relation to education. Therefore they are issues which are still very much alive in the educational scene of the 1970s.

Bouquillon's thesis was that "education belongs to men taken individually and collectively in legitimate association, to the family, to the state, to the Church, to all four together, and not to any one of these four factors separately" (1892b, Rejoinder, p. 1).

He held that the "right of educating" belonged naturally to the individual acting alone or in legitimate association, although in such case it was but "vague, general and dependent," being essentially subordinate to the action of the legitimate civil and religious authority. The parent in contrast had a "special and proper" right to educate, giving him an "inadmissible" control of the education of his child, but nevertheless subject to the control of civil and religious authority within their proper spheres. To the church was reserved the right of teaching in the religious sphere.

In his consideration of the rights of the state, Bouquillon maintained the state's right to educate not as a "vague and general right"—which was generally conceded by Catholics and subsumed such rights as the state's right to function in loco parentis—but as a "special and proper right."

> we affirm unhesitatingly, and in accord, as we think, with the principles of sound theology and philosophy, and with the testimony of the tradition of the Church, that it must be admitted, as the larger number of theologians do admit, that the State has the right to educate. The following reason, drawn from the very nature of things and, in our judgment, thoroughly apodictical, will suffice. Civil authority has the right to use all legitimate temporal means it judges necessary for the attainment of the temporal common welfare, which is the end of civil society. Now, among the most necessary means for the attainment of the temporal welfare of the commonwealth is the diffusion of human knowledge. Therefore civil authority has the right to use the means necessary for the diffusion of such knowledge, that is to say, to teach it, or rather to have it taught by capable agents [Bouquillon 1892b, p. 12].

From the general principles laid down, Bouquillon drew a number of logical inferences as regards the state's power to control parochial as well as public school education that were not in line with the positions taken by a number of his coreligionists.

Thus he concluded that the state has the power of exacting "ordinary and reasonable conditions of qualification" from those who would teach; this would imply that the state had the right to require state certification of those who would teach in parochial schools. In addition, he not only accepted the state's right to institute compulsory education but allowed it the right to set minimum standards of instruction:

> If the State may coerce parents who neglect the education of their children, so also may it determine a minimum of instruction and make it obligatory. Who admits the former must admit the latter. The consequence seems to us logically necessary and we are surprised that all do not see it. Consider, when are parents called negligent? Evidently, when they do not give their children a minimum of education. If then you grant the State power over cases of neglect, you at once give it power to define what is the minimum of education, and to exact that minimum by way of prevention and of general precept. A law prescribing a minimum of instruction is nothing else, it seems to us, than the application of a principle of natural law to the given circumstances of this or that country [Bouquillon 1892b, p. 26].

Many within the Catholic Church feared that Bouquillon's theological and philosophical arguments would in practical application make the parochial school and the family subservient to the state—and their rights contingent upon the whim of that secular power. There followed a bitter controversy in which conservative Church leaders denounced Bouquillon and those Americanizing Bishops who supported his views.

Bouquillon, stung by the attacks, made several attempts to clarify his position and to distinguish between what he advocated in principle and what might be feasible in practice.

> Now, what I undertook to show in my pamphlet was that parent, individuals, Church, state, may if they find it necessary or convenient, be school teachers and managers; . . . that education is, in the language of the Church, a mixed matter. Suppose the parent is the educator of his child, he must take into account the authority of the state and the Church in the work of his child's schooling. Suppose an individual or corporation is the parent's agent in the education of the child, they must take into account the parent, the state, and the Church. Suppose the state is the agent chosen by the parent, it must not forget that the parent and the Church have something to say in the matter. Suppose that the Church is the educator the parent trusts his child to, she must remember that, while she is independent in matters religious, in secular teaching she must pay due regard to the parents, and also, in cases instanced above and in others of like nature, to the state. Thus, it is that education is a mixed matter, and this is precisely what I hold. Church, state, parents, individuals physical and moral—all these are co-workers in this complex business of education. The parent is first; it matters little to me whom you put last [Bouquillon 1892a, p. 373].

This analysis of the individual, family, church, and state rights in educational matters is clear and cogent and not without its relevance for our own time. For we need only substitute "subculture" for "Church" and "cultural" for "religious," and the argument is applicable to the respective educational rights of individuals, family, state, and minority groups in general. It is of interest that the higher courts of the land in decisions upon educational rights from the 1890s to our present day have generally moved into a position consistent with Bouquillon's philosophical analysis.

Compulsory Education

In Tyack's (1976) analysis of the history of compulsory education in the United States he distinguishes two phases. The first was from 1852 when Massachusetts adopted its compulsory attendance law to about 1890 when most states adopted compulsory-attendance legislation which was generally unenforced if not unenforceable. This stage which he calls *symbolic* was characterized by ideological dispute rather than practical implementation. The second phase, designated the *bureaucratic* phase, began shortly before the turn of the century. It was a time in which American school systems grew in size and complexity, techniques of bureaucratic control evolved, compulsory schooling laws were strengthened, and enforcement was increasingly effective. This latter phase of compulsory education shall be of concern when we study the development of special education in the public schools since such laws were a primary factor leading to the development of special classes. But here we would like to focus on Tyack's *symbolic* phase, for although the phase may well have ended in the 1890s, the ideological conflicts are not extinct and have forced a continuing redefinition of state versus minority educational rights to our own day.

In the 1890s, the right of the state to enforce compulsory education was still under challenge, primarily a Catholic challenge. One of the most important of these challenges and one which attracted much national attention was to occur in relation to the Ohio compulsory education law of 1879. Father Quigley, pastor of a Catholic school in Toledo, chose on constitutional grounds not to comply with that section of the law which required him to make quarterly reports to the state. He was arrested and brought to trial and convicted. When on appeal the case finally reached the Supreme Court of Ohio in 1892, Bouquillon's pamphlet had already appeared. The state's attorney made effective use of it to indicate that within the Catholic camp itself support could be found for the legitimacy of the state's right to legislate compulsory education. Judge Dunne, counsel for the defense, made a long and learned rebuttal of Bouquillon's thesis but to no avail. In a precedent-setting decision the Court found in favor of the state (Burns 1969).

Tyack is probably right in stating that during the second phase of bureaucratic compulsory education ideological conflict over compulsory attendance diminished. But other aspects of the state's right to control education did continue to provoke ideological conflict, particularly in the area of state control over private and parochial schools, and these conflicts were at times intertwined with the compulsory attendance issue. For if the state could require compulsory school attendance—and even Catholics following the court rulings of the 1890s, reluctantly or not, had to grant that—did that not also imply that the state might determine the kind of school and the nature of the instruction that would fulfill the compulsory attendance requirement?

These further encroachments of the state on the rights of the family, church, and ethnic groups were to coincide with yet another periodic upheaval of nativist sentiment that developed about the time of World War i. From the year 1905, when the annual immigration first exceeded the one million mark, through 1914, approximately 10,000,000 immigrants came to the United States. Increasingly after the turn of the century this immigration had become dominated by eastern and southern European national groups. In addition to the social concerns such large numbers of immigrants might reasonably evoke, there was much alarm in nativist circles—reinforced by the developing eugenics movement—that this influx of inferior blood would dilute, if not wash away in a flood, the superior Nordic blood of the founding fathers.

If the outbreak of World War I gave some temporary relief by drastically reducing the number of new immigrants, it also made the nativists more concerned about the loyalty of the foreigners already in their midst. As a result, there developed simultaneously a clamor for restrictive immigration laws and a vigorous program for Americanizing the immigrant. To the public schools, naturally, was assigned a major role in this Americanizing program. Grade school and high school programs increasingly emphasized the cultivation of patriotism and good citizenship and even became involved in adult education programs for the immigrant (Thompson 1971, Atzmon 1958). What is of particular interest to us in this Americanization program is the fact that by 1919, some sixteen states had passed laws prohibiting the teaching of foreign languages in all public *and* private primary schools (O'Brien 1961).

The crucial legal test of these laws began in Nebraska when Robert Meyer, a teacher in a parochial school sponsored by the Zion Evangelical Lutheran Church, was convicted of having taught a ten-year-old child to read in German through the use of Bible stories. In reversing Meyer's conviction in 1923, the United States Supreme Court based itself on the clause of the Fourteenth Amendment which holds that a state may not deprive an individual of "life, liberty, or property, without due process of law." In explicating the word "liberty," the Court held that it included not merely freedom from bodily restraint but the right "to enjoy those privileges long recognized at common law as essential to the orderly pursuit of happiness by free men." Within this construction the court held that the rights of Meyer to teach the German language as part of his occupation and the rights of the parents to engage him to so instruct their children had been violated by the state. The Court took this position while it explicitly indicated it did not intend to question the power of the state "to compel attendance at some school and to make reasonable regulations for all schools" (Stokes 1950, pp. 737–41). Like Bouquillon, the Court was recognizing the need for balancing the rights of individual, family, and state. But in the spirit of the times, attempted encroachment by the state on individual, family, and church rights continued.

In 1920, the Scottish Rite Masons, Southern Jurisdication of the United States, publicly proclaimed their belief that the only sure foundation of our free institutions was the education of all children in public primary schools in which instruction should be restricted to the English language (Tyack 1968). With Scottish Rite support, a proposed amendment to the Michigan constitution requiring public school attendance for all students was advanced in the same year but soundly defeated in referendum (Holsinger 1968). The scene of activity in this campaign to destroy the parochial schools then shifted to the Northwest where, with Masonic support and vigorous backing by the Ku Klux Klan, Oregon voters exercised that favorite democratic device of the progressive era, the initiative, to pass a law in 1922 essentially requiring all children between the ages of 8 and 16 to attend public schools. Penalties of fines and imprisonment were to be imposed on parents who failed to comply. Sponsors of the law had aimed it specifically at the Catholic school system but with populist and patriotic fervor they extended their rhetoric to the snobbish private schools of the bluebloods and those private schools which were designated to further the cause of Bolshevism (Holsinger 1968, Tyack 1968).

Prior to the projected date of implementation of the law, the Society of Sisters of the Holy Names of Jesus and Mary which operated a parochial school and the Hill Military Academy sought a court injunction. Before the U.S. District Court, counsel for the sisters argued that the law would, among other things, deprive the society of property without due process of law and deprive the parents of the right to control the education of their children. The state argued that increased attendance at nonpublic schools had been accompanied by an increase in juvenile delinquency and that compulsory attendance at public schools was necessary as a "precautionary measure against the moral pestilence of paupers, vagabonds, and possibly convicts," that children educated in nonpublic schools would be exposed to the doctrines of "bolshevists, syndicalists, and communists" (Jorgenson 1968, p. 462). Further, if any one denomination were permitted to conduct schools, others would do so and that would lead to the destruction of the public school system. The state therefore freely admitted that the intent of the law was to destroy nonpublic schools. "The necessity for any other kind of school than that provided by the State has ceased to exist" (Jorgenson 1968, p. 462).

The District Court issued an injunction restraining the state from putting the law into effect. The state appealed to the Supreme Court. Meanwhile,the excesses of nativism and nationalism of the World War period began to subside; immigration was well below the pre-War levels and the Ku Klux Klan mentality was beginning to recede. On the whole, the national press was vigorous in its denunciation of the Oregon law and the court challenges of the Sisters were vigorously supported by Protestant and Jewish groups.

In its decision of June 1, 1925, to uphold the lower court's decision, the Supreme Court indicated that:

> No question is raised concerning the power of the State reasonably to regulate all schools, to inspect, supervise, and examine them, their teachers and pupils; to require that all children of proper age attend some school, that teachers shall be of good moral character and patriotic disposition, that certain studies plainly essential to good citizenship must be taught, and that nothing be taught which is manifestly inimical to the public welfare [Jorgensen 1968, p. 463].

But the court denied the state's right to exercise arbitrary, unreasonable, and unlawful interference with the property rights of the appellees, and with wider scope and implication the Court stated:

> we think it entirely plain that the Act of 1922 unreasonably interferes with the liberty of parents and guardians to direct the upbringing and education of children under their control. As often heretofore pointed out, rights guaranteed

by the Constitution may not be abridged by legislation which has no reasonable relation to some purpose within the competency of the state. The fundamental theory of liberty upon which all governments in this Union repose excludes any general power of the state to standardize its children by forcing them to accept instruction from public teachers only. The child is not the mere creature of the state; those who nurture him and direct his destiny have the right, coupled with the high duty, to recognize and prepare him for additional obligations [Stokes 1950, vol. 2, p. 740].

Certainly, nationwide press reaction indicated this to be one of the most popular of Supreme Court decisions, ever. Leo Pfeffer (1958), an outstanding attorney and scholar of constitutional law would subsequently consider the decision "the Magna Carta of private schools in America and perhaps as well the Magna Carta of cultural pluralism" (p. 83).

A Pluralistic Society and the Schools

In our account of the Public School Society's experimental primary schools where German immigrant children were instructed in basic English before transfer to the regular school program, we noted the rejection of such accommodation to cultural diversity when it was proposed to extend the program to Italian immigrant children. At that point we discussed the role of minority value systems within a complex culture. We recognized that a multiplicity of value systems might be of such degree that it could vitiate the cohesiveness necessary for communal survival; but we also note that a diversity in value systems may be a necessary precondition for a society's survival. A multiple value system might give a society reserves to draw upon as conditions change and call for new responses upon the part of the culture. If, then, we accept Pfeffer's suggestion that *Pierce* v. *Society of Sisters* can be considered a Magna Carta of cultural pluralism it behooves us to look at it more closely in this role.

First, it is striking that a court decision on the educational rights of a religious corporation and the parents contracting with that corporation for the education of their children should be the basis of a Magna Carta for cultural pluralism. This would suggest that the nature and extent of the state's control of education is the key to either cultural pluralism or homogeneity. Second, this Magna Carta did not say that families had a right to be Catholic, Protestant or Jewish—presumably guarantees of religious freedom already provided for that—but that families may direct the upbringing and education of their young and have the right, and the high duty, to prepare them for obligations beyond those owed to the state. In the context of the case this obviously included the right of religious training, but by implication it extends to a broader range of values.

Indeed, in 1927, the Court in the case of *Farrington* v. *Tokushige* reviewed Hawaiian Territory legislation aimed at the Japanese-American foreign language schools and explicitly indicated that the parental rights affirmed by Pierce had constitutional strength independent of any religious rights that might be involved. In this case the Court held that the state had denied "owners and patrons reasonable choice and discretion in respect of teachers, curriculum and textbooks" (Arons 1976, p. 85). Thus, not only do the parents have the right to transmit a religious subculture but even subcultural values independent of their religious context.

Finally, this Magna Carta implicitly recognizes that formal education in public or nonpublic schools is a basic transmitter of culture and it therefore denies to the state the monopolistic right to form all children in one cultural mold. At the same time it guarantees parents the right to utilize formal schooling as the means of transmitting a subculture. It needs to be underlined that this Magna Carta does not give the parents an absolute right in the matter of cultural transmission via formal schooling, for the court's opinion allows the state reasonable control of all schools, public and private.

The question then moves to the one which Bouquillon in his theoretical analysis did not address. Granted that education is a mixed matter in which individuals, families, church, and state have shared rights, how in practice does one define the limits of those rights? In other words, what constitutes "reasonable regulation" by the state?

Presumably what is reasonable will be determined by such factors as legal precedent, customs, traditions, and public opinion. In times of cultural change and conflict we may expect continual reassessments and court challenges of what at that particular moment constitutes "reasonableness." As the society as a whole feels secure, the standards for reasonable regulation relax and broaden and the cultural pluralism of our society is singled out for praise. In periods of internal or external threat we assume that what is reasonable will be stringently and narrowly defined and emphasis will be on the need for a uniformity of civic values to maintain the well-being of society.

But regardless of the climate of security or insecurity, which will ultimately determine what is "reasonable," it behooves educators, historians, and practitioners of the social and behavioral sciences to study more closely the interaction between education and cultural pluralism. How wide a range of pluralistic values can the state tolerate between its public and nonpublic schools? Assuming that cultural pluralism within the limits required by the overall cohesiveness of the society is a desirable end, to what extent can education serve that cause of cultural pluralism? Can it be served only by something similar to the present dual system of public and nonpublic schools? Or is it possible that within the framework of public education it would be possible to foster the transmission of different cultural values without traumatic change in the specific cultural Gestalts in which they occur? Insofar as the experts—educator, historian, social or behavioral scientist as the case might be—can throw light on these questions, society will be in a better position, when it must decide in the course of events to alter its definition of "reasonable regulation," to do so with less arbitrariness and possibly more wisdom.

The Extent of State Control Over the Secular Education of Children

There is obviously no precise answer to the definition of "reasonable regulation," as it will vary with the times and the society's perception of the degree of internal or external threat to its security. Examples of court decisions, however, can give some idea of the limits that "reasonable regulation" has taken in recent decades.

In Pfeffer's (1967) account of *People v. Donner,* a group of Hassidic Jewish parents were found in violation of New York State's compulsory education law because their children attended a religious school in which English was not the medium of instruction and in which the curriculum was limited to the study of the Bible, the Talmud, and elementary Jewish law. No instruction was provided in the common branches of secular learning required by state law. In their defense the parents argued that according to the religious belief of their particular Jewish sect, Jewish law prohibited all systematic, secular education and the enforcement of the compulsory school attendance law therefore violated their First Amendment rights.

In overruling this contention, the Domestic Relations Court argued the importance for the total society that all its children receive a basic secular education in the English language and added that:

> Compulsory education laws constitute but one of the many statutes of a government, dedicated to the democratic ideal, which are universally enacted for the benefit of all the children within the realm of government. Child labor laws and laws making it criminal to abandon or neglect children, are similar instances of governmental intervention for the protection of children. Religious convictions of parents cannot interfere with the responsibility of the State to protect the welfare of children . . . [Pfeffer 1967, pp. 715-716].

When the case was appealed to the Supreme Court in 1961, the Court held that the States' constitutional power to require all children to receive a minimum secular education was so plainly evident that the case did not warant a hearing.

In such instances as the above, the courts would hold that the right of the state to ensure its own safety and to protect the welfare of children overrides even the "preferred position" the courts ordinarily assign to First Amendment rights. Our second instance indicates some of the restraint that First Amendment rights place, in turn, on the state's right to ensure its safety and protect the welfare of children. For this, we turn to a consideration of the Old Order Amish and their recent difficulties with state departments of education.

The Old Order Amish are a Mennonite Christian group in which family, social, and economic life are tightly integrated by religious beliefs. Generally, they are settled in small agricultural communities where they aspire to conduct a simple life style in as much isolation as possible from the surrounding technical, industrialized society. In material ways their life is not much different from that which their ancestors knew on the farms of the nineteenth century. The tractor has not yet supplanted the horse, nor has the automobile replaced the horse and buggy. In dress, customs, folkways, and value systems, they remain much as they were a hundred years ago. Of all our immigrant peoples, the Amish have been the most successful in resisting assimilation. Nevertheless, the Amish comprise a thriving and economically successful culture. Want for the necessities of life are at a minimum and the Amish are recognized by their neighbors as competent farming people who make up in knowledge and hard work for their lack of motorized machinery and the gadgetry of modern farming. Their ethos emphasizes mutual help within the community. They abhor violence and shun contention even to the extent of often refusing legal redress for wrongs inflicted upon them.

Although some of their number might occasionally protest the materialistic, worldly spirit of the common school, the Amish in general accepted the public schools of rural nineteenth century America. The one-room elementary school, dedicated to the teaching of the basic skills of reading, writing, and arithmetic met all their needs for formal education. The family and the community would do the rest.

This not unsatisfactory state of affairs began to change about the turn of the century when compulsory schooling laws extended the educational years, rural schools began to consolidate, and secondary education became a standard feature of public schooling. These new developments gradually supplanted the old one-room schoolhouse with its neighborhood control and replaced it with large, consolidated schools, remote from the influence of the home and equipped with new curricula designed to prepare the child to take part not in the simple life of the family farm but in a highly industrialized, technical society (Keim 1975).

These developments were no longer acceptable to the Amish, and so with increasing frequency during the course of the twentieth century they found themselves in violation of the compulsory education laws. These clashes were to climax in Iowa, Kansas, Nebraska and Wisconsin in the 1960s, where the disputes attracted national attention and became the spur to much serious thought, discussion, and debate among educators, lawyers, politicians, churchmen, and concerned citizens (Erickson 1969, Keim 1975). All the old thorny questions of state, church, minority, and family rights that had plagued the courts since the 1890s were opened up again, and despite Amish reluctance to engage in civil dispute, the matter was before the courts.

The Amish consider themselves forbidden by the precepts and example of Christ to participate in war or violence in any form; their routine response to the military draft is to apply for the status of conscientious objector. Faced with hostility from the surrounding community, their inclination is to move on to new locations without attempting to defend their rights. Therefore the Amish have been reluctant to search aggressively for legal redress in the face of the encroachment of compulsory education upon their religious culture. They have chosen to remove themselves from school districts with overly conscientious enforcement of compulsory education laws, to adopt strategies of passive noncompliance, to build parochial grade schools, and to attempt some compromise with the letter of the law by establishing their own "vocational high schools." These require but a few hours' attendance per week and hence permit the adolescents to continue their real training for adulthood by participating in the work of the farm and the home.

But some other Americans, less troubled by St. Paul's admonitions against legal contentiousness, indignant at the sight of the apparent injustice, and concerned that the cause of Amish freedom is the cause of all of us, have proven more ready to join issue. Thus, Rev. William C. Linholm, a Lutheran pastor troubled by the Amish school controversy in Iowa, was moved to found in 1966 the National Committee for Amish Religious Freedom, an organization composed of a dedicated handful of scholars, lawyers, and religious leaders. Following a number of legal interventions on the behalf of the Amish, the committee made its most significant effort in a case in the New Glarus community of Wisconsin in 1968. Here, public school officials chose to cause the arrest of several Amish parents under a criminal complaint for refusal to enroll their children in high school. The children had completed an elementary school education but the law required that they continue school until the age of sixteen.

Linholm's National Committee engaged William Ball, a Catholic lawyer long concerned with state-church constitutional issues, to defend the Amish parents before the Green County Court. In Ball's (1975) account of the trials, he makes it clear that on the basis of previous court decisions it was apparent that a state violation of religious liberty could only be justified on the basis of a "compelling state interest." The legal strategy then dictated demonstration of the religious basis of the Amish objection to compulsory education beyond the elementary school level and the lack of a "compelling" state interest requiring such extended compulsory education for the Amish children. Expert testimony was presented according to that strategy and such authorities as Dr. John Hostetler were called upon to explicate the interrelatedness of Amish communal life.

Ball recounts with relish the prosecutor's cross-examination of Hostetler: "Now, Doctor, let's talk about education. What's the point of education? Isn't it to get ahead in the world?" To which Dr. Hostetler's superb and simple answer: "It all depends upon which world" (p. 118). How better to underscore that education is only in part the training of skills. Its larger part, covert and incoherent though it may often be, concerns the "ultimate values" — as secular or spiritual as they might be.

Nevertheless, the court, though granting the violation of the religious liberty of the Amish, held that a superior state interest necessitated the attendance of the children at school, and found the parents guilty. On successive appeals the Supreme Court of Wisconsin was to reverse the lower courts and hold that the Amish children should be exempt from compulsory attendance at secondary schools.

With such a decisive ruling, Ball expressed his surprise that the State of Wisconsin elected to appeal the case to the Supreme Court of the United States. He probably underestimated the obsessive need with which the bureaucratic mind pursues the welfare of others. At any rate, the Supreme Court in May of 1972 upheld the decision of the Wisconsin Supreme Court, holding that secondary schooling contravened the basic religious tenets and practice of the Amish faith, and that foregoing a few additional years of compulsory education would neither impair the child nor materially detract from the welfare of society. In the Court's opinion:

> a State's interest in universal education, however highly we rank it, is not totally free from a balancing process when it impinges on other fundamental rights and interests, such as those specifically protected by the Free Exercise Clause of the First Amendment and the traditional interest of parents with respect to the religious upbringing of their children so long as they, in the words of Pierce, "prepare [them] for additional obligations" [Keim 1975, pp. 155–156].

But lest this decision cause us to underestimate the educational powers of the state, it need be noted that the Amish were vindicated not on the basis of rights pertaining to any secular subcultural value system but very specifically on the basis of rights according to a religious belief. Again, in the words of the Court:

> We come then to the quality of the claims of the respondents concerning the alleged encroachment of Wisconsin's compulsory school attendance statute on their rights and the rights of their children to the free exercise of the religious beliefs they and their forebears have adhered to for almost three centuries. In evaluating those claims we must be careful to determine whether the Amish religious faith and their mode of life are, as they claim, inseparable and interdependent. A way of life, however virtuous and admirable, may not be interposed as a barrier to reasonable state regulation of education if it is based on purely secular considerations; to have the protection of the Religion Clauses, the claims must be rooted in religious belief. Although a determination of what is a "religious" belief or practice entitled to constitutional protection may present a most delicate question, the very concept of ordered liberty precludes allowing every person to make his own standards on matters of conduct in which society as a whole has important interests. Thus, if the Amish asserted their claims because of their subjective evaluation and rejection of the contemporary secular values accepted by the majority,

much as Thoreau rejected the social values of his time and isolated himself at Walden Pond, their claim would not rest on a religious basis. Thoreau's choice was philosophical and personal rather than religious, and such belief does not rise to the demands of the Religion Clause [Keim 1975, p. 157].

If Pfeffer's suggestion that *Pierce* v. *Society of Sisters* was not only the Magna Carta of private schools but of cultural pluralism is correct, and if we are right in contending that such an interpretation implies the state's control of education is the key to either cultural pluralism or homogeneity, then *Wisconsin* v. *Yoder* would underscore the power the state wields in exercising its control of education. To repeat the words of the Court: "A way of life, however virtuous and admirable, may not be interposed as a barrier to reasonable state regulation of education if it is based on purely secular considerations."

In an increasingly secular age, if religion alone can withstand the state's will to homogenize its children by "reasonable regulations," how important is the definition of "reasonable"; and how much wisdom is required by the state if its educational goals of promoting its security and the welfare of its children is not to run the risk of sacrificing the long-term survival values of social pluralism for the short-term values of social cohesiveness? In this view of *Wisconsin* v. *Yoder* there is less comfort in the well deserved protection that the Court offered to the rights of the Amish than concern that we as an entire people are not yet assured that the state will exercise its court approval powers for the control of education with the restraint and wisdom that are necessary for solving the complex and crucial educational problems that beset us in this half of the twentieth century.

Looking Back

The great school war of the 1840s, which was in large part the challenge of a minority to the majority's claim of an exclusive right to determine the values which should be transmitted in the schools, has cast a long shadow. We have seen how it sharply delineated the problem of providing public education in a democratic, pluralistic society. To solve the problem it was necessary to secularize the public schools, develop a dual system of public and nonpublic education, and settle in the courts the respective rights of family, individuals, church, minority groups, and the state.

But despite gratifying successes we cannot say the problem has been solved. The building of parochial schools may have helped meet the needs of the immigrant Catholic and Lutheran groups. In addition, by providing an alternative schooling for minority groups, nonpublic schools may also have pressured the public school systems into meeting the competition with wiser accommodations to the needs of the immigrant child and his family. In fact one of the few, and probably the most successful instance, in which nineteenth century public schools permitted the use of an immigrant language in the schools occurred in St. Louis from 1864 to 1887, when the threat of patronizing a rival German parochial school system was employed by the immigrant group (Troen 1975).

Such an alternative can exist only when a minority, impoverished though it may be, can find the resources to build its nonpublic school system. The Catholics, in the engendered passions of religious rivalries and bigotries, sacrificed to find such resources and their dedicated religious teachers further aided the cause by working for salaries of one-third to one-half the prevailing norms (Burns 1969). But just as important, they built schools at a time when the state had not fully developed its minimal standard requirements for staff certification, school building specifications, and quality and extent of curriculum. The immigrant groups under these conditions could begin the building of school systems, with trust to the future to provide increased resources.

Whether minorities of today need alternatives to the present system of public schools and whether such alternatives should be publicly or privately financed and what would be the gains and losses of such alternative schools are questions which we need to address. It is beyond a doubt that the education of minority groups is the pressing issue for education in the second half of the twentieth century, and as we resume the development of the public schools in the following chapters we shall see how in the last one hundred years, the education of minorities and the development of special education programs became a confusing entanglement that remains unsnarled.

12

The Pestalozzian Rationale in the Evolving, Complex American School System

As THE PREVIOUS chapters suggest, one cannot understand the development of the public school system without trying to describe the nature of our society and how it has changed in relation to diverse forces and ideologies. That is no less true for special education than for "regular" education. Indeed, we have gone to some length to illustrate that in our social history there has been an intimate relationship between social characteristics of our society and the criteria employed for judging the intellectual worth and status of its citizens. For a good part of the nineteenth century, judgments about intellectual inferiority did not have the potent educational consequences they later came to have if only because the common schools did not yet possess a highly complex organizational structure.

As the schools began to increase in size, and economic considerations came to the fore, efficiency in teaching and administrative structure became central concerns. Not surprisingly, many of these efforts at reform were administrative in nature. That is to say, they were only minimally derived from changing perceptions and understanding of the "nature" of children and learning. However, such changing perceptions and understanding were in the wings, and when they made their entrance on the educational stage, they had a discernible impact in two ways. First, they influenced the organization of classrooms and schools as well as the nature of teacher training. Second, and more lasting, they created a controversy centering around the aims and processes of schooling. More specifically, the momentous question was raised: what should characterize the relationship between pupil and teacher? And when that question came into center stage in ever growing school systems struggling to educate widely differing immigrant groups, systems reflecting the tensions and prejudices of the larger society, that question inevitably guaranteed controversy. Indeed, the quest is still center stage today. Because that question was so fateful for education, and, consequently, for special education, this chapter is devoted to how that question came on the scene and why it remains there. And, as we shall shortly see, Pestalozzi is the chief actor in this act of the educational drama.

Following their introduction in New York City by the Free School Society in 1806, Lancastrian schools spread from Massachusetts to Georgia and from the east coast to the Mississippi Valley. The cheapness, the husbanding of scarce teaching resources, the apparent success in imposing military-like order upon boisterous and unruly youth, and the relative effectiveness as a teaching method made the Lancastrian school attractive to those civic leaders concerned with the problem of educating the hordes of children of the urban poor. It mattered little whether that concern sprang from humanitarian zeal, a fear of impending civil disorder arising from the disaffected, unsocialized poor, or a mixture of both. The Lancastrian system seemed to offer an economically feasible solution to the problem, and many citizens were drawn into an active support of education as a cure for the social ills of the time. The success of the Lancastrian schools in eliciting support for the development of the tax-supported common school has been generally conceded by educational historians. In addition, the monitorial training schools that developed in conjunction with Lancastrian schools played an important role in the early development of teacher training programs. With the schools of the Christian Brothers, the Lancastrian schools were important in fostering the development of group instruction methods which were much more efficient than the old techniques of individual instruction (Griscom 1825, Parker 1970, Cubberley 1919).

Nevertheless, even in their heyday the Lancastrian schools were not without their critics and as the nature of pedagogy underwent change in the first half of the nineteenth century, the inadequacies of the school system became more apparent. As we may remember from the autobiographical accounts of the late colonial and early national schools, emphasis was on the mastery of reading, writing, and simple arithmetic. Rote memorization and recitation from the alphabet through the catechism and the computational rule of three was the method and measure of achievement. For such a curriculum and such achievement it was theoretically possible to program small steps in learning where monitors, but little advanced over the pupils, might teach that which they themselves had only recently mastered.

But critics such as Henry K. Oliver—whose boyhood experience in the Boston schools was previously cited—pointed out that in all but the most mechanical departments of knowledge the Lancastrian system led to superficial and inaccurate learning (Oliver 1831). Even the Public School Society, generally steadfast in its adherence to the monitorial system, had come to recognize the limitations of the Lancastrian system for younger age groups. As we previously noted, in its proposal to develop infant schools it had acknowledged the superiority of the system utilized by the Infant School

Society—a system that was influenced by Pestalozzian educational theory and practice.

The fact was that the Lancastrian system like the system of De La Salle had made a notable contribution to educational practice by substituting group methods for the inefficient individual instruction of the eighteenth century schools. But their educational aim, like that of the schools utilizing individual instruction, had remained focused on book knowledge. In the indictment by Pestalozzi, it was a "Monkish" education, one characterized by a reverence for the authority of the word. Not surprisingly, rote memorization and mechanical mastery of a body of bookish knowledge were the method and the goal. The cognitive skill aspect of this education was mastery of the word in reading and writing with the more abstract language of arithmetic introduced at the higher levels. The development of character, that other great aim of education, was to be achieved by the reading of religious, moral, and ethical texts.

Even as the eighteenth century techniques of instruction began to give way before these new methods of group instruction, society was accelerating its rate of change. The industrial revolution had begun; the urbanization of culture increased, knowledge expanded explosively, and social and political forms of life underwent both continuing development and disruptive upheavals. The home and community which had carried the major burden of inculcating cognitive skills and character training seemed ever less adequate in their ability to prepare youth for their adult roles in society. But if the state were to make up for the shortcomings of family and community in our western civilization, could the school systems of Europe and America furnish the vehicle? The prevalence of the belief that they could is attested to by the increasing involvement of the state in education throughout the nineteenth century both in Europe and America. We have in part attempted to illustrate this in our selective consideration of schooling in the United States.

But state sponsorship and control of education were only part of the projected solution. What was needed was reform in the aims and the philosophy as well as the content, methods, and organization of formal education. So the nineteenth century was characterized by continual educational reform. Since a number of these reforms were to have fateful consequences for both the origin and character of special education programs, we will consider such varied developments as the Pestalozzian movement, and the bureaucratization of education including the grading of schools.

The Pestalozzian Movement

In listing causes for the decline of the monitorial system of education, Kaestle (1973b) indicates its incompatibility with new educational developments such as Pestalozzian pedagogy with its demand for an individual relationship between adult and child and the development of the infant school movement. In these infant schools, which were under Pestalozzian influence, monitorial regimentation and memory drill proved unsuitable to the nature of the younger children.

It is true that some advocates of the monitorial system had attempted to wed the Pestalozzian methods of object teaching to the Lancastrian framework (Fowle 1826), but as the Public School Society's experience with infant schools would suggest, Kaestle is probably correct in pointing to the incompatibilities of the two systems as the reason for the decline of the Lancastrian system. Certainly, the incompatibilities of the systems are readily enough apparent in even a cursory glance at Pestalozzi's educational theory and practice.

Like Lancaster and De La Salle, Pestalozzi was concerned with the education of the poor. His first educational experiment in 1774 was in the industrial education of vagrant children in which he attempted to teach them to support themselves by farming and spinning. His previous unsuccessful efforts at farming, which had dissipated much of his own and his wife's resources, had provided him with considerable practical experience for the enterprise. Nevertheless, the experiment failed and there followed a period in which he undertook various writings on education and social reform, including his famous novel on peasant life, *Leonard and Gertrude* (1906), in which there is limned much of his educational and social philosophy.

The French invasion of Switzerland in 1798, and its resultant social upheaval, brought Pestalozzi back into an active role in teaching, and his interest moved from industrial education to elementary school methods. At Burgdorf in the years 1799-1804, he developed his object method of teaching, undertook the training of teachers, published his influential educational text, *How Gertrude Teaches Her Children* (1912) and became internationally famous. His activities were then transferred to Yverdon where from 1805-1825 his institute became a mecca for educators from all parts of Europe. Many, like Froebel of subsequent kindergarten fame, spent time as assistant teachers in the institute and then returned to spread the Pestalozzian principles in their homelands.

Pestalozzi's system of education is extensive and complicated. Nor is its overall comprehensibility aided by his generally informal presentation and oftentimes confusing blend of religion, humanistic philosophy, romanticism, idealism, pedagogical science, and just plain common sense. Fortunately, for our limited purposes, we need concern ourselves with only a few aspects of Pestalozzi's system in order to demonstrate its importance for the development of elementary education and to show its affinity to developments in the education of retarded and handicapped individuals that were also taking place in the first half of the nineteenth century.

Pestalozzi's system was conceived as a reaction against the prevailing practices of his day, and as is not uncommonly the case with those who have a revolutionary impact upon their times Pestalozzi considered himself to be advocating a return to the ways of our forefathers. He objected to an education divorced from life, and maintained that in former times the child as soon as possible became involved in the work of the adult. With such an education, the child was appropriately prepared for its role in society.

Pestalozzi felt that the family rather than the school should be the center of education and that the successful school should be modeled upon the home — particularly that the relationship of the teacher to the pupil should be as a loving parent to its child. True education would involve educating the whole person in all of his intellectual, physical, and moral capacities; the development of mind, hand, and heart should proceed together. He was particularly incensed at the verbalness of formal schooling and, somewhat anticipatory of McLuhan's *Gutenberg Galaxy* (1962), noted that the invention of the printing press was not an unmixed blessing. While, on the one hand, it facilitated the development of the arts and sciences, on the other hand the foundations of natural education were lost. In a paraphrase of Pestalozzian thought Pinloche states:

> That Europe should overrate the influence of the invention of printing on learning was natural enough, also that it should have let this invention dazzle it and make it giddy; but it is incomprehensible that it should still be affected by that giddiness, and let it grow to a nervous fever which ruins body and mind. It is unheard of that the use of the five senses, and especially the sense of sight, the most general tool of *sense-perception*, should have been reduced to contemplate the idol of the new knowledge, letters and books, so that the eyes, and even men themselves, are become mere instruments to read letters [Pinloche 1901, pp. 140–141].

Such bookish idolatry went against nature, presenting abstractions to the child that were beyond his grasp. True education would conform to the real, natural world and to the developing nature of the child. Progress would start with the most concrete experience and only by gradual steps move on to abstract ideas and judgment. Such education would involve an inductive methodology.

This theory of instruction was based upon a theory of knowledge, prevalent in pre-Platonic Greece and formulated and reformulated down through the ages from Aristotle through Locke. In its simplest form it holds that knowledge is obtained through sensory-perception. The mind begins as a tabula rasa upon which experience is to impress an accumulating fund of knowledge. A theorist such as Locke might hold that ideas derived from externally evoked sensations are supplemented by the ideas derived from the mind's reflection upon its own operations, but the essential cast of such theories in contrast to Platonic intuitive theories of knowledge is the emphasis placed upon the role of sensory input. From such a theory of knowledge, it is reasonable that one deduces the importance of sensory experience for learning, and in making such a deduction Pestalozzi was not unique as an educator.

Comenius in his *Great Didactic* had argued:

> the commencement of knowledge must always come from the senses (for the understanding possesses nothing that it has not first derived from the senses). Surely, then, the beginning of wisdom should consist, not in the mere learning the names of things, but in the actual perception of the things themselves [Comenius 1896, p. 337].

> Those things, therefore, that are placed before the intelligence of the young, must be real things and not the shadows of things. I repeat, they must be *things;* and by the term I mean determinate, real, and useful things that can make an impression on the senses and on the imagination. . . . From this a golden rule for teachers may be derived. Everything should, as far as possible, be placed before the senses. Everything visible should be brought before the organ of sight, everything audible before that of hearing. Odours should be placed before the sense of smell, and things that are tastable and tangible before the sense of taste and of touch respectively. If an object can make an impression on several senses at once, it should be brought into contact with several . . . the truth and certainty of science depend more on the witness of the senses than on anything else. For things impress themselves directly on the senses, but on the understanding only mediately and through the senses. This is evident from the fact that belief is at once accorded to knowledge derived from the senses, while an appeal is always made to them from *a priori* reasoning and from the testimony of others. We do not trust a conclusion derived from reasoning unless it can be verified by a display of examples (the trustworthiness of which depends on sensuous perception) [Comenius 1896, pp. 336–337].

Comenius's *Great Didactic,* completed about 1632, was not published until the middle of the nineteenth century and so had no direct influence on Pestalozzi. Nevertheless, Pestalozzi was aware of Comenius's use of sensory experience as an instructional method (Walch 1952, p. 99). A more direct and obvious influence was however provided by Rousseau's *Emile* where a Lockean theory of knowledge appears as follows:

> As all that enters the human understanding comes through the senses, the first reason of man is a sensuous reason; and it is this which serves as a basis for the intellectual reason. Our first teachers of philosophy are our feet, our hands and our eyes. To substitute books for all these is not to teach us reason, but to teach us to use the reason of others; it is to teach us to believe much and never to know anything [Rousseau cited in Parker 1970, p. 194].

Basing himself on such a theory of knowledge and assuming the corruptness of the existing society and the innate goodness of individual man, Rousseau attempted to set forth in his fictionalized account of the upbringing of a young gentleman the principles and practice of the ideal education.

There is much in the Pestalozzian system, from the emphasis on experiental learning to the adaptation of instruction to the developmental level of the child, that directly reflects Rousseau and went counter to the prevailing educational practice of the eighteenth century. "The moment *Emilé* appeared my highly impractical and speculative mind was enthusiastically impressed by this equally, impractical book of fantasy" (Pestalozzi cited in Walch 1952, p. 11). But Pestalozzi was original in devising the methods and techniques for changing a fantasied educational system into reality. In so doing he expanded, altered, and rejected specific ideas of Rousseau. In particular, Pestalozzi was not concerned with the education of the young gentleman but of poor children, and his educational system did not involve a withdrawal to nature from the corrupting influence of society, but rather an education of children in groups, socially oriented in its means as well as its ends.

Although Pestalozzi was primarily concerned with this social and moral aspect of education, and less with its intellectual and physical aspects, his actual impact upon the practices of his day was to be much greater in those areas of formal schooling specifically concerned with intellectual education. This may have been due to the more glaring deficiences of the eighteenth century schools in this area of instruction. But it is also likely that Pestalozzi, like countless other educators, found it most difficult to formulate the principles and techniques of moral education in ways that permit ready application to classroom practice. It is easier to prepare and implement a curriculum and a methodology to help a child to master facts and to reason well than to teach him to live with love and wisdom. Nevertheless, Pestalozzi's rejection of the then all too prevalent corporal punishment in the schools, his insistence on intellectual education proceeding in an atmosphere of loving care for the child, and his demand that the instruction adapt itself to the developmental level of the child, could not but foster a teacher-pupil relationship in which moral education had at least opportunity to occur.

In the area of intellectual education, Pestalozzi's method has been variously referred to as object teaching, the objective method, the inductive method, and oral instruction. Actually, each of these terms can be used to refer to overlapping, complementary, and interdependent modes of instruction that neither originated in nor are confined to the Pestalozzian system. But each of these terms does categorize important aspects of the Pestalozzian system that contrast it to the prevailing verbalism of the eighteenth century schools and foreshadow developments in instructional methods that were to take hold in the nineteenth century.

Thus the use of objects was characteristic of Pestalozzi's instructional methods. Natural history objects such as plants and rocks gathered in walks with the children would be examined and described by the teacher and children together. Lessons in arithmetic were accompanied by collections of objects such as pebbles or beans, to be manipulated by the child as he sought to grasp the abstract relationships of number. Excursions to the hills and valleys about the school were the beginnings of geography lessons; attempts to construct and interpret maps would come later. In all subject matter, the movement was from the known to the unknown, the simple to the complex, the concrete to the abstract (Parker 1970, Green 1969).

This teaching through observation and experience was aimed at the formation of real ideas and their expression in precise language rather than the mastery of hollow words reflecting only the haziest of notions. According to Parker (1970), it led to the subordination or elimination of book study which in turn caused the teacher to become an active instructor of groups of children instead of a hearer of individual recitations. At the same time it led to the training of the children in oral expression—an innovation in the schools of that day. Thus, object teaching was naturally wedded to oral instruction in which the knowledge of teacher and children was shared and expanded. Such instruction required a teacher with both breadth and depth of knowledge, skilled in leading the children to abstract from their experiences and to reason upon them. Such teacher competence and skill could not be expected in the youthful monitors of the Lancastrian schools; hence the system's incompatibility with monitorial instruction.

These principles and practices of Pestalozzi as developed by his followers were to revolutionize the curricula and instruction of nineteenth-century schooling. To note just some of the more important areas of innovation and change we would list language instruction, elementary science, geography, and arithmetic. The interaction of teacher and child in the method of oral instruction offered the child both instruction and practice in the use of his native language, regardless of the specific subject matter. Object teaching, which in its origin was an informal use of objects, experience, and the natural world in order to exercise sensory-perception, to increase the children's fund of knowledge and improve their command of language, developed into curricula of elementary and natural science.

Karl Ritter, the great German geographer, who was instrumental in replacing the dictionary-encyclopedic geography of the schools with principles relating physiographic conditions to economic, social, and historical conditions, directly attributed his pedagogical contributions to the personal influence and inspiration of Pestalozzi. It was Guyot, Ritter's student, who first developed geography textbooks with this orientation for the American schools in the 1860s (Parker 1970, Monroe 1907).

Pestalozzi's impact on the teaching of arithmetic was revolutionary in a number of ways. In contrast to prevailing custom, he introduced the teaching of arithmetic into the curriculum of the youngest of elementary school children, and greatly increased the amount of schooltime devoted to the subject. He applied the object method to arithmetic instruction in order to give the child clear and precise concepts of number and placed great emphasis on mental arithmetic (Parker 1970, Krüsi 1875).

Warren Colburn's book *First Lessons in Arithmetic on the Plan of Pestalozzi* was published in 1821. Its adoption was so widespread and its continued use so prolonged in nineteenth-century America that it has been ranked in historic importance with such textbooks as the *New England Primer* and Webster's speller (Parker 1970). Colburn advocated the acquisition of number concepts through observing and manipulating objects. Problems were to be performed mentally or by the manipulation of objects such as beans or nuts. Ciphering or the solution of problems using written numerals was delayed until mastery of simple arithmetical computation was achieved. In fact, in the 1842 edition, entitled *Intellectual Arithmetic, upon the Inductive Method of Instruction,* the ordinary arabic numerals used in ciphering are not introduced until the mental solution of simple problems in addition, subtraction, multiplication, and division are mastered and fractional numbers have been introduced (Colburn 1842).

Pestalozzian Influence in Prussia and the United States

The first attempt to introduce the Pestalozzian system into the United States was undertaken by Scottish businessman and philanthropist William Maclure—co-sponsor of Robert Owen's socialist community of New Harmony and "Father of American Geology." Impressed with his firsthand observation of the work at Yverdon, he induced Joseph Neef, one of Pestalozzi's former assistants, to come to America and open a school in Philadelphia in 1806. The school was short-lived as were several additional schools established by Neef, including one at New Harmony. Nevertheless, through the writings of Maclure and Neef, Pestalozzian ideas began to take hold in America (William Monroe 1907). It is apparent that directly—by visits of Americans to Yverdon, Pestalozzian writings, and occasional importation of Pestalozzian-trained teachers such as Neef and Herman Krüsi, Jr.,—and indirectly via the example of the Prussian school system which had adopted Pestalozzian methods, most leading American educators in the common school revival were deeply influenced by the Pestalozzian system and philosophy of education.

Henry Barnard, leader of school reform in Connecticut and Rhode Island, and subsequently appointed the first U.S. Commissioner of Education in 1867, came under the influence of Pestalozzian thought early in his career. His highly influential *Journal of American Education* did much to publicize the new methods and theory of education. Calvin E. Stowe—a leader of the common school movement in Ohio and husband of Harriet Beecher Stowe—and Horace Mann, leader of the common school revival in Massachusetts, wrote influential and widely distributed reports on the Prussian school system which praised those aspects of it directly reflecting Pestalozzian theory and practice (Stowe 1837, Mann 1844).

Not all the Pestalozzi-like features of Prussian instruction derived directly from the Swiss educator. German educators such as Basedow, and those who followed him such as Salzman and Baron von Rochow, had in the latter part of the eighteenth century likewise been influenced by the theories of Locke and Rousseau and by the educational ideas of Comenius; and they had developed schools in which various aspects of object teaching and oral instruction were present (Parker 1970, von Raumer 1863).

However, Pestalozzi's influence on nineteenth century German educational thought and practice was truly immense. Monroe (1907) maintains that nearly every really great German educator in the first half of the century could lay claim to personal relationships with Pestalozzi. Certainly, many of them, including Fichte, Froebel and Herbart, had either visited with Pestalozzi or undertaken training at his institution.

When Prussia sought to recover from the disastrous defeat inflicted by Napoleon in the battle of Jena in 1806, the country turned to social reform and in particular to popular education as one means of attaining national regeneration. The philosopher of idealism, Fichte, delivered his *Addresses to the German Nation* in French-occupied Berlin in brave, if culturally chauvanistic, terms, calling upon the German people to rejuvenate themselves and accept their manifest destiny as spiritual leaders of mankind. The means of this rejuvenation would be the complete reorganization of education: Education—universal and compulsory—must be recognized as the proper function and mission of the state. The rights of the state to control and supervise the education of the child are absolute. To produce the new, spiritually rejuvenated German man the child must even be removed from the custody and the contaminating influence of the parent. The basis of this new education in general aim and method was already at hand in the system of Pestalozzi (Fichte 1922).

Fichte had been close friends with Pestalozzi and knew his educational practice firsthand. Nevertheless, the romantic idealist of Yverdon whose system of education was based on the model of the loving relationship of parent to child might have been startled at the lengths to which the Prussian idealist would go to ensure the spiritual revitalization of the German people. But Fichte had only succumbed to the temptation to which educational theorists have always been susceptible since the time of Plato. It would be so easy to educate the ideal man in any generation if only parents did not interfere by the example and practice of their humanity!

Fortunately, not all of Fichte's educational prescription was accepted but it is of interest in the way it reflects the prevalent nineteenth century assumption that universal, compulsory education, state-supported and controlled, was the panacea for the ills of society. At any rate, Prussia did embark on a reorganization of its educational system, with particular impetus given by

Wilhelm von Humboldt in his brief tenure in the ministry of ecclesiastical affairs and education. Although the King of Prussia had shown interest in introducing Pestalozzian methods into his country as early as 1803, it was during this period of educational renaissance and at the special intercession of Queen Louisa that Prussia first sent a number of its young men to Yverdon for extended periods of training in the Pestlozzian method. On their return, these young men, as teachers and principals of normal schools, did much to quickly infuse Pestalozzian ideas into the Prussian system (Krüsi 1875, Paulsen 1908, Parker 1970).

It was this revitalized Prussian system that so impressed Stowe and Mann not only in its methods of instruction, but in a wide variety of features. What appealed to the leaders of the American common school revival were the range of curriculum which included much practical subject matter, a Christian atmosphere with hymn singing and extensive nonsectarian Bible instruction, the grading of students according to age and ability, and the near absence of corporal punishment. In addition, the system was also appealing to the Americans in its thorough-going organization. The whole consisted of interrelated elementary schools, secondary schools, teacher seminaries, and universities. Despite the extensive degree of local control and support, there was overall state supervision at all levels for public and private schools alike, with a foundation of compulsory attendance enforced by the courts for all children though the age of fourteen.

In particular, Mann was impressed with the training of teachers. A system of numerous, publicly supported normal schools with admission by examination provided two or three years of intensive training closely monitored by examining committees who controlled teacher certification. Often, elementary schools were annexed to these training schools to provide opportunity for practice teaching under experienced supervision (Mann 1844, Cousin 1835).

Mann's enthusiastic review of the Prussian system and the excellence of its teacher preparation, as contained in his *Seventh Annual Report* (1844) to the Massachusetts Board of Education, helped provoke an acrimonious public conflict with the schoolmasters of Boston who felt maligned by the implied comparison. The controversy, however, only served to give wider publicity to the newer educational ideas and to arouse public interest in the cause of education and so furthered Mann's crusade for common school reform.

Teacher Training in the United States

Generally speaking, in the early years of the nineteenth century there was little or no specific teacher training available in the United States. Little as did exist was in connection with the monitorial schools of the Lancastrian system or as a small part of the general course of studies available in the academies. The academies were the primary vehicle of secondary education and were generally under private or church control, although not infrequently assisted by state financial aid. Unlike the Latin grammar schools which were college preparatory, emphasizing the study of Latin and Greek, the academies offered a broader and more practical education featuring English, history, mathematics, and science. It was an education better suited to those who after graduation would assume the roles of farmers, businessmen, merchants, and mechanics. In addition, the academies generally differed from the Latin grammar schools in offering enrollment to young women as well as to men.

Although these academies were to be largely replaced by public high schools in the post-Civil War era, while they lasted they formed an important source of supply of teachers for the developing common school system. As early as the 1820s, some academies began introducing lectures on the "principles of teaching," and in 1834, the State of New York legislated financial aid to those academies that would undertake the training of teachers for the common school. Such teacher training classes in the academies, and subsequently in the public high schools, were not highly successful in supplying teachers in sufficient numbers or with sufficient training to meet the needs of the common schools (Harper 1939).

Other efforts for improving training took the form of teachers' institutes. The first of these was organized by Henry Barnard at Hartford in 1839. This was a class of some 26 young men, several of whom had already taught in the common schools, brought together for six weeks of instruction in the subject matter and the methods of teaching appropriate for the common schools. The idea of the teachers' institute took rapid hold and in the 1840s, various states undertook their financial support as a means of upgrading the quality of teaching in the common school. Instruction was usually provided by leading educators of the day including men of such caliber as Thomas Gallaudet, former principal and moving force behind the first American institution for the education of the deaf at Hartford; Warren Colburn, famed for his arithmetic textbook; Louis Agassiz, the renowned Harvard science teacher; and Herman Krüsi, Jr., a Swiss educator trained in the Pestalozzian system. At times these institutes, with sessions lasting anywhere from several days to several weeks, took on the characteristics of peripatetic normal schools as they were held successively in various parts of the state. In Rhode Island the institutes even included "model lessons" on different elementary school subjects. For these the instructor and his pupils were conveyed about the state in a covered wagon in order to provide the institutes with live demonstrations on "how to teach" (Monroe 1912).

In one form or another, institutes became a part of the developing state educational systems and survived down into the twentieth century. Their direct descendants may be seen in the teachers' workshops of today.

In addition to all of the foregoing efforts, beginning as early as the 1820s, there was increasing demand on the part of the leaders of common school revival for the provision of state-supported normal schools. In this agitation, effective argument was made using the various reports on the success of the Prussian training system. Legislative action was finally taken in Massachusetts in 1838, and in the following year schools at Lexington and Barre were opened in close succession. Enrollment at Lexington was limited to female students while Barre accepted both male and female candidates. Tuition was free and the projected course of study one to three years (Mangun 1928).

By 1860, twelve state normal schools existed in nine northern states, and these were supplemented by six private schools for the training of teachers. After 1865, the rate of establishment of normal schools, public and private, rapidly increased with the latter diminishing in number toward the turn of the century (Cubberley 1919).

The early normal school provided a varied curriculum of English, mathematics, geography, vocal music, physiology, philosophy, and Bible study as well as instruction in methods of teaching. As with the Prussian seminaries, elementary schools for observation and practice teaching were usually annexed to the training institution.

From the beginning, the normal schools were associated with the spread of Pestalozzian methods. All of the four Massachusetts schools existing prior to 1860 instructed in the art of teaching according to the Pestalozzian method, but the normal school at Oswego, New York, which developed from the efforts of Edward Sheldon, the city's superintendent of education, has credit for introducing and widely disseminating a more formalized type of Pestalozzian teaching which became known as the Oswego Movement (Monroe 1907, Parker 1970).

Organizational Growth and the Grading of Schools

In the course of the nineteenth and early twentieth centuries, the American public school system was to develop features other than normal schools which would increase its similarity to the much admired Prussian system. The common school, in theory open to all the children of the community (if one ignored exclusion or segregation of nonwhites*), supported by

---

*Beginning in the middle of the eighteenth century a number of Southern colonies and states had passed laws prohibiting the education of slaves, and in the 1830s some of these states even extended the prohibition to the education of free blacks. Instances of the exclusion of blacks were not unknown in the North—in 1833 a Connecticut law made it a crime to open a school for blacks in that state—but the more typical pattern in the North was the establishment of segregated schools. Following the Civil War, the South developed its segregated system of education while the North began its efforts at desegregation (Washington 1913).

public funds, and controlled by the community through its representatives was the central feature. Toward the latter part of the nineteenth century, public high schools had come to supplement the elementary grade schools even though their numbers were relatively small until their great expansion in the early twentieth century. Normal schools increased in numbers throughout this period and were transformed into degree-granting teachers' colleges. The various states—through increasing financial support of the local public schools, by the passage of school legislation relating to curriculum, attendance, academic standards, teacher certification, and by the creation of supervisory agencies and personnel—had succeeded in developing the kind of integrated public school systems that would have delighted the hearts of the leaders of the common school revival and from which Prussians themselves might have learned the art of organization.

Systematization was of course inevitable in view of the gargantuan task confronting educators and legislators alike. In 1850, when the first phase of the development of the public school system was nearing completion in the sense that universal education of the young had become generally accepted as the responsibility of the whole community, the public schools enrolled approximately 3.3 million students (Cremin 1951). In 1871, public school enrollment was slightly in excess of 7.5 million, and by 1900 it had topped 15.5 million. Of the total enrollment at this latter date, only slightly more than one-half million were enrolled in the public high schools; so the personnel and economic resources were preponderantly devoted to elementary education.

Although the private schools enrolling 1.3 million students in 1900 were independent of the mammoth public school system, we indicated how they came increasingly under state regulation and control, and so despite the dual system the general uniformity of the education process and its products were ensured (U.S. Bureau of the Census 1965).

Of the various aspects of this increased systematization of schooling there are two that are of critical importance for the development of special education. These are the grading of schools and compulsory attendance. We have already considered various aspects of the development of compulsory schooling and need now only give some attention to the grading of the school.

The Grading of the Schools

We have noted how Mann's report on the Prussian system praised the age and ability grading of the schools; grading of the American school system was one of the major objectives of the leading schoolmen prior to the Civil War.

The instructional methods of Lancaster and De La Salle had necessitated classification of pupils in terms of their levels of achievement in order to make efficient use of the techniques of simultaneous teaching. Pestalozzi had also advocated simultaneous teaching. In general the leaders of educational reform in the nineteenth century were convinced of its efficacy. But if simultaneous teaching demanded classification and grading of pupils, the organization of the common school as it existed needed extensive adjustment. The case for grading of the common school was clearly expressed by Henry Barnard in his 1845 *Report on the Condition and Improvement of the Public Schools of Rhode Island.*

Something should be done to reduce the multiplicity and variety of cares and duties which press at one and the same time, upon the attention of the teacher, and to introduce more of system and permanency into the arrangement of classes and studies in all the schools. No matter whether the school be large or small, there will be found collected into one apartment, under one teacher, children of both sexes, and of every age from four years and under, to sixteen years and upwards. This variety of age calls for a multiplicity of studies, from the alphabet to the highest branches ever pursued in well regulated academies. The different studies require at least a corresponding number of classes; and in most schools the number of classes actually required is more than doubled by the diversity of books, and of different editions of the same book, in which the same studies are pursued by different scholars. The number of classes are again increased by the differing attainments of scholars in the same study, arising out of differences in school attendance, parental cooperation, individual capacity and habits of attention. Each class requires a separate recitation, and in those studies, such as arithmetic and penmanship, in which no classification is attempted, the teacher will be obliged to give individual assistance to as many scholars as may be pursuing them, which is never less than one-half of the whole school. With so many causes at work to prevent the teacher from acting on any considerable number at a time, he is obliged to carry forward his school by individual recitations and assistance. Out of one hundred and sixty schools, from which information on this point was obtained, in 1844, there were fifty schools containing more than seventy scholars, in which the number of distinct recitations, including the classes in reading and spelling, and excluding the attention given to pupils in arithmetic and penmanship, averaged as high as twenty-three in each half day; there were one hundred and ten, numbering over fifty scholars, in which the average exceeded seventeen. The amount of time in a half-day's session, which can be made available for purposes of recitation, in most schools, with the utmost diligence on the part of the teacher, does not exceed one hundred and fifty minutes, and much of this is lost in calling and dismissing the classes, and in beginning and ending the lessons, so that an equitable distribution of the teacher's time and attention, gives but a small fragment to each class, and still less to each individual. The disadvantages under which pupils and teachers labor, in consequence of this state of things, are great and manifold. . . .

The work of education going on in such schools, cannot be appropriate and progressive. There cannot be a regular course of discipline and instruction, adapted to the age and proficiency of pupils — a series of processes, each adapted to certain periods in the development of the mind and character, the first intended to be followed by a second and the second by a third, — the latter always depending on the earlier, and all intended to be conducted on the same general principles, and by methods varying with the work to be done, and the progress already made [Barnard, cited in Brubacher 1965, pp. 78–80].

Excepting the Lancastrian schools, the ungraded school described by Barnard was the norm for school organization not only in the rural areas and small villages but even in the larger towns and cities during the first decades of the nineteenth century. Gradation of these public schools was to begin in the cities and was to obtain first between schools of different levels rather than within a school level. Despite some features unique to itself, the Boston system of public schools is illustrative of this.

Originating in Colonial times, the Boston Latin School offered college-preparatory instruction with emphasis on the study of classical languages.* Entrance into the Latin School assumed mastery of English grammar which was provided at a lower step in the system by writing and reading schools. These latter schools were organized separately under different schoolmasters even when housed in the same building and were attended alternately by the pupils. In the reading or grammar department, the students were taught spelling, reading, English grammar, and geography; in the writing department, they were taught writing and arithmetic, and at times bookkeeping. Although this vertical organization into reading and writing schools was not widely copied in other cities (its administrative inefficiency and economic wastefulness were probably all too obvious) the development of grammar schools in which the function of reading and writing schools were combined occurred from 1840 to 1862 in all of those 22 cities which the 1860 census indicated had a population of 40,000 or more. Boston itself, in 1855, was to complete its integration of the last of the reading and writing schools into a single grammar school under the direction of but one master (Rickard 1947).

According to school regulations adopted in Boston in 1789, grammar schools were intended for children from 7 to 14 years of age; the child's ability to read was a criterion for admission. The teaching of reading was left to the parents or to private enterprise such as that provided by the Dame schools which women would operate in their homes for instructing children in the elements of reading. In an earlier section we gave Henry K. Oliver's reminiscence of his attendance at such a school.

The system as described by Rickard (1948) obviously prevented the children of poor and uneducated parents from obtaining the necessary preparation for entrance into the grammar schools. There were those who expressed their concern over this state of affairs and after prolonged agitation the selectmen of Boston appointed a primary school committee in 1818 for the purpose of establishing primary schools. In its first year of operation, the committee established 18 presumably one-room schools for children between four and seven years of age.

---

*The first publicly supported English high school was established in Boston in 1821 (Brown 1918).

The committee's regulations of 1829 provided that the pupils, though housed in a single room, were to be arranged in four classes. The first or highest class was to be reading in the New Testament; the second class read easier material; the third class worked on spelling and still easier reading material; and the fourth or entrance class was to learn to read words of one syllable. There were specific requirements for promotion from one class to the next. Thus, no child was to be advanced from the fourth to the third class who would not "read deliberately and correctly in words of one and two syllables" (p. 327). No one was to be recommended by the Examining Committee for entry into the English Grammar schools "unless he or she can spell correctly, read fluently in the New Testament and has learned the several branches taught in the second class; and also the use and nature of the pauses; and is of good behavior" (pp. 327–28). Until 1855, it appeared to be the general rule that one teacher had charge of all classes in the primary school even though there might be anywhere from six to nine grades in the single room.

While gradation of the school was following such a line of development in Boston, the Lancastrian schools of New York City were following a somewhat different course. From the beginning of the Public School Society's monitorial schools, classification of students in terms of their achievement was part of the system, and students moved from one classification to the next as they mastered each step in the course of instruction. The first step, and hence the first class, consisted of those children learning to write the alphabet upon the sand tables. From there the children moved, upon the recommendation and examination of monitors, to the higher levels, with flexible grouping and regrouping of pupils according to their achievements in different subject matter areas, a system not unlike some of our recent innovations in elementary education. However, all the grading and classification of students was in a large room under the supervision of one master. The first differentiation in this system was the development of separate departments for girls and boys in 1818, although coeducation continued in some schools where the number of students and teachers made it uneconomical to run separate departments.* (Boese 1869)

The further departmentalization of the Society's schools waited until 1827, when a "Junior Department" was organized in the basement of Public School No. 8 for children as young as two years of age. This department, with an enrollment of 300 children, was placed under a woman principal assisted by a paid monitress. The Lancastrian system of organization and instruction was utilized. Around this date, the women composing the Infant School Society organized a school for children in the first years of life, under

---

*Rickard (1947) notes that this social bias for separation of the sexes in grammar schools led to some retardation in the development of graded classes. Teacher and physical plant resources that might have been utilized in the sorting of children by academic levels were spent instead on maintaining the social distinction of the sexes. As late as 1883, eight of the 22 cities in his study still made some provision for separate education of the sexes in their grammar schools.

the Pestalozzian system as they understood it. We have already given the account of the committee that the Public School Society appointed to judge the relative merits of its Junior Department run on the Lancastrian plan and this infant school. Comparison was all in favor of the Pestalozzian type school and when this was coupled with the Society's study of the Boston primary schools, it eventually led to extensive development of primary departments and schools by the Society in the 1830s.

The primary departments were housed in the same buildings with the monitorial schools for older children, but occupied a different floor level and operated independently. Rickard (1948) makes a useful distinction between the informal education of the infant school and the formal education, particularly in reading, which characterized the primary school. The infant school movement which had begun to make headway within New York City during the late 1820s soon faded not to be revitalized until the kindergarten movement toward the end of the century. Its demise was apparently due to the greater public demand for formal education of the young, and because state funds were available only for the enrollment of children over four years of age.

The primary schools were conducted in the various wards of the city and had the advantage of bringing schooling closer to the homes of the small children than the large and widely scattered public school buildings. In these primary schools, conducted by women teachers, the course of study included reading, spelling, the simple elements of arithmetic, and geography. On completion of studies in the primary departments and schools, the children were promoted to the higher departments of the public school system, where the course of study had been extended to include such secondary school topics as algebra, geometry, trigonometry, and bookkeeping. Assistant teachers and paid monitors were hired to aid the principal in the teaching of this more diversified curriculum (Boese 1869, Bourne 1870).

Thus, at the time schoolmen such as Mann and Barnard were agitating for a more efficient grading of the schools, the development was already underway in terms of the gradation of public school levels into primary and grammar schools. By 1860, all the major cities had established a system of primary and grammar schools and in some cities intermediate schools were inserted between the primary and the grammar school levels. There was also considerable variability among the cities in terms of the number of years encompassed in the course of each level of schooling. Sometimes these schools, as in Boston, had been established independently of each other. In other instances they came about simultaneously by simple division of the old one-room school into two departments (Rickard 1947, 1948).

But Mann and Barnard had been advocating an ideal of even finer grading as exemplified in the Prussian system. In Mann's *Seventh Annual Report* (1844) he pointed out how in Prussia, when numbers permitted, the teacher was placed in charge of a single class or as small a number of classes as possible, the ideal being a single class with its own teacher, housed in its own room. This too, insofar as it was feasible, became the ideal of American educators.

As indicated in Barnard's description of the one-room school, and in the description of the monitorial schools of the New York Public School Society, it is obvious that classification of pupils within a school level existed from the earliest years of the nineteenth century. Simultaneous teaching was impossible without some grouping of the children in terms of their level of achievement. What was missing was a systematic graded organization of classes conducted independently of each other, in separate rooms, each with its own teacher. Gradation between school levels such as that of primary and grammar school had prepared the way and gradually, within the different levels of school, the classes became graded. In Cubberley's description of the process:

> The third and final step in the evolution of the graded system was to build larger schools with smaller classrooms, or to subdivide the larger rooms; change the separate and independent and duplicate school on each floor, which had been the common plan for so long, into parts of one school building organization; sort and grade the pupils, and outline the instruction by years; and the class system was at hand. This process began here and there in the decade of the thirties, and was largely accomplished in the cities by 1860. In the smaller places it came later, but usually was accomplished by or before 1875. In the rural districts class grading was not introduced until the last quarter of the 19th century [Cubberley 1934a, p. 311].

John D. Philbrick, Principal of the Quincy School in Massachusetts, is generally given credit for establishing the first fully graded school in 1847. This he accomplished by the reorganization of his school on the Prussian model as espoused in Mann's report. In the following year, a new Quincy school was established under Philbrick's direction. Housed in a new building, whose design was to set a model of school architecture for years to come, this school provided for 660 pupils. There were 12 classrooms arranged on three floors, each equipped with 55 individual desks and seats, an innovation for the time. The fourth floor was entirely devoted to a large assembly hall. According to Cubberley (1934a), this was to be the standard type of city elementary school building for the next fifty years and it was to play a major role in the introduction of the graded classroom form of school organization.

In 1885, Philbrick was to write a report on the city school systems of the United States for the Commissioner of Education (Philbrick 1885). The report indicates that the general principles of the grading of schools and classes existed in all cities at that date.

> The characteristic fact in the pedagogical organization of our city schools is the division of the schools into three grades: the high, gramar, and primary. The demarcation between the primary and grammar division has no foundation in the nature of things. The grammar and primary courses of study taken together constitute the elementary course and should be considered as a whole. On the other hand, the elementary and high schools constitute two distinct categories of instruc-

tion. The high school belongs to secondary instruction, or the first stage of liberal education. Elementary education is that which is deemed essential for every citizen, whatever may be his destination, and hence it is that which is generally considered as obligatory. The high school, on the other hand, while it is desirable that it should be open to all, is not expected to give instruction to the masses of pupils. In theory there is a very considerable approximation of uniformity in respect to the upper limit of the elementary course, or, what amounts to the same thing, in respect to the line of demarcation between the grammar and high school courses. In general it is intended so to frame the elementary course, as to its stages and the amount of work to be done, that the average pupil may complete it at the age of fourteen, provided the system of instruction is conducted with sound judgment and efficiency. . . . While the lower limit of elementary education is, of course, substantially uniform in respect to the substance of the matters taught, in respect to the age it is not so, the lower limit as to age being six in a large proportion of the cities, while perhaps in a nearly equally large proportion it is five [Philbrick 1885, pp. 19-20].

The report goes on to indicate considerable variability among city systems in terms of the number of one-year divisions in each of the three grades of schools. In Western schools, there was a preference for four divisions of one year in the primary, grammar, and high schools. In New England cities, the primary course generally comprised three years and the grammar school six. Gradually, over the next two decades this variability lessened. The primary schools and grammar schools were consolidated in New York in 1897, and Boston, 1906, to form a standard eight-year elementary program of instruction capped by four years of high school.

The ideal graded common school of the reformers had now been achieved but, almost at once, difficulties appeared. A graded school system, taking a new crop of children every year at six years of age, moving them through their studies in "lock-step" fashion till graduation at fourteen makes an assumption about the equality of ability, motivation, and performance for children of similar age that the reality of individual differences was to rudely challenge. Despite all our innovations in methods, techniques, and organization of instruction, this challenge remains with us today. We shall have occasion to deal with it again in this book when we discuss the current educational scene. but now we should like to consider the problem as it appeared to the educators about the turn of the century, and to examine some of their attempted solutions in the hope that it will enrich our discussion of present-day struggles.

William Torrey Harris, the superintendent of the St. Louis school system, was one of the first to articulate the difficulty and to propose a solution. He first raised the issue in his report for the school year of 1868-69, and it was a prominent feature of his reports in subsequent years. Harris was clearly aware of the advantages of graded schools, such as increased efficiency in instruction and recitation afforded by the classification of pupils. He also prized the social stimulation that was added to the learning process when children were taught in groups of similar age and ability. But at the same time he maintained that grading and simultaneous instruction provided a kind of Procrustean bed, holding back and cramping the talented students at the same time it overstretched the abilities of duller children. In the case of talented children, there was the danger that boredom would lead to the development of poor habits of study and application. The duller child would suffer from discouragement and lowered self-esteem that might even lead to his withdrawal from school.

Harris was aware of the many factors making for different levels of performance in the graded classes. Children differed in ability and in perseverance for study. Children were started at different ages, with some more mature and better able to cope with the course of studies. Attendance figures indicated high rates of absenteeism. A child returning to school after several weeks' absence could hardly be expected to catch up on the missed work while trying to keep abreast of the new work. And if he could cover the missed work on his own, would that not disprove the efficacy of group teaching? The economic conditions of families forced some of the children to work and attend for only part of the school year. All of these factors made it impossible for a class to move along in its studies with even pace. And if a child fell behind, should he repeat a whole year even though he might have already mastered 50 or 75 percent of the work? If it happened once, it was a bitter disappointment to a child and his family. If it happened twice, the discouraged child might withdraw. There was no doubt—and subsequent investigators would bear it out—that grade retardation was correlated with withdrawal from school.

Harris's solution to the problem was to make classifications of finer gradation: to develop a system of classes not by steps of a yearly interval of work, but by irregular intervals of six to twenty weeks. Thus, a student would be moved up or down, or fall behind, by only small steps. Reclassification of the pupils would be made throughout the year. The stability of class groupings would not be too threatened because with each reclassification period a part of the more advanced students in a class would be moved up to the next higher class at the same time that a number of students would join the group from the class one step below. Harris thus envisaged a flexible, fluid progress of pupils through the graded school (Harris 1900, pp. 303-330).

Harris's system was similar to several other systems adopted in various cities during the last quarter of the nineteenth century. However, the irregular intervals for reclassification was not a feature of the plan that achieved any wide acceptance. The need for somewhat closer intervals between classes was more readily granted, and a survey included in the Report of the Commissioner of Education for 1890-1891 indicated that of 465 responding cities, 237 had adopted class intervals of less than a year with the modal interval among these being one-half year (Boykin 1894).

A different approach to the problem of individual differences and the grading of instruction was first attempted by Colonel Parker in the late 1870s in Quincy, Massachusetts, but more fully developed by John Kennedy, superintendent of schools in Batavia, New York (Cubberley 1934a; Kennedy 1914). In the Batavia plan, the simultaneous instruction, which is the raison d'être for the graded system, is supplemented by individual instruction. Kennedy first devised his plan as a solution to an overcrowded classroom situation. Instead of separating the 60 pupils into two smaller classes he opted to put an additional teacher into the room. This teacher, a Miss Lucie Hamilton, was not an assistant to the room teacher but a coordinate teacher serving a different function. While the regular classroom teacher conducted class, Miss Hamilton's role was to devote her attention to those pupils who were lagging behind in their studies in order to bring them up to grade. W. H. Holmes relates her success to a rare personality and a superior teaching power, and he notes:

> From this individual teacher, class-individual instruction took its rise. For the first time in the history of education a teacher had been assigned to deal with backward pupils in a humane way. Up to this time they had been neglected or else classed by themselves in rooms for backward pupils and with the spur that comes from an aggregation of dullness they were supposed to succeed. Now they were to be kept with their fellows and given the opportunity to succeed. And they did succeed. After a few months of class-individual instruction, it was evident that a marked change had taken place in the first of two-teacher room. Pupils who had been considered very dull began to improve, and some of them were soon up among the leaders. There was only one way to explain the really marvelous change. The reason lay in the work of the teacher, who hour after hour, and day after day, had called the retarded and backward pupils to her side to find the difficulties, and to encourage them to overcome these difficulties.
>
> There was a change not only in the working ability of the pupils, there was a change in their attitude as well. The whole atmosphere of the room was changed. all were happily at work. There were no bright pupils with nothing to do, and no dull pupils who could do nothing. The standard of work was gauged by what the ablest pupil could do, and all the pupils were soon well up to the standard [Holmes 1911, pp. 513–14].

The plan was extended to other overcrowded rooms by the use of additional coordinate teachers and the success was equally good. But reflecting upon the results, Kennedy arrived at the conclusion that the results were not due to the two-teacher plan but to the blending of two different kinds of teaching—individual instruction with group instruction. He then undertook to introduce the utilization of both kinds of teaching into the single teacher classroom (Holmes 1911).

In these single teacher classrooms, with enrollments of 50 or less, the teacher was expected to divide her time between individual instruction for those pupils having difficulty with their work and class instruction for the group as a whole. When the teacher was engaged with individual students, the remainder of the class were expected to be "working independently at their seats." Holmes assured his readers that the plan worked equally well with one or two teachers. Jones, commenting more realistically on the plan, noted that:

> It is commonly conceded that the study period is one of the most serious problems confronting us. The teacher who had tried the plan of spending a half hour instructing students singly at her desk, with forty others to be kept "engaged at their seats," will readily conceive the difficulty of supplying independent work, under such conditions, for forty students of widely varying abilities, to say nothing of the problem of discipline [Jones 1911, p. 90].

It is perhaps unfortunate that the economics of the situation was such that the Batavia plan spread more in its single teacher form that in the two-teacher form. But it does not take too much imagination to see the resurrection of the two-teacher plan in our present day use of support teachers in mainstreaming programs, which we shall discuss in detail later in this book.

A third type of solution to the individual versus class grading problem is exhibited in the Cambridge (Massachusetts) plan which provided for alternate tracks proceeding through the same course of study during a different number of years. In its final form, as utilized in Cambridge, it provided for two different divisions of students, sorted by their performance shortly after entry into school, to proceed through the same course of study in six or eight years, respectively. Thus, at the end of the third year the accelerated students would have covered as much work as the slower group would cover at the end of four years. The total course of study would be completed in six years by the accelerated group and in eight years by the slower students. There were a number of points in the parallel progression at which it was possible to switch from one track to the other without loss or repetition of work with the course then requiring some time interval between six and eight years of completion. Thus, at the end of three years a child in the fast track might be moved to the slow track or at the end of four years the child on the slow track could be moved to the fast track. In either case the child would then complete the program in seven years [Cubberley 1919: Holmes 1911].

These plans were only a few among the many which were experimented with around the turn of the century and which in various guises continue to be offered today as solutions to the thorny problem of individual differences in a class-graded educational system. It should be noted that all of these plans were essentially designed for children within the range of ability or achievement that we would generally call normal. They all assumed that the child would be capable of mastering the usual course of studies—the duller or less persevering children taking somewhat more time or requiring somewhat more teaching effort, the brighter or more motivated child capable of more rapid advancement.

We shall need to consider next the children who were not capable of mastering the usual course of study without an extension of schooling years long past those required by the compulsory education laws. For these, a special class needed to be formed—the so-called ungraded class. And the next chapter is devoted to its emergence and development.

13

The Functions of Special Education and Its Origins

IN PREVIOUS CHAPTERS we described the interaction of the various social and economic forces that powered the development of our common school system. At the turn of the century the system was essentially complete, with the class-graded school and the group method of instruction forming its very foundation. One might have assumed that it only required the effective enforcement of compulsory education laws to ensure the schoolmen's dual aim of preserving and perpetuating our society while fostering the welfare of the individual child.

We have discussed compulsory education at earlier points in this book particularly in terms of ideological conflicts between the state and minority groups. From Tyack's (1976) point of view, if not ours, much of this ideological conflict ended with the passage of compulsory education legislation and in the following bureaucratic phase, which began in the 1890s, this compulsory education legislation began to be effectively enforced. As Ensign's (1921) classic study plainly indicates, the adoption and enforcement of effective compulsory schooling laws were intimately linked with the adoption and enforcement of child labor legislation. The two issues were so interlocked that states often addressed themselves to both within the same legislative act. In Ensign's opinion, the prime movers behind this joint campaign for compulsory schooling and restrictions on child labor were not educators, but rather philanthropic interests and organized labor.

It may be that Ensign's humanitarian and economic motivational pattern is too simple an explanation for the advent of effective compulsory schooling laws. Certainly the more sophisticated analysis of Tyack (1976) demonstrating how various political, bureaucratic, and economic explanatory models are needed to depict the different levels of social reality is more compelling. However, we suspect that Ensign was at least partially right in his contention that schools and teachers had an inconspicuous place in the development of public support for the passage of more adequate laws for the protection and education of children. As he bluntly charged, "Teachers have

261

not been anxious to receive in their well-ordered classes those who, by taste or necessity, placed foremost the bread-winning pursuits," and "school officials empowered to enforce attendance laws often have persistently declined to discharge their duty" (Ensign 1921, p. 234).

Burgess (1976) has recently added another perspective to our understanding of the development of compulsory schooling laws by placing such laws in a broad social context of a general societal response to the disorder brought about by the Civil War and the subsequent rapid industrialization and technological growth. This response is viewed as an attempt to foster social stability and promote a sense of nationhood by the utilization of legislation to define "loyalty" and Americanism according to a consensus. The legislation was designed to supplant local informal persuasion and local formal regulation of behavior by state and federal standards. During the half century between the Civil War and World War I, there were repeated attempts to legislate compulsory voting, monogamy, national rules on divorce, obscenity, and compulsory teetotaling. Compulsory schooling was only one of the endeavors to legislate behavior that formerly was left to individual or local control. Burgess notes that Herbert Spencer, observing these efforts to establish new codes of standardized behavior across the land, had called it an American penchant for "moral trespassing."

At any rate, the effective enforcement of school attendance in the 1890s posed a problem to educators and presented an immediate need for a radical adjustment upon the part of the "lock-step," class-graded common school. This was to take the form of the development of ungraded classes for truants, discipline problems, backward children, and non-English speaking children. Previously, children with such traits or tendencies had either drifted out or were forced out of the class-graded school. It is to the development of these ungraded classes, particularly as they became specialized for the educationally backward child, that we now turn our attention.

Functions and Definitions of
Special Education Programs and Ungraded Classes

To the educators at the turn of the century, the relationship between compulsory education laws and the development of special education programs was readily recognized and admitted. James Van Sickle, Superintendent of the Baltimore Public Schools, noted in an article prepared for the *Psychological Clinic* (1908–9), that before attendance at school was enforced by law the superintendent of Philadelphia had reported that there were not enough backward children in any neighborhood in his city to form a special class. But by 1900, there were 1,122 children in his schools too backward for the usual grade instruction. Van Sickle acknowledged that the experience of

Philadelphia was the experience of Baltimore and doubtless of all large communities, and he maintained that "Before the attendance laws were effectively enforced there were as many of these special cases in the community as there are now; few of them, however, remained long enough in school to attract serious attention or to hinder the instruction of the more tractable and capable" (p. 102).

Van Sickle went on to explicate further the motivation for special classes:

> If it were not for the fact that the presence of mentally defective children in a school room interfered with the proper training of the capable children, their education would appeal less powerfully to boards of education and the tax-paying public. It is manifestly more expensive to maintain small classes for backward and refractory children, who will profit relatively little by the instruction they receive, than to maintain large classes for children of normal powers. But the presence in a class of one or two mentally or morally defective children so absorbs the energies of the teacher and makes so imperative a claim upon her attention that she cannot under these circumstances properly instruct the number commonly enrolled in a class. School authorities must therefore greatly reduce this number, employ many more teachers, and build many more school rooms to accommodate a given number of pupils, or else they must withdraw into small classes these unfortunates who impede the regular progress of normal children. The plan of segregation is now fairly well established in large cities, and superintendents and teachers are working on the problem of classification, so that they may make the best of this imperfect material. Whether or not school boards really approve spending money upon the education of mentally defective children, the enforcement of the compulsory attendance laws leaves no other course open. We are committed to their education so far as their capacity permits. The movement for their education is supported on other grounds by those who are not very much, if at all, concerned with the financial side and the need of protecting the rights of the more capable children. The investigations of modern science, as well as the philanthropic sentiments that actuate people in every community, have reinforced the practical and economic arguments which were the primary considerations whenever public school authorities have formed special classes [Van Sickle, 1908-09, pp. 102-103].

Prominent in Van Sickle's argument for special classes are first, the economic consideration that special children can be taught in regular classrooms only if the total number of pupils in such classes are reduced, and second, teaching effectiveness: "the rights of normal children cannot be safeguarded when 50 percent of the energy of the teacher is expended on 5 percent of the pupils in the class" (p. 111). But Van Sickle was not unmindful of the advantages that might accrue to the special child when such classes were organized according to the nature of the difficulty and the proper training prescribed to make the child—backward, defective or refractory as the case might be—a self-supporting, useful citizen.

This general perception of the twofold utility of special classes appears in much of the literature on special education programs appearing shortly after the turn of the century. In many of these reports, teacher narratives would also suggest that a prime mover for the setting up of special classes must have been the regular classroom teacher who in her overcrowded urban classroom was driven to distraction by disciplinary problems with unwilling pupils and the frustration of trying to bring laggards up to the pace of the rest of the class.

A little noted derivative value of special education classes rarely alluded to in the literature of the time was their influence on educational practice in the regular classroom. Martin Barr, Chief Physician at the Pennsylvania School for Feebleminded Children at Elwyn, Pennsylvania, although not considering special classes in the public schools, had at an earlier time expressed himself on what teachers of normal children could learn from the teachers of defective children. Chief among those lessons was the studying of each child's individuality, and the adjustment of the teaching to that individuality. His prescription was: "To individualize standards for the day's work; requiring not so rigidly that each shall accomplish the same task, as that each shall exercise his or her capacity to its full measure in the given task. In other words, to require the best the child can do and to demand no more" (Barr 1903, p. 55). It was not a prescription easily adapted to the overcrowded, lock-step urban classroom.

That such influence on the regular classroom did exist and might well provide an additional rationale for the establishment of special classes was argued before the National Education Association in 1908 by E. R. Johnstone, Superintendent of a residential school for the feebleminded at Vineland, New Jersey. Beginning about 1903, Vineland had become actively involved in the training of public school teachers for special education classes and Johnstone spoke with considerable knowledge and experience.

> The special class must be what the up-to-date institution of today endeavors to be; viz., the laboratory for the public-school classes. Already it is interesting to note how the teachers in the primary grades go to the special class teacher to learn how she accomplishes, with subnormal children, results which they find difficult to obtain with their normal children. It is interesting to note how easily the truant is kept in school as soon as he gets to the special class. Here his interests are made paramount and the routine of the school is secondary. Working with special children makes us realize and see in a new light the statement of the Master, "A little child shall lead them." I firmly believe that our most advanced ideas on educational procedure will come from the study of "special" children and their mental processes. . . . The normal child observed by its teacher is seen as is the automobile going at twenty miles an hour. His mental processes are so rapid that she can learn but little of them. It is a fleeting glance and he is gone. Our children are slowed down and some go at four miles an hour, some at two, and some are standing still. We study them as we please. We may get to understand many of their mental processes. But their mental processes are the same as those of the normals. The difference is one of degree, not of kind. That is why we teachers of feeble-minded people are bold enough to come to you and say, "It should be done this way." We have been in the automobile. We have driven it. Because we dare

not undertake to teach a child something which in our case takes two or three years, but with the normal child would take only two or three months, and fail, we must constantly ask ourselves of what use will this be to the child. It seems to me that this is a question that might well be asked of many things in the curriculum for the normal child. We are not quite ready to prove, altho nearly so, that your courses of study for primary and intermediate children must be radically changed. There is so much stuff in the course which will never be used excepting to pass an examination for a teacher's license in order that the teacher may impose it upon her pupils so that they may pass a teacher's examination, and teach other pupils, etc. We are sure that your arithmetic with first- and second-year pupils is wrong, and as the Scotch woman said, "we hae our doots" of your reading and geography, etc.

The special class is showing the great value of industrial training and demonstrates at every turn that normal children must get more away from book-learning and do things. We do not claim great knowledge because we asked for this many years ago. It was simply forced upon us because of the class of children with whom we work. Is it not fair to say that no matter when a child leaves school, he should know those things which will best equip him for the life he will probably lead, and is it not part of the work of the educator to find out what kind of life most of his children will lead, if they leave school before the college period?

Perhaps the greatest lesson the special class has for the regular class teacher is the need of making the children happy in their work. If the children do not want to go to school, surely there is something wrong with the school [Johnstone 1908, pp. 1116-1117].

There is undoubtably considerable evidence to support Johnstone's contention that the special education class — whether in an institution or in a public school — can serve as a testing laboratory to develop educational practices adaptable to the normal child. One need only recall how work with the mentally subnormal performed by Seguin, Howe, and Montessori influenced educational practices in the nineteenth and twentieth centuries, particularly at the primary grade levels. And certainly in our own time, the work of clinicians and educators on the problems of the dyslexic child have not been without influence on our new approaches to teaching reading to the normal child (Money 1966).

However, we suspect that the development of the self-contained special education class in the public school around the turn of the century prevented the kind of input from the special educator to the regular classroom teacher that Johnstone envisaged. It remains to be seen if the present-day trend for mainstreaming special children will promote the kind of communication between the special educator and the regular classroom teacher that will facilitate the latter's work not only with her special pupils but with her normal children as well. This issue of mainstreaming which essentially challenges the legitimacy of the arguments which educators made at the turn of the century for the segregation of special children into ungraded classes, is one to which we shall return.

A function of the special class that appears more frequently in the early literature is that which Johnstone refers to as that of a "clearing house."

> The special class must become a clearing-house. To it will not only be sent the slightly blind and partially deaf, but also the incorrigibles, the mental deficients, and cripples. In the beginning it must be expected that more than one of these types will be found in the same classroom, and indeed all of them may drift in. The teacher must not become discouraged. As a better understanding comes there will be closer differentiation and separation will be more complete. In the case of the mental deficients, many children of comparatively low grade will drift into the classes. Indeed there are now in special classes thruout the country many who are actually feeble-minded and imbecile [Johnstone 1908, p. 1115].

Explicating this further, Johnstone recognized the inadequacy of institutional provisions for the care of all defectives.

> Public-school men may say, "This is not our problem." To say this means nothing. The children are here; they are present in the public school in large numbers. They cannot be turned out. What are they going to do about it? The only thing to do is to give them the best care and training possible. Keep them in the special classes until they become too old for further care in the school, and then they must be sent to the institutions for safety, or they must be transferred to their homes, if they are such as can be trusted there. As I said, the special classes must be the clearing-houses [Johnstone 1908, p. 1115].

Others using this concept of a "clearing house" for the special class apparently did not think of the child remaining in the school for any great length of time but rather that the special class was to form a sort of "way stop" on the route to the institution. David Lincoln (1903, 1909) of the Boston school system, W. C. Martindale (1912-13) of Detroit, and Grace Boehme (1909-10) of Cleveland, all accepted this clearinghouse function as one of the aims of their special classes. As expressed by Grace Boehme:

> We appreciate fully the inheritance these children always give their offsprings and if these special classes were to be used only as "clearing houses" they would more than pay for themselves each year by the removal of several cases a year who would not only eventually end in the almshouse or institution but take their offspring with them, if left at large. It may be of interest to note here that each year during the past four years, from four to six children have been placed in institutions through our special classes. Of course there are many who can never and should never be placed in an institution. Many of these are the children of illiterate parents — hard-working but ignorant people. Doubtless their fathers could not read before them and the problem is still harder for the children. But by our special methods used we do teach them to read and "count their letters" independently, and enough arithmetic to get along in their small world [Boehme 1909-10, p. 84].

A final argument for the education of the defective child in the public school, not often expressed in those days when so many advocated residential care as the ideal solution, was voiced by S. P. Goodhart (1904, p. 200) who argued that in the newly developing special schools "the defectives shall have the advantage of home environment and parental, family, and friendly encouragement." This argument in advance of its day was eventually, after World War II, to be extended to the care of even the more severely retarded institutionalized child and helped to bring about the development of day-care and training facilities in close proximity to the populations for which they were designed.

A major problem confronting us, as we review this early literature to perceive the pattern of growth in special education, is the often vague and shifting terminology employed in the description of both children and programs. The term auxiliary school may refer to one or more classes housed in the same building with regular public school classes or it might mean a class or several classes for special pupils housed separately and administered independently of the regular public schools. Or, such a setup as the latter might be referred to as a "center" for special classes with no clear indication of its administrative tie to the neighboring public school. The same kind of pupils might be referred to as backward, feebleminded, defective, or atypical, or these terms might be used for more or less clearly differentiated categories of children. Other favorite terms in the literature are ungraded classes or opportunity rooms. In one school system the ungraded classes might include slow learners, the mentally subnormal, epileptics, learning disabilities, chronic truants, behavior problem children, physically handicapped or immigrant children suffering from language or cultural handicaps. In another school system, or even within another school in the same district, the term might be used for a class quite homogeneous in the nature of its handicaps.

When one is lucky, the context of a term is sufficiently rich to permit a reasonable estimate as to the nature of the special education program and the type of child enrolled. In reviewing some of the literature we will try to concern ourselves with the development of special education classes—whatever they might be called—in the narrow sense of the term used by Whipple in Monroe's *Encyclopedia of Education* (1913): "public day school classes for children of mental subnormality."

As the reader will shortly see, these classes were often not the first ungraded or special classes to be founded in American school systems. The first classes set up outside the graded classes were most frequently for discipline problems or truants who were forced into the system by the compulsory education laws. Only gradually did various specialized education programs such as that for the mentally subnormal differentiate themselves from these first classes which had become repositories for all kinds of children who did not fit into the regular classroom. Therefore, the reader may experience confusion when an ungraded class such as that first established by Miss Farrell in New York City is referred to in one article as a class for truants and in another as a class for the mentally subnormal. Both types of children were present and depending upon a particular author's purpose or knowledge it will be designated as either a class for truants or feebleminded children.

European Influences

The formation of special education classes originated in Germany. Even England, though lagging behind Germany, got off to a slightly faster start than the United States, and the development of both these European special education programs had sufficient influence on our progress to give them some brief attention. This is not to say that our development was not basically endogenous. If the common school system itself was a response to the development of the modern, industrialized state, the development of special education programs was just as inevitably a response to the development of the common school system itself. Without any influence from abroad our system would have originated and developed much in the way it did. On the other hand, there is no doubt that European ideas, curricula, instructional methods, and principles of organization did facilitate the growth of our programs. It is also interesting to note, even in our necessarily brief account, how the European experts could be as divided in their perception of the problem of special education and its proposed solutions as we ourselves.

The most likely origins of the special class for mentally subnormal children occurred in Halle, Prussia, in 1859, when Principal Haupt received permission from his school board to establish "a special class for defective children." Those children who were not making progress in the regular folk school were provided with two hours of daily instruction by a folk school teacher specifically assigned to this task (Maennel 1907, Kanner 1964). From this there gradually developed within Germany a system of "auxiliary" classes and schools for the education of the mentally retarded so that by 1905, there was estimated a total number of 583 classes in 181 cities giving instruction to 11,923 pupils (Maennel 1907).

The rationale for the formation of these special education programs within the German public school system, as reviewed by Maennel, is not very different from that which was formulated in the development of the American system of special education for the retarded. It included such components as relieving the child of the frustration and stigma of repeated failure in the regular grades; giving the child's needs special attentions in smaller classes with a program of instruction specifically matched to his abilities; and increasing the efficiency of the regular classroom by removing those children who by their behavior or need for extra tutoring reduced the time and effort the teacher could devote to the progress of the large majority of the class. But even then the segregation of these children in either special classes or special schools was not without its critics, and some of the controversies are still being sounded out anew in our own time.

One of the early controversies concerned the organization of auxiliary schools versus auxiliary classes closely integrated within the folk schools. The city authorities of Berlin resisted the general trend represented by other German cities which opted for separation of the special classes from the folk schools. In an official report of 1898-99, they argued for the education of the retarded as follows:

> A considerable number of cities have sought to obtain this philanthropic object by the establishment of special schools (auxiliary schools). We have not undertaken this for two reasons: In the first place, the distances to school would become too great; but in the second place, the definitive assignment of children to such a school would place upon them the stamp of inferiority for all time, and often prematurely. We follow the plan of retaining the child as a pupil in his own district, of placing him for instruction in small classes, and of bringing him back into association with the other children as soon as possible. While we now begin special instruction with the children of the lowest classes, our plan is, step by step and according to the quality of the pupils, to add to the lowest auxiliary class a higher one, and so on, but always with the purpose of replacing the special instruction as soon as possible by the regular [Maennel 1907, pp. 14-15].

Pupils were assigned to these auxiliary classes only if they had attended the regular classes for two years without progress. Class size did not exceed 12 children, markedly below the 70 or so pupils that might be assigned to the primary class of a folk school of this period. Nevertheless, Maennel argues that these classes did not achieve the fixed purpose of Berlin's school officials, which was the return of the children from the special instruction back to the regular class. In 1903, from 91 special classes with an enrollment of 1,302 pupils, only 65 were returned to the regular classes. Therefore, Maennel was in favor of the independent auxiliary school and the advantages that could accrue from consolidation of staff, pupils, and facilities in an independent unit.

In addition to the controversy as to how special instruction should be organized, there were some who objected in principle to the segregation of the mentally subnormal in any form, and Maennel presents the arguments of J. H. Witte even as he rebuts them. Witte, objecting to the establishment of auxiliary schools, maintained that these schools withdrew the mentally deficient pupils from the helpful influence of the more gifted and he advocated mixing "one-third weak-minded pupils among two-thirds strong" (Maennel 1907, p. 28).

It is interesting that these German school systems so far in the advance of the rest of Europe in identifying the problem of the mentally subnormal in the public schools and in seeking an appropriate response to the need should have been so long content to draw the needed teachers of the auxiliary schools either from the staffs of the folk schools or from the educational institutions and asylums for the blind, the deaf, and the mentally defective. At any rate, it was not until after Zurich in 1899 had established a course for teachers in special schools, that Jena in 1904 developed in the pedagogical department of the vocational schools a training program specially designed to meet the needs of auxiliary school teachers. This program "Presented lectures regarding defects of character in childhood and youth, child psychology, the auxiliary schools system, difficulties of speech in childhood, the physiology of the brain, and demonstrations by reference to meagerly endowed and defective children" (Maennel 1907). Our own American efforts at training special class teachers were to follow a not dissimilar development with heavy reliance on summer school programs attached to institutions for the retarded, the normal schools, and colleges.

Subsequent to the initial developments in Germany, special classes and day schools for the mentally subnormal spread throughout much of Europe (Kanner 1964). We need to glance briefly at the programs in England for these, in general following the German model (Pritchard 1963, p. 121) were a more direct influence upon our efforts.

Beginning in the 1890s, the *Journal of Psycho-Asthenics* presented for American professionals a series of articles on the development of special classes both within the States and in Europe. One of the earliest of these was a report based on information supplied by Dr. Shuttleworth (1899), indicating that the London school board opened its first "Special Class" for the instruction of the feebleminded in 1892.* By the spring of 1899, London had special class accommodations for over 1,800 children. The London Board regulations restricted class size to 20 pupils and the per pupil cost of this special education was estimated to be twice that of regular students. This is one of the earliest indications in the journal literature of the economic factor in special education programs. The development of special education in England was furthered by an 1899 act of Parliament indicating that where defective children existed in a district, education should be provided by one of several methods, including classes in public schools certified by the education department as special classes, establishing schools certified for defective children, by boarding out children near such schools or class (Shuttleworth, 1899).

These European special classes and schools had their influence on our American programs not only by their reports in the American journals but also by extensive visits to Europe by a number of the leaders of the education of the retarded in this country, such as Walter Fernald, superintendent of the Massachusetts School for the Feebleminded; Henry H. Goddard, Director of the Research Laboratory at the Vineland Training School; and Elizabeth Farrell, the moving force in the development of New York City's ungraded classes for the mentally subnormal.

*According to Pritchard (1963), the establishment of the first class for the feebleminded in a British Board School occurred in Leicester several months before the opening of the London special class.

The reports of Fernald (1903–04) and Goddard (1908) are interesting for the rather jaundiced view they displayed at that time of the potential effectiveness of the education and training of the mentally subnormal in the public schools. The work of both men was principally related to institutional care and they shared a eugenical concern about the dangers of the unlimited reproduction of hereditary feeblemindedness. Both men felt that the lifelong care and segregation of the feebleminded was necessary if society was to have any hope of controlling the social problems of vice, crime, and poverty stemming from feeblemindedness. In that fear and in their proposed solution of permanent institutionalization for the feebleminded they reflected attitudes common to many professional and intellectual leaders in the first decades of the twentieth century. We refer the reader to Sarason and Doris (1969) for a fuller account of this period in our social history when the mentally subnormal were seen as a major menace to society.

To Fernald and Goddard, although they were subsequently to modify their positions, the only reasonable place for the care of the mentally subnormal was in the residential training institution. They accepted training in the public schools only because the sheer numbers of the retarded as they perceived them precluded the construction of sufficient institutional housing to provide for them all. Failing the ideal solution of permanent segregation, they accepted the need for training in public schools to reduce to some extent the propensity of the mentally subnormal to engage in lives of vice and crime in a setting of vicious poverty.

Since the literature is not always specific as to the traits possessed by the children in the special classes, it is of some interest to note the descriptions that Fernald and Goddard applied to the children they observed in the English special classes. According to Fernald, the defective children were designated by the teacher if unfit for promotion after two years in one grade. They were then examined by a medical expert who certified to the mental defect and the need for instruction in the special schools. These children were classified in the English system as feebleminded, ranking above the imbecile or idiotic classification (consigned to the state institutions) but not capable of being properly taught in ordinary elementary schools by ordinary methods. They appeared able to benefit from the individual attention and modified instruction of the special classes, and at the age of thirteen or fourteen achieved a stage of elementary instruction equal to that of ordinary children at eight or nine years of age. In addition, they were often capable of being trained in some manual occupation. Fernald records his impression as follows:

In the schools that I examined the pupils seemed distinctly inferior, both mentally and physically, to the pupils found in the school departments of the American institutional schools for the feeble-minded. I saw very few pupils of the same degree of intelligence as the brighter school classes at Elwyn, Syracuse and Columbus; and the standard of nutrition and bodily vigor seemed decidedly below that of pupils in American institutions or in the English institutions [Fernald 1903–04, p. 31].

This unfavorable comparison of elementary pupils in the English special classes to the American institutionalized children can be explained in part by the fact that nearly all of the American institutions for the mentally subnormal were organized as strictly educational institutions. Fernald quotes Samuel G. Howe's description of his institution for the mentally subnormal as "a link in the chain of common schools, the last link indeed, but still a necessary link in order to include all the children in the state" (Fernald 1903–04, p. 32). From the time of Howe's beginning work in 1848 until the time of Fernald's article, nearly all of the American institutional schools gave preference to the new pupils with lesser degrees of mental defect as offering greater opportunity for improvement. The admission of lower grade defective children and the retention of adults in custodial care came about only gradually over the course of the existence of these institutions.

Goddard, making a visit a few years after Fernald, noted that in 1908 London as a result of compulsory education had 6,000 children in its special education classes, all "feebleminded or highgrade imbeciles." Of these, 5,000 were in the opinion of the chief medical examiner institution cases. In one class Goddard noted two hydrocephalic cases, two microcephalic, and one mongoloid. In another class he noted a cretin. Goddard felt constrained to agree with the medical examiner that fully five-sixths of the children in the special classes were institutional cases. At this point in his career Goddard had considerable experience with mental subnormality and we are inclined to accept his specific diagnoses of hydrocephalic and microcephalic children. But when he refers to five-sixths of the children as institution cases we have to keep in mind Fernald's description of what the usual American institutional case was in those days. It was what we would call in our current terminology an educable child. We need also keep in mind that this is the same Goddard whose trained field workers had such "uncanny" success in selecting by cursory inspection mental defectives from the lines of immigrants at Ellis Island! But such success was probably not all that uncanny in view of the fact that Goddard's Binet testing of the same immigrant groups indicated from 40 to 80 percent as feebleminded (Sarason and Doris 1969).

The work of Elizabeth Farrell in the New York City school system will shortly concern us in detail but at this point we would like to limit ourselves to her report on the special classes of Great Britain that she submitted to the city's Department of Education in 1903. In that report she had particular focus on "a large body of children who, after an examination more or less scientific, were set apart as fit subjects for classes of special instruction" (p. 244). Her interest derived from the setting up of the first of New York City's ungraded classes. This had caused her to question "what particular kind of child could be educated only in a special class" (p. 244).

She presumed that such a child must not be of too low a mental power because then he would properly belong in an institution, and that he must not be a truant unless his truancy was the result of "some lack in his own make-up and not to poor teaching and unpleasant school surroundings" (p. 244). With that question and those presumptions she observed some 1,000 children in twenty Board Schools with particular attention given to four schools comprising 250 children. Her observations are of particular interest in that in contrast to Fernald and Goddard she resorts less to summary diagnostic labels of feebleminded and imbecile and gives more detailed descriptions of the children and their environments.

> Since it was the child and not the methods used in educating him which was of primary importance, His Majesty's Inspector of Special Schools in England and Wales gave me a list of Board Schools where he considered the children to be types of mental defectives. In the Hugh Myddleton Schools, the children came from one of the slum districts of London, and the mental defect probably arose from the poor physical environment, poor food, lack of care, and badly ventilated sleeping rooms. The St. Clements Road School, Nottingdale, London, had children from a neighborhood known as being the home, if home it may be called, of the criminal classes. These children, with an inheritance of crime and lawlessness coming through generation after generation, seemed to have no moral sense at all and were classified as moral imbeciles. The Bloomsbury Road Board School in Birmingham had the children of skilled workmen, children whose condition was supposed to be the result of illness or accident [Farrell 1903, p. 245].

The description of these particular schools, insofar as they might be representative of the English Board Schools designed for "mental defectives," would suggest that in large part they were schools in the slums of the cities. Miss Farrell continues with a description of the children themselves:

> After a careful consideration of all these children of varying degrees of mental power, the impressive fact was that in many if not most cases it was not mental power alone that was lacking, but that there was a most positive and pronounced lack in the child's whole physical organism. In nearly every school were startling evidences of neurosis. Many children were suffering from St. Vitus's dance, infantile paralysis, epilepsy or meningitis, and the child tainted with tuberculosis or some other hereditary disease was always in evidence. As a whole the children were anemic—children with thin arms and legs; pinched, old-looking, sad little faces; large unwieldy joints, which told of malnutrition early in life; children stunted, unkempt, and uncared for—these were the subjects of special school instruction. With all the evidences of sin and poverty and ignorance were other more or less pronounced physical marks of mental deficiency. The cranial and facial abnormalities, the malformed palate, the protruding, flaplike ears, the open mouth, the suggestion of drooling and the diseased misshapen teeth, all told a truth to one whose experience allowed him to read and interpret [Farrell 1903, p. 246].

We lack the experience to read mental deficiency from malformed palates, flaplike ears, open mouths, and diseased misshapen teeth, and only the extremes of cranial and facial abnormalities would lead us to suspect mental subnormality but then we would never have been able like Goddard and his field workers to pick out *at a glance* the feebleminded from the waiting lines of immigrants at Ellis Island. This is not to say that we would suspect that all or even a large proportion of the children observed by Fernald, Goddard, and Farrell in the British special education classes were not mentally subnormal.

What we would be willing to say about the detailed description that Farrell provides is that these are in large part the children of poverty; malnourished, ill, and neglected. The degree to which poverty, malnourishment, illness, and neglect were accompanied by mental subnormality is in our estimation moot. However, in fairness to Miss Farrell and perhaps to Goddard it ought to be pointed out that at that time, prior to the introduction of the Binet tests, it was widely believed that mental subnormality was almost invariably accompanied by physical defects and signs. Thus the importance assigned to the role of the medical examiner in this developing English system of special education. To a considerable extent the importance of the physician's role was also accepted in the early programs set up in American city school systems. The physician was not only expected to identify real problems of health or sensory defect that might account for the child's educational backwardness, but he was also to note in the healthy child those subtle signs that were indicative of feeblemindedness or imbecility. In discussing the position of some English physicians — expert in the area of mental subnormality at the turn of the century — Pritchard notes:

> doctors . . . believed they could detect imbecility by physical signs. Moreover, they declared that the same signs, in a less marked degree, would indicate that the children concerned were feeble-minded and could not be taught in the ordinary schools by the ordinary methods. Thus, educational judgments were being based upon physical manifestations. Warner had already reduced to a system the means of detecting weak-minded children by nervous signs, and he would only admit to a special class those children who had visible defects. Fletcher Beach, who had been Medical Superintendent of Darenth, had also devised a test of feeble-mindedness. Among other things, he looked for malformation of the head, a V-shaped palate, large, coarse, outstanding ears, a fixed stare, a curved little finger, and distractibility noticeable by a constant movement of the eyes. Beach felt that his test was more efficient than Warner's for detecting feeble-mindedness, but agreed with Warner that only a medical man was capable of diagnosing mental weakness. However, he cast some doubt on the practicability of his system when he stated that there were not more than six doctors in England capable of discriminating between imbeciles and feebleminded children [Pritchard 1963, p. 137].

With such physicians having the final say in the placement of English children in the special classes, Farrell's observations on the physical condition of the children could only be a reflection of the reality; and her inference that these physical signs and conditions were evidence of "mental deficiency" was in accord with some of the best expert opinion of the day.

This pathognomonic touchstone of physical stigmata in the diagnosis of the mental subnormality of school children would in the course of the next decade give way to the intelligence test score. One may have some question as to whether this provided an increase or decrease in the validity of the diagnostic criterion but the reliability with which it singled out the children of poverty seems to have remained constant!

Developments in Special Education in the United States: 1896–1910

The Establishment of Special Education Classes in the Public Schools

Whipple's (1913) wider and more generic definition of a special class designated "any form of class provided for a group of children who are in some way exceptional and who cannot, therefore, be instructed to advantage in the regular classes of the school system, either because they fail to receive the instruction suited to their special needs or because they receive such instruction at the expense of the remainder of the class" (p. 384). Special classes falling under this designation were established at least as early as the 1870s. Wallin (1924) notes the opening of a public school special class for the deaf in Boston in 1869, a truancy class in New York in 1874, and a disciplinary class in Cleveland somewhat later in the seventies.

Cleveland also may have made the first attempt—abortive though it proved to be—to establish a special class in Whipple's narrower sense of a public day school class for children of subnormal mentality. According to Steinbach's account, in 1875:

> About fourteen of the most serious cases of imbecility in the most congested quarters of the town were gathered together and a superior, conscientious teacher placed in charge. The good folk responsible for this inauguration were united in their belief that the pupils would soon become as normal children, once they were properly taught. The teacher heroically attacked the problem, but before the close of the year, all were aware that their experiment was doomed to failure. At the close of the term the class was disbanded—the imbeciles returned to their homes, probably not much the worse for their "schooling," but the poor teacher suffered a mental collapse which necessitated a sojourn at our State Hospital [Steinbach 1918-1919, p. 104].

Further attempts to develop programs specifically for the mentally subnormal were delayed to the 1890s. And the history of such efforts are with rare exceptions quite difficult to follow. Generally speaking, special classes, ungraded classes, opportunity rooms or whatever they might be called, were often repositories for many different kinds of children who could not adapt to the regular graded classes. Even when they were initially designed for a homogeneous group—and most often this was for truancy or discipline cases — other types of special children were soon assigned to the group. This is clearly indicated in the history of the Providence, Rhode Island, special classes and it was Providence's attempt in 1896 to reassort the children in its disciplinary classes that originated the first successful program of special education for the mentally subnormal in American public schools. Rhoda Esten, supervisor of special schools in Providence gave the following account not long after the establishment of the program:

> These schools are an outgrowth of our schools for special discipline and instruction. Our teachers in the regular schools found so much relief when disorderly pupils were transferred to the disciplinary schools, that they were not slow to request the removal of backward or mentally deficient children, who were receiving comparatively little benefit in their schools, to the same school for special instruction. There were soon collected in Hospital street and Ashmont street schools a number of pupils of this class. It was at once apparent that the discipline, instruction and physical exercises necessary for the development of the bright, healthy, active and mischievous boys, who constituted the great majority of the pupils in these schools, were ill-adapted to these feeble plodding ones; also, that it was not well in other respects for these pupils to be thrown together; hence in December, 1896, a special school was opened on Burnside street for the better treatment of these pupils. Fifteen pupils were placed here under the charge of Miss E. Gertrude Tift, a teacher selected from our corps of primary teachers on account of her special adaptability for the work. The same condition obtaining in Mt. Pleasant disciplinary school the following year, another school was opened in December, 1897, also a third in Orms street in December, 1898. A fourth room in Harrison street school is now used partly for this purpose [Esten 1900, pp. 11-12].

Neither Esten's report nor Legarde's (1903) subsequent report on the Providence schools would suggest in the description of the students or the nature of the curriculum that these schools constituted special classes in other than Whipple's narrow sense of classes for the mentally subnormal. But it would also appear evident from the reports that these children were functioning at a level that would be termed educable by today's standards. Esten specifically states that:

> The high grade of feeble-minded or backward children found in our schools are but slightly mentally defective; indeed, so nearly normal are some of them that their defects would only be noticeable to a discerning teacher or to the persons who made a study of this class, and many are bright and attractive in appearance, but all are weak in will power, deficient in reasoning power and judgment, hence, easily influenced for evil. Unless they are properly cared for and educated, they will retrograde, fall into evil ways and become victims of the vicious [Esten 1900, p. 13].

Ellen Legarde (1903), director of physical training for the Providence schools, makes much of the lack of coordination of these children, and the frequency of speech defects. She notes also "the pale, flabby-face, the dull or ever-shifting eye, the protruding ears, open mouth, low receding forehead, the restless or apathetic body, and other physical evidence of poor bodily or mental stamina" (p. 38). She is concerned about their nutritional status and recommends they be given a midday meal. But she describes a curriculum which includes reading, numbers, geography, and language work, albeit with appropriate adjustments to the backwardness of the pupils. In addition there is sewing, weaving, and basketry for hand and eye training, and Swedish exercises in gymnastics for coordination. With such a program she maintains that 80 percent of the children are cured.

> By cured one does not mean made into Edisons, Marconis or Roosevelts, but lifted up to better things. Oscar, who greets me in the big department shop where he is a cash-boy, is able to be an intelligent cash-boy, slow of speech to be sure, but patient and painstaking. Angelina May, who at fourteen used to follow me noisily on the streets and insist I note her new gown or shoes, is now at twenty in a jewelry shop packing cheap jewelry and putting what was once a restless, talkative, never concentrated self into quiet, well directed, energetic labor. Jacob and Annie will never be any better, but they can read and write, know right from wrong and have been taught that cleanliness is a necessary part of life, as well as good manners. John and Susie and Maude are back in the grades, not brilliant but doing as well as their limited abilities will allow. Not disgraced because they were "born short" but aided and encouraged to make the best possible of what is in them. Such are the types. Few are lost, many saved, all improved [Legarde 1903, p. 38].

With such a success story, it is not surprising that other cities attempted to follow suit. However, in most of these cities the separation of different types of special children into different classes was not as clear-cut as was apparently the case in Providence. Springfield, Massachusetts, may have been as close to the Providence model of homogeneity in a class for the mentally subnormal as is possible to find in those early years. Springfield is generally given credit for establishing the second class for the mentally subnormal in an American school in 1898. Frances Cheney's (1903–04) account of five years' experience "in teaching a class of mentally defective children" is instructive in providing details on the nature of the children enrolled in the program. In five years, thirty boys and five girls were in attendance. Ages upon entrance were from six to fourteen years. Eighteen of the children attended the school for one year or less. Seventeen remained two to five years.

> Eleven were not distinctly feeble-minded, but appeared to be hopelessly behind the work of the grade they were in, and were too old to be placed in lower grades. One of these eleven soon left school to go to work, and the remaining ten were promoted, six of them to grade schools and four to ungraded grammar preparatory schools. The six who were promoted to grade work are doing well in grades from second to sixth. Nine have gone to work and are earning in factories from sixty cents to one dollar a day. Of these nine, three were distinctly feeble-minded, and the remaining six below the average in mental ability. One only who has left school is unemployed. This boy is a low-grade defective and should be placed in the state institution at Waverley. Three have been lost track of by removal from the city.

One has been sent to Waverley, the mother having died and the father deserting his children [Cheney 1903-04, p. 39].

These early accounts of the pupils in special classes frequently indicate that they are preponderantly children of the poor. Cheney's account is of additional interest in that it is one of the few that give complete details on ethnicity. Under the heading of nationality she indicates that "twenty were Irish, six were Americans, six were Russian Jews, one was German Jew, one was Swede, one was Assyrian" (p. 39).

Another program in this early period which was specifically designed for "backward or feebleminded" children was established in Boston in 1899. David Lincoln (1903) makes a sharp distinction between "special" classes—as he termed them—and Boston's system of ungraded classes which were for "those who may be ignorant of our language, or who from neglect for slight backwardness require some individual training to enable them to re-enter the grades" (p. 85). The educational retardation of the children in these special classes would seem readily apparent:

> By way of illustration of the history of such a class, let us take the one originally formed by Miss Daniels. During the four and a half years of its existence it has had twenty-seven pupils, of whom fifteen remain; two have been sent to Waverley, three transferred to other classes of this type, and two to private schools for the feeble-minded, while one has died, one disappeared, one left on account of ill-health, one for home employment, and one on account of reaching the limit of age, sixteen years. They have been admirably taught, and yet, at the average age of nearly twelve years none can now do first-grade primary work efficiently and at the normal rate of speed, and none are in any single study much beyond the attainments of that grade, except in manual work [Lincoln 1903, p. 84].

The educational backwardness is clear enough but a listing of the health problems of the children makes one wonder about the range of etiologies underlying the educational retardation:

> In the same class three years after its foundation, there being at the time fifteen members, it is stated that two had had rickets, six convulsions, one epilepsy, three were seriously deaf, four had difficulty with the ordinary movements of walking and skipping, ten spoke with defective articulation, two had deformed palates and only three had good teeth [Lincoln 1903, pp. 84-85].

In a later report on these special education classes, Lincoln (1909) notes that of 264 pupils who had been taught, 26 had reentered the regular public schools of which number probably one-half were satisfactory pupils receiving promotion in the usual way.

Proliferation of Classes for Exceptional Children, 1900-1910

Though there are only isolated instances of special classes for handicapped or problem children before 1900, their increase in the following decade, as the graded schools sought to adjust to the compulsory schooling laws, was phenomenal. In 1911, the U.S. Bureau of Education published a Bulletin of the Provison for Exceptional Children in Public Schools prepared by James H. Van Sickle, then superintendent of schools in Springfield, Massachusetts, Lightner Witmer, founder of the first psychological clinic in America, and Leonard Ayres of the Russell Sage Foundation. In March 1911, these authors had sent survey questionnaires to 1,285 city school superintendents inquiring whether or not their school systems provided special classes for defective, blind, deaf, epileptic, foreign or gifted pupils. Eight hundred and ninety-eight replies were received.

For purpose of interpreting the results, the responses were treated as referring to provision made for children categorized as morally, mentally, physically or environmentally exceptional. One hundred and fifty-two, or 17 percent, of the responding cities had classes or residential schools for delinquent, incorrigible, and refractory children. Ninety-one cities, or 10 percent, provided classes for the physically handicapped such as the blind, the deaf, the dumb, the crippled, the speech-handicapped, and the weak or sickly child. The sickly child was provided for in open air classrooms which presumably stimulated the children and protected against lung diseases. Three hundred and forty-six cities, or 39 percent, provided for the environmentally exceptional, primarily non-English speaking pupils or late entering students. Somewhat misleading in these figures is the fact that most of the non-English speaking classes were evening classes rather than an integral part of the day school program.

The school systems providing for the mentally exceptional—our special interest—numbered 373 or 43 percent of the total number. Ninety-nine school systems had classes for the mentally defective, 220 had classes for the backward child, and 54 had classes for the exceptionally gifted. The data are difficult to interpret because there was no clear-cut definition of either mentally defective or backward children and, to compound the difficulty, classes for epileptics were categorized with the mentally defective and the figures for classes for backward children include the cases in which the reports stated that special teachers were employed to assist the slow pupils. Oddly enough the authors did not make any attempt to determine the actual number of classes in each school district or the number of pupils enrolled. But the survey at least offers ample evidence that the idea of special classes as ancillary to a graded school system had been widely accepted by urban school districts following the enforcement of compulsory schooling laws [Van Sickle, Witmer and Ayres 1911].

14

The Social Work Function
of the School and
the New Immigration

ALTHOUGH WE HAVE emphasized the inevitable development of ancillary special classes, given the combination of the lock-step graded schools and compulsory education, we must recognize that there were other factors that also influenced the formation of various categories of special education programs. These factors had to do with a changing perception of the role of the school that was occuring about the turn of the century. This was what Ravitch has referred to as "The social-work concept of schooling—that is, the school as an institution that 'takes charge' of children in view of an incompetent family and a disintegrated community. . ." (Ravitch 1974, p. 171).

It is of course true that this concept of the school did not originate at the turn of the century; much of it can be seen in the activities and motivations of the Public School Society and the nineteenth century schoolmen. Certainly, in their reports and public statements on the relationship of the common school to the society at large, the incompetence of poor families and the disintegration of the community were often stated. But the concept of the school's role in relationship to the children of the poor and to the apparent disintegration of the community did undergo extensive development if not radical change following the Civil War.

It was during this period that Cremin (1964) places the origins of progressive education: "a many sided effort to use the schools to improve the lives of people." [p. viii] To the Progressives, it meant

> broadening the program and function of the school to include direct concern for health, vocation, and the quality of family and community life. . . . applying in the classroom the pedagogical principles derived from new scientific research in psychology and the social sciences. . . . tailoring instruction more and more to the different kinds and classes of children who were being brought within the purview of the school [Cremin 1964, pp. viii-ix].

In the first and third of these meanings there is:

the social work impulse of the progressive movement [that] brought into the schools programs which had originated in settlement houses. Evening trade high schools and industrial schools of elementary grade were opened, primarily for young immigrants and Negroes who worked at manual labor during the day. The public schools inaugurated a medical inspection of all school children. Libraries were established in every school building. Special classes were created for those who were overage or slow learners; some of these classes were for non-English-speaking pupils, others for children who intended to leave school at age fourteen to go to work. Summer classes were opened, as well as evening study classes in recreation centers. And, in a complete break with the past, the school buildings were made available to their surrounding communities for after-school use for academic, recreational, and social programs [Ravitch 1974, pp. 168-169].

These expanding functions of the school may have begun, as Cremin argues, "as part of a vast humanitarian effort to apply the promise of American life — the ideal of government by, of and for the people — to the puzzling new urban-industrial civilization that came into being during the latter half of the 19th century" (1964, viii). On the other hand, if one views the situation with a more jaundiced eye, it may have been part of the effort of the dominant groups in our society to use the school to control and mold the newer waves of urban immigrants in ways that would propagate the existing control of society. Since society has an order of complexity that at its minimum exceeds that of the individual it is reasonable to assume that here too the motivation was in the jargon of the psychoanalyst, "overdetermined."

This "social work" role of the school was addressed to many of the same problems to which the common school addressed itself earlier in the century: the weakening role of the family and the community in the rearing of children in a developing complex, industrial, urban society — poverty, slums, immigration, vice, and crime. All the social problems that Jacob Riis (1890, 1892, 1902) made so vivid with word and picture were there in the urban ghettos prior to the Civil War.

The accounts of urban problems existing prior to the Civil War reviewed in earlier chapters would suggest that the problems in the postbellum period may have looked larger and more threatening. But if so, it was probably not because of a relative increase in their size but because of changes in the perceptions society had of itself.

For example, the immigration problem, so closely interwoven with other urban social problems and viewed with such alarm by nativists and eugenicists in the first decades of the twentieth century (Sarason and Doris 1969), was undoubtedly large in terms of absolute numbers. In 1905, the annual immigration to the United States for the first time exceeded the one million mark. From that year through 1914, the total immigration was in excess of 10,000,000. Such numbers must have seemed and in fact are awesome. But a close look at the data—if one were concerned with the relative impact of this immigration—might have reduced some of the alarm. As Carpenter (1927) was to indicate in his study of immigrants and their children, from 1860 to 1920, the proportion of foreign-born white stock in the total population varied from 13.0 to 14.5 percent with peak years occurring in 1890 and 1910. From 1870, the year when parental stock was first recorded, to 1920, the total proportion of foreign white stock, including the foreign-born and the native born of foreign or mixed parentage varied from 32.2 to 39.5 percent with the peak year occurring in 1910. The relative size of the immigrant stock does not appear to have altered all that much in these years.

What might have caused the changed perception that society had of itself and its problems? Surely the closing of the frontier must have been a major factor. Westward expansion could no longer be perceived as a safety valve for relieving the pressure of the urban melting pots. One wonders to what extent the rapid development of communications after the Civil War—the railroad, telegraph, telephone, rotary press, photography—helped society to perceive its social ills with an immediacy that had been lacking at mid-century. To paraphrase McLuhan, by the turn of the century we were well on our way to becoming a "national village." Whatever the complex pattern of multiple causes, there is no question that the concerned citizen perceived himself facing social ills unique in both size and nature. The optimistic view of the schoolman of mid-nineteenth century that the common school would be the panacea for the ills of society was now much harder to maintain. The common school was in place and, with the exception of the small percentage of children attending parochial and private schools, it reached most children of school age. Still there was poverty, vice, and crime.

If one was to retain faith in the common school one had to assume that the problems themselves had grown at a faster rate or become qualitatively different. Fortunately, for those who would retain their faith in the common school, it was possible within the climate of the times to assume that the problems had become qualitatively different. The children of the impoverished immigrant were no longer the same, for the old immigration from northern and western Europe had been supplanted by a new immigration from southern and eastern Europe in the 1870s. The old immigration, compatible—as it now seemed—with the stock of the founding fathers had been replaced with a breed inferior both intellectually and morally.

Subtle and overt acts of prejudice and hate were directed toward the new immigrant. They were not essentially different from those we have recorded for other ethnic groups earlier in the century. For vivid accounts of the prejudice directed toward the Italian and Jewish components in this new immigration we would recommend: *"Wop!"—A Documentary History of Anti-Italian Discrimination in the United States,* (1973) edited by Salvatore J.

LaGumina, and *"Kike!"—Anti-Semitism in America,* edited by Michael Selzer (1972).

We think it appropriate in the present context of educational developments at the turn of the century to call attention to some familiar passages from Ellwood P. Cubberley's *Public Education in the United States.* In 1919, this most popular textbook, widely used in normal schools and college training programs for teachers, presented contrasting views of the old and the new immigration. In summarizing the characteristics of the old immigration Cubberley maintained that:

> While these different people frequently settled in groups and for a time retained their foreign language, manners, and customs, they have not been particularly difficult to assimilate. Of all these early immigrants the Germans had shown the greatest resistance to the assimilative process. All except the Irish came from countries which embraced the Protestant Reformation, where general education prevailed, and where progressive methods in agriculture, trade and manufacturing had begun to supersede primitive methods. All were from race stock not very different from our own, and all possessed courage, initiative, intelligence, adaptability, and self-reliance to a great degree. The willingness, good-nature, and executive qualities of the Irish; the intellectual thoroughness of the German; the respect for law and order of the English; and the thrift, sobriety, and industry of the Scandinavians have been good additions to our national life [pp. 336–337].

Gone are the attitudes of the Know-Nothing movement from this description of the Germans and the Irish, and there is only a whisper of the Klan in Cubberley's regret that the wonderful work of the assimilation of these peoples was retarded "by the coming of such numbers, by city congregation and segregation, by the coming of so many male adults without their wives and children, by the work of the Germans in trying to preserve their language and racial habits and *Kultur,* and by the work of the Catholic and Lutheran churches in endeavoring to hold nationalities together" (p. 342). In contrast was Cubberley's perception of the new immigration:

> These Southern and Eastern Europeans were of a very different type from the North and West Europeans who preceded them. Largely illiterate, docile, lacking in initiative, and almost wholly without the Anglo-Saxon conceptions of righteousness, liberty, law, order, public decency, and government, their coming has served to dilute tremendously our national stock and to weaken and corrupt our political life. Settling largely in the cities of the North, the agricultural regions of the Middle and Far West, and the mining districts of the mountain regions, they have created serious problems in housing and living, moral and sanitary conditions, and honest and decent government, while popular education has everywhere been made more difficult by their presence. The result has been that in many sections of our country foreign manners, customs, observances, and language have tended to supplant native ways and the English speech, while the

so-called "melting-pot" has had more than it could handle. The new peoples, and especially those from the South and East of Europe, have come so fast that we have been unable to absorb and assimilate them, and our national life, for the past quarter of a century, had been afflicted with a serious case of racial indigestion [p. 338].

For educators possessed with such a perception of the new immigrant stock, incompetent and morally corrupt, how fierce a challenge! If the common schools were to rise to the challenge, how broad and intensive an attack it must mount! So the school systems of our urban centers pressured the immigrant child to conform to its "American" mold at the same time it gave ground more or less grudgingly and developed new programs for the educational misfits. In these new programs was much of the progressive educators' social work programs. Looking at it from the point of view of the immigrant, one might well have perceived this quality of a social work agency but one might also have perceived the quality of a correctional institution. Certainly, the proliferation not only of day classes but residential schools for truants and delinquents would give some credence to the latter perception.

Leonard Covello's recollection of his introduction to the "Soup School" in Italian East Harlem in the mid-1890s gives much of that double image. While the school was not a public elementary school, it had enough of the characteristics of a public school, that Covello's account of the entrance experience of a nine-year old immigrant child with but one or two words of English at his command might not be deemed very different from what he might have experienced in his neighborhood public school:

> The Soup School got its name from the fact that at noontime a bowl of soup was served to us with some white, soft bread that made better spitballs than eating in comparison with the substantial and solid homemade bread to which I was accustomed. The school itself was organized and maintained by the Female Guardian Society of America. Later on I found out that this Society was sponsored by wealthy people concerned about the immigrants and their children. How much this organization accomplished among immigrants in New York City would be difficult to estimate. But this I do know, that among the immigrants of my generation and even later *La Soupa Scuola* is still vivid in our boyhood memories.
>
> Why we went to the Soup School instead of the regular elementary public school I have not the faintest idea, except that possibly the first Aviglianese to arrive in New York sent his child there and everyone else followed suit — and also possibly because in those days a bowl of soup was a bowl of soup.
>
> Once at the Soup School I remember the teacher gave each child a bag of oatmeal to take home. This food was supposed to make you big and strong. You ate it for breakfast. My father examined the stuff, tested it with his fingers. To him it was the kind of bran that was fed to pigs in Avigliano.
>
> "What kind of a school is this?" he shouted. "They give us the food of animals to eat and send it home to us with our children! What are we coming to next?"
>
> By the standards I had come to know and understand in Avigliano, the Soup School was not an unpleasant experience. I had been reared in a strict code of

behavior, and this same strictness was the outstanding characteristic of the first of my American schools. Nor can I say, as I had indicated to Vito, that a blow from Mrs. Cutter ever had the lustiness of my teacher, Don Salvatore Mecca. But what punishment lacked in power, it gained by the exacting personality of our principal.

Middle-aged, stockily built, gray hair parted in the middle, Mrs. Cutter lived up to everything my cousin Vito had said about her and much more. Attached to an immaculate white waist by a black ribbon, her pince-nez fell from her nose and dangled in moments of anger. She moved about the corridors and classrooms of the Soup School ever alert and ready to strike at any infringement of school regulations.

I was sitting in class trying to memorize and pronounce words written on the blackboard—words which had absolutely no meaning to me. It seldom seemed to occur to our teachers that explanations were necessary.

"B-U-T-T-E-R-butter-butter," I sing-songed with the rest of the class, learning as always by rote, learning things which often I didn't understand but which had a way of sticking in my mind.

Softly the door opened and Mrs. Cutter entered the classroom. For a large and heavy-set woman she moved quickly, without making any noise. We were not supposed to notice or even pretend we had seen her as she slowly made her way between the desks and straight-backed benches. "B-U-T-T-E-R," I intoned. She was behind me now. I could feel her presence hovering over me. I did not dare take my eyes from the blackboard. I had done nothing and could conceive of no possible reason for an attack, but with Mrs. Cutter this held no significance. She carried a short bamboo switch. On her finger she wore a heavy gold wedding ring. For an instant I thought she was going to pass me by and then suddenly her clenched fist with the ring came down on my head.

I had been trained to show no emotion in the face of punishment, but this was too much. However, before I had time to react to the indignity of this assault, an amazing thing happened. Realizing that she had hurt me unjustly, Mrs. Cutter's whole manner changed. A look of concern came into her eyes. She took hold of my arm, uttering conciliatory words which I did not understand. Later Vito explained to me that she was saying, "I'm sorry. I didn't mean it. Sit down now and be a good boy!"

Every day before receiving our bowl of soup we recited the Lord's Prayer. I had no inkling of what the words meant. I knew only that I was expected to bow my head. I looked around to see what was going on. Swift and simple, the teacher's blackboard pointer brought the idea home to me. I never batted an eyelash after that.

I learned arithmetic and penmanship and spelling—every misspelled word written ten times or more, traced painfully and carefully in my blankbook. I do not know how many times I wrote "I must not talk." In this same way I learned how to read in English, learned geography and grammar, the states of the Union and all the capital cities—and memory gems—choice bits of poetry and sayings. Most learning was done in unison. You recited to the teacher standing at attention. Chorus work. Repetition. Repetition until the things you learned beat in your brain even at night when you were falling asleep.

I think of the modern child with his complexes and his need for "self-expression"! He will never know the forceful and vitalizing influence of a Soup School or a Mrs. Cutter [Covello 1958, pp. 24-27].

The high-handed Americanization of the immigrant is beautifully and poignantly portrayed in another scene from Covello's book. It also presents us with the way in which the Americanization process could foster alienation between the immigrant and his child:

Our kitchen table was covered by an oilcloth with a picture of Christopher Columbus first setting foot on American soil. It was the familiar scene of Columbus grasping the flag of Spain, surrounded by his men, with Indians crowding around. More than once my father glared at this oilcloth and poured a malediction on Columbus and his great discovery.

One day I came home from the Soup School with a report card for my father to sign. It was during one of these particular bleak periods. I remember that my friend Vito Salvatore happened to be there, and Mary Accurso had stopped in for a moment to see my mother. With a weary expression my father glanced over the marks on the report card and was about to sign it. However, he paused with the pen in his hand.

"What is this?" he said. "Leonard Covello! What happened to the *i* in Coviello?"

My mother paused in her mending. Vito and I just looked at each other.

"Well?" my father insisted.

"Maybe the teacher just forgot to put it in," Mary suggested. "It can happen." She was going to high school now and spoke with an air of authority, and people always listened to her. This time, however, my father didn't even hear her.

"From Leonardo to Leonard I can follow," he said, "a perfectly natural process. In America anything can happen and does happen. But you don't change a family name. A name is a name. What happened to the *i?*"

Mrs. Cutter took it out," I explained. "Every time she pronounced Coviello it came out Covello. So she took out the *i*. That way it's easier for everybody."

My father thumped Columbus on the head with his fist. "And what has this Mrs. Cutter got to do with my name?"

"What difference does it make?" I said. "It's more American. The *i* doesn't help anything." It was one of the very few times that I dared oppose my father. But even at that age I was beginning to feel that anything that made a name less foreign was an improvement.

Vito came to my rescue. "My name is Victor — Vic. That's what everybody calls me now."

"Vic. Sticka. Nicka. You crazy in the head!" my father yelled at him.

For a moment my father sat there, bitter rebellion building in him. Then with a shrug of resignation, he signed the report card and shoved it over to me. My mother now suddenly entered the argument. "How is it possible to do this to a name? Why did you sign the card? Narduccio, you will have to tell your teacher that a name cannot be changed just like that. . . . "

"Mamma, you don't understand."

"What is there to understand? A person's life and his honor is in his name. He never changes it. A name is not a shirt or a piece of underwear."

My father got up from the table, lighted the twisted stump of a Toscano cigar and moved out of the argument. "Honor!" he muttered to himself.

"You must explain this to your teacher," my mother insisted. "It was a mistake. She will know. She will not let it happen again. You will see."

"It was no mistake. On purpose. The *i* is out and Mrs. Cutter made it Covello. You just don't understand!"

"Will you stop saying that!" my mother insisted. "I don't understand. I don't understand. What is there to understand? Now that you have become American-ized you understand everything and I understand nothing."

With her in this mood I dared make no answer. Mary went over and put her hand on my mother's shoulder. I beckoned to Vito and together we walked out of the flat and downstairs into the street.

"She just doesn't understand," I kept saying.

"I'm gonna take the *e* off the end of my name and make it just Salvator," Vito said. "After all, we're not in Italy now."

Vito and I were standing dejectedly under the gas light on the corner, watch-ing the lamplighter moving from post to post along the cobblestone street and then disappearing around the corner on First Avenue. Somehow or other the joy of childhood had seeped out of our lives. We were only boys, but a sadness that we could not explain pressed down upon us. Mary came and joined us. She had a book under her arm. She stood there for a moment, while her dark eyes surveyed us questioningly.

"But they don't understand!" I insisted.

Mary smiled. "Maybe some day, you will realize that *you* are the one who does not understand" [Covello 1958, pp. 29-31].

Adele Shaw in her 1903 article on the New York City schools gives several instances of immigrant children spontaneously Americanizing their given and family names. Shaw apparently attributes the practice to the children's eagerness to become Americans. Considering that at another level it might reflect the shame and insecurity the children associated with their immigrant heritage, one might legitimately ask what was there in the climate of the schools that made them so ashamed and insecure in relation to that heritage.

The completeness of Covello's Americanization in the various schools he attended in the City of New York makes his story somewhat unique for an immigrant child, as does his academic success within that educational system. He ended up principal of Benjamin Franklin High School in East Harlem. In his doctoral dissertation at Columbia, he made a most penetrating study of southern Italians and their adjustment to the American school system, a study that we will refer to later as we try to understand how this ethnic group ranked lowest among immigrants in the first decades of this century on so many measures of school achievement and intellectual ability. But before addressing this problem, we would like to look more closely at the school system of New York City as it existed about the turn of the century and the development of its special education programs.

The New York City School System and the Development of Its Ungraded Classes

In an earlier chapter we described the Pestalozzian reforms in elementary education that began to influence American schooling in the decades prior to the Civil War. Covello's vignettes of the Soup School of East Harlem, however, would hardly reflect the ideals of the Swiss educator. One might not be surprised at the absence of "the loving relationship of parent to child," as even in the home that is an ideal to be pursued rather than an ever present reality; but the absence of object teaching in all its varied forms is striking, considering the many decades Pestalozzian methods had been advocated by leading educators and school administrators. In fact, Covello's schooling would appear to trace its lineage more directly to Lancaster than to Pestalozzi, not only in its group instruction, its verbalism, drill, and emphasis on rote memorization, but also in its regimentation and rigid discipline.

Nor was Covello's education in a charity school in any way essentially different from the kind of education prevailing in many of the public school systems of the large cities. That such was the case is attested to by J. M. Rice's report on his observation of classroom teaching in the schools of 36 cities. In all, over 1,200 teachers were observed at their work. In addition, Rice gathered information on the management of the schools from perusal of official documents, attendance at school board and teacher meetings, and personal interviews with superintendents, principals, and teachers.

The results of his study were published in *Forum* and subsequently in book form (Rice 1893). Their publication caused much stir and indignation in educational circles as well as concern in the public at large. In an era that was to become renowned for the quality of its muckraking journalism, Rice's investigation of the schools was a first-rate success. In the preface to the book, Rice maintained:

> As to the criticisms that will be found, I beg that they be accepted in the spirit in which they are written, it being far from my purpose to inflict injury on any one. It is to be hoped, however, that the reader will bear in mind one thing, which, though frequently forgotten, I never forget, as it is the foundation upon which this work rests, — namely, that the school exists for the benefit of the child, and not for the benefit of boards of education, superintendents, or teachers. In this work the child's side will be presented, and the spirit in which it is written is the same as that in which an advocate pleads for his client [p. 4].

Though he often chose the worst examples of teaching that he could find, Rice defended the adequacy of his sampling in each city and added:

In my opinion, however, one would not go very far wrong by condemning the school system of any city after visiting only one school building, if he should find the teaching throughout that building exceedingly poor. It is only in cities where the conditions are extremely unfavorable that a school building can be found in which the teachers are accustomed to conduct sing-song recitation in spelling and arithmetic, hear children recite lessons verbatim from a textbook, or conduct concert recitations in geography. In every city where one such school is tolerated, many similar ones can be found. One is liable to find in any city a teacher here and there who follows such methods of instruction, but in no city where the school system is conducted on scientific principles can a single school building be found in which even one of the teachers is allowed, year after year, to instruct in that manner. In the progressive schools these methods are never tolerated for any length of time after they have been detected, the teacher who follows them being obliged either to abandon them or to forfeit her position . . . . And a school system must be judged not by what particularly energetic teachers are, of their own accord, willing to do, but by what each teacher is required to do in order that she may retain her position [pp. 6–7].

Rice classified the school systems he evaluated in three groups as determined chiefly by differences in the conduct of the primary grades where he felt the differences between systems were most marked. The best and the smallest of these groups comprised Indianapolis, Minneapolis, St. Paul, and La Porte, Indiana. In these schools, Rice praised what we have identified earlier as Pestalozzian reforms: from the beginning, the work centers on the development of the child, the acquisition of ideas rather than the memorization of words, the endeavor of the teacher "to render the instruction thoughtful and the work interesting by conforming their methods to the laws of mental development" (pp. 221–22), and all instruction embedded in the kindly and considerate treatment of the children.

Much of these characteristics were also found in Rice's second classification but what particularly distinguished his highest class was the way in which the walls between the various branches of knowledge tended to disappear: "the mind is no longer regarded as consisting of a number of independent compartments—one for penmanship, a second for reading, a third for arithmetic, a fourth for geography, etc.; but the ideas gained regardless of subject are led to support each other, and they become clearer by being seen in the light of each other" (p. 222).

At the other extreme of Rice's classificatory system were the schools designated as antiquated, "that is, the purely mechanical schools, the schools that aim to do little, if anything beyond crowding the memory of the child with a certain number of cut-and-dried facts" (p. 220). Among schools of this order were those of Baltimore, Buffalo, Cincinnati, New York, Milwaukee, Chicago, Boston, St. Louis, Brooklyn, Worcester (Massachusetts), and Peoria (Illinois). In the matter of discipline, the schools of St. Louis were particularly singled out as being the most barbarous in the country.

The schools of New York had the dubious honor of being the first discussed in detail by Rice, for they could be regarded in his opinion as typical of the schools of all our large cities, showing the elements that led to an inferior order of schools.

It is to be remembered as we look more closely at this "typical" large city school system, that at the turn of the century such were the school systems in which the bulk of immigrant children began their Americanization. In 1908, the Immigration Commission, as part of its general study of the immigration problem, undertook a large-scale survey of the school children in 37 cities with the intent of determining "to what extent children of the various races of immigrants are availing themselves of educational facilities and what progress they make in school work" (Immigration Commission 1911, p. 4). Of 1,815,217 public school pupils included in this survey, 1,048,490 had fathers of foreign nativity, a rate of 57.8 percent.

Knowing from the previously cited study of Carpenter (1927) that the total foreign stock, both native and foreign-born, for all ages did not exceed 40 percent in the census of 1910, it appears likely that by and large the children of the new immigrants were educated in the city school systems. Of course the percentage of the immigrant children varied from city to city, the lowest among the cities sampled being New Orleans with 18 percent. New York City and Chicago were among the leaders with 71.5 percent and 67.3 percent respectively.

There was also considerable variation in ethnic composition of pupils in different cities. The Russian Jews and the Italians accounted for 19.2 percent and 10.5 percent of New York City pupils respectively, but were only 6.8 percent and 4.3 percent of Chicago's pupils. In looking at the academic performances and intelligence scores of these immigrants, at a later point, it will be important to keep in mind the school systems in which they were educated, as the different ethnic groups adapted with varying degrees of success to those school systems.

Rice's description of the "typical" New York City school system began with a particularly flagrant example of a school conducted according to the "antiquated and mechanical" methods of instruction. He justified his choice on the grounds that the work of the principal of this school during her long tenure had uniformly been graded "excellent." In describing the pedagogical views of this principal, Rice notes:

> She believes that when a child enters upon school life his vocabulary is so small that it is practically worthless, and his power to think so feeble that his thoughts are worthless. She is consequently of the opinion that what the child knows and is able to do on coming to school should be entirely disregarded, that he should not be allowed to waste time, either in thinking or in finding his own words to express his thoughts, but that he should be supplied with ready-made thoughts as given in a ready-made vocabulary. She has therefore prepared sets of questions and answers, so that the child may be given in concise form most of the facts prescribed in the course of study for the three years of primary instruction. The instruction

throughout the school consists principally of grinding these answers *verbatim* into the minds of the children. . . .The spirit of the school is "Do what you like with the child, immobilize him, automatize him, dehumanize him, but save, save the minutes." In many ways the minutes are saved. By giving the child ready-made thoughts, the minutes required in thinking are saved. By giving the child ready-made definitions, the minutes required in formulating them are saved. Everything is prohibited that is of no measurable advantage to the child, such as the move-ment of the head or a limb, when there is no logical reason why it should be moved at the time. I asked the principal whether the children were not allowed to move their heads. She answered, "Why should they look behind when the teacher is in front of them?"—words too logical to be refuted [Rice 1893, pp. 30-32].

Not only was the content of the lessons mastered by mechanical drill and rote memorization, the very movements of the children in passing out materials, in rising to recite, or returning to place were prescribed and ex-ecuted with the speed and exactness of automatons.

In reading, the word method is followed. The pupils are taught to read the number of words prescribed for the grade and no more, and they are taught to spell the words as they learn to read them. They are not encouraged to acquire the ability to read new words, each new word being developed before it is shown to the child, which means practically that the child is told what the word is before he is allowed to name it. But this method is typical of the New York primary schools. I asked the principal whether the children in the highest grade (third-year class) were not able to read new words without being told what they were. She answered in substance: "How can they know what a word is when they have never seen it before? Could you recognize a thing that you had never before seen?" . . .

The typical New York City primary school, although less barbarous and ab-surd than the one just described, is nevertheless a hard, unsympathetic, mechanical-drudgery school, a school into which the light of science has not yet entered. Its characteristic feature lies in the severity of its discipline, a discipline of enforced silence, immobility, and mental passivity. The differences found in going from room to room and from school to school—I have seen many of them—are differences in degree only, and not in kind. One teacher will allow her pupils to move their heads a little more freely than the standard, another will allow a little more freedom to the shoulder-joints, but less freedom in moving the head, and a third will require the children to keep their hands in their laps, instead of behind their backs.

The character of the instruction is identical with that found wherever this false system of discipline prevails, being of that form which appeals to the memory alone. The aim of the teacher is simply to secure results by drilling the pupils in the facts prescribed for the grade. The public-school system of New York City of-fers, therefore, a striking example of how, under unwise management, a trained teacher may be reduced to the level of one who has no training. Many New York school-teachers have told me that the New York school gave them no opportunity to put their knowledge of psychology and pedagogy to practical use, and that they consequently felt the normal-school influence vanish soon after beginning to teach [Rice 1893, pp. 38-39].

Rice identified various factors adversely affecting the functioning of the schools such as public apathy, political interference and corruption, and teaching and administrative incompetence. He called for the complete separation of politics from the operation of the school system and the upgrading of administration by the appointment of able educators. The latter should devote their time to the education and guidance of the teachers under their charge rather than to the routine examination of classes which only ensured the continuance of the mechanical rote memorization methods of instruction. He also called for the development of a corps of teachers who were themselves students, constantly endeavoring to grow in professional and general intellectual strength. He was, as Cremin (1964) indicates, not the first to speak out against the condition of the schools but prior to Rice, protest was local, intermittent, and generally ineffective.

> By contrast the nineties brought a nationwide torrent of criticism, innovation, and reform that soon took on all the earmarks of a social movement. And it is at this point that Rice's articles appear to mark a beginning. His *Forum* series was the first to weave the many strands of contemporary protest into a single reform program; it was the first to perceive the educational problem as truly national in scope; and it was the first to apply the technique of muckraking in attacking the political corruption and professional intransigence infecting the schools. The progressive movement in education begins with Rice precisely because he saw it as a movement. It is this growing self-consciousness more than anything else that sets the progressivism of the nineties apart from its sources in previous decades.
>
> Once under way, the movement manifested itself in a remarkable diversity of pedagogical protest and innovation; from its very beginning it was pluralistic, often self-contradictory, and always closely related to broader currents of social and political progressivism. In the universities it emerged as part of a spirited revolt against formalism in philosophy, psychology, and the social sciences. In the cities it was but one facet of a wider program of municipal clean-up and reform. Among farmers it became the crux of a moderate, liberal alternative to radical agrarianism. It was at the same time the "social education" demanded by urban settlement workers, the "schooling for country life" demanded by rural publicists, the vocational training demanded by businessmen's associations and labor unions alike, and the new techniques of instruction demanded by avant-garde pedagogues. It embraced the kindergartens of St. Louis and the State University of Wisconsin, venerable Harvard, and an *arriviste* New York professional school named Teachers College, Columbia University. It enlisted parents and teachers, starry-eyed crusaders and hardheaded politicians. And in less than two generations it transformed the character of the American school [Cremin 1964, p. 22].

Transformation may well have begun in the 1890s, but the advance of the progressive movement in the schools was slow and uneven. In 1903, Adele Marie Shaw undertook for *The World's Work,* an evaluation of the schools similar to that of Rice. According to Cremin, her series of articles, appearing in that magazine from 1903 to 1904, "testified eloquently to the persistence of the conditions that Rice had exposed a decade earlier" (p. 21). Our own reading of the series suggests that Shaw was either of a more sanguine and benign temperament than Rice or that considerable improvements, though uneven and scattered, had occurred in the interim. Nevertheless, the picture as a whole, particularly in those schools serving the immigrant poor, was still grim. Unlike Rice who focused on the conduct of the schools, and the public apathy and political corruption that tolerated such inept instruction, Shaw was also sensitive to the physical conditions of the school as well as the various socioeconomic causes underlying the conditions she observed. The difficulties of designing a school building program to keep up with the rapidly expanding and shifting population, the overcrowded classrooms, the deterioration of the physical plants, the polyglot nature of the students, all made the difficulty of the teacher readily apparent. Viewing the New York City Schools, she made such notes as:

There were enrolled in the public schools last year 588,614 pupils. This year there is an increase in the day schools of 40,408 (enrolled pupils). September 30th there were 89,316 children in part-time classes (Shaw 1903, p. 4205).

In a Brooklyn School not far from the Bridge I visited a room where sixty-five very small children were packed into a space properly intended for twenty. A bright faced young woman was steadying a sleeping baby upon his third-of-a seat while she heard the remaining sixty-four recite. . . . "He and his brother here are little Cubans," she explained. "They speak no English, but the brother can already imitate anything the rest can do." (Shaw 1903, p. 4206).

New York children do not have equal chances, physically, in the New York schools. Yet the custom of seating two children (and in crowded classrooms I frequently saw *three*) at the same desk cannot be done away with till money can be spared for new furniture and space allowed for single desks (Shaw 1903, p. 4209).

Good air in the months of September and October is not hard to obtain, yet in nearly every classroom that I entered the atmosphere was foul. Sometimes even the assembly hall and the corridors were distinctly offensive. A room in which forty-six little girls live and work five hours in the day contained only one outside window. The miserably flickering gas over their heads consumed the oxygen needed by starved lungs, and yet on the three warm days during which I visited this class I did not once see the window open more than a few inches (Shaw 1903, p. 4209).

The playground space was a small dark basement divided so as to give the girls the larger share. Sunken between the tenements and the school building was a narrow court not so large as a good city back yard, where 500 boys "went out to play." On rainy days they are often crowded so close in the hopeless darkness of the basement that there is barely standing room. The teacher in charge of the playground must stay in this cell, though to see what is going on is impossible, and although on winter days the place is miserably cold for her and the boys.

Four schools I came upon that had been condemned six or seven years ago, but as fast as new buildings had replaced them they had been filled to the brim with an overflow (Shaw 1903, p. 4210).

Nor is there any greater equality in the conditions in which the New York public-school child develops mind and character.

The well-to-do, who furnish the principal support of the public schools, send their children elsewhere. Three-fourths of New York's elementary teachers could not get positions in private schools.

"Who told you to speak out?" "*You've* paid attention!" scolded or sneered at a boy who is struggling to express an independent thought, will not make him a ready user of the gifts with which he is endowed.

The tone of continual exasperation in which more than one class is addressed would blight the forthputting powers of a Macaulay. Truancy from some of these classes should be imputed to a child for righteousness (Shaw 1903, p. 4210).

In one school in which I spend the better part of two days I did not once hear any child express a thought in his own words. Attention was perfect. No pupil could escape from any grade without knowing the questions and answers of that grade. Every child could add, subtract, multiply, and divide with accuracy; every child could and did pronounce his reading words with unusual distinctness. The chant in which recitations were delivered was as uniform as everything else. . . . It was the best and the worst school I ever saw. The best, because no pains, no time, *nothing* had been spared to bring it up to the principal's ideal; and the effort had been crowned with entire success. The worst, because it ignored absolutely any individuality in the pupils and fitted them for nothing more than a mechanical obedience to another's thinking [Shaw 1903, pp. 4210–4211].

Shaw summed up her observations on the New York City schools as follows:

1. New York City has the most difficult educational problem in the country. It stands in a class by itself and has difficulties that no other city presents.

2. Under the present school administration it is doing wonderful work toward solving that problem.

3. But conditions still exist that put the complete solution of the problem beyond the reach of any normal effort and expense.

4. The only remedies for such conditions are the restriction of immigration and a vast increase in expenditure—larger than has yet been dreamed of (Shaw 1903, p. 4221).

Scattered through Shaw's article on the New York City system are glimmerings of a brighter educational scene. New school buildings equipped with roof playgrounds, school nurses and doctors, schools with shower baths for the unwashed and vermin-infested children of the ghettoes, evening study rooms in recreation centers, free evening lectures for adults, and ungraded classes for the mentally retarded.

Such schools are making self-supporting men of probable paupers, good men and women of probable criminals, and good American citizens of thousands and thousands of children whose parents speak no English, and learn loyalty to government only by seeing what it does for their offspring [Shaw 1903, p. 4207].

In all of this can be seen the influence of the settlement house and the development of the social work movement within the schools.

15

The Growth and Development of Special Education Programs

IN NEW YORK CITY, the 1890s were characterized by political reform and reorganization, much of which affected the structure and organization of the city's school system. Ravitch (1974) has detailed this activity in *The Great School Wars*. For our purposes it suffices to note that the reform and reorganization of city government, as culminated in the Greater New York Charter (1897), provided for the consolidation of the city of New York (Manhattan and the Bronx), the city of Brooklyn, Richmond County (Staten Island), and part of Queens County (as it then existed). This charter also provided for a new Board of Education for the consolidated city made up of representatives from the school board of Manhattan and the Bronx, and the school boards of Brooklyn, Queens, and Richmond (Palmer 1905). Revision of the charter in 1901 abolished the borough boards and established a Board of Education of 46 members appointed by the mayor. The office of City Superintendent was retained with greatly enlarged powers.

In token gesture toward local control, school boards were established in each of forty-six districts. These local boards could inspect the schools and give voice to local concerns but had no power to directly affect the administration of the schools. The cumulative result of these changes was, as Ravitch indicates, a highly centralized and professionalized educational system that in this institutional form was to persist for almost seventy years with but minor changes. In Ravitch's view:

> The most important impact of centralization was a remarkable burst of energy and innovation, unparalleled before or since in the New York schools. The reformers had a program, a social-work approach to children's lives, and the new concentration of authority made it possible to introduce massive changes in the schools. The first victim of change was the traditional notion that school was a place to learn reading, writing, and arithmetic, and that students who failed had only themselves to blame. In its place was substituted what was then called "the new education" and later known as "progressive education"—amorphous terms which covered a range of antitraditional approaches [Ravitch 1974, p. 167].

Shaw's (1903) description of the city's schools, which we reviewed in the last chapter, suggests that the changes were not immediate but there is no doubt that the first city superintendent of Greater New York, William Henry Maxwell, pursued a program of innovative reform in the city's schools. In support of this contention, one finds a section on special schools for defective children in his first annual report to the Board of Education for the school year ending July 1899. After a brief review of London's special education program and an expression of eugenical concerns about the state's duty to prevent the marriage of people who are incapable of producing mentally and physically sound offspring, he asserts that as long as such defective children are brought into the world, humanity demands and the state requires that "such children should receive that training which will, as far as possible, neutralize inherited evil tendencies and develop the good seed that otherwise will have fallen among thorns or by the road-side" (p. 131). He then indicated that he would take steps to ascertain the number of mentally and physically defective children within the city's schools and recommend that a "center" for the training of such individuals be established.

In that same year, and with apparent independence of the superintendent's plans, the first ungraded class was established by Elizabeth Farrell. Her account follows:

The special classes in the public schools of the city of New York had their beginning in Public School, 1, Manhattan, in 1899. It is interesting to know that this class, which was to demonstrate the need for further classification of children in public schools, was not the result of any theory. It grew out of conditions in a neighborhood which furnished many and serious problems in truancy and discipline. This first class was made up of the odds and ends of a large school. There were over-age children, so-called naughty children, and the dull and stupid children. They were taken from any and every school grade. The ages ranged from eight to sixteen years. They were the children who could not get along in school. They were typical of a large number of children who even today are forced directly or indirectly out of school; they were the children who were interested in street life; many of them earned a good deal of money in one way or another. While some of them had been in trouble with the police, as a class they could not be characterized as criminal. They had varied interests but the school, as they had found it, had little or nothing for them. If these boys were to be kept in school they had to be interested. They had to be shown that school could be more than mere study of books in which they had no interest. They had to be convinced that to attend school was a privilege not a punishment. This "about face" on the part of these boys was accomplished after many months.

They came to school and while they were doing interesting things, making toy wagons and wheelbarrows, they became a human laboratory in which many observed, studied. Some anthropometric measurements were taken, reaction to given stimuli was observed. This study showed that the physical condition of these children in nearly every case was as bad as it could be. All phases of bad nutrition and its effects were exemplified by those children. Sense defects were of course, common; one hemiplegic, one epileptic, one so-called moral defective were included in this first class. The mental equipment was not more promising. There were children who could read and those who could not; children who could count and those who could not. One would hardly believe that children could attend school for two, three, four or more years and still be so beautifully ignorant of most that had been done there. The mental habits were of the worst kind—little power of attention to abstract notions, will-power of a wishy-washy character or else so obstructed that action was frequently paralyzed [Farrell 1908-1909, pp. 91-92].

If Miss Farrell's initial efforts in special education started independently of the plans of Superintendent Maxwell and the social work movement of the settlement house, it did not go long without support from both those quarters. Lillian Wald's *Windows on Henry Street* recounts the involvement of the Henry Street Settlement with Miss Farrell's work:

a resident of the House brought the glad tidings that there was a young teacher in her school who had an "idea." "The girl," she submitted, "needed looking after," as if having "an idea" laid her open to study if not suspicion. This was our introduction to Elizabeth Farrell, the girl with "the idea." And when she had shared it with us it was borne in upon us that she had been vouchsafed a vision, though not till later was it developed by study and experience into the programme which has been praised and followed by educators the world over. . . .

Miss Farrell's "idea" was that *every* individual should be developed to the highest level of which he was capable. This was no startlingly new concept: Miss Farrell's originality lay in applying the idea to the education of the atypical in the public schools. She was optimistic enough to believe that the largest and most complex school system in the country—perhaps in the world—with its hundreds of thousands of children, its rigid curriculum, its mass methods, could be modified to meet the needs of the atypical—often the least lovely and potentially the most troublesome of its pupils. . . .

With the approval of the principal of Public School Number 1 on Henry Street, Miss Farrell selected from its "chronic truants," the members of the first Ungraded Class, one of the first in any public school system in the world. There were said to be at that time fifty thousand truants in New York City, boys and girls who had set themselves in opposition to society. Miss Farrell held that the children who were unwilling to attend school constituted a challenge to our whole scheme of public education; for she knew that this was not a problem peculiar to New York City—"it is doubtless the same in every city, in every town, perhaps in every village."

These subnormal and occasionally supernormal children were in the regular grades. They were getting little or no profit from their attendance, and held back their classmates who approached "the norm." Miss Farrell's experiment was based upon her certainty that the reason these atypical children played truant was that there was nothing which attracted them in the school. The docks, the streets, the empty lots, even the ash cans and the garbage provided them with interest, if not education, as our elaborate school system failed to do. Miss Farrell discarded the old routine and brought into the classroom the materials, or their equivalent, that absorbed the boys and girls outside. In her hands, tin cans, picture puzzles, paints and brushes, wood and tools, became implements of education. Her children brought food to school and a luncheon was served—the first so far as I know, in a city schoolroom. Friends of the Settlement gave pretty dishes and other necessary equipment, and the mothers were invited to visit the class, sometimes to take lunch. When an Italian mother was asked to prepare spaghetti for the children "like the old country," it dignified Italian parentage and custom in the eyes of these oncoming American citizens. We often overlook how important it is for children to hold to their traditions. Sometimes their loyalty and respect are greatly imperiled by the appeals to be "one hundred percent Americans." . . .

Two members of the Board of Education—Charles Burlingham, the president and Felix Warburg, his friend and colleague—were invited to meet Miss Farrell at Henry Street. In that sympathetic environment she forgot her shyness and presented her idea with glowing vigor and enthusiasm. With the superintendent of schools, Dr. Maxwell, one of the educational statesmen of the day, these socially minded board members paid tribute to her as a genius whose vision was essentially practical. She was given freedom and thoughtful encouragement to develop her project [Wald 1935, pp. 134-137].

In relation to Wald's account of luncheon in this ungraded class we note that among the settlement workers at the turn of the century there was some agitation about introducing a program of school lunches for poor children. The special education teachers within the school system were particularly anxious for this innovation for they frequently expressed concern about the poor state of nutrition of their charges. Some school administrators such as Van Sickle (1908–09) were of the opinion that the problem was not that the parents could not afford to supply their children with proper food but that parental carelessness and ignorance resulted in the improper nourishment of the children.

Elizabeth Farrell became a long-time resident of the Henry Street Settlement House and:

insisted that she found in the House a living spring of inspiration. The Settlement's rich understanding of people, life, events, its multicolored and changing activities, provided her, she said, with a background which helped keep her own thought and emotions fresh and vital. She never considered herself the dynamo that generated the power for her great achievement, though she had the unusual experience of recognition by colleagues in many fields. Professor Edward L. Thorndike testifies to his indebtedness to her when she was teaching a course at Teachers College, Columbia University: "She never forgot that schools do not exist chiefly to serve some vague doctrine of education or some abstract ideal of the state, but to make life happier for actual living children in school and through life. She was the defender of the interests of dull, thwarted, imperfect children whom she loved" [Wald 1934, p. 138].

Under the section entitled "Abnormal Children," in Maxwell's *Fourth Annual Report of the City Superintendent of Schools* (1902), the developing special education program of New York City is discussed with particular reference to the problem of the classification of students.

The question of providing special instruction in the elementary schools for pupils classed roughly as defective, backward, or dull children, has been considered for some time prior to this year in a more or less desultory fashion. In Public School No. 1, in Henry street, there has been, for some years, a class for such children who showed also tendencies to become habitual truants. In Girls' Department, P.S. 77, also, certain experiments in classifying unusual children have been made. This year, however, the problem has been considered more formally and in detail. The principals were asked to report the number of such children in each school. They reported about 8,000. A careful scrutiny of their answers indicated that the total number of children now in the schools, who should properly be classed as defective, is not more than a fourth of that reported.

In dealing with children who come under the general titles, "abnormal" or "atypical," it is necessary to distinguish carefully between incorrigible and truant children and those who are to be considered as defective in mental ability. In dealing with this second group a further subdivision of the various classes is essential to intelligent treatment. The following subdivisions seem to include almost all children of the atypical class:

(a) Dull children; those who are behind in any or all studies; those who exhibit abnormal precocity in one or more studies; those who have lost time because of irregular attendance or frequent transfer; those who are deficient in English because of foreign birth and residence.

(b) Defective children, whose minds may be clouded; those whose defects are partial; those whose defects may be cured; those who, because of some abnormal growth, such as adenoids in the throat, and deafness, are behind the other members of their class.

(c) Idiotic or permanently defective children.

Before recommending any general rule to establish special instruction for these children, the Board of Superintendents thought it wise to experiment in several schools with classes affording various courses of study or other special features. Several of these experiment stations have been established in Manhattan and the results obtained are being studied closely with a view to the extension of the work. The experimental stations, none of which, however, is dealing exclusively with any one class of children, are located in Public Schools No.s 1, 40, 77, 111, 113, and 180, Manhattan [Maxwell 1902, pp. 108-109].

Maxwell closed this section of the report with iterated emphasis on the importance of the proper classification of children. Nevertheless, progress in classification was slow. A few years later Lydia Chace, reporting before the National Conference of Charities and Corrections, was to note:

The work in New York for mentally deficient children is in a formative but chaotic state at the present time. The terms "ungraded" and "special" classes are used synonymously, and cover those for wayward, backward, and mentally deficient children. It is impossible to tell how many there are for the latter, for backward and mentally deficient children are often in class together. There are, however, at least five where the majority of the children are mentally deficient, and where the work is planned for such pupils [Chace 1904, pp. 397-398].

This report of Chace has an additional interest in that it gives an independent view of the operation of Miss Farrell's ungraded class:

> The class has been a difficult one to teach: in the first place, it has usually numbered eighteen or twenty; then the boys have been very ungraded, at times, some more wayward than backward. At present, there are nineteen in the class, twelve of whom are mentally deficient. The youngest is six and a half years of age and the oldest seventeen. In work they range from "sub-kindergarten" to the second year of the grammar school. Notwithstanding these difficulties, each child is studied individually and his education fitted to his needs.
>
> The chief aim is to create in the boys a love of work so that when they go out into the world, they will not join the ranks of the criminal class. For this reason, everything is related to manual training and made subordinate to it. They always have some subject as a center; at present it is the farm. In woodwork, they are making a house and barn, fences, furniture, and flower-boxes. They are weaving the rugs for the floor, making a hammock, doing raffia work and basketry. They went to the country for the soil to plant their miniature fields, and sent to Washington for the seeds. In painting, their subjects have been apple blossoms and violets with an illustrated trip to Bronx Park. In picture study, they have taken "Oxen Plowing," "The Angelus," etc. In arithmetic, the older boys measure in a concrete way, the rooms of the house and the fields. In their written work in English, they are having stories of farm life, and reports of personal observation; in reading, stories of dogs, horses, making hay, and so on; in spelling, words relating to manual occupations, e.g., "soil, seeds, leaves, barn." In nature work, they are studying soils, the earthworm, buds and seeds. This is simply suggestive of the excellent work that the boys are taking up at present. The subjects are chosen and the different studies related to the center with the purpose of developing the social instincts in the boys [Chace 1904, pp. 339-400].

The reader need hardly be reminded to note the resemblance of this project-oriented curriculum for mentally subnormal children to the similar reforms of progressive educators designed for the education of normal children, several examples of which can be found in Dewey's *The Schools of Tomorrow* (1915).

Within two years following Chace's report, the special education program of New York City underwent rapid growth and differentiation. Julia Richman (1907), a district superintendent in lower Manhattan, summarized that development as it applied to special students other than defective or mentally subnormal.

> Almost all the cities in the United States now have an eight-year course of instruction, which is planned for a child beginning school at five or six, at the outside limit seven, and is intended to be completed by the time the child reaches fourteen or fifteen. In the last annual report of the city superintendent of schools of the city of New York, for the year ending July 31, 1906, on pages 51 to 59 inclusive, there are tables showing the classification of the children in the New York public schools

according to age and year of school. From that table it will be seen that more than thirty per cent of the children in the New York public schools are above the normal age, notwithstanding the fact that within the last two years more than 20,000 children were taken from the regular grades and put into special classes, in order to give them the individual help that they require to advance more rapidly. (In this classification of special classes I do not include the classes for mental defectives. They were the first special classes to be organized, but in order to remove from such grading any stigma, it was decided that such classes be called "ungraded.")

The board of education has authorized the establishment of three other kinds of special classes, known as Special C, Special D, and Special E classes. The C classes are known in Boston as "Steamer Classes." They are designed solely for the recently arrived immigrant from non-English speaking countries. The chief function of the C class is to give these children a working vocabulary and an ability to read in the English language, so that after a few months every child can be placed in a grade suited to its age, general mentality, and previous education. Before the establishment of classes of grade C, the fate of the little immigrant depended upon the intelligence or lack of intelligence of the individual principal or teacher. Although some principals did their full duty by these newcomers, in many schools it was customary to place such children in the lowest grade, basing such classification upon the fact that if a child can not read or speak English, the primer of the lowest grade is fitted to his needs. As a result of so stupid a classification it was found when the child labor law in New York State was put into operation in October, 1903, that thousands of boys and girls thirteen or fourteen years of age were still in the first four years of school life, because of injudicious grading and bad judgment on the part of those who should have known better. Occasionally an extremely bright boy or girl was pushed forward, but that was the exception. . . .

There are causes for backwardness in school other than being foreign-born, or being dull and inattentive. There are the partially backward children, who through illness, lack of language, irregular attendance, frequent removals causing change of school, or other causes, have lost time. Such children need individual help, which is practically impossible to be given in the large class and with the many obligations placed upon the average public school teacher. In order to provide for such cases the Special E grade was established. The work of the Special E grade can not be confined to one class. Instruction of this kind is necessary for the backward, over-age children of every year of school life from the first to the sixth. It would be of value in the seventh or eighth years and might even serve a good purpose in the high school. Every child that is two years beyond the normal age of a given grade should be taken from that room to receive the personal attention that his mental needs require. It will be found that the removal of the over-age children from the regular grades will practically solve the discipline problems in those grades, because it is generally the older, backward child who is the truant and the school incorrigible. . . .

The Special D grade was formed for those boys and girls of fourteen, or well past thirteen, whose parents desire them to go to work, but who are far behind the academic requirements of the child labor law. In the D classes an earnest effort is made to arouse the child's ambition to make up the deficiencies in his earlier school life, and to give him a solid foundation along the lines of the "Three R's" and such manual work as will arouse and maintain his interest, and which may possibly have a utilitarian value.

So much for the general plan now in operation in most districts in the city. In the schools under my personal charge the special class was first introduced by special permit, granted upon my application early in 1904, although as principal of a school in another district I had organized such classes fully ten years ago. The plan has been in operation, under my personal supervision, for more than three years. In three or four of my schools the results have gone beyond my most sanguine expectations. In some of the other schools the work is being satisfactorily done, and in all the schools something is being done in that direction [Richman 1907, pp. 234-236].

Richman went on to note that although the Special E classes took from the regular classes practically all the truants and incorrigibles, there remained the lawless and defiant, the chronic truant, arrested for delinquency and paroled by the children's court. Upon her recommendation the board of superintendents had approved the establishment of a special school, Public School 120, where such boys were isolated in order to keep their bad example from influencing the behavior of other children.

A variety of special classes for the physically handicapped—the crippled, the blind, the deaf and dumb, the tuberculous and the anemic—were also established. The Fourteenth Annual Report of the City Superintendent of Schools for the year ending 1912 indicates that as of June of that year there were 71 classes for these various physically handicapped children in which 1,514 children were registered (Maxwell 1912, p. 173). The ungraded classes were now left free to focus on the mentally subnormal.

However, in spite of the greatly improved sorting of children with special needs, it is not to be assumed that uniformity of handicap prevailed in the ungraded classes. In 1912, Henry H. Goddard of *Kallikak* fame was induced to make an official study of the ungraded classes in New York City. At the time of his investigation and according to his figures—which are slightly different from those in the superintendent's report for that year—there were 131 ungraded classes registering nearly 2,500 children. After visiting 125 of these classes Goddard concluded that the children were largely feebleminded and institution cases—we must bear in mind Goddard's rather loose criteria for diagnosing feeblemindedness and institutional cases—but nevertheless they included, "some that are really of normal mentality and should not be in these classes but should rather be in the progress classes—the E classes— among those children whom special attention will bring up to grade" (Goddard 1914, p. 3).

Goddard was of the opinion that the inclusion of mentalities ranging from that of a three-year-old to that of a normal child could only make the work of the teacher unduly difficult and expensive for the system. What is of interest to us is that Goddard, whose career activity at this point was generally characterized by an overreadiness to diagnose mental retardation on the basis of the flimsiest of evidence, should nevertheless have considered some of the children in the ungraded classes of normal intelligence. This at the same time that he maintained that there must be on the basis of an assumed 2 percent retardation rate among school age children some 15,000 feebleminded children in the New York City schools. It was Goddard's opinion, based on some sampling of the children's intelligence that he undertook with the Binet-Simon test of intelligence, that many of these children were to be found in the special D, E, and C classes.

Accepting the fact that the ungraded classes of this period probably included some children who were of normal intelligence does not mean that we would assume that the children were not by and large appropriately classified even if we were to use today's standards of classification. It does suggest that one could argue then as now that classes for educable children are a mixed bag.

Returning to Farrell and her ungraded class, we recall the resemblance in Chace's description of the conduct of the class to the kind of curriculum and methodology that was being advocated by progressive educators of the day for normal children. Farrell, however, in presenting the conduct of the ungraded class before the National Education Association in 1908 traces the roots of her system not to contemporary progressive education but directly back to original sources.

It has been said that the treatment of mentally defective children in the public schools and the treatment of the average normal boy or girl differ in no essential particular. It is a difference of degree, not of kind. We do not have any new methods, sentence, word and phonic; we have no new device for developing the sense of quantity or of quality: we weigh, measure, compare, reckon; we have only such means as are open to all for the training of childhood. Like the teacher of the normal child we go back to Locke for his philosophy. "Nothing can enter the mind except thru the senses; to Comenius we go for a sequence in training—sense, memory, intellect; to Rousseau we go to realize again and again the supreme importance of knowing the child, and his development which is to come, if at all, thru his experience with things, things, things; to Pestalozzi we go to learn that our aim is not that the child should know what he does not know but that he should behave as he does not behave, and the road to right action is right feeling." And again he says: "I have proved that it is not regular work that stops the development of so many poor children but the turmoil and irregularity of their lives, the privations they endure, the excesses they indulge in when opportunity offers; the wild rebellious passions so seldom restrained; and the hopelessness to which they are so often the prey." To Froebel we go for his philosophy of the unity of all life, even encumbered as it often is by disease, defect, ignorance and crime. From these, the master teachers, we learn to look from the defective mind to the cause of it—the defective eye, the defective ears, the poor control, will explain much and indicate more; instead of nagging and scolding the child for seemingly careless work we seek causes for it in the badly nourished anaemic body, the victim perhaps of our modern slavery—child labor—and likely as not the inheritor of such nervous instability as comes from the parent, who may be the slave of some intoxicant, or the victim of that sad and miserable poverty which undermines the power and usefulness of men.*

In general it is true that mental life of greatest reach and possibility is directly dependent on physical efficiency; so our treatment of the mentally defective child must begin in a complete diagnosis of his case. It must proceed along those lines which nature unimpeded takes with the average human infant. We have to do with the "misfit" in the schools, the child out of tune, the child isolated by his inabilities and often by his teacher. It is ours to fit the school to him; to restore the harmony; to socialize him and make him feel with his more fortunate brothers the unity of all life [Farrell 1908, pp. 1134–1135].

Addressing herself more specifically to the education of the mentally ·defective child Farrell states:

The general principle upon which all education of mentally defective children is based is: "Begin where the defect of disease impeded the normal development." This point may be determined in either of two ways: the teacher may begin with those exercises which naturally a boy of given years should be able to do, and from that work backward to the point where the child can accomplish a given exercise. This may be called the negative procedure. The opposite process is that which begins with the most elementary workings of the child's neuro-muscular system, and climbs upward by means of very short, definite, more complex workings until the arrest in development has been reached. This process of localization is a positive procedure. I need not state to this audience which is the more valuable to the child. A process which leaves any child, or adult for that matter, flushed with his own success, his own great achievement, is the process which makes for future advance by giving the individual faith in his own power to do. With the mentally defective child, conscious often of his own shortcomings, realizing frequently that he is different from his fellows, the negative procedure is positive cruelty and when practiced in the school defeats, or at least delays, the achievement of the very purpose for which the school exists [Farrell 1908, pp. 1132–1133].

Farrell then illustrates the application of the principle in the case of a child with neuromuscular handicap. Indicating that control of fine motor movements is more complex and difficult, she maintains that the training exercises should begin with large muscle exercises such as climbing a ladder, playing with a basketball, or using large tools such as a saw or plane. Only later in the child's training should one undertake work requiring fine muscle control such as sewing and weaving: "Our help must be given along the lines of natural development" (p. 1133).

Similarly she notes, "there is another sequence to be observed in the training of mentally defective children, and this is the sequence based upon the natural order of mental development" (p. 1133). Here she cites Preyer on the

---

*In this etiological explanation of mental subnormality Farrell is utilizing the popular nineteenth century "degeneration theory" of Auguste Morel, vestiges of which still appeared in the writings of the experts in the first decade of the twentieth century. See Sarason and Doris (1969).

basic importance of imitation in the development of the child. "Imitation gives rise to language . . . imitation is the first step in mental development" (p. 1133). She admonishes:

> The teacher of mentally defective children must realize that much, if not all, of her first work with a child must be based on this principle of imitation. The teacher of mentally defective children must realize that often she must show the child the movement he is to make. She must put his body into the position she wants him to assume until he feels that position, and so be able to imitate the seen movement reinforced by the "felt movement" of his own body [p. 1133].

Summarizing her views on imitation she gives William Torrey Harris as authority for the statement that "imitation develops into habits, customs, morals, that is, the will side of the human mind, and on the other it develops into perception, memory, ideas and insights, which is the intellectual side of the human mind" (p. 1134).

We have spent time on Farrell's philosophy and methods of teaching the mentally subnormal because of the important role she played in training the first public school teachers of ungraded or special education classes. In 1906, she was appointed to the position of Inspector of Ungraded Classes with the duties of supervising the work of existing classes, aiding in the formation of others, and the training of teachers for this special work. She first used her own class as a training class for prospective teachers of ungraded classes; in 1911 she was instrumental in establishing a training program for special teachers in the City's Maxwell Training School for Teachers. She also participated in the newly developing summer training programs for special teachers at the University of Pennsylvania, New York University, and Teachers College. Her professional influence was furthered by founding and subsequently editing *Ungraded,* a magazine published by the Ungraded Class Teachers' Association. This journal from 1915 to 1926 was an important disseminator of information relevant to the teaching of the mentally subnormal. In 1922 she organized and was the first president of the International Council for the Education of Exceptional Children (Phillips 1934).

During Miss Farrell's twenty-five years of leadership in the department of ungraded classes it grew rapidly in size and diversification of programs. The fourteenth Annual Report of the City Superintendent of Schools (1912) tabulated 110 ungraded classes for "mental defectives" with a register of 2,253 pupils. In that report the superintendent indicated that two assistant inspectors and two physicians had been appointed to aid Miss Farrell in her work. As early as 1909, Miss Farrell had begun the conduct of a clinic in her office where children were tested to determine the level of their physical and mental development. This was the beginning of the first psycho-educational clinic to be established within a public school system in the United States.

From the earliest years of her work Farrell was to emphasize the interdisciplinary nature of the diagnosis of mental subnormality. She worked with physicians at first; later social workers and psychologists became part of her departmental staff. Social workers first joined the Department of Ungraded Classes under the designation of visiting teachers. The first such visiting teacher was actually supported and sponsored by the Public Education Association, a reform organization founded in 1895 which advocated evening schools, playgrounds, vocational studies, free lunches, visiting teachers, and special classes for mentally and physically defective children (Cremin 1964). In 1912, this first field-worker's activities have been described as follows:

> Many children who appeared to be hopelessly defective were taken by this visitor to hospitals or clinics where they were examined and found to be more normal than at first supposed. Others who were regarded by teachers as unruly and difficult were found to be handicapped by some slight physical trouble which might easily be remedied. In cases where the pupil was clearly unequal to the task of grappling with public education, the investigator attempted to explain the situation to the family and to have the child placed in an institution where it could be taught and cared for [Training School Bull.; 1913–14, 105].

In the following year the Board of Education, convinced of the need to correlate the school life of the child with its home life, undertook the hiring of additional visiting teachers. By 1914 the selection of candidates for the ungraded classes involved a consideration of the following data:

1. The report of the school principal or other person proposing the child for examination.
2. The social service report made by a social worker who visits the home to get the various phases of the environmental setting of the child's life.
3. The clinical study of the child which includes a physical, psychological, and pedagogical examination [Walsh 1914, pp. 59–60].

Stationary clinics had been established at the New York and Brooklyn offices of the Board of Education, and traveling clinics were held for several days at a time in different centers throughout the city. As we shall see when we look at the criteria for assignment to special education classes in other cities of this period, New York's approach appears quite sophisticated. How thoroughly the examinations were carried out might be another question, for Walsh notes that "the obvious cases are given relatively little time." The emphasis of the clinic was upon the "border-line" cases: "those children who deviate only slightly from the normal, the child who can grasp arithmetic but who cannot learn to read, and vice versa, the child who is strongly ear-minded or motor-minded and who has fallen behind because the instruction given in most schools is based on the fact that the majority of children are eye-minded" (Walsh 1914, p. 60). Apparently, by Walsh's account, children that today's educator would label "learning disabled" might end up in a ungraded class with the teacher alerted to their special patterns of learning strengths and weaknesses.

Walsh's article is of further interest in that she indicates that the school system was now beginning to classify the children in ungraded classes. "There are classes for high grade older boys, for high grade older girls and classes for low grade children. To one of the above types of classes a child approved for ungraded class work is assigned. Many of the cases examined are too low to receive any benefit by attendance at a public school. For such, institutional care is recommended" (Walsh 1914, pp. 62–63).

It was not until 1928, again as a result of Miss Farrell's efforts, that these latter children with IQs below 50 were provided with classes in the city's school system (O'Shea 1929, Phillips 1935). In these classes, according to O'Shea's account, no formal school work was attempted. The children were taught simple, practical activities with the emphasis on motor training.

Superintendent O'Shea's report on the progress of the city schools from 1924 to 1929 also details the further growth of the ungraded department under Miss Farrell's direction. During this period, the number of ungraded classes had increased from 305 to 409 with a corresponding increase of registered pupils from 5,898 to 8,109. In 1925, trade extension classes were organized in cooperation with the Manhattan Trade School for Girls. These classes designed for girls of 15 years of age or more were intended to train the girls for various trades which would permit them to enter the job market as skilled workers. Again, on Farrell's recommendation similar classes were subsequently developed for boys.

Elizabeth Walsh, an Assistant Inspector under Miss Farrell, was to succeed to leadership in the early 1930s. By the outbreak of World War II, the responsibility for providing specialized educational training and health care for all types of handicapped school children was organized as a division within the Department of Education of the City of New York. The Division in turn was organized into seven bureaus, namely, the Bureau of Child Guidance, Bureau for Children with Retarded Mental Development, Bureau for Physically Handicapped Children, Bureau of Speech Improvement, Bureau of Industrial and Placement Work for Physically Handicapped Children, Classes for the Blind, Sight Conservation Classes, and the School for the Deaf (McCooey 1940–41).

The Bureau for Children with Retarded Mental Development by this time was responsible for 621 classes serving 12,000 children. In accordance with state regulations, children were recommended for placement in these classes as follows:

1. Children with intelligence quotients between 50 and 75 and mental ages between 5 and 10, based on adequate individual examination, may be placed in elementary ungraded classes.
2. Children of appropriate age with intelligence quotients between 50 and 75 and mental ages between 8 and 12 may be placed in junior high school ungraded classes.

3. Children whose intelligence quotients fall below 50 and who are socially adjusted and able to profit by such training may be placed in low IQ classes. Classes for mentally retarded children are as far as possible homogeneous. According to state regulations, registers of classes having a four year chronological age range are limited to twenty-two pupils; if the age range is wider, the maximum register is 18. Because of this limitation in size, provision for individual guidance and instruction can be made [Smith 1940-41, p. 169].

This account of the organization of classes by Rose Smith who at that time was the Bureau's acting director is of interest, first, because of its indication of the dominating and rigid role the IQ score had come to assume in educational decisions regarding the care and training of the mentally subnormal; and secondly, in the indication of the important role that state regulations had assumed in the education of the mentally subnormal. Our account of the beginnings of special education classes for the mentally subnormal had focused on city school systems because the education of the mentally subnormal was at first a city school system problem. It was within the cities that these children occurred in sufficient numbers to constitute a problem for the class-graded schools.

Beginning in 1911, New Jersey legislated obligatory provision of special classes for mentally subnormal children. New York State followed suit in 1917 (Wallin 1924). The New York State law made it obligatory on all school districts within the state to ascertain the number of children in attendance in their schools who were three years or more retarded in mental development, and to establish in those districts in which there were ten or more such children special classes of not more than fifteen pupils each, as might be necessary to provide instruction adapted to the mental attainments of the children. Districts in which there were less than ten such children might exercise the option of contracting for the education of these children with neighboring school districts providing such classes (Cornell 1919). From this beginning the state took on a more and more active role in the regulation and support of public school programs for the mentally subnormal.

The Growth of Special Education
on the National Scene

The rapid growth of New York City's program for the mentally subnormal, the diversification of programs, and the increasing state involvement in the regulation of such classes were duplicated on the national scene. In our account of the U.S. Bureau of Education Report of 1911 on the provision for exceptional children in the public schools, it was noted that of 898 city school systems responding to a survey, 99 had classes for the mentally defective, and

220 had classes for the backward child. There were, however, difficulties interpreting the data for no clear definition was given for differentiating mental deficiency from backwardness and there were no data on the number of children registered in such classes (van Sickle, Witmer and Ayres, 1911).

In contrast to that survey, a 1924 Bureau of Education *Bulletin* presents statistics showing city school systems providing special classes or day school programs for the mentally subnormal increasing from 54 in 1914, to 133 in 1922, with corresponding changes in enrollment from 10,890 to 23,252 pupils (Phillips 1924). Why the Bureau should have reported fewer school systems with special classes in 1914 than reported by the 1911 survey is not readily apparent. But Wallin (1924) cogently argues the unreliability of these early statistics partly due to the difficulty in getting survey returns and partly due to the improper utilization of the returned data. Nevertheless, he accepted the rapid growth of special education programs in this period and attributed it not only to the stimulus of state enactments of educational measures promoting the interests of the mentally handicapped but also, interestingly enough, to the increasing use of the Binet scale. The widespread utilization of this instrument in the second decade of the twentieth century had done much to facilitate "the discovery of the moron" (Davies 1930).

In 1921, V. V. Anderson, Associate Medical Director for the National Committee for Mental Hygiene, reported in that Society's journal the results of a 1919 survey of special education classes in the public schools. The report is of interest in that it addressed itself to issues other than the number of classes. Of the school administrators contacted in 155 cities, 125 replied to the questionaire. Only seventeen cities indicated that they had no provision for special classes. In the remaining 108 cities, there were 1,177 special classes providing for 21,251 "mentally defective" pupils. In those cities in which public school population — exclusive of high schools — exceeded 90,000 (Chicago, St. Louis, Cleveland, Boston, New York, and Philadelphia) the number of special class pupils varied from 0.5 percent of the total number of pupils in St. Louis to 1.2 percent in Cleveland. Boston was the only other city to reach the 1 percent level.

Given Anderson's assumption of from 1 to 2 percent mental defectives in public school populations, it becomes apparent that only Cleveland and Boston among the major cities were approaching adequate provision for the mentally subnormal in the schools. In 53 of 86 cities responding to an inquiry regarding the training of special-class teachers, there was some requirement of specialized training. In the remaining 33, there was no criterion of selection other than some indication of "interest," "adaptability," "efficiency," etc., upon the part of the teacher to distinguish her from the regular teachers.

Anderson noted that the demand for specially trained teachers far exceeded the supply and stated that the greatest need was for training courses in normal schools and universities, supplemented by practical work in state institutions for the feebleminded. There were, in his opinion, very few places in the United States where teachers could receive anything like adequate training in special education, a problem which continued to persist. Twenty percent of the total number of cities studied were equipped with special schools in which all of the special classes were grouped. This was disappointing to Anderson who felt that all who had given much thought to the subject were agreed that the defective child should not be placed in separate classes in the regular schools; not only does grouping of the classes in a special school provide for better organization, systematization, and grading but the defective child is protected from comparison with normal children as well as taunts from those more capable than himself. It is interesting that Farrell (1908) during the same era was arguing against special schools and for integration of the school program for the mentally subnormal with the regular program in order to protect the child from the stigma of being different. This issue is not dissimilar to the pros and cons of mainstreaming which we shall discuss in Chapter 17.

The average class size was 16 for all cities combined, with a range from 7 to 40 plus. Anderson's average class size appears to have been obtained by dividing the total number of pupils (21,251) by the total number of teachers (1,292) which would give 16.4 pupils per teacher. If we use the total number of classes (1,177) as the denominator, the result would be 18.0 pupils per class. St. Louis, Missouri, was outstanding with only eleven classes for 471 pupils although its listed complement of 26 teachers suggests that more than one teacher was assigned to a class. Anderson was concerned about the lack of distinction between classes for backward and feebleminded children in some 35 cities and warned the reader that it was quite likely that many of the special classes in his report contained a mixture of both kinds of children. The backward children were those who because of language difficulties, health problems, irregular attendance, etc. were academically lagging and could be returned to the regular grades with proper study and treatment. Compounding this difficulty of not distinguishing between feeblemindedness and backwardness were the criteria being used for the diagnosis of mental deficiency.

> This investigation shows that 16 of the 108 cities that replied to the questionnaire had no examinations whatever, the children being selected by teachers and principal purely on the basis of school work in the regular grades; that in 54 cities, or about 54 percent of the total number, special-class teachers, principals, and supervisors gave Binet tests and made diagnoses upon children selected by the grade teachers. With no examination other than these tests, a child is diagnosed as defective or not defective. In 36, or 32 percent, of the cities studied, psychiatrists or psychologists passed upon the question of mental condition before the child was placed in the special class. In 3 cities trained nurses gave Binet tests [Anderson 1921, p. 114].

Anderson concluded that in 68 percent of the cities, children were being placed in special classes for mental defectives without being properly diagnosed by adequately trained experts. His review of the training programs of the various special classes was equally harsh:

> The greatest criticism we have to offer from a careful study of the returns of the questionnaire is that school authorities all too frequently see in the special class only a chance to segregate a greater or lesser number of the children from the regular grades; to remove from the wheels of the educational machine a certain amount of grit that disturbs the smoothness of its running gear. Too often it was obvious that there was little or no purpose in view in the training given. Weeks and months of a defective child's time might be taken up on the making of a basket or the weaving of a rug, or in doing many things that would never lead to self-support. To be sure, these kept the child employed, provided good exhibit material, and relieved teacher of the necessity of much planning; but as for fitting the child to do some useful thing by means of which he could earn a living, that was a consideration that apparently had received very little thought and attention in the majority of instances [Anderson 1921, pp. 117–118].

A concluding concern of Anderson was the lack of supervision and after-care provision for the children. In only five cities was anything like a serious attempt made to keep in touch with the defective children after they left school and entered employment.

The increase in the number of pupils enrolled in special education programs for the mentally subnormal since 1922 has been concisely summarized by Dunn (1973). Compiling data from a number of official government sources, he reports that the number of mentally retarded pupils in local public school systems in 1922 was 23,252; by 1940 it had reached 98,415; and in 1972 totaled 872,113. Breaking the total number of mentally subnormal down into educable and trainable groups reveals that in 1948 there was an enrollment of 4,509 trainable children in the public schools, and in 1968 it had reached 55,000. Dunn's tabulation indicates no trainable children in the public schools as of 1940. However, we noted that New York City opened its first class for children with IQs below 50 in 1928 (O'Shea 1929, Phillips 1935). Furthermore, Rose Smith as acting director for the Bureau of Children with Retarded Mental Development in New York City reported in 1941 that at that time there were 34 classes for such children in the city's school system. Apparently, Wallin's 1924 complaint about the reliability of government statistics on special education programs still had some validity.

Throughout this period the rate of growth in provision for the mentally subnormal child was greater than the growth rate for the school population as a whole. This discrepancy became more marked in the period following World War II, and probably reflected the increased public attention to mental subnormality. In the chapter on mainstreaming, we will have occasion to consider some of the social factors stimulating that increased public awareness.

What we would like to consider next is an issue that the reader must immediately recognize when considering such remarkable growth rates in special education classes—the problem of teacher training. Assuming that children in special classes were there because they could not profit from the teaching that took place in the regular grades, it was reasonable to assume that the special education teacher required different training from that required by the teacher of the regular grades.

The Training of Special Education Teachers for the Mentally Subnormal

As was apparent in our accounts of the formation of some of the earliest special classes for the mentally subnormal, teacher preparation consisted of an interest in working with the children who were to be assigned to such classes. In the account of Farrell (1908), who was one such self-selected teacher, the philosophy, principles, and methods of such teaching were derived from Locke, Comenius, Rousseau, Pestalozzi, Froebel, and others who had in fact shaped the general form of modern education. If that were completely true, one might wonder why then the need for special education? Recalling the descriptions of Rice and Shaw of the city school systems around the turn of the century, the obvious answer might be that their classes were not, in general, taught according to the principles and methods of Farrell's master-teachers. To work with such principles and methods in the cities at the turn of the century was indeed a utilization of a special kind of teaching.

But Farrell's application of the principles and methods of the masters had also undertaken in part a special form which allied it to the educational system of Edouard Seguin. This in spite of the fact that she makes only one brief tangential mention of Seguin. On the other hand, it is true that while placing herself within the generally accepted educational philosophy of the times—indicating that the treatment of the defective child is to differ from the normal only in degree and not in kind—she does note that within that framework the special education teacher is to recognize the point at which the child's defect has impeded normal development and, beginning at that point, undertake the training of the child along the lines of natural development. In doing that with a severely motor-impaired child, the account of her teaching practice which we have previously given does take on a resemblance to Seguin's system of education. Nevertheless, taking the account of her philosophy and principles of teaching at face value she apparently was little influenced by the educational programs that had for over a half of a century been utilized in the institutions for the mentally subnormal. It was in these institutions that the philosophy and principles of Edouard Seguin were practiced. That his work and these institutions did directly influence the special education programs and the training of special education teachers for the public schools is easily enough documented even for the City of New York.

Elizabeth Walsh, an Assistant Inspector of Ungraded Classes under Farrell, gave direct tribute to the influence of Seguin on the classroom teaching of the mentally subnormal:

> The method employed is the one expounded by that wonderful man, Dr. Seguin, which he called the physiological method of education. The method is largely motor. It includes all forms of motor expression employed in teaching reading, writing, drawing and physical training, as well as the manual exercise used in gardening, weaving, pattern making or carpentry. Seguin said, "Our instruments of teaching must be those that go directly to the point. We must use objects, pictures, photographs, cards, patterns, clay, wax figures, scissors, compasses, pencils, colors, even books." It is Dr. Eliot who says that it is through practice with eye, ear, nose and touch, that the same nerves and ganglia that transmit and record our sensations and set going our movements that we all get our minds to work in childhood and acquire not only skill with eye and hand but also skill in thinking. The normal child gets this practice through his own activity and curiosity. For the defective child, especially if he is of low mentality, provision must be made in order that he shall get it. To this end the low grade children are given work in sense training. The purpose of this is not to make the senses sharper, but to get the children to attend to impressions received through their senses. Through careful training of the senses, and through reasoning on the testimony of the senses, the processes of reasoning are brought as near perfection as may be. Exercises for the training of touch, hearing and vision have been carefully worked out. They include many devised by Seguin. To avoid formalism in this work, we give the child a motive for what he does. Instead of buttoning and unbuttoning strips of cloth, he buttons and unbuttons his companion's coat, or if a little girl, she buttons and unbuttons her doll's clothes. If the sense training is separated from real needs and accepted motives, it degenerates into mere mental gymnastics and the children get little real training from it [Walsh 1914, pp. 63–64].

Ignoring the somewhat confusing reference to Dr. Eliot, this concise account gives some idea of Seguin's principles and methods. Although Seguin's methods and apparatus give prominence to the motor and sensory training components of his educational system, he aimed at a comprehensive and harmonious development of the moral, intellectual, and physical capacities of the child. For a fuller account of his system, the reader is referred to his *Idiocy: Its Treatment by the Physiological Method* (1866).

Mabel Talbot's 1964 study of Seguin ought to be consulted as well, to place the man and his work in a proper historical context which will indicate his indebtedness to Itard, to the specialized field of the education of the deaf, particularly as represented by the work of Pereire, to the gymnastic teaching of Amoros, and also to the developments within eighteenth century pedagogical theory, notably those of Rousseau and Rollin.

Among these predecessors of Seguin there was the advocacy of a teaching method involving activity and sensory experience and a de-emphasis on the highly verbal instruction that was common to the schools of the eighteenth century. Thus Seguin, like Pestalozzi, although drawing his inspiration from different sources—with the exception of Rousseau who was common to both—was approaching the problem of the education of the defective child as Pestalozzi approached that of the normal child with a bias against verbalism and towards an interaction between the self and the world of things and events. In that sense, it was possible for Farrell to attribute the principles and methods utilized in the ungraded classes of New York to the tradition of general education represented by Pestalozzi, while at the same time Walsh could attribute it to Seguin's work with institutionalized defectives.

The time at which each entered the field of special education in the public schools might also account for the difference in perception: Farrell near the beginning and before she had made any contact with the institutions for the retarded; Walsh later, after contact with the training schools had been established. Certainly by the time Walsh wrote in 1914, the influence of the institutions in the preparation of public school teachers was well advanced.

Seguin entered the field of mental subnormality as a pupil of Itard in that he began the education of an idiot child under the latter's tutelage in 1837. Esquirol, the great French alienist of the period, attested to the success of the work by affirming that a child nearly mute and "resembling an idiot"—his preconception as to the incurability of idiocy necessitated the qualifier—had in a period of eighteen months been taught "to use his senses, to remember, to compare, to speak, to write, to count, etc." (Talbot 1964, p. 59).

Subsequently, Seguin treated idiot children at the Hospice des Incurables (Saltpêtrière) and the Hospice de la Vieillesse (Bicêtre) in Paris. His success was acclaimed by colleagues and in reports of official commissions assigned to evaluate his work. In the space of a few years he gained international renown. In the political climate of 1850, with Louis Napoleon's ambitions becoming more evident, the liberal-minded Seguin emigrated to the United States (Talbot 1964). This was the formative period of the state residential schools for the mentally subnormal and Seguin's influence had already preceded him by the reports of those Americans who had visited his schools in Paris.

In 1848, Samuel Gridley Howe set up the first state-supported school for the mentally subnormal in a wing of the Perkins Institute for the Blind in Boston. Seguin spent his first months in this country advising on the organization of its work. Hervey B. Wilbur, director of New York State's first training school, was in close contact with him and after the school was permanently located in Syracuse in 1854, Seguin was a continual help in the development of its program. For a brief period, he was connected with the Pennsylvania Training School for Idiots.

He advanced the idea of a cooperative association of superintendents of training schools and in 1876, when the Association of Medical Officers of

American Institutions for Idiotic and Feebleminded Persons was formed, he was elected its first president. The organization was to change its name in 1906 to the American Association for the Study of the Feebleminded and in 1933, to the American Association on Mental Deficiency. The *Proceedings of the Association,* first published in 1877, fulfilled Seguin's hope for an organ of communication for those interested in mental subnormality. In 1896, the annual proceedings were replaced by the *Journal of Psycho-Asthenics* which was to serve an important role in communicating new developments in special education within the public schools (Davies 1930, Kanner 1964, Talbot 1964).

Thus, Seguin had enormous influence on the development of training programs in the state institutions. When special education classes first began to develop within the public schools, educators looked to the institutions for guidance and training, and Seguin's influence flowed into the public schools. Seguin felt that his physiological method was appropriate for the education of the normal child and he had also published on the problems of general education but his influence on general education is more directly traced through the work of Maria Montessori who used his methods first with defective children and subsequently with normal children (Talbot 1964).

According to the accounts of Lincoln (1903, 1909), Boston made very direct use of the resources of residential training schools in the development of its special classes, the first of which was established in 1899:

> The original plan was very simple. The best possible teachers were selected — women of experience in their profession, acquainted with kindergarten methods, some of whom had been trained by regular service at Barre and Mrs. Seguin's school, while others had been sent by the Board to spend three months in residence at Elwyn previous to taking classes in Boston. The teachers thus chosen were practically allowed to act as their own judgment dictated. There was no requirement, scarcely even a suggestion, as to the results to be sought, or the methods to be used; the work to be done is very much the same as in state schools for feeble-minded, and such differences as may be observed between individual classes are chiefly matters of detail and personal preference.
>
> Previous to the appointment of the first teacher, Miss Daniels, the names of two hundred pupils had been secured from the masters of schools as unsuited for being taught in the regular classes. From these, after examination, she picked out fifteen of the most urgent cases and became their teacher. Other classes were formed at intervals; and, about three years later, a second inquiry elicited a new series of cases, of which about two hundred have been studied by Dr. Arthur C. Jelly, acting as an unpaid volunteer. A considerable number of the latter have been sent to the State School at Waverly, and others have been placed in the "special" classes we are now describing. It may be well to state here that no properly descriptive name had been attached to these classes; they go by the rather indeterminate designation of "special" classes [Lincoln 1903, p. 84].

In this account, Barre apparently refers to the private school for the mentally subnormal founded by Hervey B. Wilbur in Massachusetts in 1848. Mrs.

Seguin's school was the private school founded in New York City by her husband shortly before his death in 1880. Dr. Martin Barr, superintendent of the Pennsylvania State School at Elwyn, recalled his role in the training of Boston's public school teachers:

> When Mr. Seaver, of Boston, first proposed sending me teachers to train I was appalled. I consented to do it on condition that I could have them under my absolute control and could have women of cultivation and refinement. He sent me most delightful women in every way, earnest, thoughtful, capable, hard workers. I insisted that they should follow our classification. I gave them clinics and laid out a course of reading for them and had them spend a great deal of time in manual training and sloyd work.* It was a valuable experience to them. They stayed three months and I hear from Boston that they are doing very well using Weir Mitchell's motto that "the working hand makes strong the working brain" [Lincoln 1903, p. 90].

Other state training institutions participated to a greater or lesser extent in the training of public school teachers but it was left to the private institution of the Vineland Training School to play the most active role in the institutional training of public school teachers. According to E. R. Johnstone, who was director of the institution during this period, the first summer school for training public school teachers was held at this institution about 1903. Five students attended. Gradually, enrollment increased and by 1909, some thirty students attended a six-week session, in which according to Johnstone:

> Dr. Goddard has a course of lectures and much laboratory work that the teachers are required to do. They have one hour each day in the school rooms teaching various lines. There are two periods a week in which Mrs. Nash, the principal of the schools, teaches them the elements of various lines of industrial work that are valuable in teaching backward children. I myself give a lecture one hour each day. The principal gives a period each day where practical work of the school room is discussed and methods taken up. What we are after is to try to teach these folks what seems to be the best mode of procedure with backward children and in order to do that we try to get at the bottom of things; we try to forget all that we would be taught in the public schools and taught in the institutions and try to begin with the child and after all these years I am more than ever convinced that we must get down in our institutions to a little lower starting point before we are building our training on a solid foundation. Therefore, the very first thing we speak of to our teachers is the question of happiness. There is no institution man who is not sure that happiness is the ruling element in the work of his institution. Every one of us believes that our institution is the happiest place we know of but it can't be so unless we make a definite point of that thing, unless we require our teachers to say, not, "How can I best get my children to obey me or to understand me?" but, "How can I have these children as happy as they can be made in the day room, at the entertainments in the schoolroom and anywhere else they may be?" This has been

---

*Sloyd work refers to a system of manual training originating in Finland and Sweden, based on the premise that the active occupations of kindergarten should be retained throughout the grades (Parker 1970).

a definite business of the institution and wherever it is made a definite business everything else is easy [Johnstone 1909-10, p. 125].

In the apparent folksy yet kindly philosophy that Johnstone reveals in this account of his school, there may be one of the ingredients that made the Vineland summer school one of the most — if not the most — effective special teacher training institutions of that period. But among other assets must certainly be listed Henry H. Goddard and the *Training School Bulletin* that he and Johnstone helped edit.

Henry H. Goddard, who had obtained his Ph.D. under G. Stanley Hall at Clark University in 1899, was appointed director of the Research Laboratory at the Vineland Training School in 1906. He was an active researcher, a prolific writer, and a major force in the development of the field of mental subnormality. His books *The Kallikak Family* (1912,), *Feeble-mindedness: Its Causes and Consequences* (1914), and his articles on feeblemindedness among immigrants (1913, 1917) and among delinquents (1911) were to make him prominent in the American eugenics movement. He invented the term moron to designate those higher grades of mental subnormality whose diagnosis was to rely so heavily upon the use of intelligence tests. On a visit to Europe in 1908, he became acquainted with the 1905 form of the Binet-Simon scales, translated it, and with some reservation about its adequacy began utilizing it at Vineland. His immediate reaction to the 1908 revision was also reserved. It looked too simple to provide an adequate evaluation of intelligence. However, he decided to give it a trial and was soon convinced that the classification of children based on this 1908 revision agreed with the classification of the children as based upon the experience and observation of the Vineland staff. In 1910, Goddard published a summary of the scale and from that time on the Vineland Laboratory became a major center for disseminating knowledge of the scale and for the training of teachers in its use.

By 1914, the Vineland summer school was restricting its enrollment to sixty students and was offering an advanced course for teachers of backward or mentally deficient children; eligibility for enrollment required a previously attended course at Vineland or elsewhere. In this six-week program, the work included lectures by staff members, study and observation of children and methods in school, and testing and examination of children in the laboratory. In this advanced course it was intended to give special attention to fitting students for supervisory position (*Training School Bulletin, 10*, p. 46; *11*, p. 13).

Goddard's training of special class teachers was not limited to Vineland, for he appears on the faculty listings of other summer school programs of that time including New York University, and the State Teachers' College of Colorado (*Training School Bulletin*, 1913, *10*, p. 153). To have been a pupil of H. H. Goddard in that period surely must have been the highest certification of one's training in the field of mental subnormality.

Certainly, there is no question but that graduates of the Vineland Summer Training program were prominently placed in supervisory roles in the developing special education programs in the major cities, and the names of many of them appear as frequent contributors to the professional literature of that time. Whether due to the kindly, homespun philosophy of Johnstone or the dynamic leadership of Goddard, there appears to have been an outstanding esprit de corps among the young women graduates of the Vineland Training School. They formed the Summer School Alumni Association (*Training School Bulletin*, 1914, *11*, p. 72) and the *Training School Bulletin* served to keep them aware of each others' activities. A section of the *Bulletin* entitled "Special Class" became a regular feature and in it there would be notices of developments of new special education programs and the activities of alumni.

The *Bulletin* also served a useful function for all interested in training for public school teachers by periodically listing available programs and their curricula. Thus a 1914 article in the *Bulletin* lists summer schools for teachers at New York University, the University of Pennsylvania, State Teachers' College of Colorado, University of Washington, University of Pittsburg, Teachers College of Columbia University, The Minnesota School for Feeble-Minded and Colony for Epileptics, The Rome State Custodial Asylum, and of course the Training School at Vineland. Looking over the faculty listing of such programs one cannot help but he impressed with the quality of the teaching staffs. New York University listed Dr. Arnold Gesell as well as Dr. Goddard. State Teachers' College of Colorado lists Lightner Witmer, H. H. Goddard, G. S. Hall, and D. S. Jordan, the latter an outstanding biologist and leading eugenicist.

Gradually, some normal schools, colleges, and universities began to train special teachers in their regular programs. One of the most extensive of such programs appears to have developed at New York University. This is described by James E. Lough, the University's Director of the Department for Teachers of Backward and Defective children, in a 1915 issue of *Ungraded*. It was a two-year program and presumed that the students would have taken a two-year course in a normal school, or city training school, followed by some experience as a teacher of normal children.

A more typical training program was that introduced by the Oswego State Normal School and announced by its principal James Riggs in the *Proceedings of the National Education Association* in 1916. As more fully described by Riggs in 1922 the course of study and faculty were as follows:

Fundamentals of mental deficiency, principles of mental testing, abnormal psychology, sociology, special methods in arithmetic, reading, English, physical education, handwork of various kinds, weaving, chair-caning, wood-working, etc.

The faculty in charge consists of: Flora E. Otis, Head of Department. Adelaide Fitch, Assistant in Department. Dr. Richard K. Piez, Psychology. C. L. G. Scales, Sociology [Riggs 1922, p. 9].

Otis and Fitch were both graduates of the Vineland Summer School and adequately trained by the standards of the day. However, something of a makeshift character in the program is suggested by the listing of Piez for psychology and Scales for sociology. Both had long and distinguished teaching careers at Oswego, but neither had training in the disciplines they were to represent for the program. Piez was a jack-of-all trades as an educator but in the consensus of students made his least effective teaching contribution in the area of psychology. Scales was considered a brilliant teacher of literature and composition but had neither preparation nor extensive experience for presenting her offerings in sociology. Practical experience in connection with the program was provided by the Rome State School. The program was not particularly popular with students and was dropped in 1934 to save expenses (Riggs 1922, Rogers 1961).

Despite developing programs in normal schools and colleges, the preparation of teachers for special classes lagged behind the need. In a review on the education of exceptional children prepared for the Office of Education in 1931, Elsie Martens noted that "All too frequently teachers are assigned to teach mentally deficient children who have had little or no preparation for the work." She cited the preliminary report of the Committee on Special Classes of the White House Conference to the effect that "of the teachers preparing to teach mentally deficient children, five-eights have *six weeks or less* of training, and three-eights have had 18 weeks or more" (p. 410).

As to training facilities for teachers, she again cites the Committee's report, "Including all institutions granting certificates to special class teachers during the past 5 years, there have been trained an average yearly total of 189 teachers for the mentally deficient . . . " (p. 410). On Martens's assumption that the public schools were providing for only one-tenth of the 500,000 children who needed special education because of mental handicap, the growing supply of trained teachers seemed pitifully inadequate. She indicated that of 549 institutions responding to an Office of Education questionnaire asking for information as to specialized courses offered in any one of the fields of special education, only 61 stated that they included among their objectives the special preparation of teachers of one or more types of exceptional children. In many of these institutions the "special preparation" was limited to a few courses given in psychology and measurement.

The 1930s saw a sharp increase in the number of educational institutions offering more or less intensive training for special education teachers (Martens 1937) but somewhat disappointing efforts on the part of the states to extend and upgrade special-class teaching certification (Wallin 1937).

16

The Challenge
to Special Education
and the Problem
of Minority Discrimination

WE HAVE LIMNED the development of special education for the mentally subnormal with broad, selective strokes caring more to enhance understanding of that development than to provide the student with a balanced history of all its component parts. Thus we have dealt with curriculum development only tangentially. For the reader wishing some systematic introduction to curriculum development for the mildly retarded we would suggest Rothstein (1971) and Kolstoe (1972).

Nor will we spend much time on the explosive development that occurred in special education in the first two decades following World War II; by 1970, there were 728,000 mentally subnormal pupils in public elementary or secondary schools receiving special instruction either in special classes, which numbered 54,300, by ancillary instruction within the regular school program, or by independent instruction (Grant and Lind 1976). Given the foundations that we have outlined, much of that development up until the late 1960s was essentially quantitative growth of what was already in place.

The training of teachers was no longer conducted at the institutions; summer schools were less important; and preparation for careers in special education was more incorporated into the curriculum proper of the colleges and universities. But nothing new in teacher training had developed. State certification requirements, limited in the 1930s, had been adopted by 41 states in 1963. But the most frequently required courses for the endorsement of teachers of the educably retarded were Methods of Teaching Mentally Retarded, the Psychology of Exceptional Children, Arts and Crafts, and Psychological Tests and Measurements—nothing that would have seemed innovative in a summer school catalog of 1915 (Krause 1963). Even the inclu-

sion of the trainable retardate in the public school special education programs, so often represented as a postwar development, was begun at least as
early as 1928 in New York City, and by 1941 that city had 34 of its total of
621 special classes reserved solely for the trainable child (Smith 1940-41).
This would have to be considered more than an experimental or trial program for educating the trainables prior to World War II.

But even as the system matured it began to show cracks. Some cracks
seemed the natural result of too rapid a growth. The training of special
teachers never seemed to catch up with the increasing demand. Addressing
himself to the need for teachers of the handicapped in all areas of excep-
tionality, Bruce Balow, as director of the division of training programs in the
Bureau of Education for the Handicapped, noted:

> Manpower need, based on a ratio of approximately 20 handicapped pupils per
> teacher, is estimated currently at 370,000 qualified teachers to adequately serve
> the six million school-aged handicapped in the U.S. With some 125,000 teachers
> employed, of whom one-half are estimated to be not certified for such teaching,
> there is a current need for 245,000 teachers of school-age children plus another
> 60,000 to serve about one million preschool handicapped. Thus about 300,000 ad-
> ditional teachers of the handicapped would be needed immediately if the states
> were to fulfill the commitment of equal educational opportunity for the handi-
> capped [Balow 1971, p. 44].

While Balow addressed himself to the teacher needs for all exceptional
groups, the figures apparently reflected accurately enough the manpower
situation with the mentally subnormal. Dunn (1973) cites as a probably
typical picture one state director of special education reporting in 1970 that
89 percent of his teachers of the retarded were not adequately prepared — 39
percent were not certified and 50 percent needed upgrading (p. 155). At
another point, Dunn notes that "Gallagher has estimated that it would take
until the year 2770, at least, to bridge the gap between manpower needs and
training programs in the area of the mildly handicapped, assuming current
special education prevalence figures and using current categories, instructional models, and teacher-education programs" (p. 22).

Other cracks appeared to be in the faulty design of the system itself, particularly as applied to the educably retarded. One of the more forceful
arguments for the development of segregated special class placement for
Goddard's newly discovered "morons" at the turn of the century was that in
segregated classes such children would profit from teaching specially designed for their limitations. The teachers of such segregated classes were
mindful of the need to demonstrate that effectiveness, and some even undertook formal follow-up studies of their graduates (Farrell 1915, Taylor 1925).
They made no claims and stressed the need for longer-term follow-ups. Still,
in view of the high percentage of employment and adequate social adjustment among many of the boys and girls, the studies must have been satisfying

at a time when expert prediction was that feebleminded individuals were foreordained to lives of pauperism, crime, and vice.

Taylor's study had the added interest of weekly wages and IQ scores for 122 of the young people. While the distribution of wages and IQs suggested a definite positive correlation for the boys, such did not appear to be the case with the girls. What was particularly of interest was that nineteen employed young retardates, a not inconsiderable number of the total sample, had IQs under 55. But in spite of these early promises, as such studies became more refined and utilized suitable control groups of children with equally limited IQ scores, who for one reason or another were not given the opportunity of being assigned to a special class, it became difficult if not impossible to demonstrate either better academic achievement in school or better social and economic adjustment subsequent to leaving school (Kirk 1964, Johnson 1962, Heber and Dever 1970).

Again the argument was advanced that segregation of such children protected them from the taunts of their peers with superior endowment. As the reader may remember, the dispute in the first decades of the century was whether segregation in special classes in the regular school was sufficient to protect the child's self-esteem or whether he should in fact be segregated into special schools for his own protection.

Beginning in the 1960s, research findings (Meyerowitz 1965, 1967; Jones 1972) opened up the issue to debate (Dunn 1968; Kolstoe 1972). Researchers began fumbling for appropriate measurements, designs, and analyses, as all the while it became more apparent that clear-cut answers to the question of lowered self-esteem would not be easy to establish. Nevertheless, summing up the state of the field, one might, as Dunn did in his seminal article in 1968, raise the ultimate question: "Special Education for the Mildly Retarded — Is Much of It Justifiable?" The article set off quite a furor, but for many reasons Dunn had sensed the changing wind and his article pointed in the direction of that change.

In reviewing some of the controversy stirred up by Dunn's article, Hammons (1972) correctly indicated that the article was "only symptomatic of a growing disenchantment with emerging practices of special education" (p. 565). Concerns had begun to appear at least as early as the 1930s; the issue of the deleterious effects of labeling a child mentally retarded had often been raised and the question of the appropriateness of classifying handicapped children by medical criteria instead of social and educational needs was not new to the literature. Nevertheless, Dunn's article articulated the disenchantment at a time when that disenchantment was combining with other social discontents to provoke a fundamental challenge to the system of special education which had gradually been built up over three-quarters of a century.

What we would like to focus on at this point is one of the aspects of special education for the mildly retarded that caused Dunn to question its validity. This aspect concerns the overrepresentation of impoverished minority group children in special education classes, and the appropriateness of such educational placement for these children. Dunn had opened his argument by stating that:

> A better education than special class placement is needed for socioculturally deprived children with mild learning problems who have been labeled educable mentally retarded. Over the years, the status of these pupils who come from poverty, broken and inadequate homes, and low status ethnic groups has been a checkered one. In the early days, these children were simply excluded from school. Then, as Hollingworth pointed out, with the advent of compulsory attendance laws, the schools and these children "were forced into a reluctant mutual recognition of-each other." This resulted in the establishment of self contained special schools and classes as a method of transferring these "misfits" out of the regular grades. This practice continues to this day and, unless counterforces are set in motion now, it will probably become even more prevalent in the immediate future due in large measure to increased racial integration and militant teacher organizations. For example, a local affiliate of the National Education Association demanded of a local school board recently that more special classes be provided for disruptive and slow learning children [Dunn 1968, p. 5].

In Dunn's estimation 60 to 80 percent of the pupils taught by special education teachers "are children from low status backgrounds—including Afro-Americans, American Indians, Mexicans, and Puerto Rican Americans; those from non-standard English speaking, broken, disorganized, and inadequate homes; and children from nonmiddle class environments" (p. 6). It was Dunn's thesis that such deprived children should not be labeled mentally retarded.

Independently of Dunn, others were concerned about the disproportionate representation of minority group children in special education classes. For example, a number of surveys and research studies undertaken in California in the 1960s clearly demonstrated the overrepresentation of Spanish-surname and black children in the special education classes of that state. In 1966, a survey of enrollment in special classes by ethnic group membership revealed that for every county having 5 percent or more black or Spanish-surname children enrolled in school, the percentage of such children in special class placement exceeded the percentage of such children in the total school population for that county. In the 35 counties involved, the percentage of these minority children in the special classes was often two to three times what it was in the total school population (Mercer 1970). Again, in 1969-70, 15.2 percent of the total school population of California's public day schools were of Spanish surname, while 28.3 percent of all pupils classified as educable mentally retarded were of Spanish surname. Blacks constituted 8.9 percent of the total school enrollment but 25.5 percent of the educable pupils. In contrast, white, non-Spanish-surnamed children were underrepresented in the classes for educable children. While such white children constituted 72.4 percent of the total school population they represented only 44.3 percent of those classified as educable (Dunn 1973). It is hardly surprising that Mexican-American and black parents brought court challenge to the diagnostic and classificatory system utilized by the public schools in setting up their special education classes.

A series of articles written by Jane Mercer in the early 1970s, based upon her years of research on the special education programs of California, gives some excellent insights into the workings of that diagnostic and classificatory system. Mercer's approach to the understanding of educable retardation rejects the medical or "disease" model — however appropriate that might be for moderate or severe forms of retardation — and utilizes instead a social systems approach:

> From a social system perspective, mental retardation is not viewed as individual pathology but as a status which an individual holds in a particular social system and a role which he plays as an occupant of that status. In this context, mental retardation is not a characteristic of the individual, but rather, a description of an individual's location in a social system, the role he is expected to play in the system, and the expectations which others in the system will have for his behavior. Mental retardation is an achieved status. It is a position in the group that is contingent upon the performance or, in this case, the lack of performance, of the individual. Thus mental retardation is specific to a particular social system. A person may hold the status of a mental retardate in one social system and may play the role of a mental retardate in that system, yet may also participate in other social systems in which he is not regarded as mentally retarded and does not hold that status. If a social system does not place a person in the status or role of mental retardate then he is not retarded in that system, although he might qualify for the status of mental retardate if he were participating in some other system. Consequently, the "prevalence" rate for mental retardation is relative to the level of the norms of specific social systems and will vary with the expectations of the definer [Mercer 1970, pp. 383-384].

Using a social system analysis Mercer then identified a number of clearly differentiated stages through which a child may move in progressing from the status of a normal student to that of an educable mentally retarded child (EMR). The first step toward acquiring EMR status is enrolling in the public schools. Mercer makes it clear that this is not a trivial statement. In the community she was studying there were 2,500 elementary school students in Catholic parochial schools. These schools had no special classes for mentally retarded children, and although there were several dozen children in these parochial schools who by intelligence test scores would have been eligible for EMR status in the public schools, they could not achieve that status in the parochial school because the status of mental retardate did not exist within that system. The best that could be achieved was to be classified as a "slow learner."

In a public school, the child is assumed a "normal" student if not visibly defective. A normal student remains as such until he fails to meet the role expectations of the teacher. He may then be required to repeat a grade and achieve the status of a "retained" student. Seventy-two percent of the EMR students in the study had repeated one or more grades in the course of their educational careers. As a retained student the child may meet expectations and again move ahead as a "normal" student. Failing expectations, the teacher exercises one or two options: "an unearned social promotion" which sidesteps EMR status, or a referral to the principal as an "academic problem." At this point he is evaluated by teacher and principal and may be assigned some label such as "reading problem," "speech problem," or "underachiever," which keeps his status in the regular class but may make special educational resources available to him.

Alternatively he may be sent to the psychologist for evaluation. The psychologist then exercises one of several options. He might decide the child is "emotionally disturbed" or "situationally distressed" and the child might return to regular class status. On the other hand, he might decide to give the child an individual intelligence test. If the child scores too high for EMR class placement, he returns to the regular grade. If, however, the child scores below the accepted standard he is a possible candidate for EMR status. A parental conference and a staff planning session now determine whether or not he will be assigned to a special class. Adamant parents and a borderline IQ may cause the staff to decide the child is emotionally disturbed and his IQ not really representative of his potential. He returns to his regular class. Otherwise, and barring the parents removing the child from the school, the child has achieved the status of a mental retardate. Very few are reassigned to regular classes once such status is achieved. As Mercer notes, "The limited nature of the special education curriculum makes reassignment to the regular class curriculum virtually impossible after a period of time" (p. 388).

The reader will note that in this detailed analysis there are many decision-making points where subjective judgments of teacher, principal, and psychologist can affect the labeling of the child.

> We have found that, at every stage in the labeling process, a child of Spanish surname is exposed to a higher probability of going on to the next stage in the process than is an English-speaking Caucasian child or a Negro child. Those children most likely to complete the sequence are those who have many academic problems, who come from homes where little English is spoken, and who have difficulty communicating in English. The English-speaking Caucasian children who are most likely to escape the label after initial referral are those with mental health problems, with many interpersonal problems, and with poor social adjustments. Those with physical handicaps, neurological involvements, and poor speech facility complete the course. These factors did not differentiate labeled from nonlabeled children of Spanish surname. Negro children who were eventually placed in EMR classes tended to have significantly more interpersonal problems than did English-speaking Caucasian children who were placed [Mercer 1970, p. 388].

The subjective element in EMR placement is further indicated by data from a desegregation study that Mercer reports in the same article. The

Wechsler Intelligence Scale was administered to all Spanish-surname and black children in three segregated elementary schools, and to a random sample of English-speaking Caucasian children in the predominantly Caucasian schools in the same district. While 1.2 percent (N = 6) of the Caucasian children tested had IQs below 80, 15.3 percent (N = 78) Spanish-surname, and 12.4 percent (N = 36) black children had similar IQ scores. Nevertheless, all of these children were holding the status of "normal" children in the regular classroom. Furthermore, *there was no significant difference between the average IQ of these children who were holding a "normal" student status and children of the same ethnic group, in the same schools, who were in special education classes.*

What is evident in this account of Mercer and several other reports on her work (Mercer 1971, 1974) is that in California, in the late sixties, an IQ score equal to or less than 79 was a sine qua non for the diagnosis of mental retardation within the public school system. That is, one could not achieve the status of a mental retardate without obtaining such a score on an individually administered intelligence test such as the Wechsler Intelligence Scale for Children. What is equally evident is that such a low IQ score was not pathognomonic, i.e., the possession of such an IQ score was not in itself indicative of mental retardation.

It is also clear in Mercer's reports that once the status of mental retardate is achieved within the public school system it is rarely lost, and from this Mercer concludes:

> The social system perspective highlights the extent to which the medical perspective in mild mental retardation may be implicated in creating and perpetuating the very condition it seeks to prevent. Once assigned the status of a mental retardate, an individual soon becomes socialized to play the role and to meet the lesser expectations of his retarded status. When being mildly retarded is viewed as a social process in which a person moves from one status to another, new approaches to prevention and intervention are revealed. There are many alternative labels and programs available. By what rationale should some children be placed in an EMR status in the public schools when . . . other children of equivalent intellectual attainment remain unstigmatized? [Mercer 1970, p. 391].

Mercer does not detail the way in which the child becomes socialized to play the role of a mental retardate. But she does indicate that the different and less academic curriculum of the special class guarantees that the longer one remains in EMR status the further one falls behind one's peers in the regular class track. We would also wonder at the extent to which attitudes and motivations toward academic achievement are modified by the special class in ways which affect not only learning but also performance, e.g., test-taking attitudes.

In many respects Mercer's analysis supports the iatrogenic role of the public schools in the etiology of mild mental retardation that we advanced earlier in this book as part of our rationale for studying the development of the public school system.

Approaches to the Problem
of Overrepresentation of Minorities
in Special Education

Concerned about this overrepresentation of minority groups in special education classes, both Dunn and Mercer have offered solutions to alleviate the problem. In evaluating these solutions it should be noted that both authors assume a cultural causation not only for the selective assignment of such children to special education classes but also for the disproportionate number of low IQ scores obtained by these minority groups in relationship to the population at large. That is to say, they assume the cultural bias of our standard tests of intelligence.

For Dunn, the solution to the problem would involve the schools discarding the terms "educable" and "mentally retarded" and adopting the designation of "mild general learning disabilities":

> To be classified as having a mild general learning disability for purposes of receiving special education services, a pupil (1) must have reached the age of six years; (2) must score no higher than the second percentile for his ethnic subgroup based on local school district norms on both verbal and performance types of individual intelligence tests administered in his most facile language, yet not in the lower one half of 1 percent; and (3) must be achieving in all basic subjects, as measured by age norms on an individual, nationally standardized test for school attainment administered in the language of instruction, no higher than his capacity as determined by the average mental age expectancy score derived from his scores on both the verbal and performance types of nationally standarized intelligence tests administered in the language of instruction. [Dunn 1973, p. 128].

While retaining the intelligence test as a diagnostic tool these recommendations would presumably mitigate or abolish its cultural bias; and the use of a nationally standardized test of school attainment would serve as a check on the subjectivity of the classroom teacher's opinion. This correction for the assumed cultural bias of the standardized intelligence test and the provision of a control for teacher bias could of course change the ethnic ratios in special classes in the direction of greater conformity to the ethnic ratios in the entire population of school age children. If assignment of a child to an educable special education class has, ipso facto, a negative effect on the education of that child, then Dunn's selection procedure would at least have the advantage of distributing this educational handicap fairly across ethnic groups. On the other hand, if assignment to a special class should have positive value for a child with a low IQ score and poor academic performance, then we are not so sure what the effect of the adoption of Dunn's criteria of selection would have upon the ultimate educational progress of minority students. Fortunately, for our dilemma, the essential component of Dunn's proposals for reform in the education of the mildly retarded — and it is in line with subsequent developments in the field — was not concerned with labels and the criteria for the assignment of labels but a basic reorganization of the structure, methods, and curriculum of special education. As expressed in his 1968 article:

> Existing diagnostic procedures should be replaced by expecting special educators, in large measure, to be responsible for their own diagnostic teaching and their clinical teaching. In this regard, it is suggested that we do away with many existing disability labels and the present practice of grouping children homogeneously by these labels into special classes. Instead, we should try keeping slow learning children more in the mainstream of education, with special educators serving as diagnostic, clinical, remedial, resource room, itinerant and/or team teachers, consultants, and developers of instructional materials and prescriptions for effective teaching.
>
> The accomplishment of the above *modus operandi* will require a revolution in much of special education. A moratorium needs to be placed on the proliferation (if not continuance) of self contained special classes which enroll primarily the ethnically and/or economically disadvantaged children we have been labeling educable mentally retarded. Such pupils should be left in (or returned to) the regular elementary grades until we are "tooled up" to do something better for them [Dunn 1968, pp. 11–12].

Basing herself on an intensive twelve-year study of mental retardation in the city of Riverside, California, Mercer approaches the problem of an over-representation of minority children among those classified as mentally retarded from a civil rights point of view.

> We believe that psychological assessment procedures have become a civil rights issue because present assessment and educational practices violate at least five rights of children: a) their right to be evaluated within a culturally appropriate normative framework; b) their right to be assessed as multi-dimensional, many-faceted human beings; c) their right to be fully educated; d) their right to be free of stigmatizing labels; and e) their right to cultural identity and respect [Mercer 1974, p. 132].

We would refer the reader to the original article for the full explication of these violations of children's rights. We now selectively call attention to part of the argument to provide insight to issues considered in this book. Mercer, like many others, notes that the cultural bias of the standardized intelligence test violates the right of the child to be evaluated within a culturally appropriate, normative framework. But she warns that:

> Establishing separate norms for an entire racial/ethnic group or developing culture-specific tests for each racial/ethnic group is not the solution. Important socio-cultural differences exist not only between but within racial/ethnic groups. In the sample of Black and Chicano children mentioned earlier, we were able to identify five levels of socio-cultural modality, ranging from a group completely assimilated into the Anglo-American culture to a group having little contact with modern industrial America. Such cultural heterogeneity must somehow be

recognized in psychological assessment. . . . We found little evidence that clinicians consider cultural factors in interpreting standardized test scores. We believe that each child has a right to be evaluated within a culturally appropriate normative framework. Children should not be classified as abnormals because they have been socialized into a non-Anglo cultural tradition [Mercer 1974, pp. 133-134].

This suggests the difficulty that might be involved in attempting to implement Dunn's suggestion of utilizing local school district norms for each ethnic subgroup when within the one city Mercer identifies five levels of sociocultural difference within an ethnic subgroup. Would one be better off to be guided by the ethnic group norms or by sociocultural norms? Of course, logically one ought to norm by sociocultural modality within ethnic group but even with the aid of the computer, the local school district's psychologist might be sorely tried. In regard to being assessed as a multidimensional human being, i.e., as one fulfilling roles in several different social systems simultaneously, Mercer notes:

When we interviewed the mothers of children labeled as mentally retarded by the schools, we found that many were situationally retarded. Their retardation was confined to the six hours in school. In the eyes of their family and friends, they were normal. Some were carrying a heavy load of responsibility in the home. Others were known in their neighborhoods for their mechanical aptitude and ability to solve problems.

Our studies convinced us that a child has a right to be assessed as a multifaceted person playing roles in many social systems. Children who succeed in non-academic roles are *not* comprehensively retarded even though they score as subnormal on a standardized intelligence test [Mercer 1974, p. 134-135].

Considering the right of the child to be fully educated, Mercer states:

One of the most persistent complaints we heard from parents of children inappropriately placed in classes for the mentally retarded was their concern about the limited and repetitious nature of the educational program. For example, one Black mother in our study said, "Bill is being retarded in special education. . . . We have to make Bill go to school because the class does not offer a challenge to him. What they do is repetitious—the same thing over and over. . . . He does not like school."

Many of these children, given prompt assistance early in their educational career, would eventually be able to progress without special help. Placed in a special education class for the mentally retarded, they will never be fully educated [Mercer 1974, pp. 135-136].

The complaints of these parents about the limited and repetitious nature of the educational programs may have reminded the reader of the complaint of V. V. Anderson about the training of special class students in 1921, in which he bemoaned the weeks and months spent in making a basket or weaving a rug. The curriculum may have changed in content but how much in educational value?

Mercer has the following to say on the right to be free from stigmatizing labels:

Sixty-seven percent of the children in special classes in our labeling study were not viewed as subnormal by other social systems. This disparity was especially marked for minority children. Forty-eight percent of the children labeled as mentally retarded in the public school were Anglo-American, while 36.5 percent were Chicano and 11.9 percent were Black. Conversely, the ethnic proportion for those labeled mentally retarded in all social systems in which they participated were 78 percent Anglo-American, 13 percent Chicano, and 5 percent Black. This closely approximates the ethnic proportions in the general population. Minority children were particularly burdened with school-specific stigmatizing labels [Mercer 1974, p. 136].

Finally, on the right to ethnic identity and respect, Mercer says:

Achievement and intelligence tests are designed to predict a child's probability of success in American public schools which are culture-bearers for the Anglo-American tradition. The public schools have been a mechanism for the Americanization of non-Anglo migrants to the United States. Speaking a language other than English has been consistently discouraged. For example, 32 percent of the 5,800 schools surveyed recently in five southwestern states opposed the use of Spanish in classrooms. Schools having the highest percentage of Chicano children and the highest percentage of children from lower socio-economic levels were the *most* likely to discourage the use of Spanish. Children from Spanish-speaking homes are expected to learn English with no special assistance from the schools. In 1970 there were only 131 bilingual programs in public schools to serve the entire Spanish-speaking population in the United States.

When some parents protested that present psychological assessment procedures were "a conspiracy to keep minorities down" and were "most unfair," they were expressing feelings of systematic exclusion from the dominant society. Intelligence testing perpetuates the subordinate position of non-Anglos in American society. Standardized testing provides a mechanism for blaming children and their families when the educational program of the school fails [Mercer 1974, pp. 136–137].

Some Historical Perspective
on the Overrepresentation of Minorities
in Special Education

As the reader recalls we introduced the approaches of Dunn and Mercer to the problem of overrepresentation of minority children in special education classes with the indication that both authors assumed the cultural bias of standardized tests of intelligence. But from the generally conceded point that all intelligence test items are culturally loaded to the assumption that such cultural loading introduces a significant degree of bias, into a given intergroup comparison utilizing a given test, is not a foregone conclusion

(Smith 1974, Jensen 1974). Loehlin, Lindzey, and Spuhler (1975), in their careful and balanced review of the literature on race differences in intelligence, warn that "All in all, while the existence of some amount of cultural bias in some IQ tests for some intergroup comparisons can hardly be doubted, we are a long way from being able to assess with confidence the precise importance of such biases for particular group comparisons" (p. 71). It is worth noting the two generalizations these authors make regarding the quality of the evidence available in regard to racial-ethnic differences in intelligence:

1. The design, execution, and reporting of studies concerned with racial-ethnic differences in intelligence often leave much to be desired. The conclusions that we have attempted to draw from these data are necessarily limited by this fact.

2. We have been concerned privately by the number of instances in which the political and social preferences of the investigators apparently have grossly biased their interpretation of data. Such distortions appear to be at least as prevalent at environmentalist as at hereditarian extremes. While we have preferred in this book to report findings directly rather than their authors' interpretations of them, we must face the possibility that the influence of the investigators' preconceptions may in some instances have crept in earlier in the scientific process, and affected the gathering of the data as well. Consequently, any evidence deriving from a single unreplicated study must be viewed with more than the normal caution stemming from statistical considerations [Loehlin, Lindzey, and Spuhler 1975, p. 232–233].

In regard to this second generalization we would refer the reader to the Sarason and Doris (1969) discussion of sociopolitical factors in science as well as the observations we have made on Albee's etiological view of familial retardation earlier in this book. What then are the general conclusions to which these authors are led?

Given the empirical findings, and the theoretical arguments we have discussed, what conclusions about racial-ethnic differences in performance on intellectual tests appear justified? It seems to us that they include the following:

1. Observed average differences in the scores of members of different U.S. racial-ethnic groups on intellectual-ability tests probably reflect in part inadequacies and biases in the tests themselves, in part differences in environmental conditions among the groups, and in part genetic differences among the groups. It should be emphasized that these three factors are not necessarily independent, and may interact.

2. A rather wide range of positions concerning the relative weight to be given these three factors can reasonably be taken on the basis of current evidence, and a sensible person's position might well differ for different abilities, for different groups, and for different tests.

3. Regardless of the position taken on the relative importance of these three factors, it seems clear that the differences among individuals *within* racial-ethnic (and socioeconomic) groups greatly exceed in magnitude the average differences between such groups.

Let us emphasize that these conclusions are based on the conditions that have existed in the United States in the recent past. None of them precludes the possibility that changes in these conditions could alter these relationships for future populations. It should also be noted that the probable existence of relevant environmental differences, genetic differences, and psychometric biases does not imply that they must always be in the same direction as the observed between-group differences.

On the whole, these are rather limited conclusions. It does not appear to us, however, that the state of the scientific evidence at the present time justifies stronger ones [Loehlin, Lindzey, and Spuhler 1975, pp. 238-239].

Regardless of the limitations of the scientific evidence and the restricted and tentative conclusions such evidence will allow, we are left with the undoubted facts that were of concern to Dunn and Mercer. Certain minority groups obtain average IQ scores that are lower than that of the population at large and those minority groups are overrepresented in our special classes. If science offers controversy rather than understanding for social facts, we can at least glance at our social history for the suggestions that it might offer.

In recalling the history of the common school, it is obvious that impoverished minorities, so often the object of the solicitude of the schoolman and his philanthropic and humanitarian supporters, have often in considerable numbers ignored, fought, or rejected the very institution designed for their welfare. From the schools of the benevolent Public School Society, the impoverished Irish and German immigrant children stayed away in droves. Stubborn and proud in their poverty, their popish idolatry and alien ways, they wandered the streets or they attended the makeshift parochial schools their parents erected in rivalry to the common school system. The Public School Society was left to care for those larger numbers of children who were part of, or wished to become part of, the dominant Anglo-Protestant culture. For all the undoubted reasons of efficiency and economy that caused the Public School Society to adopt the Lancastrian system for its charity schools, it may not have been without an additional gratification that it was the system of an English schoolmaster with a strong adherence to Quakerism — a form of Protestantism simple enough in dogma and rites to be quintessentially pan-Protestant.

But the Irish and German children were lucky — and in a way so was the Public School Society. In that era prior to compulsory schooling there was no need for a direct confrontation within the schools. The immigrant children could elect to stay outside the public schools, and the public school had no need to adapt itself to these cultural heretics. Therefore, when the clash occurred between the minority and majority culture it did not occur primarily within the public school itself but rather in the external political arena as the Public School Society and the rival parochial schools fought over the distribution of public school funds. This was the first of the great school wars and the fight was essentially a stand-off. Those in the minority culture resistant to assimilation withdrew into their own enclaves — to assimilate themselves to America and to cause America to accommodate them, all in good time, without the benevolent pressure of the Public School Society.

All of this description is of course an oversimplification and it is focused on New York City. Nevertheless, we would submit that in general outline this constitutes the relationship between the immigrant child and the public schools throughout much of the nineteenth century not only in New York but in all the large cities where the immigrant poor congregated. It explains why the immigrant child—no matter how much the immigrant group might be vilified in the public press—was never assigned the status of mental retardate during this era. However, once compulsory education laws were effectively enforced, the relationship between the public school and the immigrant child underwent a change.

In an earlier chapter, we took note that the problems of diagnosis do not arise until there is a disruption within a social context. Looking back on the development of the class-graded common school system, we can see how the enforcement of compulsory education laws at the turn of the century disrupted the social context of the common school. Those children who because of intellect, temperament, motivation, physical traits, and cultural heritage, would previously have been forced out of the social context of the school system were being kept within the system.

It was necessary for society to make a diagnosis of the problem, and naturally enough society chose as diagnosticians those who were essentially in charge of maintaining the system: the teachers, the administrators, the Boards of Education, and the various experts that they consulted for advice upon the maintenance of the system, such as physicians. It is not surprising therefore that the diagnostic process lacked Sameroff's transactional approach. The emphasis was primarily upon the child and his shortcomings. He was physically or morally, or intellectually defective. If at times and for particular children, "defective" seemed too strong an appellation then it was necessary to assign the child's shortcomings to his rearing prior to entry, or to influences persisting outside the beneficial ambience of the school. In poverty or minority cultures—and in the cities both factors were as one—it was easy enough to identify malnourishment and ill-health, poor racial stock, inferior cultural values, and life styles, all contributing to the child's incapacity to profit from the intellectual, social, and moral training of the school. With such a diagnostic approach it was reasonable not to make any fundamental change in the school system but rather to build an auxiliary system—the special education programs designed for the defective or incapable child—and this was essentially what was undertaken in way of intervention. Then, as now, these special classes were predominantly filled with the children of the impoverished minorities. That is evident whenever the literature on these early special education classes undertakes a listing of the ethnic origins of the children (Cheney, 1904, Farrell, 1921, Taylor, 1925). The significance of this, however, is not straightforward. During the first decades of the century, the children of the immigrants constituted a high percentage of all the pupils in the larger cities. For example, a 1908-1909 survey undertaken in 37 cities by the Immigration Commission indicated that 57.8 percent of the fathers of all public school pupils were foreign-born. Since the special classes in the first few decades of the twentieth century were found almost entirely in city school systems, even a random assignment of children to the special classes would have caused the children of immigrants to be a majority of the special education students. Therefore, when Farrell's 1921 survey of the nationality of children in ungraded classes reveals that 76.6 percent of the fathers of 4,771 children are foreign-born, it is not possible to conclude that immigrant stock is overrepresented.

We would need to know not just the proportion of immigrant stock among the pupils of the New York City public school system as a whole, we would need to know the proportion in the school districts where these special classes were located. These data may be available somewhere in the archives of the city's schools but, insofar as we know, it is not found in the professional literature of that period. Lacking those data, all we may be justified to conclude is that special classes were an inevitable product of city school systems, and their ethnic makeup probably represented the general ethnic makeup of the city in which they occurred.

In such circumstances the approach to studying ethnic factors in special education in that era must be somewhat indirect. In this indirect approach we need to look at several different indices of the adjustment of the immigrants' children to the American schools, including retardation in grade, dropout rates, as well as special class placement. We also need to look at them not only from the point of view of the immigrants' children taken as a single group but with specific comparisons for different subgroups of immigrants. Doing this we may be able to see what analogies if any exist between the educational problems of the immigrant's child in the early years of this century and the educational problems of the impoverished minority groups of today.

In comparing subgroups of immigrants, we will be taking cognizance of the fact that the immigrant experience with the American school system was not a homogeneous experience. That is obviously true when we compare the old immigrations with the new. Not only did the Irish of the pre-Civil War period bring a different cultural heritage to the public schools of their day than did the Italians in the decade prior to World War i, but the American school system itself changed. The Italian did not meet the degree of institutionalized religious prejudice in the American school of his day that the Irish had found, but on the other hand he came with a linguistic handicap. The language of the home was not the language of the school, a problem that had not confronted the Irish.

Even if we limit our consideration to one cultural group, secular changes might radically alter the experience the child would face in the school. The

Irish immigrant's child in the 1900s would not be troubled by the religious issue as was his predecessor in 1840. The likelihood was also that a considerable proportion of his public school teachers were likely to be young women of his own nationality and creed. The Irish child of a previous generation had, to a considerable extent, become assimilated. Again, he was likely to be in a city where Irish political power had to be reckoned with and economic opportunities, while not yet equal to that of the native American, had vastly improved. Compared to the Irish immigrant's child of the 1900s, the Italian child was sadly handicapped. So in looking at the indices of retention, elimination from the schools, and special class membership, we will need to look at subgroups lest the average performance for immigrants as a whole blur the acute difficulties of some cultural groups.

Retardation and Elimination of Pupils in the Public Schools

Retardation defined simply as being overage for one's grade placement was viewed by educators in the first decades of the twentieth century as a major problem. The efficiency of group instruction which was the keystone of economical mass education depended upon a lock-step progress of pupils from the first grade entered at approximately six years of age through the eighth grade completed at approximately 14 years of age—the upper age limit for compulsory education. Thus a pupil who is older that the "normal" age for his grade is ipso facto a "retarded" pupil. A first-grader is assumed to have a "normal" age of seven; if he is eight or older he is retarded. The normal age for a second-grader is eight; if he is nine or older he is presumed retarded for that grade and so on through the various grades of the school. Obviously, such a statistic counts equally students who are overage because of slow progress and the student who is overage because of entering school at a later age than that considered normal. Nevertheless, the statistic was widely used in the evaluation of the schools:

> The method has come into general acceptance because, all things considered, it is the most satisfactory standard by which to measure retardation. Statistics based on the time pupils have spent in each grade are exceedingly rare, often unreliable, and usually are non-cumulative. That is, they deal with each grade as a separate unit and fail to tell us how much time the pupil has gained or lost in the entire course.
>
> Statistics giving us figures as to grade and age distribution on the other hand, are simple, certain, easy to gather, and embody valuable information as to many conditions and results of school work. Their application to the problem of retardation is so easy that the process may be employed by anyone, however unversed in statistical procedure [Ayres 1909, pp. 36-37].

Retardation so measured was indeed a sizable factor in the efficiency of the schools. For example, in the survey of 37 cities by the Immigration Commission previously discussed, approximately 36 percent of the students in the elementary public school grades were "retarded." Ayres (1909) reviewing data from the school system of 31 cities arrived at a similar retardation rate of 33.7 percent. Such high rates of retardation had both educational and economic implications:

> Wherever we find that the retarded children constitute a large part of all of the school membership we find that many of the children do not stay in the schools until they complete the elementary course. Children who are backward in their studies and reach the age of fourteen (which is generally the end of the compulsory attendance period) when they are in the fifth or sixth grade instead of the eight, rarely stay to graduate. They drop out without finishing. The educational importance of this fact is great. We are apt to think of the common school course as representing the least amount of schooling that should be permitted to anyone, but the fact remains that a large part of all our children are not completing it. As retardation is a condition affecting all of our schools to some extent, so too elimination, or the falling out of pupils before completing the course, is an evil found everywhere but varying greatly in degree in different localities. In Quincy, Massachusetts, of every hundred children who start in the first grade eighty-two continue to the final grade. In Camden, New Jersey, of every hundred who start only seventeen finish. The other eighty-three fall by the wayside. The general tendency of American cities is to carry all of their children through the fifth grade, to take one-half of them to the eight grade and one is ten through the high school [Ayres 1909, pp. 3–4].

One explanation some educators had offered for the high percentage of overage children in the schools was that so many of them entered school at comparatively advanced ages. Ayres dismissed this explanation with the contention that only a small part of all retarded children entered school late. In New York City, where he had conducted an intensive study, he maintained that the retarded children whose backwardness could be attributed to late entrance constituted less than one-third of the total number and concluded:

> If the lower grades of our schools contain many children who are not going ahead at the normal rate, this means that there are large numbers of pupils who are doing the work of the grades they are in for the second or third time. These children are repeaters. The study of the figures from different cities reveals the importance of this class from both the educational and economic view points. The computations show that in the schools of Somerville a little more than 6 per cent of the children are repeaters. From this figure the records of the cities range upwards until we reach Camden, New Jersey, with 30 per cent of the children in the repeating class. The average percentage is a little over 16. This means that in the country as a whole about one-sixth of all of the children are repeating and we are annually spending about $27,000,000 in this wasteful process of repetition in our cities alone [Ayres, 1909, p. 5].

Ayres attributed this retardation to late entrance, irregular attendance, illness, physical defects, and the difficulty of the course of studies. He recommended better compulsory attendance laws and more effective enforcement, better medical services, a course of study better adapted to the student of average ability, more flexible grading, and improved administrative practices. His cost-effectiveness approach to education was to earn him plaudits in his own day and criticism from school historians of a latter day as a factory-management view of school administration.

But what is of interest to us is the light that the Ayres study throws on minority group adjustment. In a chapter entitled, "The Nationality Factor," Ayres addressed himself to this issue. He noted first that the school population of foreign parentage approximated 34 percent for the country as a whole, but that it was unevenly distributed, being largest in the North Atlantic, North Central, and Western states. In general, Ayres appears to have an optimistic view of the adjustment of the immigrants' children in our schools. He noted that illiteracy was smaller in this population than among children of native white parentage, and that in the country as a whole the children of foreign parentage between the ages of five and fourteen were found in greater proportion in the schools than were their native white counterparts. But with those findings — which may have simply reflected the fact that the foreign stock was largely located in cities easily serviced by urban schools — Ayres's account gives no more advantage to the immigrants' children.

Examining school reports from a number of cities, he noted that the child of foreign parentage occurred in decreasing proportion from the first grade through the eighth and on into high school. In Worcester, where the data had the advantage of breaking the foreign stock down into the native child of immigrant parents and the immigrant child itself, Ayres noted that in kindergarten, native Americans were only 36 percent of the total grade population but were 60 prcent of the high school population. The native-born of foreign parentage started kindergarten a robust 56 percent of the total population and finished with 37 percent at the high school level. The foreign-born child started at 7.3 percent and ended up at 3.8 percent. Obviously the foreign stock was eliminated from the schools at a faster rate than the native-born.

This pattern of elimination of foreign stock pupils in their progress through the common school is also substantiated by the 1911 *Report of the Immigration Commission* which indicated that while 57.6 percent of all the immigrants' children attending the public schools were in the primary grades, only 4.7 percent were in the high schools. In contrast, while 52.1 percent of the native-born white children attending public schools were in the primary grades, 9.1 percent were in the high school (p. 25). If we accept Ayres's contention that retardation played a major role in elimination of pupils, we would expect the data on retardation of the immigrants' children in relationship to children of native white parentage to offer support for this contention.

Actually, the Commission's data do lend some support to this expectation. Throughout the first six elementary grades, the percentage of retarded among immigrant stock exceeds that of the children of white native parentage. But the real difference between the white native children and those of foreign stock in both Ayres's study and the Commission's report was in the proportion of children who started high school. Whether this was basically an economic factor, with more immigrant families in need of the income of their adolescent children, or whether it was in part a cultural factor, resulting in greater difficulty in the immigrants' children adapting to the demands and values of the school, these studies offer little direct information.

A more recent study by Olneck and Lazerson (1974) sheds some further light. These authors undertook an analysis of the school achievement of immigrant children from 1900 to 1930, and although they caution that their study is limited by the inadequacy of available data, they nevertheless maintain, "that the data we report and try to explain, suggest important conclusions about patterns of immigrant adaptation which might otherwise be ignored in the absence of 'hard' data" (p. 454). Of first interest in this study is that the authors accept and extend into succeeding decades the patterns of adaptation to the schools noted by Ayres and the Immigration Commission:

> During the first three decades of the twentieth century, the younger children of immigrants were as likely to be in school as children of native-born whites. At older age levels, however, they neither attended nor completed school in the same proportions as children of native whites. Throughout the schooling process, they were more likely to be older than other children in the same grade and were more likely to drop out when legally permitted, though the trend after 1920 was for most children to stay in school longer. These findings suggest that while attendance in elementary school was roughly similar for immigrants and non-immigrants, rates of progress through school varied. Nevertheless, the differences between native-born and immigrant were not large, and they were especially small for immigrant children from English-speaking homes. Only at the point of high school entrance did substantial disparities become evident [Olneck and Lazerson 1974, pp. 454–455].

Where Olneck and Lazerson are particularly of value is in their insistence that there was no single immigrant experience in the schools: "Nationality groups varied substantially on such measures as elementary school retardation, grammar school continuance, high school entrance, continuance and completion, and in the ratio of males to females in high school" (p. 458). These differences had been noted in earlier studies but where Olneck and Lazerson differed is in their recognition of the importance of attempting to understand and explain such differences.

Ayres had recognized that the school's "immigration problem" was not unitary and that educational questions relating to the Scotch or English immigrant children were different than those relating to the Italian or Russian child. In 1908, he undertook a study of the comparative success of the children of different nationalities in 15 public schools of New York City. Twenty thousand pupil records were sorted in terms of the degree of advancement of the children in comparison with their ages. A liberal criterion for "retardation" was established. All children up to the age of nine were considered as of normal age for the first grade. Ten years of age was considered the cut-off for the second grade and so on. So classified, 23 percent of the children were "retarded." The percentage of retardation was then determined by the nationality of the children with the following results: German 16 percent; American 19 percent; Mixed 19 percent; Russian 23 percent; English 24 percent; Irish 29 percent, and Italian 36 percent. Striking was the fact that the German children did slightly better than the American children whereas the Italians had nearly twice the percentage rate of retardation of the Americans.

The conclusion that Ayres drew from these results was that language difficulty was of relatively slight importance in the educational assimilation of the non-English speaking immigrant child. The fact suggesting this conclusion was that the German children did better than the American children and the Irish — an English speaking group — performed almost as poorly as the Italians. This conclusion is important to bear in mind when we come to consider national differences in IQ scores for it presumably formed part of the intellectual climate which permitted investigators of intellectual differences among national groups to ignore language factors.

The report of the Immigration Commission also supported these data on the poor school performance of the Italians. Of twenty-six national groups examined, Southern Italians had the highest rate of retardation with 48.6 percent. Northern Italians did slightly better with 45.9 percent. Polish, Portuguese, French Canadian, French, and Slovak were the only other foreign groups registering retardation rates in the 40 percent range. On the other hand a number of other groups including the English, Dutch, Finnish, Swedish, and German Jewish recorded retardation rates somewhat below the 34.1 percent rate of the children of native-born white parentage (Report of the Immigration Commission 1911).

Differential Representation of Immigrant Groups in Special Education Classes

Before we consider some possible factors involved in the differential school performance of immigrant groups, we would like to look at their differential representation in special education classes and their differential performance on tests of intelligence. Just as it can be shown that there is a consistency in poor school performance, overrepresentation in special education classes, and low average IQ scores for certain minorities of today, we believe that there is evidence for the existence of the constellation in other white minorities earlier in this century, the most easily documented case being the children of the Italian immigrant. The same case could probably could be made for certain other immigrant groups of that period but in the case of the Italians, there are not only more readily accessible data but, thanks to the work of Covello, there is a detailed sociocultural history of the Southern Italian that can go far to explain why this group had so much more difficulty in adjusting to the American school system than other groups of that period.

In our earlier discussion of Miss Farrell's survey of the nationality of children in New York City's ungraded classes we noted that without data on the distribution of such national groups in the regular public school classrooms of the city, and particularly in school districts where ungraded classes were established, it would be difficult to estimate the extent to which the foreign stock children were overrepresented in the ungraded classes. Fortunately, for our present problem of the differential adjustment of national groups to the American school systems, Miss Farrell does provide relevant information.

First it should be noted that although 76.6 percent of the fathers of the 4,771 children were foreign-born, it can be ascertained from Farrell's tabulation that of the 3,657 children with foreign born fathers only 575 of the children were themselves foreign-born. Therefore, of the total foreign stock pupils, approximately 84 percent were themselves native-born. It is not to be thought, however, that the total foreign stock, approximately 75 percent of the ungraded class pupils, represented the total minority group representation in those classes. For among those pupils, counted neither as of native white parentage nor of white foreign parentage, were 96 blacks. Miss Farrell was of the opinion that the number of blacks was understated for many of them having been simply listed as "American." A true estimate of minority membership in these ungraded classes might have more closely approximated 80 percent of the total.

What is of chief interest to us is the breakdown of Farrell's data in terms of national groups. Using census data from 1920 she notes the number of foreigners of each nationality in the city and then compares this with the number of children in the ungraded classes with foreign-born fathers from each of the national groups.

The sign of plus or minus after each national group in column two provides Farrell's estimation of whether or not a given nation is represented more frequently than would be expected from the numbers of that nation in the city. By this measure, Italy clearly stands out as being overrepresented. In fact, the 1,627 children of Italian stock are almost half of the total 3,657

FOREIGN POPULATION U.S. CENSUS 1920		FOREIGN FATHERS OF UNGRADED CLASS CHILDREN AS OF JANUARY 1921		
Russia	479,481	Italy	1627	+
Italy	388,427	Russia	859	−
Ireland	202,833	Germany	264	+
Germany	193,558	Austria	241	+
Poland	145,257	Ireland	221	−
Austria	126,447	Hungary	78	−
England	71,288	Poland	69	−
Hungary	64,235	England	47	−

children of foreign stock in all the ungraded classes. There are, of course, a number of faults one can find in Farrell's statistical analysis. What one really needs to know is the number of children of Italian, Russian, German, Irish, etc., extraction who were attending the New York City school system. Without such data there is always room for error in the inference that one wishes to make. On the other hand, even allowing for the looseness of the statistical analysis, the preponderance of Italian children in the ungraded classes is striking and one suspects that even with appropriate statistical corrections the Italians would remain overrepresented in these special classes. If one had serious doubts about that, one could consider that by 1920, a major diagnostic criterion for assignment to the ungraded classes of New York City was a low IQ score; and we then turn to a consideration of the investigations into ethnic and racial IQ differences that were made during this period.

Early Studies on Ethnic and Racial IQ Differences

Earlier in this book we mentioned Pintner's summaries of studies on ethnic and racial differences in IQ scores. The first of these summaries to concern us appeared in his book *Intelligence Testing* (1923). In the chapter on the foreign-born, there is a separate section on Italians in America in which he tables the median IQ scores obtained by Italian children in five studies. These median IQ scores ranged from 77.5 to 84, with the number of children tested ranging from 25 to 313. Two of these studies using control groups of American children reported median IQs of 106 and 95.

Another study, utilizing the Army Alpha, compared 402 American children with 248 Italian children. The approximated IQs obtained from converting the Alpha scores were 107 and 88 respectively. On the Army Beta test — a nonverbal form of the Alpha — the Americans obtained an IQ of 109 (N = 393) and the Italians 96 (N = 246). As Pintner points out, this would suggest the importance of the language factor in determining the scores of the Italian children. In discussing the results of the Army testing program of World War I, Pintner notes that with these foreign-born draftees:

> The difference between the northern European and the southern and eastern European group is marked. With reference to the Italian group it is interesting to note that if we assume age 14 as the average mental age of adults and divide the Italian mental age of 11.2 by this, we arrive at an I.Q. of 80, which agrees well with the I.Q. of Italian children found by means of the Binet [Pintner 1923, p. 355].

For a brief review of the Army's testing program in World War I and the political and social usages — or rather misuses — to which it was put the reader is referred to Sarason and Doris (1969), chapter 16.

Pintner's book was designed for use as a college text and it was the author's hope — he was then a prestigious professor in Columbia's Teachers College — that it would prove useful in serving as a guide to the thousands of teachers who were then becoming interested in the use of intelligence tests within the schools. The book was apparently successful enough to warrant a new edition in 1931. Again, there was special consideration given to the IQ scores of Italian children. Twenty-three studies are tabulated, using various IQ tests of either the verbal or performance type. For seventeen of the studies, results were reported in the form of IQ scores which for the various groups of Italian children ranged from 76 to 100, with a midpoint around 87. For the fourteen studies reporting IQs for American control groups, the IQs ranged from 85 to 107, with a midpoint around 102. In no study was the IQ of an Italian group equal to or superior to its American control group. These studies all of which had been conducted between 1921 and 1929, were summed up by Pintner:

> Some would hold that this difference between 87 and 102 represents roughly the difference in the mentality of the two races. The writer would contend that this difference is probably exaggerated because of the predominance of verbal tests used. Wherever we have non-language and language tests given to the same groups we find the Italians drawing close to the Americans on the non-language tests. The results of Young, Pintner and Kirkpatrick show this. Nevertheless, even on these tests, the Italian groups are below the Americans. If the median I.Q. of American children in general is 100, then that of the Italians is undoubtedly below this. In all probability it is not as low as 87. A rough estimate might place it between 90 and 95 [Pintner 1932, P. 451].

Pintner is somewhat misleading in heading his chapters in which these data are reported as "The Foreign Born." Our own check of a number of these studies indicates that none ever dealt with an exclusively foreign-born group of Italian children in the American schools. In many of the studies it is reasonable to suppose that there was a mixture of immigrant Italian children and native-born children of Italian immigrants. One of Pintner's (1923) own studies used as selection criterion for the Italian group the mere possession of an Italian surname. That would apparently guarantee a mixture of native-born and immigrant Italian children, plus some unknown number of second or third generation children of Italian extraction, plus some offspring from cross-national marriages.

Fortunately, in several studies pains were taken to make sure that the children were in fact American offspring of Italian immigrant parentage. Thus, Hirsch (1926) reported a large-scale study of racial and ethnic groups that involved the testing of 5,504 children ranging in school placement from the first through the ninth grades. All the children were American-born of foreign-born parentage, with the exception of the white and black American groups. All of the children of immigrant stock were first generation Americans educated in the English language. But even more important to Hirsch than equality as to language was the similarity of the emotional attitude of the testees: "our testees were all 'Americanized,' feeling that they were as good as the next fellow, and unconscious of any national or racial animosity. Furthermore, they were nearly all interested in taking 'the games and puzzles.' All children took them voluntarily; no coercion was applied" (p. 246).

The Pintner-Cunningham Primary Mental Test was used for the first-graders. It was considered a nonverbal test requiring no ability to read or write letters or numbers. The Dearborn Form A, a largely nonverbal test, was used for the second and third grades. The Dearborn Form C, a partly verbal and partly nonverbal test, was used for the higher grades. On these tests 1,030 Americans obtained an average IQ of 98.3 whereas 350 children of Italian parentage obtained an average IQ of 85.8, a finding clearly in line with other studies that had not chosen native-born Italian children with equal care.

It was also of interest to Hirsch that a number of other immigrant groups whose parents spoke foreign languages did better than the Americans. Polish Jews and Swedes both averaged over 102. Germans and Russian Jews also performed slightly better than the Americans. Apparently, language handicap was not the explanatory factor for the poor showing of the Italians. Of the 16 ethnic and racial groups, only the French Canadians, the blacks, and the Portuguese performed more poorly than the Italians, and then only by differences of one to three points.

In view of Pintner's contention that language difficulties were part of the explanation of the poor performance of Italian children—even though he felt there was a real residual difference between the intelligence of American and Italian children—it might be worthwhile to take a close look at one more study he cites, especially since it does not appear to offer support for his hypothesis. This is a study by Florence Goodenough (1926) who used her newly developed Draw-a-Man test of intelligence—a short nonverbal test in good repute and frequent use by clinicians and researchers up until the time of its replacement by the revised and more adequately standardized Harris-Goodenough test in 1963 — to study ethnic and racial differences in intelligence.

Her results were based on the testing of 2,451 public school children, "practically all of whom were American-born but in whose immediate ancestry a number of racial stocks are represented" (p. 393). Children of mixed parentage were not included except for blacks and American Indians. Her 500 American children obtained a median IQ of 100.3 with a mean of 101.5, whereas the 456 Italian children in the study obtained a median IQ of 87.5 and a mean of 89.1. These were the lowest scores of any group of either European or Oriental ancestry. These scores were roughly of the same order as those of the Spanish-American children, a trifle better than the scores of California blacks and Indians, and noticeably superior to the southern blacks who obtained a median score of 76.5 and a mean of 78.7, the poorest performance among the various groups. Goodenough concluded that since her test was entirely nonverbal the obtained differences could not be attributed to linguistic handicap. She also noted that although the test was completely independent of language, the rank-orders of the various racial groups corresponded closely to the results of other investigators who used verbal tests.

Since part of our interest in reviewing the school adaptation of the children of the Italian immigrant is to point out analogies to the school adjustment of our present-day minority groups, it may not be amiss to quote Goodenough's perceptions of the similar plight of the Italians and the blacks:

> Two theories have been offered to account for these differences. The first ascribes the inferior showing made by the South Europeans and the negroes to such postnatal factors as inferior environment, poor physical condition and linguistic handicaps. The second point of view, while it recognizes that the factors named may to some degree affect the test-results, nevertheless holds that it is impossible to account for all the facts which have been observed upon any other hypothesis than that of innate differences among the groups under consideration.
>
> It is unquestionably true that the home surroundings of certain racial groups, notably the Italians and negroes, are, as a rule, far less favorable than those of the average American children. Not only is this true of the foreign-born Italians, but their American-born descendants frequently continue to live in the same neighborhoods and with little or no improvements in social or hygienic conditions. In this respect a notable difference may be observed between the Italian and the Jew. Both find a home in the slum on first coming to this country; but while the Italian remains there, the Jew soon moves to a better neighborhood.
>
> "Social pressure" or "race prejudice" is often urged as a reason for the segregation of certain racial groups within the poorer neighborhoods. In this connection it should be remembered that while racial prejudice may bring about segregation, the character of the neighborhoods thus set off is primarily dependent upon the people living within them. It is doubtful whether even the Southern negro has more to contend with in the way of this prejudice than the Chinese or Japanese in

California; yet the contrast between the typical Oriental neighborhood and the Italian or negro district is marked. Poverty there may be; but the squalor which is characteristic of the Italian and the negro sections is lacking.

It seems probable, upon the whole that inferior environments is an effect at least as much as it is a cause of inferior ability, as the latter is indicated by intelligence tests. The person of low intelligence tends to gravitate to those neighborhoods where the economic requirement is minimal and, once there, he reacts toward his surroundings along the line of least resistance. His children inherit his mental characteristics [Goodenough 1926, pp. 388-391].

Goodenough was undoubtedly one of the most outstanding psychologists of her day and one might be inclined not to dismiss her opinions lightly especially when they appear based on such solid empirical data. We would only note that the above paragraphs might well appear in any one of the present-day polemical discussions of the nature-nurture controversy and racial differences in intelligence. We would further submit that the designation of the Italians as one of those less well-endowed groups who are of marginal economic success and the creators of their own slums simply would not occur. Yet, it would not be unlikely to find the blacks or the Spanish Americans still at the center of weighty professional debates involving the subtleties of ever more recondite hereditability quotients. We are tempted to speculate on the present absence of the Italians from such discussions. Did their genes begin to mutate somewhere in the 1930s? Has it simply become politically unwise to investigate the abilities of that ethnic group? Or is it possible that somewhere in the 1920s, if not earlier, the sociocultural history of Italo-Americans took a turn from the blacks and the Spanish Americans which permitted their assimilation into the general undifferentiated mass of Americans, at least to an extent approximating that of the Irish and Germans who had preceded them?

Sociocultural Factors in School Adjustment

It would be unfair to assume that all investigators of differences between the intelligence of Italian and American children in the 1920s assumed that the basis of the empirical findings resided entirely in the genes. As early as 1921, Arlitt cautioned on the need to take social status into account in the establishment of racial norms. She reported Binet average IQs for groups of white (N = 191), Italian (N = 87), and blacks (N = 71) as being 106.5, 85, and 83.4 respectively. Then she removed from the white group those children of superior social status, so that the resulting group more nearly resembled the social status of the Italians and blacks. In this case, the average IQ of the whites fell to 92 or to approximately one-third of its original superiority over the Italian and black groups.

Margaret Mead (1927) attempted a more subtle analysis of the intellectual differences between her sample of 276 Italian children and 160 American children as obtained on the Otis group intelligence test. For the Italian children, she took into account the degree to which English was spoken in the home, the number of years the father was resident in the United States, and the social status of the family. Each of these variables influenced the size of the differences between the scores of the Italian and the American children in the expected direction.

Controlling for such gross socioeconomic variables in a comparison of intellectual differences between two groups can of course be reassuring to those who would maintain an environmentalist interpretation of such differences. Unfortunately, as the history of the nature-nurture debate has repeatedly shown, they are not conclusive. If the environmentalist notes that intelligence scores vary with family income, the hereditarian responds, of course, what did you expect? Intelligent people have the edge in the economic marketplace. If in the twenties the amount of English spoken in the home correlated with the test scores of the children, a Goodenough could and did reply that, of course, the more intelligent the group the more quickly the parents and children pick up the second language. Therefore, we would think that there is something to be gained not in cross-sectional studies of different ethnic groups but in some attempt to grasp the temporal dynamics of the sociocultural adjustment of a minority group as it copes with American society.

The question we would like to ask is: Assuming that the children of the Italian immigrant in the early decades of the twentieth century did not appear to cope any more successfully with the school and its academic demands than did black or Spanish-American children—and we think we have reasonable evidence for that assumption—how is it that we no longer perceive the adjustment of the child of Italian extraction as a special problem as we continue to do with the black and Spanish American child? We think some of the answer lies not in a study of the Italian child of today but rather in understanding the Italian child of yesteryear and the cultural heritage which he brought to an American school system that was not designed to adjust to children from cultures different from those possessed by the nineteenth century schoolmen who shaped our common school.

Covello's Study of the Social Background of the Italo-American School Child

Leonard Covello, whose experience as an Italian immigrant school boy has been recounted, undertook for this doctoral thesis a monumental study of the southern Italian family mores and their effect on the adjustment of the

Italian immigrant and his children in America. The study was primarily focused on East Harlem in New York City, but it is reasonable to suppose that the findings and insights of the author would be more or less applicable to similar large urban Italian communities in any American city in the decades prior to World War II. We do not have the space to do full justice to this work, but we shall try to indicate with appropriate references to the book why our understanding of the adjustment of the minority child to our school system cannot begin at the time he enters school; nor can a successful adjustment of the child be achieved by centering the problem on the child and the ways in which we can change him in order that he may adjust to the school system already in place. Of course, historically that is what we have tended to do, and to some extent it has worked. The career of Covello himself is an example of how in some instances it can work splendidly, but by and large such an approach to the education of a minority child is not only wasteful but inhuman: Wasteful in the expenditure of scarce resources for little gain; inhuman in the degradation and loss of dignity it imposes not only upon the children but upon ourselves.

According to Covello's account, the Italian immigration to America which began its surge in the 1880s was primarily from southern Italy—the lower part of the Italian boot and the island of Sicily. It was an impoverished country with great landed estates and absentee landlords. The *contadini*—who formed the bulk of the emigrées to the United States—were essentially a propertyless peasantry, employed in an archaic agricultural system utilizing archaic tools. They were not farmers in the American sense of the word and were equally unsuited and ill-adapted to the industrial component of the American economy. The peasants of southern Italy were not rural dwellers, but lived instead in small towns from which they went out each day, often at considerable distance, to work upon the land. Within the densely populated towns was a rigid caste system with the *contadini* at the lowest level.

> The social characteristics of this *contadino* society were: illiteracy, lack of organization, lack of leadership, political immaturity, suspicion of authority and legalized government, and lack of civic experience and responsibility.
>
> Functioning as a unit member of a *famiglia*, the chief and often only concern of the *contadino* was the maintenance of a state of equality with other peasant families and the rigidity of class lines. "Once a peasant always a peasant." Social, educational, and professional advancement were considered hostile elements which would upset the *status quo* and therefore the peace of the *contadino* community. In spite of a community of interests, peasant life had only the appearance of a closely integrated society; there was little or no spirit of a group-conscious peasantry.
>
> Such social concepts were brought over to America where, confronted with an overtly democratic and classless society, they were bound to produce additional difficulties in the process of adjustment. (Covello 1967, p. 399).

The concept of family that prevailed in South Italy was that of *la famiglia*, a family group which included all blood and in-law relatives, and which was an inclusive social world in itself. Family solidarity within the family, and against the outsider, was its basic code. . . . All members of the southern Italian *contadino* family were bound rigidly by the family mores. The male members, who assumed the dominant role of the family, from the *capo di famiglia* practically to the youngest male, were accorded a certain freedom of action completely denied to the female members of the family. . . . Since the Italian girl's sphere of activity was confined strictly to the home, . . . it made the problem of adjustment of the Italian girl to prevailing American mores particularly acute.

The position of children in the family was in great measure controlled by economic necessity to use the labor of the whole family in the struggle for existence. Boys and girls were taught to help at an early age, and were early employed in gainful labor. This situation led to early social maturity for the child, and this feature of the family pattern became a fruitful source of conflict in the school situation in America [Covello 1967, pp. 400–402.].

The educational system in southern Italy was controlled from and based upon norms applicable to the more modernized and industrialized north of Italy, and hence essentially alien to *contadino* society. In 1901 the illiteracy rate among men in the various regions of southern Italy ranged from 70 to 79 percent. The rates were much higher for women, and since the rates were calculated on the basis of all the social classes in a region we can readily suppose that they would be considerably higher for the *contadini*.

Long after various policies were inaugurated by the central authority in Italy toward education in southern Italy, the rate of illiteracy continued to be high in comparison with the rest of the country. That this was so was in part due to the poorly organized educational system, in the light of the conditions and the needs, but mainly because of the conflict between the mores of the *contadino* family and the principles governing school education in Italy. To the *contadino* parent, education was the handing down of all the cultural, social and moral value of his society through the medium of folklore, or the teaching, generation after generation, of the child by the parents. The peasant's desire for security in his way of living was directly opposed to education from outside the family circle. Further, education in South Italy was aimed at achieving early social and economic competence, which was not compatible with long schooling.

This antagonism toward the school, which was definitely manifested in Italy and which constituted a part of the cultural tradition, was carried over to America and paved the way for the still current lack of rapprochement between the American school and the Italian parents [Covello 1967, pp. 402–403].

With such a cultural background the Italian immigrant and his child confronted the American school. We have indicated in our earlier review of the data on the immigrants' adjustment to the schools that the Italian children were repeatedly conspicuous by ranking among those ethnic groups with the highest retardation rates. In addition, their IQ scores—which if nothing else must be considered among the better predictors of academic success—were among the lowest obtained among the various European ethnic groups and of an order not distinguishable from those obtained by northern blacks, Indians, and Spanish-Americans.

The U.S. Immigration Commission Report of 1911 gave further evidence of the greater likelihood that Italian children in comparison to other ethnic groups would drop out before the completion of the elementary school course, be less likely to enter high school, or having entered high school be less likely to finish. Thus, for the combined cities of Boston, Chicago, and New York, only 58 percent of the southern Italians in the seventh grade went on to enter the eighth grade. In comparison, 66 percent of the native blacks and 80 percent of the native whites did so. Of other ethnic groups, only the Polish rate of 62 percent even approximated the Italian rate. In a ranking of ethnic and racial groups in terms of the percentage of eighth-graders that entered high school in the same cities, the Italians were again at the bottom of the list with 23 percent. The native whites achieved 58 percent and native blacks 49 percent. Finally, for the same three cities, the ratios of seniors to freshmen for the various groups places the Italians at the bottom of the list with .08, the next higher ratio was obtained by the Irish at .18, native whites and native blacks were .22 and .20, respectively (Olneck and Lazerson, 1974).

As one would expect from the *contadini's* attitudes toward the education of females their representation among high school students was in striking contrast to that of other ethnic groups. For Boston, Chicago, and New York in 1908, only Russian Jewish, Polish, and southern Italian groups had a smaller ratio of females to males attending high school. The southern Italian group was lowest with only 48 females to 100 males attending high school. Among other groups, for example, the native white and the Irish, the ratio was markedly reversed, being in these two instances 135 and 137 females to 100 males, respectively.

It might well be, as Olneck and Lazerson suggest, that it was economic sense for boys not headed toward college to enter the job market in the high school years, whereas employment opportunities for girls opening up in the areas of secretarial, office work, and teaching required their continuance to a high school degree. But, if so, attitudes against the education of women, in the Russian-Jewish, Polish, and particularly the Italian groups, must have outweighed these economic advantages.

Covello's study indicates that the difficulties of the Italian child did not end with the beginning of the 1930s. Rather, there was a shift in difficulty from the elementary school level to the high school level.

> On the whole the conspicuity of Italo-American school children shifted during the last fifteen or twenty years from the elementary school to the junior and senior high schools. In former years, elementary school teachers rather frequently expressed their perturbation that

. . . . Italian children were usually more crude in manner, speech, and dress than non-Italian children. . . . It was common for Italian boys and girls to leave school to help out the family income. Parents were openly opposed to the long educational period of the elementary school. . . . Boys and girls were truants. . . . These children, especially the boys, were a source of constant irritation to teachers. . . . These children were disliked both by teachers and non-Italian pupils . . . they created difficulties for the school.

(F.M.B.-N.Y.U.-89)

The situation in the elementary schools seems to have changed for the better, and this is being attested by a great number of teachers. One states, for example:

In restrospect, certain things stand out as I compare our present Italo-American pupils with those that have come to us over a nineteen-year period. They are much less unlike the non-Italian children than their oldest brothers and sisters were. . . . Except for the difficulty of making Italo-American children bring their parents to visit the school, there is practically no reason to accuse Italo-American pupils of being different from the rest.

(L.C.-E.H.-1942)
[Covello 1967, p. 283]

In spite of this improvement in the adjustment of the Italian child in the elementary school, there was an increase of "problem cases" in the secondary schools.

A study made by the High School Division of the New York City Board of Education in 1926 shows that an average of 42.2 per cent of all high school students in New York City graduate. It is of immediate interest to contrast this with the results obtained in a study made in 1931 which showed that only 11.1 per cent of Italo-American high school registrants graduate.

Truancy, absence, cutting classes, lateness, and disciplinary infractions are problems of much greater frequency among high school students of Italian origin than among non-Italians [Covello 1967, p. 285].

Covello presented data from a number of studies that he had conducted in the early 1930s to support this contention of a disproportionate amount of problem behavior among the Italo-American high school students. There was some suggestion of improvement in the 1940s, but Covello was skeptical.

The true situation in 1944 would be difficult to ascertain, but in the absence of available objective data, it is of interest to note that the consensus among high school teachers is to the effect that "during the last ten years there has been an improvement in the school attitude and behavior of the Italian students." Changes, if any, appear, however, to be so imperceptible as to be scarcely measurable. Up to the beginning of the Second World War the situation remained, in comparison with 1930-34, and for all practical purposes, the same. This latter situation applies to students who live within the centers of Italian cultural survival; i.e., the large Italo-American communities. Significantly enough, reports from culturally heterogeneous areas of New York City indicate "a rather rapid disappearance of an Italian type of student who used to be outstanding in doing just the opposite of what an average high school boy ought to do" [Covello 1967, p. 286].

To Covello, the difficulties in the accommodation of the Italo-American child to the public schools was a direct result of the cultural clash between the *contadino* society and the values of American culture as reflected in the schools. The slow resolution of the difficulties was due to the assimilative lag of the Italian immigrant, bolstered as he was by old-world traditions persisting within large, self-contained Italo-American communities.

The educational inheritance of the southern Italian immigrant—the concepts of and attitudes toward education—has been described . . . in sufficient detail to give a general idea of its significance in his process of accommodation. From the immigrant's point of view there was no obvious need for more than a trifling amount of formal education. All practical arts and skills should be acquired at an early age by working either in the parental household or through apprenticeship. . . . The moral code in his simple and homogeneous society had also been simple. A uniform body of rules of behavior was learned in daily contacts with relatives and neighbors. All moral customs, unshaken for centuries, were effectively transmitted without any stimulation of critical and logical faculties. School learning was, therefore, at a great distance from popular comprehension and consumption. . . .

Such an attitude toward school education inevitably found itself in conflict with the prevailing American mores that govern education and, particularly, with the compulsory character of school education in America. The impulse to resist compliance, which meant the exposure of his children to a world of strange ideas, was rooted in the desire to entrench them in parental ways of thinking and doing things. School education in America, as the southern Italian peasant found it, not only had no appeal to him; it was conceived to be an institution demoralizing youth and disorganizing their traditional patterns of family life. . . .

There was undoubtedly fear of indoctrination of alien concepts, and the peasant felt rather keenly the danger to his traditions. But the most overt area of conflict arose in the economic and social patterns of family life. For next to the difficulties of the parents themselves in making the necessary economic and social adjustments, the prospects of compulsory school education for their children threatened the very foundations of orderly family life.

Under the southern Italian cultural patterns, all children were useful and effective members of their families from an early age. As the child became older and increased in physical strength and experience, in judgment and dependability, he performed more numerous and more difficult tasks and shared more and more fully in the counsels of the family group. There was no sharp age divisions; each shaded into the older and younger. So general was the pattern of life where children fitted into family life and its economy that all people were divided into two groups: children and adults. There was no adolescent group, so to speak. There were helpless infants and playful tots, young men and women, feeble folk, but there was never a group of adolescents.

The first reaction to the American school system was based on the immigrant's discovery in American [sic] of a group which, though evidently adult in physical growth, was a child-group since it attended school and indulged in childish activities, such as playing ball. The status of American youth amazed him but also filled him with apprehension [Covello 1967, pp. 287-289].

The way in which these cultural factors and attitudes toward schooling upon the part of the *contadini* were translated into the poor school performance that our review of school statistics revealed is often poignantly illustrated in Covello's volume by anecdotes of adults relating their frustrations over compulsory education laws that deprived their families of the economic input of their adolescent children and their anger at schools that alienated their children from the traditional mores of the *contadini*. Other anecdotes by children, or adults recalling their childhood, reveal the agonizing conflict of young people caught in guilt and shame, bewilderment and anger, between the opposing cultural demands of the school and the home. No wonder these children were so often problem children given to truancy, absence, cutting classes, lateness, and disciplinary infractions.

We have detailed the school adjustment of the children of Italian immigrants to a considerable extent in order to evoke a number of serious questions in regard to both special and general education. In regard to special education we noted earlier that the most frequent diagnostic category applied to educable children is that of familial retardation. Although it is possible that some of those children to whom we apply such a designation are in fact children at the tail end of a normal distribution of genetic ability, there may be others for whom the designation is inappropriate. We indicated that some such errors in labeling might occur when the children have suffered from one of the many factors, occurring in an environment of poverty, that can interfere with the development of children in ways that leave no gross neurological signs but nevertheless deleteriously affect the development and function of the central nervous system. We also suggested that cultural factors, per se, might mimic a genetically based familial retardation by the ways in which a given culture might affect the development of those skills which are both exercised and tested in school performance.

Thinking back on the overrepresentation of Italian children in the ungraded classes of New York City in 1921, and recalling the large number of studies in the 1920s indicating that Italian children obtained average IQs in the mid-80s, and remembering their high rates of grade retention and school elimination, we wonder to which type of familial retardation we would be willing to assign those Italian children in the ungraded classes? Surely in the impoverished environment from which they came, there would be reason to expect that some would have suffered insult to the central nervous system; some severe enough to warrant a label of mental defect, others perhaps mild enough to go unnoted, and they would be considered familial retardates. And of the remainder, in all probability the larger number, would one opt for genetically determined familial retardation? Or would one call into question the appropriateness of considering them retarded at all—unless one utilized a new designation, that of *iatrogenic retardation:* a form of intellectual retardation that is induced by the very system devised to foster intellectual development?

The remaining question evoked by the experience of the Italian children is the question posed throughout our history of the development of the common school and its special education offshoot. Given a society of varied groups—of ethnic, religious, racial, social, and economic differences—to what extent can we devise a common education capable of transmitting intellectual skills and moral values that does not have built into it the potential for becoming a procrustean bed to terrify or deform the children of one minority group or another? We suspect, as we recall the Amish children being chased through the cornfields of Iowa and the stoning of bus loads of black children, that the potential will always be there. The best we may be able to do is to maintain the sensitivity to identify those instances when the potentiality threatens to become reality, and to respond with firm commitment and balanced judgment to adjust not the child to the school but to adjust the interaction of the school, the subculture, and the family for the benefit of the child.

17

Mainstreaming: Dilemmas, Opposition, Opportunities

THE SPEED WITH which mainstreaming as a concept, value, and public policy has emerged in our society is little short of amazing. Indeed, the change has come about so fast and with such apparent general approbation as to raise a question about what people understand about mainstreaming and its implications for schools. Let us try to gain some historical perspective on this question in the hope of avoiding an oversimple stance to a very complicated set of issues. Because we may think mainstreaming is desirable is no excuse for assuming that institutional realities will accommodate our hopes. To confuse change with progress is to set the stage for disillusionment.

Mainstreaming before 1950

Imagine that it is anytime before 1950 and you are attending a convention of people who work in the field of mental retardation. Suppose that at the general meeting someone requests the floor and makes the following statement:

> This is the first time I have attended this kind of meeting and I am impressed and encouraged by what I have heard. Thank God there are people like you who are fighting for justice for mentally retarded people. For too long society has ignored the needs of these people. Our state institutions are, as many of you have said, overcrowded and understaffed: We call them training schools but for the most part they are custodial institutions, and pretty bad even at that. What really gave me a lift was to hear so many of you call for many more community facilities to reduce the need for institutionalization. For example, you favor more special classes in our schools, want to attract more and better people into special education, and in general upgrade training programs in colleges and universities. But one thought has been nagging at me: why do we have to segregate mentally retarded individuals in our schools? Why are we so ready to separate them from

355

> the mainstream? Why can't they be accommodated in the regular classroom? Are you in favor of separate but equal facilities in exactly the same way as we treat blacks? Does not this type of segregation affect the retarded person adversely, and does it not rob the normal student of a kind of knowledge and experience that will make the student a better moral person? I would like to go on record as opposed in principle to the segregation of mentally retarded children in our schools. Indeed, I move that we go on record as opposed to segregation anyplace.

The speaker would have been regarded at best as a misguided idealist of the bleeding heart variety, and at worst as a dangerous mentally disordered person, out of touch with social reality and the nature and needs of mentally retarded people. The speaker would have been met by a stony silence and the meeting would have moved on to more "realistic" considerations. It would be an egregious injustice to judge the response as a symptom of callousness, immorality, or narrow self-interest serving the status quo. The fact is that these were dedicated people sincerely trying to get society to be more responsive to what the advanced knowledge, research, and experience suggested about the nature and needs of mentally retarded people. Indeed, the people well understood societal prejudice because they devoted themselves to the welfare of mentally retarded people! Why would anyone "choose" to work with "them"?

Let us do some more imagining. One of the people at the meeting feels badly that no one bothered to respond to the speaker, and feels an obligation to seek the speaker out to explain why his recommendation was so misguided, however lofty the motivation. So, this person gets the speaker aside and says:

> You are an idealist and there is a part of me that accepts what you said about segregation, although in the case of mentally retarded people you are simplifying the complexity of the issues. But let's assume that everyone at this meeting agreed with you. How do you think the "outside world" would react?
>
> I'll tell you how they would react: either with the same stony silence you received at this meeting or with anger because we are telling them that their communities have been immoral, callous, and irresponsible. And how do you think the school people would respond? They don't even want the special classes they now have; so how do you think they would cotton to the idea of putting mentally retarded people into the regular classrooms? Put them into the mainstream? It would be unfair to say they would like them to drown, but it is not unfair to say they want them on isolated islands surrounded by an awful lot of water. Mainstream them? If we came out and said *that*, it would be used as evidence that *we* were mentally retarded.

Twenty-five years later, mainstreaming became public policy. Did opposition melt away? Was there an unprecedented attitudinal and moral change in our society? Were welcome signs erected by schools and communities? Or were we dealing with a variation of the 1954 Supreme Court desegregation decision: racial segregation in schools was unconstitutional but changing practice to accord with that decision turned out to be beset by a host of obstacles, deliberate and otherwise. There were some naive people who greeted that decision with a sigh of relief: thank God the moral cancer was spotted and could now be excised—maybe not tomorrow or next year but certainly in a decade or so. We have learned otherwise. Deeply rooted attitudes, ingrained and reinforced by tradition, and institutional and social structure and practice, are not changed except over a long period of time (Sarason 1973). And mainstreaming is no exception.

Let us examine more clearly what contributed to this change in attitude and policy. The first set of facts represented a convergence of events and forces: the quick growth and power of a national parents' group; the Kennedy family's personal and political interest in mental retardation powered by the financial resources of the Kennedy Foundation; and exposés in the national media of degrading conditions in state institutions that made mental retardation a topic of public interest. But this change is not comprehensible unless one sees it in the context of an even more drastic social change accelerated by the Great Depression: the widespread acceptance of the idea of governmental responsibility for citizens rendered dependent or handicapped for reasons beyond their control (Sarason 1976).

Before the thirties, it was not seen as the federal government's responsibility to intervene in matters of education and health. There were a few handicapping conditions such as blindness for which there were modest programs, but they were the exceptions and not to be considered forerunners of an increased federal role. The philosophy of "that government is best that governs least" made it extremely difficult to sustain national attention on issues in education and health. At best, they could receive attention in the states but even the states were guided by the prevailing philosophy. It took a national economic calamity to start the process of philosophical change, so that today our prepotent response to a social problem is to think in terms of federal policy and programs.

At the time that mental retardation started to receive national attention and the pressures for a federal role began to mount, there were social forces, at first unrelated to policy issues about mental retardation, that later had the most influence on how these issues were to be transformed. We refer here to the civil rights movement, which came from the desire to eradicate racial discrimination but which soon spread far beyond these confines to include the rights of women, homosexuals, older people, members of the armed forces, children. What were their constitutional rights? What constituted their equality before the law, and how had tradition and practice come to rob them of their basic constitutional rights as citizens? On what constitutional grounds can mental patients be confined in a state hospital? What are the legal restrictions to the use of psychological tests as a basis for job promotion? What legal procedures must be observed before a child can be suspended or expelled from school?

One could ask scores of similar questions, all testifying to a resurgence of attention to individual liberties and rights. Put in another way, the law and therefore the courts became agents of social change. The most pervasive changes have been through judicial decisions essentially reinterpreting or enlarging the scope of laws and existing constitutional language. And many of these decisions were not greeted with anything like unanimous approval, involving as they did radical changes in institutional thinking and practice. And that is the point; although these court decisions were stimulated by "plaintiffs" seeking change, they were opposed by "defendants" who were by no means few in number if lacking in strength. To interpret a decision in favor of the plaintiff as a "victory" is understandable but one should never underestimate how long it can take for the spirit of victory to become appropriately manifest in practice.

When mental retardation first became a topic of public discussion, moral-humane rather than legal-constitutional matters were in the forefront. Mentally retarded people "deserved" as much attention and programmatic support as other groups with disabling conditions. In fact, advocates for the mentally retarded wanted no more, and certainly no less, than "separate but equal facilities." No one was calling for elimination of state training schools or special classes. However, it did not take long before the rationale behind the historic 1954 Supreme Court desegregation decision began to influence the thinking of advocates for the mentally retarded.

Central in that rationale was the argument that segregation has pernicious effects both on the segregant and the segregationist. The 1954 decision marked the first time that the Supreme Court had ruled the findings of social science research admissible as evidence, and the weight of that evidence was that segregation had adverse effects on white and black children (Fellman 1969). Generalizing from that rationale, it is not surprising that its judicial relevance to mentally retarded people began to be examined. As a consequence, the status of mentally retarded people became a focus of legal scholars.

Lawyers did not have to be sophisticated about mental retardation to see, study, and write about legal-constitutional issues long ignored by everyone. And once the forces behind the movement for more and better facilities started to go down the legal-constitutional road, their goals became more encompassing and radical—radical in that they found themselves at a familiar root: segregating mentally retarded people in schools or elsewhere was demeaning to all involved. Blatt and Kaplan's (1966) *Christmas in Purgatory*—a pictorial essay of scandalous institutional conditions that was given such a big play in the mass media and placed in the hands of every United States Congressman—told only what happened to those who were segregated. In his subsequent books (*Exodus from Pandemonium*, 1970; *Souls in Extremis*, 1975; *The Revolt of the Idiots;* 1976) Blatt rounded out the picture by telling us what happens to the segregators.

The literature on the impact of court decisions on mentally retarded people in schools, institutions, the community, and work is vast. It is also staggering in complexity of details and the niceties of legal argument to those unfamiliar with constitutional law and the workings of the judiciary. But to someone interested in history and social change it is a fascinating literature. We recommend to the reader *The Mentally Retarded Citizen and the Law* (1976) edited by Kindred, Cohen, Penrod, and Shaffer. This book discusses the major court decisions as well as suggests the major problem areas whose legal-constitutional status has yet to be clarified. Another important and instructive book is *The Right to Education* by Lippman and Goldberg (1973), describing the development and consequences of the landmark Pennsylvania court decision affirming the right of all handicapped children to an education. It is interesting that the authors, who participated in the litigation, saw the case as a variation of 1954 Supreme Court desegregation decision.

Opposition

We have given this very brief overview in order to make a point too easily overlooked: the change in societal attitude and social policy was spearheaded by a dedicated minority relying on political pressure and the courts; at every step of the way this minority encountered opposition, especially from those in schools, institutions, and state agencies who saw how drastic the proposed changes would be for them. This opposition, of course, is quite understandable. After all, few people look with relish at the necessity of redefining their roles, activities, and values. Those who opposed the proposed changes were not evil or unintelligent people. Far from it. They were people engaged in public service, carrying out their tasks in ways that their professional training as well as long-standing custom said was right and effective. To be told that their values were wrong, that they had been contributing to evil, and that they would have to accommodate to new procedures and practices, it is no wonder that opposition did not dissolve. It may have had an opposite effect.

Consider the structural-administrative relationship of the field of mental retardation to the field of education, beginning with colleges and universities. In our schools of education, mental retardation has always been "special" or "exceptional," in that whatever it was, it was pretty much by itself, away from the mainstream of "real" education. Faculty and students in mental retardation were rarely viewed with a sense of pride, as an indispensable part of a department or school of education. It is not by chance that in our private colleges and universities mental retardation was hardly represented, and most of the time was completely unrepresented. If it was represented in our state colleges and universities, it was less because it was viewed as indispensable and more as a reaction to pressure or legislation for preparing the teachers to take positions in state institutions. Even then, the department of mental retardation or special education tended to be small and politically weak. If these departments were more tolerated than warmly embraced it bespoke of snobbishness reinforced by and reflecting societal attitudes.

The field of mental retardation was seen as an unrewarding one in which to work. The field had a "hopeless" quality and if people entered it, it was either because the could not make it in the mainstream of education, or they were misguided, or they were noble, self-sacrificing individuals.

But there was a more fundamental assumption that undergirded all of these perceptions and it was one that everyone accepted: to understand and educate mentally retarded students required theories and techniques different from those required for "normal" human beings. There is or should be one human psychology based on principles applicable to all people. Women are different from men, Republicans from Democrats, and Catholics from Protestants, but to conclude that these differences arise on the basis of psychological-developmental-social principles and processes unique to each of these groups is gratuitous and a massive misinterpretation of what we have learned about human behavior. Because people develop differently does not mean that their development was governed by different processes. Diversity in behavior among people does not require resorting to diversity in underlying principles.

In any event, the separation between special and "regular" education, a separation accepted by both, was based on the assumption that retarded individuals required special theories: they were different kinds of human beings. Therefore, people trained to understand and work with retarded children could not work with normal children, and vice versa. For all practical purposes, the could not talk with each other! They segregated themselves from each other, and the thought that perhaps they should be together in the mainstream was considered ludicrous. The opposition to mainstreaming children was long contained in the political-administrative-social structure of departments and schools of education in our colleges and universities.

When we look at the public schools we would have seen much the same set of relationships, except that special class teachers *and* their students were now isolated from the mainstream. It is only in recent years that the special classroom was physically as well-appointed and situated as the regular one. Not all schools had special classes, and some children were bused to a school which did have one. To the rest of the school faculty, the special class teacher was a second-class citizen, someone who was expected to be a good custodian rather than an effective educator. Students were placed in the special class "for life"; there was no expectation that they would be returned to the regular class. And it was by no means infrequent for children to be placed in the special class because of their behavior rather than their academic inadequacy. Special classes were not numerous enough to accommodate all retarded children, and it should not be surprising that these classes were used selectively for purposes of behavioral control.

Aside from the special teacher, no one was concerned about what the children learned or at what rate, because they were not expected to learn very much and even that would take years. The school principal, who either by tradition or administrative regulations came from "regular" education, considered himself incompetent to advise the special class teacher and, not infrequently, the principal saw the special class either as an unasked for burden or a blemish on the school's image. In urban settings, there was a supervisor of special education who would visit the classroom occasionally. If the special class teachers felt alone and unwanted, they were feelings warranted by reality. It would be a gross mistake to see their situation in personal terms, or, better yet, to react to it in personal ways. *It was a situation pretty much viewed as "natural" by almost everyone, including the special class teacher who if she felt otherwise was careful not to articulate it. At best, the special class teacher would have been delighted to achieve separate but equal status.* Nor must we overlook the fact that what we have described had the sanction of the community.

The pressures for mainstreaming did not come from within educational institutions and that fact alone allows one to predict that these pressures would be resisted. It is not a case of the "good guys and the bad guys." Personalizing the polarities in such ways overlooks how both sides are reflecting tradition, history, *and* a fast-changing society. Institutional custom and practice are effective bulwarks to forces for change and this, we too easily forget, has both good and bad features. On the one hand, we do not want our institutions to change in response to every new fad or idea and, on the other hand, we do not want them blindly to preserve the status quo. In regard to mainstreaming, how one regards the oppositional stance of our schools and university training centers will depend on how one feels about mainstreaming. If one is for mainstreaming, then one will tend to view opposition as another instance of stone-age attitudes. If one is against mainstreaming, one will tend to view it as another misguided effort that will further dilute the quality of education of everyone.

The important point is that opposition to mainstreaming was predictable. To proceed as if that would not be the case is to deny the obvious about institutional custom and practice, especially when they have always been congruent with societal values and attitudes. What happens when societal attitudes begin to change, at least among segments effectively organized to bring about change, and that change, like mainstreaming, is generally seen as related to many other matters involving basic constitutional issues? As we indicated earlier, the legal and human issues emerging from segregation practices in regard to mentally retarded individuals can only be understood in the context of an upswell of protest against discriminating practices in regard to many other groups.

What frequently happens is that legislation is passed and public sentiments are translated into public policies having the force of law. From that point on, institutional opposition must conform to the law's intent and requirements or suffer sanctions. This, of course, does not mean that by virtue of the law, long-standing attitudes and practices have been dissolved and reconstituted to willingly accept its new thrust. One has to expect that ways will be sought to circumvent the new intent or to implement it minimally. This was true in the case of discrimination against any minority. Passing laws is far easier than getting them implemented consistent with both their spirit and their letter. This says less about human capacity to be socially perverse than it does about the strength of institutionalized custom and practice. We are not dealing with opposition based on "personality" but on institutional custom, organization, and values.

For example, Andelman (1976) writing about the Massachusetts mainstreaming law (Chapter 766) which served as a model for the federal law 94-142 passed in 1975, says:

> Teachers are also concerned with the accountability factor in 766. The law stipulates that parents of a child with special needs must approve the educational program designed for the child before such a program is implemented. Once the parents approve and sign the plan, the local school committee is legally bound to its specifications and required to produce the educational outcomes specified for the child. Teachers believe that they will be held responsible for failing to produce in children certain desired educational outcomes, when in fact, it is the larger system of public education which has failed to provide adequate resources for such outcomes even to be approximated . . . .
>
> For almost a decade teachers in our state have been negotiating their wages, hours, and conditions of employment. Hundreds of local collective bargaining agreements (a number of them negotiated on a multi-year basis) have established the structure of the teachers' work day and the nature of working conditions as they pertain to instructional assignments, preparation time and responsibilities, access to professional development resources, in-service education, participation in curriculum development, and many other issues.
>
> Aware of the fact that there was bound to be some conflict between their present collective bargaining agreements and what the requirements of the new Chapter 766 might be, teachers hoped that regulations for the new law could be promulgated sometime during the school year of 1972-1973 so that the collective bargaining required for the 1974-1975 school year could take into account the shape and scope of the new mandate. However, regulations for Chapter 766 were not promulgated until the spring of 1974, and many of the provisions of those regulations did prove to be incompatible with many collective bargaining agreements.
>
> For example, Chapter 766 requires that meetings to plan special-needs programs for children are to be scheduled at the convenience of the child's parents. In

an industrial state like Massachusetts, where both parents usually work, this means that many such school meetings have to be held after the school day and sometimes in the evening or on weekends. The requirements of a new state mandate that certain things may have to take place after the normal work day of the teacher are incompatible with collective bargaining agreements which define the structure and nature of the teacher's work day. After two years of collective bargaining, the problem is still not resolved in many communities [pp. 20–21].

Let us become concrete. We give below most of a summary of the federal law. It was prepared by the Children's Defense Fund (1976), an agency which, as its name implies, seeks to protect and enlarge the rights and opportunities of children.

On November 29, 1975, the Education for All Handicapped Children Act (Public Law 94-142) was signed into law. This law builds upon, expands, and will eventually replace the Education of the Handicapped Act, including Part B which provides assistance to states, as amended by the Education Amendments of 1974 (Public Law 93-380). P.L. 94-142 will become fully effective on October 1, 1977 (Fiscal Year 1978).

Both laws are extremely important for children who are handicapped, or misclassified as handicapped by their school districts, and for parents of these children because the laws (1) require states to provide special education and related services to children with special needs, (2) provide financial assistance to states and local school districts to develop appropriate programs and services and (3) establish and protect substantive and procedural rights for children and their parents.

State Plan

To be eligible for money under EHA-B, a state must develop policies and procedures in a "state plan" to insure that the requirements of the law are carried out in every school district in the state (whether or not that school district actually receives EHA-B money). State plans must be available to the public for comment and then submitted for approval to the Federal Bureau of Education for the Handicapped (BEH) in the U.S. Office of Education. The state plan must demonstrate that the state has established and will enforce the following:

1) *Full Services Goal*—a goal of providing all handicapped children with "full educational opportunities"; at least 50% of the EHA-B funds must be given to children who are receiving *no* education at all (i.e., are not in school) and children who are severely handicapped. The plan must provide a timetable showing how services, personnel, equipment and other resources will be developed and assigned in order to reach "full services".

2) *Due Process Safeguards*—policies and procedures describing due process safeguards which parents/children can use to challenge decisions of state and local officials about how a child has been identified, evaluated or placed in a special education program.

   These safeguards must include:
   a. prior notice before a child is evaluated or placed in a special program;
   b. access to relevant school records;

c. an opportunity to obtain an independent evaluation of the child's special needs;

d. an impartial due process hearing to challenge any of the decisions described above; and

e. the designation of a "surrogate parent" to use these safeguards for each child who is a ward of the state or whose parent or guardian is unknown or unavailable.

3) *Least Restrictive Alternative—local and state procedures to assure that handicapped children are educated with non-handicapped children to the extent possible. Separate schools, special classes or other removal of any handicapped child from the regular program are only allowed if and when the school district can show that the use of a regular educational environment accompanied by supplementary aids and services is not adequate to give the child what he/she needs* [emphasis in original].

4) *Non Discriminatory Testing and Evaluation*—procedures showing that tests and other materials or methods used to evaluate a child's special needs are neither racially nor culturally discriminatory. The procedures should also assure that whatever materials or methods are used, they are not administered to a child in a discriminatory manner.

5) *Confidentiality of Information about Handicapped Children*—procedures to guarantee that information gathered about a child in the process of identifying and evaluating children who may have special educational needs, is kept confidential. State procedures must conform to regulations, issued in the February 27, 1976 Federal Register by the Commissioner of Education, which include requirements that parents must be given the opportunity to see relevant school records before any hearing is held on a matter of identification, evaluation or placement of a special needs child. These regulations also apply to the requirements for confidentiality of information under the Education for All Handicapped Children Act.

1) *Full Service Goal*—"free appropriate public education" must be available to all handicapped children ages 3-18 by September 1, 1978 and to all handicapped children 3-21 by September 1, 1980 unless, with regard to 3-5 year olds and 18-21 year olds, "inconsistent" with state law. States must place a priority in the use of their funds under this Act on two groups of children: 1) handicapped children who are *not* receiving an education, and 2) handicapped children with the most severe handicaps, within each disability, who are receiving an inadequate education.

2) *Due Process Safeguards*—as of October 1, 1977 the policies and procedures describing due process safeguards available to parents and children in any matter concerning a child's identification, evaluation or placement in an educational program must include:

a. prior notice to parents of any change in their child's program and written explanation in their primary language, of the procedures to be followed in effecting that change;

b. access to relevant school records;

c. an opportunity to obtain an independent evaluation of the child's special needs;

d. opportunity for an impartial due process hearing which must be conducted by the SEA or local or intermediate school district, but in no case by an employee "involved in the education or care of the child." In any hearing, parents have the right to be accompanied by a lawyer or any individual with special knowledge of the problems of special needs children, the right to present evidence, to confront, compel and cross-examine witnesses, and to obtain a transcript of the hearing and a written decision by the hearing officer. Parents have the right to appeal the hearing decision to the SEA and, if they are still dissatisfied the SEA ruling in federal or state court;

e. the right of a child to remain in his/her current placement (or, if trying to gain initial admission to school, in the regular school program) until the due process proceedings are completed; and

f. the designation of a "surrogate parent" to use the procedures outlines above on behalf of children who are wards of the state or whose parents or guardians are unknown or unavailable.

3) *Least Restrictive Alternative*—handicapped children including children in public and private institutions, must be educated as much as possible with children who are not handicapped.

4) *Non-Discriminatory Testing and Evaluation*—the tests and procedures used to evaluate a child's special needs must be racially and culturally non-discriminatory in both the way they are selected and the way they are administered, must be in the primary language or mode of communication of the child, and no one test or procedure can be used as the sole determinant of a child's educational program.

5) *Individualized Educational Plans*—written individualized educational plans for each child evaluated as handicapped must be developed and annually reviewed by a child's parents, teacher, and a designee of the school district. The plan must include statements of the child's present levels of educational performance, short and long-term goals for the child's performance, the specific criteria to measure the child's progress. Each school district must maintain records of the individualized education plan for each child.

6) *Personnel Development*—comprehensive system to develop and train both general and special education teachers and administrative personnel to carry out requirements of this law must be developed by the state, and each local school district must show how it will use and put into effect the system of personnel development.

7) *Participation of Children in Private Schools*—free special education and related services must be provided for handicapped children in private elementary and secondary schools if the children are placed or referred to private schools by the SEA or local school districts to fulfill the requirements of this law. The SEA must assure that private schools which provide programs for handicapped children meet the standards which apply to state and local public schools, and that handicapped children served by private schools are accorded all the same rights they would have if served in public schools.

To the reader unfamiliar with how Congress passes a law we recommend Bailey's (1950) *Congress Makes a Law*. It conveys well how legislation emerges from a welter of forces, past and present, leading inevitably to compromise and ambiguity. Those of us not saddled with responsibility for legislation underestimate the role of compromise, conflict, and competing values in shaping legislation. More recent and relevant to educational policy and implementation is Gallagher's (1975) brief but highly instructive article, *"Why the Government Breaks its Promises."* Gallagher had an important post in the federal bureaucracy concerned with education and, as the title of the article suggests, he came away from that experience with a very realistic view of the inevitable gulf between the spirit and consequences of legislation.

> If a well-informed citizenry is the basis for a democratic society, we are in trouble. My own experience of three years in Washington convinces me that not one in a thousand citizens has even a rudimentary knowledge of how things get done in government. This section and the one following give a brief indication of some of the decision-making points in both the legislative and executive processes that determine the shape and magnitude of educational programs supported by the federal government.

Gallagher goes on to describe "The Rise and Fall of the National Institute of Education."

> The establishment of the National Institute of Education (NIE) in 1972 grew out of disappointment with the existing education research program within the U.S. Office of Education and a desire to set up an independent organization on the model of the National Institutes of Health. Some rhetoric to the effect that this institute would be a key to reform in American education was helpful in getting legislation establishing NIE through Congress.
>
> Two highly contradictory goals were presented at the same time: NIE would support major investigations into basic research on the learning characteristics of the child, and it would finance innovation programs testing major alternative educational strategies and procedures.
>
> Advertised as a big new $100 million-a-year education program, it actually turned out to have less than $20 million of new money, a sum inadequate for the ambitions or needs of American education. The rest were funds required merely to continue or complete already committed efforts.
>
> Three years ago, in testimony before the Select Sub-committee on Education in the House, I predicted a corrosive cycle of *overexpectation-underfunding-disillusion* for NIE unless limitations were squarely faced. One way to come to grips with reality is to examine the price tag for various educational products. Experience has given reasonable guidelines on what programs cost. With $20 million of new money, NIE could fund one major curriculum project, one experimental school, and some miscellaneous smaller projects. That is all. Obviously, legislators or budget examiners would be ill-advised to express quick disappointment that American education has not been reformed by NIE in one or two years' time.
>
> NIE found itself in another catch. The authorizing legislation provided that a National Council of Education Research be established as the policy-making board. But appointment to the board was made only through the White House, and this procedure was delayed until almost one year after the legislation was passed. The professional leadership of NIE was forced to choose between two courses, either of which was highly dangerous: they could embark on major new

directions clearly intended by the legislation and risk criticism for ignoring the intent of Congress that policy be determined by the National Council; or they could wait until the National Council was established and risk criticism for being unresponsive to the clear need to get started in innovative directions. The NIE leadership engaged in a little of each and was predictably criticized on both counts.

Two years after its initial funding the National Institute of Education lies in shambles, struggling against administrative mishaps and lack of money. The Senate Appropriations Committee report recently suggested that NIE disband. What now? Again, there are two courses, neither of which holds much promise. One is to fire the whole leadership cadre of NIE on the "persona devil" theory; the other is to reorganize NIE into some other slot in the HEW complex in hope that some benefit will be gained by changing the label on the door Meanwhile, cries for reform in education persist.

In discussing Public Law 94-142 we must constantly bear in mind that we will be dealing with ambiguities, compromises, expectations, and history. Before taking up a few of the provisions of Public Law 94-142 we should warn the reader that this federal law is very complex, containing many provisions for priorities, time schedules, funding levels, diagnostic and testing practices, advocacy for children, parental role, etc. This law, superceding a previous federal law, went into effect in October 1977. In late 1976, the *federal* regulations, spelling out in detail the criteria by which the law would be administered, were published. Those regulations determine the confines and substance of required *state* plans and regulations which, in turn, determine the plans and regulations required of *local* districts. Congress passed a law, the executive interprets and administers it, and so down the line. At every step of the way one is dealing with interpretations of interpretations. At this time, it is obviously impossible to evaluate the law's consequences. Some states such as Connecticut, California, and Massachusetts already have legislation consistent with Public Law 94-142, but most do not.

In the discussion that follows we examine some of the possible implications of a few of its provisions on two grounds: the historical background; and discussions with teachers and administrators in local school districts as well as with staff of state departments of education from several states.

In digesting these discussions we could come to only three firm conclusions. First, there was unanimity that the law would have massive consequences for public education, although there was no unanimity on what these would be. Second, implementation of the law would require an equally massive increase in time, energy, and paperwork for everyone. Third, despite the funding provisions in the law, the long-range effect would be to require local school districts to increase their school budgets. Less firm than these three conclusions was the view that one has to nurture a healthy skepticism about the relationship between what school people say they will do and what they actually do.

What follows has to be regarded not as an effort at prediction or evaluation but as a kind of analysis seeking to determine how past historical trends interacting with emerging attitudes and practices in today's realities can give us a glimpse of the future. Acceptance of mainstreaming as a concept and value is a socially moral triumph, but just as we had no good reason to accept the Supreme Court's 1954 desegregation decisions as "solving" a problem, we have no reason to view Public Law 94-142 as a solution to other forms of educational segregation. Social pendulums swing from one pole to the other, in part because of our tendency to underestimate how deeply ingrained practices and habits of thinking manage to subvert our better intentions. If what follows cannot be characterized as sunshine and light, it is not because we are cynics but because we cannot let our hopes blind us to obstacles.

Legislation is often a strange mixture of inkblot and unambiguous statements about intent, consequences, time tables, payments, and punishments. Public Law 94-142 is no exception. Far from being a criticism of this law, our characterization is intended to suggest that there is sometimes wisdom in the ambiguities. For example, take the item concerned with *Personnel Development*. Why is personnel development necessary? If the aim of the law is to mainstream handicapped children, why is personnel development necessary for special and regular education teachers? If mainstreaming is an effort to eradicate discriminating segregation, should not the law be explicit about phasing out special class teachers and classrooms? And why does the law require so many procedures and controls in an effort to insure that the law's intent will be implemented? Have the schools been so lawless about the rights of handicapped children, so discriminating, or so unresponsive as to require all of these new procedures and controls?

One might come away from a reading of the law with the conclusion that schools have not been for handicapped children but against them. The fact is that the contents of the law only make sense if one assumes that the forces for the law understood quite well the opposition on the part of school personnel, and that school personnel would have to be "helped" to adjust to new conditions not of their making. Indeed, without federal money as an incentive and a few years as a kind of grace period, the implication seems to be that mainstreaming would be impossible to institutionalize.

Where the law is most clear the rationale is the most implicit. This is another way of saying that those who wrote the law knew well that a radical transformation of the schools was being called for and that it would encounter opposition for some time to come. Mainstreaming, like school desegregation, would take place with "deliberate speed," a phrase from the 1954 Supreme Court desegregation decision. That phrase in the decision was ambiguous and wisely so, although none of the Supreme Court justices expected that a quarter of a century after the decision, school desegregation would still be encountering mammoth obstacles. A reading of Public Law

94–142 suggests that although its writers may have been aware of the nature of the opposition, their time perspective was far more optimistic than those of the Supreme Court justices in 1954.

What we have just said assumes that the intent of the law was to end segregation practices. That this is an unwarranted assumption is clearly suggested by the item *Least Restrictive Alternative.* What this item boils down to is that when a school district can show that the use of a regular educational environment accompanied by supplementary aids and services is not adequate to give the child what he or she needs, educational segregation is permissible. Given the law's implicit recognition of the opposition to mainstreaming, one does not need to be a cynic to predict that school districts would find ways to justify the continuation of special classes. It would be a rejection of every theory of individual and institutional behavior if school districts did not seek ways to continue what they regard as right and proper. This is not because they wish to discriminate in the pejorative sense against handicapped people, but because the law and the schools agree that there will be many cases where mainstreaming is impossible. The law and the schools are not in opposition about principles. *What the law intends is that the number of segregated individuals should be reduced somewhat.* We should then amend our prediction in this way: The schools will seek to mainstream more handicapped people but the bulk of these people will continue to be segregated. Public Law 94–142 intends a modest quantitative change and, in that respect it is miles apart from the 1954 decision which ruled segregation unconstitutional.

The word "mainstreaming" never appeared in the federal legislation, lending support to the position of some people who were influential in developing 94–142, that the law is being misinterpreted by different individuals and groups. It is a position fully congruent with our observations that in practice the law is not being implemented in the spirit of "separate but equal facilities are inherently unequal." Indeed, many of our observations suggest that in many school districts economic-budgetary considerations are far more potent than anything else in determining whether a handicapped child is mainstreamed or not mainstreamed to any extent.

This is a point that Scull (1977) emphasizes in relation to the decarceration movement. It is precisely when economic-budgetary considerations become primary that one has to set drastic limits to the relationship between the spirit and the consequences of legislation like Public Law 94–42.

Equally distressing, professional rivalries among school psychologists, teachers, guidance counselors, and other educational specialists frequently appear to be having adverse effects on the formulation and implementation of a handicapped child's individualized educational program (IEP), a "program" mandated by the law but the contents and processes of which are vague. We know of instances where professionals participating in the formulation of a child's IEP have not made recommendations to mainstream a child because of conflict with the school district's policies, raising the thorny, ethical question: Who is the client?

From a narrow, legalistic standpoint, it may be inappropriate to view Public Law 94-142 as an attempt at mainstreaming. But it is clearly not inappropriate to say that the law never could have been written and passed except in a climate suffused with the mainstreaming considerations explicitly contained in the 1954 desegregation decision. If the law is being "misinterpreted" as mainstreaming legislation, it is due less to what the law actually says and more to a perception of some people that the law was a derivative of anti-segregation sentiment. Given our observations about how the law is being implemented, the silence of the law about mainstreaming, as well as its emphasis on due process and least restrictive alternative, suggests that the law's evasiveness about mainstreaming is setting the stage for future court battles about mainstreaming as a value and practice.

Gallagher (1972) regards the controversy about labeling as fruitless and makes the case that from the standpoint of influencing and developing public policy, "labelling is a standard first step in trying to provide needed services" (P. 529). History is on Gallagher's side. Gallagher then goes on to emphasize what he considers more important than labeling: How opposition to mainstreaming is based on long-standing attitudes, practices, and school structure.

> There is yet another problem that has been swept gently under the educational rug, but that community activists and parent groups have called to our attention again. It is that special educational placement is too often an exclusionary process masquerading as a remedial process. The regular educational program is only too happy to refer their most troublesome cases to special education. In too many instances general educators only ask one thing of the special educational program—that it take those troublesome children and not give them back.
> The special educator has long held to a philosophy that he has been unable to implement in the educational system. A fine example of the theoretical position is presented by Reynolds (1971):
>
> Special education should be arranged so that the normal home, school, and community life is maintained whenever feasible. Special education placements, particularly those involving separation from normal school and home life, should be made only after careful study and for compelling reasons. [p. 425].
>
> The learning requirements of exceptional pupils, not only their etiological or medical classification, should determine the organization and administration of special education [p. 429].
>
> These are sentiments that most educators could easily subscribe to, yet data collected informally by the Office of Education suggested that special education was de facto, a permanent placement. In a number of large city school systems far less than 10 percent of the children placed in special education classes are ever re-

turned to regular education. When one considers that the referral error could well be that high, it is easy to conclude that the bridge that should exist between special and regular education is, in fact, not really there. The traffic all goes in one direction.

Ten parents have recently sued the state of Pennsylvania for excluding their retarded children from educational services, thus violating their right to equal educational opportunity, and have received a favorable judgment. The concept of *zero reject,* that no child shall be denied educational services appropriate to his level of development and need, seems to be on the verge of acceptance in our society. But such a victory will be a hollow one if what happens is merely a more sophisticated version of exclusion, this time to a special educational program that cannot deliver effective services and cannot negotiate that child back into the regular program when appropriate [Gallagher 1972, p. 529].

A note of reality. To someone unfamiliar with schools, Public Act 94-142 will appear as a step to initiate mainstreaming. The fact is that most handicapped pupils have always been mainstreamed in the public schools. In whatever ways schools may have defined a handicapped child there were never enough special classes in the schools to accommodate all the children so defined. Special classes for the mentally retarded go back a long way in our society but never has there been other than a very small fraction of these children in these classes. This was not because school personnel wanted few special classes but rather an unwillingness to bear the costs. In recent decades, due to state or federal subsidies special classes have been developed for other types of handicap such as perceptually impaired, learning disabled, and emotionally disturbed, but the number of children in these classes has always been a very small percent of those considered to have a handicap.

Why, then, this new push for mainstreaming? Several factors have been at work. First, it is obvious that if a handicapped child is placed in a special class it is not because of the diagnosis. If it were, how did the schools decide to place one handicapped child in the special class and not many others with the same diagnosis? The most frequent answer has been that the children placed in the special class were disturbing in the regular class. And not infrequently that said as much about teachers as it did about handicapped children. In short, special classes were a kind of dumping ground for "behavior problem" children, and the dumping was not always deserved. Second, the dramatic increase in special classes of all sorts in the past two decades was a direct consequence of state and federal subsidies that made it "profitable" for school systems to set up these classes. As one teacher said: "Now we have a lot of places to dump children." Third, particularly in our urban areas, special classes tended to have a disproportionate number of children from ethnic or racial minorities, a tendency that did not go unnoticed by more militant members of these minority groups. Fourth, if the trend for increased numbers of special classes continued, both the state and federal budgets would have to expand considerably. In a sense the process came full circle: Local school districts would not increase the number of special classes unless a good part of the costs came from the state or federal governments, and now these governments were concerned about the increasing costs. Not surprisingly, economics has been a potent factor. Economics, dumping, overrepresentation of minority groups—these together with a heightened sensitivity to civil rights account for the recent push for more mainstreaming. As for economics, let us listen to part of an editorial by Ryor (1976) as president of the National Education Association:

> For effective mainstreaming, regular classroom teachers must have the strong and coordinated backing of special education teachers and support personnel. Yet in these economically perilous times, the threat that boards will fire special education teachers as they put handicapped into regular classrooms hangs like a pall. What an ironic twist it will be if, in implementing this potentially valuable movement for the handicapped, we dispose of the teachers now best prepared to help them!
>
> If mainstreaming is to receive NEA support, it must emphasize thorough preparation of regular and special teachers for their roles. Mainstreaming is one of the most complex educational innovations ever undertaken, and for boards and administrators to plunge their schools into it without advance preparation carries great potential harm for regular and special students and for teachers as well. Without question, this basically good program, riding a wave of enthusiasm, has sometimes been pushed far too fast. Few states yet have carefully organized programs for making mainstreaming work. . . .
>
> Finally, it is pie-in-the-sky fantasy to envision effective mainstreaming without increased funds for additional teachers, auxiliary services, special supplies, and other necessities. Locally, mainstreaming reportedly threatens to bankrupt some districts that are already teetering on the brink of insolvency. Perhaps from a broader view, the answer is the same as for much other school financing: America must get its priorities lined up right. NEA's goal of one-third federal funding for education speaks eloquently to that point [Ryor 1976. p. 1].

The reader should not assume that opposition to mainstreaming only exists within the schools. In some communities opposition to mainstreaming has come from parents of handicapped children, either because they are satisfied with what their children are getting in segregated classes, or because they have little confidence that the regular classroom teacher will be able to integrate handicapped children. The parallels between the reactions of different groups in the 1954 desegregation decision (and the consequent busing) and to Public Law 94–142 are striking and should serve as a base for fashioning a realistic time perspective in regard to accomplishing goals of legislation (or court decisions) that require people to modify their attitudes, behavior, and practices. This, in fact, was a major consideration in the decision to acquaint the reader with some of the issues in the history of our educational system, a history that tells us again and again, that societal values, institutional practices, and blatant prejudice change slowly, and that these changes are always stormy. Someone once said that the ruling "law" of the fate of a public policy (its formulation, acceptance, and implementation) is "whose ox is being gored?" In regard to 94–142, as in the case of the 1954 desegregation decision, the oxen of many groups will be gored. For a concrete example of the real problems 94–142 brings in its wake, the reader should consult an article by Greenberg and Doolittle in The New York Times Magazine (December 11, 1977). The main heading is: "Can schools speak the language of the deaf?"; the subheading is : "A new federal law requires public schools to educate deaf children, but in states where 'mainstreaming' has been tried, it's created many problems."

One other factor deserves mention and it is no less potent for its lack of clear and direct explication. The polarization between school and community has become deeper and stormier. The fact is that school personnel have more and more become the objects of community hostility, derogation, and rejection. Never before have school programs and practices been so scrutinized and criticized. It is only somewhat of an exaggeration to say that school personnel are perceived as guilty until proven innocent. If that is an exaggeration of how the community views the school, it is nevertheless how school personnel feel.

It should occasion no surprise, therefore, that in the course of criticizing schools (e.g., types of tests used, confidentiality of files, criteria for suspension and explusion, racial discrimination, accountability) the questions of how handicapped children are diagnosed, managed, and educated would at some point come to center stage in a drama of deep and opposing currents of feeling. Mainstreaming in the past, as well today, cannot be seen as an educational issue or problem. It has always reflected the nature of the larger society, if only because deviancy or handicap are consequences of societal norms.

Our analysis has indicated that opposition to mainstreaming has characterized the history and structure of our educational institutions. One may, therefore, ask what has been the reception accorded Public Law 94–142? Before trying to answer that question, however, let us look at possible implications of the very title of the law: Education for *All* Handicapped Act.

All Handicapped Children

Public Law 94–142 is not only for those diagnosed as mentally retarded. To anyone familiar with the recent history of advocate groups for the mentally retarded, what is remarkable is not the law itself but the lack of strong opposition by these advocate groups to the law. Ever since the early fifties, when the advocate groups became formidable, their efforts have been directed to spotlighting the need of retarded people for more equitable and humane public support. Put in another way, they were opposed to administrative setups that had responsibility for all handicapped people, which in practice meant that the mentally retarded would be, so to speak, low man on the totem pole.

For example, it was long the practice that the state department of mental health had responsibility for state programs, residential or otherwise, for mentally retarded people. This meant that they had responsibility for the mentally ill and the mentally retarded. It also meant that the latter got far less attention and support than the former, if for no other reason that the heads of these state agencies were psychiatrists who by virtue of their training had far greater interest in mental illness than in mental retardation. In *Exodus from Pandemonium* (1970), Blatt describes and discusses the "politics" of a state department of mental hygiene, and there is every reason to believe that his story is not atypical. A special act of the legislature was required for Blatt himself to be appointed in the Massachusetts Department of Mental Hygiene as Deputy Director for Mental Retardation because he was not a physician. It is small wonder that advocate groups began to fight for the administrative independence of programs for mentally retarded people. Two examples:

1. Up until the late fifties, Connecticut had no central state department of mental health. Each institution for mentally ill or mentally retarded people had a board of trustees appointed by and responsible to the governor. Pressure for a centralized agency began to mount for three reasons: growing public awareness of the extent of the mental health problem, the inadequacies of existing mental hospitals, and the combination of rising costs and the desire for efficiency. Plans were developed for the proposed state agency to have responsibility both for the mentally ill and the mentally retarded. A variety of advocate groups, aware as they were from other states of the consequences of this administrative arrangement, mounted a campaign for mental retardation to be placed in the department of health rather than in the new department of mental health. It is not accidental that between 1935 and 1960, Connecticut pioneered in new programs for mentally retarded people (Sarason, Grossman, and Zitnay 1972). During this period Connecticut may well have been the only state in which mental retardation was "independent." Within the past decade, the administrative separation of mental retardation from mental health has become more frequent.

2. In 1966, a subcommittee of the House of Representatives conducted a hearing on a proposed bill which contained funding provisions for special education which then meant mental retardation. The bureau head (Dr. Donald N. Bigelow) from the Office of Education who was testifying in favor of the bill made an eloquent plea the thrust of which was to bring special education, especially in regard to the training of teachers, into the mainstream of American education. This plea did not sit well with the subcommittee chairman who had fought for greater and separate recognition of

the field of mental retardation. He interpreted, wrongly in this instance, the bureau chief's plea as a kind of power grab that would have the familiar effect of robbing the field of its need for increased support. The hearing was on a Friday. By the end of the next Monday, mental retardation programs had been separated from the bureau.

On the surface the All Handicapped Children Act appears unobjectionable. Indeed, it appears a tremendous stride forward. But from the standpoint of partisans for mentally retarded children, especially those with a sense of history and knowledge of the culture of schools, there are grounds for unease. This stems from the fact that in the past fifteen years there has been an exponential growth in special classes for the emotionally disturbed, the learning disabled, the perceptually handicapped, and the hyperactive child. The push for those classes came from within and without the schools and among the leaders from without were those from the mental health professions who heretofore had never exercised such leadership on behalf of the mentally retarded. This is not said in criticism but simply as a matter of fact.

The array of special classes was for the most part for pupils not regarded as retarded but whose handicaps were either in some way disruptive of the normal class routine or put undue burdens on teachers who felt inadequate to deal with these children. These special classes and programs were also costly because they required a variety of educational and mental health specialists than was ever deemed necessary for special classes for the mentally retarded. The unease in all this stems from the fact that powering the passage of Public Law 94-142 was far less a concern for mentally retarded children than for the bewildering assortment of children the schools considered "handicapped" and in need of segregated programs. We put quotes around handicapped because the bases for such a label are ambiguous, prejudicial, and even invalid in many instances.

For example, few topics can engender more heated controversy than trying to get agreement on the criteria of emotional disturbance or the nature of learning disabilities. The unease can be now put in the form of a concrete question: is it not likely that in implementing the mainstreaming intent of Public Law 94-142, less attention and effort will be given to mentally retarded children than to the others encompassed by the act? This question has to be raised not to alert anyone to a conspiracy against mentally retarded children but to suggest that public laws are reactions to current perceptions of social problems. In the case of Public Law 94-142, the problems in our schools that seemed to need correction did not primarily center around mental retardation. This, of course, does not mean that the law was not concerned in an important way with mentally retarded children but rather that *in the process of implementing the law schools would tend to give greater attention to other kinds of children.* Traditions, structure, and perceived priorities will determine the law's effects. Individuals and institutions are rather adept at transforming a law's intent to their purposes. If that were not the case, legislative bodies would spend far less time than they do amending laws and writing remedial legislation.

Let us give attention to an article by Milofsky in the magazine section of the *New York Times* for Sunday, January 2, 1977. The heading of the article is as follows:

Schooling for Kids No One Wants

A new Federal law requires "mainstreaming" of handicapped children into regular classes. It could prove as controversial as busing.

The heading reflects the feelings of many people. Milofsky's article is based on observations of mainstreaming in Massachusetts consequent to the passage of a 1972 state law containing "Chapter 766" on which federal law 94-142 was later based. Mainstreaming has been in effect for five years in Massachusetts.

It requires local school districts to take responsibility for the education of all children who suffer from handicaps "arising from intellectual, sensory, emotional or physical factors, cerebral dysfunctions, perceptual factors, or other specific learning disabilities or any combination thereof." Chapter 766 discourages the labeling of handicapped children as much because of the "stigmatizing effect" this can have and instead emphasizes the individual needs of each child, determined through a "core evaluation" by a team consisting of a psychologist or social worker, doctor, or nurse, the child's present or most recent teacher, and a parent. The law mandates the involvement of parents and lay groups in "overseeing, evaluating, and operating special education programs" through regional and state advisory committees, a majority of whose members are parents of handicapped children.

The Massachusetts law has enabled the mainstreaming of the "vast majority" of handicapped children into public schools, says Dr. Robert Audette, Associate Commissioner for Special Education in Massachusetts. Most of these children divide their time between regular and special classrooms, with only the most severely afflicted children in segregated classes.

Before giving some of Milofsky's observations, it should be noted that he gives examples of mainstreamed pupils: cerebral palsied, learning disabled, emotionally disturbed, and perceptually handicapped children. Mental retardation is never mentioned in the entire article. This may be an oversight but that is our point: The mentally retarded may well be overlooked. One could argue that it is a real step forward that our society is recognizing that there are many handicapped children with different types of conditions, and that no more attention should be given to one group such as the mentally retarded than to others. We agree.

However, as we pointed out in earlier chapters, ours is a society that places such a high value on "intelligence" that those who are considered to have less of it are devalued more than those who don't but have other characteristics interfering with school learning. As soon as a child is diagnosed as mentally retarded, the social-educational-productive worth of that child tends to be seen as less than if the label given the child was "emotionally disturbed" or "learning disabled"; the latter labels implying a more hopeful prognosis.

Every teacher has been told: "You teach children, not subject matter." If that admonition is so often honored in the breach, it is for the same reason that we so often react not to children but to labeled children, and the label does not have to be based on a formal diagnosis. So, if we seem to be partisans for mentally retarded pupils, it is not because we feel they are owed more than other children, which is as silly as saying that we should devote more attention to "gifted" than to "run-of-the-mill," but rather because in our society they are likely to get less than other children.

Let us turn to what Milofsky (1977) reports:

1. Mainstreaming means being in the mainstream part of the time: "Most of these children divide their time between regular and special classrooms, with only the most severely afflicted children in segregated classes." What that statement means is that some children are more segregated than others.
2. Many teachers feel unprepared for the responsibilities the Massachusetts law gives to them, and those school personnel who might be of help to teachers are too busy meeting their new responsibilities under the law. Some teachers, in the minority, report being able to cope with their new responsibilities.
3. Emotionally disturbed children are most disturbing, and school personnel feel that they are being required to deal with these children with very inadequate resources and no expectation that these resources will ever be available to them. In the City of Springfield "Most of these children are boys and many of them are black or Spanish-speaking [and] there is little hope of returning them to regular classes."
4. It is difficult for parents to assert their rights, in part because they do not know the law and in part because "they are intimidated by the whole thing."
5. For some towns and cities the law, despite its funding provisions, has created financial hardships.

Consequences of Public Law 94–142

Passed in 1975, Public Law 94–142, building on a law passed in 1974, required that each state "has in effect a policy that assures all handicapped children the right to a free appropriate public education   by October 1977 when funding was to begin. Even if one were writing many years after October 1977, it would be difficult to judge the law's consequences for reasons we will take up later. What is possible at this point is to present observations of how some school districts have reacted and prepared for the deadline. We do not claim that our observations are based on any kind of representative sampling. We have observed and talked to numerous school teachers, administrators, and policy makers — sufficient to give us some sense of the diversity of reaction and program.

The consequences of Public Law 94-142 will vary in terms of urban, suburban, and rural settings. Put in another way, the consequences will vary not only in terms of the size of the school district but also in terms of factors highly correlated with size: racial and ethnic composition, average achievement levels, serious problems of management and discipline, class size, frequency of families moving within a school district, teacher morale, and level of conflict between school personnel and the community. Only if we were living in another world, could one avoid predicting that the consequences in our urban settings will very likely be different from those in suburban and rural settings.

Someone once said that our urban school systems are really two systems, regular and special, and that the regular exceeds the special in size by a surprisingly small amount. In 1968, the President's Committee on Mental Retardation found that children from poverty and ghetto areas are fifteen times more likely to be diagnosed as mentally retarded than children from higher income families, and that nationally most of the retarded are found in our slums.

From the standpoint of urban school personnel, these and other types of special classes contain only a fraction of pupils who would be in them if more funds were available. As more than one urban school teacher has said: "I am a *regular* classroom teacher but don't kid yourself, I have a *special* class." This feeling on the part of urban school personnel increases in frequency and depth as one moves from elementary to middle to senior school levels.

These feelings have deepened in the past few years as cutbacks in funds have made for larger classes. But even before these cutbacks, teacher unions in our urban settings sought, often successfully, to insure that regular classroom teachers would not have to cope with children who in one way or another disrupted classroom routine and academic goals. From the standpoint of urban school personnel, the provision in Public Law 94-142 restricting funding to a small percent of pupils diagnosed as handicapped is a gross misperception of the size of the problem. Furthermore, from the standpoint of urban school personnel, the provisions of the law safeguarding the rights of children and parents will not only be costly in time but may well heighten the level of existing conflict between school and community. The fact that the law provides in-service training for school personnel to enable them to cope with the consequences of increased mainstreaming is explicit recognition that what is at issue is changing the attitudes of school personnel.

Our observations and discussions lead to the unfortunate conclusion that urban school systems are hardly prepared to implement Public Law 94-142. There are some school systems that had no plan at all several months before the deadline of October 1977. As one administrator in a large urban school system, who shall go unidentified, said:

> It's not that we don't want to be prepared but simply that we have not had the time, and frankly the energy, to think through what we should do and how we should do it. And to be completely truthful, I have not read the law and no one I know has either. We thank God when we get through a day or a week with our hearts and bodies intact, so when you ask what we are doing about the law, I get a sinking sensation. But then again that's exactly the way we feel, sinking.

We have quoted this nameless person's reactions not for the purpose of criticizing, or evaluating, or excusing, but to underline the stance of beleaguerement that urban educators project.

Several urban school systems reported that they had already instituted mainstreaming. Although the reports differed in a number of respects, they tended to have several features in common. First, the creation of centers to which handicapped children were sent for academic subjects and in which they spend a significant portion of the day. Second, these pupils were "mainstreamed" with the other children in the gymnasium, lunch, music, etc. In some instances, children were bused daily to the center and the mainstreaming took place there; in other instances the center was in the school which the child would normally attend by virtue of place of residence. In one instance the center was in a mobile unit parked next to the school. Third, in almost every instance the descriptions provided us indicated that primary attention was being given to those labeled as emotionally disturbed or learning disabled. In other words, they seemed to be defining mainstreaming, far less in regard to mentally retarded pupils and far more to those with labels less suggestive of an intellectual deficit.

Mainstreaming: Begging the Question

Mainstreaming is a concept powered by a value: Every effort should be made to allow a handicapped child to be an integral member of his peer age group and only when this is not possible should one employ the least restrictive alternative. The question arises, however, by what criteria should one resort to a least restrictive alternative? The answer to this question, of course, will in practice determine what mainstreaming is. It is relatively easy to get agreement on a verbally stated value, it is far more difficult to keep the agreement once that value is acted upon. Between intent and performance is a wide area mined by obstacles that often destroy the intent. Because you want to do "good" does not mean you will, or that if you do good that others will agree that your actions have been consistent with your values.

In practice, on what basis is the least restrictive alternative being decided and how consistent is it with the underlying value? The very fact that Public Law 94–142 was enacted, that it calls for in-service training, is testimony to the widespread belief that too frequently schools defined least restrictive alternative in ways congenial to their accustomed perception of their mission rather than what was in the best interests of certain children. This is not peculiar to schools but is characteristic of the way most organizations deal with troublesome individuals. Public Law 94–142 does not tell school systems how to decide the question; it puts the burden of proof on schools to justify resort to a least restrictive alternative. How do some schools seem to be justifying resort to the alternative? Keeping in mind that mainstreaming is in its infancy, and that our observations and discussions cannot be assumed to be representative, although they may turn out to be, the answer to the question is: relatively sincere tokenism. And by that confusing and self-contradictory answer we mean that there is sincere desire to comply with the law at the same time that a tremendous amount of time and energy go into the development and maintenance of the new type of segregated setting.

The very existence of these settings requires justification and use, and this often plays into the tendency to avoid asking to what extent the child is removed from the regular classroom because of the inadequacies of the classroom. This is not to say that the child labeled as handicapped is no problem in the classroom but rather that classroom problems are always a consequence of the interaction among characteristics of the child, the teacher, and other children. Problem behavior always has a situational component. Problem behavior is not "inside" or characteristic of a child, but a feature of a complex situation. For example, the most dramatic and sustained change in behavior we have ever seen has been when we could change a child's classroom, no mean diplomatic feat (Sarason, Levine, Goldenberg, Cherlin, and Bennett 1966). Consider the following case description:

> Tommy was a seven-year-old boy enrolled in the second grade. He was a well developed, goodlooking child of above-average intelligence who had entered the elementary school one year before when his family had moved into the area. Both academically and socially his performance and adjustment at the time were more than adequate and consistent with his abilities and talents. Although initially noted to be somewhat shy, he quickly made friends and was highly regarded by his first grade teacher.
>
> Tommy had had several of the usual childhood diseases (chicken pox and measles) and his last complete physical examination had been essentially negative. His teeth required attention, his vision was 20-20 and his hearing was normal. Thus, until the summer of 1964, Tommy was a relatively healthy, attractive and bright seven-year-old whose developmental and medical history was essentially

unremarkable. Although he experienced some minor difficulty when he entered the new school situation, his adjustment, both academically and socially, was completely satisfactory.

During the summer vacation Tommy, delivering newspapers, was viciously attacked and bitten by a dog. As he went up to one of the houses on his paper route, the dog leaped on him, ripped his clothing, and bit him on the back and wrist. Tommy's screams eventually brought the dog's owner, who had to beat the dog repeatedly with a club in order to make him let go of the child.

Tommy was taken immediately to the office of a local doctor. His mother was notified and met Tommy there. His wounds were cauterized and injections administered for possible infection, and he was given sedatives. Soon after this experience Tommy became very quiet and extremely withdrawn, not talking or playing with other children, and refusing to leave his home. About three weeks later, he developed a cold and what was described as an "asthma attack" in which he was short of breath and had difficulty breathing. According to Tommy's mother it was during this time immediately following the incident with the dog that Tommy "woke up nights screaming and crying and at times running out of the house. He complained of a pounding in his head and imagined seeing things."

With the passage of time and the approach of the new school year Tommy's posttraumatic symptomatology appeared to become more involved and frightening. He began actively hallucinating and talking about "the ugly little man who's coming and putting bad feelings in my head." He became extremely frightened by loud sounds and constantly sought his mother's attention, reassurance, and protection. The only way in which she could calm him down would be to hold him and speak to him in a soft quiet manner. After numerous consultations with the family doctor, it was decided to put Tommy under the care of Dr. S., a "nerve specialist in town." Dr. S. placed Tommy on a regimen of medication (phenobarbital) to be taken three times a day after meals. It was his feeling that Tommy's condition was "an emotional reaction related to the strain stemming from his traumatic episode with a brutal dog." Tommy was told that the "pill he took to school would help him get rid of the spells."

It will be recalled that when Tommy initially entered the first grade he had experienced some minor difficulties in adjusting to his new living and school settings. It was during this period that he first came into contact with the school nurse. According to her he "often would come to me during the first few weeks of school complaining of a cold or stomach upset, but would be satisfied to just talk with me, have his temperature taken and return to class." Following his successful adjustment in school he contented himself with visiting the nurse whenever the holidays were drawing near, at which time he would wish her a happy holiday, and would often give her a card that he had made for her.

On returning to school this year Tommy was assigned to a second-grade class. At this time he was extremely nervous and upset, often running away from the loud noises in the schoolyard, and frequently hallucinating. His single anchor of security in school appeared to be the faith he placed in "the pill that would help my spells."

Tommy's second-grade teacher was an essentially unresponsive and reserved person. Her approach to teaching and to the children was all business. Her previous teaching experience had been confined to the parochial school setting and it was difficult for her to tolerate any interference with the academic standard and expectations she set for her students. Our observations in her classroom always revealed an academically competent teacher who was a stern and controlling disciplinarian and who utilized methods of shaming and rejecting to ensure the maintainance of an orderly efficient classroom. Although never harsh or uncontrolled in her interpersonal dealings with the children, neither would she allow herself or them to minimize their personal distance in a physical or psychological manner. In short, however competent her preparation and however well-intentioned her philosophy of teaching, she was a teacher who was essentially unable or unwilling to deal with the particular and idiosyncratic needs of her children. She tended to perceive these needs as unwelcomed and unrelated interruptions in the processes and aims of second-grade education.

In terms of the teacher's relationship with Tommy, although upset and somewhat frightened by his behavior, she perceived his spells as essentially interfering; that is to say, as discrete behaviors that erected unwanted barriers for her in her attempts to present specific material to the rest of the class. As far as his pills were concerned, she viewed the responsibility for his taking them as a matter of concern for Tommy, his parents, and his doctor. It was not within the scope of her definition of her professional responsibilities to become involved in a problem that was distracting in nature and took time away from her teaching duties. This being the case, and because she was unable to materially reorganize her perception of the situation, she was content to allow Tommy to utilize the nurse and her office as the appropriate setting for such interactions. This removed Tommy from her classroom during his periods of stress, and at the same time enabled her to maintain her firm position regarding the limited and relevant areas of responsibility for a teacher.

From this point on Tommy began spending more and more of his time at the nurse's office, and it was here that we first met him. According to the nurse, whenever Tommy was in school—his absence rate for the months of September and October were extremely high—he would come to her office to take his pill or "whenever he felt a spell coming on." They would spend these periods of time talking and Tommy would describe vividly his feelings and tell her about the "things he saw." Often when his crying and trembling subsided she would call his mother, talk with her at length, and eventually have Tommy taken home. Although the nurse knew about the incident with the dog, Tommy himself soon brought it up during one of his particularly difficult days. They spoke about it at some length and the nurse, in the context of sharing and understanding his fear, related to him several other such incidents involving other children. It was during the next day that we met Tommy. On that occasion Tommy had come to the nurse's office and wanted to go home. He was sobbing uncontrollably and seemed extremely nervous when we came into her office. After he calmed down a bit we all sat around while Tommy told us about "the little man I saw in my class who was coming to put bad things in my head." Once more he spent a good deal of time talking about the past summer, but finally began speaking of the terrible difficulty he had whenever he felt a spell coming on and would have to ask his teacher about letting him go out of the class to take his pill. He ended by informing us of his desire not to come to school anymore. After speaking with Tommy's mother and the teacher we decided eventually to change his class, and, for the interim, we put him on half days, both to minimize his anxiety-arousing contact with his teacher and to enable us to have the time to search for an appropriate second-grade teacher. During the time that he was attending school only in the afternoons he spent most of his time doing his schoolwork in the nurse's office after his teacher had given him his assignment. We were, as yet, relatively new in the school. Although we felt the need to have Tommy's class changed, we wanted time to get a better idea of exactly which teacher would be most appropriate for him. Since neither Tommy's current teacher nor the school nurse minded him using the nurse's office as his interim "classroom," everyone agreed to this arrangement. This enabled the nurse and ourselves to utilize that period of time to search for, become acquainted with, and brief whoever was to become Tommy's new teacher.

The following week we were in the lunchroom during a time of the day when the school nurse usually is not in her office. Tommy entered the lunchroom looking obviously upset and a bit bewildered. He was grasping his bottle of pills tightly in his hand as he looked around for his teacher. Before we could reach him or he could see us he turned to another teacher and hesitatingly began asking her permission to take his pill. The teacher, noting his degree of upset and the air of panic pervading his speech, immediately took his hand and accompanied him out of the lunchroom. They proceeded down the hall to a fountain where she helped Tommy take the pill. Once this was accomplished the teacher took Tommy to her room where he calmed down in a relatively short period of time. With her arm draped gently around his shoulders she then took him back to the lunchroom where he sat at her class's table for the remainder of the period. In this very short time we knew that we had found Tommy's next second-grade teacher.

This teacher was a young and attractive woman who was relatively inexperienced in terms of the number of years she had been teaching. Her class was generally a bit more noisy than others but always jumping with activity. She was an extremely warm and accepting person who seemed most effective and efficient when she became intimately involved with and in the ongoing activities of her children. Although she never lost control of her class there was a prevading atmosphere of disjointedness in the sense that many activities might be going on at the same time. This looseness quickly subsided whenever she raised her voice a bit above the well-modulated tone in which she usually addressed individual students. Her lessons were not always totally prepared and sometimes were lost in organizing particular events. She was extremely patient with the children and utilized well both verbal and nonverbal cues to communicate her feelings to them. More than anything else she seemed to enjoy teaching and being with her children, and this enjoyment appeared to be reciprocal.

We immediately met with the nurse and the "new" teacher to consider the transfer of Tommy to her class. We discussed Tommy's difficulties and the reasons we felt she might be helpful. The teacher, in turn, communicated her desire to have him placed in her class and informed us that, indeed, she had a great affection for him and hoped she would be able to help him. It was decided that the school nurse would be the most appropriate person to handle the transition in the sense that she would both help present the idea to Tommy and would remain the available resource whenever he felt the need to leave the classroom for any reason relating to his difficulties. It was also decided that the teacher would meet with us on a weekly basis to discuss Tommy's progress or lack of progress.

Tommy was transferred to his new class and immediately placed on a full-day schedule. During the first day the teacher spoke with Tommy about his difficulties and communicated to him how important it was to her that he get better and take his "spell pills." They established a procedure whereby he would not have to make any public statements in class prior to the granting of permission to leave the room to take his pill. Whenever Tommy was absent the teacher immediately called his home and spoke with him and his mother. Although Tommy was informed of the availability of the school nurse the teacher made it clear to him that his health, as well as his school work, was now also a joint venture between him and herself. To Tommy this meant that she very much wanted him to be able to talk with her about his feelings and his symptoms, and that her interest in him was as a "little boy" and not just as a "little student."

Tommy's progress after entering his new class was speedy and marked and was manifested in virtually all of the areas in which he had been experiencing profound difficulties. For purposes of clarity we describe these areas separately, although the reader should note that his behavior in each of these areas was influenced by, and interrelated with, his experiences in the others. Tommy's absence rate from school decreased almost immediately after he was placed in his new class. In terms of academic performance, Tommy rose to be one of the top five students in his class. According to his grades as well as his teacher's observations, he was beginning to fulfill the above-average potential noted in the first grade. Although before his shift he was unable to concentrate, had difficulty maintaining attention, and was unwilling to work at anything but his reading material, he was now actively involved in the varied projects occurring in his classroom. In general his over-all academic performance, as well as his social adjustment, was at a higher level, occurred in a context relatively free of the debilitating effects of undue loss of attention or the inability to concentrate, and appeared to have become more inner-directed and self-satisfying than externally imposed.

Of greatest import were the changes that occurred in Tommy's symptomatology and schedule of medication. The week before his transfer was particularly difficult for him. His symptoms (fearfulness, phobic reactions to loud noises, periods of fitful crying, and apparent hallucinatory experiences) were quite pronounced, and the occasions necessitating his approaching his teacher to request attention for his "spell pills" seemed to exacerbate these symptoms. At that time he was on phenobarbital. During the time after his transfer to his new class he showed evidence of a steady and progressive reduction in the intensity and duration of his psychotic symptomology. Soon after entering his new class the periods of fitful crying accompanying his pill-taking behavior subsided. He was gradually able to tolerate loud noises, although this aspect of his difficulty has been only recently eliminated. His hallucinatory experiences became less frequent and frightening, the more he spoke about them with his teacher. They, too, have not been reported for some time. In mid-December, approximately one month after his transfer, his medication was decreased to every other day and by late January was further reduced. At present all medications have been discontinued. In a recent meeting of the school nurse, the teacher, and ourselves the teacher informed us that she had not noticed any changes since Tommy has been off medication. Tommy's mother reported similar progress at home and except for the fact that "he occasionally has nightmares and wakes up crying," felt that "the worst is over." Our latest classroom observations and information would support this point of view.

As far as Tommy's relationship with the nurse was concerned, this soon underwent a change. Although we made it clear to Tommy that the nurse was available to him whenever he felt he needed her, the frequency and duration of his visits to her, decreased steadily after mid-November. Although he had been in her office virtually every day that he was in school and had remained there for significant periods of time, subsequent to his shifting of classes he began showing up less often and would remain for shorter periods. This change was a gradual process and occurred over a long span of time. By late December the nurse observed that Tommy "still comes to see me about little things and many times just to say 'Hello'." Her most recent report indicated that, "Tommy has not visited my office in almost three weeks, except to look for a hat in the lost and found box!" [pp. 221-26].

This case was described long before mainstreaming was in the air and also before there were classrooms for emotionally disturbed children. Today, the chances would be high that Tommy would not be in a regular classroom but in a "least restrictive alternative." The presence of such alternatives, together with Tommy's behavior and blatant psychopathology, would probably effectively short-circuit thinking of alternative ways to maintain him in the regular classroom.

We are not asserting that all children can be maintained in the regular classroom; we are asserting three things. First, no teacher is equally effective with all kinds of children. It may sound like an extreme statement but we have never seen a child labeled as a serious classroom problem who could not be effectively managed by another teacher in that school if one disregarded grade levels. Just as we emphasized in Chapter 2 that some parent-child relationships founder because of a mismatch between child and parental vulnerabilities, the same principle holds between pupil and teacher. To resort to a least restrictive alternative without considering this principle is to subvert the intent of mainstreaming. The first question is not what is the least restrictive alternative, but how seriously has one attempted to match the child to a regular classroom teacher.

The second point, illustrated by Tommy's case, is the significance of the role of "consultant" in the school, whose task it is to support both teacher and child, but who essentially acts as an advocate for the child. The third point is that when least restrictive alternatives are not available, necessity can truly become the mother of invention. And while not all such inventions are successful, the rate of success has been quite encouraging. What we have observed about mainstreaming is that it has led to procedural and administrative inventions that are obviously different from the inventions described in Tommy's case.

There is another significance to Tommy's case and it has to do with the Yale Psycho-Educational Clinic, which was in existence between 1962–1972 (Sarason, et al. 1966; Kaplan and Sarason 1970). Clinic personnel worked in the schools and in the classrooms. To understand the role of the clinic member in the school, as well as to glimpse the significance of the rationale for mainstreaming, we give the introductory comments of a clinic member to the faculty of a school before any relationship between school and clinic was assumed.

> For a number of years some of us in the Department of Psychology at Yale have been engaged in different research projects involving elementary schools. In addition to our experiences in the elementary schools, some of us have long been interested in various aspects of special education and in the preparation of teachers. As a consequence, we became increasingly interested in the day-to-day problems facing schools in general and teachers in particular. Let me say right off that there are two conclusions to which we have come. The first is that anyone who teaches in the public schools for less than $15,000 per year ought to have his head examined. The second conclusion is that a law ought to be passed making it mandatory for each parent to teach a class by himself for a day each year. Although these recommendations may not solve all problems, they would certainly help bring about changes that all of us would agree are necessary. All of this is by way of saying that our experiences have given us an understanding of what is involved in teaching and managing a large group of children, each of whom is a distinct character, for several hours each day over a period of 10 months. It is not flattery but rather strong conviction underlying the statement that the classroom teacher performs one of the most difficult tasks asked of any professional person. It would indeed be nice if all a teacher had to do was to teach. You know, and I know, that a teacher is a parent, a social worker, a psychologist, and a record-keeping clerk. Hopefully there is time to teach once the duties associated with these other roles are discharged. We are living at a time when everyone seems to be an expert on the schools and ignorance seems to be no barrier to articulating strong opinions. There is no doubt, as I am sure you will agree, that there is much one can criticize about schools, but there is also no doubt that unless one understands what a school is like and what it is faced with in its day-to-day operation the benefits we would like to see from these changes will not be so great as they should be.
>
> One of the most staggering problems facing our society concerns the degree of serious maladjustment in many people. One has only to look at the size and number of our mental hospitals, psychiatric clinics, reformatories and the like to begin to grasp how enormous a problem this is. We are talking about millions of people and billions of dollars. What needs to be stressed is that in the foreseeable future we will have neither the personnel nor the facilities to give these troubled people the quality of treatment they need. In all honesty I must also say that for many of these people our knowledge and treatment procedures leave much to be desired.
>
> As a result of our experiences, we at the Psycho-Educational Clinic in the Yale Department of psychology have come to two conclusions: first, far too little is being done either to try to prevent the occurrence of problems or to spot them at those points in the individual's life where with a little effort a lot may be ac-

complished. Second, if we believe what we say, we ought in a very limited kind of way to attempt to see what we can do. I do not have to emphasize to a group of elementary-school teachers the significance of a preventive approach to problems in the early grades. As I am sure all of you know as well as, if not better than I, you are faced daily with children whose behavior, learning difficulties, and interpersonal relations, (with you or other children) arouse in you concern, bewilderment, anger, and a lot of other reactions. On the basis of all the talks and meetings we have had over the years with teachers there would seem to be in any one classroom of 25 children anywhere from three to six children about whom the teacher is concerned in the sense that she has a question about their academic learning and personal adjustment in the school setting.

What do we propose to do? It is easier for me to tell you what we do *not* intend to do. For one thing, we do not intend to come into a school in order to see how many problem children we can refer out to various agencies. There is no doubt that you know a lot of children who could utilize the services of a child-guidance clinic or family service society. To come in with the intent of referring them out is both unfair and unrealistic because these agencies, particularly the child-guidance clinics are overwhelmed with cases and generally have long waiting lists. Even if the child-guidance clinic could take the child on, it would take them quite a while to get to first base with the child and in the meantime you still have that child in your class. Treatment procedures are neither that quick nor effective to allow you to expect that your difficulties with the child are over once you know he is being seen in a clinic. The question we have asked of ourselves is how can we be of help to the teacher in the here and now with whatever questions and problems she raises with us. In short, we want to see how we can be of help within the confines of the school.

It is not our purpose to come into a school to sit and talk to teachers, however helpful and interesting that might be. When we say we want to be helpful in the here and now within the confines of the school, we mean that in addition to talking with the teacher about the child we have to be able to observe that child in the context of the classroom in which the problem manifests itself. For help to be meaningful and practical it must be based on what actually goes on in the classroom setting. For example, it is in our experience no particular help to a teacher to be told that a child needs individual attention, a need which differentiates him not at all from the rest of us. What a teacher wants to know is when, how, and for what goals this "individual attention" will occur, and this requires a first-hand knowledge of what is going on.

We do not view ourselves in the schools as people to whom questions are directed and from whom answers will be forthcoming. Life and the helping process are not that simple. We have no easy answers, but we have a way of functioning that involves us in a relationship to the teacher and the classroom and that together we can come up with concrete ideas and plans that we feel will be helpful to a particular child. We are not the experts who can come up with solutions even though we have no first-hand knowledge of the context in which the problem has been identified.

I hope I have made clear that when we say we want to help it means that we want to talk to the teacher, observe in the classroom, talk again to the teacher, and together come up with a plan of action that with persistence, patience, and consistency gives promise of bringing about change. It is not a quick process and it is certainly not an easy one.

I cannot state too strongly that we are not coming into the schools with the intent of criticizing or passing judgment on anyone. We are nobody's private FBI or counterintelligence service. We are not the agent of the principal or some other administrative hierarchy or power structure of the school system. We have no special strength or power except that which flows from our being able to establish a situation of mutual trust between teachers and ourselves. To the extent that we can demonstrate to you by our manner, gesture, and verbalization that we want to help, to that extent we make the development of this mutual trust more likely and quickly to occur.

There is one aspect of the way we function that I think needs some elaboration. I have already told you why it is essential for us, if our efforts are to be maximally useful, that we spend time in the classroom. Another reason this is essential resides in the one advantage we have over the teacher, i.e., we do not have the awesome responsibility of having to handle a large group of young characters five days a week for several hours each day, a responsibility that makes dispassionate observation and clear thinking extraordinarily difficult. We can enjoy the luxury of being in the classroom without the responsibility of the teacher for managing and thinking about 25 or more unique personalities. We do not envy you although I am quite sure that you will envy us for not having your responsibilities. It is precisely because we are "free" that we can observe what is going on in a way not usually possible for a teacher.

In order for us to help in a school it is crucial that we know that school as a physical entity and as a kind of social organization. Consequently, we usually make the request that for the first six weeks or so we visit classrooms and get to know you and what you do in different grades without any obligation to get involved with any problem. A school and a classroom are not simple settings and it takes several weeks until we get the feeling of familiarity. We will be here on certain days of the week so that you can count on when we will be here. We try to spend a day and a half a week in each school.

We do not know to what extent we can be of help to you. We do not present ourselves as experts who have answers. We have much to learn about this helping process. If our previous work with teachers is any guide, the type of service we want to develop is one that they feel they need. The only thing we can guarantee you is that we want to learn and to help. We have much to learn from you, and together we may be able to be of help to children in school [Sarason et al. 1966, pp. 59–62].

The thrust of the clinic's rationale was, obviously, to keep children in the regular classrooms. There were some special classes for the mentally retarded but none for any other type of handicap; children were not placed in special classes because they were retarded but because they were troublesome, and if state regulations did not set a limit to the size of these classes they would have been crowded in the extreme. Those were the days when pressure was mounting for more types of special classes and more community facilities to deal with children with school problems. The clinic's aim was to see if the pressure to segregate and refer could be blunted. Those were also the days when suspensions and expulsions were frequent and not subject to the legal, civil rights procedures of today.

In early 1977, we interviewed Mr. Murray Rothman, long the Director for Special Education in the New Haven schools, to discuss what was being done about mainstreaming. What is relevant to the present discussion is that for several years before Public Law 94-142 was enacted, he had been able to place in each of nine schools a person whose major function was to be whatever help possible to classroom teachers in regard to their pupils. This he had done, he said, spontaneously as a result of his close working relationship with the Yale Psycho-Educational Clinic, and witnessing firsthand how the role of a clinic member in school helped teachers to maintain handicapped children in the regular classroom. He then reported that the nine schools which had a person who functioned in the cliniclike role referred significantly fewer children to "least restrictive alternatives." It was his opinion that if he were able to have such a person in each school, the need for these alternatives would not be eliminated but discernibly diluted in strength. This opinion finds clear support in an experimental study by Cantrell and Cantrell (1976), based on a rationale quite similar to that employed by the Yale Psycho-Education clinic and Mr. Rothman.

Finally, mention must be made here of a recent study by Lorion (1977) on individualized education for learning disabled children. The study is noteworthy in three respects that bear directly on mainstreaming. First, formulating a diagnostic-prescriptive program for each schoolchild took between three to four hours. Second, the prescriptive core took into account the child, the teacher, and the classroom, and was very specific and concrete. Third, the prescribers were available to teachers to answer any questions and, equally important, came into the classroom to observe and help.

At the end of the first year of the project, the educational gains of the students were remarkable and general. The significance of Lorion's study is in its demonstration of how integrated diagnosis, prescription, and follow-through must be if the individual needs of students and teachers are to be met. Public Law 94-142 mandates an individual educational prescription for each handicapped child, but to be done well this not only requires time but harmonious relationships among school personnel. "Harmoniousness" is only possible when each person makes a contribution at the same time that the person makes a contribution at the same time that the person feels his or her needs are being recognized and met. Such an ambience cannot be legislated and it is no secret that it is only rarely found in our schools. An individual educational prescription is not a collection of test scores and generalizations so vague and nondiscriminating as to remind one of the glittering generalities of a horoscope. It is, as in the case of Lorion's study, a formulation specific to the student and the teacher. It does not assume the teacher to be a mind reader but someone who needs to know what is expected and why.

The individual prescription is a plan of action not for a student by a teacher but for a student and diverse personnel in need of each other. As we pointed out in an earlier chapter, Binet knew this but those who came after him riveted their attention on his tests and missed what he called "mental orthopedics." For Binet, tests had no meaning if they could not be translated into specific actions in the classroom, and he knew this was no easy task. He never dreamed his test would become a task so routinized, so devoid of specificity for action, so assembly line in character, as to defeat everyone's purposes. Public Law 94–142 may well lock this routinization in concrete, not because that is its purpose but because it does not confront some of the major realities of the culture of schools.

In summary, mainstreaming, both in terms of its current conceptual status and possible consequences, has to be seen from a historical perspective that brings together long-standing educational practices and attitudes, reflecting the larger society and the forces for social change. Until recently, the conflict between forces for tradition and change had little impact on segregation practices within schools, so educational segregation of the mentally retarded went unchallenged.

However, as the conflict gathered strength, and began to be manifested in schools, segregation of other "handicapped" groups became much more frequent. The forces against educational segregation practices came primarily from outside the schools. Public Law 94–142 is the culmination of their efforts. However, these forces may have vastly overestimated the power of legislation to change the structure of schools in ways appropriate to the intent of mainstreaming or the attitudes of school personnel. This must be understood not in moral terms but in light of the weight of long traditions.

Preliminary observations suggest that many school systems are unprepared to deal with mainstreaming. Some are approaching it in ways that only minimally begin to meet the intent of mainstreaming: to avoid the negative effects of stigmatizing labels: and to foster tolerance and mutual understanding between handicapped and nonhandicapped youngsters. These preliminary observations also suggest that school personnel are perceiving mainstreaming largely in terms of nonretarded, handicapped pupils.

It appears that, in the future as in the past, those stigmatized with the label mentally retarded will benefit least from the intended benefits of mainstreaming. But as one school administrator in a large urban setting said: "Why not say that the mentally retarded will be harmed the least from the coming chaos!" Such a comment may well be unduly cynical but it does reflect the mixture of anxiety, impotence, puzzlement, and pressure which school personnel in our urban settings feel. To overlook such feelings is to do an injustice both to school personnel and to those who fought for mainstreaming. Between enactment of a law and practices consistent with it is the whole, poorly understood problem of how to effect institutional change.

A Major Deficiency of Public Law 94–142

We have already said that the law can be construed as criticism of what our schools have been. Handicapped and nonhandicapped students are human beings, not different species, and their basic makeup in no way justifies educational practices that assume that the needs they have for social intercourse, personal growth and expression, and a sense of mastery, are so different that one must apply different theories of human behavior to the two groups. If we respond to the handicapped as if basically different, we rob them and us of the experience of similarity and communality. We can no longer allow schools to segregate children and educational personnel, based on conceptions that are invalid and morally flawed. That is the message that Public Law 94–142 implies.

But where did school personnel learn such conceptions? There are two answers, one general and one specific. The general answer is that they learned those conceptions, and justified them morally, by growing up in a society in which these conceptions and moral precepts were seen as valid, right, and proper. In short, they learned them in the same ways everybody else learned them.

The specific answer is that school personnel are graduates of our colleges and universities. It is there that they learn there are at least two types of human beings and if you choose to work with one of them you render yourself *legally* and conceptually incompetent to work with the others. As we pointed out earlier in this chapter, what we see in our public schools is a mirror image of what exists in colleges and universities. *One of the clearest implications of Public Law 94–142 is that the gulf between the special and regular education has to be bridged, and yet the law requires no change in our college and university training centers.*

We, therefore, have the situation in which the law mandates changes in our schools. School personnel must change in attitude, thinking, and practice, at the same time our training centers educate school personnel in the traditions of the "most restrictive alternative." As an educational administrator in Milofsky's article says:

"It's fine to pass laws," he says, "but it's the teachers who are stuck trying to implement them. Nothing in the law requires in-service training on a systematic basis and a lot of the teachers have no experience in dealing with handicapped kids. We think 766 should require major changes at the undergraduate level. If there are going to be laws like this, they should be taken into account during a teacher's educational training."

At its root, mainstreaming is a moral issue. It raises age-old questions: How do we want to live with each other? On what basis should we give priority to one value over another? How far does the majority want to go in accommodating the needs of the minority? The emergence of mainstreaming as an issue raises but does not directly confront these questions. To the extent that we put discussion of mainstreaming in the content of education and schools, we are likely to find ourselves mired in controversies centering around law, procedures, administration, and funding. These are legitimate controversies because they deal with practical, day-to-day matters that affect the lives of everyone. But the level of difficulty we encounter in dealing with these matters will ultimately be determined by the charity with which the moral issue is formulated. At the very least it should make us more aware of two things: So-called practical matters or problems are always reflections of moral issues, and differences in moral stance have very practical consequences.

18

What Are Schools For?

IN THE PREVIOUS CHAPTER we expressed concern about how mentally retarded children would fare under mainstreaming, not from partisan considerations but rather on the basis of the relationship between the values in our society and reactions to people with a perceived intellectual deficit. Few things are as highly valued as "smartness"; to be called a genius is high praise. As a society, however, we do not value high intelligence as such unless it leads to socially approved achievement. If we know someone of high intelligence who contents himself with a lowly job, we consider it a tragedy because he is not "using" his intellectual gifts. When we say that a person "should make something of himself," we mean that he should use his mind to achieve goals on which *we* put our stamp of approval. If a person decides to make something of himself through a life of crime, we consider that a tragedy. What we look for is productive, socially valued achievements. It is hard to overestimate the importance we place on achievement, and the psychologically debilitating consequences the lack of such achievement so frequently has in the lives of people. The sense of unworthiness people may have because of their lack of achievement reflects how well society inculcates in us its importance.

In the abstract, we are sympathetic to people who are unable to achieve because of conditions beyond their control. They did not ask to be dependent and nonproductive. But our sympathy has limits and one of them is reached when caring for the dependent person interferes with the productive goals of other people. At that point, we tend to segregate the dependent person. The justification is usually phrased in terms of his best interests, downplaying the fact that a decision was made on moral grounds: the productive achievements of the many should not be interfered with because a few people require special attention. That is to say, the interests of those who lead "productive" lives justify segregating those who are "unproductive."

Nowhere has this been taken as seriously as in our schools. There have always been some dissenters who have pointed out that there were other values no less important than ability that should be heeded in deciding who shall live in what ways with whom. The long-standing controversy about homogeneous versus heterogeneous classes in schools is a case in point. Those

393

who favored homogeneous classes put forth three arguments. First, heterogeneous classes penalized students who could learn at a faster rate than less capable students. Second, the less capable students were at an unfair competitive disadvantage and could not get the kind of attention they needed. Third, heterogeneous classes were a major source of frustration to teachers who were put in the moral dilemma of deciding who should get the inevitably limited time and attention. There was really a fourth argument: the needs of our society required capable citizens, especially highly capable ones, and it would be socially self-defeating to dilute their education in any way. The minority who argued for heterogeneous classes presented these arguments: the importance of pupils to learn to live amicably and democratically with different kinds of people; the dangers of producing an elite group isolated from other people; and the injustice that would be done to pupils who would be misplaced in lower "tracks" but who might have flourished if stimulated by more able students.

The controversy about homogeneous versus heterogeneous classes was about "normal" children. A similar controversy, far less frequent and heated in its eruptions because it took place outside of "regular" education, concerned the efficacy of special classes for "high functioning" mentally retarded children. Did children placed in these classrooms perform better than comparable children in regular classrooms? Although the preponderance of studies failed to establish advantages of the special class, they had no effect on school practice. Neither controversy could change the belief in and practice of tracking and segregation. It would have been strange if they had, because educational beliefs and practices reflect dominant features in the larger society. We like to think that schools are "outside" of society, somehow untouched by the harsh realities of the "real world," a kind of protected retreat in which the child can learn and grow so that when leaving school, his or her individuality will not be overwhelmed by the harsh realities of living and working. However, many people who hold such beliefs do not find it inconsistent to act on another belief: It is a major function of the schools to determine the capabilities of students and to so organize the schools that children of different capabilities do not interfere with each other's educational growth. In other words, *the perceived limits of capabilities are the major criterion for determining with whom they live in schools. At its root, this rests on production-achievement as the major criterion for judging people.* This went virtually unchallenged until the 1954 desegregation decision; and the passage of Public Law 94-142 joins the issue even more clearly because it has to be confronted independent of race. Mainstreaming puts back on the discussion table the question of how we want to live together. What are schools for? How shall we judge them? If we want to judge them differently than in the past, if we want them to change, where are the major obstacles and what constitutes a realistic time perspective for overcoming them? In the remainder of this chapter we will examine some of these obstacles.

Myth of Homogeneity

If one examines the products coming off the assembly line, it is virtually impossible to discern differences among them. By definition and intent an assembly line produces products that are homogeneous in appearance, content, and function. Obviously, when we talk of homogeneous classrooms we do not mean homogeneous in the assembly line sense. Take the situation where a sixth grade classroom consists of children all of whom have an IQ of 160. One does not have to see the children, only the tests, to know that it is most unlikely that any two of the children got their scores by passing or failing exactly the same test items. The fact that they have identical test scores says more about the test than it does about the children. Indeed, if one gave them a different intelligence test, it would be most unlikely that they would end up with similar test scores.

Now, if we were to sit for a few days in the classroom, the word homogeneous in anything like its literal sense would not easily come to mind. In fact, in regard to some of these children we might find ourselves wondering where their "IQ of 160" was because they would not match our picture of brightness in action. But we really do not have to sit in the classroom; we only have to interview the teacher. In what ways, we would ask her, are the children homogeneous? We would likely be greeted with staring disbelief. John is lazy, Andy is imaginative, Harold is hostile, Robert does not do his homework, Ruth is manipulative, Richard is really not bright at all, Susan is bright but doesn't believe it, Allan is a predelinquent, Cathy and Herbert are delightful, and so on. From the standpoint of the teacher, the students may be homogeneous according to a psychological test but in the classroom she sees a bewildering array of educational, intellectual, intrapersonal, and interpersonal styles.

It is a cliche to say that each human being is unique. No proponent of homogeneous classrooms would argue that individual differences do not exist. What they do argue is that these classrooms reduce the range of these differences. To our knowledge no one had demonstrated that the *range* is discernibly lessened. That is to say, from the standpoint of the teacher, the range of differences is always great and troublesome. What the teacher has to deal with is not IQs but "whole" people, the "parts" of whom are embedded in that whole in dramatically different ways. So in the case of two students with IQs of 160, the teacher may be in no doubt that one is "dumb" and the other is "smart." The writers of this book have decades of experience working with graduate students: high test-scoring people with superb undergraduate records, and with glowing letters of recommendation from their undergraduate teachers, so that they are "homogeneous" on more than test scores. Given the competition to get into graduate school, those who are finally accepted have as good paper credentials as one could desire. And yet, within weeks after beginning graduate school, the faculty is reminded that despite its screening procedures the entering class is fantastically varied in personal style, creativity, curiosity, work efficiency, and any other characteristic the faculty considers predictive of future achievement.

If homogeneity in the classroom is a myth at variance with the realities of these classrooms, what sustains the myth? The answer is in the belief that intellectual excellence, predictive of future socially valued productivity, should be accorded top priority by society. Society needs many kinds of individuals and among them it needs the intellectually superior individual the most — this is the value on which the argument rests. What is wrong with such a view? There is nothing wrong with such a view as long as one recognizes and articulates that some people will be more valued by society than others, that the farther away an individual is from the top of the intelligence scale the less society needs him or her. There is nothing inherently wrong in stating that our society should treasure one value more than others and, therefore, that it needs some people more than others. Does society need a seriously retarded child as much as it needs a budding "genius"? How can you justify putting them into the same classroom? How can society justify penalizing the more intelligent person by robbing him of the kinds of stimulation and ambience appropriate to his potential? How can society justify any waste of talent? It is, the argument continues, a sad fact of life that individuals differ in how much they have to contribute to society and to deny that fact, to organize our schools as if that were not true, is a form of societal suicide. It is not an argument for the survival of the "fittest"; it is not intended to deny the needs and rights of others, but rather a clear assertion that some people are valued more than others.

For some, the argument presents no problem; it has a self-evident plausibility. For others, the argument creates unease because it smacks of an elitism to which they are opposed. To handle this dilemma they would say: Schools have two major functions: One is to foster the academic-intellectual growth of children, and the other is to inculcate in them those values appropriate to life in a democracy. If the inculcation of these values is done well, we have nothing to fear from homogeneous classrooms. There is no conflict between ability groupings and learning the values of a democratic society. This argument, however, leads to an issue that far transcends ability groupings in importance. What are schools for? How should we evaluate how they meet their purposes?

The Goals of Education

The dilemma of homogeneous classes is resolved by saying that schools have two major purposes. In effect, what is said is that values underlying the argument for homogeneous classrooms should not be given priority over the values of democratic living. The values are coequal. However, there is every reason to conclude that coequality has been taken seriously only on the level of rhetoric. For example, although schools have been criticized over the decades for many things, no criticism comes close in frequency or heat to that about the schools' failure to educate students properly in academic skills and content.

When Russia was the first country to orbit a satellite in 1956, there was an uproar in the United States as a reaction to this wound to national pride. A ready explanation was at hand: Our tradition-bound schools were doing a poor job, and a thoroughgoing revamping of the academic curriculum was in order. The criticism directed at the schools also spoke to the stifling atmosphere in schools, but the importance of that lay primarily in its consequences for academic learning.

A more current example concerns why so many children cannot learn to read. There is no point in multiplying examples. From society's standpoint, schools are expected to give top priority to the educational-intellectual development of children in order for them to "take their places" in society. That value has no coequal. We are reminded of a story, related by Dr. Edward Zigler, one of the early formulators of the Head Start program and the first director of the Office of Child Development. One of the items in his budget was for meals for Head Start children. Early on, he learned that when he went before a congressional committee to justify his program and budget, he could not say that Head Start children should be fed because they may be hungry. He had to say that if these children were fed they would be better learners! It is not very much of an exaggeration to say that any proposal about formal schooling has to be justified in terms of its contribution to the intellectual-academic development of children.

One can look at the issue from the standpoint of educational research. A modest sampling of books, journals, and technical reports would quickly show that the bulk of educational researchers devote themselves to evaluating the effects of all sorts of things on cognitive skills and academic performance, or the relationship of personality and social class with academic progress. Relatively speaking, there has been very little research on the effects of formal schooling on children's absorption of democratic values and modes of adapting to group living. The studies spearheaded by Lewin and his colleagues (Lewin 1948; Lewin, Lippitt, and White 1939: Lippitt 1939: Lippitt 1940) almost forty years ago in experimentally created social climates (democratic, autocratic, laissez-faire) had little impact on the direction and methodology of educational research. There is no evidence at all that it had any impact on school personnel.

During the turmoil of the turbulent sixties, when the controversies in the larger society were also manifest in our schools, the whole issue of the quality of group-classroom living came to the fore, and the group dynamics move-

ment, its rationales and techniques, was eagerly embraced by school personnel. What was not known was that the group dynamics movement, growing
in splinter-fashion and holding out promise of being a panacea for the problems of individual and group living, had several origins and one of the most
important was the early work by Lewin and his colleagues on social climates
in schools. It is both ironic and saddening that the frantic and unsuccessful
attempts in the sixties to change the quality of group living in schools were a
consequence of massive social unrest, not a reflection of values and traditions
indigenous to schools.

Similarly, it should be noted that this work by Lewin and his colleagues
was in the most direct way a reaction to the worldwide force of fascism and
the approaching Second World War. It was not by chance, of course, that
Lewin, a refugee from Nazi Germany, riveted on the responsibility of schools
for inculcation in children of the values of group living in a democratic society. As Gordon Allport (1948) noted:

> There is a striking kinship between the work of Kurt Lewin and the work of John
> Dewey. Both agree that democracy must be learned anew in each generation, and
> that it is a far more difficult form of social structure to obtain and to maintain
> than is autocracy. Both see the intimate dependence of democracy upon social
> science. Without knowledge of, and obedience to the laws of human nature in
> group settings, democracy cannot succeed. And without freedom for research and
> theory as provided only in a democratic environment social science will surely fail.
> Dewey, we might say, is the outstanding philosophical exponent. More clearly
> than anyone else has he shown us in concrete, operational terms what it means to
> be a democratic leader, and to create a democratic group structure (p. xi).

Unfortunately, neither Dewey nor Lewin have had an influence on the
quality of formal schooling. Each is a highly respected and quoted person but
that should not be confused with having an impact on classroom organization and practice. We would not agree with Allport that Dewey was only the
chief philosophical exponent of democracy; he was also an educator who
took his philosophy seriously and put it into practice. Like Lewin later,
Dewey understood that theory without practice could be an arid and
dangerous affair. In 1896, at the University of Chicago, Dewey put his ideas
to the test by starting his own school. How little we have traveled since that
time can be seen by comparing the detailed description of his school
(Mayhew and Edwards 1966) with that of a school today.

Jencks's book *Inequality: A Reassessment of the Effect of Family and
Schooling in America* (1972) is relevant here and not because of his conclusion, based on a literature review, that far more important in its effects than
formal school on inequalities in cognitive-academic development of children
are their families: the influence of family on what a child is like when he or
she begins schools, what the child brings, so to speak, to school. Even if one
believes that Jencks and his colleagues are not fully justified in such a conclusion, there is no room at all for complacency about how well schooling has in-

tended cognitive benefits for children. More directly relevant for our purposes is Jencks's assessment of the effects of schooling on non-cognitive traits.

> Cognitive skills are not the only outcome of schooling. Educators claim schools teach virtues ranging from patriotism and punctuality to curiosity and creativity. Critics claim that schools teach an equally wide range of vices, ranging from competition and conformity to passivity and authoritarianism. None of these traits is well measured by cognitive tests.
>
> We would like to be able to give the factors influencing each of these traits as much attention as we give cognitive skills, but we do not know enough to do this. We do not even have generally agreed upon names for these traits, much less a system for measuring them. Our discussion of them must therefore be largely conjectural [Jencks, p. 131].

> The evidence of our senses tells us that non-cognitive traits also contribute far more than cognitive skills to the quality of human life and the extent of human happiness. We, therefore, believe that the non-cognitive effects of schooling are likely to be more important than the cognitive effects. But we do not know what these non-cognitive effects are likely to be [Jencks 1972, p. 134].

Jencks finds himself able to devote only one chapter to noncognitive traits. A chapter of four pages! There is no better evidence that the preponderance of educational researchers implicitly consider cognitive-academic achievement of children to be the most important criterion by which to judge schools. So, let us listen to one of Jencks's final recommendations:

> These arguments suggest that the "factory" model which pervades both lay and professional thinking about schools probably ought to be abandoned. It is true that schools have "inputs" and "outputs," and that one of their nominal purposes is to take human "raw material" (i.e., children) and convert it into something more "valuable" (i.e., employable adults). Our research suggests, however, that the character of a school's output depends largely on a single input, namely the characteristics of the entering children. Everything else—the school budget, its policies, the characteristics of the teachers—is either secondary or completely irrelevant.
>
> Instead of evaluating schools in terms of long-term effects on their alumni, which appear to be relatively uniform, we think it wiser to evaluate schools in terms of their immediate effects on teachers and students, which appear much more variable. Some schools are dull, depressing, even terrifying places, while others are lively, comfortable, and reassuring. If we think of school life as an end in itself rather than a means to some other end, such differences are enormously important. Eliminating these differences would not do much to make adults more equal, but it would do a great deal to make the quality of children's (and teachers') lives more equal. Since children are in school for a fifth of their lives, this would be a significant accomplishment [p. 256].

And so Jencks brings us back to the concerns of Lewin in the thirties and John Dewey at the turn of the century. How shall we live with each other? This question is given further force by Rosenbaum's (1976) detailed study of the effects of tracking on ability groupings in a high school very homogeneous in terms of the social class background of students. We shall only concern ourselves here with the effects of tracking on students' perception of themselves and others.

> The interviews asked respondents to describe the students in each track . . . because all students come from the same social background, we might expect that most respondents would say that students are all pretty similar. Furthermore we might expect that if they offered distinctions, their distinctions would be related to the official definition of tracking. Thus they might say that college-track students are "academically oriented," "interested in college," or "want a job that requires college." But if administrators have succeeded in imparting the official definition of tracking as an open contest, then we would not expect students to say that students in different tracks differ in personal capacities.
>
> My interviews reveal results quite discrepant from the expectations. More than three-quarters of the Grayton respondents provide stereotypes of the students in each track, and the stereotypes refer to personal capacities of the students. College-track students are characterized as smart or "brains" by more than a third, these descriptions being offered by a substantial number of respondents from each track. College-track students are also characterized as "snobs" and as "conformists" ("momma's kids," "brown nose") by one-sixth of the students.
>
> The most common descriptions for non-college students are the opposites of the precedings. They are described as unmotivated (or "lazy," "goof-offs," or "don't care about school") by more than half of the respondents, as negativistic (trouble-making or tough) by more than one-third, and as not very smart (or stupid) by more than one quarter [Rosenbaum 1976, p. 163].

As for students' perceptions of themselves, Rosenbaum presents data and observations indicating the negative effects of tracking. When one puts together the findings of Coleman (1966), Jencks (1972), and Rosenbaum (1976), one comes to the unpleasant conclusion that our schools leave much to be desired in terms of meeting their two major goals: to nurture the cognitive-academic development of pupils; and to provide them with experiences in classrooms informed by the values of a democratic ethos. Since the values behind mainstreaming, as those behind the efforts at racial integration, are identical to those of a democratic ethos, it is obvious that mainstreaming would confront serious obstacles. This is not because schools are evil places, or school personnel insensitive people, but rather because schools are instruments of the larger society in which these same obstacles have long been a feature. Let us try to get a glimpse of how this may work in regard to mainstreaming.

An Imaginary Mainstreamed Classroom

Let us imagine the situation in which all special classes are abolished, and in any one classroom there would now be, in addition to the "regular" children, one child labeled mildly mentally retarded, one emotionally disturbed, and one learning disabled. To make the situation even more difficult, if not seemingly outrageous, let us add a fourth child who in addition to being *profoundly* retarded also has defects in motor coordination. The class size may be between twenty-two to twenty-seven pupils. How should the teacher be thinking about his or her tasks and goals? What new elements, principles, and problems have to be confronted? If one takes seriously that learning to live with others is no less a goal of schooling than acquiring academic knowledge and skills, how does this determine the teacher's thinking and actions? This question does not arise because of the heterogeneous composition of the class; that factor only complicates the answer. It is a question that should always be center stage.

To illustrate what we are getting at, let us turn to a study we report elsewhere in some detail (Sarason, 1971). The focus of the study was how a teacher and students forged the "constitution" on the basis of which they were going to live together. More specifically, we were interested in the process by which classroom "laws" were discussed and implemented, and how in the process predictable issues in group living were anticipated. When we say that a classroom is organized, we mean that there are explicit rules by which members are expected to govern themselves in interaction with others. It will not surprise very many readers to learn that the constitution was never forged by teachers *and* students; the constitution was, so to speak, written and promulgated by the teachers. Students "received" the constitution; they had no part in its development. Invariably, the constitution was clear about what the teacher expected of students. There was little or no clarity about what students could expect of teachers. For example, the one thing that both teachers and students could count on—the one thing the teacher knows will be the greatest single source of problem and challenge—is that the students will differ in all kinds of ways. How does one deal with these differences? How does one get students to recognize these differences and how can they be helpful in regard to them? How does one create a sense of mutuality among students and between students and teachers?

It is obvious that our observations and questions reflect several assumptions. First, students are desirous of being treated as if their opinions were worthy of attention and respect. Second, students are capable of learning about and adapting to the dilemmas and complexities of group living. Third students can be counted on to be curious about themselves and others, and to be willing to try to be helpful to others. Most students love to be helpful to the teacher, if only because the reward system encourages it, but that also provides the basis for assuming that students can be helpful to each other. Fourth, the process of being helpful is one of the most potent ways of feeling respect for oneself and those one helps. Fifth, the recognition, understanding, and acceptance of diversity are among the most important experiences any person can have.

When applied to the classroom, these assumptions in no way imply a philosophy of permissiveness, and they are not intended to conjure up images of the teacher as a passive leader of student opinion. On the contrary, to act consistently on these assumptions requires the teacher to be a leader sensitive to and respectful of students' needs and opinions, at the same time enlarging their experience with the opportunities of being part of a group with a purpose. Such a leader does not abdicate responsibility or mindlessly do what others want. But neither does such a leader deny others a role in matters affecting their lives or shield them from problems in group living that they will confront throughout their lives. If school is not a preparation for life but life itself, then the teacher together with the students must cope with the obvious: Classroom living contains almost all of the problems and opportunities of group living.

These observations were made in regular elementary school classrooms, and they talk directly to the question of the purposes of formal schooling. The thrust of our answer is no different than the one to the question we asked earlier: How should a teacher think and act when her classroom will contain some handicapped children? *Mainstreaming raises no new questions. It brings to the fore old and poorly answered questions.* But let us listen to one of the teachers to whom Milofsky (1977) spoke about mainstreaming.

> "I don't have any real problems, I think some of these teachers make too much of all this." He is impressed with the way the children take care of each other. "I have one kid who has C.P. (cerebral palsy)," he says, "and he comes down here with the rest of the class. He has some trouble cutting paper, and whenever we have a project that requires cutting I go to help him. But before I can get there some kid is already helping. The other thing is that he drools. At first, you know, it was kind of revolting to me. The first half-hour or so, maybe more, it bothered me to see it. It's not nice to say, but it's the truth, and I think it bothered the kids, too. But now if he drools the kid sitting next to him cleans it up. It's amazing."

It is "amazing" only if one operates on assumptions about children different from those we stated earlier. In the case of the teacher Milofsky quotes, one would predict that if we could observe him and his students we would conclude that he does operate on these assumptions, however implicit and unverbalized they may be.

The introduction of four handicapped children into our imaginary regular classroom has to be viewed not as a problem but as an opportunity that allows one to put to the test a basic value and goal of the classroom. If most teachers do not see it in this way, it says less about teachers and more about how the emphasis on cognitive-academic goals in teacher training accurately reflects what the larger society considers primary. To see our imaginary classroom as a problem and burden is the clearest testimony that schooling is viewed as having one superordinate value and goal. If teachers generally feel this way, how should we expect the parents of the children in our imaginary classroom to feel and to react?

Before addressing this question, however, two aspects of teachers' reality have to be noted. The first of these aspects is that mainstreaming is being mandated at a time when school personnel, particularly those in urban settings, perceive cutbacks in school budgets as making a bad situation worse. The second aspect is that school personnel feel under attack because articulate members of their communities are dissatisfied with the education their children are receiving, and the criticism has to do with academic skills and achievement. In short, it is hard to overestimate the strength of the pressures coming from the community for improving children's academic achievement; and the effects of these pressures tend to make teachers focus even more of their efforts in these directions.

One must expect, therefore, that our imaginary mainstream classroom may even heighten tensions and pressures in that parents of "regular" children may protest against what they would see as a further dilution in academic standards and goals. Nor should we overlook the fact that some parents of handicapped children would fear the consequences for their children being in a classroom where academic goals are of primary importance. Mainstreaming not only raises the "internal" question of how children should live together in our schools but, no less important, the question of how differences among parents can be confronted and reconciled.

In 1946, Taylor wrote a book *Experiments with a Backward Class.* This class in a British elementary school consisted of thirty-two boys, some of whom we would call mentally retarded, some we would call emotionally disturbed, and others we would call learning disabled. As Taylor states: "as miscellaneous an assemblage of boys as one might hope to find, but a group bound together by the one characteristic of its prevailing mental dullness" (p. 14). Taylor justifies the book in these words (the italics are hers):

> The primary aim of this account is to demonstrate how, in an actual case, the activities described came into being, to show how they sprang *from the suggestions and ideas of the boys themselves,* and to record the manner in which, by the combined energies of teacher and class, it was possible to translate them into useful and acceptable vehicles of education, revealing the potentialities inherent in even dull children if given the opportunity to display and to pursue their natural bent, and to follow a curriculum which takes into consideration their particular needs and adapts itself to their ascertained interests [p. xii, italics in original].

Taylor's is a remarkable account, starting with her descriptions of each boy, describing the usual classday, then zeroing on one event that opened Taylor's eyes to the necessity of radically changing her conceptions of learning and the nature of classroom living. She devotes the remainder of the book to the transformation of classroom life and its relation to cognitive achievement.

> Indisputably, there emerged one factor of the greatest value. If nothing more had been achieved than that change of heart to which every act, every word, and every cheery face of these boys bore constant witness, the work of the year would have

been largely justified. This new attitude to school life and schoolwork was the fundamental preliminary to any progress whatsoever. The horse can be brought to the water but cannot be forced to drink, nor will the dull boy be coerced, or even persuaded, into effective learning, unless a means can be found of creating in him an active desire for it in some form or other. For in boys like those of IIIB, there is much else to be combated than mere dullness of intellect. Even more fatal than that is the accumulation of all those deadening influences which tend to stagnate still further the slow-moving, erratically flowing streams of mental activity—the lethargy, the indifference, the positive aversion which arise from compulsory preoccupation with uncongenial tasks; the discouragement and the breakdown of confidence which come from constant failure, erecting insurmountable barriers to progress and blunting the sharp edge of understanding.

The new spirit of lively enthusiasm and healthy enjoyment had rapidly permeated every aspect of the life of the classroom. A breath had breathed upon the valley and the dry bones had assumed a sudden, unexpected vitality. Boys who were not members of the class would now have been glad of the opportunity to come in, and those who belonged to it were reluctant to leave [p. 71].

Taylor's accomplishments, as she well recognized, could only be understood as a consequence of the insight that if she changed the constitution governing classroom living (if its goals of classroom living were granted the same importance as those of academic achievement), she and the student might be saved from boredom, frustration, and hopelessness. But why did Taylor have to be hit over the head to gain this insight? One part of the answer is that she, like many others, was teaching labels not children. Indeed, even at the end of the book she expressed surprise that "dull" children could have done what they did, rather than asking what "dullness" means, if it serves any other purpose than as an administrative basis for segregating students? But the other part of the answer is that Taylor had been trained to give priority to academic achievement. That she managed to escape from the baleful consequences of such training is a tribute to her. Some people do overcome their training. But in overcoming it Taylor opened herself to another source of sadness. At the end of the book she says: "The story of IIIB was now ended, and the boys passed on to the next standard. They returned once more to the old regime—to the collective class-instruction, the dictated syllabus, the formal timetable, and the classroom restrictions of former times" (Taylor 1946, p. 98).

The Definition of Resources

A major objection to our imaginary classroom and the elimination of special classes could be put in this way: Your imaginary classroom reflects the spirit of fairness in that it does not deny a child the opportunity to live with his peers; by not segregating one type of child from another you minimize the chances that educational resources will be distributed unequally. Your utopian example breathes fairness but it creates injustice in that it would be impossible for the teacher to respond to the needs of the children. Granted that how children live together is as important as the academic knowledge and skills they acquire; in practice your classroom will end up giving far more attention to living together than to the acquisition of formal knowledge and skills. You are asking the teacher to do the impossible.

There are several ways of replying to this objection. It is an objection that can be raised in relation to any classroom. It is the rare teacher who will not say that in order to do justice to the individual differences of pupils, additional resources should be available. As long as we view mainstreaming as raising a resource problem, we miss the obvious point. From the standpoint of teachers, there has always been a resource problem in that they have never felt that students received what they needed.

The guilt that many teachers have felt has two sources. First, like the rest of humanity they have been aware that they have limitations in knowledge, understanding, and skills, an obvious enough point to anyone who has had to deal with groups of children. For a long time the community expected teachers to be equally effective with all children; and if teachers knew otherwise, self-serving professionalism or misguided pride prevented them from saying so. The second source of guilt was less personal but no less significant. It had to do with the frequent clash between the needs of children and the structure and organization of schools and, in the case of the latter, teachers resented having no voice.

One cannot understand the meteoric rise of teacher militancy unless one recognizes the strong feeling of teachers that the community and school administrators did not comprehend the plight of the classroom teacher in dealing with diverse children with diverse problems. If teachers were criticized for the authoritarian way they ran their classrooms, it was the same criticism that teachers directed at administrators and boards of education. The turmoil of the post-World War II period, the population explosion, and the increasing role of the federal government in public education combined to dramatically increase new resources available to schools.

There were two characteristics of these developments that are central to our present purposes. The first was that needed resources were defined as they always were: specially trained, highly educated professionals who had to be paid. Put more generally, a resource was that for which one paid and therefore controlled. And if one had no money, one could not obtain the resource. The second characteristic was the belief that the money necessary to purchase these resources, indeed to obtain even more, would always be forthcoming. The myth of unlimited resources was not exposed for what it was until the seventies.

The events of the past few years not only exposed the fact that resources are always limited but also emphasized the need to reconceptualize what we mean by resources. More specifically, as long as schools define resources as those for wnich they can pay, the discrepancy between what schools can and should do will always be large. This is not only a problem for schools but for almost every type of human service that by tradition and public sanction is dominated by professionalism. The disease of professionalism is in the tendency to define human problems in ways that require highly educated professionals for their solution, thus rendering the problem unsolvable. This statement should not be construed as antiprofessionalism. The antidote to the disease is to see its limitation. There are two circumstances when the limitations of professionalism are recognized and willingly circumvented. One is war time the requirements of which make strict adherence to professionalism dangerous. One cannot accept the criteria of professionalism if they do not produce the necessary human resources. Therefore, the question becomes not "who has the qualifications?" but rather "who can quickly learn to be helpful?" The other circumstance is in those rare times when there is a dramatic shortage of professional personnel to perform a function deemed vital by society. This happened during the sixties when the demand for teachers far exceeded the supply. As a result, there was a willing relaxation of the formal requirements for becoming a classroom teacher. There is no evidence whatsoever that in either of these circumstance the redefinition of resources had adverse effects. But as soon as the "crises" are over, there is a reversion to professionalism.

We will pose a question in terms of our imaginary mainstreamed classroom: How can additional resources be made freely available to that classroom in ways that are not only helpful to teacher and pupils but at the same time contribute to the education, growth, and worth of those who will become part of the classroom scene?

Fortunately, it is a question for which a rather large body of experience and research is relevant. Whether it is older pupils helping younger ones, or using college students, or community people, the evidence is rather clear that resources can play a very valuable role in the classroom. We are not discussing "volunteerism" which in practice usually means that the giving is in one direction. What experience and research demonstrate is that there has to be an exchange of resources so that all parties feel that they are learning and changing, not only "doing good" for others but expanding knowledge of self and the world. This cannot be accomplished unless several conditions are met:

1. One has to accept the fact that professional resources will never be made available to the degree required by the traditional definition of resources. The problems of schools have not been and will not be resolved by reliance solely on professionals.

2. One has to believe that there are diverse types of people who can be helpful in the classroom even though they have no professional credentials. This in no way means that those who lack these credentials have, as a group,

a kind of folk wisdom absent in professionals. Wisdom and imaginativeness are distributed in the same way among professional and nonprofessional groups.

3. The crucial task is how to locate, select, and train these new resources so that their needs for new and productive experiences are met at the same time they are helping to meet those needs in others.

4. School personnel have to see themselves as resource locators and coordinators, constantly scanning school and community in order to match needs in a mutually productive manner.

These are not pious statements of virtue but directions substantiated by research and experiences.* They permit us to look at our mainstream classroom not as a creature of well-intentioned but unbridled imagination, but rather as a real possibility, the obstacles to which are in our ways of thinking. The teacher in that classroom need not be "alone" in the struggle to meet the needs of children to learn more about the world of ideas, skills, and social living.

It has been pointed out that although a school is one of the most densely populated settings on earth, "teaching is a lonely profession" (Sarason, Levine, Goldenberg, Cherlin, and Bennett, 1966; Sarason, 1971). It is not the loneliness of solitude but a feeling compounded of isolation, frustration, and the pressure to appear competent to handle any and all problems. It is a sense of loneliness that gnaws, debilitates, feeds on itself, and frequently leads to a sense of stagnation. The reasons for this are many but chief among them is the traditional way of defining roles and resources. This is not to suggest that by redefining roles and resources problems will disappear and the educational millennium will be in sight.

What we suggest is a redefinition that takes several things seriously: Diversity, even extreme diversity, in the classroom is as much an opportunity as it may be a problem. Schooling has two coequal goals: productive learning and mutuality in living. The classroom teacher should not be expected to meet these goals alone; additional resources in the classroom are required. These resources as traditionally defined have never been available in anything resembling adequate numbers. The needs of children and teachers can be met in part by matching these needs with those of other people in or

---

*Without question, Cowen et al.'s (1975) project in the Rochester schools is the most systematic, longitudinal effort to detect and prevent school problems. It is a project that developed over a period of nineteen years. Cowen and his colleagues describe a series of studies on the selection, use, and contributions of nonprofessionals in classrooms and in their contacts with children. Books by Rappaport (1977), Zax and Specter (1974), and Zax and Cowen (1972) contain sections reviewing the research on the use of nonprofessionals with diverse clinical populations. The reviews leave little doubt that carefully selected and trained nonprofessionals can be of great value. In an article, "Keeping Exceptional Children in Regular Classes," Christoplos (1973) asserts that "the first critical condition for successful integration of exceptional children into regular classes is the use of interstudent tutoring so that (a) teachers will not be overwhelmed by the variety of children, curricula, and materials; (b) children will have one to one relationships in learning relationships . . . ; and (c) fostering cooperative attitudes and mutual self respect . . . ."

out of school. Classrooms are not only for children but can serve as a resource for others who also strive for productive learning and social mutuality.

Mainstreaming, as mandated in Public Law 94-142, recognizes the need for additional resources at the same time that it meets those needs in the most traditional way. What is ironic in all this is the implicit assumption that the need for new resources arises because of mainstreaming. The fact is that one of the major factors maximizing the gulf between educational goals and accomplishment has been the way resources have been defined. This was the case long before mainstreaming was even an idea. Mainstreaming does not create a resource problem; it exacerbates a problem stemming from a self-defeating definition of resources. The funding provisions of 94-142 in no way challenge or seek to alter the traditional conceptions of resources, and, therefore, one has to predict that the law will fall far short of its intended goals. Further, despite its funding provisions, the other provisions of the law will have the effect of forcing increases in the budgets of local school districts, thus aggravating further what is already tense school-community relationships.

That resources are always limited is axiomatic in economics. If other fields did not recognize this, they have in recent years been rudely awakened to the significance of that axiom in all major spheres of public policy. During much of the post-World War II era, most people accepted the myth of unlimited resources; as a society we could do whatever we decided to do and whatever limitations existed were a function of a lack of national resolve. We are now faced with the issues and dilemmas of choice. This has been dubbed by some people as the "dialysis problem": how do you justify spending several millions of dollars to keep alive a very small number of people with kidney disease, and proportionately spend far less money for much larger groups with serious problems in living?

As Fuchs (1975), a medical economist points out in his book *Who Shall Survive?*, we can no longer answer this question as if we could do everything for everybody. This is not the conclusion of a political conservative or a reactionary insensitive to the real needs of real people but rather a description of the realities of the formulation and implementation of public policy in any country, however, different its political structure may be from our own.

There are two major implications of limited resources that will have to be faced. The first is that any agency, like a school or school system, can no longer define resources only in terms of purchase by money. On the contrary, agencies like schools will have to become resource locaters and developers but on a basis that meets mutual needs so that there is resource exchange without money exchange. A somewhat similar position in relation to communities has been described and implemented by Schindler-Rainman and Lippett in their book *The Volunteer Community. Creative Use of Human Resources* (1975). Although they do not directly confront the fact of limited resources, they make a very persuasive case for viewing the volunteer not only for what he or she can contribute but for what the experience can mean for the personal growth of the volunteer. Where most volunteer programs are inadequate and inefficient is in their "one way street" stance. They put far more emphasis on what they can get than what they can give to the volunteer. Their chapter "The Motivational Dynamics of Voluntarism" should be required reading for professionals and agency personnel.

In a recent book, Sarason, Carroll, Maton, Cohen, and Lorentz (1977) described the development over three years of a "barter economy" network of individuals that vastly increased resources available to any network member. If that description is not persuasive, we urge the reader to consult the monograph size testimony of Daphne Krause (1975) before a congressional committee. Taking the fact of limited resources seriously, she describes how she was able to get individuals and agencies to exchange resources without exchanging money, with everyone being benefited.

The concept of the barter economy is obviously not new and, equally obviously, it conflicts with professionalism. More correctly, the traditions of professionalism rather effectively obscure how they inevitably create a gulf between those who need a service and the numbers available to render that service.

The stance of the schools is typical of all agencies: Additional resources are needed, but it requires money to obtain them or to be the basis for an exchange of resources. As a consequence, agencies spend a good deal of time trying to get more money, in effect competing with each other for these additional financial resources. And that stance makes it inordinately difficult, and in practice almost impossible, to do three related things: to confront (if only as a possibility) that resources are and will be limited; to examine critically the accepted relationship between problems and solutions; and *to figure out possible ways in which agencies can learn to exchange resources in mutually beneficial ways and without finances being a prerequisite for discussion or the basis for exchange.* We have italicized the last point to emphasize the contrast between a typically "market" and "barter" way of viewing and exchanging resources. In the former, money is absolutely essential; in the latter, it is primarily a matter of determining whether there exists different needs that can be satisfied in mutually satisfying ways: "What do I have that somebody else can use in exchange for something of his that I need?" To be able to put the question in this way already suggests that vehicles need to be developed that not only maximize knowledge about available resources but also facilitate the processes of exchange. (As we shall see, networks can be such a vehicle.) The question is based on a way of thinking that is drastically different than that ordinarily governing relationships among agencies. In everyday practice, agencies do not seek each other out for the purposes of resource exchange; each agency sees itself as independent of all others, dependent only on its own subsidized resources to meet its goals, and energetically seeking new monies to purchase more resources. Each agency is an island, seeking ways to expand its land areas, fearing erosion from uncontrollable and unpredictable sources; and nurturing the fantasy that there must or there should exist the quantity and quality of resources that could ensure a safe and goal-fulfilling life.

Our experience led us to see how the usual way of thinking maintains or increases the gulf between what needs to be done and the resources available to do it. In suggesting that there may be other ways of thinking about the issue, we in no way are suggesting that the gulf can be eliminated, but rather that it can be reduced [Sarason et al. 1977, p. 21, italics in original].

Let us take a concrete example:

How many more physicians would be needed to give adequate medical care to all in our society? We can safely assume that there would be controversy about defining adequate care, but it is also safe to assume there would be general (but no unanimous) agreement that many more physicians would be required. Whether the increase would be of the order of 25, or 50, or 100 percent, the absolute number of new physicians would run into the thousands. These numbers could not be trained without creating a few score of new medical schools, the cost of which would run into billions of dollars. If our society were to go that route, several problems would have to be confronted. Where would one get the personnel to man these new facilities? It could be argued that existing medical schools vary tremendously in quality, in part because the number of truly first-rate physicians is small and in part because only a few medical schools have the traditions, atmosphere, and resources to attract and keep first-rate faculty. As a consequence, it would be argued, there is a concentration of such faculty in relatively few centers, and the bulk of medical schools must settle for less able people and, therefore, their students are less well prepared to give adequate care. So, if you create twenty new medical schools, the competition for scarce quality personnel could intensify with at least two possible results: The quality of the best medical schools would be diluted (they are brought closer to the mean), or the new medical schools will be unable to compete "in the market" and they will settle for second best. This line of argument could be much more developed and it is one guaranteed to arouse violent differences of opinion. But everyone would agree that quality of medical personnel was not uniform and, indeed, there is no evidence to suggest that the distribution of quality is other than a normal one; that is, a small percentage would be excellent, an equal percentage would be poor, and the bulk of personnel would be bunched somewhat above *and* below the group mean. Quality is a limited resource, and to plan as if it were in large supply is to deny reality.

One could counter this argument by saying that training physicians to give adequate care does not require a largely first-rate faculty, who for the most part are more interested in research than they are in teaching for practice. What is required are good teachers, and although they are not an unlimited resource, there are more of them than there are first-rate medical faculty and researchers. Furthermore, this argument could continue, even if the first argument had some validity, there are so many people receiving no or scandalously poor medical care that they would benefit immensely from the increase in the number of physicians who, although not receiving the highest quality of medical training, would nevertheless be far better than no service at all. The major task is to increase the number of good teachers. This argument, like the opposing one, assumes that the quality necessary for a desirable outcome is limited. Unfortunately, in the heat of controversy in which the proponents of one position try to demolish the proponents of the other position, both manage to overlook their area of agreement: The quality of human resource considered by each to be desirable and necessary is in short supply. And by overlooking this agreement, they no longer are in a position to confront the implications of a major obstacle to a desirable outcome.

But let us assume there is no controversy and everyone agrees that we need more physicians, more medical schools, and the only obstacle to overcome is finding the addition billions per year such an expansion would cost. Can we afford to do it? There are those who would say that the more appropriate question is: How can we justify not doing it? That is to say, the problem is at root a moral one and, when seen in that way, what is required is an act of national will and the problem will be solved. Some who take this stance would maintain that, given our riches as a country, we could mount such a program without taking away resources from other programs. (This is like the sixties, when some people said we could afford to go to the moon and conduct the war on poverty at the same time we were conducting a foreign war.) By formulating the solution in moral terms, the assumption about adequacy of resources goes unexamined. Furthermore, this moral stance about a particular program glosses over the fact that other people take a similar stance about other programs. Moral stances are not in short supply and when one arrays the programs to which such stances give rise, the assumption of unlimited resources is seen for what it is: an uncritically accepted assumption.

When proponents of a new program confront the reality of limited resources, they accept (or are forced to accept) a scaling down of their plans. So, instead of twenty new medical schools, they may be willing to settle for five, hoping that in the future they will gain new resources. After all, five does represent an incremental gain, even though the discrepancy between what needs to be done and will be done is still large. Morality has, so to speak, won a battle in a long war. But this sense of satisfaction is based on the assumption that available resources will either remain constant or increase. What if available resources decline or the competition for existing resources becomes more fierce because new needs arise from within or without our society? Anyone familiar with our history knows that our economy has long had the characteristics of a yo-yo. And anyone familiar with recent international history knows the degree to which the definition of the scope of our society's resources has become dependent on what happens elsewhere in the world. Therefore, to assume that resources available to us will be constant or increase is, to say the least, dangerous. Yet that assumption has been given a wide degree of acceptance. The exposure in practice of its invalidity has caused widespread disappointment and even cynicism, but, unfortunately, there continues to be a resistance to the idea that among the reasons for program failure or inadequacy, the assumption of unlimited or increasing resources occupies an important place.

The size of available resources to deal with any social problem is a function of many factors, but certainly one of the most important is how the problem is defined. For example, in presenting the problem of providing adequate medical care, the problem was defined in a way so that its solution *required* training many more physicians. *Such a definition contains the "solution," but, as we tried to demonstrate, it is a solution that renders the problem unsolvable.* Put in another way, resources are always limited, but the discrepancy between what needs to be done and resources available to do it is frequently widened by our definition of what needs to be done [Sarason, et al. 1977, p. 16].

For the spirit of mainstreaming to be appropriately reflected in schools, the dilemmas of limited resources cannot be ignored. And this leads us to the second major implication of limited resources and that is the importance of a community approach by which we mean scanning, understanding, and relating to the community so that the possibilities of resource exchange are considerably enlarged. To rely only on those resources within one's setting is to doom one-self to never ending disappointment. As a society, we are beginning to face, albeit reluctantly, the fact of limited resources. It should in no way be surprising that in analyzing recent public policies affecting mentally retarded people the centrality of that fact should emerge. And, we must conclude, if that fact is not faced squarely, we are likely to find that the more things change the more they remain the same.

19

Mental Retardation
and Society: Four Themes

SOMEONE RECENTLY SAID that it is no longer possible to write a text on mental retardation that does justice to all of the major substantive issues of the field. If we had any doubts about that, they were dispelled in the course of writing this book. As we look back over the ground we have covered, being sensitive to what we did not cover, we are more impressed than ever before with how intimidating a venture it is to try to see the "whole" field. However, we have discerned several major themes that deserve summary, if only in the hope that they will stimulate others to go beyond us.

The first of these themes is as fascinating as it is obvious: mental retardation, be it in its etiological, definitional, diagnostic, or treatment-educational aspects, is not comprehensible apart from American society, culture, and history. When one takes into account how intertwined our history has been with European history, with Africa in connection with slavery, and with the repercussions of Africa's emergence from colonial domination, the social history of mental retardation has staggering dimensions. Immigration, slavery, religious conflict, and urbanization have been dominant factors influencing how we conceive of the nature of retardation, in how we think we understand and deal with it, and how our views have changed as these forces have changed.

There are many perspectives from which one can view our society and history. There is no one valid way, especially if we believe that our knowledge of ourselves, as individuals or a society, inevitably changes with time and we find ourselves perceiving and coping with new worlds. Mental retardation is one of those perspectives, and an illuminating one for at least two reasons. First, it enables us to see our past differently, even though in the distant past mental retardation was not the "issue" it is today; yet we see how the stage was being set for it to become a matter of public policy and discussion. Be it in our individual or collective lives, we know that our actions have consequences, and one of the unintended consequences of universal compulsory education was the need to develop special education. It is fair to say that only in recent years have we began to confront how the composition of these classes was correlated with immigration, urbanization, and poverty. Like other features of our schools, these classes historically reflected enduring features of our society.

Why has it taken so long for these correlations to gain general recognition? In our opinion, a large part of the answer has been the tendency to conceptualize mental retardation in an ahistorical manner; the failure to conceptualize it as possessing a social historical influence. This theme, however, should not be interpreted as advocating a respect for the past but rather as a plea to become more sensitive to the fact that within the boundaries of the present are the influences of the past.

We like to think that our values, ideas, and practices are "modern" and sharply differentiated from those that came before. We are also prone to believe that today's problems are basically different than those of previous generations. There is, of course, a kernel of truth to this, but in the case of mental retardation the history we have traced suggests that we, as individuals and a society, have much in common with those of earlier times.

But, it could be argued, look at all the legislative and judicial actions taken in the past decade to treat mentally retarded individuals as *citizens* entitled to all constitutional rights? Haven't we *finally* recognized how we used to segregate them in dehumanizing institutions, to separate them from the educational "mainstream," and to stigmatize them with pejorative labels? From a social-historical perspective, the answer has to be that we must be wary of confusing change with progress; at the same time, there are grounds for satisfaction in the recent trends. But that satisfaction must be tempered by the knowledge that institutions, prejudice, and tradition do not quickly change. They adjust to impacts, changing their overt stance but prepared to reassert themselves. This will be as true for the changing scene in mental retardation as it was for racial discrimination, even with the 1954 Supreme Court decision.

A second major theme has to do with the changing role of public policy. Up until the end of the last century one could say there was no public policy in regard to mental retardation, except on a local and state level for the purpose of institutional segregation. If a federal role were nonexistent, that should not be taken to mean that there were not other federal policies that mightily influenced people's reaction to "intellectual inferiority." The most fateful of these policies, and one that became more focused and discriminatory as the decades went on, had the aim of keeping out "poor stock." It was a policy that had general support and reflected the tendency to devalue people who appeared intellectually inferior. It was a policy that was influenced by and in turn influenced the different versions of the nature-nurture controversy. There can be no doubt that what prevented the emergence of a clear federal public policy in regard to mental retardation was the shared distrust of federal intervention and power. That view of a federal role changed as a result of the Great Depression. It was not until after World War II that a federal policy truly began to develop, but even then it was directed to education generally, not mental retardation.

We would like to believe that public policy reflects a rational process in which facts, experience, and research are primary determinants. In the case of mental retardation there were two factors that influenced the formation of a public policy. The first was the amazingly swift and effective fashion with which parents of retarded individuals became a potent lobbying force in the national scene. The second was that at the height of the parents' movement, President Kennedy had taken office. Given his family's interest in mental retardation, it was only a matter of time before a policy would emerge.

The stage had already been set by federal policy to change and support public education. Just as universal compulsory education set the stage for the emergence of special education, so the post-World War II development of a federal policy for education set the stage for one specifically directed to mental retardation. One could not have predicted when this would happen, or what the scope of the policy would be.

A decade ago, few people would have thought that the mainstreaming legislation, Public Law 94-142, would be enacted. As we look back over the past ten years, we can see that what was being underestimated was the strength of the diverse forces seeking equality before the law—racial and ethnic minorities, women, homosexuals, older people, mental patients, the physically handicapped. Rarely is a public policy in regard to one problem or group independent of policies being forged for other problems or groups. The term public policy is a kind of shorthand for societal forces and movements pervading the society at a particular time, and they get reflected in public policies in different ways. That is why the 1954 desegregation decision and the mainstreaming legislation of 1975 have to be seen as related reflections in a public policy of changing moods and opinions.

It was not by chance that the mainstreaming legislation was not specifically directed to the needs of mentally retarded individuals but to those of *all* handicapped students, a recognition of the fact that we are living at a time when there is a heightened sensitivity to the implications and consequences of past denials of constitutional rights of diverse "minorities." From the standpoint of mentally retarded people, it is a distinctive and momentous change to be given recognition in public policy.

But there is one aspect to the emergence of public policies that requires special emphasis, for what it may portend for the future. We refer here to the seemingly inexorable momentum for public policies to be initiated, implemented, and require funding support from the federal government. Up until the end of World War II, public policy in regard to education generally, and mental retardation in particular, was "local." Indeed, the idea that the federal government should play other than the most minor of roles in this area was considered anathema. "That government is best that governs least" was a widely shared belief.

Times have changed, and there are people who feel that the federal government should get even more involved in shaping a differentiated, standardized national education system. Such a suggestion may sound today no less strange than the idea of universal compulsory education did to people in the early nineteenth century. Without trying to forecast the future, one has to note that the increased federal role has not been without its problems and critics. The fact is that even supporters of an increased federal role are aware of the dangers of dependence upon the control by centralized authority. The dangers do not inhere in the motivations and personality of individuals but in a fantastically intricate and often ambiguous system of federal-state-local interrelationships in which the shape of actions take precedence over the substance and spirit of actions. We must not forget that where we are today is in large measure a response to the perception that local authority was unwilling or unable to cope with pressing educational problems, some of them of a constitutional nature that the federal government could not ignore. Professor Murray Levine's maxim "problem creation through problem solution" characterizes the fate of all public policies.

What we have said about policy brings us to a third theme: the changing views and policies about institutions for the mentally retarded. The idea that most mentally retarded individuals can and *should* live in their natural community has only recently taken root in our society, and only in the past few years become part of public policy. But, as in the case of mainstreaming, it is one thing to proclaim a policy, and quite another thing to implement it appropriately.

The fact is that the continued existence of the residential institution receives support not only from ingrained values and perceptions of what mental retardation "is" but from two other sources. The first of these is the economic stake that states have invested in these institutions, i.e., buildings, staff, and state administrative bureaus and departments. The second is diverse, and often subtle, resistances from local communities. Here again it would be a mistake to interpret this in individual terms as if those in opposition are morally perverse.

Rather it has to be seen as a principled and opening battle in a long war, the social-historical background of which goes back a long way. What is involved in deinstitutionalization is a social change that will have reverberations in our major social institutions, and change always encounters obstacles. The strength of the obstacles is proportionate to the number of people and institutions that will be affected. It is precisely because deinstitutionalization requires community change that it will continue to be opposed by many people.

Religious bigotry and racial and ethnic discrimination are less potent today than during the nineteenth century when our society was riddled with hot and cold wars: Catholics versus Protestants, German Catholics versus Irish Catholics, ethnic group versus ethnic group, South versus North, and "natives" versus immigrants. But who will say that these wars are over? How can one argue that the wars were avoidable? When people are arrayed in opposition to each other because they see the world differently, because their definitions of themselves stem from differing perceptions of what is right and wrong, truth and heresy, a social change is begun in the form of social conflict.

In the case of institutionalization the conflict has begun among state departments, community groups, and the courts. We must not forget that the move to deinstitutionalization, as was the case with so many of the conflicts around education, came from court decisions and not from a ground swell of outraged public opinion.

In the middle of the last century, Dorothea Dix described for the Massachusetts legislature the inhumane conditions in that state's "humane" institutions. A century later, to the same legislature, Dr. Burton Blatt gave a similar description with pictures. And a decade later, in his presidential address to the American Association on Mental Deficiency, he demonstrated again with the pictures that relatively little had changed except in a superficially esthetic way.

If we have emphasized the institutional issue, it is because it has a long seamy history explainable by the fact that mental retardation has never been a "thing" but a conceptual invention bearing the imprint of society's structure, traditions, values, and prejudices. If today that imprint does not seem to give priority to institutionalization, to the tendency to segregate, we will only be deluding ourselves if we believe that an opposing tendency supported by near and long-term social history has been extinguished. We say this not to dampen the spirit of those who have led the deinstitutionalization movement, but to remind them that modes of thinking reinforced over the centuries are not easily changed. The change has begun and it will take future Dorothea Dixes and Burton Blatts to consolidate past accomplishments and accelerate the pace of change. The time to be discouraged is when there is no Dorothea Dix, Burton Blatt, or Thomas Szasz on the scene.

The final theme is one with which this book began: mental retardation is never a thing or a characteristic of an individual but rather a social invention stemming from time-bound societal values and ideology that make diagnosis and management seem both necessary and socially desirable. The shifting definitions and management of mental retardation are not understandable in terms of the "essence" of the "condition" but rather in terms of changing social values and conditions.

We are beginning to comprehend that in the case of the mentally retarded individual, regardless of etiological considerations, development is *always* transactional; the individual affects and is affected by the family setting into which he or she is born. We are not dealing with simple cause and effect relationships but dynamic transactions in a complicated familial web. This may be obvious but it is another instance where the obvious has not penetrated into clinical practice.

When one looks at diagnostic and treatment-management programs, one finds a concentration on the *individual* rather than on those who comprise the family network. The result is that one drastically reduces the understanding one can gain and the help one can provide to all who are part of the network. How much we are unwitting prisoners of conceptual tunnel vision is most clearly illustrated by the custom of only seeing the mentally retarded individual in our offices and clinics, robbing us of valuable information and opportunities to alter what needs to be altered in the natural setting.

Criticism of customary practice has received substantial empirical support from research on home-based observations and the use of parents as "therapists." As in the case of institutionalization, the obstacles to change are rooted in habits of thinking, professional training, and the economic-political structure of human services. To translate the transactional approach appropriately into practice is no less than to encounter the relationships among culture, social history, organizational structure, and the constraints of existing ideologies. So we see again that in pursuing the societal context in which mental retardation becomes defined and managed, we are provided a perspective from which to look at the nature of our society. When we study mental retardation we are studying our society, and the failure to understand that goes a long way to explaining the seamy history of mental retardation in our society.

Bibliography

ABBOTT, E. *Historical Aspects of the Immigration Problem: Select Documents.* Chicago: University of Chicago Press, 1926.

ABBOTT, E. *Immigration: Selected Documents and Case Records.* Chicago: University of Chicago Press, 1924.

ACKERMAN, N. *The Psychodynamics of Family Life.* New York: Basic Books, 1959.

ADAMS, F. K. "Comparisons of Attitudes of Adolescents towards Normal and Retarded Brothers." *Dissertation Abstracts,* 1966, *27* (3-A), 662-63.

ALBEE, G. W. "Let's Change Our Research Priorities in Retardation." *The Journal of Special Education,* 1970, *4* (2), 139-147.

ALLPORT, G. Foreword to *Resolving Social Conflicts,* by K. Lewin. New York: Harper & Row, 1948.

ANDELMAN, F. "Mainstreaming in Massachusetts under Law 766." *Today's Education,* March-April, 1976, 20-22.

ANDERSON, M. L. *Education of Defectives in the Public Schools.* Yonkers-on-Hudson, N.Y.: World Book Company, 1917.

ANDERSON, V. V. "Education of Mental Defectives in State and Private Institutions and in Special Classes in Public Schools in the United States." *Mental Hygiene,* 1921, *5,* 85-122.

ARLITT, A. H. "On the Need for Caution in Establishing Race Norms." *Journal of Applied Psychology,* 1921, *5,* 179-183.

ARONS, S. "The Separation of School and State: Pierce Reconsidered." *Harvard Educational Review,* 1976, *46* (1), 76-104.

ATZMON, E. "The Educational Programs for Immigrants in the United States." *History of Education Journal,* 1958, *9* (3), 75-80.

AUSUBEL, D. P. *Ego Development and the Personality Disorders.* New York: Grune & Stratton, 1952.

AYRES, L. P. *Laggards in Our Schools.* Philadelphia: Press of W. F. Fell Co., 1909.

BABSON, S. G. and R. C. BENSON. *Management of High-Risk Pregnancy and Intensive Care of the Neonate.* St. Louis: Mosby, 1971.

BAILEY, S. K. *Congress Makes a Law.* New York: Columbia University Press, 1950.

BAILYN, B. *Education in the Forming of American Society: Needs and Opportunities for Study.* Chapel Hill: University of North Carolina Press, 1960.

BAKER, B. L. "Parent Involvement in Programming for Developmentally Disabled

Children." In L. L. Lloyd (ed.), *Communication Assessment and Intervention Strategies.* Baltimore: University Park Press, 1977.

Baker, B. L. "Support Systems for the Parent as Therapist." Paper presented at the convention of the Fourth International Congress of the International Association for the Scientific Study of Mental Deficiency, Washington, D.C., August, 1976a.

Baker, B. L., A. J. Brightman, L. J. Heifetz, and D. Murphy. *READ Project Series: Ten Instructional Manuals for Parents.* Cambridge, Mass.: Behavioral Education Projects, 1972, 1973a.

Baker, B. L., A. J. Brightman, L. J. Heifetz, and D. Murphy. *Steps to Independence Series: Behavior Problems; Early Self-Help; Intermediate Self-Help; Advanced Self-Help.* Champaign, Ill.: Research Press, 1976c.

Baker, B. L., and L. J. Heifetz. "READ Project Series: Teaching Manuals for Parents of Retarded Children." In T. D. Tjossem (ed.), *Intervention Strategies for High Risk Infants and Young Children.* Baltimore: University Park Press, 1976b.

Baker, B. L., L. J. Heifetz, and A. J. Brightman. *Parents as Teachers: Manuals for Behavior Modification of the Retarded Child.* Studies in Family Training. Cambridge, Mass.: Behavioral Education Projects, 1973b.

Ball, W. B. "Building a Landmark Case: Wisconsin v. Yoder." In A. N. Keim (ed.) *Compulsory Education and the Amish: The Right Not To Be Modern.* Boston: Beacon Press, 1975.

Balow, B. "Teachers for the Handicapped." *Compact,* 1971, *5* (4), 43–46.

Barnard, H. "Biography of Ezekiel Cheever with Notes on Early Free or Grammar Schools of New England." *American Journal of Education,* 1855–56, *1,* 297–314.

Barr, M. W. *Mental Defectives: Their History and Treatment and Training.* Philadelphia: Blakiston, 1904.

Barr, M.W. "What Can Teachers of Normal Children Learn from the Teachers of Defectives?" *Journal of Psycho-Asthenics,* 1903–04, *8,* pp. 55–59.

Barry, C. J. *The Catholic Church and German Americans.* Milwaukee: Bruce Publishing Co., 1953.

Becker, E. *The Denial of Death.* New York: Free Press, 1973.

Bereiter, C. "Schools without Education." *Harvard Educational Review,* 1972, *43* (3), 390–413.

Berkowitz, B. P., and A. M. Graziano. "Training Parents as Behavior Therapists: A Review." *Behavior Research and Therapy,* 1972, *10,* 297–317.

Biklen, D. *Let Our Children Go: An Organizing Manual for Advocates and Parents.* Syracuse, N.Y.: Human Policy Press, 1974.

Billington, R. A. "Maria Monk and Her Influence." *Catholic Historical Review,* 1936–37, *22,* 283–296.

Billington, R. A. *The Protestant Crusade 1800–1860.* New York: Macmillan, 1938.

Birch, H. G., and J. D. Gussow. *Disadvantaged Children: Health, Nutrition and School Failure.* New York: Harcourt, Brace & World, 1970.

Blatt, B. *Exodus from Pandemonium.* Boston: Allyn & Bacon, 1970.

Blatt, B., A. Ozolins, and J. McNally. *The Family Papers: Documentation from the Hidden World of Mental Retardation.* Glen Ridge, N.J.: Exceptional Press, 1978.

BLATT, B. *The Revolt of the Idiots.* Glen Ridge, N.J.: Exceptional Press, 1976.

BLATT, B. *Souls in Extremis.* Boston: Allyn & Bacon, 1975.

BLATT, B., and F. KAPLAN. *Christmas in Purgatory.* Boston: Allyn & Bacon, 1966.

BLOCK, J. H. "Debatable Conclusions about Sex Differences." Review of *The Psychology of Sex Differences* by E. E. MACCOBY and C. N. JACKLIN. *Contemporary Psychology,* 1976, *21* (8), 517–522.

BLOM, G. E. "Principles of Normalization: A Case Study." Unpublished paper available from author, Department of Child Psychiatry, Michigan State University, East Lansing, Michigan.

BOEHME, G. M. "Special Classes in the Cleveland Schools." *Journal of Psycho-Asthenics,* 1909–10, *14,* 83–88.

BOESE, T. *Public Education in the City of New York.* New York: Harper & Bros., 1869.

BOGDAN, R., and D. BIKLEN. "Handicappism." *Social Policy,* March–April, 1977, 14–19.

BOGDAN, R. and S. TAYLOR. "The Judged, Not the Judges: An Insider's View of Mental Retardation." *American Psychologist,* 1976, *31,* 47–52.

BORROWMAN, M. L. *Teacher Education in America.* New York: Teachers College Press, 1965.

BOUQUILLON, T. "The Catholic Controversy about Education." *Educational Review,* 1892a, *3,* 365–373.

BOUQUILLON, T. *Education: To Whom Does It Belong?* (with a Rejoinder to Critics.) 2d ed. Baltimore: John Murphy, 1892b.

BOURNE, W. O. *History of the Public School Society.* New York: W. Wood & Co., 1870.

BOYKIN, J. C. "Class Intervals in City Public Schools." *Report of the Commissioner of Education for the Year 1890–91, Vol. 2.* Washington: Government Printing Office, 1894.

BRAGINSKY, D., and B. BRAGINSKY. *Hansels and Gretels.* New York: Holt, Rinehart & Winston, 1971.

BRAINE, M. D. S., C. B. HEIMER, H. WORTIS, and A. M. FREEDMAN. "Factors Associated with Impairment of the Early Development of Prematures." *Monograph Social Research and Child Development,* 1966, *31,* (4), 1–92.

BRAZELTON, T. B. "Anticipatory Guidance." *Pediatric Clinics of North America,* 1975, 22, 533.

BRONFENBRENNER, U. "Early Deprivation in Mammals: A Cross-Species Analysis." In *Early Experience and Behavior.* Springfield, Ill.: Charles C. Thomas, 1968.

BRONFENBRENNER U. "The Origins of Alienation." *Scientific American,* 1974, 231, 53–61.

BROWN, E. E. *The Making of Our Middle Schools.* New York: Longmans, Green, 1918.

BRUBACHER, J. S. (ed.). *Henry Barnard on Education.* New York: Russell & Russell, 1965.

BRUNER, J. S. "Nature and Uses of Immaturity." *American Psychologist,* 1972, *27,* 687–708.

BURGESS, C. "The Goddess, the School Book, and Compulsion." *Harvard Educational Review*, 1976, *46* (2), 199–216.

BURNS, J. A. *The Catholic School System in the United States: Its Principles, Origin and Establishment*. New York: Benziger Brothers, 1908.

BURNS, J. A. *The Growth and Development of the Catholic School System in the United States*. New York: Arno Press, New York Times, 1969 (reprint of 1912 edition).

BURT, C. "The Inheritance of Mental Ability." *American Psychologist*, 1958, *13*, 1–15.

BURT, C., and M. HOWARD. "The Multifactorial Theory of Inheritance and Its Application to Intelligence." *British Journal of Statistical Psychology*, 1956, *9*, 95–131.

BUSEY, S. C. *Immigration: Its Evils and Consequences*. New York: De Witt & Davenport, 1856. Reprint, New York: Arno Press, New York Times, 1969.

CALLAHAN, R. E. *Education and the Cult of Efficiency*. Chicago: University of Chicago Press, 1962.

CALLAHAN, R. E. "Leonard Ayres and the Educational Balance Sheet." *History of Education Quarterly*, 1961, *1*, *(1)*, 5–13.

CANTRELL, R. P., and M. L. CANTRELL. "Preventive Mainstreaming: Impact of a Supportive Services Program on Pupils." *Exceptional Children*, 1975–1976, *42*, 381–386.

CARPENTER, N. *Immigrants and Their Children 1920*. Washington, D.C.: Government Printing Office, 1927.

CARVER, J. J., and N. E. CARVER. *The Family of the Retarded Child*. Syracuse, N.Y.: Syracuse University Press, 1972.

CASLER, L. "Perceptual Deprivation in Institutional Settings." In G. NEWTON and S. LEVINE (eds.), *Early Experience and Behavior*. Springfield: Charles C. Thomas, 1968.

CHACE, L. G. "Public School Classes for Mentally Deficient Children." *Proceedings of the National Conference of Charities and Correction* at the thirty-first annual session held in the city of Portland, Maine, June 15–22, 1904. pp. 390–401.

CHASE, A. "The Legacy of Malthus." *The Social Costs of the New Scientific Racism*. New York: A. A. Knopf, 1977.

CHENEY, F. E. "Five Years' Experience in Teaching Mentally Defective Children in a Public School." *Journal of Psycho-Asthenics*, 1903–1904, *8* 39–41.

Children's Defense Fund. *Your Rights under the Education for All Handicapped Children Act*. Washington, D.C.: Children's Defense Fund, 1976.

CHISOLM, J. J. "Poisoning Due to Heavy Metals." *Pediatric Clinics of North America*, 1970, *17* (3), 591–615.

CHRISTOPLOS, F. "Keeping Exceptional Children in Regular Classes." *Exceptional Children*, 1973, *39*, 569–572.

CIANCI, V. "Home Supervision of Mental Deficients in New Jersey." *American Journal of Mental Deficiency*, 1947, *51*, 519–524.

CLARK, K. B. "Alternative Public School Systems." *Harvard Educational Review*, 1968, *38* (1), 100–113.

CLARKE, A. D. B. and A. M. CLARKE. "How Constant Is the I.Q.?" *Lancet,* 1953, *2,* 877–880.

COHEN, H. J. "Critical Issues in the Development of Services for the Developmentally Disabled Child: Implications for Public Policy." Paper delivered at working conference on long-term care requirements concerning the needs of people disabled early in life. Philadelphia: Temple University Sugarloaf Conference Center, February 13–16, 1977.

COLBURN, W. *Intellectual Arithmetic, upon the Inductive Method of Instruction.* Boston: Hilliard, Gray & Co., 1842.

COLE, E. G. *Handbook of American History.* New York: Harcourt, Brace & World, 1968.

COLEMAN, J. *Equality of Educational Opportunity.* Washington, D.C.: U.S. Government Printing Office, 1966.

COMENIUS, J. A. *The Great Didactic of John Amos Comenius—Now for the First Time Englished with Introduction, Biographical and Historical.* Trans. KEATINGE. M. W. London: Adam and Black, 1896.

CORNELL, W. B. "The New State Law Relating to Retardation of Public School Children and Its Application." *Ungraded,* 1919, *5* (3), 55–59.

CORNELL, W. S. "Mentally Defective Children in the Public Schools." *Psychological Clinic,* 1908–9, *2,* 75–86.

COTTLE, H. J. *Barred from School 2 Million Children.* Washington, D.C.: New Republic Book Company, 1976.

COUSIN, M. V. *Report on the State of Public Instruction in Prussia.* Trans. S. AUSTIN. New York: Wiley & Long, 1835.

COVELLO, L. *The Heart Is the Teacher.* New York: McGraw-Hill, 1958.

COVELLO, L. *The Social Background of the Italo-American School Child.* Leyden: E. J. Brill, 1967.

COWEN, E., M. A. TROST, R. P. LORION, D. DORR, L. D. IZZO, and R. J. ISAACSON. *New Ways in School Mental Health: Early Detection and Preventions of School Maladaptation.* New York: Human Sciences Press, 1975.

CREMIN, L. A. *The American Common School: An Historic Conception.* New York: Bureau of Publications, Teachers College, Columbia University Press, 1951.

CREMIN, L. A. *The Transformation of the School: Progressivism in American Education 1876–1957.* 1st Ed. New York: Knopf, 1961. Reprint, New York: Vintage Books, 1964.

CROSS, R. D. "Origins of the Catholic Parochial Schools in America." *American Benedictine Review,* 1965, No. 26, 194–209.

CUBBERLEY, E. P. *Public Education in the United States.* Boston: Houghton Mifflin Co., 1919. Rev. Ed., 1934a.

CUBBERLEY, E. P. (ed.). *Readings in Public Education in the United States.* Boston: Houghton Mifflin Company, 1934b.

CURRAN, F. X. *The Churches and the Schools: American Protestantism and Popular Elementary Education.* Chicago: Loyola University Press, 1954.

DAVIE, R., N. BUTLER, and H. GOLDSTEIN. *From Birth to Seven: A Report of the National Child Development Study.* London: Longmans, 1972.

DAVIES, S. P. *Social Control of the Mentally Deficient.* New York: Crowell, 1930.

DAVIS, D. B. "Some Themes of Counter-Subversion: An Analysis of Anti-Masonic, Anti-Catholic and Anti-Mormon Literature." *The Mississippi Valley Historical Review,* 1960, *47,* pp. 205-224.

DE LA SALLE, J. B. *The Conduct of the Schools of Jean-Baptiste De La Salle.* Trans. and intro. F. DE LA FONTAINERIE. New York & London: McGraw-Hill, 1935.

DEWEY, J. *The School and Society.* Chicago: University of Chicago Press, 1915.

DEWEY, J., and E. DEWEY. *Schools of Tomorrow.* New York: E. P. Dutton, 1915.

DEXTER, L. *The Tyranny of Schooling.* New York: Basic Books, 1964.

DOHAN, J. M. "Our State Constitutions and Religious Liberty." *American Catholic Quarterly Review,* 1915, *40,* 276-322.

DOLL, E. A. *The Vineland Social Maturity Scale: Manual of Questions.* Vineland, N.J.: Training School, 1935.

DORIS, J. "Science, Action, and Values in Familial Retardation." *The Journal of Special Education,* 1970, *4* (2), 161-170.

DRILLIEN, C. M. *Growth and Development of the Prematurely Born Infant.* Edinburgh and London: Livingstone, 1964.

DUNN, L. M. "Special Education for the Mildly Retarded—Is Much of It Justifiable?" *Exceptional Children,* 1968-1969, *35,* 5-22.

DUNN, L. M. (ed.) *Exceptional Children in the Schools: Special Education in Transition.* 2d Ed. New York: Holt, Rinehart & Winston, 1973.

DWIGHT JR., T. "Management of a Common School." In *The Introductory Discourse and the Lectures Delivered before the American Institute of Instruction in Boston 1835.* Boston: Charles J. Hendee, 1836.

EAST, E. M. *Heredity and Human Affairs.* New York: Scribner's, 1927.

EATON, J. W., and R. J. WEIL. *Culture and Mental Disorders: A Comparative Study of the Hutterites and Other Populations.* Glencoe, Ill.: Free Press, 1955.

EDSON, T. *Memoir of Warren Colburn.* Boston: Brown, Taggard & Chase, 1856.

EHLERS, W. H. *Mothers of Retarded Children: How They Feel, Where They Find Help.* Springfield, Ill.: Charles C. Thomas, 1966.

ELLIOTT, C. M. "A Foreword on Teacher Training." *Journal of Exceptional Children,* 1936-37, *3,* 139-147.

ENSIGN, F. C. *Compulsory School Attendance and Child Labor.* Iowa City: Athens Press, 1921.

ERICKSON, D. A. (ed.) *Public Controls for Nonpublic Schools.* Chicago: University of Chicago Press, 1969.

ERIKSON, E. *Childhood and Society.* New York: Norton, 1950.

ERNST, R. *Immigrant Life in New York City 1825–1863.* Port Washington, N.Y.: Ira J. Friedman, 1949, Reissued, 1965.

ESTEN, R. A. "Backward Children in the Public Schools." *Journal of Psycho-Asthenics,* 1900, *5* (1), 10-15.

FANTINI, M. D. "Beyond Cultural Deprivation and Compensatory Education." *Psychiatry and Social Science Review,* 1969, *3,* 6-13.

FARBER, B. *Family: Organization and Interaction.* San Francisco: Chandler, 1964.

FARBER, B. "Family Organization and Crisis: Maintenance of Integration in Families with a Severely Mentally Retarded Child." *Monographs of the Society for Research in Child Development,* 1960, *25,* 1.

FARBER, B. "Interaction with Retarded Siblings and Life Goals of Children." *Marriage and Family Living,* 1963, *25,* 96–98.

FARBER, B. *Mental Retardation: Its Social Context and Social Consequences.* Boston: Houghton Mifflin, 1968.

FARBER, S. "Cancer Patients and Private Practice Physicians." Unpublished paper (available from author at 70 Sachem Street, New Haven, CT 06520), 1977.

FARRELL, E. E. "Survey of Nationality of Children in Ungraded Classes." *Ungraded,* 1921, *7,* 25–28.

FARRELL, E. E. "A Preliminary Report on the Careers of Three Hundred Fifty Children Who Have Left Ungraded Classes." *Journal of Psycho-Asthenics,* September–December, 1915, *20* (1,2), 20–26.

FARRELL, E. E. "The Problems of the Special Class." *National Education Association Journal of Proceedings and Addresses of the 46th Annual Meeting,* 1908, 1131–1136.

FARRELL, E. E. "Report on Treatment of Defective Children in Great Britain." *Fifth Annual Report of the City Superintendent of Schools to the Board of Education of the City of New York for the Year Ending July 31, 1903,* 243–263.

FARRELL, E. E. "Special Classes in the New York City Schools," *Journal of Psycho-Asthenics,* 1908–1909, *13* (1,2,3,4), 91–96.

FELLMAN, D. (ed.) *The Supreme Court and Education.* New York: Columbia University Press, 1969.

FELZEN, E. S. *Mothers' Adjustment to Their Mongoloid Children.* Unpublished doctoral dissertation, Cornell University, 1970.

FERNALD, W. E. "Mentally Defective Children in the Public Schools." *Journal of Psycho-Asthenics,* 1903–4, *8* (2,3), 25–35.

FICHTE, J. G. *Addresses to the German Nation.* Trans. R. F. JONES and G. H. TURNBULL. Chicago: The Open Court Publishing Co., 1922.

FINEGAN, T. "Free Schools: A Documentary History of the Free School Movement in New York State." In the *Fifteenth Annual Report of the Education Department, vol. I.* Albany: University of the State of New York, 1921.

FITCH, C. E. "Educational History: A) History of the Common School in New York, B) Biographical Sketches of the Superintendents of Public Instruction." Part of *Report of State Superintendent of Public Instruction.* State of New York Department of Public Instruction, Fiftieth Annual Report of the State Superintendent for the School Year Ending July 31, 1903. Albany: Oliver A. Quayle, 1904.

FITTS, A. M. "The Function of Special Classes for Mentally Defective Children in the Public Schools." *Journal of Psycho-Asthenics,* 1917, *21,* 94–98.

FITTS, A. M. "How to Fill the Gap between the Special Classes and Institutions." *Journal of Psycho-Asthenics,* 1916, *20,* 78–87.

FITZPATRICK, J. P. "Letters on Bilingualism: The Importance of a Child's Roots." *New York Times,* December 12, 1977.

FOWLE, W. B. "Boston Monitorial School: Instructer's [sic] Report to the Trustees." *American Annuals of Education,* 1826, *1,* 32-42, 72-80, 160-166.

FRANCIS-WILLIAMS, J., and P. A. DAVIES. "Very Low Birthweight and Later Intelligence." *Developmental Medicine and Child Neurology,* 1974, *16,* 709-728.

FUCHS, V. R. *Who Shall Live? Health, Economics, and Social Choice.* New York: Basic Books, 1975.

FULLER, J. L., and W. R. THOMPSON. *Behavior Genetics.* New York: Wiley, 1960.

GABEL, R. J. *Public Funds for Church and Private Schools.* Gettysburg, Pa.: Times and News Publishing Co., 1937.

GALLAGHER, J. J. "The Special Education Contract for Mildly Handicapped Children." *Exceptional Children,* 1971-1972, *38,* 527-535.

GALLAGHER, J. J. "Why the Government Breaks Its Promises." *New York University Education Quarterly,* 1975, *6,* 4, 22-27.

GALTON, F. *Hereditary Genius.* London: Macmillan, 1869.

GANS, H. J. *The Urban Villagers: Group and Class in the Life of Italian-Americans.* New York: Free Press of Glencoe, 1962.

GARBER, H. "Intervention in Infancy: A Developmental Approach." In M. J. BEGAB, and S. A. RICHARDSON (eds.), *The Mentally Retarded in Society.* Baltimore: University Park Press, 1975.

GARMEZY, N. "The Study of Competence in Children at Risk for Severe Psychopathology." In E. J. ANTHONY and C. KOUPERNIK, (eds.), *The Child in his Family. Children at Psychiatric Risk,* vol. 3. New York: Wiley, 1974.

GESELL, A., and C. AMATRUDA. *Developmental Diagnosis.* New York: Hoeber, 1941.

GINSBURG, H. *The Myth of the Deprived Child.* Englewood Cliffs, N.J.: Prentice-Hall, 1972.

GINZBERG, E. and D. BRAY. *The Uneducated.* New York: Columbia University Press, 1953.

GODDARD, H. H. "The Binet Tests in Relation to Immigration." *Journal of Psycho-Asthenics,* 1913, *18,* 105-110.

GODDARD, H. H. "Impressions of European Institutions and Special Classes." *Journal of Psycho-Asthenics,* 1908, *13,* 18-28.

GODDARD, H. H. *The Kallikak Family: A Study in the Heredity of Feeble-mindedness.* New York: Macmillan, 1912.

GODDARD, H. H. "Mental Tests and the Immigrant." *Journal of Delinquency,* 1917, *2,* 243-277.

GODDARD, H. H. *School Training of Defective Children.* New York: World Book Company, 1914.

GODDARD, H. H., and H. F. HILL. "Delinquent Girls Tested by the Binet Scale." *Training School Bulletin,* 1911, *8,* 50-56.

GOFFMAN, I. *Stigma.* Englewood Cliffs, N.J.: Prentice-Hall, 1963.

GOLDSTEIN, H. "Social and Occupational Adjustment." In H. A. STEVENS and R. HEBER (eds.), *Mental Retardation.* Chicago: The University of Chicago Press, 1964.

GOLDSTEIN, H., C. ARKELL, S. C. ASHCROFT, O. L. HURLEY, and M. S. LILLY.

"Schools." In N. HOBBS (ed.), *Issues in the Classification of Children, Vol. II*. San Francisco: Jossey-Bass Publishers, 1975.

GOODENOUGH, F. L. "Racial Differences in the Intelligence of School Children." *Journal of Experimental Psychology*, 1926, *9*, 388–397.

GOODHART, S. P. "The Education of Defective Children." *Journal of Psycho-Asthenics*, 1904, *9*, 200.

GOODRICH, S. G. *Recollections of a Lifetime or Men and Things I have Seen*, vol. I. New York: C. M. Saxton, 1859.

GOYER, R. A. "Lead Toxicity: A Problem in Environmental Pathology." *American Journal of Pathology*, 1971, *64* (1), 167–179.

GRANT, W. V., and G. C. LIND. *Digest of Education Statistics, 1975 Edition*. Washington, D.C.: U.S. Government Printing Office, 1976.

GREELEY, A. M. *The Catholic Experience*. Garden City, N.Y.: Doubleday, 1967.

GREEN, J. A. *The Educational Ideas of Pestalozzi*. New York: Greenwood Press, 1969. Originally published in 1914 by W. B. Clive.

GREEN, J. A. and F. A. COLLIE (eds.) *Pestalozzi's Educational Writings*. New York: Longmans, Green, 1912; London: Edward Arnold, 1912.

GREENBERG, J., and G. DOOLITTLE. "Can Schools Speak the Language of the Deaf?" *New York Times Magazine*, December 11, 1977, 50.

GRIFFITHS, W. E. *Religion, the Courts and the Public Schools: A Century of Litigation*. Cincinnati: W. H. Anderson, 1966.

GRISCOM, J. *Monitorial Instruction*. An address, pronounced at the opening of the New-York High-School, with notes and illustrations. New York: Mahlon Day, 1825.

GRISCOM, J., V. COUSIN, and C. E. STOWE. *Reports on European Education*. E. W. KNIGHT (ed.). New York: McGraw-Hill Book Company, Inc., 1930.

GROB, G. N. Introduction to JARVIS, *Insanity and Idiocy in Massachusetts: Report of the Commission on Lunacy*. Cambridge, Mass.: Harvard University Press, 1971.

Grossman, F. K. *Brothers and Sisters of Retarded Children: An Exploratory Study*. Syracuse, N.Y.: Syracuse University Press, 1972.

GROSSMAN, H. J. (ed.). *Manual on Terminology and Classification in Mental Retardation*. Washington, D.C.: American Association on Mental Deficiency, 1973.

GUILFORD, J. P. "The Structure of Intellect." *Psychological Bulletin*, 1956, *53*, 267–293.

GUTHRIE, E. R. *The Psychology of Human Conflict*. Boston: Beacon Press, 1938.

HALEY, J. *Problem Solving Therapy: New Strategies for Effective Family Therapy*. San Francisco: Jossey-Bass, 1976.

HAMMONS, G. W. "Educating the Mildly Retarded: A Review," *Exceptional Children*, 1971–1972, *38*, 565–570.

HANDLIN, O. *Boston's Immigrants 1790–1865: A Study in Acculturation*. Cambridge: Harvard University Press, 1941.

HANDLIN, O. *The Uprooted: The Epic Story of the Great Migrations that Made the American People*. Boston: Little, Brown, 1951.

HANKS, J. R., and L. M. HANKS. "The Physically Handicapped in Certain Non-Occidental Societies." *Journal of Social Issues*, 1948, *4*, 4, 11–20.

HARPER, C. A. *A Century of Public Teacher Education.* Washington: National Education Association, 1939.

HARRIS, W. T. *Report of the Commissioner of Education for the Year 1898–99, 1.* Washington: Government Printing Office, 1900.

HASSLER, F. R. "Psychiatric Manpower and Community Mental Health: A Survey of Psychiatric Residents." *American Journal of Orthopsychiatry,* 1965, *35,* 695–706.

HAWKINS, R. P., R. F. PETERSON, E. SCHWEID, and S. W. BIJOU. "Behavior Therapy in the Home: Amelioration of Problem Parent-Child Relations with the Parent in a Therapeutic Role." *Journal of Experimental Child Psychology,* 1966, *4,* 99–107.

HEAL, L., and E. GOLLAY. "An Empirical Description and Analysis of Deinstitutionalization." A paper presented at the 10th Annual Gatlinburg Conference on Research in Mental Retardation, Gatlinburg, Tenn., 1977. (Available from Dr. Laird Heal, Depart. of Special Education, University of Illinois, Urbana, Ill. 61801.)

HEBER, R. F. "Standards for the Preparation and Certification of Teachers of the Mentally Retarded." *Mental Retardation,* February, 1963, *1,* (1), 35–37, 60–62.

HEBER, R. F., and DEVER, R. B. "Research on Education and Habilitation of the Mentally Retarded." In HAYWOOD, H. C. (ed.), *Social Cultural Aspects of Mental Retardation.* New York: Appleton-Century-Crofts, 1970.

HEIFETZ, L. "From Consumer to Middleman: New Roles for Parents in the Service Delivery System." Unpublished paper, 1977.

HEIFETZ, L. "Professional Precociousness and the Evaluation of Parent-Training Strategies." Paper presented at the Fourth International Association for the Scientific Study of Mental Deficiency, Washington, D.C., 1976.

HEIFETZ, L. J. "Toward Freedom and Dignity: Alternative Formats for Training of Retarded Children in Behavior Modification." *Dissertation Abstracts International,* February, 1975, *35,* 8–B, 4175–4176.

HELLER, J. *Something Happened.* New York: Ballantine Books, 1975 (paperback).

HERBERG, W. *Protestant-Catholic-Jew: An Essay in American Religious Sociology.* New York: Doubleday & Co., 1955.

HIGHAM, J. "Another Look at Nativism." *The Catholic Historical Review,* 1958, *XLIV* (2), 147–158.

HILLIARD, D. M. "Historical Development of Grades and Departments in the Public Schools of Memphis, Tennessee." *The Elementary School Journal,* 1946, *47,* (3), 157–160.

HIRSCH, N. D. M. "A Study of Natio-racial Mental Differences." *Genetic Psychology Monographs,* 1926, *1* (3,4), 231–406.

HODGE, D. E. W., and L. F. HODGE. *A Century of Service to Public Education.* The Centennial History of the New York State Teachers Association, 1945.

HOLLAND, C. J. "Elimination by the Parents of Fire-Setting Behavior in a Seven-Year-Old Boy." *Behavior Research of Therapy,* 1969, *7,* 135–137.

HOLMES, W. H. "Plans of Classification in the Public Schools." *The Pedagogical Seminary,* 1911, *XVIII* (1), 475–522.

HOLSINGER, M. P. "The Oregon School Bill Controversy, 1922–1925." *Pacific Historical Review,* 1968, *37,* 327–341.

HOROWITZ, F. D., and L. Y. Paden. "The Effectiveness of the Environmental Intervention Programs. In B. CALDWELL and H. RICCIUTI (eds.), *Review of Child Development Research*, vol. 3. Chicago: University of Chicago Press, 1973, pp. 331–402.

"How Defective Children Are Trained in School 25." *The Training School.* 1910, *7* (4), 230–231.

HUNT, N. *The World of Nigel Hunt: The Diary of a Mongoloid Youth.* New York: Gannett, 1967.

HURLEY, R. *Poverty and Mental Retardation.* New York: Vintage Books, 1969.

IMMIGRATION COMMISSION. *Abstract of the Report on the Children of Immigrants in Schools.* Washington: Government Printing Office, 1911.

INSKEEP, A. D. *Teaching Dull and Retarded Children.* New York: Macmillan, 1926.

ITARD, J. M. G. *The Wild Boy of Aveyron.* New York: Appleton-Century-Crofts, 1962.

JENCKS, C. *Inequality: A Reassessment of the Effect of Family and Schooling in America.* New York: Basic Books, 1972.

JENSEN, A. R. "How Biased Are Culture-Loaded Tests? *Genetic Psychology Monographs*, 1974, *90*, 185–244.

JENSEN, A. R. "How Much Can We Boost IQ and Scholastic Achievement?" *Harvard Educational Review*, 1969, *39*, 1–123.

JOHNSON, A. "The Extension Department and the Association for the Study of the Feeble-Minded." *The Training School Bulletin*, September, 1914, *11*, (5), 69–71.

JOHNSON, C. *Old-Time Schools and School-Books.* New York: Macmillan, 1925 (c. 1904).

JOHNSON, G. O. "Special Education for Mentally Handicapped—a Paradox." *Exceptional Children*, 1962, *19*, 62–69.

JOHNSON, J. L. (ed.). "Special Education and the Inner City: A Challenge for the Future or Another Means for Cooling the Mark Out?" *The Journal of Special Education*, Fall, 1969, *3*, (3), 241–251.

JOHNSTONE, E. R. "The Functions of the Special Class." *National Education Association Journal of Proceedings and Address of the 46th Annual Meeting*, 1908, 1114–1118.

JOHNSTONE, E. R. "The Summer School for Teachers of Backward Children." *Journal of Psycho-Asthenics*, 1909–1910, *14*, 122–130.

JONES, M. A. *American Immigration.* Chicago: University of Chicago Press, 1960.

JONES, R. L. "Labels and Stigma in Special Education." *Journal of Exceptional Children*, 1971–1972, *38*, 553–564.

JONES, W. F. "Study of Grading and Promotion." *Psychological Clinic*, May and June, 1911, 63–96, 99–120.

JORGENSON, L. P. "The Birth of a Tradition." *Phi Delta Kappan*, 1963, *44*, 407–418.

JORGENSON, L. P. "The Oregon School Law of 1922: Passage and Sequel." *Catholic Historical Review*, 1968, *LIV*, 455–466.

KAESTLE, C. F. *The Evolution of an Urban School System: New York City, 1750–1850.* Cambridge, Mass.: Harvard University Press, 1973a.

KAESTLE, C. F. (ed.) *Joseph Lancaster and the Monitorial School Movement.* New York: Teachers College Press, 1973b.

KANNER, L. *A History of the Care and Study of the Mentally Retarded.* Springfield, Ill.: Charles C. Thomas, 1964.

KAPLAN, F., and S. B. SARASON. "The Psycho-Educational Clinic, Yale University, 1970." (Papers and research studies available from S. B. Sarason, Yale University, Institution for Social and Policy Studies, 70 Sachem, New Haven, CT 06520.)

KATZ, J. *Experimentation with Human Beings.* New York: Russell Sage, 1972.

KEIM, A. N. (ed.). *Compulsory Education and the Amish: The Right Not to Be Modern.* Boston: Beacon Press, 1975.

KEMPE, C. H. "Pediatric Implications of the Battered Child Syndrome." *Archives of Disease in Childhood,* 1971, *46,* 28.

KEMPE, C. H., and R. E. HELFER (eds.). *Helping the Battered Child and His Family.* Philadelphia: J. B. Lippincott, 1972.

KENNEDY, J. *The Batavia System of Individual Instruction.* Syracuse, N.Y.: C. W. Bardeen, 1914.

KINDRED, M., J. COHEN, D. PENROD, and T. SHAFFER (eds.). *The Mentally Retarded Citizen and the Law.* New York: Free Press. Macmillan, 1976.

KING, R. D., N. V. RAYNES, and J. TIZARD. *Patterns of Residential Care: Sociological Studies in Institutions for Handicapped People.* London: Routledge & Kegan Paul, 1971.

KIRK, S. A. "Research in Education." In H. A. STEVENS and R. HEBER (ed.), *Mental Retardation.* Chicago: University of Chicago Press, 1964, pp. 57-99.

KIRK, S. A., and B. D. BATEMAN (comps.) *Ten Years of Research at the Institute for Research on Exceptional Children.* Urbana, Ill.: University of Illinois Press, 1964.

KIRP, D. L. "Student Classification, Public Policy, and the Courts. *Harvard Educaional Review,* 1974, *44* (1), 7-52.

KLEIN, M., and L. STERN. "Low Birthweight and the Battered Child Syndrome." *American Journal of Diseases of Children,* 1971, *122,* 15-18.

KNOBLOCH H., and B. PASAMANICK. "Complications of Pregnancy and Mental Deficiency. In P. W. BOWMAN and H. V. MAUTNER (eds.), *Mental Retardation.* New York: Grune & Stratton, 1960, 182-93.

KNOBLOCH, H., and B. PASAMANICK. "Syndrome of Minimal Cerebral Damage in Infancy." *Journal of the American Medical Association,* 1959, *170,* 1384-1387.

KOLSTOE, O. P. "Programs for the Mildly Retarded: A Reply to the Critics." *Exceptional Children,* 1972-1973, *39,* 51-55.

KRAUSE, I. B., JR. "Requirements for Teachers of Mentally Retarded Children in the Fifty States." *Mental Retardation,* February, 1963, *1,* 38-40, 62-64.

KRAUSE, D. U.S. Congress. House Select Committee on Aging. Hearing before the Subcommittee on Health and Long-Term Care, 94th Cong., 1st sess., July 8, 1975. (Available from Superintendent of Documents, U.S. Government Printing Office, Washington, D.C. 20402. Stock number 050-070-02903-0.

KRÜSI, H. *Pestalozzi: His Life, Work and Influence.* Cincinnati: Van Antwerp, Bragg, 1875.

KÜBLER-ROSS, E. *On Death and Dying.* New York: Macmillan, 1970 (paperback).

LANCASTER, J. *Improvements in Education as It Respects the Industrious Classes of the Community,* 4th ed. London: Lancaster, 1806.

LANE, H. *The Wild Boy of Aveyron.* Cambridge, Mass.: Harvard University Press, 1976.

LaGUMINA, S. J. (ed.). *Wop!* A Documentary History of Anti-Italian Discrimination in the United States. San Francisco: Straight Arrow Books, 1973.

LEACOCK, E. B. (ed.). *The Culture of Poverty: A Critique.* New York: Simon & Schuster, 1971.

LEGARDE, E. "Should the Scope of the Public School System Be Broadened to Take in All Children Capable of Education?" *Journal of Psycho-Asthenics,* 1903, *8,* 35–38.

LEWIN, K. *Resolving Social Conflicts.* New York: Harper & Row, 1948.

LEWIN, K., R. LIPPITT, and R. WHITE. "Patterns of Aggressive Behavior in Experimentally Created 'Social Climates'." *Journal of Social Psychology,* 1939, *X,* 271–299.

LEVINE, M. "Some Postulates of Community Practice." In F. Kaplan and S. B. SARASON (eds.), *The Psycho-Educational Clinic Papers and Research Studies.* Monograph Series, Massachusetts Department of Mental Health, 1969. (Library of Congress Catalog Card No. 74-625106.)

LILIENFELD, A. M., and E. PARKHURST. "Study of the Association of Factors of Pregnancy and Parturition with the Development of Cerebral Palsy." *American Journal of Hygiene,* 1951, *53,* 262–282.

LINCOLN, D. F. "Special Classes for Feeble-Minded Children in the Boston Public Schools." *Journal of Psycho-Asthenics,* 1903, *7,* 83–93.

LINCOLN, D. F. "Special Classes for Mentally Defective Children in the Boston Public Schools." *Journal of Psycho-Asthenics,* 1909, *14,* 89–92.

LIPPITT, R. "Field Theory and Experiment in Social Psychology: Autocratic and Democratic and Democratic Group Atmospheres." *American Journal of Sociology,* 1939, *45,* 26–49.

LIPPITT, R., "Studies on Experimentally Created Autocratic and Democratic Groups." *University of Iowa Studies: Studies in Child Welfare,* 1940, *XVI* (3), 45–198.

LIPPMAN, L., and I. I. GOLDBERG. *Right to Education: Anatomy of the Pennsylvania Case and Its Implications for Exceptional Children.* New York: Teachers College Press, 1973.

LITTLEFIELD, G. E. *Early Schools and School Books of New England.* New York: Russell & Russell, 1965. (First Published in 1904.)

LOEHLIN, J. C., G. LINDZEY, J. N. SPUHLER. *Race Differences in Intelligence.* San Francisco: W. H. Freeman, 1975.

LONDON, M. "A Study of Interagency Perception and Cooperation." B.A. thesis, Yale University, 1977.

LORION, R. "Individualized Education for Brain-Injured (Learning Disabled) Children: The Systematic Development and Evaluation of a Diagnostic-Prescriptive Approach." Unpublished progress report, Geneva Academy, Philadelphia, 1977.

LOUGH, J. E. "A Course of Study for Teachers of Backward and Defective Children. *Ungraded,* 1915, *1,* (4), 60–65.

LOURIE, R. S. "Prevention of Lead Paint—or Prevention of Pica" *Pediatrics,* 1971, *48,* 490–491.

LOURIE, R. S., E. M. LAYMAN, and F. K. MILLICAN. "Why Children Eat Things that Are Not Food." *Children*, 1963, *10*, 143.

MACCOBY, E. E., and C. N. JACKLIN. *The Psychology of Sex Differences.* Stanford, Cal.: Stanford University Press, 1974.

MACGREGOR, F. C., T. M. ABEL, A. BRYT, E. LOUER, and S. WEISSMAN. *Facial Deformities and Plastic Surgery: A Psychosocial Study.* Springfield, Ill.: Charles C. Thomas, 1953.

MAENNEL, B. "The Auxiliary Schools of Germany." *Bulletin of the Bureau of Education.* 1907 (3), 376, 1–137.

MANGUN, V. L. *The American Normal School: Its Rise and Development in Massachusetts.* In Columbia University Dissertations, 1928, Monograph 3, Baltimore: Warwick & York, 1928.

MANN, H. *Seventh Annual Report of the Board of Education together with the Seventh Annual Report of the Secretary of the Board.* Boston: Dutton & Wentworth, State Printers, 1844.

MARNELL, W. M. *The First Amendment: The History of Religious Freedom in America.* Garden City, N.Y.: Doubleday, 1964.

MARTENS, E. H. "Education of Exceptional Children." *U.S. Bureau of Education Biennial Survey of Education 1928–1930 Bulletin*, 1931, *1*, (20), 381–418.

MARTENS, E. H. "Present Status of Opportunities for the Preparation of Teachers of Exceptional Children. *Journal of Exceptional Children*, 1936–1937, *3*, 140–142.

MARTINDALE, W. C. "How Detroit Cares for Her Backward Children." *The Psychological Clinic*, 1912–13, *6* (5), 125–130.

MATHENY, A. P. and J. VERNICK. "Parents of the Mentally Retarded Child; Emotionally Overwhelmed or Informationally Deprived?" In J. J. DEMPSEY (ed.), *Community Services for Retarded Children.* Baltimore: University Park Press, 1975.

MATHEWS, M. M. *Teaching to Read: Historically Considered.* Chicago: University of Chicago Press, 1966.

MAXWELL, W. H. "Defective Children." *Seventh Annual Report of the City Superintendent of Schools to the Board of Education of the City of New York for the Year Ending July 31, 1905. 112–119.*

MAXWELL, W. H. *Fourteenth Annual Report of the City Superintendent of Schools for the Year Ending July 31, 1912.* Department of Education City of New York.

MAXWELL, W. H. *Fourth Annual Report of the City Superintendent of Schools for the Year Ending July 31, 1902,* Department of Education, City of New York, 108–109.

MAXWELL, W. H. "Report on Special Classes for Defective Children." *Seventh Annual Report of the City Superintendent of Schools to the Board of Education of the City of New York for the Year Ending July 31, 1905,* Department of Education, City of New York, 425–439.

MAXWELL, W. H. *Seventh Annual Report of the City Superintendent of Schools to the Board of Education of the City of New York for the Year Ending July 31, 1905,* Department of Education, City of New York, 112–119.

MAXWELL, W. H. "Special Schools for Defective Children." *First Annual Report of the City Superintendent of Schools to the Board of Education for the Year Ending July 31, 1899,* Department of Education, City of New York, 130–134.

MAYHEW, K. C., and A. C. Edwards. *The Dewey School.* New York: Atherton Press, 1966.

McAVOY, T. T. *A History of the Catholic Church in the United States.* South Bend, Ind.: University of Notre Dame Press, 1969.

McCLELLAN, R. "The Institutional Phenomenon: A Socio-economic Inquiry" (available in Yale University Library, 1973). Summarized in S. B. SARASON, *The Psychological Sense of Community.* San Francisco: Jossey-Bass, 1974, Chapter IX.

McCLUSKEY, N. G. (ed.). *Catholic Education in America: A Documentary History.* New York: Teachers College Press, 1964.

McCLUSKEY, N. G. *Catholic Viewpoint on Education.* New York: Image Books, 1962.

McCOOEY, M. J. "Growth of Special Education." *Journal of Exceptional Children,* 1940-41, *1* (5), 164, 203.

McGUFFEY, W. H. *McGuffey's First-Sixth Reader.* Rev. Ed. Cincinnati: Van Antwerp, Bragg, 1879.

McLUHAN, H. M. *The Gutenberg Galaxy: The Making of Typographic Man.* Toronto: University of Toronto Press, 1962.

MEAD, M. "Educational Research and Statistics." *School and Society,* 1927, *25,* 465-468.

MERCER, J. R. *Labeling the Mentally Retarded.* Berkeley: University of California Press, 1973.

MERCER, J. R. "The Meaning of Mental Retardation." In R. KOCH and J. C. DOBSON (eds.), *The Mentally Retarded Child and His Family.* New York: Brunner/Mazel, 1971.

MERCER, J. R. "A Policy Statement on Assessment Procedures and the Rights of Children. *Harvard Educational Review,* 1974, *44* (1), 125-141.

MERCER, J. R. "Sociological Perspectives on Mild Mental Retardation." In H. C. HAYWOOD (ed.), *Social-Cultural Aspects of Mental Retardation.* New York: Appleton-Century-Crofts, 1970.

MEYERS, S. "Have You Killed a Child Recently?" Address delivered at the 24th Annual Convention of the Ohio Association for Retarded Citizens, April 30, 1976. Cleveland, Ohio: Cuyahoga Association for Retarded Citizens.

MEYERSON, L. "Physical Disability as a Social Psychological Problem." *Journal of Social Issues,* 1948, *4* (4), 2-11.

MEYEROWITZ, J. H. "Family Background of Educable Mentally Retarded Children. In H. GOLDSTEIN, J. W. Moss, and L. J. JORDAN (eds.) *The Efficacy of Special Education Training on the Development of Mentally Retarded Children.* Urbana: University of Illinois Institute for Research of Exceptional Children, 1965, 152-182.

MEYEROWITZ, J. H. "Peer Groups and Special Classes." *Mental Retardation,* 1967, *5,* 23-26.

MILOFSKY, D. "Schooling for Kids No One Wants." *New York Times,* January 2, 1977, magazine section.

MINNICH, H. C. (ED.) *Old Favorites from the McGuffey Readers.* New York: American Book Company, 1936.

MINUCHIN, S. *Families and Family Therapy.* Cambridge, Mass.: Harvard University Press, 1974.

MOHL, R. A. *Poverty in New York 1783–1825.* New York: Oxford University Press, 1971.

MONCRIEFF, A. A., O. P. KOUMIDES, B. E. CLAYTON, A. D. PATTRICK, A. G. C. RENWICK, and G. E. ROBERTS. "Lead Poisoning in Children." *Archives of Disease in Childhood, 39* (1), 1964.

MONEY, J. (ed.) *The Disabled Reader.* Baltimore: Johns Hopkins Press, 1966.

MONEY, J. "Perversion or Paraphilia?" (Review of *Perversion: The Erotic Form of Hatred,* by R. J. Stoller). *Contemporary Psychology,* 1976, *21* (8), 528–529.

MONROE, P. *Founding of the American Public School System,* vol. 1. New York: MacMillan, 1940.

MONROE, W. S. *History of the Pestalozzian Movement in the United States.* Syracuse, N.Y.: C. W. Bardeen, 1907.

MONROE, W. S. "Institutes." In P. Monroe (ed.), *A Cyclopedia of Education,* 1912, *3,* 467–469.

MORSE, S. B. *Foreign Conspiracy against the Liberties of the United States.* New York: Leavitt, Lord, 1835.

MOSIER, R. D. *Making the American Mind: Social and Moral Ideas in the McGuffey Readers.* New York: King's Crown Press, Columbia University, 1947.

MYERS, G. *History of Bigotry in the United States.* New York: Random House, 1943.

NEEDLEMAN, H. L. "Lead Poisoning in Children: Neurologic Implications of Widespread Subclinical Intoxication." In S. CHESS and A. THOMAS (eds.), *Annual Progress in Child Psychiatry and Child Development, 1974.* New York: Brunner/Mazel, 1975.

The New England Primer. A facsimile of the New England Primer published between 1785 and 1790. Boston: Ginn & Company, 1900.

NEWTON, G., and S. LEVINE (eds.). *Early Experience and Behavior.* Springfield, Ill.: Charles C. Thomas, 1968.

NIRJE, B. *The Normalization Principle and Its Human Management Implications.* In R. KUGEL and W. WOLFENSBERGER (eds.), *Changing Patterns in Residential Services for the Mentally Retarded.* Washington, D.C.: President's Committee on Mental Retardation, 1969.

NISBET, R. *The Quest for Community* Rev. ed. New York: Oxford University Press, 1970.

O'BRIEN, D. J. "American Catholicism and the Diaspora." *Cross Currents,* 1966, *XVI* (3), 307–323.

O'BRIEN, K. B., JR. "Education, Americanization and the Supreme Court: The 1920's." *American Quarterly,* 1961, *XIII* (2), 161–171.

O'CONNOR, N. "Children in Restricted Environments." In G. Newton and S. LEVINE (eds.), *Early Experience and Behavior.* Springfield, Ill.: Charles C. Thomas, 1968.

OLIVER, H. K. "On the Advantages and Defects of the Monitorial System: With Some Suggestions, Showing in What Particulars It May Be Safely Adopted into Our Schools." *The American Institute of Instruction,* 1831, 207–230.

OLIVER, H. K. "Schools as They Were in the United States." *The American Journal of Education*, 1876, *26*, 209-224.

OLNECK, M. R. and M. LAZERSON. "The School Achievement of Immigration Children: 1900-1930. *History of Education Quarterly*, 1974, 453-482.

O'SHEA, W. J. "Education of Children Who Are Mentally Handicapped." *Progress of the Schools*. Report of the Superintendent of Schools of the City of New York, 1924-29, 86-91.

PALMER, A. E. *The New York Public School*. New York: Macmillan, 1905.

PARKER, S. A. *The History of Modern Elementary Education*. Totowa, N.J.: Littlefield, Adams, 1970 (c. 1912).

PASTORE, N. *The Nature-Nurture Controversy*. New York: Columbia University Press, 1949.

PASAMANICK, B., and H. KNOBLOCH. "Epidemiologic Studies on the Complications of Pregnancy and Birth Process." In G. CAPLAN (ed.), *Prevention of Mental Disorders in Children*. New York: Basic Books, 1961.

PASAMANICK, B., and H. KNOBLOCH. "Retrospective Studies on the Epidemiology of Reproductive Casuality: Old and New." *Merrill-Palmer Quarterly*, 1966, *12*, 7-26.

PATTERSON, G. R., and M. E. GULLION. *Living with Children: New Methods for Parents and Teachers*. Champagne, Ill.: Research Press, 1968.

PATTERSON, G. R., S. McNEAL, N. HAWKINS, and R. PHELPS. "Reprogramming the Social Environment." *Journal of Child Psychology Psychiatry*, 1967, *8*, 181-195.

PAULSEN, F. *German Education*. New York: Charles Scribner's Sons, 1908.

PEINE, H. "Programming the Home." Paper presented at the meetings of the Rocky Mountain Psychological Association, Albuquerque, N.M., 1969.

PERLSTEIN, M. A., and R. ATTALA. "Neurologic Sequelae of Plumbism in Children." *Clinical Pediatrics*, 5 (292), 1966.

PESTALOZZI, J. "How Gertrude Teaches Her Children." In J. A. GREEN and A. Frances (eds.), *Pestalozzi's Educational Writings*. New York: Longmans, Green Co., 1912.

PESTALOZZI, J. *Leonard and Gertrude*. Trans. and abr. EVA CHANNING. Boston: D. C. Heath, 1906.

PFEFFER, L. *Church, State and Freedom*. Boston: Beacon Press, 1967.

PFEFFER, L. *Creeds in Competition: A Creative Force in American Culture*. New York: Harper & Bros., 1958.

PHENIX, P. H. "Religion in American Public Education." *Teachers College Record*, 1955-1956, *57*, 26-31.

PHILBRICK, J. D. "City School Systems in the United States." *Circulars of Information of the Bureau of Education, No. 1, 1885*. Washington: Government Printing Office, 1885.

PHILLIPS. F. M. "Schools and Classes for Feeble-Minded and Subnormal Children, 1922." *Bureau of Education Bulletin*, 1923 (59). Washington: Government Printing Office, 1924.

PHILLIPS, H. C. "Elizabeth E. Farrell." *The International Council for Exceptional Children Review*, February, 1935, 1 (3), 73-76.

436   *Bibliography*

PINLOCHE, A. *Pestalozzi and the Foundation of the Modern Elementary School.* New York: Scribner's, 1901.

PINTNER, R. "Comparison of American and Foreign Children on Intelligence Tests," *Journal of Educational Psychology* (1923), *14,* 292–295.

PINTNER, R. *Intelligence Testing: Methods and Results,* 1st ed. New York: Henry Holt, 1923.

PINTNER, R. *Intelligence Testing: Methods and Results,* 2d ed. New York: Henry Holt, 1932.

PRITCHARD, D. G. *Education and the Handicapped 1760–1960.* New York: Humanities Press, 1963.

QUINLAN, R. J. "Growth and Development of Catholic Education in the Archdiocese of Boston." *Catholic Historical Review,* 1936 *22, 27–41.*

RANDALL, S. S. *History of the Common School System of the State of New York—From its Origin in 1795, to the Present Time.* New York: Ivison, Blakeman, Taylor, 1871.

RAPPAPORT, J. *Community Psychology.* New York: Holt, Rinehart & Winston, 1977.

RAUMER, K. G. VON. *German Educational Reformers.* Republished from the American Journal of Education. Philadelphia: J. B. Lippincott, 1863.

RAVITCH, E. *The Great School Wars: New York City, 1805–1973.* New York: Basic Books, 1974.

REED, E. W., and S. C. REED. *Mental Retardation: A Family Study.* Philadelphia: Saunders, 1965.

REIGART, J. F. *The Lancasterian System of Instruction in the Schools of New York City.* New York: Teachers College, Columbia University, 1916.

REILLY, D. F. *The School Controversy (1891–1893).* Washington, D.C.: The Catholic University of America Press, 1943.

"Report of the Immigration Commission: The Children of Immigrants in Schools." *Abstracts of Reports of the Immigration Commission, Vol. II.* Presented by Mr. DILLINGHAM, 1910. Washington: Government Printing Office, 1911.

REYNOLDS, M. R. "Policy Statement: Call for Response." *Exceptional Children,* 1971, *37,* 421–433.

RICCIUTI, H. "Adverse Social and Biological Influences on Early Development." In H. McGURK (ed.), *Ecological Factors in Human Development.* New York: North Holland, 1977.

RICE, J. M. *The Public-School System of the United States.* New York: Century, 1893.

RICHMAN, J. "Special Classes and Special Schools for Delinquent and Backward Children." *Proceedings of the National Conference of Charities and Correction Minneapolis, Minnesota 1907.* 1907, pp. 232–243.

RICKARD, G. E. "Establishment of Graded Schools in American Cities, I. The English Grammar School." *The Elementary School Journal,* 1947, *47* (10), 575–585.

RICKARD, G. E. "Establishment of Graded Schools in American Cities, II. The Primary School." *The Elementary School Journal,* 1948, *48* (6), 326–335.

RIGGS, J. G. "Training Teachers for Special Classes." *Journal of the New York State Teacher's Association,* 1922, *9* (4), 7–9.

RIIS, J. A. *The Battle with the Slum.* New York: Macmillan, 1902.

RIIS, J. A. *The Children of the Poor.* New York: Arno Press, 1971. (Reprint of 1892 edition.)

RIIS, J. A. *How the Other Half Lives: Studies among the Tenements of New York.* New York: Scribner's, 1890.

ROBINSON, N. M., and H. B. ROBINSON. *The Mentally Retarded Child,* 2d ed. New York: McGraw-Hill, 1976.

ROFFMAN, H., and L. FINBERG. "Lead Poisoning in Children: A Disease of the Envionment. *Health News,* 1969, *46* (6), 2-5.

ROGERS, D. *Oswego: Fountainhead of Teacher Education.* New York: Appleton-Century-Crofts, 1961.

ROSENBAUM, J. *Making Inequality.* New York: Wiley, 1976.

ROSS, S. L., H. G. DEYOUNG and J. S. COHEN. "Confrontation: Special Education Placement and the Law." *Journal of Exceptional Children,* 1971, *38,* 5-12.

ROSSI, P. H., and A. S. ROSSI. "Background and Consequences of Parochial School Education." *Harvard Educational Review,* 1957, *XXVII* (3), 168-199.

ROSSITER, C. *1787: The Grand Convention.* New York: Mentor Books, 1966 (paperback).

ROTHMAN, D. J. *The Discovery of the Asylum.* Boston: Little, Brown, 1971.

RUSSO, S. "Adaptations in Behavioral Therapy with Children." *Behavior Research and Therapy,* 1964, *2,* 43-47.

RYAN, W. *Blaming the Victim.* New York: Pantheon, 1971.

RYOR, J. "Mainstreaming." *Today's Education,* March-April, 1976, p. 5.

SAMEROFF, A. J. "Concepts of Humanity in Primary Prevention." Paper prepared for the Vermont Conference on the Primary Prevention of Psychopathology. Burlington, Vermont, June, 1975.

SAMEROFF, A. J., and M. J. CHANDLER. "Reproductive Risks and the Continuum of Caretaking Casualty." In F. D. HOROWITZ, M. HETHERINGTON, S. SCARR-SALAPATEK, and G. SIEGEL (eds.), *Review of Child Development Research.* Chicago: University of Chicago Press, 1975, *4,* 187-244.

SAMEROFF, A. J., and M. ZAX. "Schizotaxia Revisited: Model Issues in the Etiology of Schizophrenia." *American Journal of Ortho-Psychiatry,* 1973, *43,* 744-754.

SANDERS, J. W. *The Education of an Urban Minority: Catholics in Chicago, 1833-1965.* New York: Oxford University Press, 1977.

SARASON, S. B. "Community Psychology and the Anarchist Insight." *American Journal of Community Psychology,* 1976, *4,* 243-261.

SARASON, S. B. *The Creation of Settings and the Future Societies.* San Francisco: Jossey-Bass, 1972.

SARASON, S. B. *Culture of the Schools and the Problem of Change.* Boston: Allyn & Bacon, 1971.

SARASON, S. B. "Jewishness, Blackishness and the Nature-Nurture Controversy." *American Psychologist,* 1973, *28,* 962-971.

SARASON, S. B. "The Nature of Problem Solving in Social Action." Invited address at the Eastern Psychological Association, Boston, 1977.

SARASON, S. B. *The Psychological Sense of Community.* San Francisco: Jossey-Bass, 1974.

SARASON, S. B. "Some Aspects of the Brain-Behavior Problem." *Boston University Journal of Education,* 1964, *47,* 53–61.

SARASON, S. B. "The Unfortunate Fate of Alfred Binet and School Psychology." *Teachers College Record,* May, 1977, *77* (4), 579–592.

SARASON, S. B., C. F. CARROLL, K. MATON, S. COHEN, and E. LORENTZ. *Human Services and Resource Networks.* San Francisco: Jossey-Bass, 1977.

SARASON, S. B., K. DAVIDSON, and B. BLATT. *The Preparation of Teachers: An Unstudied Problem in Education.* New York: Wiley, 1962.

SARASON, S. B., and J. DORIS. *Psychological Problems in Mental Deficiency.* 4th Ed. New York: Harper & Row, 1969.

SARASON, S. B., and T. GLADWIN. "Psychological and Cultural Problems in Mental Subnormality: A Review of Research." *Genetic Psychology Monographs,* 1958, *57,* 3–290.

SARASON, S. B., F. GROSSMAN, and G. ZITNAY. *The Creation of a Community Setting.* Syracuse: N.Y.: Syracuse University Press, 1972.

SARASON, S. B., M. LEVINE, I. GOLDENBERG, D. CHERLIN, and M. BENNETT. *Psychology in Community Settings.* New York: John Wiley, 1966.

SCHINDLER-RAINMAN, and R. LIPPETT. *The Volunteer Community: Creative Use of Human Resources.* Fairfax, Va.: NTL Learning Resource Corporation, 1975.

SCHNEIDER, D. M. *The History of Public Welfare in New York State 1609–1866.* Chicago: University of Chicago Press, 1938.

SCHNEIDER, D. M., and A. DEUTSCH. *The History of Public Welfare in New York State 1867–1940.* Chicago: University of Chicago Press, 1941.

SCISCO, L. D. *Political Nativism in New York State.* New York: Columbia University Press, 1901.

SCULL, A. T. *Decarceration, Community Treatment and the Deviant: A Radical View.* Englewood Cliffs, N.J.: Spectrum Books, Prentice-Hall, 1977 (paperback).

SEAGOE, M. V. *Yesterday Was Tuesday, All Day All Night: A Story of a Unique Education.* Boston: Little, Brown, 1964.

SEGUIN, E. *Idiocy: Its Treatment by the Physiological Method.* New York: William Wood, 1866.

SELZER, M. (ed.). *Kike!* A Documentary History of Anti-Semitism in America. New York: World Publishing Company, 1972.

SENN, M. E. *Anticipatory Guidance of the Pregnant Woman and Her Husband for Roles as Parents.* Transcript of the First Conference. Jos. Macy Foundation, March, 1947.

SHAW, A. M. "The True Character of New York Public Schools." *The World's Work,* 1903–1904, *7,* 4204–4221.

SHERWOOD, J. J., and N. NATAUPSKY. "Predicting the Conclusion of Negro-White Intelligence Research from Biographical Characteristics of the Investigator." *Journal of Personality and Social Psychology,* 1968, *8,* 53–58.

SHORE, M. F., and S. E. GOLANN (eds.). *Current Ethical Issues in Mental Health.* National Institute of Mental Health (National Clearinghouse for Mental Health Information). Washington, D.C.: EHEW publication No. (HSM) 73-9029, 1973. (Available from Superintendent of Documents, U.S. Government Printing Office, Washington, D.C. 20402).

SHUEY, A. M. *The Testing of Negro Intelligence.* Lynchburg, Va.: J. P. Bell Company 1958.

SHUEY, A. M. *The Testing of Negro Intelligence,* 2d ed. New York: Social Science Press, 1966.

SHUTTLEWORTH, G. E. "The Elementary Education of Defective Children by 'Special Classes' in London." *Journal of Psycho-Asthenics.* 1899, *4* (2), 58–64.

SKEELS, H. M. "Adult Status of Children with Contrasting Early Life Experiences." *Monographs of the Society for Research in Child Development,* 1966, *31* (3), ser. no. 105.

SMITH, M. W. "Alfred Binet's Remarkable Questions: A Cross-National and Cross-Temporal Analysis of the Cultural Biases Built into the Stanford-Binet Intelligence Scale and Other Binet Tests." *Genetic Psychology Monographs,* 1974, *89,* 307–334.

SMITH, R. M. "Education of Mentally Retarded Children in New York City Schools. *Journal of Exceptional Children, 1940–41, 7* (5), 168–171, 207–208.

STEINBACH, C. "Report of the Special Class Department, Cleveland, Ohio." *Journal of Psycho-Asthenics,* 1918, 1919, *23,* 104–109.

STERN, C. *Principles of Human Genetics,* 2d ed. San Francisco: Freeman, 1960.

STEVENS, R., and R. STEVENS. *Welfare Medicine in America.* New York: Free Press, 1974.

STOKES, A. P. *Church and State in the United States: Historical Development and Contemporary Problems of Religious Freedom under the Constitution.* 3 vols. New York: Harper & Bros., 1950.

STOKES, A. P., and L. PFEFFER. *Church and State in the United States.* New York: Harper & Row, 1964.

STONE, N. D. "Family Factors in Willingness to Place the Mongoloid Child." *American Journal of Mental Deficiency,* 1967, *72* (1), 16–20.

STOWE, C. E. "Report on Elementary Education in Europe" (1837). In KNIGHT, E. A. (ed.) *Reports on European Education* by John Griscom, Victor Cousin, Calvin E. Stowe. New York, 1930.

STRAUGHAM, J. H. "Treatment with Child and Mother in the Playroom." *Behavior Research and Therapy,* 1964, *2,* 37–41.

STUBBLEFIELD, H. W. "Religion, Parents, and Mental Retardation." *Mental Retardation,* 1965, *3* (4), 8–11.

"Summer School for Teachers of Defectives." *The Training School Bulletin,* 1913–14, *10,* 45–46, 153–155.

"Summer Schools for Teachers of Special Classes." *The Training School Bulletin,* 1914–15, *2,* 12–15.

Surveyor Course Manual for Intermediate Care Facility for Mental Retardation. Department of Health Services Administration, School of Public Health, Tulane University, New Orleans.

SZASZ, T. S. *Ceremonial Chemistry: The Ritual Persecution of Drugs, Addicts, and the Pushers.* Garden City, N.Y.: Doubleday, 1974.

SZASZ, T. S. *The Manufacture of Madness.* New York: Harper & Row, 1970.

SZASZ, T. S. *The Myth of Mental Illness.* New York: Harper & Row, 1974.

SZASZ, T. S. *The Theology of Medicine.* New York: Harper Colophon Books, 1977.

TALBOT, M. E. *Edouard Seguin: A Study of an Educational Approach to the Treatment of Mentally Defective Children.* New York: Bureau of Publications, Teachers College, Columbia University, 1964.

TAYLOR, E. A. *Experiments with a Backward Class.* London: Methuen, 1946.

TAYLOR, M. "Aftercare Study, 1924–1925." *Ungraded,* November, 1925, *11* (2), 25–33.

TERMAN, L. M. *The Measurement of Intelligence.* Boston: Houghton-Mifflin, 1916.

THOMAS, A., S. CHESS, and H. BIRCH. *Temperament and Behavior Disorders in Children.* New York: New York University Press, 1968.

THOMPSON, F. V. *Americanization Studies, Vol. 1: Schooling of the Immigrant.* Montclair, N.J.: Patterson-Smith, 1971.

Training School Bulletin, 1913–14, *10,* 1914–15, *11.*

TROEN, S. K. *The Public and the Schools: Shaping the St. Louis System, 1838–1920.* Columbia: University of Missouri Press, 1975.

TUER, A. W. *History of the Horn-Book.* London: London Hall Press; New York: Scribner's, 1897.

TULKIN, S. R. "An Analysis of the Concept of Cultural Deprivation." *Developmental Psychology,* 1972, *6* (2), 326–339.

TYACK, D. B. "The Perils of Pluralism: The Background of the Pierce Case." *American Historical Review,* 1968, *LXXIV,* 74–98.

TYACK, D. B. "Ways of Seeing: An Essay on the History of Compulsory Schooling." *Harvard Educational Review,* August, 1976, *46,* 355–389.

United States Bureau of the Census. *The Statistical History of the United States from Colonial Times to the Present.* Stamford, Conn.: Fairfield Publishers, 1965.

U.S. Congress, Senate, Subcommittee on Long-Term Care. Supporting paper No. 1. *The Litany of Nursing Home Abuses and an Examination of the Roots of the Controversy.* Washington, D.C.: U.S. Government Printing Office, 1974. (Available from the Superintendent of Documents, U.S. Government Printing Office, Washington, D.C., 20402. Stock No. 5270–02650. Price $1.20.)

U.S. Congress, Senate, Subcommittee on Long-Term Care. *Nursing Home Care in the United States: Failure in Public Policy.* Washington, D.C.: U.S. Government Printing Office, 1974. (Available from the Superintendent of Documents, U.S. Government Printing Office, Washington, D.C., 20402. Price $1.75.)

VAN SICKLE, J. H. "Provision for Exceptional Children in the Public Schools." *Psychological Clinic,* 1908–9, *2,* 102–111.

VAN SICKLE, J. H., L. WITMER, and L. P. AYRES. "Provision for Exceptional Children in Public Schools. *U.S. Bureau of Education Bulletin, No. 14.,* Washington: Government Printing Office, 1911.

"Visiting Teachers for Ungraded Classes." *The Training School Bulletin.* 1913–14, *10,* 105.

WADE, M. "The French Parish and *Survivance* in Nineteenth Century New England." *The Catholic Historical Review,* 1950, *XXXVI,* No. 2, 163–189.

WALCH, M. R. *Pestalozzi and the Pestalozzian Theory of Education.* Washington, D.C.: Catholic University of America Press, 1952.

WALD, L. D. "Education and the Arts." *The International Council for Exceptional Children Review,* February, 1935, *1* (3), 82-87.

WALLIN, J. E. W. *The Education of Handicapped Children.* Boston: Houghton Mifflin, 1924.

WALLIN, J. E. W. "Trends and Needs in Teacher Training." *Journal of Exceptional Children.* 1936-1937, *3,* 144-147.

WALSH, E. A. "Ungraded Class Work in New York City: Methods and Results." *Journal of Psycho-Asthenics,* September, 1914, *19* (1), 59-66.

WASHINGTON, B. T. "Education of the Negro." In P. MONROE (ed.), *A Cyclopedia of Education,* 1913, *4,* 405-408.

WATSON, J. B. *Psychological Care of Infant and Child.* New York: Norton, 1928.

WEBER, N. A. "The Rise of National Catholic Churches in the United States." *The Catholic Historical Review.* 1915-1916, *1,* 422-434.

WEBSTER, N. *American Spelling Book* With an Introductory Essay by HENRY STEELE COMMAGER. New York: Bureau of Publications, Teachers College, Columbia University Press, 1962.

WEBSTER, N. Letter to Barnard, 1840, cited in *The American Journal of Education,* 1876, *26,* 195-196.

WECHSLER, D. *The Measurement and Appraisal of Adult Intelligence.* Baltimore: Williams & Wilkins, 1958.

WELTER, R. *Popular Education and Democratic Thought in America.* New York: Columbia University Press, 1962.

WERTENBAKER, T. J. *The Puritan Oligarchy: The Founding of American Civilization.* New York: Charles Scribner's Sons, 1947. (Paperback, Grosset & Dunlap.)

WESSEL, M. A. "The Prenatal Pediatric Visit." Pediatrics, 1963, *32,* 926.

WHIPPLE, G. M. "Special Classes." In P. MONROE (ed.), *A Cyclopedia of Education,* vol. 5. New York: Macmillan, 1913, 384-386.

WOLF, T. H. *Alfred Binet.* Chicago: University of Chicago Press, 1973.

WOLFENSBERGER, W. *The Principle of Normalization in Human Services.* Toronto: National Institute of Mental Retardation, 1972.

WOLFENSBERGER, W., and R. A. KURTZ (eds.). *Management of the Family of the Mentally Retarded.* Follett Educational Corporation, 1969.

WRIGHT, B. A. *Physical Disability: A Psychological Approach.* New York: Harper & Bros., 1960.

WRIGHT, H. C. *Human Life Illustrated in my Individual Experience as a Child, Youth, and a Man.* Boston: Bela Marsh, 1849.

YEPSEN, L. N., and V. CIANCI. "Home Training for Mentally Deficient Children in New Jersey." *Training School Bulletin* (Vinel and J. J.), 1946, *43,* 21-26.

ZAX, M., and E. COWEN. *Abnormal Psychology: Changing Conceptions.* New York: Holt, Rinehart, & Winston, 1972.

ZAX, M., and G. A. SPECTER. *An Introduction to Community Psychology.* New York: Wiley, 1974.

ZIGLER, E. "Familial Mental Retardation: A Continuing Dilemma. *Science,* 1967, *155,* 292–298.

ZIGLER, E., and D. BALLA. "Impact of Institutional Experience on the Behavior and Development of Retarded Persons." *American Journal of Mental Deficiency,* 1977, *82,* 1–11.

ZUK, G. H., R. L. MILLER, J. B. BARTRUM, and G. F. KLING. "Maternal Acceptance of Retarded Children: A Questionnaire Study of Attitudes and Religious Background." *Child Development,* 1961, *32,* 525–40.

INDEXES

Name Index

A

Abbott, E., 184, 185, 186, 187, 188, 189
Abel, T. M., 53n
Ackerman, N., 52, 125
Adams, F. K., 55
Agassiz, L., 248
Albee, G. W., 139, 140, 142, 143, 144, 332
Allport, G., 398
Amoros, F., 314
Andelman, F., 362, 363
Anderson, V. V., 310, 311, 330
Aristotle, 241
Arkell, C., 138
Armatruda, C., 20
Arlitt, A. H., 346
Arons, S., 230
Ashcroft, S. C., 138
Attala, R., 146
Atzmon, E., 227
Audette, R., 376
Ausubel, D. P., 53n
Ayers, L. P., 137, 138, 279, 336, 337, 338

B

Babson, S. G., 20
Bailey, S. K., 365
Bailyn, B., 208, 220, 221
Baker, B. L., 126, 127
Ball, W. B., 233
Balla, D., 94–96
Balow, B., 322
Barnard, H., 163, 168, 170, 251, 252, 254, 255
Barr, M. W., 264, 317
Barry, C. J., 213, 218
Bartrum, J. B., 55

Bateman, B. D., 55
Beach, F., 274
Becker, E., 63
Bell, A., 170, 171
Bennett, M., 122, 380–88, 407
Benson, R. C., 20
Berkowitz, B. P., 124, 125, 126
Bijou, S. W., 124, 125
Bilken, D., 80, 130
Billington, R. A., 192, 196
Binet, A., 3, 31, 32, 33, 34, 35, 36
Birch, H. G., 21, 148, 149, 150
Blatt, B., 5, 11, 18, 84, 112, 132, 358, 374, 417
Block, J. H., 37
Blom, G. E., 97, 98, 99, 100, 102, 104, 108
Boehme, G. M., 266
Boese, T., 172, 176, 177, 253, 254
Bogdan, R., 11, 12, 80
Bouquillon, T., 223, 224, 225, 226, 227, 230
Bourne, W. O., 170, 178, 179, 180, 195, 197, 198, 202, 204, 254
Boykin, J. C., 257
Braginsky, B., 11, 26
Braginsky, D., 11, 26
Braine, M. D., 149
Bray, D., 82
Brazelton, T. B., 120
Brightman, A. J., 126, 127
Bronfenbrenner, U., 120, 152
Brown, E. E., 252n
Brubacher, J. S., 168, 252
Bruner, J. S., 72
Bryt, A., 53n
Burgess, C., 262
Burlingham, Charles, 299
Burns, J. A., 213, 217, 220, 223, 226, 236
Burt, C., 140, 142, 142n

Subject Index